INTRODUCTION TO

MEASUREMENT

in Physical Education and Exercise Science

MARGARET J. SAFRIT, Ph.D.

Henry-Bascom Professor
University of Wisconsin
Madison, Wisconsin

TIMES MIRROR/MOSBY COLLEGE PUBLISHING

St. Louis • Toronto • Santa Clara   1986

Editor: Nancy K. Roberson
Developmental editor: Michelle Turenne
Project editor: Barbara Merritt
Manuscript editor: Maureen Kenison
Book design: Nancy Steinmeyer
Cover design: Susan E. Lane

Library of Congress Cataloging-in-Publication Data

Safrit, Margaret J., 1935-
   Introduction to measurement in physical education
      and exercise science.

   Bibliography: p.
   Includes index.
   1. Physical fitness--Testing. I. Title.
GV436.S223   1986   613.7′1   85-29033
ISBN 0-8016-4291-4

C/VH/VH   9   8   7   6   5   4   3   2   03/A/299

To my parents—
Margaret Cline and Ernest Crawford Safrit, Sr.—
with grateful appreciation for their
constant support and encouragement
during my years as a student and
throughout my career in academia.

Preface

In the fields of physical education and exercise science, two concepts assume universal significance—the measurement of motor behavior and the evaluation of performance of physical skills and effectiveness of educational programs. Teachers of physical education should be able to select good tests, administer them properly, and use the results to improve student achievement. Although tests of motor behavior are of predominate interest to the teacher, knowledge tests and tests of affective behavior—such as sportsmanship—are also utilized. Further, the evaluation of instruction, curriculum, and program cannot be ignored. Specialists in fitness or sports centers have similar needs. The status of incoming clients should be evaluated. Their improvement should be monitored on a regular basis. The effectiveness of the center, both programmatically and financially, must be assessed. Indeed, without the tools of measurement and evaluation, indicators of attainment would be limited to totally subjective judgment.

This textbook was written to prepare the undergraduate student in physical education or exercise science to effectively implement measurement and evaluation techniques. Since many undergraduate students are now preparing for careers in nonschool settings, the basic principles of measurement are exemplified in both school and nonschool settings. Numerous examples of tests are provided throughout the book.

FEATURES

- One of the prominent features of this book is its *straightforward presentation of measurement and evaluation concepts*. The author has drawn upon her 20 years of experience in teaching measurement to undergraduate physical education majors to provide a clear, accurate discussion of issues appropriate at this level of instruction.
- Another strong point is the inclusion of two chapters on the use of *microcomputers* along with listings of several programs that can be used by both students and faculty. Considering the rapid increase in the use of microcomputers in the United States, this is both timely and useful material.
- An important and timely feature of the book is its *representativeness of the*

field of physical education as it exists today. No longer are most physical education majors preparing to teach or coach physical education. Many students are interested in alternative careers in a nonschool setting such as a fitness center. A practical approach to testing in this type of setting is included.

● The organization of the book provides a *practical presentation* for learning. After a general introduction to measurement and evaluation in physical education, the technical section of the book is introduced with an overview of basic statistics and measurement concepts. The next section of the book encompasses easy-to-locate material on testing and types of tests. The latter portion of the book deals with typical problems associated with the measurement of motor skills and abilities.

ORGANIZATIONAL FEATURES

The book is divided into eight parts. The first part provides an overview of measurement and evaluation, including an up-to-date coverage of the importance of these concepts in school and nonschool settings in physical education and exercise science. In the second part, statistical techniques that can be used to describe test scores are presented in a straightforward manner, with step-by-step examples and problems/answers for the student. This material is written in a simplified manner for those who have only the most basic arithmetic skills. The third part focuses on concepts in measurement, presented in understandable yet accurate terminology. Both norm-referenced and criterion-referenced measurement are covered. The textbook becomes even more practical in the fourth part with a detailed description of test construction techniques for both sports skills and knowledge tests. In the fifth and sixth parts, many examples of tests of physical performance are presented and analyzed. These include tests of sports skills, health-related physical fitness, athletic performance-related physical fitness, muscular strength and endurance, balance and flexibility, motor ability, and affective behavior. A variety of unique measurement concerns in physical education are covered in the seventh part. Examples of these concerns are tests for children, tests for special populations, and grading. In the eighth and final part, emphasis is placed on the use of microcomputers in our field. This part can easily be followed by students with no previous experience on a microcomputer. Lastly, the Appendices include statistical tables, microcomputer programs, and sources for a wide variety of sports skills tests.

PEDAGOGICAL FEATURES

The author has had over 20 years of experience teaching undergraduate students in measurement and evaluation. This experience has been used to design a book that is a genuine aid to student learning:

Key Words: Each chapter begins with a list of the most important terms that students should become familiar with while reading the chapter.

Introduction: A description of the purpose of the chapter prepares the student for each chapter's application of information to both physical education and exercise science.

Tables, Drawings, and Photographs: Tables and illustrations are used throughout to provide additional information, and to clarify concepts and activities.

Summary: Summaries at the close of each chapter carefully reiterate its major points of content.

References: Presenting the most complete and up-to-date documentation, the references provide additional sources for further study.

Annotated Readings: Selected resources are provided with annotations to enhance the learning process.

Learning Experiences: A set of learning experiences concludes each chapter, and provides student exercises to reinforce the material in the text. When appropriate, answers are provided.

Glossary: The text concludes with a comprehensive glossary in which each key word shown at the beginning of the chapter is listed and defined. Additionally, the glossary contains the page location where terms first appear.

SUPPLEMENT

An Instructor's Manual and Test Bank are available for instructors using the textbook. The manual contains supplementary information to be used at the discretion of the instructor. Included in the manual are chapter objectives; chapter overviews; additional learning experiences; microcomputer programs modified for the Commodore and the IBM; additional sample tests; 20 transparency masters of important drawings, tables, and charts; and over 660 multiple-choice, true-false, matching, and essay test questions. Separate answer keys are provided. In addition, the manual is perforated for convenience of use.

ACKNOWLEDGMENTS

No textbook can be completed without the assistance of many others, and this has certainly been true for this book. Their support is gratefully acknowledged.

Many authors and publishers granted permission to reproduce material in this text. The American Alliance for Health, Physical Education, Recreation and Dance was especially generous in this respect. Many tables and figures from their publications are reprinted herein. Two colleagues, Michael Pollock and Janet Seaman, kindly granted permission to reproduce several of their photographs.

Sincere appreciation is expressed to Linda Spraker for the artwork and Jerry M. Capps for the photography. The models for the photography were of invaluable assistance. Several were undergraduate students at the University of Wisconsin, Madison—Daniel McCourt, Sharon Novak, Spencer Kurtz, Kenneth Siedenberg, and Laurie Rabideau. M. Glaucia Costa, Linda M. Hooper, and Terry M. Wood, three graduate students who deserve special recognition, were not only models for photography sessions, but they also contributed in many other ways to the preparation of both the text and the Instructor's Manual. Thanks are extended to two of my colleagues whose expertise was of great benefit in the photography sessions and in other ways—Dr. Bonnie Chalmers-Ballsrud, adapted physical education, and Dr. Francis J. Nagle, Biodynamics Laboratory. Finally, the photography sessions could not have been completed without the indispensable assistance of Dr. Kay Harty, principal, and Ms. Christine J. Harper, physical education teacher, at Midvale Elementary School, and Mr. Jack Horton, principal, and the physical education staff at Orchard Ridge Middle School in Madison, Wisconsin, as well as the cooperation of the children at both schools.

It is expected that any book will undergo revisions after the first draft has been submitted to the Publisher. Reviewers were selected by the Publisher to evaluate not only the first draft but also the second draft of the manuscript. Their reviews were extremely useful in revising the text and, without question, contributed to improvements in the original version. A very special debt of gratitude is conveyed to these individuals for their thorough and conscientious analysis of the material herein:

Charles J. Ansorge
University of Nebraska-Lincoln

John G. Bayless
Oklahoma State University

Agnes Chrietzberg
Eastern Kentucky University

William F. Clipson
University of Alabama

Patricia A. Frye
Ithaca College

Keith C. Henschen
University of Utah

Larry D. Hensley
University of Northern Iowa

Jean McCarthy
Mankato State University

Edgar W. Shields, Jr.
University of North Carolina-Chapel Hill

Ronald A. Siders
University of Florida

Roger C. Wiley
Washington State University

Sincere thanks are also expressed to Vinni Pedersen and Sharon Ruch for their assistance in typing portions of the book. Their efficiency is hereby gratefully acknowledged.

Last but not least is well-deserved recognition to the staff of Times Mirror/ Mosby College Publishing for supplying sound direction to the preparation of the text, in particular, Michelle Turenne. Their aid contributed significantly to the quality of the final product.

Margaret J. Safrit

Contents

PART ONE AN OVERVIEW OF MEASUREMENT AND EVALUATION IN A MOTOR BEHAVIOR CONTEXT

1 The Value of Measurement and Evaluation, 2

Measurement and evaluation defined, 4
Use of tests, 5
Norm-referenced and criterion-referenced measurement, 8
Formative and summative evaluation, 10
A brief history of measurement, 11
Recent changes in measurement practices, 13
Summary, 18

2 Measurement in a School-Based Setting, 20

Do physical education teachers use tests? 22
Preparing educational objectives, 24
Conducting a needs assessment, 37
Importance of accountability, 38
Summary, 39

3 Measurement in a Nonschool-Based Setting, 42

Measuring skills in sports clubs, 43
Measuring health-related fitness in fitness centers, 44
Summary, 62

PART TWO SIMPLIFIED STATISTICS

4 Summarizing a Set of Test Scores, 66

Measurement scales, 67
Discrete and continuous variables, 68
Frequency distribution, 69
Calculation of percentiles, 75
Calculation of percentile ranks, 80
Summary, 82

5 Describing a Distribution of Test Scores, 86

Measures of central tendency, 86
Measures of variability, 89
Score distributions, 92
Standard scores, 96

Correlation, 102
Use of norms, 108
Summary, 112

PART THREE   CHARACTERISTICS OF A GOOD TEST

6   *Validity and Reliability of Norm-Referenced Tests,* 118

Validity, 119
Reliability, 130
Objectivity of scoring, 138
Summary, 140

7   *Validity and Reliability of Criterion-Referenced Tests,* 143

Mastery learning, 144
Uses of a criterion-referenced test, 146
Validity, 146
Reliability, 151
Summary, 154

PART FOUR   PRINCIPLES OF TEST CONSTRUCTION

8   *Constructing Sports Skills Tests,* 160

Steps in developing a sports skills test, 161
Development of a battery of skills tests, 165
Development of rating scales, 165
Other approaches to measuring skill, 168
Summary, 169

9   *Constructing Knowledge Tests,* 171

Table of specifications, 172
Test administration, 173
Types of test items, 174
Weighting test components, 184
Correction for guessing, 184
Item analysis, 184
Summary, 187

PART FIVE   MEASURES OF PHYSICAL PERFORMANCE

10   *Tests of Sports Skills,* 192

Examples of tests, 192
Summary, 223

11   *Tests of Health-Related Physical Fitness,* 226

Definition of health-related physical fitness, 228
Measuring health-related fitness, 229
Fitnessgram, 249
Measuring health-related fitness in a laboratory setting, 256
Summary, 262

12 Tests of Athletic Performance-Related Physical Fitness, 265

AAHPER Youth Fitness Test, 266
Examples of other tests, 285
Administration of physical fitness tests, 287
Tests of physical fitness knowledge, 296
Summary, 296

13 Tests of Muscular Strength and Endurance, 299

Techniques for measuring muscular strength and endurance, 301
Examples of strength tests, 303
Examples of endurance tests, 312
Power testing, 320
Summary, 326

14 Tests of Balance and Flexibility, 329

Measuring balance, 330
Measuring flexibility, 334
Measuring posture, 339
Summary, 342

15 Tests of Motor Ability, 345

Examples of motor ability tests, 347
Critique of motor ability tests, 358
Should motor ability tests be used for ability grouping? 359
Summary, 361

PART SIX MEASURES OF RELATED ABILITIES

16 Tests of Affective Behavior, 366

Types of measures, 367
Uses of affective measures, 371
Examples of affective measures, 372
Summary, 395

PART SEVEN UNIQUE MEASUREMENT CONCERNS

17 Measuring Motor Performance in Children, 398

Assessing basic movement patterns, 399
Tests of sports skills, 403
Tests of physical fitness and motor ability, 417
Tests of perceptual motor behavior, 419
Example of growth charts, 422
Summary, 422

18 Adapting Tests and Measurements For Special Populations, 427

Legal mandates affecting evaluation, 429
Observational techniques, 431
Performance tests, 431

Motor performance testing, 448
Summary, 452

19   *Grading in Physical Education,* 454

Use of grades, 455
Determining a final unit grade, 458
Norm-referenced approach to grading, 462
Criterion-referenced approach to grading, 465
Calculating final grades, 467
Use of weights in calculating grades, 468
Using the microcomputer to calculate final grades, 469
Other systems of grading, 469
Use of institutional grades, 470
Reporting multiple grades, 472
Summary, 472

20   *Special Issues in Measurement and Evaluation,* 475

Measuring improvement, 475
Evaluation topics, 477
Sex differences in motor performance, 489
Summary, 491

PART EIGHT   *THE USE OF MICROCOMPUTERS IN MEASURING MOTOR BEHAVIOR*

21   *Conceptual Overview of a Microcomputer,* 494

A brief history, 496
The makeup of a microcomputer, 496
Summary, 502

22   *Microcomputers Applications,* 504

Variations in microcomputers, 505
Preparing the disk, 506
Elementary computer commands, 507
Examples of programs, 510
Summary, 516

Glossary, G-1

Appendices

Appendix A, A-2
Appendix B, A-3
Appendix C, A-4
Appendix D, A-8
Appendix E, A-18
Appendix F, A-35
Appendix G, A-41

Credits and Acknowledgments, C-1

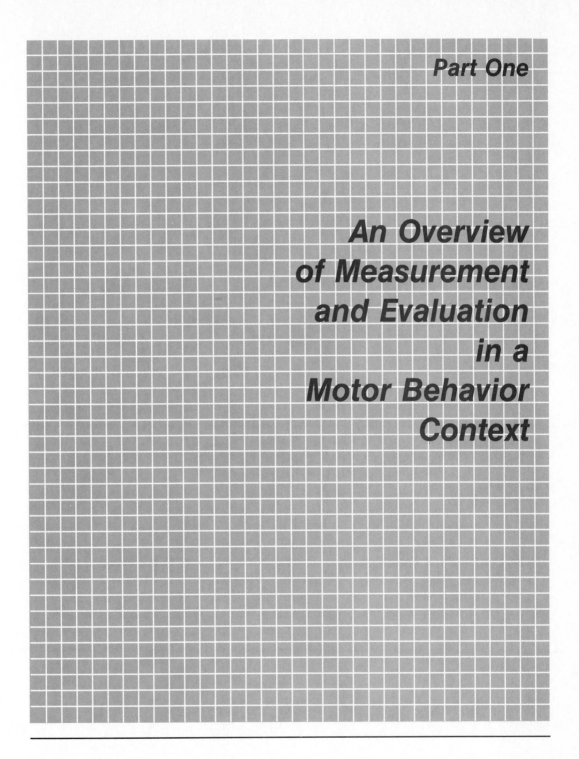

Part One

*An Overview
of Measurement
and Evaluation
in a
Motor Behavior
Context*

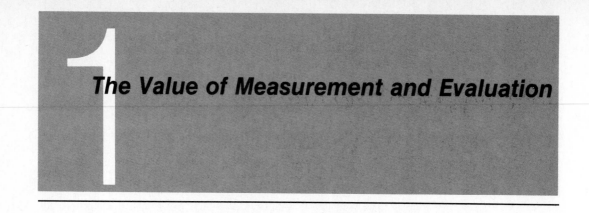

The Value of Measurement and Evaluation

KEY WORDS *Watch for these words as you read the following chapter:*

achievement	improvement	quantitative measurement
competency-based evaluation	mastery test	summative evaluation
	measure	test
criterion-referenced test	measurement	test user
evaluation	norm-referenced test	Title IX
formative evaluation	qualitative measurement	

The field of physical education is changing. From its inception to the early 1970s, the majority of students majoring in physical education planned to teach physical education in a school and perhaps coach one or two sports. During the 1970s the interests of some students began to change. As knowledge about health and fitness mushroomed in the United States, careers other than teaching in schools became available to physical education majors. For instance, as fitness clubs sprang up around the country, managers and instructors trained in physical education were sought. How has this changed the field of physical education? Even though many of the basic principles taught to physical education teachers are germane for those with other career options in the motor behavior area, the application of these principles may vary. Thus, every area of specialization in physical education is affected, including the measurement and evaluation area. For example, tests are sometimes used to motivate students in a school setting. Some students may be motivated because they realize their test score will be used in determining unit grades. In nonschool settings, such as private fitness clubs, private sports clubs, corporate fitness centers, the Young Women's Christian Association (YWCA), and the Young Men's Christian Association (YMCA), tests will not be motivating because of grades, at least in the traditional sense. On the other hand, a test may stimulate individuals to improve their performance in both school and nonschool settings. The underlying principles of measurement are the same in both settings, but the application of these principles may differ depending on the clientele and the predetermined objectives.

Measurement and evaluation are vital aspects of instruction. The importance of these processes is not diminished if the instruction takes place in a nonschool setting. This book focuses on the use of measurement and evaluation of motor behavior in school and nonschool settings, because instruction in physical education takes place in both of these environments. The basic measurement principles are equally applicable no matter where a test is administered. However, the way in which test scores are used may vary, depending on the setting.

Suppose an individual joins a fitness center. Before prescribing an exercise program for the client, an instructor administers a battery of fitness tests. These tests might be identical to those used in physical education classes in local high schools. Yet in the private club context, the constraints surrounding the measurement process can be quite different from the public school situation. In the private club, testing is often individualized. The age and needs of the client may differ from those of the high school student. Attention must be paid to appropriate motivational strategies. Techniques that are effective in the fitness center may not have the same impact in the high school, and vice versa. The importance of prior medical approval is magnified in the older population. Since private clubs are often able to administer tests on a one-to-one basis, the use of laboratory-type testing procedures is more feasible in this setting than in the schools.

Most students reading this textbook will have already spent many years in physical education classes in the school system. Can you recall whether tests were used in these classes? If so, when were tests usually administered during a unit of instruction? Did testing seem important to your physical education teacher? How were the test scores used? Were test results used for any purpose other than determining grades? The use of tests probably varied from unit to unit. The same situation exists in nonschool settings. In some instances no tests are used at all, and in others the testing program is of high quality. In subsequent chapters several of these testing programs are described. Measurement practices in both school and nonschool settings are included, with material directed to the budding exercise specialist or private sports club instructor as well as the future teacher of physical education. Since the nonschool and school settings encompass so many potential career options, each with a different title, the term **test user** will be used in a generic sense throughout this textbook to refer to an individual who selects and administers a test, regardless of his or her job title.

MEASUREMENT AND EVALUATION DEFINED

Measurement and evaluation are closely related processes. From a practical standpoint, **measurement** takes place when a test is administered and a score is obtained. If the test is **quantitative,** the score is a number. If the test is **qualitative,** the score may be a phrase or a word such as "Excellent"; or it may be a number representing a phrase or word. A more precise definition of measurement is the process of assigning a number to an attribute of a person or object. By this definition, measurement is a quantitative and not a qualitative process. If body fatness is the attribute of interest, it can be measured by determining skinfold thickness. The number assigned to this attribute represents skinfold thickness reported in millimeters (mm). This score would fit the universal definition of the term *measurement*. Throughout this textbook, however, measurement is interpreted in the broadest sense as encompassing both quantitative and qualitative indicators.

The process of **evaluation** involves the interpretation of a score. Once skinfold thickness has been measured, what does the score mean? If the sum of triceps plus subscapular skinfolds is 18 mm for a 10-year-old boy, is this a reflection of a desirable body composition? The score must be interpreted for it to have true meaning. In the strictest sense of the word, measurement is an objective, nonjudgmental process, whereas evaluation requires that judgments be made.

USE OF TESTS

Throughout this textbook the noun *test* will be used synonymously with *measure*. For example, a **measure** of maximal oxygen uptake has the same meaning as a **test** of maximal oxygen uptake. Tests have many uses in school and non-school settings. A test may be administered for one purpose or for multiple purposes, as determined by the test user. Usually, the rationale for using a test encompasses more than one purpose. The following are a few of the uses of tests in the physical education field.

Motivation

Tests are frequently administered for motivational purposes. A skills test might be administered in a physical education class to encourage students to improve their skills further. In a corporate fitness center, skinfold measures might be used to motivate overweight employees to lose weight. When a performance standard must be met in a public service setting, examinees are sometimes motivated to work toward meeting the standard by taking a test. The advance knowledge of an upcoming test can motivate students to practice a skill with greater intensity. When a test is administered more than once, students are usually interested in the extent to which they have improved. They like to compare their current score with a previous score, which, in itself, can be a motivational factor. The use of tests for motivation is most effective if scores are viewed in the context of areas needing improvement rather than in a punitive sense. In other words, the test should be used as a positive motivator rather than a negative motivator. Certainly motivation is a powerful factor in performance before, during, and after the test's administration.

Achievement

One of the most common uses of tests is the assessment of achievement. How much has an individual achieved during a specified period of time? If most of the clients in a center are below average in their levels of fitness after a year of participation in a fitness program, this points to insufficient achievement by the participants. Do students achieve a higher level of skill in several sports after participating in a physical education program year after year? Do employees in a corporate fitness center achieve the targeted amount of weight loss? **Achievement** should not be confused with **improvement.** Improvement is the difference in performance from one point in time to another. These points may or may not coincide with the beginning and end of the course. Achievement in and of itself encompasses only the final ability level at a designated point in time and is often relative to a standard or criterion.

Improvement

The idea of measuring improvement is near and dear to the hearts of many test users and understandably so. The rationale is that individuals lacking in skill cannot be expected to achieve the level a highly skilled group can attain; thus, the beginning ability level of each participant is considered and the extent to which the individual improved beyond that point is assessed. Similarly, individuals with initial low levels of fitness will be unable to achieve the same level of fitness upon completion of a training program as those who are highly fit. These are valid concerns. Nonetheless, a number of factors make the desired amount of improvement difficult to obtain when dealing with sports and other forms of physical activity. In a school setting, units of instruction are often too short to bring about desired levels of improvement. The background of the student or client can also affect the amount of improvement occurring during a unit. Those who have an adequate understanding of the underlying principles of movement can sometimes learn new skills in a shorter period than those without this knowledge. On the surface, measuring improvement seems to be a reasonable solution to the problems associated with fairly assessing individuals with varying skill levels. However, inherent problems do exist in the measurement of improvement and are discussed in Chapter 20.

Diagnosis

One of the most important uses of measurement in physical education is to diagnose weaknesses in performance. What is wrong with a student's tennis serve? Why does a racquetball club member have an ineffective backhand? Why has an individual's running performance failed to improve? In other words, the diagnostic process helps the participant learn more efficiently. Furthermore, the teacher is able to *teach* more effectively. Diagnostic procedures can be particularly potent when dealing with knowledge in our field. In this case, errors in responding to individual items or clusters of items can pinpoint gaps in the examinee's knowledge of specific content. For example, a student in a badminton class may answer incorrectly many of the test items dealing with rules specific to the singles game in badminton. This suggests a need to review that particular section of the rules book. Of course, tests are not the only means of diagnosing weaknesses, but they are extremely useful in this respect. Some diagnostic tests can be self-administered, allowing the instructor to spend more time meeting other instructional needs.

Prescription

Once weaknesses have been diagnosed, the test user formulates a prescription for correcting these weaknesses. *Exercise prescription* is a widely used term for prescribing the appropriate exercise program for an individual. Of course, teachers frequently prescribe corrective activities for students even though the term *prescription* might not be used. This usage of tests is not limited to exercise programs. When an area needing improvement has been identified on the basis of test results, a prescription for improvement is appropriate regardless of the form of sport or physical activity. Sometimes students can generate their own prescription for improving performance, based on test results.

Grading

Grading is a practice that occurs in almost all physical education programs throughout the United States. Sound grading practices are based on the use of objective tests, since grades represent symbols of achievement. Moreover, once a teacher makes the decision on grades for a given unit, the impact on students is immediate, long-lasting, and usually irreversible. However, grades are not always determined on the basis of tests. The stark reality is that grades are still determined subjectively by many physical education teachers and are frequently based on behavioral assessments such as wearing proper uniforms, effort, and sportsmanship, rather than physical performance. The use of measurement to determine grades is certainly appropriate, but to administer tests solely for the purpose of determining grades suggests a limited view of the value of measurement.

Evaluation of unit of instruction

In planning a unit of instruction, a set of objectives is typically set forth. At the end of the unit, an effort is usually made to determine whether the objectives have been met. Making this judgment is difficult without administering tests, especially if the evidence must be submitted to someone else such as the school principal, club manager, or corporation president. Test data can also be used to demonstrate the effectiveness of programs in a nonschool setting to potential members.

Evaluation of program

The evaluation of individual units of instruction, along with an assessment of the overall program, provides evidence of the effectiveness of a total program. One or two teachers in a school might have met the predetermined objectives in their classes, but overall the school might have fallen short in this respect. A system-wide program evaluation can include the evidence from this unit as well as broader evaluation procedures encompassing the program in the entire system. All of the franchises for a fitness corporation might be evaluated on the ability of the corporation as a whole to meet program objectives and financial goals. Program evaluation forces examination of the total picture rather than narrowly focusing on an isolated unit in a single location.

Classification

Over the years tests have been frequently used to place individuals into groups on the basis of their ability level in motor performance, allowing those with the same or similar classifications to be grouped for purposes of instruction. The underlying assumption is that both learning and instruction are more efficient if the learners have similar ability levels.

Prediction

One way in which tests have been used with increasing frequency is as predictors of various aspects of motor behavior. Coaches have, for many years, been interested in tests that would predict success in their sport. Since sport psychology has blossomed as an area of specialization in physical education, there has been considerable interest in attempting to predict success in a variety of physical activities using measures of psychological and physiological parameters. In some instances the prediction involved Olympic athletes; other efforts were directed to the college athlete. Efforts have also been directed to predicting long-term involvement in physical activity. In exercise physiology, scores on a fitness test might be used to estimate maximal oxygen uptake. The percentage of one's body fat can be predicted using indicators such as skinfold thickness tests. These are merely a few examples of the widespread use of tests as predictors in physical education and exercise science.

NORM-REFERENCED AND CRITERION-REFERENCED MEASUREMENT

Just as a test can be used for various purposes, it can be designed by the test developer to perform different functions. One of these functions is to measure *individual differences.* For many years sport psychologists have been interested in studying an athlete's traits, such as self-motivation. To be able to study self-motivation, it must be possible to measure it. Thus, if a sport psychologist plans an experiment on self-motivation, a test would be administered to the athletes at some point during the experiment. If all athletes obtained the same score on the test, how would the results be interpreted? It would be logical to suggest that all athletes participating in the experiment had the same level of self-motivation, yet this outcome is not very likely. A group of athletes—in fact, any group of individuals—would be expected to have differing levels of a trait. The test of the trait, in other words, is expected to detect *individual differences* in the trait. In the early part of the twentieth century, most of the advances in measurement were made by individuals interested in this approach.

Educators have also been interested in this function of measurement. One way of knowing how much a student has achieved is to examine his or her score in relation to the scores of others on the same test. In essence, a student's score is *compared* to other student's scores. Here again, individual differences are anticipated because some students are expected to perform better than others. This function identifies the test as a **norm-referenced test.** The score is compared to a set of norms. For example, scores on the American Alliance for Health, Physical Education, Recreation, and Dance (AAHPERD) Youth Fitness Test are usually compared to the national norms for the participant's gender and age group. (Refer to Chapter 11 for abbreviated forms of these tables.) Generally, the educator is interested in the performance of the students in relation to other students.

Although educators are aware that students differ in many ways, they are, however, sometimes unconcerned about individual differences. Suppose, for example, a physical education teacher identifies a cardiorespiratory function objective for his or her classes and plans to use a test of the mile run to measure this objective. A standard that reflects a satisfactory level of cardiorespiratory endurance is also set for the test. For example, a standard of 7 minutes and 15 seconds is set for 16-year-old boys. In other words, the goal for each 16-year-old boy in all classes is to run the mile in 7:15 by the end of the school year. This type of test is called a **criterion-referenced test.** A standard of performance is set that all or most students are expected to meet. The standard assumes importance because it is *referenced to a criterion behavior.* In the above example, the criterion behavior is a satisfactory level of cardiorespiratory function. Students who meet the standard are labeled *masters* and those who do not are labeled *non-masters.* Another name for a test performing this type of function is a **mastery test.** There are no restrictions on the number of students who master the test. The question of interest is whether or not the student was able to meet the predetermined standard. In a norm-referenced context, the question of interest concerns how the student's score compares with the scores of others.

Each of these types of measurement, norm-referenced and criterion-referenced, provides a valuable approach to testing. To suggest that one function is better than another is not meaningful, because one approach may be more desirable in a specific context. Most of the published tests in physical education are norm-referenced measures; however, interest in criterion-referenced testing has increased in recent years, especially in the schools. This interest should lead to an increase in the development of new mastery tests.

FORMATIVE AND SUMMATIVE EVALUATION

A number of new terms are being introduced in this chapter that will be used throughout this textbook. The term *evaluation* was defined in a previous section as the interpretation of a score. The process of evaluation can take place at any time during a program or unit of instruction. In an aerobic dance class, for instance, an informal self-evaluation often takes place several times during each session of an instructional unit. The participant engages in vigorous physical activity, stopping to measure heart rate at periodic intervals. Evaluation of the heart rate is accomplished by judging whether the rate is high enough to provide the desired physiological benefits. When evaluation occurs *during* the training period or instructional unit, it is known as **formative evaluation.** This type of evaluation is not uncommon in physical fitness units, where performance is often monitored on a daily basis. Formative evaluation is also appropriate for other aspects of the physical education curriculum in the schools but has been used less frequently in this setting. More typically, tests are administered at the end of the unit. When evaluation takes place solely at the end of a unit, it is referred to as **summative evaluation.** For example, the last 2 days of a tennis unit might be devoted to administering one or two skills tests, a written test, and a test of playing ability. The test scores are usually used to evaluate achievement. In a physical education class this may be translated to a unit grade. In a private tennis club, and perhaps in a school setting, these test scores might be used as an indicator of the effectiveness of instruction.

When only summative evaluation takes place, it is often too late to correct problems that have been identified. In a school setting students move to another unit of instruction; thus if the objectives of the previous unit were not met, it is too late to remedy the situation. Had evaluation taken place during the unit of instruction, deficiencies could have been addressed in a more positive way. The teacher could have prescribed activities to correct these deficiencies. Should formative evaluation be used in a nonschool setting? Yes, the provision of feedback to clients on an ongoing basis helps them understand their strengths and weaknesses. In fact, when *exercise* is the primary mode of physical activity, it is only through regular evaluation that the instructor can monitor the appropriateness of the exercise. When the physical activity involves a sport, private clubs are less likely to engage in formal evaluation, either formative or summative.

Although formative evaluation has been emphasized in this section of the book, one should not assume it is superior to summative evaluation. Sometimes one approach is more appropriate than the other, depending upon the reasons for evaluating. Formative evaluation is stressed here simply because it has been neglected in the past. Using either approach exclusively is not necessary. To maximize the effectiveness of evaluation procedures, both formative and summative evaluation should be used.

A BRIEF HISTORY OF MEASUREMENT

In the late 1880s a number of prominent physical educators were also medical doctors. They were primarily interested in body symmetry and proportion and prescribed exercise to modify body size. Thus anthropometric measures were used extensively during this period. In 1861 Edward Hitchcock of Amherst, Massachusetts, developed standards of age, height, and weight; chest, arm, and forearm girths; and strength of the upper arm. He was the leading authority in anthropometry between 1860 and 1880. Because of his contributions in this area, Hitchcock is often called the father of measurement in physical education. In 1878 Dudley Sargent of Harvard University developed similar tables of standards. Strength tests were also used during this early period. Sargent was an active contributor in this area as well as in anthropometry, developing the Intercollegiate Strength Test in the 1870s.

Widespread usage of both strength and anthropometric measurement lagged in the early 1900s. Although interest in the measurement of strength subsequently resumed, anthropometric measures have never regained the prominence received in the early days. Nonetheless, this type of measure still holds an important place in the physical education field in measuring growth, body composition, and body types. At the turn of the century, there was considerable interest in measuring cardiorespiratory function because of the development of measures of endurance and of heart and lung tests. At that time there was also the general perception that individuals became muscle-bound by strength exercises, thus hindering athletic performance. The first test of cardiac function, the Blood Ptosis Test, was developed by C. Ward Crampton in 1905. Crampton noted changes in cardiac rate and arterial pressure on assuming the erect position from a supine position. In the 1920s more sophisticated work was published on the measurement of physical efficiency. E.C. Schneider designed a test used in aviation in World War II to determine fatigue and physical condition for flying. The relationship between pulse rate and blood pressure in the reclining position and the standing position was determined, as well as the ability to recover to normal standing values after a measured bout of exercise. In 1931 W.W. Tuttle modified a block-stepping test similar to a step test measuring endurance and general state of training called the Tuttle Pulse-Ratio Test, a forerunner of the Harvard Step Test developed in 1943. The efficiency of the circulatory system was indicated by the increase in heart rate during exercise and the speed with which the heart rate returned to normal after exercise. Work in this area became increasingly sophisticated with the development of the Balke Treadmill Test in 1954 and other similar measures. These latter tests still represent the standard for measuring cardiorespiratory function in a laboratory setting.

The earliest tests of sports skills were developed as part of athletic performance batteries. For example, in 1913 the Athletic Badge Tests were published by the Playground and Recreation Association of America. David Brace at the University of Texas first attempted to measure a group of fundamental skills for a specific sport, basketball, in 1924. He also worked on the development of tests for indoor baseball and soccer. In a 1930 measurement textbook, Bovard and Cozens noted that the area of skill testing was relatively untouched (Bovard and Cozens, 1930). They identified 1916 as the approximate year that the physical education curriculum was broadened to include game activities. Therefore, they noted, physical educators ought to be prepared to measure sports skills as well as other aspects of physical activity. Although tests were being developed during this time, many were not published. Several outstanding measurement specialists in physical education emerged during this period, including Ruth Glassow at the University of Wisconsin. Skills test development was emphasized at Wisconsin, and Glassow and Broer published a measurement book in 1938, which was almost entirely devoted to skills tests and batteries. Charles McCloy (1939) at the University of Iowa was a strong critic of subjective measures of skill in his 1939 textbook; similarly, Harrison Clarke was a critic at the University of Oregon in his 1945 textbook (Clarke, 1945). Subsequently Gladys Scott and her students at the University of Iowa made many contributions to the development of skills tests in the field of physical education. A number of these tests were described in the 1959 textbook by Scott and French.

After a temporary lag in the use of strength tests, interest was restored with the development of new tests in this area, such as the Strength Index and Physical Fitness Index developed by Frederick Rand Rogers in 1925. This type of measurement became much more precise with the development of the cable tensiometer tests by Harrison Clarke. Clarke's innovative thinking led to the design of equipment allowing an investigator to measure the strength of many different body parts. As more sophisticated equipment such as the dynamometers and weight-training machines became available to the physical educator, other approaches to testing strength were feasible.

The history of physical fitness testing is described in Chapters 11 and 12. Up to the 1950s physical fitness was typically stressed when the United States was engaged in war. In 1954 the results of administering the Kraus-Weber Test of Minimum Strength to American and English children were published. For the first time, fitness was stressed as important to the individual's health rather than solely as an indicator of readiness for combat. (Refer to Chapters 11 and 12 for details.)

Up to this point, one type of testing in the physical education field has been ignored—the measurement of general motor ability. Motor ability is an expression that was familiar to physical educators in the early 1900s. Actually, as early as 1894 the Normal School of Gymnastics in Milwaukee and the Gymnastics Societies in Cleveland administered batteries of tests that measured ability in events such as jumping, climbing, shot-putting, lifting, and so forth. As time passed, many schools began to institute testing programs, including basic events from track and field. Most of the test batteries developed then had many similarities, and none of the original batteries was based on sound test development as we know it today. In the 1930-1940 era, a number of test batteries purporting to measure basic motor ability were published, based on a much stronger scientific rationale. However, the overall validity of these batteries was never firmly established. Yet the popularity of the concept of motor ability continued into the late 1950s. At that time the concept began to be questioned in light of emerging research evidence. This reexamination is described in greater detail in Chapter 15. Suffice it to say that the idea of general motor ability, while intuitively appealing, has never been verified scientifically.

In conclusion, the development of tests in physical education has occurred despite the absence of a strategy for systematically adding to various categories of tests and modifying tests when necessary. More attention has been paid to field and laboratory tests of various physiological attributes largely because of the existence of exercise physiology laboratories in departments of physical education throughout the United States. These laboratories provide a mechanism for systematic work on test development. No similar environment exists for the development of skills tests and tests of basic movement. As a result, there is a significant void in the availability of tests, in particular for preschool and elementary school-age children in physical education. This deficit points to the pressing need for a test service to provide the impetus for the development of tests of all aspects of motor behavior.

RECENT CHANGES IN MEASUREMENT PRACTICES

Measurement and evaluation courses have been taught for many years in physical education programs throughout the United States. Tests of sports skills, fitness, and motor ability, for example, have been advocated in these courses. Presumably, some testing has taken place in physical education programs as well as in exercise and sport programs in nonschool settings. Have measurement practices in the field changed in recent years? Although judging the extent to which changes have taken place is difficult, events transpiring over the past two decades point to the need for certain changes to occur. The most prominent events include modification of sports, the use of competency-based tests in the public schools, the accessibility of microcomputers, the passage of Title IX, and a concern for the development of health-related physical fitness.

Reflection of modification of sports

When a test of a sport skill is developed, the validity of the test rests, in part, on the degree to which the test measures the skill as it is used most efficiently in the sport. For instance, it would be illogical to design a test of the basketball jump shot that requires the examinee to take the test at a distance of 30 feet from the basket since the average student in a physical education class would not attempt a shot from that distance. On the other hand, the sport itself can be modified over the years so that tests that were previously valid are no longer appropriate. As the sport of volleyball changed to a power sport, the use of several volleyball skills also changed. Years ago, players would use an underarm serve that was returned to a front-court teammate using a pass. Power volleyball incorporated an overarm serve usually returned, again to a front-court team-mate, using a bump. The Liba and Stauff Volleyball Pass Test (Collins and Hodges, 1978) was developed for the pass as it was used in an earlier version of the sport. In the test the overhead pass was measured over a distance equivalent to executing the pass from the backcourt to the forecourt. In power volleyball, the ball is typically hit from the backcourt to the forecourt using a bump. A pass usually follows, but at a shorter distance and lower height than the dimensions required in the earlier version of the sport. This invalidates the Liba and Stauff Test as a measure of the pass in power volleyball; however, the test can easily be modified to accurately measure the constraints of the game as it is now played. Changing the constraints of a sport can invalidate a test. This does not mean the test should be discarded but rather that the test should be modified to fit the current version of the game. The implications of these changes are discussed in more detail in Chapters 8 and 10.

Competency-based evaluation

Competency-based evaluation is based on the premise that there are certain competencies identifiable for a group of examinees that ought to be mastered. A test is developed for each competency, and a test score is selected as the standard representing the criterion behavior—the behavior representing mastery of the competency. Individuals who meet or exceed the standards pass the competency-based evaluation; all others fail. Decisions made on the basis of this type of evaluation can have a tremendous impact on the individuals involved. For example, some states have developed a competency-based program for their high school students. Students who fail to meet the standards expected for a high school graduate are sometimes denied a high school diploma. These programs are highly controversial, since the decisions about those who are competent and those who are not will never be error-free. In other words, the decisions will sometimes be wrong. The most serious consequence of an incorrect decision is the classification of a student as unsuccessful in meeting the standard, when, in reality, the student is competent. At best, the student must undertake remedial work to obtain a diploma that should have been awarded in the first place. In some states competency-based evaluation is applied in the certification of teachers. A standardized test of knowledge about teaching and content areas is administered to prospective teachers. If the predetermined standard for prospective teachers in a specified area (e.g., art, physical education, or mathematics) is not met, the student will not be certified to teach in that state. As you might suspect, these programs also promote controversy because 100% accuracy is not possible when decisions are made. Criterion-referenced tests are generally used in competency-based programs, and these tests must be rigorously developed.

Microcomputers

In the early 1970s it was unusual for students in a measurement class in physical education to own minicalculators. Analyzing a set of test scores was accomplished either by hand or by using a large desk calculator, if available. Although the small, hand calculators were being sold, they were expensive and capable of only a few basic arithmetical operations. By the end of this decade, the cost of the minicalculator had dropped to an affordable price and the capability of the instrument had markedly expanded, allowing many physical education majors in measurement classes to use their own minicalculators. Now vast improvements in the microchip have resulted in the development of small desk-top computers called microcomputers, which are gradually becoming more affordable. By 1990 microcomputers will be available at a fairly modest cost. Eventually it will be commonplace for measurement students to own their own microcomputers and carry small, portable ones to class. Since the impact of microcomputers on measurement and evaluation in physical education will be significant, two chapters in this textbook are devoted to this topic. Certainly this technological advance will facilitate measurement and evaluation practices in the field.

Reassessment of physical performance standards for girls and women

When physical education programs were first promoted in the United States, providing separate programs for boys and girls was not uncommon. Many colleges and universities even established separate physical education departments for men and women. Almost all activities were taught in separate classes for males and females. In 1975 a set of regulations known as **Title IX** of the Education Amendments of 1972 became effective. This legislation required fair and equal opportunities in all phases of education, including evaluation. It pointed to the need for greater attention to ability grouping and performance standards.

Three subparagraphs in the Title IX legislation are directed specifically to physical education.

Subparagraph 86.34 (b) provides that ability grouping in physical education classes is permissible provided that the composition of the groups is determined objectively with regard to individual performance rather than on the basis of sex. Subparagraph 86.34 (c) allows separation by sex within physical education classes during competition in wrestling, boxing, ice hockey, football, basketball, and other sports, the purpose or major activity of which involves bodily contact. Subparagraph 86.34 (d), requiring the use of standards for measuring skill or progress in physical education which do not impact adversely on members of one sex, is intended to eliminate a problem raised by many comments that, where a goal-oriented standard is used to assess skill or progress, women almost invariably score lower than men. For example, if progress is measured by determining whether an individual can perform twenty-five push-ups, the standard may be virtually out-of-reach for many more women than men because of the difference in strength between average persons of each sex. Accordingly, the appropriate standard might be an individual progress chart based on the number of push-ups which might be expected of that individual (Federal Register, 1975: 24132).

More research needs to be conducted on sex differences in motor performance. Some of these differences may be caused by differences in basic physiological factors; others may be culturally induced. As opportunities increase for women to participate in athletics, their physical abilities and skills are presumably also increasing. These changes should be monitored on an annual basis.

In the summer of 1981 the Illinois State Board of Education sponsored a Physical Education Ability Grouping and Performance Evaluation Symposium. The purpose of the symposium was to identify guidelines that physical education teachers could use to develop their own objective, sex-fair standards of measures for grouping and evaluating students. An outgrowth of the symposium was a useful publication including practical tips and techniques for the teacher (Illinois State Board of Education, 1982).

Increase in the use of physical fitness tests

Historically, Americans have been concerned about physical fitness in times of war. Many young men who were drafted during previous wars were not physically fit at the time of their induction. Thus, it is not surprising that fitness received considerable emphasis when the country was involved in a war. This emphasis was also felt in the schools, especially in physical education classes. Between wars, however, the interest in fitness waned. This remained true for many years despite the stress placed on fitness by presidents such as Eisenhower and Kennedy. This pattern began to change in the 1970s when Americans became concerned about their own fitness for health-related reasons, not merely because fitness was necessary to fight in a war. The fitness explosion has led to a proliferation of fitness clubs and health spas throughout the country. Many of these organizations administer health-related fitness tests to their clients. The AAHPERD has published the Health-Related Physical Fitness Test. In 1982 this test battery was approved as one of the official fitness tests of the Alliance. The Alliance, along with the President's Council on Physical Fitness, also sponsors the Youth Fitness Test. Either the Youth Fitness Test or the Health-Related Physical Fitness Test can be used in the new FITNESSGRAM program (1983), which provides computerized test results and an exercise prescription for each child participating in the program. It is probably fair to say that the use of tests measuring fitness has increased relative to the use of other types of tests in our field.

The United States Department of Health and Human Services (1985) recently published the results of a nationwide study of youth fitness. In this study three major questions were asked: (1) How fit are American boys and girls in grades 5 through 12? (2) What are the physical activity patterns of children and youth in these grades? (3) How do differences in physical activity patterns affect measured fitness? As a result of this investigation, a new set of fitness norms was formulated. These norms are presented in Appendix F.

SUMMARY

Measurement and evaluation represent essential aspects of most careers in physical education and exercise science. Tests are used for many purposes and can range from simple field measures to highly sophisticated laboratory measures. The more recent changes in the measurement of motor behavior have resulted from the widespread use of competency-based measurement, the availability of microcomputers, modifications of various sports, the advent of Title IX legislation, and the increased interest in health-related fitness. New approaches to testing motor skills and abilities have recently been proposed. Technological advances will lead to modifications of tests and testing programs, enabling physical educators and exercise scientists to measure with greater precision and accuracy.

LEARNING EXPERIENCES

1. Try to remember when tests were used in your high school physical education program. What types of tests were used? Were they administered at the end of each unit or throughout the unit? How were the test results used?
2. Familiarize yourself with one of the tests of motor skill or physical fitness included in this textbook. Think of ways in which the test could be used (a) in a school setting and (b) in a nonschool setting. Write a brief paper summarizing your thoughts.
3. Interview a physical education teacher who teaches in a public or private school in your area, or invite one to visit one of your measurement classes. Ask the teacher about the tests used in his or her classes. Ask about the major problems a physical education teacher faces in implementing a sound testing program.

REFERENCES

American Alliance for Health, Physical Education, Recreation and Dance and the Institute for Aerobics Research. 1983. FITNESSGRAM instructor certification manual. Dallas: The Institute for Aerobics Research.

Bovard, J.F., and Cozens, F.W. 1930. Tests and measurements in physical education. Philadelphia: W.B. Saunders Co.

Clarke, H.H. 1976. Application of measurement to health and physical education, ed. 5, Englewood Cliffs, N.J.: Prentice-Hall, Inc.

Collins, D.R., and Hodges, P.B. 1978. A comprehensive guide to sports skills tests and measurement. Springfield, Ill.: Charles C Thomas, Publisher.

Illinois State Board of Education. 1982. Tips and techniques: ability grouping and performance evaluation in physical education. Springfield, Ill.: Illinois State Board of Education.

McCloy, C.H. 1942. Tests and measurements in health and physical education. New York: Appleton-Century-Crofts.

Rogers, F.R. 1925. Physical capacity tests in the administration of physical education. New York: Teachers College Contribution to Education.

Scott, M.G., and French, E. 1959. Measurement and evaluation in physical education. Dubuque, Iowa: Wm C Brown Group.

United States Department of Health and Human Services. 1985. Summary of findings from the National Children and Youth Fitness Study. Journal of Physical Education, Recreation, and Dance **56**(1): 43-90.

United States Department of Health, Education, and Welfare. 1975. Federal Register **40**(108), June 4.

ANNOTATED READINGS

Daves, C.W. 1984. The uses and misuses of tests. Washington: Jossey-Bass Inc., Publishers.

Addresses several major issues associated with the use of tests: the public stake in proper test use, professional standards for proper test use, issues in test use in schools, and test use and the law; written by experts in measurement, but in readable, nontechnical language.

Disch, J.G. 1983. The measurement of basic stuff. Journal of Physical Education, Recreation, and Dance **54**(8): 17-29.

A series of articles on the measurement of the body of knowledge in physical education as presented in the Basic Stuff Series, published by the American Alliance for Health, Physical Education, Recreation and Dance; includes articles on measurement in exercise physiology, motor development, biomechanics, humanities in physical education, psychosocial aspects of physical education, and motor learning.

Perkins, M.R. 1982. Minimum competency in testing: what? why? why not? Educational Measurement **1**(4): 5-9, 26.

Presents various definitions of minimum competency testing; describes the perceived benefits of this use of tests; discusses the perceived costs of minimum competency testing; valuable reading for teachers involved in competency-based testing.

Ross, J.G., and Gilbert, G.G. 1985. A summary of findings. Journal of Physical Education, Recreation and Dance **56**(1): 45-53.

A description of the National Children and Youth Fitness Study, which was designed to determine the fitness status and activity levels of students in grades 5 through 12; includes a brief overview of the data collection procedures, new fitness standards, and a summary of other results.

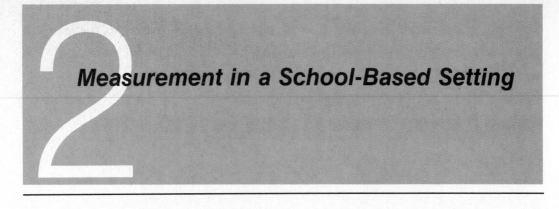

Measurement in a School-Based Setting

KEY WORDS *Watch for these words as you read the following chapter:*

accountability	curriculum objectives	needs assessment
affective domain	evaluation objectives	psychomotor domain
behavioral objectives	immediate objectives	standard of performance
cognitive domain	level of behavior	taxonomy
condition (objective)	long-range goals	terminal behavior
content (objective)		

If you plan to teach physical education in the schools, you will be expected to evaluate your students' performance on a variety of tasks. Most schools use several testing programs that have varying degrees of formality. The most formal program is the administration of standardized achievement tests, although these will not comprise a sizable part of the testing because not many standardized tests are available in the physical education field. The American Alliance for Health, Physical Education, Recreation, and Dance (AAHPERD), our national organization, has published two standardized tests for the schools: the Health-Related Physical Fitness Test, which is described in Chapter 11, and the Youth Fitness Test, which is presented in Chapter 12. A series of test manuals for several sports can also be obtained through the AAHPERD. Certain types of standardized tests have been developed for special populations, such as students with impairments or children in elementary school, although many of these tests are designed to diagnose special perceptual or motor problems. Of the tests mentioned thus far, all are measures of motor behavior. Only one standardized knowledge test has been published in the field. In 1970 the Cooperative Knowledge Test was made available as a measure of the knowledge students in grades 4 through 12 have about physical education. However, the content of a knowledge test ought to be revised periodically, and this test has not been updated since its original development. This more formal part of the testing program is usually the basis for informing people outside the school of the physical educa-

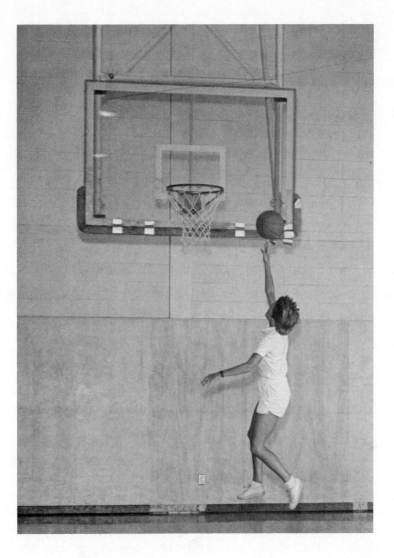

tion program's effectiveness. Reports of test results and comparisons with national norms are prepared for parents, other schools in the district, the school board, and all tax-paying citizens in the community.

Testing also occurs at a less formal level in the schools. At this level the teacher selects or develops tests to be used in his or her classes. This differs from school-wide testing in which all students at a given grade level are administered the same standardized test. For example, Mr. Moore, a physical education teacher, might use the Health-Related Physical Fitness Test to measure the fitness of his students because it is a requirement in all physical education classes in the system. In contrast, it might be Mr. Moore's responsibility to select other tests to be administered to his students throughout a unit or at the end of a unit. These tests may or may not be used by any of the other physical education teachers in his school or school system. The fact that this level of testing is less formal is not meant to suggest that the tests are handled more casually. *Less formal* in this context means that the decision to use certain tests is made individually rather than on a school-wide basis. One of the positive features of our society is that schools operate in various ways to achieve the goals of education. For instance, in some schools the entire staff of physical education teachers may decide that a certain series of tests will be used in all classes in the school. In others, each teacher makes these decisions; although this may result in different tests being used by each teacher, the objectives of the physical education program are the same for all.

In this chapter you will learn how to make some of the most basic decisions in teaching. How do you decide what to test in your physical education classes? This decision can be made in a systematic manner if behavioral objectives have been properly prepared. This process is described in the forthcoming sections after a discussion of the current status of testing in physical education.

DO PHYSICAL EDUCATION TEACHERS USE TESTS?

When you accept your first teaching position, what sort of expectations should you have about the testing program? The program may be excellent or virtually nonexistent. Probably most programs fall somewhere in-between these extremes.

In the 1958 edition of a measurement textbook by Mathews, he referred to an informal survey of 50 student teachers on the grading practices in their cooperating schools. In 80% of the systems, the student's mark was based solely on being present and in uniform daily. In 1974 Cousins gave a keynote speech at a measurement symposium at Indiana University. He cited a number of incidents reflecting the misuse of tests in our field and suggested that the greatest misuse of tests was the lack of use by physical education teachers. In 1978 Morrow conducted a survey on the use of evaluation techniques and concluded that tests were simply not being used in the schools he sampled. Assessment of students was made on the basis of dress and participation. All of these reports were published before 1980; surely the situation has improved. A 1982 survey of Florida physical education teachers (Imwold, Rider, and Johnson, 1982) suggests this is not true, however. A portion of their survey appears in the boxed material.

Skills tests were used by only 54% of the teachers; less than 40% used knowledge tests. Skills tests were administered more frequently by female teachers, junior high teachers, and those with 4 or more years of experience. In general,

---

Use of evaluation in Florida public school physical education programs*

Use of tests

Skills tests	54%
Written tests	Less than 40%
Measurement model	Predominantly norm-referenced
Major users	Women teachers
	Junior high teachers
	Teachers with more experience
	Teachers with coaching responsibilities
Least frequent users	Elementary physical education teachers

Determination of grades

Bases for grading	Performance scale (less than 50%)
	Subjective assessment
Type of grade	Letter (high school)
	P-F (elementary school)

---

*Modified from Imwold, C.H., Rider, R.A., and Johnson, D.J.

---

norm-referenced tests were selected more frequently than criterion-referenced tests, with the latter being used primarily by senior high school teachers with 4 or more years of experience. Few teachers graded on the curve. The most popular method of grading was a performance scale; however, this was used by less than 50% of the teachers. This survey clearly demonstrates that many teachers still use a subjective assessment of effort, sportsmanship, class attendance, and assessment of behavior to determine grades. The subjective approach was most frequently used by elementary physical education teachers, the group most likely to use no tests at all. (However, elementary physical education classes often meet infrequently and for short durations.) Although it has been suggested that coaches are too involved in athletics to be conscientious about their teaching, the Florida survey showed that teachers with coaching responsibilities used more skills tests than those without these responsibilities.

Where should the blame for this dilemma be placed? The likely culprit may appear to be the physical education teacher in the public schools. Perhaps some teachers are to blame, yet there are teachers who do use tests and use them very effectively. Before the total blame is placed hastily on teachers, the situation should be looked at from a broader perspective. King (1983) suggested that the tests available to physical education teachers are not being used because they are not appropriate for a school setting. He was not enthusiastic about these tests because most of them are norm-referenced, require too much time to administer, and often use an overly elaborate test setup. His solution to the problem is, at least in part, to develop new types of criterion-referenced tests that have satisfactory validity and reliability, and yet are practical enough to be used in schools. While there is considerable merit in King's criticisms, tests are available that are appropriate for the school setting and feasible from an administrative standpoint. However, many of these tests require the use of a special test setup, such as a target. Taking time to prepare for testing should not be viewed as a burden but simply as a part of good teaching. Certainly teachers will come across tests that require expensive equipment their schools cannot afford. If a version of the equipment cannot be constructed by school personnel, then the test cannot be used. Also, some tests require so much time to set up that they may not be reasonable options. Yet this does not mean that all tests requiring set-up time should not be used. A test requires preplanning, organization, and preparation time.

Of course, evaluating students by observing and rating their performance is always possible. This may be an effective approach if the rating scale is well defined and can be demonstrated to be valid. Unfortunately, this approach is all too often used in the worst possible way—by merely looking at the student and jotting down a score, with no breakdown of the component of skill being rated and no assurance that the teacher is rating objectively. This is a form of *subjective evaluation* that is discussed more thoroughly later in this book.

What is the best way to begin planning your testing program once you arrive at your new school? First, review the objectives that have been agreed upon for the total school as well as the physical education program. Always keep in mind that you are a part of a *total* school system and that the physical education program should contribute to the objectives of the school. The physical education objectives may be written for the program as a whole. Then you may be expected to prepare the objectives specifically for your classes. After all, how will you know what to evaluate, if you do not know what your objectives are?

PREPARING EDUCATIONAL OBJECTIVES

The process of preparing educational objectives is the first step in implementing the concept of **accountability,** that is, holding teachers in a school accountable for the results of their program. An educational objective can be defined as a statement of proposed change in the learner (Mager, 1962). This change will presumably take place as the result of planned learning experiences. When an objective is stated in terms of the performance or behavior that the student will exhibit when the objective is successfully attained, it is referred to as a **behavioral objective.** Note that the reference is to the behavior of the *student*. Objectives can be written in two ways: a description of the expected behavior of the teacher and a description of the expected behavior of the student. The latter type is of interest in a behavioral objective because the primary interest in education is the student's achievement. The assumption is that educators will teach in such a way that the desired results will be attained. Thus, the following is the first rule of thumb in writing behavioral objectives: Incorporate the behavior the student is expected to display when the objective has been successfully met. By stating objectives in terms of student response rather than teaching material, both the student and the teacher will know precisely what to expect. Also, stating objectives in behavioral terms helps to establish evaluation procedures that relate to student performance as it has been described.

In a school setting both long-range and immediate objectives are usually identified. **Long-range goals** usually specify the behavior of a fully educated person and are by nature general. Typically these goals are first established within the school system. To learn whether students are moving toward the long-range goals, **immediate objectives** are determined that provide guidance for the selection of activities to be incorporated into a unit of instruction. These objectives can be attained in a relatively short period.

Many terms have been used to describe different types of behavioral objectives. In this book the terms **long-range goals, curriculum objectives,** and **evaluation objectives** will be used to specify three levels of objectives that establish a link between long-range goals and immediate objectives. The relationship among these levels is shown in Fig. 2-1.

FIG. 2-1. *Relationship among levels of objectives.*

The first level, *long-range goals*, represents the long-term general goals of education that describe the final product of a complete education. For example:

1. The student will develop the fundamental movement skills and abilities.
2. The student will develop adequate interest and motivation for participation in physical activity as an adult.
3. The student shall become a citizen who is informed about community health issues and able to use this information intelligently.

These goals might be a part of the overall objectives of the school or even the school system. New teachers' orientation will probably include a review of these long-range goals.

Once the long-range goals have been established, curriculum objectives are derived from these goals. This second level, *curriculum objectives*, is the reduction of the general goals into precise behaviors that reflect the terminal performance of students successfully completing an instructional unit during a course or following an entire course. Instead of stating expectations in general terms, curriculum objectives are written for specific courses or groups of courses. These objectives represent examples of ways in which the broad-based goals can be met. Note, for example, two objectives students might be expected to meet on completing elementary school physical education:

1. Can execute the hop, skip, jump, run, throw, and other basic movement patterns.
2. Can execute the above movement patterns with varying combinations of time, space, and force.

At the third level *evaluation objectives* are used to describe at the unit or course level of specificity a step-by-step hierarchy, each step representing a behavior more sophisticated than the previous one. Evaluation objectives are derived from the curriculum objectives and specify the standards that students are expected to meet after the objectives have been implemented. An essential part is the specification of a standard of performance. The following examples of evaluation objectives are related to the second curriculum objective in the previous paragraph:

1. Can run at fast and slow speeds.
2. Can run while the body is at high and low levels in space.
3. Can run using heavy and light force.
4. Can run with body at different levels in space, using a slow speed and heavy force.

Usually the curriculum and evaluation objectives will have been written previously by the physical education staff. However, you may be responsible for writing the evaluation objectives. Notice that the evaluation objectives may not specify exactly how the skills should be measured. This may be determined either by the physical education staff as a whole or by the individual teacher. In a large high school it is not unusual for the physical education teachers to work cooperatively to develop a testing program. In an elementary school where the physical education teacher often works on a part-time basis, the testing program is usually developed by the individual teacher.

Behavioral objectives become increasingly specific and require different levels of decision making. Since the third level of objectives, the evaluation objectives, are most likely to be developed by individuals, details on expanding them into legitimate behavioral objectives are described in detail in the next section.

Selection of objectives

Covering all aspects of the physical education program within a school program is impossible; therefore, choices must be made before writing objectives. Before beginning, ask two important questions: What are the bases for the choices? Are the choices sound?

Curriculum developers often use the following information as a basis for making choices:

1. Data regarding the students themselves, their pretest abilities, knowledges, skills, interests, attitudes, and needs.
2. Data regarding the demands society is making on the graduates, opportunities and defects of contemporary society that have significance for education, and similar data.
3. Suggestions of specialists in various fields regarding the contribution they think their subjects can make to the education of students. (Tyler, 1951:50)

You may find these suggestions useful in writing objectives for your classes. Of course, considering that information could still lead to an excessive number of objectives, but the final choice should be based on a sound philosophy of physical education, the school's philosophy, and principles derived from motor learning. If other physical education teachers are in your school, a mutually agreeable approach to the formulation of objectives should be reached.

Decision making based on the previous information may take place at the district level, but a number of choices are still left as the daily instructional program is planned. Certainly these choices will be influenced by personal interests and values. In a soccer unit, for example, an educator must decide which skills to teach, how much time to devote to learning skills, how much time to devote to playing the game, and so on. Most teachers and coaches would agree that several soccer skills are essential to the game. Beyond these, the teacher makes choices based on personal values, interests, knowledge of course content, and level of students, as considered in the perspective of the expectations of the physical education staff within a school and the school district as a whole.

Writing one's own objectives is not always necessary. Another teacher or a staff of teachers may have written behavioral objectives for specific units of instruction in physical education, and these objectives may be suitable for you, especially as a new teacher. However, you may wish to individualize those objectives, which requires writing your own. Even if you initially use someone else's objectives, you will probably want to modify these objectives after you become a more experienced teacher. Of course, this assumes that objectives have not been predetermined for physical education within your school. If you feel the objectives should be modified, you should recommend your proposed revisions to the other teachers. Objectives should be so clearly stated that anyone could read them and understand exactly what is required. Keep this in mind as you clarify your values, set goals, and define standards.

Writing objectives in behavioral terms

Writing sound objectives is not an easy task, and there is no substitute for actual practice in writing them. It is helpful to begin by working with other colleagues in small groups, having each person write an objective and then share it. To write the objective, follow these three basic steps:

1. Identify the **terminal behavior.**
2. Further define the desired behavior by describing the important conditions under which the behavior will be expected to occur.
3. Specify the criteria of acceptable performance by describing how well the learner must perform to be considered acceptable. (Mager, 1962:12).

In the first step, *student behavior,* not teacher behavior, is described since student achievement is of greater concern than the material the teacher will present. The second step deals with the *surrounding circumstances.* Any given behavior could occur under many possible conditions. The third step refers to evidence that the student has *achieved* the objective.

The basic attributes of a good objective—content, behavior, condition, and standard of performance—are shown in Fig. 2-2. **Content** is the material or skill the student is expected to learn. **Behavior** refers to the process the learner is

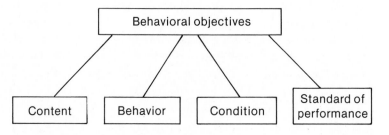

FIG. 2-2. *Attributes of a behavioral objective.*

presumed to use in learning the content. (Levels of behavior are described in the next section.) **Condition** refers to the situation in which the behavior is expected to occur. **Standard of performance** is the degree to which the student is expected to meet the objective.

Objectives are always written for a specific age group at a specified level of skill. Sometimes a list of objectives like those in the boxed material is developed. What is wrong with these objectives? Certainly the list delineates exactly what students would be expected to learn in a basketball unit. However, the statements of objectives are *incomplete*. Only *content*, one of several necessary attributes, is included.

Content of a basketball unit

1. Development of skills: passing, catching, dribbling, shooting, guarding, etc.
2. Development of ability to play game.
3. Knowledge of rules.
4. Knowledge of safety factors.
5. Knowledge of appropriate principles of movement.

Let's look at the basketball unit more closely. If you plan to teach the basketball chest pass, you undoubtedly have specific skill goals in mind. If not, this is where you should begin. Ask yourself questions concerning how well the student should be able to pass and under what conditions. If there is no statement of learner behavior, too many interpretations of an objective are possible. Let's assume you are teaching a basketball unit to beginning basketball players in the eighth grade. Start by asking yourself to describe the situation in which the student will be expected to perform. Presumably you will want to see good passes in the game situation, but you do not begin by placing beginning students in a game. Besides, in a game setting, the players may not have an equal chance to use the pass. You probably still feel the pass is a skill everyone should be exposed to, so you will undoubtedly teach the skill to your students and have them practice it in a drill setting. The following objective, then, might be appropriate for all students in the class:

Objective—basketball pass: Given the ball and a partner in a practice situation, the student will be able to pass the ball 15 feet to a partner with both speed and accuracy. (In this example, the partner is stationary. An intermediate objective might be desirable where the partner is moving in a practice situation.)

Even though this objective includes both content and student behavior, its interpretation might differ. Questions like the following arise: How much speed and accuracy are desired? Is every student expected to master the objective? How often should the student be able to meet the performance standard?

It is obvious that no standard of performance is given in the above objective. In a properly written behavioral objective, a minimal level of performance that most students should be able to attain is specified. How fast and how accurately should the basketball be thrown? The following is one revision of the objective:

Objective (1st revision): The student will be able to pass the basketball with a flat trajectory and with enough accuracy to place the ball at a partner's mid-chest level 8 out of 10 times. The ball will be passed over a distance of 15 feet.

Now there is a clearer picture of the desired ball path. It is also clear that the student will throw the ball 10 times and is expected to meet the standard 8 of those times. Although the objective has been improved, it still might not satisfy some teachers. How, they might ask, does one decide whether the trajectory is flat enough or not? Look at another revision:

Objective (2nd revision): The student will be able to pass the basketball to a partner's chest area in x seconds or less, 8 out of 10 times. (The ball is timed from the point of release to the moment the partner contacts the ball.) The ball will be passed over a distance of 15 feet.

A further criticism might be that the "chest area" is not a very precise standard. How could a more specific accuracy goal be developed? A common procedure is to use a target to measure accuracy. Assume that a target is available to evaluate this objective. A third revision follows:

Objective (3rd revision): The student will be able to pass the basketball to the center of a target in x seconds or less, 8 out of 10 times. The ball will be passed over a distance of 15 feet.

If you were the teacher in this situation, you would determine the standard of performance based on the skill level of the students at the beginning of the unit, along with the length of time of the unit. If final standards are set by the school system, your standards must ensure that the students are progressing in the proper direction.

Be sure the standards set are within the students' reach. Keep in mind that you are not setting standards for varsity basketball players on pass performance but rather for the average student in your classes. The standard should force students to improve their skill but should not be so demanding that they could never hope to meet it. Setting standards is difficult even for the experienced teacher, so be prepared to go through a process of trial and error in determining this part of the objective. The validity of the test standard is essential to the overall validity of the test. (The topic of setting performance standards is treated more extensively in Chapter 7.) An entire class should not be expected to attain the standard described in an objective. Most teachers are satisfied if 80% of their students achieve a standard, although the expected percentage typically ranges from 70% to 90%.

COGNITIVE DOMAIN. Tests are often described as measures of a certain type of behavior, usually cognitive, affective, or psychomotor. The classification of educational objectives for the **cognitive domain** is a result of the work of Bloom and his associates (1956). These were presented in the form of a **taxonomy,** which is defined as a *classification scheme.* The taxonomy represents **levels of** intellectual **behavior** ranging from a low level (memorization of facts) to a higher level (application of these facts). In other words, the levels of the taxonomy are hierarchical, with each one building on the other. It is assumed that mastery of a designated level of cognitive behavior must be preceded by mastery of all lower levels. For example, to be able to apply facts, one must be able to recall them. Bloom has classified cognitive behavior into six levels: *knowledge, comprehension, application, analysis, synthesis,* and *evaluation.*

The domain of cognitive behaviors is broken down into two major categories: *knowledge* and *intellectual skills and abilities.* The first category contains only the initial and most basic level of cognitive behavior—knowledge. The remaining five levels fall into the second category. As behavior increases in complexity, the degree of abstraction also increases. The higher level behaviors depend on the sequential development of all the behaviors in the lower part of the sequence.

This taxonomy can be used in a physical education setting to develop knowledge tests. The teacher must decide on the levels of cognitive behavior that should be mastered by a class; then objectives can be written for each level. Otherwise, undue emphasis may be placed on the lowest level of cognitive behavior, knowledge, which requires the memorization of facts. The learning of factual material is important but should not be tapped to the exclusion of other important behaviors. How many tests have you taken that required pure memorization of facts? When the taxonomy is used, a test of factual knowledge is developed by design rather than by oversight.

Learning to recognize cognitive objectives at low and high levels is the first step in learning to write objectives at several levels. Practice writing objectives at low and high levels, then try to write objectives within subdivisions of the higher level. Several examples of objectives written for different levels of cognitive behavior are shown in the boxed material. Note that the statements of objectives are not worded in behavioral form but are designed to demonstrate differences in the levels of cognitive behavior.

Examples of cognitive objectives at different levels of behavior

1.25   Knowledge of kinesiological techniques for studying patterns of motor skill.

2.10   Skill in translating symbolic statements given as statistics into verbal material, and vice versa.

3.00   Ability to describe the important components of a specific construct, such as physical fitness.

4.20   Ability to explain the relationship between test validity and test reliability.

5.20   Ability to plan appropriate evaluation techniques for a learning situation.

6.00   Ability to judge the validity of a test based on criteria for the selection of a good test.

Writing objectives at various levels of cognitive behavior is easier said than done. Take another look at the boxed material, in particular the fourth objective. This objective is written at the *analysis* level of cognitive behavior. This level represents the *analysis of relationships*. The objective deals with the relationship between validity and reliability. Suppose a student is able to master this objective by meeting a predetermined standard. How does the teacher know the student answered correctly because he or she was able to analyze the relationship between validity and reliability? The teacher does not know; in fact, the student could have memorized the answer. Perhaps this relationship was discussed in a study session, and another student figured out the correct answer. This does not mean, however, that the idea of a taxonomy of educational objectives should be discarded, by any means. However, recognizing the limitations of using this system in writing objectives is important. Do not try to make fine discriminations in levels of cognitive behavior. Write objectives at low and high levels of behavior. Then, as you become more accomplished, add medium levels of behavior. The evaluation of each objective can then be geared to the appropriate level. If students are expected to master material at different levels of cognitive behavior, they should be tested at these levels.

AFFECTIVE DOMAIN. A taxonomy for the affective domain was developed by Krathwohl and associates (1964). An *affect* is defined as an emotional behavior. The **affective domain** encompasses the levels of emotional behavior, including interests, attitudes, or personality characteristics. At a low level of affective behavior, an individual may display acceptable affective behavior because an authority figure (e.g., parent or teacher) is present. At higher levels of affective behavior, the individual's actions are based on personal beliefs about the value of a certain response. This belief is often strongly influenced by societal standards of affective behavior. In a sports setting players are expected to maintain acceptable levels of sportsmanship. If sportsmanlike behavior occurs only when an official is nearby, the player is operating at a low level of affective behavior. If the desired behaviors are displayed consistently, regardless of the situation, a higher level has been incorporated by the player.

Writing objectives for affective behaviors often seems more difficult than writing cognitive and psychomotor objectives. The major problem lies in identifying precise evaluation procedures, in particular, the determination of a standard of performance. For instance, Ms. Smith, a physical education teacher, has written a behavioral objective in the affective domain dealing with sportsmanship. How will she evaluate this objective? In fairness to the students, clearly defined evaluation procedures should be established. Ms. Smith develops a rating scale that she uses during class to record sportsmanship-type behaviors. When a student has displayed specified behaviors a certain percentage of time, the objective has been met. How is this percentage determined? How are the specific behaviors identified? How is a discriminating scale developed? These tasks plainly are not easy. Some examples of curriculum objectives for the affective domain are shown in the boxed material. These objectives are not written in behavioral form but are used to demonstrate the differences in *levels* of affective behavior.

Examples of affective objectives at different levels of behavior

---

1.3   Observes a modern dance with some recognition of the use of space, time, and force.
2.1   Accepts umpire's decision in a baseball game.
3.3   Encourages team members to work together by setting an example.
4.0   Weighs team tactics against standards of fair play rather than winning at any cost.
5.0   Consistently honorable in observing training rules.

Popham and Baker (1970) recommend the following steps for writing objectives for measurable affective behaviors. For a given affective behavior, think of an individual who possesses the behavior and an individual who does not. Describe a situation in which the two individuals would be expected to react differently with regard to the behavior in question. Use that situation to write the affective objective. Ms. Smith would first identify an individual whom she classifies as a *good sport* and one whom she classifies as a *poor sport*. Many-situations could be described in which the two individuals would probably behave differently. For instance, an individual who is a good sport would probably play by the rules in a game situation, while a poor sport might attempt to break or "stretch" the rules on every possible occasion. An affective objective could be written incorporating this situation.

PSYCHOMOTOR DOMAIN. Of course, the **psychomotor domain** is of greatest interest to the readers of this textbook. It is probably fair to state that very few people outside of the field of physical education have been interested in the development of a taxonomy for this domain. However, several classification schemes for motor behavior have been proposed for physical education. An excellent example of one of these schemes is a taxonomy developed by Jewett (Nixon and Jewett, 1980).

Jewett's taxonomy more closely parallels the cognitive and affective schemes than any other taxonomy of motor behavior. Her categories are hierarchical and deal with process rather than content. The Jewett classification scheme is presented in the boxed material.

How do you learn to write psychomotor objectives? Writing objectives at a low level and then rewriting the same objectives at a high level may be easier. In other words, the taxonomy is reduced to two gross categories, as suggested for the cognitive domain, when learning to write objectives. Once you feel comfortable working with two levels of motor behavior, try writing objectives for specific categories of the Jewett taxonomy. Sample objectives (Jewett and Mullan, 1977) are given in Table 2-1.

For further clarification of the use of this taxonomy, let's examine the objective written for the basketball chest pass in the previous section. The objective is repeated here:

The student will be able to pass the basketball to the center of a target in x seconds or less, 8 out of 10 times. The ball will be passed over a distance of 15 feet.

Since the objective is written for eighth-grade boys and girls, it is assumed the overarm throw has already been *patterned* (level A.2 in the boxed material entitled "Jewett Taxonomy of Educational Objectives: Motor Domain"). Now the student is being asked to *adapt* (level B.3 in Jewett's taxonomy) the overarm throw to meet specific task demands, namely force and accuracy. When this objective has been met, the student would be expected to perform the skill under more complex conditions, such as in a game. Jewett has labeled this higher level of behavior as *refining* (level B.4 in Jewett's taxonomy).

What if our initial assumption concerning the *patterning* of the overarm throw is not valid for all students? This would require the preparation of an objective in which students learn to pattern a skill. Within a class setting students may be working at different levels, requiring the planning of appropriate learning experiences and standards for each.

Jewett taxonomy of educational objectives: motor domain*

A. *Generic Movement:* Those movement operations or processes which facilitate the development of characteristic and effective motor patterns. They are typically exploratory operations in which the learner receives or "takes in" data as he or she moves.
  1. *Perceiving:* Awareness of total body relationships and of self in motion. These awarenesses may be evidenced by body positions or motoric acts; they may be sensory in that the mover feels the equilibrium of body weight and the movement of limbs; or they may be evidenced cognitively through identification, recognition, or differentiation.
  2. *Patterning:* Arrangement and use of body parts in successive and harmonious ways to achieve a movement pattern or skill. This process is dependent on recall and performance or a movement previously demonstrated or experienced.
B. *Ordinative Movement:* The processes of organizing, refining, and performing skillful movement. The processes involved are directed toward the organization of perceptual-motor abilities with a view to solving particular movement tasks or requirements.
  3. *Adapting:* Modification of a patterned movement to meet externally imposed task demands. This would include modification of a particular movement to perform it under different conditions.
  4. *Refining:* Acquisition of smooth, efficient control in performing a movement pattern or skill by mastery of spatial and temporal relations. This process deals with the achievement of precision in motor performance and habituation of performance under more complex conditions.
C. *Creative Movement:* Those motor performances which include the processes of inventing or creating movement which will serve the personal (individual) purposes of the learner. The processes employed are directed toward discovery, integration, abstraction, idealization, emotional objectification and composition.
  5. *Varying:* Invention or construction of personally unique options in motor performance. These options are limited to different ways of performing specific movement; they are of an immediate situational nature and lack any predetermined movement behavior which has been externally imposed on the mover.
  6. *Improving:* Extemporaneous origination or initiation of personally novel movement or combination of movement. The processes involved may be stimulated by a situation externally structured, although conscious planning on the part of the performer is not usually required.
  7. *Composing:* Combination of learned movement into personally unique motor designs or the invention of movement patterns new to the performer. The performer creates a motor response in terms of a personal interpretation of the movement situation.

---

*From Jewett, A.E., and Mullan, M.R.

TABLE 2-1. *Sample objectives for the Jewett motor domain**

Movement process	Balance beam	Soccer
Perceiving	The child walks on the balance beam hesitantly, stops frequently to maintain balance; may hang onto partner or teacher. Experiments with body and arm positions. Child may use a shuffle step or slide step.	After a demonstration, the student replicates a kicking pattern. A fundamental striking pattern (swing) with the foot is the goal performance. Neither accuracy nor distance is brought into focus.
Patterning	Child walks on the balance beam using an alternating step pattern with a well balanced body position. Some hesitancy or slowness in performance may still exist.	The student executes a kicking pattern. The force, point of contact, and follow through is the focus.
Adapting	Child walks on a balance beam with an alternating step pattern. He/she walks over a wand and through a hula hoop. May lack smoothness in performance.	The student adjusts his kicking pattern to perform an instep kick.
Refining	Each time the child walks on the balance beam, he/she performs the task smoothly with an alternating step pattern and good body position. He/she is able to move over the wand and through the hula hoop with no hesitation or loss of body control.	The student performs efficiently the instep kick in soccer. The pattern of the kick is performed smoothly with the same force and accuracy each time.
Varying	The child while walking on the balance beam varies the walk by adding a hop. The child is trying to perform a movement in a different way.	The student alters his kicking pattern to perform several variations. The student tries to perform the soccer kick from varying distances and positions from the goal.
Improving	The child while walking on the beam uses a leap to go over the wand instead of a step.	The student in a game of soccer modifies the pass pattern to take advantage of his opponent's being pulled out of position.
Composing	The child designs and performs a series of moves on the balance beam.	The student will be able to design an offensive strategy (kick at goal), responding to a set pattern of play developed with teammates.

From Jewett, A.E., and Mullan, M.R.

Although the criticisms of behavioral objectives have been numerous, emphasis on their tie to taxonomies has brought about a reexamination of teaching and learning in the classroom. As the motor domain is developed in a useful way for physical educators, a similar reexamination of what is being taught in the gymnasium should take place. This reexamination may show that a teacher spent an entire unit patterning basic skills, emphasizing a low level of motor behavior in spite of the fact that a number of students in class should actually be working at higher levels. If the objectives for this class were written in behavioral terms, it would be clear that either instruction ought to be modified so that all students were learning patterning skills or that objectives ought to be written to reflect actual student behavior. This type of information, when carefully analyzed, can lead to improved instruction.

CONDUCTING A NEEDS ASSESSMENT

Once your objectives have been written in behavioral form, your expectations of students are clearly defined by the standards of performance. Setting standards is, at best, an arbitrary procedure. What if your standards are inappropriate for your students? How will you know? If the standards have been used in the school for a number of years, the other teachers have probably established that

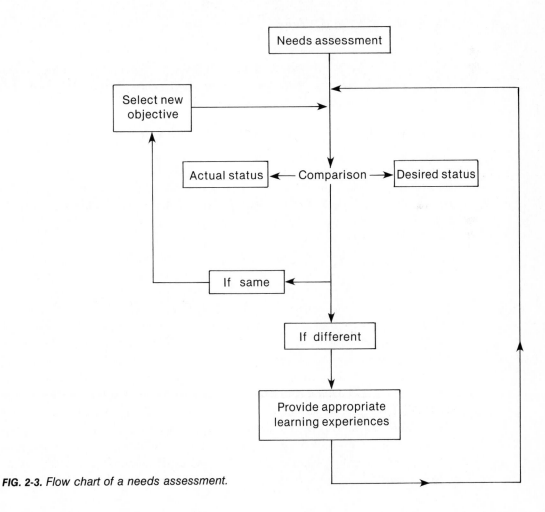

FIG. 2-3. *Flow chart of a needs assessment.*

they are reasonable for the students. If not, data can be collected to assist in the preparation of objectives. It might be wise to consider conducting a *needs assessment* before writing a set of objectives. This is a process for determining the appropriateness of the objectives for the targeted group of students. Each objective has a built-in evaluation procedure. In a needs assessment, students are evaluated on each objective at the beginning of the school year. This determines their *actual* status on each objective. These results are compared with the standards already specified in the objectives, referred to as their *desired* status. If the actual status is equal to or better than the desired status, the objective should be rewritten. In other words, students should be expected to improve beyond their actual states from the beginning of the year to the end. The definition of a **needs assessment,** then, is a comparison of actual and desired states. See Fig. 2-3 for a flow chart of this process.

IMPORTANCE OF ACCOUNTABILITY

If you become a physical educator, you can expect to hear a great deal about accountability in the schools. Although emphasis may be placed on the so-called basic skills of reading, writing, and so forth, the physical educator is expected to be equally accountable for the learning outcomes of his or her students. Teaching students new skills and knowledges about physical activity is not enough; you must be able to demonstrate that your students have actually accomplished these abilities at the expected level. Perhaps physical fitness is one of your major goals, and you have stressed its importance throughout the year. The important question concerns your success in emphasizing this concept by changing student behavior. Remember—it's not what *you* do but what *your students* are able to do after instruction is completed. Thus, to be accountable you must show how your students have changed behavior. To do so, a testing program must be implemented. Of course, the tests you select must be feasible for a school setting. In the context of your fitness goal, although you realize a maximal test of cardiorespiratory function (shown in the illustration) is the most valid measure you could use, it is not realistic to consider using this test in a school. Instead, a battery of physical fitness tests might be administered at the end of the year. A written test could be used to provide evidence of knowledge about physical fitness. The scores could then be compared with national and local norms, if they are available. Data could also be collected at the beginning of the year so that changes in performance could be plotted. This information provides you with evidence that you are accountable for your work with students in their physical education classes. The accountability concept is not going to disappear, so expect to deal with it throughout your teaching career. Make it work for you rather than against you by planning ahead. It is difficult to demonstrate that you are accountable for your teaching when you do not think about it until the end of the year. Accountability is a sound educational concept and a reasonable job expectation. Even if communities did not demand accountability in school systems, good teachers and schools would still hold themselves accountable for their teaching.

SUMMARY

New teachers of physical education face a formidable task in planning for their classes. This includes the formulation of behavioral objectives along with evaluation procedures for each objective. Even if a set of objectives has already been written for the physical education teachers in a school, writing more specific objectives for classes may be necessary. Of course, these must be in line with the broader objectives of physical education. A new set of objectives should be tested on students by first conducting a needs assessment. Objectives should remain flexible and able to be modified if necessary. Objectives also serve as evidence of the accountability of a physical education teacher. By following these steps, one can establish a firm basis for enhancing measurement practices as teaching experience is gained.

LEARNING EXPERIENCES

1. Choose one of your favorite sports. Select a skill and write an objective at a low level of motor behavior. (Use the sample objectives in this chapter as a guide.) Include all of the important components of an objective as described in this chapter. Don't hesitate to use detailed descriptions. Most people are much too brief when they first begin writing behavioral objectives.

2. Form small groups in your class. First review the objectives written by members of your group. As changes are suggested, revise the objectives. Then pass your objective to someone else in another group, and take someone else's objective. As a homework assignment, carefully evaluate the objective you received from someone else. Write suggestions for improving the objective, as well as good points about it. Return the objective to the instructor at the beginning of the next class period.

3. Using the sport skill you selected in *1*, write an objective for a group of individuals operating at a high level of motor behavior. Be specific, especially in your description of the performance standard. Compare the standard with the one you described in *1*. Be sure both testing situations are clearly explained. On what basis did you determine the more difficult standard? How do you know it will not be too difficult? In other words, justify the standards you identified.

REFERENCES

Bloom, B., and others. 1956. Taxonomy of educational objectives: Handbook I: the cognitive domain. New York: David McKay Co., Inc.

Imwold, C.H., Rider, R.A., and Johnson, D.J. 1982. The use of evaluation in public school physical education programs. Journal of Teaching in Physical Education **2**, 13-18.

Jewett, A.E., and Mullan, M.R. 1977. Curriculum design: purposes and processes in physical education teaching-learning. Washington, D.C.: AAHPER.

King, H.A. 1983. Measurement and evaluation as an area of study: a plea for new perspectives. In Tipton, C.H., and Hay, J.G., editors, Specialization in physical education: the Alley legacy. Iowa City: University of Iowa.

Krathwohl, D.R., and others. 1964. Taxonomy of educational objectives: Handbook II: the affective domain. New York: David McKay Co., Inc.

Mager, R.F. 1962. Preparing instructional objectives. Palo Alto, Calif.: Fearon Publishers.

Nixon, J.E., and Jewett, A.E. 1980. An introduction to physical education, ed. 9, Philadelphia: W.B. Saunders Co.

Popham, W.J., and Baker, E.L. 1970. Establishing instructional goals. Englewood Cliffs, N.J.: Prentice-Hall, Inc.

Tyler, R.W. 1951. The functions of measurement in improving instruction. In Lindquist, E.L., editor, Educational measurement. Washington, D.C.: American Council on Education.

ANNOTATED READINGS

Bain, L.L. 1980. Program evaluation. Journal of Physical Education and Recreation **51**(2): 67–69.

Proposes a framework for program evaluation that includes both an internal and external perspective; emphasizes criterion-referenced measurement for internal evaluation and either normative or criterion-referenced measurement for external evaluation; includes an excellent summary of the total framework in chart form; discusses how to use the results to revise a physical education program.

Bayless, J.G. 1978. Conflicts and confusion over evaluation. Journal of Physical Education and Recreation **49**(7): 54-55.

Describes a study of the evaluation of physical education programs in Oklahoma and the success of the evaluation; shows that students and physical education teachers had different perspectives of the types of evaluation taking place in class; discusses the overemphasis on dress for class, attitude, and participation in determining grades; points to the need for tests appropriate for school-age children.

Gronlund, N.E. 1985. Stating objectives for classroom instruction, ed. 3, New York: Macmillan Publishing Co.

Provides a practical guide for stating instructional objectives as intended learning outcomes, then defining the objectives by student performance; presents sample objectives for all three taxonomy domains—cognitive, affective, and psychomotor; includes sample specifications for computer banking of objectives.

Jewett, A.E., and Bain, L.L. 1985. The curriculum process in physical education. Dubuque, Iowa: Wm C Brown Group.

Presents an updated version of the Jewett Purpose-Process Curriculum Framework, which encompasses the Jewett taxonomy of motor behavior; includes examples of behavioral objectives written for various levels of the framework.

Pflug, J. 1980. Evaluating high school coaches. Journal of Physical Education and Recreation **51**(4): 76-77.

Describes a comprehensive, objective coaching evaluation program; includes a self-appraisal by the coach, evaluation by the head coach (if an assistant coach is present) and the building athletic administrator, and a conference with the building coordinator and the district athletic director; program encompasses evaluation in five areas: administration, skills, relationships, performance, and self-improvement.

Vargas, J.S. 1982. Writing worthwhile behavioral objectives. New York: Harper & Row, Publishers Inc.

Self-instructional text; teaches students to recognize and classify behavioral objectives and to write quality objectives; presents fundamentals of writing behavioral objectives; includes examples from different subject areas and grade levels.

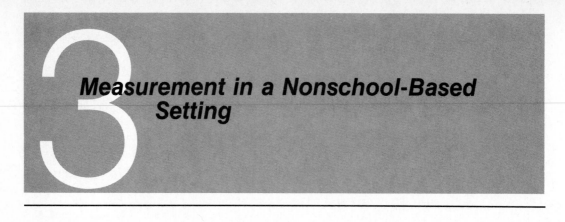

Measurement in a Nonschool-Based Setting

KEY WORDS *Watch for these words as you read the following chapter:*

bicycle ergometer	circumference measure	pulse rate
body composition	maximal oxygen uptake	skinfold thickness
carotid artery	(max $\dot{V}_{O_2}$)	step test
	MET	

Formal instruction in many types of physical activity can take place outside the school setting. Even in the early part of the twentieth century, it was possible to take dance courses in private studios, receive private lessons in sports like tennis and golf, learn a wide variety of skills in summer camps, and participate in activities at a YMCA or YWCA. Today many other opportunities are also available in private sports and fitness centers. In this textbook only the instructional aspects of these organizations are considered, since our primary interest is the measurement and evaluation techniques used in these settings. The recreational opportunities, although a valuable component of a nonschool setting, are not discussed.

Sound measurement practices are as important in nonschool settings as they are in the school setting. For example, the objectives of a private club may differ from those of a school, but a well-run organization will be accountable for its outcomes. While objectives vary from club to club, the bottom line for each club is to show a profit. This cannot be done unless members are recruited and retained. If a member chooses to enroll in a class, an additional fee is usually charged. Once in class, the client is presented with the *opportunity* to learn. It is assumed that a level of motivation initially exists, but often it is the instructor's responsibility to maintain this motivation. There is virtually no control over the "students" in these classes. They cannot be required to attend, study rules, practice skills, or take tests, for that matter. However, evaluation cannot be ignored for these reasons. The club, not the client, sets the standards. If the client wishes to ignore the standards, it is his or her prerogative.

MEASURING SKILLS IN SPORTS CLUBS

Joining a sports club for recreational purposes only is not unusual. Advantages include the availability of court space when desired and the offering of instructional programs, which usually includes private and group lessons. Undoubtedly each instructor plans objectives for these classes. They may be general or specific, including skills the instructor plans to introduce during the unit of instruction. In some instances these objectives may not be available in written form. Unless the instructional program is rather poor, the instructor has probably thought through the instructional plans and has loosely formed objectives in mind. If the club is a part of a franchise, a set of objectives, able to be modified to meet the needs of the club, might be distributed by the home office. Regardless of the source, objectives should be prepared in writing. The small size of the classes and the individualized nature of instruction create an ideal opportunity for tailoring objectives to clients' needs.

Writing objectives for class members in a private club is no different than preparing objectives for students in a school. The major difference is that, because of a smaller class size, the instructor in the private club often has the luxury of formulating objectives for each student. Individualized objectives also support the club as a business. The closer the class comes to meeting the student's needs, the more likely it is that others will enroll in future classes. If a student benefits from a class, the word will be passed on to other prospective students; some of them will sign up for a future class. Word-of-mouth is a powerful factor in sustaining this type of private enterprise.

Although the process of *writing* objectives is the same in school and non-school settings, the process of *implementing* them can differ. Although objectives have been set and the instructional process delineated, the client may not be concerned about meeting the predetermined objectives. Clients' needs in a class setting may differ. Since some sign up for a class simply to learn a little more about the sport, developing skills to a specified level may be of little interest to them. They may care little about specific objectives, as long as the basic skills needed for the game are covered. On the other hand, skill development may be important to other individuals, who often respond positively to the use of objectives that include specific evaluation standards. For them, the setups for skills tests provide an excellent opportunity to practice their skills. Furthermore, the student has a set of specific goals to work toward. Any published test of a skill can be used in a private club setting, as long as test validity and reliability are adequate for the situation and clientele. In fact, using tests requiring elaborate setup materials in a private club is far more feasible than it is in a school.

Since a private sports club is a business, the needs of the client must be met while ensuring a quality program. A multifaceted approach to preparing objectives is recommended. Objectives should be developed for the class as a whole. For example, in a beginning racquetball class objectives could be written for the serve, forehand and backhand drive, playing the game, and so forth. Each of these objectives should include specific evaluation standards. At the first meeting of the class, these objectives should be reviewed. Then, the class members could be given choices regarding their own objectives. At the very least, the client should be encouraged to adapt the class objectives to his or her own needs. This allows testing to take place during the unit of instruction, as described in the objectives. Ideally, the instructor would work closely with each client to tailor the class objectives to the individual. However, it should be made clear that all clients wishing to progress to a higher level course must meet the class objectives at the current level. It is possible that individual modifications can be even more stringent than the class objectives. At the other extreme, some class members may not care about being evaluated and may object to taking any type of test and to any formalized rating by the instructor. As long as these clients do not hinder the rest of the class, the instructor will probably allow them to remain in the class. In small clubs the number of members is often insufficient to allow several classes to take place at the same time, each with different objectives. Flexibility and individualization are the keys to success in the private club.

MEASURING HEALTH-RELATED FITNESS IN FITNESS CENTERS

Many exercise specialists are being trained to assume jobs as directors of private fitness clubs, corporate fitness centers, and other similar organizations. In these settings the objectives tend to be health-related rather than skill-oriented. Also, objectives are usually individualized since the fitness level of new clients can vary greatly. A typical objective is the reduction of body fat. The desired amount of weight loss is dependent on the client's distribution of fat and lean body mass at the time he or she joins the program. The client's **body composition,** consisting of bone, muscle mass, and fatty tissue, must be *measured* to determine the individual's current status. Types of measures of body composition vary from one organization to another; however, some methods, such as weighing the person, are surprisingly not the best measures to use. (Valid measures of body composition are discussed in detail in Chapter 11.) Once the client's body composition has been determined, a reasonable goal can be set for that individual. Note that this is another example of *needs assessment.* The *actual* level of body fatness is compared with the *desired* level.

The testing programs used in fitness centers vary widely, ranging from no tests at all to a relatively sophisticated series of measures. A review of the entrance tests used by several organizations follows. (Refer to Chapter 11 for specific information on the tests mentioned in these sections.)

Private clubs

The number of private fitness centers in the United States has proliferated over the past 10 years. Although all clubs have as their goal the improvement of a client's fitness level, various methods are used to achieve this goal. Some clubs merely provide organized workouts for their clients, with no information on the effectiveness of the exercise sessions. Others test basic physiological and physical capacities of all new clients who join their club and, on the basis of these results, prescribe an exercise program for each individual. Obviously, the latter approach is preferable. Not only is the program geared to the individual's needs, but also the client becomes more knowledgeable about his or her health-related fitness state. The testing programs used in two private clubs are described first.

VIC TANNY INTERNATIONAL OF WISCONSIN, INC. The Vic Tanny clubs in Wisconsin administer two tests of health-related fitness to their new clients. The first is a Body Fat Analysis, in which percent body fat and ideal body weight are

FIG. 3-1. *Administration of step test.*

estimated from body circumferences. The rationale for using body **circumference measures** to estimate body composition has been discussed by Katch and McArdle (1983). Three body sites are used, although the sites differ with one's gender and age. For women under 30, circumferences are measured at the midabdomen, right thigh, and right forearm. The right calf is substituted for the right forearm for women over 30. For men under 30, the sites measured are the right upper arm, midabdomen, and right forearm. The buttock is substituted for the right upper arm for men over 30. The second test is the Pulse Recovery Step Test, a modification of the **step tests** described in Chapter 11 (see Fig. 3-1). The client exercises for 3 minutes on a 12-inch bench, using a cadence of 24 steps per minute. The **pulse rate** is then measured for 10 seconds immediately after the end of the 3-minute period.

Fig. 3-2 is a portion of the form used to record fitness test information. This record is then used to plan an exercise program for the client.

OLYMPIC HEALTH AND RACQUET CLUB. The Olympic Health and Racquet Club administers the Kasch Pulse Recovery Test. This is another modification of the step test, in which the heart rate is measured during recovery. The bench height is 14 inches for women and 16 inches for men. The duration of the test is 3 minutes, with one step taken every 2 seconds. The heart rate is measured at the **carotid artery.** This rate is recorded in 10-second increments during the first minute of recovery after the completion of exercise. The total score is the sum of the ten 10-second recordings. Body composition measures are made available through other sources.

The score sheet for the Kasch Test is shown in Fig. 3-3. Notice that suggested standards for men and women are included on the score sheets used by both clubs.

Corporate fitness centers

Many large corporations provide fitness centers to enable their employees to exercise during working hours as well as before and after work. These centers are often directed by a person with at least a Master's degree in exercise physiology. Extensive testing is usually available in these settings.

CUNA MUTUAL INSURANCE GROUP. An example of one of these programs is the Exercise Resource Facility of the CUNA Mutual Insurance Group, made available to all employees of CUNA Mutual. The test package includes measurement of body composition, functional capacity, strength, and flexibility. Body composition is assessed by measuring the skinfold thicknesses at three sites. The men's sites are pectoral, abdominal, and thigh; the women's, triceps, suprailiac, and thigh. The **skinfold thickness** values are used to estimate percent of body fat and lean body mass. To measure functional capacity, a **bicycle ergometer** test is used (see Fig. 3-4). A bicycle ergometer is a stationary bicycle that can be used

CLUB TOUR   DR. PAUL WARD   3/16/82

¤ Facilities   ¤ Workout Floor and Program Explanation

¤ BODY FAT ANALYSIS

¤   I. INTRODUCTION: Body weight as shown on the scale is not a good indi-
         cator of body composition. One does not know what portion of their
         body is fat and or muscle. Therefore, it is necessary to determine
         an individual's % body fat and strive to reduce this percentage by
         proper diet and exercise programs. Percent fat determination using
         selected body circumferential measurements has been scientifically
         proven to give accurate estimates of body fat.

¤   II. MEASUREMENTS: (measurements will be different for each sex and
         age group)

                              WOMEN

              Under 30   Over 30

         (A) Mid-Abdomen: _____   (A) Mid-Abdomen: _____
         (B) Right Thigh: _____   (B) Right Thigh: _____
         (C) Right Forearm: _____   (C) Right Calf: _____
         (D) Age Const: 19.6   (D) Age Const: 18.4

                              MEN

              Under 30   Over 30   BODY BUILDERS

         (A) Rt Upper Arm: _____   (A) Buttocks: _____   (A) WAIST: _____
         (B) Mid-Abdomen: _____   (B) Mid-Abdomen: _____   (B) BUTTOCKS: _____
         (C) Right Forearm: _____   (C) Right Forearm: _____ (C) WRIST: _____
         (D) Age Const: 10.2   (D) Age Const: 14.9   (D) NECK: _____

¤   Locate the constant that corresponds to each of the three
        measurements on reference chart.

¤ III. PERCENT FAT = _____ + _____ - _____ - _____ = [_____ %]
                          A   B   C   D

¤   IV. DETERMINATION OF IDEAL BODY WEIGHT

         1. % fat from formula = _____% Convert to a decimal = [_____]

         2. Fat Weight = Body Weight X % Fat (in decimal form) = [_____]

                = _____ X _____ = [_____ lbs.]

         3. Lean Weight = Body Weight in lbs. - Fat Weight in lbs. = [_____]

                = _____ - _____ = [_____ lbs.]

         4. STANDARDS Endurance Athletes 5-9% Suggested % fat for men = 12-15%

             Suggested % fat for women = 16-20%
             Optimal % fat used = 100 - _____ % = [_____]
             (change to a decimal)

Continued.

FIG. 3-2. *Form used in exercise program planning.*
From Vic Tanny International of Wisconsin.

5. Optimal Body Weight = Lean Weight ÷ Optimal % Fat (in decimal form)
   (assuming lean weight remains the same)

   = _____ ÷ _____ = [lbs.]

6. Pounds of fat to lose = Body Weight - Optimal Body Weight =

   = _____ - _____ = [lbs.]

□   V.   These fat formulas are the exclusive property of Dr. Frank Katch and
         Dr. William McArdle and the Lea & Febiger Publishing Company,
         Philadelphia, Pa. Permission for their use has been exclusively
         given to the Health and Tennis Corporation of America. These formulas
         are protected by U.S. copyright regulations.

         Reproduced by permission
         FRANK I. KATCH and WILLIAM D. McARDLE
         Nutrition, Weight Control, and Exercise
         2nd Ed.
         Lea & Febiger Publishers
         Philadelphia, Pa.
         1983

□   PULSE RECOVERY STEP TEST

□   The three minute pulse recovery step test consists of a 12-inch
         bench, 24 per min. stepping rate for exactly three (3) minutes
         duration. Its purpose is to broadly determine the exercise
         tolerance or exercise classification of human subjects. It is not
         intended to be a diagnostic test, but for the screening and classi-
         fication of fitness as a means of prescribing an exercise program;
         (2) evaluating the subject's fitness in comparison to normals; and
         (3) to follow the progress of a person undergoing training or re-
         cuperating from a low fitness level or illness.

□   Resting pulse rate (beats per minute) _____

□   Number of heart beats exactly 0 to 10 seconds after the step-up
         exercise _____

□   "TENTATIVE" CLASSIFICATION OF HEART RATE RECOVERY

Classification	Men	Women
Excellent	17 or less	16 or less
Good	18 to 20	17 to 18
Average	21 to 23	19 to 22
Fair	24 to 26	23 to 25
Poor	27 or more	26 or more

                                                  [Subsidiary of
                                                    HEALTH & TENNIS CORP.
                                                    OF AMERICA]

FIG. 3-2, cont'd. *Form used in exercise program planning.*
From Vic Tanny International of Wisconsin.

KASCH PULSE RECOVERY TEST

NAME _____

ADDRESS _____

	TEST 1 Date: _____	TEST 2 Date: _____	TEST 3 Date: _____
Resting heart rate	_____	_____	_____
Recovery	0-10 _____	0-10 _____	0-10 _____
Heart rate	11-20 _____	11-20 _____	11-20 _____
0-1 Min	21-30 _____	21-30 _____	21-30 _____
Post exercise	31-40 _____	31-40 _____	31-40 _____
	41-50 _____	41-50 _____	41-50 _____
	51-60 _____	51-60 _____	51-60 _____
	TOTAL _____	TOTAL _____	TOTAL _____

CLASSIFICATION: (Check one)

Superior	_____	_____	_____
Excellent	_____	_____	_____
Good	_____	_____	_____
Average	_____	_____	_____
Fair	_____	_____	_____
Poor	_____	_____	_____
Very poor	_____	_____	_____

SUGGESTED STANDARDS FOR MEN AND WOMEN

Men (over 30 yrs)	Men (18-30 yrs)	Classification	Women (18 yrs & over)
67	68	Superior	70
68-78	69-80	Excellent	71-82
79-90	81-90	Good	83-94
91-105	91-104	Average	95-109
106-115	105-114	Fair	110-119
116-125	115-124	Poor	120-129
126	125	Very poor	130

FIG. 3-3. *Kasch Test score sheet.*
From the Olympic Health & Racquet Club.

FIG. 3-4. *Administration of submaximal bicycle ergometer test.*

to measure physical work capacity. Since this is a submaximal stress test, the results provide an indirect measure of maximal oxygen uptake (**max V̇O₂**). The score is also recorded in **METS**, which is an energy value somewhat like a calorie. Three measures of strength are administered: a leg press, a bench press, and a sit-up test. To measure flexibility, the Sit and Reach Test is used.

The results of this thorough testing program are used to prescribe an exercise program for the employee. Note that the employee record shown in Fig. 3-5 includes training data, the level at which each individual should be exercising.

EMPLOYEE TEST DATA

EXERCISE RESOURCE FACILITY

NAME _____   DATE _____/_____/_____

CHECK ONE: Original Test _____ Retest   Examiner _____

AGE _____ WEIGHT _____ lb _____ kg   OPTIMAL WEIGHT _____ HEIGHT _____
                                                (Estimate)

BODY COMPOSITION

(Circle one)

MEN   WOMEN

Pectoral   Triceps _____

Abdominal Suprailium _____

Thigh   Thigh _____

Sum of three   _____

% Fat   _____

Lean body mass   _____

16%   23%   _____

Abdominal girth   _____

Other: 1.   _____

2.   _____

3.   _____

STRENGTH DATA

1. Leg Press   _____
2. Bench Press _____
3. Sit-Ups Test _____

FLEXIBILITY DATA

Sit and Reach Test _____

COMMENTS:

FUNCTIONAL CAPACITY

Original workload _____

Resting HR   _____

Resting BP   _____

Workload _____ kg@ _____ RPM= _____ KPM

EXERCISE   HR   BP

Min. 1 _____ _____

2 _____ _____

3 _____ _____

4 _____ _____

5 _____ _____

6 _____ _____

Steady State HR

TRAINING DATA

METS Max   _____

METS Training   _____

Heart Rate Training _____/min

_____/15 sec

FIG. 3-5. *Employee record of training data.*
From the Exercise Resource Facility, CUNA Mutual Insurance Group, Madison, Wis.

Employee taking treadmill test at Sentry World Headquarters, Stevens Point, Wis.

Employee using Nautilus equipment for self-testing at Sentry World Headquarters.

SENTRY WORLD HEADQUARTERS. The Physical Fitness Center at the Sentry World Headquarters in Stevens Point, Wisconsin, is designed for the benefit of all Sentry Insurance employees. Physical fitness is viewed as a key element in maintaining personal health. The Sentry Wellness Program was developed to improve the quality of life for employees. It provides for an appraisal of the employee's current state of health as well as education regarding exercise, rest, nutrition, and other elements affecting one's health. Screening for potential problems such as high blood pressure is available on an ongoing basis. Assistance is provided for well and relatively well people, those with acute illness or injury, and those suffering from a chronic disability. A "flexible time" principle permits the employee to arrange working hours to allow scheduling of health promotion activities during a regular work day.

Three steps must be completed by any employee wishing to use the Physical Fitness Center. First, an orientation program is undertaken to instruct the employee in identifying good health habits and taking control of his or her personal fitness program. Next, the employee receives a medical screening, completes the form shown in Fig. 3-6, and takes the form to the medical department before participating in an organized program. Finally, a trained physical fitness specialist provides the employee with specific instructions for an individualized program consisting of two parts—Cardiovascular and Nautilus Strength and Flexibility training (Sentry World Headquarters, 1979). Each participant keeps a daily record of personal activities using the form shown in Fig. 3-7.

Other organizations

Many hospitals have their own fitness center that includes an exercise physiology laboratory. These facilities are frequently available only to patients with cardiac disease or hypertension and employees of the hospital. However, services are sometimes extended to special groups of patients such as pregnant women and elderly individuals. It is not unusual for hospitals to promote a wellness program, although exercise facilities may not be provided for those in reasonably good health. A physical education department in a university may provide fitness programs for faculty and staff. Basic assessments such as stress testing and skinfold measurement are often provided. If collaboration with a nearby hospital is solidified, a cardiac rehabilitation program may be established.

YMCA. The YMCA uses an extensive battery of tests in the Y's Way to Physical Fitness. Body composition is determined by measuring skinfold thicknesses at either four or six sites for men and three or five sites for women. The number of sites measured depends on the formula to be used in estimating percent fat. The measures of skinfold thickness are summed across the sites and an estimate of percent body fat is calculated. Furthermore, percentile norms for each skinfold site are available. The Body Composition Rating Scale for males 35 years and younger is shown in Fig. 3-8.

FITNESS AND STRESS TEST PROTOCOL

Date_____

This form is to be completed and brought to the Medical Department prior to participating in an organized program in the Physical Fitness Center or a stress test.

1. Name _____ Address _____

2. Sentry employee _____ Spouse/Dependent (State employee's name) _____
   Other _____

3. Age _____   4. Sex _____   5. Phone: (Home) _____ (Bus.) _____
                                                                       Location _____

6. Exercise program interested in _____

7. Previous stress test? _____ If so, date: _____ A copy should be on file in the Medical Department.

8. **HABITS THAT AFFECT QUALITY AND QUANTITY OF LIFE:**   **PLEASE LIST TYPE OF EXERCISE**

   A. **Exercise** _____ At least 3-5 times weekly for at least 15 minutes of vigorous exercise each time.

       _____ Less than above.   _____
                                                                    _____
       _____ None   _____
                                                                    _____

   B. **Rest:**   Average number of hours of sleep per night_____

   C. **Smoker:** _____ If so, what? _____ For how long? _____

       How much have you been averaging per day? _____

       If you quit smoking, CONGRATULATIONS! How long ago? _____

   D. **Nutrition:**   Do you eat breakfast? _____
                       Do you eat at least three meals per day? _____
                       Do you snack between meals? _____
               Average number of alcohol drinks per week? _____
               (1 drink = 1 can of beer, 1 glass of wine, 1 shot of hard liquor)

               Average number of cups of caffeinated coffee per week _____
               Average number of 8 oz. cola drinks per week _____

   E. **Stress:**   Do you feel you take adequate relaxation time? _____
                    Do you usually feel you are "in control" of how life is going? _____

9. Allergies to materials or drugs? _____ If so, what? _____

   _____

10. Use of medications, pills or shots? This would include either prescription drugs or "over the counter" prescriptions such as sleeping aids, tension-reducers, diet pills or vitamins. No _____   Yes _____ Please list: ____

    _____

11. Presently receiving care for any conditions? No _____   Yes _____

    Explain: _____

FIG. 3-6. *Fitness and stress test protocol form.*

12. If you have ever had problems with any of the following, please describe below:
    Heart or blood vessels (blood clot, murmur, rheumatic fever, chest pain, irreg. heart beat) _____

    _____

    High blood pressure _____

    Lungs, asthma, chronic bronchitis _____

    Seizure disorder/epilepsy _____

    Muscles, joints, or back _____

    Thyroid gland or metabolism _____

    Diabetes _____

    Balance or dizziness _____

    Any previous surgery/pregnancy _____

13. Have any blood relatives (parents, brothers, sisters) died before age 60 of any of the above problems? Yes _____ No _____ Explain: _____

    _____

14. Do any living blood relatives have any of the above health conditions? _____
    Explain: _____

15. Have you ever had a cholesterol or triglyceride test? _____ If so, when and what were the results? _____

    _____

    I understand that the information on this form will be released to the Physical Fitness Center.
    Signed_____

    _

    THIS PORTION TO BE FILLED OUT BY MEDICAL DEPARTMENT STAFF

    Height _____ Weight _____ Ideal Weight _____

    Blood Pressure _____ Resting Heart Rate _____

    Stress Test Date _____ Physical Condition _____

    Age-Adjusted Maximum Heart Rate (220-Age) _____

    65% _____ 75% _____ 85% _____

    RECOMMENDED INITIAL TARGET HEART RATE _____

    Conditions to be Aware of: _____

    _____

    _____

    Restrictions: _____

    _____

    Reviewed by _____ _____
    Date sent to PFC _____

NAME: _____   Target Heart Rate: _____ % _____ or _____ beats/10 sec. 8 weeks
_____ % _____ or _____ beats/10 sec. 12 weeks
_____ % _____ or _____ beats/10 sec. Stay

	Weight	Resting H.R.	Warm Up & Stretching	Treadmill	Rowing	Ergometer (Cycle)	Jump Rope	Abdominal Boards (Sit-Ups)	Balance Beam	Cool Down	Recovery H.R.

For optimum cardiovascular benefits (those for your heart, lungs, and blood vessels), three factors must be incorporated:

FREQUENCY — exercising a minimum of four times per week

INTENSITY — while exercising achieve your target heart rate.

DURATION — Keeping your target heart rate for 30 minutes of continuous exercise.

If at any time you are unsure about any phase of your program, or if you feel that you might need additional help or guidance — please — Contact ANY MEMBER OF THE STAFF — AT ONCE!!

57-3 (SWH) 2-80   *See Physical Fitness Assistant for New Card and Program Assessment*

FIG. 3-7. *Each participant keeps a daily record of personal activities.*

LEGS: Progress to 20 repetitions then increase weight unit by one the next session while decreasing the repetitions.

ARMS: Progress to 15 repetitions then increase weight unit by one the next session and decrease repetitions.

	Compound Leg				Double Chest		Double Shoulder		Bicep-Tricep			Multi-Exercise								
Hip & Back	Leg Ext.	Leg Press	Leg Curl	Pullover	Arm Cross	Decline Press	Lateral Raise	Overhead Press	Bicep Curl	Tricep Extension	4-Way Neck	Chin Ups	Calf Raises	Dips	Wrist Curl	Side Bends	Knee Tucks	Balance Beam	Cool Down	Recovery H.R.
Wt Rep	Wt Rep	Wt Rep	Wt Rep	Wt Rep	Wt Rep	Wt Rep	Wt Rep	Wt Rep	Wt Rep	Wt Rep	Wt Rep									

Y's WAY TO PHYSICAL FITNESS

Rating Scale

Norms   Males   35 Years and Under

Name ——————————   Dates: T$_1$ ——————   T$_2$ ——————   T$_3$ ——————

Percentage ranking	Rating	Percent fat	Chest mm	Abdomen mm	Skinfolds Ilium mm	Axilla mm	Tricep mm	Back mm	Thigh mm
95	Very lean	6	3	4	4	4	3	4	4
85	Lean	9	7	8	6	8	6	8	6
75	Leaner than ave.	14	12	16	11	13	10	12	10
50	Average	18	15	21	16	17	11	15	14
30	Fatter than ave.	22	18	27	20	21	13	19	16
15	Fat	25	22	34	26	25	16	24	21
5	Very fat	30	28	44	33	33	21	33	33
YOUR SCORE T$_1$		___	___	___		___	___	___	___
T$_2$		___	___	___		___	___	___	___
T$_3$		___	___	___		___	___	___	___

FIG. 3-8. *Body Composition Rating Scale.*

From Y's Way to Physical Fitness. Lawrence A. Golding, Ph.D., Clayton R. Myers, Ph.D., and Wayne E. Sinning, Ph.D., editors. Published by National Board of YMCA of USA, 1982, Chicago. Copies available YMCA of the USA, Program Resources, 6400 Shafer Court, Rosemont, IL 60018. By permission of the YMCA.

FIG. 3-9. *Estimation of heart rate by palpating the carotid artery.*

A physical work capacity (PWC) test is included as a measure of cardiorespiratory function. The male client begins exercising on a bicycle ergometer at 300 kilometers per minute (kpm) (150 kpm for the female client), and the workload is increased as dictated by the client's level of fitness. Two scores are calculated: max $\dot{V}O_2$ and METS. To measure flexibility, a trunk flexion test is administered. Two measures of muscular strength and endurance are included: an 80-pound bench press and a 1-minute timed sit-up test. These scores are recorded on the Physical Fitness Evaluation Form reproduced in Fig. 3-10. This version of the form includes the norms for females 35 years and under. The YMCA has developed separate forms for males 35 years and under, females 35 years and under, males 36 to 45 years old, and females 36 to 45 years old.

Once all tests have been administered, scores are recorded on a master score sheet, shown in the version for women in Fig. 3-11, and then transferred to the Physical Fitness Profile.

At this point the steps used in determining fitness objectives for a client should be understood. The client's *desired* level of physical fitness is compared with his or her *actual* level. Then a program of physical activity is prescribed. The appropriate physiological parameters are monitored on a regular basis to

Y's WAY TO PHYSICAL FITNESS

Rating Scale

Norms   Females   35 Years and Under

Name _____

Dates: T₁ _____   T₂ _____   T₃ _____

Percentage ranking	Rating	PWC max kgm	Liters/min	ml/kg	Mets	Trunk flexion ins	Bench press repetitions	Sit-ups 1 min reps	3-Min step test post Ex. HR 1 min BPM	Resting HR BPM
95	Excellent	1700	3.32	55	15.	23	30	39	79	59
85	Good	1500	2.74	45	13.	21	24	34	94	63
75	Above Av.	1300	2.42	39	11.	20	20	30	109	68
50	Average	1100	2.09	34	10.	18	16	25	118	72
30	Below Av.	900	1.76	30	9.	15	13	20	122	80
15	Fair	700	1.44	26	7.	14	10	15	129	84
5	Poor	500	.86	20	6.	11	5	10	137	92

YOUR SCORE

T₁ ___ ___ ___ ___ ___ ___ ___
T₂ ___ ___ ___ ___ ___ ___ ___
T₃ ___ ___ ___ ___ ___ ___ ___

	Test 1	Test 2	Test 3
Target Weight	___	___	___
Actual Weight	___	___	___
Difference	___	___	___
% Body Fat (23% Target)	___	___	___
Blood Pressure	___/___	___/___	___/___

Your actual weight should be within 10% of your target weight.

Any values over 140/90 are considered high, and below 110/65 are considered low. Values exceeding 160/95 are labeled as hypertensive.

FIG. 3-10. Physical Fitness Evaluation Form.

From Y's Way to Physical Fitness. Lawrence A. Golding, Ph.D., Clayton R. Myers, Ph.D., and Wayne E. Sinning, Ph.D., editors. Published by National Board of YMCA of USA, 1982, Chicago. Copies available YMCA of the USA, Program Resources, 6400 Shafer Court, Rosemont, IL 60018. By permission of the YMCA.

```
                    Y's WAY TO PHYSICAL FITNESS

                       SCORE SHEET FEMALES


    NAME _____   DATE _____

                                             TIME _____

    Temp. F°
          Age _____ years   Weight _____ lbs _____ kg   Height _____ ins

          Resting Blood Pressure ____/____ mm Hg   Resting Heart Rate _____ bpm
```

---

1. SKINFOLDS   2. PERCENT FAT

                                             Sum of 5   (or)   Sum of 3

   Chest   _____ mm
   Abdomen   _____ mm   Thigh   _____   Ilium   _____
   Ilium   _____ mm   Ilium   _____   Abdomen _____
   Axilla   _____ mm   Abdomen _____   Axilla   ========
   Scapula   _____ mm   Tricep   _____   Sum   _____
   Tricep   _____ mm   Scapula ========
   Thigh   _____ mm   Sum   _____

                                      Percent fat ___ %   Percent fat ___ %

3. TARGET WEIGHT (23%) _____ lbs

4. PHYSICAL WORK CAPACITY TEST

   Seat Height _____ Predicted Max Heart Rate _____ B/M

   85% of Predicted Max Heart Rate _____ B/M _____ Seconds for 30 Beats

        WORKLOADS   HEART RATE

        1st Workload 150 kgm   _____ 2nd min
                                          _____ 3rd min
                                          _____ 4th min (if needed)

        2nd Workload _____ kgm   _____ 2nd min
                                          _____ 3rd min
                                          _____ 4th min (if needed)

        3rd Workload _____ kgm   _____ 2nd min
                                          _____ 3rd min
                                          _____ 4th min (if needed)

        NOTE: Transfer above results to the PWC Graph and Compute

5. FLEXIBILITY   6. MUSCULAR STRENGTH & ENDURANCE

   Trunk flexion _____ ins   Bench Press (35 lbs) _____ reps

                                     1 min Timed Sit-ups _____ reps

        Transfer all results to Physical Fitness Profile

FIG. 3-11. Master score sheet.

From Y's Way to Physical Fitness. Lawrence A. Golding, Ph.D., Clayton R. Myers, Ph.D., and Wayne E. Sinning, Ph.D., editors. Published by National Board of YMCA of USA, 1982, Chicago. Copies available YMCA of the USA, Program Resources, 6400 Shafer Court, Rosemont, IL 60018. By permission of the YMCA.

determine progress toward the desired level of fitness. *Remember that the general procedure is no different in a private sports club or a school setting.* The *implementation* of the objectives may differ, because the client chooses to join a private club while the student is required to be in school. Evaluation assumes an important role in instruction in school and nonschool settings.

Accountability is as important in a nonschool setting as it is in the schools. Because private clubs are profit-making organizations, they must gear their operation to attracting a large membership contingency. To retain this appeal, the club is often evaluated at several levels. For instance, the cleanliness and decor of the club are factors in retaining new members, as is the efficiency of the day-to-day operation. The nature of the publicity and the attractiveness of the club membership packages affect the club's ability to secure new members. All of these elements must be evaluated periodically by the club manager. One of the best ways to retain members is to improve their skills. Theoretically, if individuals can play better, they will enjoy it more. This is why it is so important to attempt to individualize objectives in instructional settings in a private club. By creating a more personal atmosphere, the instructor is providing a rare opportunity for the member to receive individual attention from the club staff. Furthermore, the private club that is part of a franchise will be expected to demonstrate its accountability to the home office. Every effort should be made to satisfy the needs of the member while retaining high standards set by the club.

SUMMARY

Many instructional opportunities exist in nonschool settings. The process of writing objectives for these classes is similar to preparing objectives in a school setting. Individualizing objectives in a private club is often easier, however, and these objectives may be implemented differently in this setting. In a private sports club the objectives might be tailored to the skill level of class members having similar levels of skill. In a fitness center objectives are expected to be individualized, since the level of fitness of the clients typically varies markedly. Any test of sports skills or physical fitness can be adapted for the nonschool setting. In practice, some organizations evaluate their clients' progress only in the most subjective manner, while others have instituted formal testing programs.

LEARNING EXPERIENCES

1. Visit a private fitness or sports club in your community, and ask for information on the entry-level testing for new clients. Secure the printed evaluation form from the club manager, if possible. Ask for clarification of any aspect of the testing you do not understand. Bring this information back to class, and report it to your classmates.

2. Write one behavioral objective for a hypothetical new member of a private fitness club. Be sure to include all the important components of a behavioral objective as described in the previous chapter.

3. Write one behavioral objective for a beginning tennis class in a private tennis club. Then modify the objective for a new member of the class who seems to have natural ability in tennis and is highly motivated.

REFERENCES

Golding, L.A., Myers, C.R., and Sinning, W.E. 1982. The Y's way to physical fitness. Chicago: National Board of YMCA.

Katch, F.I., and McArdle, W.D. 1983. Nutrition, weight control, and exercise, ed. 2, Philadelphia: Lea & Febiger.

Pollock, M.L., Schmidt, D.H., and Jackson, A.S. 1980. Measurement of cardiorespiratory fitness and body composition in a clinical setting. Comprehensive Therapy **6**:12-27.

Sentry World Headquarters. 1979. Sentry physical fitness handbook. Stevens Point, Wis.: Sentry World Headquarters.

SUPPLEMENTARY READINGS

Heyward, V.H. 1984. Designs for fitness. Minneapolis: Burgess Publishing Co.

Pollock, M.L., Wilmore, J., and Fox, S.M. 1984. Exercise in health and disease: evaluation and prescription for prevention and rehabilitation. Philadelphia: W.B. Saunders Co.

ANNOTATED READINGS

Baun, W., and Baun, M. 1984. A corporate health and fitness program. Journal of Physical Education, Recreation and Dance **55**(4):42-45.

Describes the use of a computer system to achieve objectives in a corporate fitness setting; discusses the use of initial screening of employees followed by daily assessments; provides immediate feedback to the participant as well as a monthly activity program; uses monthly statistics to evaluate the program continuously and to develop a data base for longitudinal analysis.

Baun, W.B., and Landgren, M.A. 1983. Tenneco health and fitness: a corporate program committed to evaluation. Journal of Physical Education, Recreation and Dance **54**(8): 40-41.

Lists the objectives of the model fitness program at Tenneco Inc. in Houston; describes the program and program statistics; emphasizes the evaluation process, which includes four principal areas: (1) health and fitness monthly statistics, (2) fitness and wellness program evaluation, (3) special projects, and (4) longitudinal projects; uses information from the evaluation process to increase awareness of and commitment to positive health habits and improve the overall quality of life.

Cooper, K.H., and Collingwood, T.R. 1984. Physical fitness: programming issues for total well-being. Journal of Physical Education, Recreation and Dance **55**(3):35-36, 44.

Describes the involvement of the Institute for Aerobics Research in developing and evaluating employee health and fitness programs within the private and government sectors; notes that accountability is the major issue in program implementation; based on their evaluations of many programs, identifies several factors contributing to the success of a program, thereby facilitating participant adherence to the program; describes several program models.

Crossley, J.C., and Hudson, S.D. 1983. Assessing the effectiveness of employee recreation/fitness programs. Journal of Physical Education, Recreation and Dance **54**(8): 50-52.

Discusses a practical approach to assessing the effectiveness of employee recreation/fitness programs; labels this type of approach as "controlled comparison"; describes data collection (1) to construct an employee profile and (2) to measure employee perceptions of program benefits; substitutes survey questions for objective data; data collection also includes employee perceptions of the effectiveness of a recreation/fitness program; discusses how the data can be used to improve the program.

Farley, M. 1984. Program evaluation as a political tool. Journal of Physical Education, Recreation and Dance **55**(4):64-67.

Examines program evaluation as it applies to public service agencies; suggests program evaluation can become a persuasive political tool if viewed as a communication device; proposes ways of using program evaluation as a political tool; discusses evaluation as a means of linking the agency and elected officials in the tasks of planning and delivering services and accounting for the use of public funds.

Howell, J. 1983. Wellness for the practitioners. Journal of Physical Education, Recreation and Dance **54**(8):37, 55.

Describes hospital wellness program for hospital employees; uses an aerobic circuit modeled after Kenneth Cooper's concept; discusses fitness advisor assisting participants in establishing personal goals and monitoring progress; uses two fitness assessments as a part of membership: initial testing and the Lifestyle-Health Audit; evaluates program using class evaluations and exit questionnaires.

Part Two

Simplified
Statistics

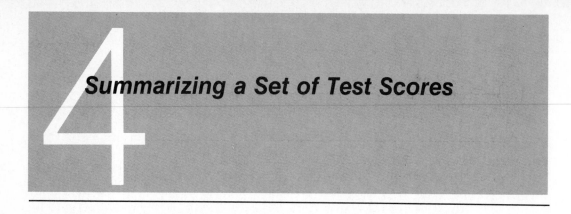

Summarizing a Set of Test Scores

Watch for these words as you read the following chapter:

cumulative frequency (cf)	frequency polygon	percentile rank
	histogram	range (R)
cumulative percent (c%)	interval (i)	real limits
descriptive statistics	measurement	score limits
frequency (f)	median	statistics
frequency distribution	percentile	tally

It is not uncommon for the terms *measurement* and *statistics* to be used interchangeably by students who are not majoring in either area. Although both disciplines deal with sets of scores, **measurement** encompasses the process of obtaining test scores and **statistics** provides the methodology for analyzing the scores. Measurement was defined as the process of assigning numerals to an object or a person in the first chapter. Statistics, on the other hand, is defined as a method of analyzing a set of scores to enhance its interpretation. While an extensive coverage of statistics is not necessary in a measurement textbook, a few basic concepts must be covered to provide an understanding of certain measurement practices described later in the book. The type of statistics covered in this book is limited primarily to **descriptive statistics,** those that can be used to describe a data set. Basically, statistics will be used in the following ways in this book:

1. *To describe a set of test scores.* Having obtained a set of test scores, what kind of information can be attained from these scores? The scores can be ordered in *frequency distribution* form, and a measure of the *center* and *spread* of the distribution can be calculated. (These terms are defined later in this chapter.)

Testing elementary school children.

2. *To standardize a test score.* Sometimes standardizing a person's score on a test is useful so that the score can be compared with those of other people. This can be accomplished by transforming scores to a different scale such as a z-score or a **percentile** scale.

3. *To estimate the validity and reliability of a test.* In measurement theory a test has certain characteristics such as *reliability* and *validity*. These test characteristics are often estimated using a statistic known as the *correlation coefficient*.

MEASUREMENT SCALES

Whenever a measurement instrument is used, some type of score is obtained. To interpret the score, knowing what it represents is necessary. An accurate interpretation depends in part on the type of scale the score reflects. Four types of scales are commonly described: *nominal, ordinal, interval,* and *ratio.*

A nominal scale is a set of mutually exclusive categories. Each category represents one aspect of the attribute being measured. If a score can legitimately be placed in more than one category, the categories are not mutually exclusive. In a properly developed nominal scale, a score can fit one and only one category. However, there is no meaningful order to the categorization. Classifying football players by number is an example of nominal scaling. A player who is assigned number 42 is not necessarily better than a player assigned number 12.

An ordinal scale is determined by ranking a set of objects with regard to some specific characteristic. A basketball coach might be asked to rank the basketball teams in a league on the basis of predicted success at the end of the season. If ten teams are in the league, a rank of 1 is assigned to the team predicted to win the league title and a rank of 10 to the team expected to be at the bottom of the league. Since a rank of 1 is better than a rank of 2, the order of the numbers is important. However, the top-ranked team might be considerably better than the teams ranked 2, 3, and 4, while the latter three teams might be similar in ability. These differences are not reflected in the differences between ranks. Ordinal scales can also characterize scores that are not in the form of actual ranks. For example, when all-star teams are selected by a national press, sportswriters are asked to vote for the player of their choice. Suppose Player F receives 232 votes; Player R, 190 votes; and Player N, 93 votes. Clearly, Player F is considered outstanding by the largest number of sportswriters, but the number of votes does not disclose how much better Player F is than Player R. Because the distance between numbers does not have a meaningful interpretation, the scores represent ordinal data. Although the actual number of votes may be reported by the press, future reference to the all-star players generally centers on the ranks of the players.

In an interval scale the scores have a meaningful order, and units of measurement are an equal distance apart on the scale. On a test of motor behavior, the distance between 93 and 90 represents the same range of ability as the difference between 53 and 50. If an interval scale contains a score of 0, the 0 score does not reflect total absence of the attribute being measured. In contrast, the ratio scale uses a 0 score that represents absence of the attribute. For example, a score of 0 on a vertical jump would be interpreted as the total lack of ability to execute the vertical jump. The ordering of numbers is meaningful (larger numbers represent higher jumps), the distance between numbers is equal (the difference between 15 and 12 inches is equal to the difference between 10 and 7 inches), and the ratio of numbers is meaningful (12 inches is twice as long as 6 inches). Of course, if two examinees are of equal height, 3 inches at higher heights may represent a greater performance increment than 3 inches at lower heights. Ratio scales include measures of length, weight, and time, which are frequently used in measuring motor skills.

DISCRETE AND CONTINUOUS VARIABLES

A variable may be classified as either *continuous* or *discrete*. A continuous variable is one which, in theory, can be measured to continuing finer degrees. Many physical measures, such as distance, time, and weight or mass, are examples of continuous variables. A long jump, for example, can be measured to the nearest foot, the nearest inch, the nearest half-inch, and so on. Variables that are not continuous are known as discrete variables, since these variables can assume values only at distinct or discrete points on a scale. A baseball team might score 8 runs during a game, but never 8½ or 8¼ runs. Other examples of discrete variables are the number of students in a class, the number of teams in a league, and the number of books in a library.

FREQUENCY DISTRIBUTION

Suppose, as the instructor of a newly formed health and fitness class, you administer several tests to the class members before beginning instruction. These tests include body composition measures, a test of physical work capacity, and a measure of flexibility. Close examination of each data set is essential before beginning work with these individuals. A simple way of making sense of the data sets is to develop a **frequency distribution** for each set. A frequency distribution is a method of organizing data having two basic characteristics. First, the test scores must have a meaningful order. For instance, assume that you have chosen two test scores out of one of the data sets and that each score has a different value. If the score with the higher value represents a greater amount of the attribute being measured, the scores in this set meet the criterion of having a meaningful order. Using the triceps skinfold as an example, it is obvious that a skinfold of 9 mm represents a thicker skinfold than a skinfold of 6 mm. On the surface, all numbers may seem to have a meaningful order, but sometimes objects are given numerical labels merely for convenience. This is almost always the case with lockers in gymnasium dressing rooms, for example, since numbers are frequently used for identification. A locker with a higher number does not represent a better locker than one with a lower number. Thus it would be inappropriate to build a frequency distribution of locker numbers. The second characteristic is that categories in a frequency distribution must be *mutually exclusive*. Assigning a score to more than one category should not be possible. The scores in one category, then, should never overlap with those in other categories.

Frequency distribution with intervals of size 1

Now let us turn to the task of actually building a frequency distribution. When the number of scores is small, the procedure is very simple. As the number of scores increases, the procedure becomes more complex although it is certainly not difficult.

ORDERED SCORES NOT IN FREQUENCY DISTRIBUTION FORM. When a test is administered to a small number of people, forming a frequency distribution is probably not needed. However, no matter how small the data set, the test user should interpret the test scores. Administering a test and failing to use the data in any way is a waste of time for the examinee as well as the test user. Thus with a small data set the scores might simply be ordered from highest to lowest. Consider the following set of scores, representing subscapular skinfold thicknesses for 9-year-old girls:

Data set of 10 scores (in mm): 6, 9, 7, 10, 2, 4, 9, 5, 3, 6

Listing these scores from highest to lowest would yield the following order:

10–9–9–7–6–6–5–4–3–2

Such an ordering can be useful, but this is *not* a frequency distribution. If the characteristics of a frequency distribution in the previous section are reviewed, the reason this representation of the data is not a frequency distribution should be clear. The numbers have a meaningful order, but there are no mutually exclusive categories. To convert this data set into a frequency distribution, every possible score from 10 to 2 would be listed once; thus each score would form a category.

CONSTRUCTION OF FREQUENCY DISTRIBUTION. These scores are scores from a test of throwing accuracy taken by 24 elementary school children:

Data set of 24 scores (in points): 6, 1, 8, 7, 5, 5, 9, 6, 4, 10, 3, 6, 6, 5, 4, 7, 7, 8, 6, 4, 6, 5, 7, 5

The symbol for the number of test scores (or the number of people obtaining scores on a test) is N. In this example, $N = 24$. Note that the range is still small $(10 - 1 + 1 = 10)$; thus it would be appropriate to use intervals of size 1 to form a frequency distribution. Of course, listing each possible score in the data set, from highest to lowest, is possible; however, the data would not be in frequency distribution form. With 24 scores, building a frequency distribution would be simpler. In addition, the description of the data would be more concise.

Score	Tally	f	cf	c%
10	x	1	24	100.0
9	x	1	23	95.8
8	xx	2	22	91.7
7	xxxx	4	20	83.3
6	xxxxxx	6	16	66.7
5	xxxxx	5	10	41.7
4	xxx	3	5	20.8
3	x	1	2	8.3
2		0	1	4.2
1	x	1	1	4.2

Note the columns in the above distribution. One is labeled **Tally,** which represents the recording of a score in the appropriate interval. Each *x* designates one score in an interval. The next column, *f*, consists of the **frequency** of scores in each interval. This can be more simply expressed as the number of scores in each interval and is obtained by summing the tallies in each interval. The next column is labeled *cf*, the symbol for **cumulative frequency.** The numbers in this column are obtained by summing the frequencies from the bottom interval to the top. In the above example the *cf* for interval 6 is *16*. This indicates that 16 out of 24 people obtained scores of 6 or below on this measure. The *c%* or **cumulative percent** column displays the conversion of the *cf* column to percentages. Take another look at interval 6. A *cf* of 16 is converted to a *c%* of 66.7% by dividing 16 by the total number (N) of test scores, in this case, 24. The result must then be multiplied by 100. Thus, c% = cf/N × 100, or cf divided by N times 100. Referring to the interval 6, it would be appropriate to say that 66.7% of the group of 24 obtained scores of 6 or below. The percentages in this column are known as *percentiles*, which are described later in this chapter.

With a larger range of score values, however, this procedure would become very cumbersome. For instance, if the highest score in a data set is 80 and the lowest is 21, the range would be 60. It would be tedious and very time-consuming to list 60 intervals of size 1 in forming a frequency distribution. It would be expedient to use intervals greater than size 1. This is sometimes referred to as a *group frequency distribution.* The major purpose of forming a frequency distribution is to summarize the data for easier interpretation. If too many intervals are used, the original purpose may be defeated. A large number of intervals often spreads the data too much to be interpretable, while a very small number of intervals can mask important trends in the data. The **range** (R) is determined by subtracting the lowest score from the highest score and adding 1 as symbolized in Formula 4-1:

$$R = (\text{Highest score} - \text{Lowest score}) + 1 \qquad \text{Formula 4-1}$$

Frequency distribution with intervals greater than size 1

When a set of test scores is distributed over a wider range, grouping the data into intervals greater than size 1 is preferred. As noted previously, this is sometimes referred to as a group frequency distribution. Additional steps must be followed when the interval size exceeds 1, such as the determination of an appropriate interval size and a suitable number of intervals.

DESCRIPTION OF PROCEDURE. Consider a data set of 22 scores on a physical fitness knowledge test, with the scores ranging from 80 to 99. The range of this set is 99 − 80 + 1 = 20. It would be more efficient and provide a better representation of the data if a frequency distribution with intervals greater than 1 were used. How many intervals should be formed? The general rule is to use *no fewer than 10 and no more than 20 intervals.* How large should the interval size be? Many interval sizes are legitimate possibilities, but the most widely used options are 2, 3, 5, 7, 10, and multiples of 5 thereafter. Since it has been determined that the range of this set of scores is 20 and that no fewer than 10 intervals should be used, the best interval size for this data set is 20/10 = 2.

Data set of 22 scores: 89, 86, 91, 82, 80, 93, 96, 87, 82,
(Fitness Knowledge   98, 96, 99, 95, 90, 89, 91, 88, 92,
Test)   93, 87, 89, 91

$$N = 22; R = 99 - 80 + 1 = 20$$

Intervals	Tally	f	cf	c%
98-99	xx	2	22	100.0
96-97	xx	2	20	91.0
94-95	x	1	18	81.8
92-93	xxx	3	17	77.3
90-91	xxxx	4	14	63.6
88-89	xxxx	4	10	45.5
86-87	xxx	3	6	27.2
84-85		0	3	13.6
82-83	xx	2	3	13.6
80-81	x	1	1	4.5

Traditionally frequency distributions are constructed so that the highest scores are at the top of the column and the lowest scores are at the bottom. Displaying an interval with the lowest score in the interval on the left and the highest score in the interval on the right is also customary. The reason higher scores are usually placed at the top of the **Interval** (i) column is that higher scores typically represent better performances. However, this is not always true in measuring motor behavior, especially when the score is recorded in time. When measuring running speed, for example, faster times (smaller scores) represent better performances. In these cases, building the frequency distribution with the smaller scores at the top of the interval column would be appropriate. Keep in mind that the purpose of a frequency distribution is to present a meaningful summary of the data.

SUMMARY OF STEPS. The following steps are taken in constructing a frequency distribution with intervals of size 1. (Other equally effective approaches may also be used to accomplish the same purpose.)

1. Calculate the range of the set of scores (highest score − lowest score + 1). List all possible scores in the range, regardless of whether the score actually occurs in the data set. The score representing the best performance should be placed at the top of the list, and the score reflecting the poorest performance should be at the bottom of the list.
2. Tally each of the scores in the data set, using *x*'s or *1*'s as tallies.
3. Develop the frequency (*f*) column by summing the tallies for each interval.
4. Generate the cumulative frequency (*cf*) column by adding the frequencies, beginning with the bottom interval.
5. Develop the cumulative percent (*c%*) column by dividing *cf* by $N \times 100$.

If the frequency distribution includes intervals greater than size 1, two additional steps *1a* and *1b* must be taken between steps *1* and *2* above.

1a. Select an appropriate number of intervals to ensure that the distribution will contain no more than 20 intervals and no fewer than 10.

1b. Select an appropriate interval size. Remember that typical interval sizes are 2, 3, 5, 7, and 10. To determine the interval size, the number of intervals can be divided into the range.

Another way to approach this is to estimate the interval size, taking into account the range; then divide the range by the interval size to obtain the number of intervals. Even with a cursory examination of the frequency distribution data on p. 72, it is obvious that the number of intervals will be relatively small. This is evident since the range (20) itself is small. Thus a reasonable estimate of an appropriate number of intervals is 10, and 20/10 = 2. The distribution, then, would have 10 intervals with an interval size of 2. To take the other approach, simply reverse your thought process as follows. Since the range is small, the number of intervals can be maximized by keeping the interval size small. Since this example deals with intervals greater than size 1, the smallest possible interval size is 2. Dividing the range (20) by 2 yields 10 intervals. This is basically a trial and error process. The interval size and the number of intervals are adjusted until both numbers are acceptable.

Graphing distributions

Although the frequency distribution is a simple method of summarizing a set of scores, it may not be the most effective way of displaying the summary to others. Graphical representations are sometimes more powerful when presenting your data to principals, club managers, laboratory directors, clients, parents, and so forth. Two popular types of graphs are the **frequency polygon** and the **histo-**

FIG. 4-1. *Frequency polygon of scores on Physical Fitness Knowledge Test.*

gram. In Fig. 4-1 the frequency distribution on p. 72 is shown in frequency polygon form. Since the intervals in this distribution are greater than size 1, the points used to plot the frequency polygon are the midpoints of the intervals shown on the horizontal axis. On the vertical axis of the graph, the frequency of cases (number of test scores) is depicted.

The histogram is a type of bar graph. The width of the bar represents the width of the interval displayed on the horizontal axis of the graph. As with the frequency polygon, the frequency of cases is shown on the vertical axis. Fig. 4-2 depicts the distribution on p. 72 in histogram form. The choice between using a histogram or a frequency polygon is largely a matter of personal preference.

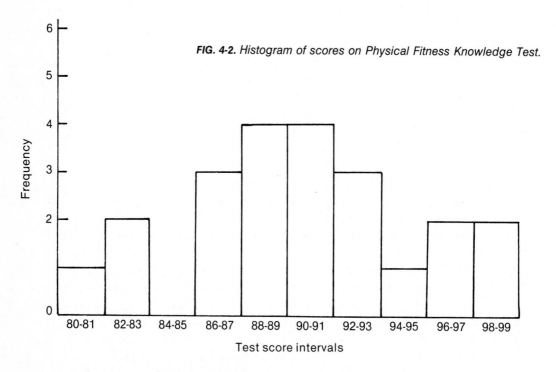

FIG. 4-2. *Histogram of scores on Physical Fitness Knowledge Test.*

Special case of frequency distribution

In situations where lower scores represent better performances, such as golf and running events, the frequency distribution may be modified accordingly. When a frequency distribution or a graph of the distribution is of primary interest, the lowest scores can be placed at the top of the distribution. This provides a clear presentation of the set of scores, since many people expect to see better scores at the top of a frequency distribution. However, if a distribution is formed in this way, the percentile and percentile rank formulas (presented later in this chapter) should not be used with this distribution of scores. Varying the formulas is possible so that they yield the correct answers, but these variations are beyond the scope of this textbook. Consider the following set of time scores on a shuttle run test, where test performance is timed to the nearest tenth of a second.

Data set of 20 scores (in seconds): 9.2, 11.1, 9.7, 10.3, 10.5, 9.8, 10.9, 11.6, 11.3, 9.0, 10.0, 10.3, 10.0, 9.8, 9.8, 10.3, 9.7, 10.5, 10.0, 10.1

$$N = 20; \text{Range} = 11.6 - 9.0 + 0.1 =$$
2.7, or 27 scores recorded to the nearest tenth of a second

Interval	Tally	f
9.1 – 9.0	x	1
9.3 – 9.2	x	1
9.5 – 9.4		0
9.7 – 9.6	xx	2
9.9 – 9.8	xxx	3
10.1 – 10.0	xxxx	4
10.3 – 10.2	xxx	3
10.5 – 10.4	xx	2
10.7 – 10.6		0
10.9 – 10.8	x	1
11.1 – 11.0	x	1
11.3 – 11.2	x	1
11.5 – 11.4		0
11.7 – 11.6	x	1

Even though these scores are recorded to the nearest tenth of a second, each tenth can be considered as a score to determine the interval size. Thus the range for this set of scores is 27. If an interval size of 3 were selected, the number of intervals would be 9, which would not fit the rule of thumb of 10 to 20 intervals. If an interval size of 2 were chosen, the number of intervals would be 14 ($27/2 = 13.5$, rounded to 14). Note that lower scores represent better performances on the shuttle run test. Therefore these scores are placed at the top of the *Interval* column. Furthermore, within each interval the lower (better) score is placed at the top of the interval (to the right) and the higher (poorer) score is placed at the bottom (to the left). If the data were presented in graphical form, the scores would be plotted in the same manner, with the lower scores placed to the right of the horizontal axis and the higher values to the left. Remember, however, that the formulas described in the remaining sections of this chapter are not appropriate to use with this distribution unless they are modified.

CALCULATION OF PERCENTILES

After a test has been administered to a group of examinees and a frequency distribution has been developed using a set of scores, using the distribution to calculate one or more percentiles is often helpful. For example, the **median** is frequently of interest because it represents the center of the distribution of scores. The median is the 50th **percentile,** often expressed by the symbol $X_{.50}$.

The median is the score that divides the distribution so that 50% of the scores fall above this point and 50% fall below. Of course, other percentiles also provide useful information, especially when standards of performance are needed to interpret a set of scores. In the following sections the format followed in describing the development of a frequency distribution is used. First, the calculation of percentiles for ordered scores (not in frequency distribution form) is described. Then, the procedures for calculating percentiles are presented for the simple frequency distribution (intervals of size 1) and the group frequency distribution (intervals greater than size 1).

Calculation from ordered scores

Using ordered scores (not in frequency distribution form), calculating the median or any other percentile is simple, especially if the number of cases is small. Consider, for example, this set representing scores on a pull-ups test.

Data set of 17 scores (no. of pull-ups): 7, 4, 10, 1, 6, 6, 4, 3, 7, 10, 1, 7, 4, 10, 7, 4, 8

These scores can simply be ordered from highest to lowest, not in frequency distribution form:

10–10–10–8–7–7–7–7–6–6–4–4–4–4–3–1–1

There are 17 scores in this data set. By definition, the median will be represented by the score dividing the distribution into equal halves. The median, then, will be the ninth score since this score divides the distribution in halves of 8 scores each. Counting up from the bottom (or down from the top), the ninth score is a score of 6. Thus the median is 6 in this example. Let's identify another percentile—the 75th percentile or $X_{.75}$. This is the score separating the top one fourth of the distribution from the bottom three fourths. Four scores fall above this point and 12 fall below; thus, the 75th percentile is 7.

Calculation from frequency distribution with intervals of size 1

This same set of 17 scores can also be displayed in simple frequency distribution form, with intervals of size 1.

Interval	Tally	f	cf
10	xxx	3	17
9		0	14
8	x	1	14
7	xxxx	4	13
6	xx	2	9
5		0	7
4	xxxx	4	7
3	x	1	3
2		0	2
1	xx	2	2

SCORE LIMITS. Up to this point, the numbers used to represent intervals have been the scores an examinee might actually obtain on a test. These numbers are called the **score limits** of the interval. For example, the top two intervals in the above distribution can be displayed as follows:

$$[\underline{\hspace{3em}}] \quad [\underline{\hspace{3em}}]$$
$$9 \qquad\qquad 10$$

Conceptually, a set of test scores is viewed as a distribution of scores. The shape of the distribution is determined by the way the scores are spread throughout the possible range of scores. If most of the scores are grouped in the center of the distribution with a smaller number of scores at each end, the distribution will resemble a normal curve. The only point to keep in mind now is that the space under the curve is the area represented by the test scores. When score limits are used to represent a data set, the representation is incomplete because a small amount of area is left out between the score limits of the intervals. Notice in the above display of score limits that all scores in the interval of 9 are considered to be in the middle of the interval. The same is true for the interval of 10. These scores represent the score limits of the two intervals. A small amount of space is unaccounted for between the intervals. In this case, the space between the two midpoints of each interval, 9 and 10, is unaccounted for. For this reason, real limits must be used to calculate percentiles more precisely.

REAL LIMITS. To obtain **real limits,** first examine the score limits for any two adjacent intervals. A real limit is determined by taking half of the distance between any two adjacent score limits representing the upper score limit of one interval and the lower score limit of the adjacent interval. In this case (intervals of size 1), the upper score limit and the lower score limit are the same for each interval. Look back to the two score limits in this section. The distance between the score limits is 1. By taking ½ of 1 and adding to and subtracting from the score limits, real limits of 8.5 to 9.5 and 9.5 to 10.5 are obtained. (Real limits are never used for purposes of tallying; only score limits are used for the placement of tallies.) Compare this representation with the one for score limits:

$$[\underline{\hspace{3em}}] [\underline{\hspace{3em}}]$$
$$8.5 \quad\; 9.5 \quad\; 10.5$$

When real limits are determined for every interval in a distribution, the entire area under the curve is taken into account. Real limits are also used in calculating percentiles using a group frequency distribution (intervals greater than 1) as well as in calculating percentile ranks.

PERCENTILE FORMULA. To use the following percentile (%ile) formula, Formula 4-2, the data must be in frequency distribution form.

$$\%\text{ile} = \text{lrl} + \frac{.x(N) - \Sigma fb}{fw} \text{ (i)} \qquad\qquad \text{Formula 4-2}$$

where %ile = percentile; for example, $X_{.50}$ = 50th percentile or median

    lrl = *lower real limit* of interval containing the score representing the desired percentile

    .x = *percentile* displayed as a proportion; for example, the 50th percentile is displayed as .50

    N = total *number* of scores; total frequency in data set

    Σfb = *sum* of *frequencies below* the interval containing the score representing the desired percentile

    fw = *frequency within* this interval

    i = size (width) of the *interval*

Now Formula 4-2 is used below with the frequency distribution on p. 76 to calculate the 75th percentile.

Be certain you are working in the correct interval before you begin calculating. In this case, the correct interval is identified by determining 75%N or .75(17), which equals 12.75. This is the calculation for .x(N) in Formula 4-2. The 12.75th score is the 75th percentile in this set of scores. Checking the *cf* column of the frequency distribution, the 12.75th score is located in the interval 7, since 12.75 is larger than 9 but no greater than 13. Although the interval has now been identified, the score must still be calculated. The formula is completed as follows:

$$\text{75th \%ile} = 6.5 + \frac{12.75 - 9}{4} \quad (1)$$

$$= 7.4375$$

Calculation from frequency distribution with interval greater than size 1

When calculating percentiles using frequency distributions with intervals greater than size 1 (group frequency distribution), Formula 4-2 *must* be used. The frequency distribution presented below is used to demonstrate this calculation. The data represent scores (in inches) on the standing long jump for a group of 14-year-old boys, where N = 60.

Interval	f	cf
80-82	1	60
77-79	3	59
74-76	5	56
71-73	6	51
68-70	9	45
65-67	12	36
62-64	9	24
59-61	6	15
56-58	5	9
53-55	3	4
50-52	1	1

Before describing the steps in this calculation, a review of the concept of real limits is appropriate since larger (wider) intervals are being used. The score limits for the top two intervals in the above distribution can be displayed as follows:

$$[\text{_____}] \; [\text{_____}]$$
$$77 \qquad 79 \; 80 \qquad 82$$

When score limits are used to represent the data set, the distribution of the scores is not completely displayed. A small amount of area is left out between the score limits of adjacent intervals. Notice in the above display of score limits that the area between 79 and 80 is not represented. To be precise in calculating percentiles, *all* of the area must be taken into account.

In this case, the lower score limit of the top interval of the above example is 80, and the upper score limit of the lower interval is 79. The distance or area between these limits is 1. Taking ½ of 1 and adding to and subtracting from the upper and lower score limits, real limits of 76.5 to 79.5 and 79.5 to 82.5 are obtained. The real limits are depicted as follows:

$$[\text{_____}] \; [\text{_____}]$$
$$76.5 \qquad 79.5 \qquad 82.5$$

The median and other percentiles can be calculated using Formula 4-2. Since the median is frequently of interest to a test user, let's calculate this value first.

$$X_{.50} = 64.5 + \frac{30 - 24}{12} \quad (3)$$
$$= 66$$

Be certain you are working in the correct interval before you begin calculating. In this case, the correct interval is identified by determining 50%N or .5(60), which is 30. Thus, the 30th case is the median in this set of scores. Checking the cf column of the frequency distribution, the 30th score is located in the interval between 65 and 67 since 30 is larger than 24 but no greater than 36. Now that the interval has been identified, the score must be calculated. Since the range of scores in the interval equals 3, the score representing the median is unknown. To determine an interval size, subtract the lower score limit from the upper score limit and add 1 to the result. For instance, if 65 were subtracted from 67, the result would equal 2. However, it is clear that the interval 65-67 contains *three* scores—65, 66, and 67. By adding 1 to the result, an interval size of 3 is obtained, which is correct. Of course, the correct size could also be obtained by subtracting the lower real limit from the upper real limit.

As another example, let's calculate the 80th percentile, or $X_{.80}$. To identify the correct interval, find 80%N or .8(60), which equals 48. Since 48 is larger than 45 in the cf column but no greater than 51, the interval 71-73 contains the

48th case, which in turn represents the 80th percentile. Now the percentile formula can be used to calculate the score representing the 80th percentile.

$$X_{.80} = 70.5 + \frac{48 - 45}{6} \quad (3)$$
$$= 70.5 + 1.5$$
$$= 72$$

CALCULATION OF PERCENTILE RANKS

The answer to the question, "What is the nth **percentile**?" is always a test score. A teacher may wish to provide summary information on students' test performance for review by the principal. The manager of a fitness club may ask for information on specific percentiles for certain measures of fitness administered to clients at some point in their program. On the other hand, from the standpoint of the client or the student, the most useful information might be the

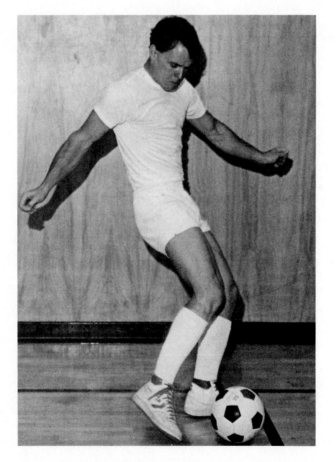

Testing soccer kick.

percentile rank representing his or her own score. Here the known factor is the student's score, and the unknown factor is the percentage, now called the **percentile rank.** Now the question is, "What is the percentile rank for a score of X?" Now the score is known and the percentile rank is unknown; in the previous section the percentile was known and the score was unknown. Keep in mind that percentiles and percentile ranks are reciprocal concepts.

Calculation from ordered scores

You will recall that it was possible to calculate a percentile without forming a frequency distribution at all. The scores were simply ordered from highest to lowest, which is reasonable if the number of scores in the data set is small. Let us use the example on p. 76 to show how percentile ranks can also be calculated from an ordered set of scores. Consider a score of 8; what percentile rank does this score represent? By counting from the lowest score upward, we find that the score of 8 is the 14th score in the data set. Since N = 17, the percentile rank can be calculated by dividing 14 by 17, which equals 82%. Therefore, a score of 8 reflects a percentile rank of 82%, meaning that 82% of the examinees in this sample obtained scores of 8 or below on this test. Only 18% of the examinees scored higher than 8; thus, 8 is a very good score. Using the same set of ordered scores, calculate the percentile rank for a score of 3. The answer you should have obtained is 18%. A score of 3 is the 3rd score in the ordered data set and the percentile rank is 3/17 = 18%. Percentile ranks can also be calculated from frequency distributions, either with intervals of size 1 or intervals greater than size 1.

Calculation for frequency distribution with intervals greater than size 1

Formula 4-3 is used to calculate more precise estimates of the percentile rank. This formula, as well as Formula 4-2 on p. 77, has many variations that will yield the same answer. Although the calculation will be exemplified using a frequency distribution with intervals greater than size 1, the formula is equally applicable when the intervals are of size 1.

$$\text{PR for } X = \frac{\dfrac{\text{cf in int.}}{\text{below}} + \dfrac{\text{Score} - \text{Lower real limit}}{\text{Int. size}}(f)}{N} (100) \qquad \text{Formula 4-3}$$

where PR = percentile rank
  X = score

You should be familiar with the other symbols from reading previous sections of this chapter. It is not necessary to perform any calculation to locate the interval since the examinee's score is provided, which automatically locates the interval. Let's calculate the percentile rank for a score of 69, using the distribution on p. 78.

$$\text{PR for } 69 = \frac{36 + \dfrac{69 - 67.5}{3} (9)}{60} (100)$$

$$= \frac{36 + \dfrac{1.5}{3} (9)}{60} (100)$$

$$= 67.5\%$$

A score of 69 has a percentile rank of 67.5.

Note that the real limits must be used in calculating this statistic. A table of percentiles and scores can easily be set up for a test, and then either the percentile or the percentile rank can be read from the table. If a test is used frequently, such a table is useful. Sample tables of percentiles are included in several chapters of this textbook. A microcomputer program for calculating a table of percentiles is included in the Appendix.

SUMMARY

Once a test has been administered to a group of examinees, a set of test scores is available to be interpreted. Several types of questions might be of interest. How are the test scores distributed for the entire group? To answer this question, a frequency distribution can be constructed and graphed for easier analysis. For example, what is the 50th percentile? For any percentile, the corresponding test score can be calculated. How good is a score of X? The percentile rank of any score in the distribution can be determined. At the very least, a frequency distribution should be formed for each set of test scores unless the number of scores is small; then a simple ordering of scores will often suffice. Test information should not be wasted. If administering the test is important enough, analyzing the scores properly is certainly worthwhile.

REFERENCES

Glass, G.V., and Stanley, J.C. 1980. Statistical methods in education and psychology. Englewood Cliffs, N.J.: Prentice-Hall, Inc.

Hopkins, K.D., and Stanley, J.C. 1981. Educational and psychological measurement and evaluation. Englewood Cliffs, N.J.: Prentice-Hall, Inc.

Mattson, D.E. 1981. Statistics: difficult concepts, understandable explanations. St. Louis: The C.V. Mosby Co.

Stahl, S.M., and Hennes, J.D. 1980. Reading and understanding applied statistics: a self-learning approach, ed. 2, St. Louis: The C.V. Mosby Co.

ANNOTATED READINGS

Gutman, A. 1984. Computerized instruction in statistics. Lavallette, N.J.: Holt, Rinehart & Winston General Book.

Consists of comprehensive courseware package; explains and illustrates the major concepts found in introductory statistics textbooks; class-tested for user-friendliness and ease of operation; eight tutorial disks cover statistical concepts; interactive exercises; eight stat-paks; available for Apple II+ or IIe.

Hills, J.R. 1983. Interpreting percentile scores. Educational Measurement 2(2):24.

Ten true-false items on the interpretation of percentile scores; provides correct answers and brief explanations for all items; useful way to review the concept of percentiles.

Spatz, C., and Johnston, J.O. 1984. Basic statistics: tales of distribution, ed. 3, Belmont, Calif.: Brooks/Cole Publishing Co.

Designed for use in a one-term introductory course; emphasizes conceptualization and interpretation of statistical results; uses distinctive pedagogical devices to stimulate interest and facilitate understanding; covers both descriptive and inferential statistics; presents problems and answers with all necessary steps and explanations.

Weinbery, S.L., and Goldberg, K.P. 1979. Basic statistics for education and the behavioral sciences. Boston: Houghton Mifflin Co.

Written for beginning students; presents case studies from education and the behavioral sciences at the end of each chapter; provides realistic examples of each concept; reviews basic mathematics in an appendix; instructor's manual includes eight sample examinations with complete solutions.

Wike, E.L. 1985. Numbers: a primer of data analysis. Columbus, Ohio: Charles E Merrill Publishing Co.

Lays the foundation for the underlying concepts of statistics; designed for the beginning student; avoids the characteristic dryness of many statistics texts; includes a computer addendum at the end of each chapter, relating material to the MINITAB computer program; uses practical examples and problems.

PROBLEMS

1. Answer the following questions *without* forming a frequency distribution:

   Data set of 15 scores (on push-ups test):
   28, 19, 30, 15, 19, 9, 20, 28, 33, 10, 14, 32, 27, 24, 19

   a. Order the scores from highest to lowest.
   b. Calculate the median.
   c. Calculate the 66⅔ (round to 67th) percentile.
   d. What is the percentile rank for a score of 15?

2. Use the following data set to form a frequency distribution:

   Data set of 15 scores (on sit-ups test):
   62, 60, 59, 66, 60, 57, 61, 65, 58, 59, 65, 60, 64, 61, 60

   a. Form a frequency distribution with intervals of size 1. Include columns for tally, f, cf, and c%.
   b. Calculate the median.
   c. Calculate the 75th percentile.
   d. What is the percentile rank of a score of 58?

3. Use the following data set to build a frequency distribution:

   Data set of 30 scores (on tennis serve test):
   63, 59, 76, 60, 44, 41, 59, 68, 64, 55, 79, 65, 65, 58, 48,
   65, 40, 72, 68, 70, 59, 46, 66, 51, 52, 69, 75, 46, 59, 58

a. Form a frequency distribution with intervals of size 4. Include columns for real limits, tally, f, cf, and c%.
b. Calculate the median.
c. Calculate the 25th percentile.
d. What is the percentile rank for a score of 66?
4. Use the following data to form a frequency distribution:

Data set of 20 scores (on the 50-yard dash):
7.4, 7.5, 6.8, 8.1, 8.7, 7.2, 9.1, 8.4, 7.2, 6.5,
8.2, 7.5, 8.1, 9.4, 8.0, 6.9, 7.5, 9.0, 6.7, 7.0

Form a frequency distribution with intervals of size 3 (actually .3, since the data are recorded in tenths of seconds). Remember that you are working with time scores and lower scores represent better performances. Include columns for real limits, tally, f, cf, and c%.

ANSWERS TO PROBLEMS

1. a. 33–32–30–28–28–27–24–20–19–19–19–15–14–10–9
   b. $X_{.50} = 20$
   c. $X_{.67} = 27.5$
   d. PR for score of 15 = 26.67%

2. a.

Interval	Tally	f	cf	c%
66	X	1	15	100.0
65	XX	2	14	93.3
64	X	1	12	80.0
63		0	11	73.3
62	X	1	11	73.3
61	XX	2	10	66.7
60	XXXX	4	8	53.3
59	XX	2	4	26.7
58	X	1	2	13.3
57	X	1	1	6.7

   b. $X_{.50} = 60$
   c. $X_{.75} = 64$
   d. PR for score of 58 = 13.3%

3. a.

Interval	Real limits	Tally	f	cf	c%
76-79	75.5-79.5	XX	2	30	100.0
72-75	71.5-75.5	XX	2	28	93.3
68-71	67.5-71.5	XXXX	4	26	86.7
64-67	63.5-67.5	XXXXX	5	22	73.3
60-63	59.5-63.5	XX	2	17	56.7
56-59	55.5-59.5	XXXXXX	6	15	50.0
52-55	51.5-55.5	XX	2	9	30.0
48-51	47.5-51.5	XX	2	7	23.3
44-47	43.5-47.5	XXX	3	5	16.7
40-43	39.5-43.5	XX	2	2	6.7

b.
$$X_{.50} = 55.5 + \frac{15 - 9}{6}(4) = 55.5 + \frac{6}{6}(4)$$
$$= 59.5$$

c.
$$X_{.25} = 51.5 + \frac{7.5 - 7}{2}(4) = 51.5 + \frac{.5}{2}(4)$$
$$= 52.5$$

d.
$$\text{PR for } 66 = \frac{17 + \dfrac{66 - 63.5}{4}(5)}{30}(100)$$
$$= 67.1\%$$

4.

Interval	Real limits	Tally	f	cf	c%
6.7-6.5	6.75-6.55	xx	2	20	100
7.0-6.8	7.05-6.75	xxx	3	18	90
7.3-7.1	7.35-7.05	xx	2	15	75
7.6-7.4	7.65-7.35	xxxx	4	13	65
7.9-7.7	7.95-7.65		0	9	45
8.2-8.0	8.25-7.95	xxxx	4	9	45
8.5-8.3	8.55-8.25	x	1	5	25
8.8-8.6	8.85-8.55	x	1	4	20
9.1-8.9	9.15-8.85	xx	2	3	15
9.4-9.2	9.45-9.15	x	1	1	5

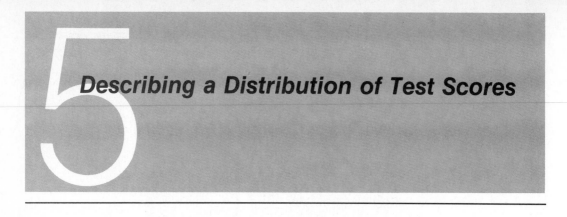

Describing a Distribution of Test Scores

central tendency	median	standard scores
correlation	mode	T-scores
correlation coefficient	normal curve	variability
interpercentile range	raw score	variance
interquartile range	skewness	z-scores
mean	standard deviation	

In the previous chapter a detailed description of the process of building a frequency distribution to summarize a data set in an orderly manner was emphasized. Procedures were also set forth for calculating percentiles and percentile ranks with or without a frequency distribution. Test users and test developers frequently use two other pieces of information: a measure of **central tendency** and a measure of **variability.** The focus of the first section of this chapter is on measures of central tendency. This material is followed by a discussion of standard scores, correlation, and the use of norms. At its best, test development includes the generation of norms. Although you may not develop these norms yourself, be certain that the normative information is appropriate for the examinees.

MEASURES OF CENTRAL TENDENCY

A measure of central tendency provides information about the center of a distribution of test scores. Three measures of central tendency are commonly used to describe a set of test scores—the **mean,** the **median,** and the **mode.** Remember from Chapter 4 that the *median,* or the 50th percentile, is the score dividing the distribution into equal halves. The *mode* is the score occurring most frequently in a distribution. Consider the following set of test scores.

Data set of 13 scores: 39, 33, 31, 29, 27, 27, 26,
26, 26, 24, 23, 23, 21

In this case, the mode is *26*, the most frequently occurring score. The *mean* is the arithmetic average of a set of scores. The mean is emphasized in this section since the calculation of the median has already been described and the mode can be determined in a straightforward manner.

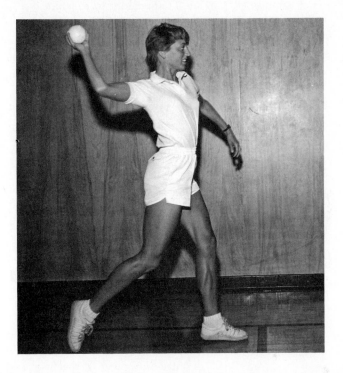

Recall that the median could be calculated for a data set that was ordered from highest to lowest scores, even when the data were not in frequency distribution form. Neither developing a frequency distribution to compute the mean nor ordering the scores is necessary. Examine the five test scores below.

Data set of 5 scores: 20, 10, 14, 18, 15

By using elementary arithmetic, a simple average can be determined by summing the scores and dividing by N. This is represented by Formula 5-1:

$$\overline{X} = \frac{\Sigma X}{N} \qquad \text{Formula 5-1}$$

where $\overline{X}$ = the *mean* (referred to as *X-bar*)
     Σ = *sum of*
     X = *score* for one examinee
   ΣX = *sum* of all *scores* in data set
         (20 + 10 + 14 + 18 + 15)

For the data set given on p. 87:

$$\bar{X} = \frac{77}{5} = 15.4$$

Sometimes it is more convenient to calculate the mean from a set of scores in frequency distribution form, especially when the raw scores for the test are not available. A **raw score** is the actual score an examinee obtains on the test. Usually these scores are available; therefore, only the simplest case of a frequency distribution is described here. This is the frequency distribution with interval sizes equal to 1. To keep the example simple a frequency distribution of only 6 intervals is used. (Keep in mind, however, that a proper distribution should have no fewer than 10 and no more than 20 intervals.)

X	f	fX
10	2	20
9	3	27
8	4	32
7	6	42
6	3	18
5	1	5
	N = 19	144

With the data in this form, Formula 5-1 must be slightly changed to take into account that more than one person obtained a score in most of the above intervals. If all of the scores in the X column were merely added and the sum were divided by N, the answer would be incorrect. The frequency column, as shown in Formula 5-2, must also be considered.

$$\bar{X} = \frac{\Sigma f X}{N} \qquad \text{Formula 5-2}$$

where X = *score* in a frequency distribution

f = *frequency* of scores in interval of frequency distribution

fX = *frequency multiplied* by score representing interval
[e.g., for top interval, $fX = 2(10) = 20$]

ΣfX = sum of *frequency multiplied* by score for all intervals
$[2(10) + 3(9) + \ldots + 1(5) = 144]$

By multiplying the X column times the f column, a score for each person is included in the calculation. In this case:

$$\bar{X} = \frac{144}{19} = 7.58$$

The calculation of the mean for data sets in frequency distribution form with intervals greater than size 1 is omitted from this chapter. This calculation is not difficult, but it is cumbersome. With the ready availability of minicalculators, punching in the raw scores and computing the mean are simple transactions. A discussion of more complex procedures is unnecessary at this level; the formulas presented in this section should be adequate. Although information about the center of a distribution is useful in itself, a more accurate interpretation of the data set is possible by obtaining information on the *spread* of the scores.

MEASURES OF VARIABILITY

Suppose two friends, Jim and Paul, bowled five lines apiece and obtained the following scores:

Jim: 138 142 140 139 141
Paul: 120 140 160 100 180

Let's order these scores to compare them more easily.

Jim: 138 139 140 141 142
Paul: 100 120 140 160 180

Which score represents the center of Jim's set of scores? Which represents Paul's set of scores? In this example both the mean and the median of each set of scores equal 140. Does the fact that these measures of central tendency are the same for both boys suggest that they have similar levels of ability in bowling? If only the means and medians were available, this conclusion might be drawn. Since all five scores are available for each boy, let's look at them closer in their ordered form. Jim's raw scores are similar, but Paul's vary to a great degree. One might say Paul is a more erratic bowler than Jim. Thus, even though the sets of scores have one characteristic in common—their centrality—they are quite different in another way—their variability.

Range and interpercentile range

Three measures of variability are described in this section. The first is the **range** (highest score − lowest score + 1). The second measure is the **interpercentile range,** which provides an indication of how scores vary around the median, the 50th percentile. The most frequently used interpercentile range is the absolute value of $X_{.75} - X_{.25}$, known as the **interquartile range.** The method for obtaining interpercentile ranges involves removing a small percentage of scores from both ends of the distribution. As a result, the most extreme scores are not allowed to affect the indicators of variability. If $X_{.75} = 50$ and $X_{.25} = 27$, the interquartile range is $50 - 27 = 23$. The number 23 is expressed in raw score units. Smaller numbers represent smaller ranges, with more scores clustering around the center of the distribution. Many other interpercentile ranges may be used, such as $X_{.90} - X_{.10}$ or $X_{.85} - X_{.15}$, as long as equal portions of the distribution are deleted from both ends.

Standard deviation

When the mean is used as the measure of the center of the distribution, variability is estimated using the **standard deviation.** This statistic provides information about the extent to which scores deviate from the mean. In statistics σ is sometimes used to represent the standard deviation of a population of examinees, and s is used to represent the standard deviation of a sample of examinees drawn from that population. For convenience and simplicity the symbol s is used in this chapter.

CONCEPTUAL FORMULA. Earlier in this chapter, Formula 5-1 was used to calculate the mean of 15.4 for a set of five scores. The same set of five scores is listed below, this time in order from highest to lowest.

X	X − X̄	(X − X̄)²
20	4.6	21.16
18	2.6	6.76
15	− .4	.16
14	− 1.4	1.96
10	− 5.4	29.16
	0	59.20

$$[\Sigma(X - \overline{X})] \qquad [\Sigma(X - \overline{X})^2]$$

Since the standard deviation reflects the deviation of scores from the mean, it seems logical to calculate this statistic by subtracting the mean from each score and summing the deviations. This calculation is demonstrated in the second column in the above example. Note the result of obtaining the deviations and summing them. The answer of 0 would be obtained regardless of the data set used. Look back and examine the individual deviations from the mean. Although an answer of 0 indicates no variability in the data set, this is obviously not true for this set of scores. An answer of 0 would only *accurately* reflect no variability in a data set if all of the scores were identical. Thus, to obtain a deviation score that provides an accurate indication of the deviation of scores from the mean, these deviations are squared. The squared deviations are shown in the third column of the above example. The sum of these deviations is 59.20.

Now that we are working with *squared* deviations, the statistic being calculated is s^2, which is known as the **variance.** Once the variance is known, the standard deviation can be calculated by taking the square root of the variance. Formula 5-3 for the variance follows:

$$s^2 = \frac{\Sigma(X - \overline{X})^2}{N} \qquad \text{Formula 5-3}$$

The sum of the squared deviations is divided by N to determine the average of the deviations. The numerator of this formula has already been determined for the set of 5 scores and, of course, $N = 5$. Thus,

$$s^2 = \frac{59.20}{5} = 11.84$$

Although calculating the variance to obtain the standard deviation is necessary, the numerical value for the variance is not useful because it is not expressed in the original raw score units of the test. The square root of this value, which is the standard deviation, is more useful in describing a set of test scores since it is expressed in the actual score units of the test. Formula 5-4 for calculating the standard deviation follows:

$$s = \sqrt{\frac{\Sigma(X - \overline{X})^2}{N}}$$ Formula 5-4

A variance of 11.84 yields a standard deviation of 3.44. To summarize for the set of five scores, the mean is 15.4 and the standard deviation is 3.44. Assume that the five scores were obtained by administering an agility test to five students. The scores are expressed in seconds. A small standard deviation means that the scores tend to cluster around the mean. In this case the standard deviation indicates that the scores are spread out on both sides of the mean rather than clustered. Since the time scores are for a test of short duration, a deviation of 3 seconds or greater is considerable. In a measure of much longer duration, such as a long-distance run, a deviation of 3 seconds would carry much less significance. The standard deviation must be interpreted in light of the actual score units of the test. In the previous example the examinees would not have similar abilities on the attribute being measured. If the standard deviation were smaller (e.g., 1.1 seconds), the scores would be spread much more closely around the mean. In this case the ability levels of the examinees would be similar. Formula 5-4 is known as a conceptual formula rather than a computational formula. In other words, it depicts in a clear-cut manner the meaning and derivation of the standard deviation. (Do not use Formula 5-4 in the actual calculation of the standard deviation.)

If you have previously taken an elementary statistics course, you might have used a formula for the standard deviation with $N - 1$ in the denominator rather than N, as shown in Formulas 5-4 and 5-5. When $N - 1$ is used, the test user wishes to use a set of test scores to estimate the standard deviation of a population of individuals like those in the group being tested. For example, a teacher might administer a standing long jump test to a group of fourth grade girls randomly selected from the entire school district. The mean and standard deviation calculated for the set of test scores could be interpreted as representative of all fourth grade girls in the district. Under these circumstances, the standard deviation formula should be used with $N - 1$ in the denominator so that the estimate of the standard deviation will be unbiased. In contrast, the more typical situation encountered in test administration is the use of a test with a specific group. Of greatest interest is the mean and standard deviation for this specific group. Generalizing to a population of individuals may not be important or, more often, may not be feasible. In this case the standard deviation formula with N in the denominator is appropriate. Thus, throughout this text, any version of the standard deviation formula will include N in the denominator. If you use a minicalculator that is programmed to calculate the standard deviation, determine which term is used in the denominator. Many minicalculators provide two estimates of *s*, one calculated using N in the denominator and the other using N − 1 in the denominator.

COMPUTATIONAL FORMULA. The standard deviation can be easily calculated from a set of raw scores by using many of the inexpensive minicalculators now on the market. In some cases after the scores have been entered, the standard deviation can be calculated with the push of a button. In others, the sums of squares needed in the computational formula are automatically calculated. The computational formula for the standard deviation used in this textbook is Formula 5-5. (A number of equivalent formulas that are equally appropriate may be used.)

$$s = \sqrt{\frac{N\Sigma X^2 - (\Sigma X)^2}{N(N)}}$$

Formula 5-5

where ΣX^2 = the *sum* of each *number squared;* for the data set of 5 scores, this would be $20^2 + 18^2 + \ldots + 10^2$

$(\Sigma X)^2$ = the *square* of the *sum* of all *scores;* in this example $(20 + 18 + \ldots + 10)^2$

Let's apply Formula 5-5 to the small data set on p. 87.

$$s = \sqrt{\frac{5(1245) - (77)^2}{5(5)}}$$

$$= \sqrt{\frac{6225 - 5929}{25}} = \sqrt{11.84} = 3.44$$

To summarize, the standard deviation is the square root of the variance. The variance must be calculated first because the sum of the deviations of scores from the mean is *0*. However, the standard deviation is the statistic of greater interest since it is expressed in raw score units. Now both the mean and standard deviation of this small set of five scores have been calculated. Interpreting these values is easier if the normal curve and its characteristics are clarified.

SCORE DISTRIBUTIONS

When data obtained from a test administration are graphed in the form of a curve, the shape of the curve will depend on the way in which the scores are distributed. The most common types of curves represented in data sets at this level are the normal curve and the skewed curve.

Normal curve

In the previous chapter test scores were graphed in frequency polygon or histogram form. If it were possible to administer a test to a large number of examinees, perhaps several thousand, and the test scores were graphed, the resultant curve would approach the **normal curve** for most physical performance tests.

The normal curve (Fig. 5-1) has several characteristics that can be of assistance in interpreting a set of scores. First, the curve is symmetrical. If the curve were lifted at one tail and folded over on top of the other side, the two halves of the curve would match precisely. In this case the mean, median, and mode would be identical. Second, the area under the curve represents 100%. It is possible to calculate the area for any portion of the curve. On the baseline of the curve, a mark is placed in the center to represent the center of the distribution. In addition, three marks are placed equidistant from each other above the center (in this context, the mean), and three marks are placed below the mean. These marks, representing 3 standard deviations both above and below the mean, divide the normal curve into six portions. The percentage of area between these points is calculated and provides useful information for test users and developers. These portions and the percentage of area in each are displayed in Fig. 5-2. Note that the tails of the curve do not touch the baseline. Obtaining scores representing 4 or more standard deviations above or below the mean is possible. For example, a genius might have an IQ that is greater than 5 or 6 standard deviations above the mean of the distribution of IQ scores. However, the likelihood of obtaining extreme scores is remote; thus the normal curve is usually described as being characterized by ±3 standard deviations.

FIG. 5-1. *Normal curve.*

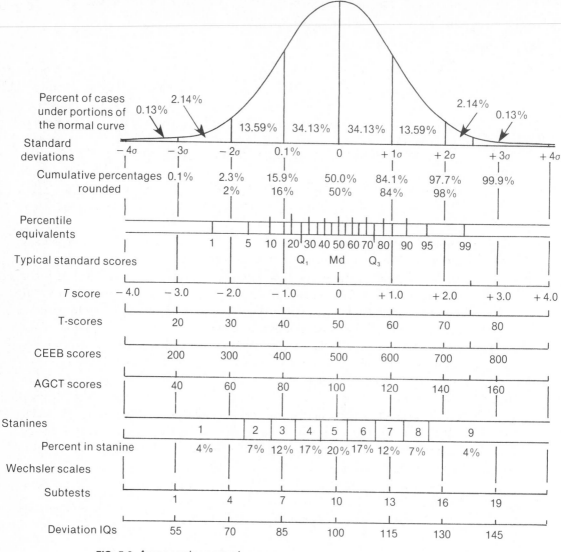

FIG. 5-2. *Areas under normal curve.*
From Text Service Notebook 148.

What kind of information can be obtained from Fig. 5-2? Look at the point designated as +1s, or 1 standard deviation above the mean. If an examinee's score falls at exactly this point, approximately 84% of the group taking the test scored below this point. The 84% was approximated by adding the percentages in each section to the left of +1s. A distribution of scores for a sit-ups test is depicted in Fig. 5-3. The mean for this set of scores is 40, and the standard deviation is 7. One standard deviation above the mean is a score of 47 (40 + 7).

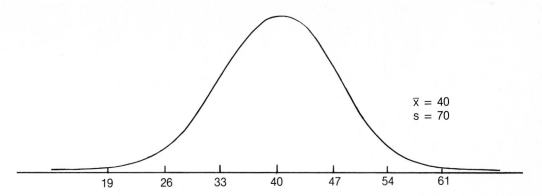

$\bar{x} = 40$
$s = 70$

FIG. 5-3. *Normal curve with standard deviations expressed in score units (number of sit-ups).*

One standard deviation below the mean is a score of 33 (40 − 7). Thus 84% of the group of examinees received scores at or below 47, while scores for approximately 16% of the group were at or below a score of 33. Of course, many scores fall between standard deviations expressed as whole numbers (e.g., +2, −1). For example, how should a score of 35 be interpreted? Certainly this score is below average, falling between the mean and 1 standard deviation below the mean. However, the score cannot be interpreted with precision unless it is converted to standard score form.

Skewed distributions

The bell shape typically associated with the normal curve shows that most of the examinees obtained scores in the middle of the distribution, with a few people scoring at each end. The two ends of the distribution are referred to as *tails* of the distribution. In short, the majority of the examinees represented under the normal curve obtained scores surrounding the average, while a smaller number received high and low scores. However, in real-life testing situations the test scores do not always approximate the normal curve. Sometimes most of the examinees will do well on a test or sometimes most will perform poorly. Then these scores form **skewed** distributions, with most of the area clustered at one end of the distribution.

When most of the examinees receive low scores on the test, the distribution is positively skewed. As shown in Fig. 5-4, the majority of scores falls in the lower portion of the distribution, with a small number of high scores occurring in the long tail stretching out to the right. The *skewed* end of the distribution is the one with the long tail. If the skewness is located to the right, as in Fig. 5-4, the distribution is labeled positively skewed. If the skewed end is located to the left, the distribution is labeled negatively skewed, as depicted in Fig. 5-5. In this case a large portion of the examinees received high scores on the test, and

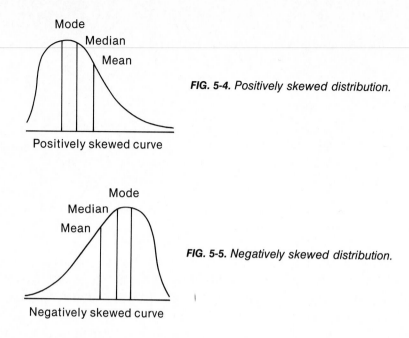

FIG. 5-4. *Positively skewed distribution.*

FIG. 5-5. *Negatively skewed distribution.*

only a few scored at the lower end of the distribution. When mastery tests are used, a negatively skewed distribution is often a desirable result. If most individuals master the material, they will do well on the test.

Consider the best way to describe these distributions. Should the mean and standard deviation be used as measures of central tendency and variability, or should the median be used? How is this decision made? First, a set of test scores should be summarized in frequency distribution form and graphed as a frequency polygon. Next, the graph (frequency polygon) should be examined. If the distribution of scores appears to approximate the normal curve, the mean and standard deviation should be used since these values have stronger mathematical properties than the median and interpercentile range. If the distribution of scores is skewed, the mean will be closer to the skewed tail of the distribution than the median, because the mean is affected by the extreme scores in the tail. Therefore, the median is a better representation of the center of the distribution when it is skewed. Since the median is a percentile, the corresponding measure of variability is one of the interpercentile ranges.

STANDARD SCORES

In Chapter 4 you learned how to convert test scores to percentile ranks. Two rules of thumb apply when transforming scores to standard scores. First, the median and the interpercentile range are used together. If these statistics are used to describe the center and spread of the distribution, percentile ranks should be used to convert scores. Second, the mean and the standard deviation are used together. When these statistics are used to describe a data set, a standard score transformation should be used.

The z-score transformation

Standard scores may take many forms, but all are based on the **z-score transformation,** which is the basic standard score transformation. Another term for this unit of transformation is the standard deviation unit. Formula 5-6 converts test scores to z-scores.

$$\text{z-score} = \frac{X - \overline{X}}{s} \qquad \text{Formula 5-6}$$

All of the symbols in Formula 5-6 should look familiar. Refer back to the data from the sit-ups test. The mean of 40, the standard deviation of 7, and the precise interpretation of a score of 35 were of interest. The z-score transformation is one way of providing greater precision. Let's apply the data to Formula 5-6 and calculate the z-score for a score of 35.

$$\text{z-score} = \frac{35 - 40}{7} = -.72$$

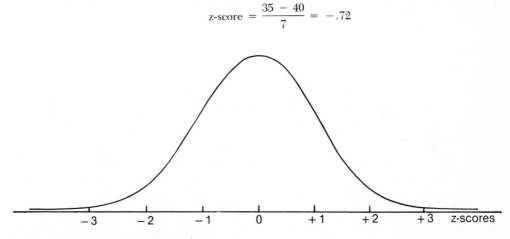

FIG. 5-6. *Graph of z-score distribution.*

The z-scores form a distribution with fixed parameters—a mean of 0 and a standard deviation of 1. Examine the z-score distribution in Fig. 5-6. The mean of the distribution is 0, and 1 standard deviation above the mean is +1. One standard deviation below the mean is −1. The z-score values above the mean are all positive; those below the mean are all negative. Whatever the metric of the test score, the z-score formula converts it to the standard z-score metric. In other words, across a wide variety of distributions the mean of each distribution is converted to a z-score mean of 0. One of these tests might be scored in feet and inches, and another may be scored in minutes and seconds; yet the z-score means of the two tests will both be 0. The standard deviations are standardized in the same way.

Certain raw scores can be easily determined without the use of Formula 5-6, if the score is equal to 1 or more standard deviations above or below the mean. In the previous example it is apparent that a z-score of +1 equals 47 and a z-score of −1 equals 33. Both a z-score of +1 and a raw score of 47 equal 1 standard deviation above the mean. A z-score of −1 and a raw score of 33 both equal 1 standard deviation below the mean.

Refer to the interpretation of a score of 35 on the sit-ups test; the z-score for this score is −.72. The negative sign indicates that the score falls below the mean, and the size of the z-score (.72) indicates that almost three quarters of a standard deviation is represented. Thus, a score of 35 is approximately three quarters of 1 standard deviation below the mean.

When interpreting only a few test scores from a single data set, it is possible to interpret the scores without converting them to z-scores if the mean and standard deviation of the data set are known. However, in the physical education field several tests are often administered to a group of examinees during a single testing session. Each of the tests may be scored in different units. For example, a set of tests might include a test of skinfold thickness, a 1-mile run, and a sit-and-reach test of flexibility. The first measure is scored in millimeters; the second, in minutes and seconds; and the third, in centimeters (cm). How can an examinee's scores on these three tests be compared? For this purpose, the z-score transformation is a very useful tool. Assume that the examinee who performed 35 sit-ups in the previous example also took the sit-and-reach test and obtained a score of 25 cm. The mean and standard deviation of the group on this test was 23 cm and 2 cm, respectively. It is rather cumbersome to graph a distribution and mark the mean and standard deviations for the sit-ups test and the sit-and-reach test so that the two test scores could be compared. If the score transformations of many examinees are needed, then the graphing approach is totally inefficient. What is the z-score for a sit-and-reach score of 25 cm?

$$\text{z-score} = \frac{25 - 23}{2} = +1$$

Now the score on the sit-ups test can be compared with the score on the sit-and-reach test. The score of 35 on the sit-ups test is represented by a z-score of −.72 and the sit-and-reach score of 25, by a z-score of +1. Referring to any other information about either of the two data sets is not necessary when comparing the two z-scores. This particular examinee is below average in abdominal strength and above average in low back flexibility. This same procedure could be used to compare the scores of two or more individuals on the same test.

The T-score transformation

A practical reason for converting test scores to standard scores is to inform others of the examinees' performance on a test. For instance, a comparison of scores on different tests is information that is often requested by parents of a child in a physical education class, by the principal of a school, or by the manager of a fitness club. While z-scores provide a logical means of comparison, the z-score scale itself is not the easiest standard score to explain. This difficulty is primarily because the negative scores occur below the mean and the scores with decimal points can be found both above and below the mean. Most test developers resolve this problem by transforming the z-scores to another standard score that is easier for the layman to interpret. Generally these transformations remove the negative sign and the decimal point from the z-scores. All of these transformations, however, are based on the z-score distribution.

The **T-score distribution** is a popular conversion with developers of sport skills and basic motor abilities tests. The T-score distribution has a mean of 50 and a standard deviation of 10. To convert z-scores to T-scores, Formula 5-7 is used.

$$\text{T-score} = 10z + 50 \qquad \text{Formula 5-7}$$

Since two z-scores were calculated in the previous section, let's use these to calculate T-scores.

$$\text{T-score (for sit-ups score)} = 10(-.72) + 50 = 42.8$$
$$\text{T-score (for sit-and-reach score)} = 10(1) + 50 = 60$$

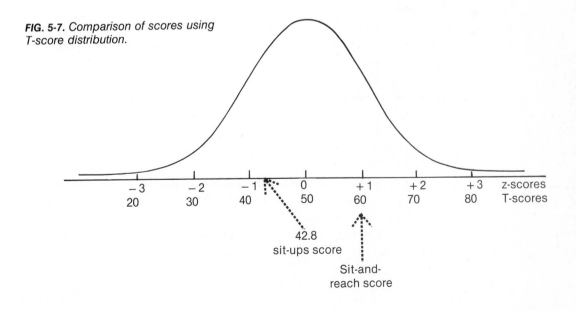

FIG. 5-7. *Comparison of scores using T-score distribution.*

Compare these scores using the T-score distribution presented in Fig. 5-7. Note that no transformed score begins with a negative sign or a decimal. At the same time the information obtained from the T-score calculations does not conceal anything previously secured from the z-scores themselves. However, T-scores have a few inherent qualities that allow this distribution to be explained more easily to the public. In general, the scores range between 0 and 100. Although scores exceeding a −3 or +3 standard deviation (exceeding T-scores of 20 or 80) are rare, a range of scores from 0 to 100 seems plausible. Many laymen think of a perfect score on a test as 100, although clearly a perfect score could take on any number of values, depending on the test length. Furthermore, the mean of the T-score distribution is 50, which seems like a reasonable average for a test to many people.

CONSTANT-VALUE METHOD. Frequently a test user is more interested in determining the T-scores for an entire set of test scores than in calculating individual T-scores. If so, the *constant-value method* can be used to construct a T-score table for the data set. This table can be used to convert raw scores to T-scores, not only for this year's examinees but also for those who take the test in future years. Of course, these types of tables must be recalculated periodically so that they remain updated. The following steps are used in the constant-value method.

1. Calculate the mean and standard deviation for a set of test scores. For the sit-ups test the mean was 40 and the standard deviation was 7.
2. Calculate $s/10$. In our example, $7/10 = .7$. This is the constant used to add and subtract from the mean.
3. List each possible T-score from 20 to 80.
4. Add the constant to the mean (40) to obtain the raw score for a T-score of 51. In this case, $40 + .7 = 40.7$. Proceed in the same manner for T-scores of 52-80. Note that the addition is cumulative. For example, to calculate the raw score for a T-score of 52, add the constant (.7) to the raw score for a T-score of 51 (40.7). The raw score for a T-score of 52 is 41.4.
5. For all T-scores below the mean, subtract the constant. For a T-score of 49, subtract the constant (.7) from the mean (40) to obtain an equivalent raw score. The raw score for a T-score of 49 is 39.3. Proceed in the same manner for T-scores of 48 down to 20.
6. Round off the raw scores to correspond with the actual test scores. In this case the actual test scores are in whole numbers (number of sit-ups); therefore, the raw scores should be rounded to the nearest whole number.

As an example, the use of the constant-value method is exemplified for T-scores of 45 to 55.

T-score	Corresponding raw score	Rounded raw score
55	43.5	44
54	42.8	43
53	42.1	42
52	41.4	41
51	40.7	41
50	40	40
49	39.3	39
48	38.6	39
47	37.9	38
46	37.2	37
45	36.5	37

To complete the table of T-scores, raw score values must be calculated for all T-scores from 20 to 80. Note that several T-score values have the same raw score values. This is not unusual, especially when the standard deviation is a small number. Once the completed T-score table has been developed, it can be used to convert all scores in a data set, assuming the test examinees are similar to those whose scores were used to prepare the table. This method is much simpler than calculating T-scores for each raw score in a set of test scores.

LOWER SCORES/BETTER PERFORMANCES. For certain measures of motor behavior, higher scores reflect poorer performance. If the data set consists of scores on a shuttle run test, lower times are faster times and thus reflect better performance. When a z-score is calculated for a time score that is actually better than the mean in a performance context but lower than the mean in a numerical context, the result may be confusing. As an example, the mean of a set of shuttle run test scores is 11.2 seconds and the standard deviation is 0.4 second. What is the z-score for a raw score of 11.8? Use Formula 5-4 to solve this problem.

$$\text{z-score} = \frac{11.8 - 11.2}{.4} = +1.5$$

The result is a $+1.5$ z-score, which indicates that the score is above the mean. This, of course, implies above average performance. Yet, in a performance context this is not true. A shuttle run score of 11.8 is slower than the average score for the group; it is a below average score. The formula for calculating z-scores, as with any other statistical formulas, only deals with numbers and not with their interpretations. Therefore, whenever lower scores equal better performances, change the sign of the z-score to the opposite; the result will then represent the correct *interpretation* of the score. Instead of obtaining a $+1.5$ z-score for a shuttle run score of 11.8, the answer would be -1.5. When the z-score is transformed to a T-score, it will also be correct in an interpretive sense. A z-score of -1.5 is equal to a T-score of 35, a below average score.

When lower scores represent better performances, an easier method of calculating the z-score is to use a variation of Formula 5-6 shown in Formula 5-8.

$$\text{z-score*} = \frac{\overline{X} - X}{s}$$ Formula 5-8

The shuttle run test scores will again be used as an example. The mean is 11.2 seconds; the standard deviation, 0.4 second. What is the z-score for a raw score of 11.8?

$$\text{z-score*} = \frac{11.2 - 11.8}{.4} = -1.5$$

Using Formula 5-8, the resulting answer corresponds with the interpretation of the score in a performance context. In other words, a time score larger than the mean actually represents poorer performance; thus, the negative z-score provides the correct interpretation.

CORRELATION

To be able to analyze a test, a basic understanding of test reliability and validity is necessary. To estimate these two test characteristics, a statistic known as the **correlation coefficient** is often used. The term **correlation** refers to the *relationship between two variables, X and Y*. The symbol X already represents a score on a test; now Y will be used to represent a score on another test. Is the ability to perform one skill related to the ability to perform a second skill? To gain insight into this type of question, a correlation coefficient can be calculated.

Pearson product-moment correlation coefficient

The **Pearson product-moment correlation** coefficient, the most commonly used correlation coefficient, is symbolized as r_{xy}. Correlation coefficients can range from $+1.00$ to -1.00. These extremes are depicted in the data sets below.

*This formula is a special case of the usual z-score formula.

Two data sets

	Data set A			Data set B	
	Leg strength	Standing long jump		Leg strength	Arm strength
A	42	7 ft, 5 in	A	42	8
B	40	7 ft, 0 in	B	40	10
C	38	6 ft, 5 in	C	38	12
D	36	6 ft, 0 in	D	36	14
E	34	5 ft, 5 in	E	34	16

In both data sets the leg strength measure (X) is an indicator of leg extensor strength measured in foot-pounds. In Data set A the second variable (Y) is the standing long jump, and in Data set B arm strength is measured by a test of pull-ups. All of these data sets are formed hypothetically to demonstrate the extreme range of correlation coefficients, $r_{xy} = +1.00$ and $r_{xy} = -1.00$. In Data set A the first examinee, A, has the highest scores on both tests, and the fifth examinee, E, has the lowest scores. This pattern can be observed across all examinees. Thus it is intuitively obvious that a high relationship exists between leg strength and the ability to perform the standing long jump (i.e., those with greater leg strength are able to jump longer distances). If r_{xy}, the Pearson product-moment correlation coefficient, were calculated for this data set, it would equal $+1.00$. A correlation coefficient of $+1.00$ represents a *perfect positive correlation*.

Now examine the two sets of scores in Data Set B. Note that precisely the reverse trend is evident in the arm strength and leg strength scores. As the leg strength scores decrease, the arm strength scores increase. The correlation between these two sets of scores is negative. In fact, in this example, the correlation coefficient is -1.00, a perfect negative correlation. Normally, it is not appropriate to calculate the correlation coefficients for such small data sets. With only five examinees, the resultant coefficient may not be an accurate indicator of the relationship between two variables, since the idiosyncrasies of one person could drastically affect the coefficient. Even in the next example, the number of cases is too small; 30 or more examinees would be desirable. However, a small data set is convenient for demonstrating the calculation of the correlation coefficient. In this example the correlation coefficient for scores of eight examinees on two variables, pull-ups and push-ups, will be determined.

Examinee	Pull-ups (X)	Push-ups (Y)	X^2	Y^2	XY
A	10	15	100	225	150
B	2	5	4	25	10
C	5	11	25	121	55
D	6	10	36	100	60
E	7	14	49	196	98
F	1	3	1	9	3
G	9	16	81	256	144
H	5	8	25	64	40
	45	82	321	996	560

The Pearson product-moment correlation coefficient, r_{xy}, is calculated using Formula 5-9.

$$r_{xy} = \frac{N\Sigma XY - (\Sigma X)(\Sigma Y)}{\sqrt{[N\Sigma X^2 - (\Sigma X)^2][N\Sigma Y^2 - (\Sigma Y)^2]}} \qquad \text{Formula 5-9}$$

where ΣXY = the *sum* of the products of XY for each examinee;
in this example, $(10)(15) + (2)(5) + \ldots + (5)(8) = 560$

$(\Sigma X)(\Sigma Y)$ = the *product* of the *sum* of the X *scores* and the *sum* of the Y *scores;* in this example, $(45)(82) = 3690$

ΣX^2 = the *sum* of each X value *squared;* in this example, $(10^2 + 2^2 + \ldots + 5^2) = 321;$ use same concept for Y^2

$(\Sigma X)^2$ = the *square* of the *sum* of all X values; in this example, $(10 + 2 + \ldots + 5)^2 = 5025;$ use same concept for $(\Sigma Y)^2$

Now Formula 5-9 will be used with the pull-ups and push-ups data.

$$r_{xy} = \frac{8(560) - (45)(82)}{\sqrt{[8(321) - (45)^2][8(996) - (82)^2]}} = 0.96$$

A coefficient of 0.96 represents a high positive relationship between push-ups and pull-ups, suggesting that performance of each measure is dependent to a large extent on a similar type of arm and shoulder girdle strength.

Rank difference correlation coefficient

Ranking the scores in each data set on p. 103 is also possible. The highest scores in each data set would be given ranks of 1, and so forth. In the pull-ups data set Examinees C and H received the same score of 5. The scores represent two rank positions, yet the ranks for the two scores should be identical. These ranks are calculated by *averaging* the two rank positions, in this case 5 and 6, and assigning the average rank of 5.5 to each score of 5. Without performing any type of calculation on the ranks, it is possible to obtain a general feeling about the degree of relationship between two variables from a visual examination of the ranks. For example, Examinee A would be assigned ranks of 1 on pull-ups and 2 on push-ups; Examinee F would be assigned ranks of 8 and 8, respectively. Although the ranks are not identical for each person, they are similar; this points to a substantial relationship between the two variables. Of course it is known that the relationship is high, since r_{xy} has already been calculated using the raw scores. Calculating a correlation coefficient using ranks only is also possible, but it requires a different statistic known as the **rank difference correlation coefficient** (ρ). Formula 5-10 is used to calculate rho, ρ.

$$\rho = 1 - \frac{6(\Sigma D^2)}{N(N^2 - 1)} \qquad \text{Formula 5-10}$$

where D = the *difference* between the two ranks for each subject

D^2 = *square* of the *difference* between ranks for an examinee

ΣD^2 = *sum* of D^2 for all examinees

The push-ups and pull-ups data will be used again, and for purposes of convenience the raw scores will be reproduced as well as ranked. Note that ΣD equals 0. This is always true, regardless of the data set. This calculation is a convenient way to check the numbers in the D column.

X	Rank (X)	Y	Rank (Y)	D	D²
10	1	15	2	−1	1
2	7	5	7	0	0
5	5.5	11	4	1.5	2.25
6	4	10	5	−1	1
7	3	14	3	0	0
1	8	3	8	0	0
9	2	16	1	1	1
5	5.5	8	6	−0.5	0.25
					5.50
					(ΣD^2)

$$\rho = 1 - \frac{6(5.50)}{8(8^2 - 1)} = 0.935$$

Note that the result of the rank difference method is not the same as the result obtained using r_{xy}, although the values are similar. This is expected since the process of converting raw scores to ranks leads to a loss of information about the original data sets.

To summarize, when two sets of scores are available for the same set of examinees, the relationship between the two variables can be estimated using a correlation coefficient. When the raw scores are continuous or discrete data (not initially in rank form), the Pearson product-moment correlation coefficient (r_{xy}) is appropriate under most circumstances. When the scores are converted to ranks, or obtained as ranks initially, the rank difference correlation coefficient (ρ) may be used. The rank difference formula is easier to use, but its result is not as accurate as r_{xy}. For all practical purposes, however, the discrepancy between estimates is not serious.

Graph of relationship between two variables

Correlational information is often presented in graphic form by plotting the *coordinates* of the X and Y scores, with the Y scores represented on the *vertical* axis and the X scores represented on the *horizontal* axis. Lower or poorer scores are located on the lower portion of the Y axis and higher or better scores, on the upper portion. On the X axis lower or poorer scores are placed to the left; higher or better scores are to the right. A coordinate is a point on the graph representing the paired X and Y scores for each examinee. The push-ups and pull-ups scores for 8 examinees are presented in graphical form in Fig. 5-8.

FIG. 5-8. *Graph of relationship between push-up and pull-up scores.*

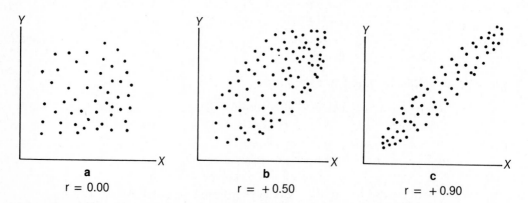

FIG. 5-9. *Graph of various sizes of correlation coefficients. A,* No relationship between *X* and *Y. B,* Moderate relationship. *C,* High relationship.

Each point on the graph represents two scores for an examinee. If the X and Y scores increase proportionally, that is, as the X scores increase the Y scores also increase by the same proportion, the coordinates will fall on or close to a straight line that slants from the lower left corner of the graph to the upper right corner. While the increase in X and Y scores is not precisely proportional in Fig. 5-8, the tendency can be observed. This is an example of a high positive correlation represented in graphical form. Examples of other sizes and signs of correlation coefficients are displayed in graphical form in Fig. 5-9.

Interpretation of correlation coefficients

Opinions vary about how the size of a correlation coefficient should be interpreted. How high should a coefficient be to be classified as high? Moderate? Low? A general rule of thumb is presented below, but under certain circumstances the interpretation may vary even from this general rule.

$\pm.80$-1.00 High
$\pm.60$-0.79 Moderately high
$\pm.40$-0.59 Moderate
$\pm.20$-0.39 Low
$\pm.00$-0.19 No relationship

Another way of interpreting the coefficient is to square it. This statistic, r_{xy}^2, is known as the *coefficient of determination*. As an example, assume the correlation between two measures of arm strength is 0.80. The square of the correlation coefficient is an indication of the *shared variance between two variables*. In other words, this is the variance the two variables share. For the two measures of arm strength, the shared variance is 0.64. This means that 64% of the variance between these two measures taps a common element, which can be assumed to be arm strength. With higher correlation coefficients the shared variance is substantial. However, with correlation coefficients of moderate and small sizes, the coefficient of determination is affected to a greater extent. For example, if $r_{xy} = 0.50$, the square of the coefficient equals 0.25. Another advantage of using the squared correlation coefficient in interpreting r_{xy} is that squared coefficients can be compared as ratios, unlike the regular correlation coefficient. For example, a coefficient of 0.90 does not represent twice as much of a relationship as a coefficient of 0.45. However, when r_{xy} is squared, coefficients can legitimately be compared in this manner. For example, a coefficient of determination of 0.50 represents twice as much variance as a coefficient of 0.25.

USE OF NORMS
Raw scores and derived scores

A raw score is the score an individual obtains on a test. If the only information available about an examinee's test performance is the raw score, interpreting it meaningfully can be difficult. For instance, if Mary runs the 50-yard dash in 7.8 seconds, is the score good? To answer this question the score can be transformed to another scale, yielding a *derived score*. In Chapters 4 and 5 procedures are described for developing both percentile and standard score norms. Even better, the raw scores can be compared to a table in which derived scores have already been calculated for the raw scores.

Types of norms

Norms are derived scores determined from the raw scores obtained by a specific group on a specific test. Whenever percentile norms are determined for a group of examinees, half will score above the middle of the distribution and half will score below. No inherent value is attached to any given norm score. The norm describes an examinee in relation to a large sample of people who have taken the test. Any judgment made about the norm is made by the test user. Several types of norms might be used, including grade norms, age norms, percentiles, and standard scores.

   GRADE NORMS. *Grade norms* are calculated by determining the average of the raw scores for a grade and using the grade equivalent in place of that average. For example, if the average distance that a class of fifth grade boys could throw a softball were 96 feet, a score of 96 feet would represent a grade norm of 5. However, scores on measures of physical performance are rarely transformed to grade norms because each grade includes children of different ages; the older children, more advanced in physical growth and development, have a natural advantage in many motor skills.

The use of grade norms has several other limitations. The units from one grade to another are not equal over different parts of the scale. Thus achievement from grade 2 to grade 3 may be greater or less than achievement from grade 8 to grade 9. Performance on physical fitness items, for instance, usually increases consistently from grade to grade for elementary school girls. However, this performance increment may level off before entrance into high school. Thus the significance of a grade norm of 11 for a ninth grade student is not nearly as great as a grade norm of 4 for a second grade student.

Furthermore, grade units may be unequal from test to test. A seventh grade student with grade norms of 11 on the distance run and 9 on the sit-and-reach test would appear to have more cardiorespiratory endurance than flexibility. However, there may be a greater range of distance run scores than flexibility scores for the sixth grade, and the student might actually have high percentile ranks on both tests.

Grade norms are useful for reporting growth in basic skills at the elementary school level. Since this type of norm can be misinterpreted so easily, other types are often preferred.

AGE NORMS. *Age norms* are determined by calculating the average score for a given age. A raw score is then interpreted in terms of an age equivalent. If the average performance by 17-year-old boys on the standing long jump is 7 feet 2 inches, then a raw score of 7 feet 2 inches is used to represent an age norm of 17. Although this type of norm has been used with tests of physical performance, in reality skeletal maturation may play a more significant role than age. In growth and development scales a form of age norms is sometimes used to describe sequences of motor behavior.

PERCENTILE RANK NORMS. The standardized tests published by AAHPERD include tables of norms based on percentile ranks. These include the Health-Related Physical Fitness Test (1980), the Youth Fitness Test (1976), the Cooperative Physical Education Tests (1970), and the Sports Skills Tests (1967). Both fitness test manuals present norms by age and gender. Grouping by age or grade should not be confused with age norms and grade norms. In the latter case ages or grades represent the norms; in the former case percentiles represent the norms.

In Chapter 4 you learned how to calculate percentile ranks. The *percentile rank norm* is based on the position of the person's score relative to others in the group. Whatever the range of raw scores, the percentiles can only range from 1 to 99. Percentiles divide a distribution of scores into 100 groups of equal size. Although a set of raw scores often forms a bell-like distribution, percentiles form a rectangular one, as shown in Fig. 5-10. Percentiles are not equally spaced

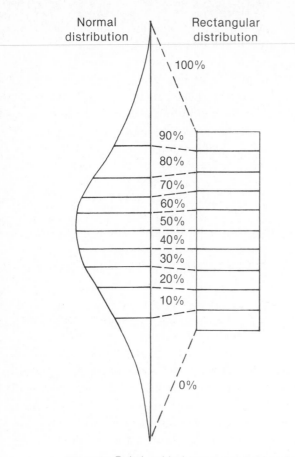

FIG. 5-10. *Relationship between normal and rectangular distributions.*

throughout the distribution, because more people are clustered at the middle of the distribution than at the extremes. Only if the same number of examinees obtains each score are the percentiles equally spaced. However, such a distribution is not likely to occur. Therefore, although percentiles seem simple to interpret, it is easy to overemphasize differences near the median and underemphasize differences near the extremes.

Sometimes averaging percentile ranks for several tests is desirable. To do so, the percentiles must first be converted to z-scores. This conversion can be made using tables that are available in most statistics textbooks. The z-scores are then averaged, and this average is converted back to a percentile rank using the same table. The raw score distribution is assumed to be normal for each set of raw scores. Also, the same norm group should be used to generate the percentiles.

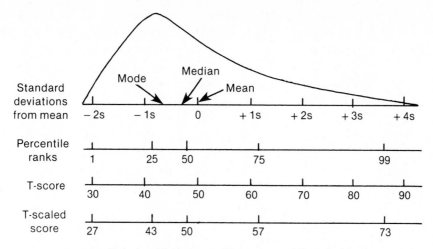

FIG. 5-11. *Relationship between T-scores and T-scaled scores.*

STANDARD SCORE NORMS. *Standard score norms*, like percentile norms, are widely used for measures of physical performance, although they have typically not been used to determine national norms in the physical education field. Fig. 5-2 represents the relationship between percentiles and standard scores. All standard scores are based on the z-score distribution, which was described earlier in this chapter. Most test users prefer to use a transformation of the z-score because this score is expressed in decimal places and, in some instances, is a negative number. The most widely used transformation in the field is the T-score, also described earlier in this chapter.

T-scores are sometimes confused with T-scaled scores, which are also standard scores, or percentiles, because all three use similar ranges of numbers. However, the T-score reflects the raw score distribution; the T-scaled score alters (normalizes) the raw score distribution unless it is normal to begin with. If the raw score distribution is normal, the T-scores and T-scaled scores will be identical. To obtain a T-scaled score, first convert the raw scores to percentiles. Then the median of the percentile distribution is set at a z-score of 0 (or a T-score of 50, now referred to as a T-scaled score of 50), and standard score values are set for other points on the distribution. The T-scaled distribution, like the T-score distribution, has a mean of 50 and a standard deviation of 10. Fig. 5-11 shows the relationship of the T-scaled score to T-scores and percentiles.

Local and national norms

National norms, if properly developed, can be useful for certain purposes. A physical education teacher may wish to compare students' test scores with a national sample as partial evidence of a successful program. If the test scores match high norms, the program is obviously achieving satisfactory results in the area tested. If the norms are low, perhaps certain aspects of the program need to be improved. National norms are also useful for comparisons among distinct subpopulations within an area. For example, in a large metropolitan area comparisons of performance levels of "inner city," "fringe-area," and suburban students with national norms could yield interesting results.

On the other hand, national norms are limited in the type of information they can provide. In a school with a good physical education program, all of the students may score above the middle of the distribution using a table of national norms. Although this information may be useful in justifying a physical education program, the individual student receives little feedback on personal performance relative to other students in the same school. *Local norms* would provide more useful information in this case. A student who is above average using national norms may be average or even below average compared with local norms. Teachers within a school district can develop local norms by collecting test scores over a period of several years to obtain adequate data; these norms should also be revised periodically so that they remain up-to-date.

SUMMARY

Measures of central tendency and variability provide essential information for a concise interpretation of a set of test scores. If the test scores are distributed so that they approximate the normal curve, the mean and standard deviation are the preferred measures. When the distribution is skewed, the median is a more accurate representation of the center of the distribution. In this case the interpercentile range would be used as the measure of variability. Because tests of motor skill and physical fitness are scored in different metrics, scores are frequently transformed to a common scale using percentiles, z-score transformations, or T-score transformations. In this way scores recorded in minutes and seconds can be compared with scores recorded in feet and inches.

Sometimes it is of interest to know whether two variables bear a relationship to one another. This can be examined by calculating a correlation coefficient using the two variables. The Pearson product-moment procedure can be used to calculate this statistic; if the scores are ranked, the rank difference method can be used. These coefficients may be interpreted on both practical and statistical grounds.

The scores of normative groups should be taken into account in interpreting scores on tests of motor behavior. Information on local and national norms is useful in obtaining an overall perspective of the ability of individual examinees in relation to others.

REFERENCES

American Association for Health, Physical Education and Recreation. 1967. AAHPER sports skills tests. Washington, D.C.: AAHPER.

American Association for Health, Physical Education and Recreation. 1976. Youth Fitness Test manual. Washington, D.C.: AAHPER.

American Alliance for Health, Physical Education, Recreation and Dance. 1980. Health-Related Physical Fitness Test manual. Reston, Va.: AAHPERD.

American Psychological Association. 1984. Standards for educational and psychological tests. Washington, D.C.: APA.

Downing, D., and Clark, J. 1983. Statistics the easy way. Woodbury, N.Y.: Barron's Educational Series, Inc.

Lyman, H.B. 1978. Test scores and what they mean, ed. 3, Englewood Cliffs, N.J.: Prentice-Hall, Inc.

Mosteller, F., Fienberg, S.E., and Rourke, R.E.K. 1983. Beginning statistics with data analysis. Reading, Mass.: Addison-Wesley Publishing Co.

Rothstein, A.L. 1985. Research design and statistics for physical education. Englewood Cliffs, N.J.: Prentice-Hall, Inc.

Sprinthall, R.C. 1982. Basic statistical analysis. Reading, Mass.: Addison-Wesley Publishing Co.

ANNOTATED READINGS

Glasnapp, D.R., and Pogglo, J.P. 1985. Essentials of statistical analysis for the behavioral sciences. Columbus, Ohio: Charles E. Merrill Publishing Co.
  Introductory statistics text tailored to students with little math background and no experience studying statistics; focuses on applied statistics; problems use data reflecting children in actual situations—the "Sesame Street" data base; includes enough theory to lay a firm foundation and enough application to be genuinely practical; emphasizes key concepts.

Hinkle, D.E., Wiersma, W., and Jurs, S.G. 1979. Applied statistics for the behavioral sciences. Boston: Houghton Mifflin Co.
  Emphasizes conceptual understanding of basic statistical procedures; helps students achieve computational skills needed for statistical procedures in practical settings; examples taken from actual settings (40% from education); begins with elementary descriptive statistics and progresses to more sophisticated procedures.

Jaeger, R. 1983. Statistics: a spectator sport. Beverly Hills, Calif.: Sage Publications, Inc.
  Designed to help anyone who wants to understand statistics; includes clear explanations that enable readers to learn what statistics are, what they mean, and how they are used and interpreted; does not include any equations; applications to a wide range of research and evaluation problems, giving particular attention to studies in the computerized files of Educational Resources Information Center (ERIC).

Kirk, R.E. 1984. Elementary statistics, ed. 2, Florence, Ky.: Brooks/Cole Publishing Co.
  Introduction to statistics for students in education and behavioral sciences; emphasizes verbal rather than mathematical problems; includes in-depth treatments of individual concepts and their interrelationships; develops the underpinnings of statistics through the use of high school mathematics; a concise review of elementary math in an appendix; incorporates real-life examples in the review exercises; provides interesting introduction to the history of statistics, as well as extensive references on important topics.

Witte, R.S. 1984. Statistics, ed. 2. Lavallette, N.J.: Holt, Rinehart & Winston General Book.
Emphasizes concepts rather than just computations; covers wide range of topics in descriptive and inferential statistics without overwhelming students with mathematics; includes extensive problem sets in each chapter, ranging from simple computational tasks to questions of interpretation, with step-by-step progressions to problem-solving.

PROBLEMS

1. Use the data set below to calculate the mean and the standard deviation.

Data set of 30 max Vo_2 scores: 54, 49, 53, 56, 55, 50, 47, 60, 53, 41,
58, 53, 48, 37, 55, 62, 54, 51, 39, 54,
53, 47, 57, 55, 42, 57, 54, 45, 49, 53

2. a. Use the above data set of 30 max Vo_2 scores to form a frequency distribution with intervals of size 2. Include columns for tally, f, cf, and c%.
   b. Calculate the interquartile range for this distribution, using the frequency distribution in *a*.

3. The mean of a set of basketball test scores is 32 and the standard deviation is 3. Calculate z-scores and T-scores for the following test scores: 31, 39, 29, 27, 33, 25.

4. a. Using the Pearson product-moment method, calculate the correlation coefficient for the scores on the first (X) and second (Y) examinations given in an undergraduate course on measurement in physical education.

Student	1st test (X)	2nd test (Y)
1	47	33
2	54	49
3	48	40
4	47	44
5	50	48
6	45	36
7	50	35
8	56	50
9	54	46
10	48	37
11	53	40
12	47	39
13	38	32
14	47	42
15	48	39
16	49	37
17	53	42
18	53	40
19	49	40
20	52	47

   b. Draw a graph of the relationship between X and Y. Plot the coordinates and record their numerical values at each point, as in Fig. 5-8.

5. Thought question: Interpret the relationship between the scores on the two measurement exams that were correlated in *4*. Consider both the size and sign of the correlation coefficient. What does this mean in terms of the students' abilities on the two tests?

ANSWERS TO PROBLEMS

1. $\bar{X} = \dfrac{1541}{30} = 51.37$; $s = \sqrt{\dfrac{(30)(80211) - (1541)^2}{(30)(30)}} = 5.93$

2. a.

Intervals	Tally	f	cf	c%
61-62	x	1	30	100.0
59-60	x	1	29	96.7
57-58	xxx	3	28	93.3
55-56	xxxx	4	25	83.3
53-54	xxxxxxxxx	9	21	70.0
51-52	x	1	12	40.0
49-50	xxx	3	11	37.7
47-48	xxx	3	8	26.7
45-46	x	1	5	16.7
43-44		0	4	13.3
41-42	xx	2	4	13.3
39-40	x	1	2	6.7
37-38	x	1	1	3.3

   b. $X_{.75} = 55.25$; $X_{.25} = 48.17$
   Interquartile range $= 55.25 - 48.17 = 7.08$

3.

Score	z-score	T-score
31	$-.33$	46.7
39	2.33	73.3
29	-1.00	40.0
27	-1.67	33.3
33	.33	53.3
25	-2.33	26.7

4. a. $r_{xy} = \dfrac{20(40593) - 988(816)}{\sqrt{[20(49118) - 976144][20(33808) - 665856]}} = 0.706$

   b. Answer is depicted in Fig. 5-12, as shown on p. 116.

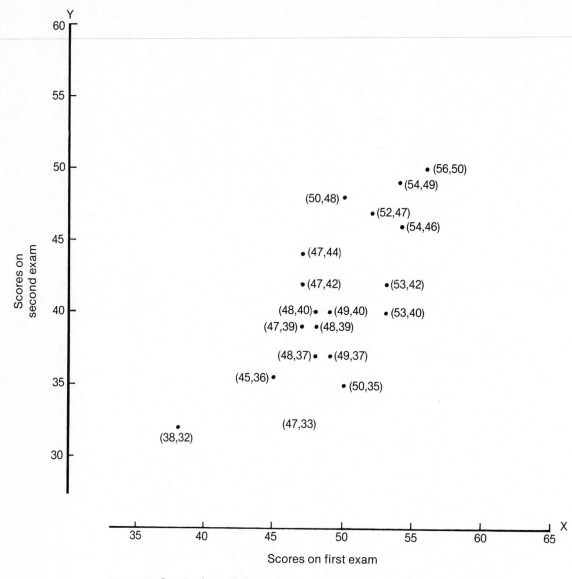

FIG. 5-12. *Graph of correlation between scores on measurement examinations.*

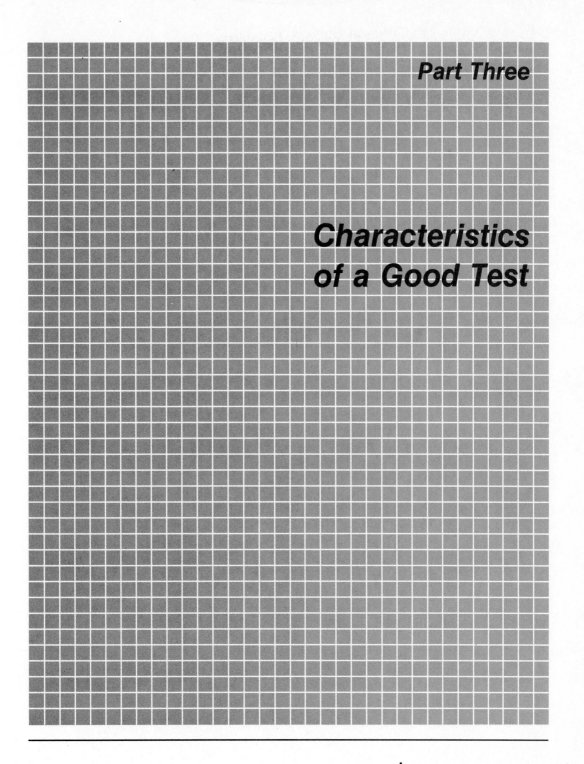

Part Three

Characteristics of a Good Test

6 Validity and Reliability of Norm-Referenced Tests

KEY WORDS   *Watch for these words as you read the following chapter:*

content validity	objective test	subjective test
contingency table	objectivity	validity
criterion-related validity	reliability	validity coefficient
logical validity	split-half reliability estimate	

In Chapter 1 the concept of *norm-referenced* measurement was introduced. This type of test, in which the *score* is interpreted by comparing it to a *norm*, is used when both the test user and the examinee want to know who has the most ability, who has the least, and so forth. Before placing any faith in the test results, it must be certain that the test is a good one: the test should measure what it is supposed to measure (**validity**) with consistency (**reliability**), using an accurate scoring system (**objectivity**). (For a discussion of these characteristics in a criterion-referenced measurement framework, see Chapter 7.)

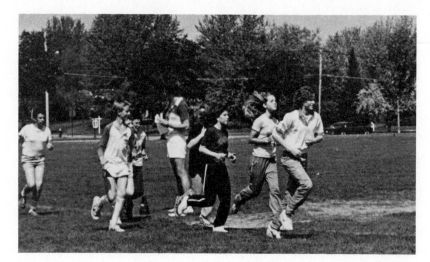

VALIDITY

Assume you are a student who has just completed a basketball unit. Mr. Miller, your teacher, announces that he will give a written test on skill execution, game strategy, and rules—the content he taught during the unit. You carefully study all three areas and feel well prepared to take the test. When the test is administered, you skim through it quickly and find that all of the items deal with rules. No questions on skill execution and game strategy are included. After completing the test, you comment to the teacher that this was not a good test, because it did not measure what it was supposed to measure. In other words, the test lacked *validity*.

A valid test can be loosely defined as a measure that is sound in terms of the purpose of the test and that meets satisfactory criteria for test construction. More broadly, validity is the soundness of the interpretation of the test. It is the closeness of agreement between what the test measures and the behavior it is intended to measure. Furthermore, to be valid a test must have reliability, or consistency of measure, which is discussed more thoroughly later in this chapter.

How does one evaluate the validity of a test? Although this is sometimes initially difficult to understand, a test can have many validities. Therefore, to state that a test is "valid" is really not accurate; rather, a test can be designated as "valid for a given purpose." For example, a test might be valid for 5-year-old girls but not 25-year-old women. It might be valid for measuring an individual skill but not game-playing ability. The first step is to think through how you plan to use the test. Then the *type* of validity of greatest interest must be determined. The most common types of validity are *content, criterion-related*, and *construct*. In the physical education field, logical validity, a special case of content validity, is frequently used (see Fig. 6-1).

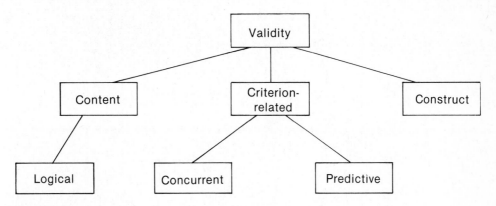

FIG. 6-1. *Types of validity.*

TABLE 6-1. *Item classification, Forms 2A and 2B, AAHPER Cooperative Physical Education Tests**

Content	Form 2A				Form 2B			
	Knowledge	Under-standing	Thinking	Numbers of items	Knowledge	Under-standing	Thinking	Numbers of items
I. *Activity performance* Basic sports skills		45, 55		2		57		1
Concepts fundamental to movement skills in strategy and activities patterns	23, 59	10	24	4	9	40, 46	15	4
Body mechanics, rules and procedures, and protective requirements		4, 11, 37	15, 26	5		14, 23, 24, 48	47	5
II. *Effects of activities* Immediate	1, 2, 12, 16, 25, 47, 52	6, 9, 13, 17, 27, 28, 36, 44, 46	48	17	20, 22, 30, 34, 35, 50, 55	6, 7, 11, 13, 32, 37, 38, 39, 58	8, 12, 59	19
Long-term health and appearance	18, 21, 42	5, 29, 30, 50	54	8	2, 25, 31	21, 29, 53, 56	19, 45	9
Capacity for effort	7, 56, 57, 58	3, 31, 32, 40	39	9	4, 10, 18, 60	26, 33, 49, 52		8
III. *Factors modifying participation in activities and their efforts*	8, 20, 41, 51	14, 19, 22, 35, 38, 43, 53	33, 34, 49, 60	15	17, 28, 44	1, 16, 27, 36, 41, 42, 54	3, 5, 43, 51	14
Number of items	20	30	10	60	18	31	11	60

*From Handbook for AAHPER Cooperative Physical Education Tests.

Types of validity

Because many definitions of validity have been proposed, the concept can be confusing to the test user. In an effort to alleviate this confusion, several national measurement organizations have developed a set of standards for educational and psychological tests. These standards include the categorization of validity into three types—**content, criterion-related,** and **construct** (American Psychological Association, 1984). The most important point to keep in mind is that validity, no matter what type, is the single most important concept in evaluating a test.

CONTENT VALIDITY. The content validity of a test is "the degree to which the sample of items, tasks, or questions on a test are representative of some defined universe or 'domain' of content" (American Psychological Association, 1984). More simply stated, when a test developer demonstrates that the items in a test adequately represent all important areas of content, the test has content validity. This type of validity is appropriate for written tests. How is the content validity of a test evaluated? This process can be demonstrated by analyzing the AAHPER Cooperative Physical Education Test (Cooperative Tests and Services, 1970), one of the few standardized written tests published for physical education students. This test was developed according to a table of specifications, sometimes referred to as a test blueprint. Table 6-1 shows the specifications for grades 10 through 12. The content areas are listed on the left side of the table and represent the content judged to be important for students in physical education classes. Across the top of the table are levels of cognitive behavior, which were described in Chapter 2. For each cell in the table, the test developer writes a predetermined number of test items. The number of items is determined by the educational importance attached to each category of content and cognitive behavior. Refer to the columns labeled "Numbers of items" at the top. The number in each cell represents the number of items written for each area of content. The largest number of items for Form 2A is 17. This suggests that the test developers viewed the immediate effects of physical activity as the most important content area. Now look at the same label "Numbers of items" at the bottom of the page. The largest number of items for Form 2A is 30, placing the greatest weight on understanding (as a cognitive behavior) the content.

Begin analyzing the test itself by evaluating its content validity. A copy of the test and the table of specifications are needed. First, take the test just as a student would be required to do. Then, arbitrarily select several items from the test and find them in the table of specifications. Answer the following question about each item: Does the item properly fit the cell designated by the test publisher? Suppose one of the items in Table 6-1 you have chosen to analyze is *42* in Form 2A. This item is written as follows:

Item 42. Which of the following represents specificity of training?
   A. Training to run distance events also improves sprinting.
   B. Practice in tennis skills improves badminton skills.
   C. Training in one sport skill limits performance in other sports.
   D. Training for one event is directed to that event alone.

According to its placement, Item *42* is a measure of knowledge about the long-term effects of physical activity. The knowledge is factual and could be learned by memorization. (See Chapter 2.) Reread the test item. Does it measure what it is supposed to measure? If so, the item contributes to the content validity of the test. If not, it is not a valid item. Obviously, this is a demanding job, but a test user is obligated to at least spot-check the test developer's decisions.

Another important aspect of content validity is whether the content areas are important in terms of the test user's educational goals. Should an area be emphasized more, deemphasized, added, or eliminated? These are judgments the test user must make. In the preceding paragraph, a substantial number of items measuring the acute effects of physical activity were noted. One might question whether the degree of emphasis on this content area is warranted. Some teachers might feel the acute effects of exercise *should* be emphasized as much as they are in the test; others might disagree. The relative importance of various areas of content might differ markedly across school districts, depending on the curricular objectives of the particular physical education program. Including a substantial number of test items on the short-term and long-term effects of physical activity might be desirable in a program where physical fitness is an important part of the curriculum. In a program where skill development is stressed in the curricular objectives, the emphasis on exercise physiology in the Cooperative Physical Education Test might be unacceptable. This variability among districts may seem to lessen the value of a standardized test. Why should a standardized test be used to judge the outcomes of a physical education program, when the content taught in the curriculum receives a different emphasis from that provided in the test? The test may not be useful for judging program outcomes, but it can still provide valuable information to the physical education staff in a school system. For example, the test might be administered to determine the status of student knowledge in the three content areas, without making a judgment on the quality of their physical education program. The test results might then be used to reexamine the current physical education curriculum. Standardized tests of this type should never be used to determine grades. They can be used appropriately as a part of program evaluation or simply to determine how well students can perform on a nationally standardized test.

To summarize, the following steps are recommended for reviewing a published test to determine its content validity:

1. Answer the test items and score your responses. This step should be standard procedure for *any* teacher with *any* test. If this step is taken seriously, detecting weaknesses in a test, including one's own test, is much easier.
2. Review the publisher's statement on content validity.
3. Examine the table of specifications.
4. Assess the appropriateness of the placement of items in the content/behavior categories.
5. Examine the universe (content and behavior categories), and respond to the following four questions:
   a. Are important elements of a content area omitted from the universe?
   b. Are unimportant elements of the content area erroneously included?
   c. Are any categories included in the content and behavior areas weighted improperly? (Weighting is reflected in the number of items included in a category.)
   d. Are all elements of the content and behavior areas educationally important?

Now that the procedure for evaluating the content validity of a published test has been described, let's examine the approach to be used when planning to develop your own test. Perhaps you are interested in developing a test of basketball rules. Obviously, including questions on all of the rules in the rule book is not possible; therefore, a representative sample of rules must be selected. The rules should be categorized in a table of specifications. Two of the categories might be offensive and defensive rules. If there are more offensive rules than defensive, the proportion of test items should reflect this difference. Levels of cognitive behavior can also be considered. When students are first learning the rules, the test might primarily measure a low level of cognitive behavior. If the rules test is intended for experienced players, you may be more interested in the degree to which students can apply the rules and thus design items measuring higher levels of cognitive behavior. Many tests include items reflecting several levels of cognitive behavior. Whatever the case, the identification of items should follow a systematic plan.

To summarize, the following steps should be taken to demonstrate content validity when you have developed the test yourself:

1. Develop a table of specifications for the test. Determine the number of items that should be written for each cell of the table. Write the appropriate number of items for each cell.
2. Prepare the test items in the format you plan to use with your students.
3. Take the test and score your responses. *This step should be taken even if the test is your own!*

4. Select 25% of the test items, and reexamine the appropriateness of their placement in the content/behavior categories of the table of specifications. Revise the items if necessary. If more than 5% (of the 25% selected) of the items were inappropriately placed, reexamine the placement of the remaining 75% of the items.

5. Determine whether the content/behavior categories should be altered in any way. Additions? Deletions? Increased emphasis? Decreased emphasis?

Often a test is developed by writing down item after item as each one comes to mind, until enough items have been written to fill the testing period. Such an approach may lead to haphazard results. The test may be heavily weighted with items in one or two categories and slighted in others. It behooves the teacher to begin by preparing a table of specifications, deciding in advance on the number of items for each category based on its relative importance. When the item-writing process is begun, it becomes a more purposeful activity. In addition, the test developer can have greater confidence that the test will be valid.

LOGICAL VALIDITY. Although written tests are used frequently in physical education and the exercise sciences, the most predominantly used tests are those measuring physical skills and abilities. The concept of content validity does not make much sense for tests of motor performance. Instead of using clusters of items to measure various content areas, the test may consist of a single item or a repetition of the same item, usually referred to as *trials* of the test. However, the initial validation of these types of tests follows a set of rules similar in concept to content validity—**logical validity.** Logical validity is defined as the extent to which a test measures the most important components of skill necessary to perform a motor task adequately.

A test of motor skill is used to demonstrate how logical validity is evaluated. If the test incorporates and directly measures the important components of the skill being evaluated, logical validity can be claimed. The concept of logical validity was proposed by Ruth B. Glassow and Marie R. Liba at the University of Wisconsin. Both were interested in developing skills tests that measured the most important aspects of skills. They had observed that many of the tests in physical education measured only accuracy in performing a skill. While accuracy is undeniably important in the execution of many skills, it is not the only important factor. Glassow and Liba reasoned that these limitations were occurring because tests were not being developed according to some logical plan, similar to the development of a good written test. Thus the idea of logical validity came into being. The general procedure to be followed in constructing a skills test is to define good performance in executing the skill, construct a test that measures the important components of skill in the definition, and score the test so that the best score represents a performance that approximates the definition of good performance.

Consider, for example, a test of the tennis forehand drive. Ms. Spencer, a physical education teacher, describes a good forehand drive as a ball hit so that it travels low over the net and deep into the backcourt. She decides to test her students on this skill using a test in which a target is placed in the backcourt. The target is sectioned so that the areas with the higher scores are closer to the baseline of the tennis court. Is this a valid test? The test measures whether the ball is hit deep into the backcourt by giving more points to the ball landing close to the baseline, but it does not measure the height of the ball flight over the net. Thus, the evidence of logical validity is insufficient and the test is not valid. Test validity could be increased by placing extensions on the standards holding the tennis nets and by stretching a rope across the middle of the court above the net. Then the examinee would attempt to hit the ball so that it passes between the rope and the top of the net.

Since logical validity is the degree to which the components of skill measured by a test correspond with those required to perform the skill adequately, the identification of important components of a skill is important. The previous section on logical validity dealt primarily with a single skills test. Although it is appropriate to measure specific skills when students are learning a sport, skills tests should not mistakenly be thought to measure playing ability. To measure playing ability, a battery of tests is often used. One of the first steps in validating a test battery of this type is to use logical validity. Logical validity, in this context, involves the definition of the important skills comprising playing ability. Tests are then selected to measure each of the skills identified as most important. Of course, each individual test must have logical validity as well.

Four major steps can be identified in assessing the logical validity of a skills test:

1. Review the test developer's statement on the purpose of the test and the components of skill the test is designed to measure. These components should be clearly stated in the test description. Make a list of these components.
2. Examine the test. List the components *actually* measured in the test.
3. Compare the two lists. Are the components identified and defined by the test developer actually measured by the test?
4. Examine the educational importance of the test:
    a. Are unimportant components of skill measured by the test?
    b. Are important components of skill omitted from the test?
    c. Do certain components of the skill receive inappropriate emphasis in the text?

Published tests of sports skills and playing ability frequently lack a statement identifying the important components of skill. In these cases, the test must be examined and the components being measured must be listed. Then, the educational importance of the test must be analyzed. If developing your own test is necessary, start with a list of the important components of skill, which will provide the basis for the design of the test.

CRITERION-RELATED VALIDITY. Criterion-related validity is demonstrated by comparing test scores with one or more external variables that are considered direct measures of the characteristic or behavior in question (known as the *criterion*). Two of the most common types of **criterion-related validity** are concurrent validity, which involves the comparison of a test with a criterion measure, and predictive validity, dealing with prediction of behavior on a criterion test. Criterion-related validity is determined by statistical methods, although content and logical validity may play a part in the initial stages of constructing the test.

Concurrent validity is used when a test is proposed as a substitute for another test that is known to be valid. This latter test is called the **criterion** test, with criterion defined as a standard of behavior. More precisely, concurrent validity is defined as the degree to which a test correlates with (is related to) a criterion test, which has already been established as a valid test of the attribute of interest. Why would one search for a substitute test when a valid test is already available? Although the criterion test's validity has been established, it may be impractical. For example, the test may require an excessive amount of time, trained personnel, or expensive equipment. Laboratory tests administered on a one-to-one basis are usually impractical in a school setting. Consider the wide variety of measures of cardiorespiratory (CR) function. It is well known that testing an examinee on the treadmill provides more valid indicators of CR function than a field test; however, trained physiologists, expensive laboratory equipment, and one-to-one testing are required. Therefore, field tests are used most frequently in fitness clubs and physical education classes. Yet, how is the adequacy of the field test determined? Usually a **validity coefficient** is reported for the test. This coefficient represents the correlation between scores on the field test (X) and the laboratory test (Y). This is the same correlation coefficient (r_{xy}) that was studied in Chapter 5, only now it is being used as an estimate of test validity. The higher the estimate, the stronger the relationship between the field test and the laboratory (criterion) test.

Three steps should be followed in evaluating the concurrent validity of a published test. To exemplify each step the 12-Minute Run Test is used as the field test of interest, and the maximal stress test on the treadmill is used as the laboratory (criterion) test.

1. Identify and examine the criterion test. Is it a logically valid measure of the attribute of interest?

Although there are other valid indicators of CR function, the measure of max $\dot{V}O_2$ obtained from maximal stress testing on the treadmill is generally accepted as a valid criterion measure. (See Chapter 11 for additional information.)

2. Evaluate the correlation (validity coefficient) between the criterion test and the test you are interested in using. Is the correlation high enough to justify substituting the test you wish to use for the criterion test?

The validity coefficient for the 12-Minute Run Test when compared with max $\dot{V}O_2$ is reported as 0.897 in one of Cooper's first published reports (Cooper, 1968). Thus, people who run longer distances tend to have higher max $\dot{V}O_2$ values, and vice versa. The validity coefficient is high enough to justify substituting the 12-Minute Run Test for the treadmill test. If you are developing the test yourself, you must calculate the validity coefficient. Use Formula 5-9 for calculating the Pearson product-moment correlation coefficient (r_{xy}).

3. If the criterion test is valid and the validity coefficient is 0.80 or above, use the test. If not, look for another test.

In general, the Cooper test appears to be an excellent field test. However, several factors should be considered before using the test. Cooper's test group consisted of adult males who were well trained and highly motivated. The test user should consider the examinee's sex, age, body fatness, and ability to pace properly and run efficiently during the test. (These elements are considered in more detail in Chapter 11.)

Predictive validity is defined as the degree to which a criterion behavior can be predicted using a score from a predictor test. Two uses of predictive validity are commonly observed in physical education and exercise science: as a *description* of the current status of an individual on the criterion behavior and as a *predictor* of the future behavior on the criterion. (The criterion again refers to the standard against which the usefulness of the test is judged.) The **predictors** are tests or variables that predict criterion behavior.

Predictive validity used to describe the current status of an individual is essentially an extension of the concept of concurrent validity. Usually the test user is interested in estimating performance on an often complex criterion variable by obtaining a score on a simple predictor variable. To be reasonably accurate in the prediction, a relationship must exist between the predictor and criterion variables. In other words, the correlation between the two variables should be substantial. Consider a prediction study by Getchell and his associates (1977) in which scores on the 1½-mile run were used to predict CR function, specifically max $\dot{V}O_2$ as measured in a treadmill test. The relationship between the two measures was determined to be -0.915. Since shorter times are associated with higher max $\dot{V}O_2$ values, the validity coefficient is expected to be negative. In this case the predictor measure, the 1½-mile run, had high validity. This is essentially an estimate of *concurrent* validity.

The application of predictive validity in *predicting future behavior* uses one or more predictor variables to predict criterion behavior at some future point. Within this context, scores on the predictor and criterion variables are not obtained at the same time. Although this may initially seem strange, it actually is the only logical way to proceed. When future behavior is being predicted, the interest focuses on the person's future performance instead of present performance. For instance, one may wish to predict the degree of success an athlete might have if selected for a team. The prediction would have to be made before the team members are selected; yet, the success of the individual would be unknown until the end of the season. Thus, this is a more difficult type of predictive validity to determine. Fortunately, a test developer will handle the difficult part. The concern here is how well the predictor works.

Let's look at an example of predicting future behavior from the sports psychology literature. A number of studies have centered on the psychological factors that can be used to predict success in sport. For example, Morgan and Johnson (1978) studied the psychological characteristics of highly skilled oarsmen. For many years all entering freshmen at the University of Wisconsin were required to take the Minnesota Multiphasic Personality Inventory. Using the scores on this inventory, Morgan and Johnson evaluated the psychological profiles of successful and unsuccessful oarsmen on the University of Wisconsin teams. Successful oarsmen tended to be less anxious, depressed, angry, fatigued, confused, and neurotic and more vigorous and extroverted. In 1974 at a training camp for potential Olympic oarsmen, the investigators administered a similar battery of psychological scales to all 57 candidates at the camp. No one, not even the investigators themselves, knew of the results of the psychological tests until the end of the training camp session. (Not until after the Olympic team members had been selected did Morgan and Johnson prepare the psychological profiles of the total group of candidates, since knowledge of these results might have influenced the coaches' decisions in making selections.)

After the team members had been selected, the psychological profiles were compared with the profiles of successful and unsuccessful oarsmen identified in Morgan and Johnson's earlier work. Based on these comparisons, each member of the group at the training camp was classified as successful (likely to be chosen for the Olympic team) or unsuccessful (unlikely to be chosen). Of course, at that point they knew who the actual team members were. Therefore, Morgan and Johnson were able to compare their predictions with the actual results, as shown in Table 6-2. This is known as a **contingency table.**

Of the 57 candidates, 10 were accurately predicted for the Success category and 31 for the Fail category. The profiles accurately predicted 62% of the oars-

TABLE 6-2. *Evaluation of the clinical (a priori) prediction model's accuracy**

Actual category	Predicted category		
	Success	Fail	Total
Success	10	6	16
Fail	10	31	41
Total	20	37	57

*From Morgan, W.P., and Johnson R.W.

men selected for the team and 76% of those rejected. Thus, psychological variables alone cannot be used to predict team membership, although knowledge of these variables can contribute to the accuracy of prediction.

(Before proceeding to the next section, be sure you understand how to read a contingency table, since they are discussed in the next chapter. Do you understand how the 62% success rate in predicting team membership was determined? The 76% success rate in rejection?)

CONSTRUCT VALIDITY. The last type of validity to be examined in this textbook is construct validity. **Construct validity** can be defined as the degree to which a test measures an attribute or trait that cannot be directly measured. Think about an attribute like athletic ability. Everyone assumes that such an attribute exists, but it cannot be measured directly. Of course certain aspects of athletic ability can be measured, but as a whole it defies precise measurement. Athletic ability can be thought of as a *construct*, a trait that cannot be directly measured.

Another example of a construct is anxiety, often a factor of concern in athletics. Measuring the sweatiness of palms, administering an anxiety inventory, and checking heart rate or blood pressure are ways to determine if a person is anxious. However, these are merely *indicators* of anxiety. Anxiety cannot really be measured directly. Although a construct cannot be measured precisely, indicators of the construct behavior are often measured. How is this type of test validated, since no criterion test is available?

Although there are many ways of determining construct validity, only one will be discussed in this textbook—the *group differences method*. Let's use Kenyon's Attitude Toward Physical Activity Inventory (Kenyon, 1968) as an example. One of the scales in the Kenyon Inventory is labeled "Vertigo." Essentially this scale is a measure of the risk-taking capacity of an individual in situations involving vigorous physical activity. How should this scale be validated? Logically, persons who participate in forms of vigorous physical activity involving risk-taking would be more likely to obtain high scores on the scale than sedentary individuals. For example, a group of mountain climbers should score significantly higher on the scale than a group of sedentary office workers. If not, the validity of the scale is questionable. Comparing two groups' scores, which should differ, is one way of providing evidence of construct validity. However, it does not establish construct validity; many pieces of evidence are required for this purpose.

Another example of the use of the group difference approach would be to compare groups on scores on the Health and Fitness scale of the Kenyon Inventory. Individuals who are known to be highly fit should score higher than those who are not. If those with a high level of CR function do not score higher than those with low CR function, the construct validity of the scale would be open to question.

Interpretation of the validity coefficient

When selecting a test, one of the factors to be evaluated is the size of the validity coefficient. How high should the coefficient be to be acceptable? If the test is being used as a substitute for a more sophisticated but impractical test, the validity coefficient should be high. Generally, coefficients of 0.90 and above are desirable, but those exceeding 0.80 are acceptable. Squaring the correlation coefficient demonstrates the amount of variance common to both tests, that is, the extent to which the two tests are measuring the same entity. Thus, a lower coefficient would not be acceptable. For a validity coefficient of 0.50, only 25% of the variance of the test and of the criterion measure overlap. For the most part, these tests are measuring different qualities.

When a test is constructed for predictive purposes, a lower validity coefficient may sometimes be acceptable. Even tests with validity estimates of 0.50 or 0.60 may be retained. The key question is whether the test does a better job of predicting than any other method, that is, is the test superior to another test or a subjective method of making the prediction? The accuracy of the prediction increases as the size of the validity coefficient increases.

RELIABILITY

One of the most confusing points in measurement to the beginning student is the definition of test reliability. The reliability of a test refers to the dependability of scores, their relative freedom from error. Reliability is popularly defined as the consistency of an individual in performing a test. Suppose an examinee took a test once and then was able to go back in time as if the test had never been taken. Then suppose the same test was administered again. We would expect the scores on the two tests to be quite similar. If not, the test would be unreliable. If a test is administered at the end of a unit of instruction, we assume the scores will represent a stable level of achievement. In other words, if the test were administered again the next day, the test scores would be similar to those obtained on the first day.

The definition of reliability as consistency is both meaningful and appropriate; however, when reliability is estimated within a norm-referenced framework, a more complex definition is implied. The term **reliability** reflects the ability of the test to detect reliable differences *between* examinees; that is, given that the test was administered on two occasions to the same students, the *same differences* between students would be detected. Remember that a norm-referenced test is designed to reflect individual differences; thus, this interpretation of reliability makes sense.

A test can be reliable without being valid, but a valid test has to be reliable. Reliability, then, refers to the consistency, not the general worthiness, or the validity, of the test. For example, suppose a physical education teacher administers a test of the football place-kick from the 20-yard line. An assistant holds the ball in place on the tee, and the student taking the test kicks the ball 10 times to complete the test. The test may be highly reliable, but its validity might be questioned, especially if the examinees have had previous experience playing football. One way of improving the validity is to snap the ball to an assistant, who must place the ball on the tee before the kick. There is a trade-off, however, in that the increased complexity of the test would probably reduce its reliability. The fewer the extraneous factors associated with the parameters of the test, the more reliable the test.

The same point can be exemplified using another test. A popular test in volleyball classes is the wall volley test, designed to measure volleying skill. Generally, the test score is the number of times the ball hits the wall, with certain distance and height restrictions. A student might be able to perform the test reliably, yet use poor form, executing the skill poorly and perhaps illegally by game rules. Reliability does not ensure validity.

Types of reliability

Most developers of motor performance tests do not provide much information about test reliability. Often a reliability coefficient is presented with little explanation. The coefficient will usually be symbolized by either $r_{xx'}$, the interclass correlation (or Pearson product-moment correlation) coefficient, or $R_{xx'}$, intraclass correlation coefficient. Both of these symbols represent correlation coefficients, but the second represents a more informative estimate. Both reflect the ratio of true scores to obtained scores. A *true score* is the score an individual would obtain on a test if there were no measurement error. An *obtained score* is the sum of true score plus error score. The scores resulting from an administration of the test are obtained scores. A true score is unknown but can be estimated by determining measurement error and subtracting it from the obtained score. The two reliability estimates mentioned represent the ratio of the true score to the obtained score.

The types of reliability described in the next sections are those most likely seen in the physical education field. These types, shown in Fig. 6-2, are single test administration, test-retest reliability, and precision of an individual test score.

FIG. 6-2. *Types of reliability.*

SINGLE TEST ADMINISTRATION. The reliability of a test can be estimated from a single administration of the test on one occasion. The resultant reliability coefficient estimates the reliability of the test at one point. There is no guarantee that an examinee's score on the test would be similar if the test were administered again the next day. However, sometimes this does not matter. For instance, sport competition anxiety can be measured using an inventory developed by Martens (1977). Test users would not use this inventory unless it measured with consistency the anxiety level of an athlete before a game. However, the athlete would not be expected to obtain the same score the next day (unless another game was being played) or even after the game ended. Anxiety levels usually fluctuate, depending on the situation.

If a student is repeatedly tested during the time a skill is being learned, one might not expect his or her scores to be consistent from one day to the next. The student has been taught more about the skill before the second testing period. One point should be clarified before proceeding. Whenever test developers administer a test more than once to establish reliability, it does not mean that test users are expected to give the test twice. However, this information is important to know when selecting a test. If test reliability was established based on one administration of the test on a single occasion, the test is expected to elicit reliable performance only for that occasion. If test reliability was established based on two administrations of the test, each one on a different occasion, the test is expected to be reliable for that general period of time. If a test is used in a different situation than that of the test developer, test reliability must be reestablished.

Now, how is the reliability of a test established when the test is administered on one occasion only? Either of two procedures for estimating reliability can be used. One is the *Pearson product-moment correlation coefficient* ($r_{xx'}$) (see Formula 5-9). The test must consist of at least two trials. If more than two trials are used, the trials must be reduced (usually by averaging) to two sets. You will recall that the correlation coefficient estimates the relationship between two sets of scores. In Chapter 5 the two sets of scores represented different variables, similar to the validity coefficients in this chapter. The reliability coefficient, however, represents two sets of scores on the *same* variable.

The second method is the **intraclass correlation coefficient,** known as $R_{xx'}$. This coefficient is estimated by calculating an analysis of variance. Generally, $r_{xx'}$ and $R_{xx'}$ are interpreted similarly. However, $R_{xx'}$ is a more accurate estimate of reliability for two reasons. One, it is not necessary to reduce the trials to two sets to calculate $R_{xx'}$. This is important because many tests of motor skill consist of more than two trials. A major portion of the test error could occur among trials, but this would not be detected when $r_{xx'}$ is used. Second, if trial scores increase or decrease systematically, this should lower the reliability of the test. Yet, these changes do not affect $r_{xx'}$. This fact can be verified by examining the scores in Table 6-3. Note that the scores on trial 2 are much higher than the trial *1* scores. However, $r_{xx'}$ equals $+1.00$, reflecting perfect reliability. It is obvious that the examinees' performances were not consistent.

TABLE 6-3. *Systematic increase in scores from day 1 to day 2*

Student	Test 1, day 1	Test 1, day 2
A	2	20
B	4	40
C	6	60
D	8	80
E	10	100
	30	300
	$\overline{X} = 6$	$\overline{X} = 60$
	s = 3.16	s = 31.62

Another way of estimating reliability on the basis of a single test administration is to divide the test into halves and correlate the two half-tests. This is referred to as a **split-half reliability estimate.** This procedure was originally devised for written tests but was subsequently used for tests in the exercise sciences. For example, the reliability of a 10-trial test of a sports skill could be determined by correlating the average of one set of five trial scores with the average of the scores on the remaining five trials. There are several ways the trials could be split. Two possibilities are a first half–second half split, where the two halves consist of trials 1 to 5 and trials 6 to 10, or an odd-even split, where the two halves consist of trials 1, 3, 5, 7, and 9 and trials 2, 4, 6, 8, and 10.

The odd-even split is used most frequently in tests of motor skill to guard against the possibility of fatigue or lack of motivation affecting performance on the last few trials of the test. To exemplify this point, let's use an extreme example. Suppose we were interested in the reliability of a 10-trial shuttle run test. If the division into halves was accomplished using a first half–second half split, the average of the first five trials is likely to be lower (better performance) than the average of the last five trials, because examinees will probably get tired before completing the test and thus receive higher scores (poorer performance) on the latter trials. This would result in a lower reliability estimate. If an odd-even split were used, the average of the odd-numbered trials would probably be similar to the average of the even-numbered trials. This comparison is demonstrated in Fig. 6-3.

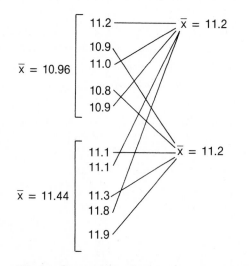

FIG. 6-3. *Comparison of odd-even split with first half–second half split using 10 shuttle run test scores (seconds).*

If a first half–second half split is used, the average of the second five trials (11.44 seconds) clearly differs from the average of the first five trials (10.96 seconds), as shown in Fig. 6-3. This is probably caused by the effect of fatigue. An odd-even split, on the other hand, yields identical averages for the odd-numbered and the even-numbered trials.

Once a test is split into halves and the averages of the halves determined, these scores can be correlated to yield $r_{xx'}$. However, since only half of the test has been correlated with the other half, the resultant reliability coefficient only estimates the reliability of half of the test. In other words, once our 10-trial test has been divided into halves, the reliability coefficient represents an estimate for a 5-trial test. We, of course, would like to know how reliable a 10-trial test would be. The formula used to estimate the reliability of the full-length (in this case, 10-trial) test, called the *Spearman-Brown prophecy formula*, is shown in Formula 6-1.

$$r^*_{xx'} = \frac{n r_{xx'}}{1 + (n - 1) r_{xx'}}$$ Formula 6-1

where n = number of times test length is increased
$r_{xx'}$ = reliability of half of the test length
$r^*_{xx'}$ = estimated reliability for the full test length

If the correlation between half-tests of a 10-trial test is 0.60, the estimated reliability of the full-length test would be 0.75. In this case, n = 2. Longer tests are expected to be more reliable than shorter ones.

TEST-RETEST RELIABILITY. If a test is used to assess achievement on a skill at the end of a unit of instruction, obtaining a test score that reflects the examinee's skill level with precision would be desirable. The assessment would be inaccurate if some examinees who obtained high scores on the day testing took place would have received low scores if the test had been administered on a second day. To avoid this possibility, the test user should look for a test with an acceptable reliability coefficient that has been established on a test-retest basis.

Either of the two correlational procedures described in the previous section would be appropriate for estimating the reliability in a test-retest context. The split-half procedure, however, is not appropriate in this setting.

PRECISION OF AN INDIVIDUAL TEST SCORE. Thus far reliability estimates that are determined for groups have been discussed. In other words, reliability is estimated by using the test scores obtained from administering the test to a group of examinees. Sometimes it is of greater interest to evaluate the reliability of an individual examinee's score. This can be done using the **standard error of measurement.** Let's assume we could administer a test to an examinee 1000 times, with each administration completely independent of the others. We would plot a distribution of these 1000 scores as described in Chapter 4. The standard deviation of this distribution of scores is the *standard error of measurement* for the examinee. As the examinee's scores become more similar, the standard error of measurement becomes smaller. Thus, a smaller standard error of measurement is associated with a more precise score. This differs from other types of reliability discussed previously, where higher values of $r_{xx'}$ and $R_{xx'}$ represent greater consistency.

Since a test cannot be administered repeatedly to an individual, the standard error of measurement is estimated using Formula 6-2.

$$SE_m = s \sqrt{1 - r_{xx'}}$$ Formula 6-2

where SE_m = *standard error* of *measurement*

s = *standard* deviation of a group of examinees

$r_{xx'}$ = *reliability coefficient*

Suppose, for example, that the standard deviation of a set of shuttle run test scores is 2 seconds and the test reliability is 0.84.

$$SE_m = 2 \sqrt{1 - 0.84} = 0.80 \text{ seconds}$$

How is an SE_m of 0.80 interpreted? First, it represents seconds, in this case. In other words, the SE_m for the shuttle run test is 0.80 second. The standard error of measurement is always presented in the actual score units of the test. Now, suppose Mary obtained a score of 9.8 seconds on the shuttle run test. How precise is her score? The SE_m can be used to form a band around the examinee's score. The smaller the band, the more precise the score. Remember that the SE_m is actually a standard deviation. Thus, if a ± 1 SE_m band around Mary's score is used, it would be expected to span her true score 68% of the time. The SE_m is subtracted from Mary's score to obtain the lower bound of the band and added to obtain the upper bound. In this example Mary's band is 9.0-10.6 seconds. If Mary repeatedly took the shuttle run, we would not necessarily expect her scores to be close to the original 9.8 seconds, since the standard error of measurement band is relatively large. As the band decreases in size, we can have more faith in the precision of Mary's score.

To summarize, the standard error of measurement provides an indicator of the precision of an individual's test score. The smaller the SE_m, the greater the reliability of the score.

Factors influencing the reliability of a test

Numerous factors influence the reliability of a test. Many of the factors are more important to test developers than test users, but knowledge of a few of these factors helps in selecting a test with acceptable reliability. See Fig. 6-4 for an overview of the factors to be described in the next sections.

TYPE OF TEST. To expect the reliability of all tests in our field to be 0.90 or above is not reasonable. The type of test must be taken into account when interpreting the reliability of a test. If performance on the test requires a maximum expenditure of effort, it is reasonable to expect reliabilities of around 0.85 or higher. For example, a grip strength test is taken by squeezing a hand dynamometer as hard as possible. This requires all-out physical effort. Performance on this test ought to be highly reliable. This is also true for measures of the long

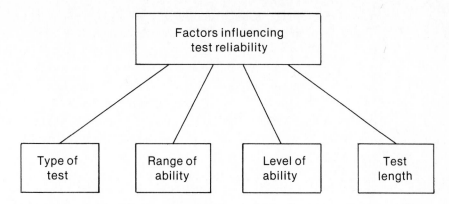

FIG. 6-4. *Factors influencing test reliability.*

jump, vertical jump, dashes, distance throw, and other similar abilities. The greater the force requirements (throw as hard as possible, jump as far as possible, squeeze the hand dynamometer as hard as possible), the higher the reliability coefficient should be.

As the accuracy demands of a test increase, reliability decreases. To expect reliability coefficients to be 0.85 or higher in most instances is not reasonable. In fact, a test primarily measuring accuracy, such as a test of the chip shot in golf or the short serve in badminton, might be acceptable with a reliability estimate of 0.70, assuming satisfactory validity. At the same time estimates below 0.70 are rarely acceptable, regardless of the type of test.

RANGE OF ABILITY. When reliability is estimated using test scores from a group with a wide range of ability, the estimate is artificially inflated. For example, assume a test of the softball throw for distance was given to a group of children in grades 2 through 6. In this case, reliability is almost guaranteed to be high. The children in sixth grade will throw the ball farther than the second graders, primarily because sixth graders are bigger and stronger than second graders. This would be true as often as the test is repeated. In a relative sense the test is highly reliable. On the other hand, it makes more sense to know whether the test is reliable for sixth graders—or second graders—and this suggests that reliability must be estimated for each grade separately. Although the scores will still fluctuate within each grade, the reliability estimate for each grade will not be an artifact of a wide range of ability. In short, when planning to test sixth graders, select a test with acceptable reliability for sixth grade children.

LEVEL OF ABILITY. Closely related to range of ability is level of ability and its effect on reliability. In physical education there has been a tendency to expect skilled individuals to perform with more consistency than beginners. Therefore, a specific skills test might be more reliable when administered to a highly skilled player. Interestingly enough, research in motor development has not totally verified this assumption. When a number of basic movement patterns are measured, poorly skilled individuals—presumably beginners in learning the pattern—tend to display highly reliable performances. They may not be very good, but they are consistent in their performance! As individuals learn more about the movement pattern—presumably moving up to intermediate level—their performances become less reliable. This may seem incongruous, but an intermediate-level performer has much more of a margin for error than a beginner. The intermediate performer is refining the movement pattern. At the advanced level these individuals become more consistent, with highly reliable performance. At this level the performer has begun to have control over the potential error and can perform with relative consistency.

TEST LENGTH. The reliability of a test can be increased by making it longer. This is a well-established fact. When measuring sports skills, increasing the number of trials will lead to a higher reliability estimate. Adding more items to a written test will have the same effect.

OBJECTIVITY OF SCORING

The degree of accuracy in scoring a test is often referred to as the **objectivity** of the test. If a test is labeled highly objective, this means there will be little error in scoring the test. Many individuals could score the test and obtain the same result. A **subjective** test might be scored quite differently, depending upon the scorer. Variability among scorers increases when the scorer is required to make judgments that are more subjective, as in rating playing ability in a sport.

When a target is used to score a test or when a distance is measured, the test can be scored at a high level of objectivity. The objectivity is so obvious that an estimate of objectivity is rarely calculated. As the subjectivity of the test increases, the test developer is obligated to report an objectivity estimate. This can be done in one of two ways, as depicted in Fig. 6-5.

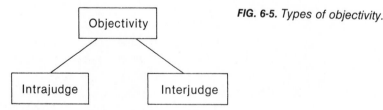

FIG. 6-5. *Types of objectivity.*

Intrajudge objectivity is the consistency in scoring when a test user scores the same test two or more times. If a written test is being considered, intrajudge objectivity can easily be determined. A set of tests can be graded once, put aside until a later date, and then graded again by the same person. Comparison of the two sets of scores would reflect the consistency of the individual in scoring the test. In testing motor skills estimates of intrajudge objectivity are more difficult to obtain because the same performance must be viewed twice. This is usually facilitated by recording the performance on film or videotape.

The second type of objectivity is **interjudge objectivity,** which is the consistency between two or more independent judgments of the same performance. Interjudge objectivity is an important part of rating events in gymnastics, diving, and figure skating, where several judges rate each performance.

Both types of objectivity can be estimated using correlational procedures similar to estimating reliability. The estimates are expected to be relatively high (0.80 or above), since lower values suggest that the judges are weighting the various components of skill differently.

A method has been proposed to objectify judging of springboard diving (McCormick, Subbaiah, and Arnold, 1982). For example, a videotape recording can be made of the front half-twist dive, and clear plastic grids are placed over the video monitor to measure various components of the dive, such as deviation of twist from 180 degrees. A total of four measures can be used to predict judges' scores—height of the diver above board (see Fig. 6-6), distance out from board, twist, and one or two angle measurements.

FIG. 6-6. *Measurement of maximum height of diver in front half-twist dive.*

To summarize, efforts to identify the sources of biasing factors in judging motor performance have been numerous. Although knowing whether or not judges agree in their ratings is useful, knowing *why* they differ is more important. The possibility of reducing the bias and increasing the objectivity of ratings then exists.

SUMMARY

The characteristics of a test should be carefully evaluated before its administration to a group of examinees. Test validity, reliability, and objectivity are of major importance. Validity is the soundness of the interpretation of the test. It can be established on logical and/or statistical grounds. Through a logical analysis evidence of content validity can be demonstrated for a written test, and evidence of logical validity can be demonstrated for a test of motor performance. Statistical evidence is used to determine criterion-related validity, and both logical and statistical information are needed to establish construct validity. Reliability is the consistency of performance on a test. Test reliability can be established for a single occasion or a general period of time. Either $r_{xx'}$ or $R_{xx'}$ can be used as reliability coefficients, although $R_{xx'}$ is generally viewed as the superior estimate. Objectivity is the accuracy of scoring a test. Statistical evidence of this characteristic should be provided when the scoring is subjective, as in gymnastics and diving. A good test will possess high levels of all three of these elements.

LEARNING EXPERIENCES

1. Select a test you might consider using in the future. (Examples of a wide variety of tests can be found in Chapters 10 to 15.) Carefully evaluate its evidence of validity, reliability, and objectivity. Suggest ways in which each of these test characteristics might be improved for the test you selected.
2. Develop a simple rating scale for a skill in a sport such as basketball. (See Chapter 8 for information on developing rating scales.) Attend a game with a friend who is also in your measurement and evaluation course, and use the scale to rate the skill. Do not try to rate more than one player. Each of you should independently rate the same person. Periodically compare ratings; if they are discrepant, discuss ways of improving the use of the scale or the scale itself.
3. Six trials of a basketball shooting test were administered to each of five students. Using this data set, answer the three questions below.

Student	Trial 1	Trial 2	Trial 3	Trial 4	Trial 5	Trial 6
A	10	11	11	12	11	12
B	14	13	14	14	15	14
C	12	12	12	13	12	13
D	9	8	8	9	9	8
E	7	9	8	8	9	9

  a. Calculate the split-half reliability coefficient for this six-trial test. Use an odd-even split.

  b. Use the Spearman-Brown formula to estimate the reliability coefficient for six trials.

  c. Briefly interpret this coefficient.

ANSWERS TO LEARNING EXPERIENCES

3a. The mean of the odd trials and the mean of the even trials should be determined for each person.

Student	Odd (X)	Even (Y)	XY
A	10.67	11.67	124.52
B	14.33	13.67	195.89
C	12.00	12.67	152.04
D	8.67	8.33	72.22
E	8.00	8.67	69.36
	53.67	55.01	614.03

Use the Pearson product-moment correlation coefficient formula to determine the correlation between the odd (X) and even (Y) means (Formula 5-9). The following values are needed for the formula:

$$\Sigma X = 53.67$$
$$\Sigma Y = 55.01$$
$$\Sigma XY = 614.03$$
$$\Sigma X^2 = 602.37$$
$$\Sigma Y^2 = 628.14$$
$$(\Sigma X)^2 = 2880.47$$
$$(\Sigma Y)^2 = 3026.10$$

$$r_{xx'} = \frac{5(614.03) - 2952.39}{\sqrt{[5(602.37) - 2880.47][5(628.14) - 3026.10]}}$$
$$= \frac{117.76}{122.70} = 0.959$$

3b. The answer to 3a is the reliability for a three-trial test, since the six-trial test was split into three-trial halves to obtain the reliability coefficient. The reliability of the six-trial test must now be estimated using the Spearman-Brown prophecy formula (Formula 6-1).

$$r_{xx'}^* = \frac{2(.959)}{1 + (2 - 1)(.959)}$$
$$= \frac{1.918}{1 + .959} = 0.979$$

3c. The estimated reliability of the six-trial test (0.979) is quite high, indicating that the basketball test is a reliable measure of performance. Since the three-trial test reliability (0.959) is also high, this suggests that administering the full-length six-trial test to measure performance reliably is not necessary. A three-trial test would be adequate.

REFERENCES

American Psychological Association. 1984. Joint standards for educational and psychological tests. Washington, D.C.: APA.

Cooper, K.H. 1968. A means of assessing maximal oxygen intake. Journal of the American Medical Association **203**:201-204.

Cooperative Tests and Services. 1970. AAHPERD Cooperative Physical Education Tests. Princeton, N.J.: Educational Testing Service.

Getchell, L.H., Kirkendall, D., and Robbins, G. 1977. Prediction of maximal oxygen uptake in young adult women joggers. Research Quarterly **48**:61-67.

Kenyon, G.S. 1968. Six scales for assessing attitude toward physical activity. Research Quarterly **39**:566-574.

Martens, R. 1977. Sport Competition Anxiety Test. Champaign, Ill.: Human Kinetics Publishers, Inc.

McCormick, J.H., Subbaiah, P., and Arnold, H.J. 1982. A method for identification of some components of judging springboard diving. Research Quarterly for Exercise and Sport **53**(4):313-322.

Morgan, W.P., and Johnson, R.W. 1978. Personality characteristics of successful and unsuccessful oarsmen. International Journal of Sport Psychology **9**:119-133.

ANNOTATED READINGS

Brown, F.G. 1983. Principles of educational and psychological testing, ed. 3. Lavallette, N.J.: Holt, Rinehart & Winston.

Thorough coverage of both theory and techniques of educational and psychological testing; presents basic concepts in testing—validity, reliability, and types of scores—and illustrates how to apply those principles in test construction, use, evaluation, and interpretation; explores rationale underlying educational and psychological testing.

Gronlund, N.E. 1985. Measurement and evaluation in teaching, ed. 5. New York: Macmillan Publishing Co.

Emphasizes principles and procedures of testing and evaluation important to elementary and secondary teachers; assumes no prior knowledge of measurement or statistics; illustrates both norm-referenced and criterion-referenced test specifications.

Mehrens, W.A., and Lehmann, I.J. 1984. Measurement and evaluation in education and psychology, ed. 3. Lavallette, N.J.: Holt, Rinehart & Winston.

Introduction to the construction, evaluation, interpretation, and uses of tests; offers a contemporary look at testing and some of its practical applications; includes updated discussion of criterion-referenced measurement; contains detailed information on the practical uses of assessment data; covers current issues in testing.

Noll, V.H., Scannell, D.P., and Craig, R.C. 1979. Introduction to educational measurement, ed. 4. Boston: Houghton Mifflin Co.

Nontechnical orientation to educational measurement; includes thorough coverage of criterion-referenced tests and national and state assessment programs.

7 Validity and Reliability of Criterion-Referenced Tests

KEY WORDS   *Watch for these words as you read the following chapter:*

contingency coefficient	domain	kappa coefficient
contrasting groups method	domain-referenced validity	mastery learning
		proportion of agreement
criterion-referenced test	instructed/uninstructed approach	reliability
decision validity		

Although most published tests in physical education and exercise science are norm-referenced, a great deal of informal testing goes on in the field that is more similar to the criterion-referenced approach to testing (Safrit, 1981). A physical education teacher, for example, may set a standard that students are expected to achieve on a test. Those whose test scores equal or surpass the test standard are classified as masters on the test; those with scores falling below the standard are labeled nonmasters (or some similar term). In a fitness laboratory clients are often placed in a category reflecting their level of fitness based on the results of a test. In a situation where there are no constraints on the number of individuals who can be classified as masters, a criterion-referenced test is appropriate. When only the top four or five examinees will be selected for a given purpose, a norm-referenced approach is more useful. A **criterion-referenced test** is defined as *a test with a predetermined standard of performance that is tied to a specified domain of behavior.* There is more to a criterion-referenced test than setting a standard, although this is an important part of this type of measure. The standard must be referenced to a criterion behavior. Suppose an exercise specialist administers a battery of fitness tests to all new clients joining a fitness club. One of these tests is a modified sit-ups measure of abdominal strength. A woman who is a new member of the club is classified as "average" in abdominal strength based on the test results. The exercise specialist suggests a series of exercises to increase abdominal strength and sets a goal of 45 sit-ups (in 1 minute) for her to achieve. How was this standard set? What does it mean? If this is a legitimate criterion-referenced test, the standard should have meaning in terms of a criterion behavior. This means that 45 sit-ups (standard) should reflect adequate abdominal strength for a woman in this fitness category. Of course, there is no way of knowing this is true. A standard could be set for any test, but it might not be clearly interpretable in light of the criterion behavior.

Even though there are problems in developing this type of test, it has certain advantages over a norm-referenced test. A norm-referenced test measures the status of the normative group, that is, "what is" rather than "what should be." For example, consider a measure of body fatness, the sum of a set of skinfold measures. Perhaps these measures are obtained from a large group of adult female examinees and used to estimate their percent body fat. The average percent fat for this group is 36%. Does this reflect a desirable standard for women to attain? This is legitimate normative data. However, it is well known that adult women tend to be overweight; therefore, normative data do not represent the most desirable standards in this case.

Furthermore, norm-referenced tests rarely provide extensive diagnostic feedback to the examinee. Think about the many tests you have taken in past years. How often did you receive meaningful feedback on your test score? In physical education few tests provide specific feedback. All over the United States students are tested on the basketball free throw by taking a predetermined number of shots at the basket. The student who makes most of these shots gets feedback on his or her skill level. The shooting technique of this individual is assumed to be good enough to be successful. However, the student who misses the shot receives little systematic feedback. If a criterion-referenced test is tied to a criterion behavior, it will provide needed feedback to the examinee. An excellent overview of the criterion-referenced approach to measurement can be found in Popham (1978, 1981).

MASTERY LEARNING

The normal distribution, as described in Chapter 5, is used in determining norm-referenced grades. Regardless of the ability levels of students, some will receive A's, B's, and so forth, according to a predetermined set of percentages. In a **mastery learning** setting (Nitko, 1984) an individual is expected to be a nonmaster before instruction or a training program. At this point, when tests are administered to the nonmasters, the distribution of scores will be skewed in a positive direction since most examinees would receive low scores and only a small percentage would receive high scores. At the end of the unit of instruction or a training program, the majority in the group is expected to master the objective. In this case, test scores will be skewed negatively, since only a few people received low scores.

Criterion-referenced testing, then, is closely associated with the mastery

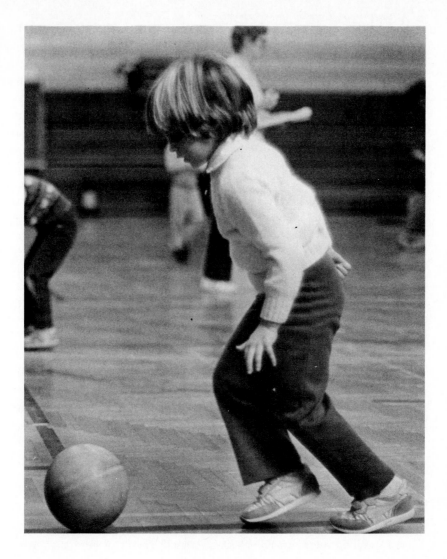

model of instruction. Frequently, teachers care little about individual differences. If many students can master the test, so much the better. (Is not the objective of education for all or most students to learn?) Many educators feel it reflects badly on education if students are taught skills, yet conclude the unit by being normally distributed on their abilities. Should not a large percentage of the students have at least minimal success in a unit? If this model of instruction is adopted, the norm-referenced approach is not quite appropriate. The criterion-referenced test is better suited to this model.

USES OF A CRITERION-REFERENCED TEST

Criterion-referenced tests have a variety of uses. Sometimes we seek information on a person's capabilities, even though we have no interest in comparing the test score to a standard. For example, an exercise specialist might be interested in determining the strength of a client by administering a strength test at various parts of the body. Yet the individual is not classified according to some predetermined standard. In the physical education field, however, the most widespread use of criterion-referenced tests is to assign people to mastery states by administering *mastery tests.*

The National Collegiate Athletic Association (NCAA) officiating examinations and the American Red Cross Swimming Tests are often used as mastery tests to estimate an individual's mastery state. In the officiating examinations cutoff scores are established for intramural, local, district, and national categories; all individuals who attain the required scores are approved to officiate at that level. In the case of swimming, specific competencies have been established by the Red Cross for beginners, advanced beginners, and so on. All who demonstrate the competencies are judged to have the ability to be classified at that level and are permitted to attempt to master the next level.

VALIDITY

The techniques for validating a criterion-referenced test are unique, although there are similarities conceptually to norm-referenced test validity methodology. Generally, the definition of validity for a norm-referenced test applies to a criterion-referenced test, that is, validity is the soundness of the interpretation of the test. However, more precise definitions must be used that are unique to the criterion-referenced test. These definitions vary according to the type of validity of interest.

Types of validity

Validity can be determined logically through domain-referenced validity or statistically, using decision validity methods. The focus here is on the mastery test, where examinees are classified as masters or nonmasters on the basis of their test score.

DOMAIN-REFERENCED VALIDITY. Remember that a criterion-referenced test has been defined as a measure of performance referenced to a criterion behavior. To develop a test of this type, the criterion behavior must be defined. Then the test is logically validated by showing that the tasks sampled by the test adequately represent the criterion behavior. This is called **domain-referenced validity,** with the term **domain** used to represent the criterion behavior. This has many parallels with both content and logical validity, which were described in Chapter 6. However, the focus of a criterion-referenced test is much narrower than its norm-referenced counterpart. A criterion-referenced test is usually de-signed to measure a single objective and is frequently used as formative evalua-tion.

How might domain-referenced validity be established for a test of a sports skill? Let's use a test of the basketball jump shot as an example. The first steps in developing the test would be to analyze the skill, identify its most important elements, and devise a test to measure these elements. This is precisely how logical validity is determined, and it is equally appropriate in criterion-refer-enced testing. Suppose the test specifies that the student take 10 jump shots from a restraining line 15 feet away from the basket. In a physical education class of high school boys, a standard of 7 out of 10 successful jump shots might be set. This is a typical approach to testing in the physical education field. How is the placement of the restraining line for the test chosen? Usually it is arbi-trary, although the distance from the basket would be expected to be realistic. Yet any one of a number of realistic locations might be selected. Would it not be a better test of the boy's jump shooting ability if he could make successful shots from several points on the court? In the context of domain-referenced va-lidity, this would be desirable. Of course, testing from every possible spot would be impossible. A procedure needs to be developed for systematically identifying several spots on the court from which the jump shot may be taken. One way of doing this would be to divide the basketball half-court into sections, as shown in Fig. 7-1.

Thinking of each of the sections in Fig. 7-1 as test items may be helpful. How many sections should be selected? For the sake of simplicity and practical-

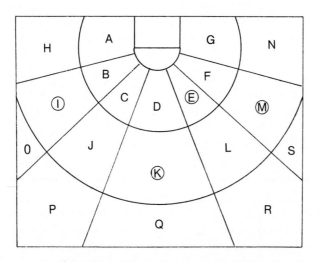

FIG. 7-1. *Sampling of basketball court areas to test jump shot.*

ity, let's use four sections. How should these sections be selected? Drawing a random sample from the entire set does not seem appropriate since a player is much less likely to attempt a jump shot from certain sections of the court than others. Areas O through S represent sections seldom used for jump shots; therefore, the sections to be sampled might reasonably be limited to A through N. These letters were converted to numbers from 1 to 14, and four numbers were randomly drawn from the set. Their corresponding letters—E, I, K, and M—are circled in Fig. 7-1.

The number of trials to be taken from each area should also be determined. Actual test scores are necessary for this purpose. Certainly more than one trial would be taken from each of the areas to have a reliable test.

Would this be a practical test to administer in a physical education class? Possibly not, in many school settings, but tests are not developed solely for use in classes. The jump shot test, with several trials taken from four spots on the court, might be useful for a basketball camp or an all-school testing program. Actually, it is not as cumbersome as it might seem for use in a physical education class. If the students are divided into four groups, they could rotate from one testing station to the other. In this way more students would be active than if only one restraining line location were used.

Domain-referenced validity, then, requires a careful description of the criterion behavior, or domain, along with evidence that the test adequately represents this domain. Although this is a logical rather than a statistical analysis, it should not be viewed as an arbitrary process.

DECISION VALIDITY. In addition to evidence of the adequacy of the test as a measure of the criterion behavior, the *accuracy of classification* as masters and nonmasters must be determined. This is done using **decision validity** procedures, which typically require the use of statistical procedures. Does the test classify people accurately? Two approaches—empirical methods and judgmental-empirical methods—are described in the next section.

As the name implies, *empirical methods* require a data base, and statistical procedures are used to estimate validity. One example of empirical procedures is a method that can be used by physical education teachers to select a valid cutoff point for a mastery test. This is usually referred to as the **instructed/uninstructed approach.** It assumes that an objective has been written, a test has been identified to measure the objective, but no performance standard has been set. The test is administered to two groups of students—one that has received no instruction on the objective and one that has received previous instruction. Then the two distributions of test scores are compared, as shown in Fig. 7-2. A degree of overlap is expected between the distributions. The best students in the uninstructed group should have scores similar to the poorest in the instructed group. The point at which the two distributions overlap represents the

FIG. 7-2. *Setting standards using the instructed/uninstructed group approach.*

cutoff score, which can be used to classify future students as masters or nonmasters.

This is a viable approach *if* the uninstructed group really is uninstructed. A unit may represent the first formal instruction the students have had in school, but many students will have learned a few skills in other settings. In the Measurement Laboratory at the University of Wisconsin, the difficulty in finding a true uninstructed group has been demonstrated in several activities. Because the uninstructed group does not consist only of nonmasters, the curves overlap too much; no meaningful cutoff point can be identified. This approach is probably most appropriate in units where more unusual activities are taught, such as self-defense or fencing, or when all students could be tested and the lower third of the distribution could be used to represent the uninstructed and the upper third, the instructed.

The second type of decision validity is *judgmental-empirical* methods. These methods require judgment on the part of the test user as well as a data base. One type of judgmental-empirical method is known as the **contrasting groups method.** Although it can be used outside a school setting, the following example is relevant for physical education teachers in a school. To use the system properly, more than one physical education teacher must be knowledgeable about the physical capabilities of the students who will be tested. Assume again that an educational objective has been set and ways of evaluating the objective have been determined, but no standard has been set. The only information the teacher needs is a list of names of the students involved. Based on his or her knowledge of the students, the teacher classifies each one as either a master or a nonmaster on the objective in question. Then the entire group of students is evaluated on the objective using the predetermined procedure. A distribution of scores is formed for those students who are expected to master the objective and

FIG. 7-3. *Setting standards using the contrasting groups approach.*

one for those not expected to master it. These distributions are then compared for overlap, as shown in Fig. 7-3. As in the previous approach, the point of overlap is the best estimate of the cutoff score.

Notice that both of the above methods use the comparison of distributions of scores to validate a cutoff score. An easier way to estimate test validity using these approaches is to set up a *contingency table.* An example of displaying the results of the instructed/uninstructed approach in a contingency table can be found in Fig. 7-4. The examinees in the instructed and uninstructed groups have already been identified. The only factor that can be varied is the cutoff score used to identify masters and nonmasters. The master/nonmaster classifications are shown on the left of the table. The teacher's job is to select a cutoff score

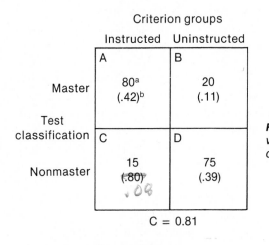

FIG. 7-4. *Procedure for estimating test validity using the contingency coefficient (C).*

[a]Number of students
[b]Proportion of students

that seems reasonable. Then the examinees are tallied in the table. For example, a student in the instructed group who is identified as a master by the test would be placed in the upper left cell (A) of the table. A student in the uninstructed group who is classified as a master would be tallied in the upper right cell (B) of the table. When all students have been tallied, the sum of the tallies in each cell is converted to a proportion. Each proportion is calculated by dividing the number of students within a cell by N, the total number of students. For example, in cell D the proportion of students is 75/190 or 0.39. The *validity coefficient* is calculated by summing the proportions in the upper left cell (A) and the lower right cell (D). The symbol for this coefficient is C, representing the **contingency coefficient.** Don't confuse this symbol with the letter C used to identify one of the cells in the contingency table in Fig. 7-4. Different sizes of the coefficient C can be examined by changing the cutoff score. The highest C value will represent the most valid cutoff score.

Review the numerical example in Fig. 7-4. Note that the whole numbers in the cells of the table represent the number of examinees; the numbers in parentheses represent the proportion of examinees. Adding the proportion of examinees correctly classified (A + D) yields C, the contingency coefficient. In this case, C equals (0.42 + 0.39) or 0.81. If a higher validity coefficient were desired, the test developer would set a different cutoff point, and develop a new contingency table. In this way the cutoff score that maximizes the differences between groups is determined.

In summary, a criterion-referenced test, like a norm-referenced test, can be validated both logically and statistically. If a mastery test is to be used in an informal setting, logical validation of the test would probably suffice. If the test is used to make major decisions about examinees, both logical and statistical validity should be established. Since the test is used to classify students as masters or nonmasters, the accuracy of these classifications should be evident.

Interpretation of the validity coefficient

Since C, the validity coefficient, is the sum of two proportions, a high coefficient is desirable. In fact, if C = 0.50, this suggests that the classification may be no better than chance. Although no hard rule has been set for evaluating the size of the validity coefficient, certainly values of 0.80 or above would be desirable.

RELIABILITY

Criterion-referenced **reliability** is defined differently than norm-referenced reliability. In the criterion-referenced context, reliability is defined as *consistency of classification*. In other words, if the examinees were classified as masters or nonmasters on one occasion, would they be classified the same way on a second occasion?

Procedures for estimating reliability

The simplest way to estimate reliability is to administer a mastery test on 2 days and tally the scores in a contingency table. The general layout of this contingency table is shown in Fig. 7-5. To the left of the table, *M* (mastery) and *NM* (nonmastery) classifications for the first day (Day 1) of testing are displayed. Across the top of the table, *M* and *NM* classifications are identified for the second day of testing. If a student is classified as a master on both days, a tally is placed in the upper left cell of the table. If a student is classified as a master on Day 1 and a nonmaster on Day 2, the tally is placed in the upper right cell. Locate the appropriate cell for the examinee who is a nonmaster on Day 1 and a master on Day 2. This is the lower left cell of the table. Once the scores have been tallied, the tallies in each cell are summed and converted to proportions.

PROPORTION OF AGREEMENT. The most popular method for estimating reliability from a contingency table is to use *P*, which is the symbol for **proportion of agreement.** The coefficient *P* is calculated by summing the proportions in cells A and D. This should sound familiar because it is the same procedure used to estimate *C*, the validity coefficient. Of course, the two coefficients have different interpretations because the contingency tables are set up differently, but the calculation is identical. Look at the data in Fig. 7-5. Of the 100 examinees taking this test, 45 were classified as masters on both days, and 35 were classified as nonmasters. There were errors in classification as well, with 12 examinees labeled masters on the first day and nonmasters on the second, while the remaining 8 students received the reverse classifications. Since *N* equals 100 in this case, the proportions will be the same numerical value as the number of students within cells preceded by a decimal point. In cell A, for example, the proportion is 45/100 or 0.45. The proportion of agreement *P* is (0.45 + 0.35) or 0.80.

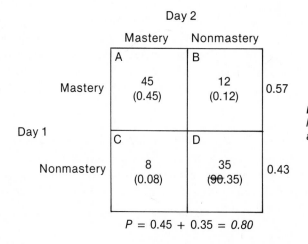

Day 2

	Mastery	Nonmastery	
Mastery	A 45 (0.45)	B 12 (0.12)	0.57
Nonmastery	C 8 (0.08)	D 35 (90.35)	0.43

Day 1

$$P = 0.45 + 0.35 = 0.80$$

FIG. 7-5. *Procedure for calculating* P, *the proportion of agreement.*

KAPPA COEFFICIENT. The coefficient P fails to take into account that some correct categorizations will be made purely by chance. Given that this is true, what degree of agreement has been obtained beyond the expectation of chance? One approach to this problem is to use k, **kappa coefficient,** to estimate reliability (Swaminathan, Hambleton, and Algina, 1974). Formula 7-1 is used to calculate k.

$$k = \frac{P_o - P_c}{1 - P_c}$$
Formula 7-1

where P_o = *proportion* of *agreement*
P_c = *proportion* of *agreement* expected by *chance*

or

$P_c = \Sigma \, (P_i)(P_i)$
where P_i = marginal proportion

To calculate P_c, follow this rule of thumb. Determine the marginal proportions by adding the proportions for each column and row of the contingency table. For example, in the first row of the table, the proportions for cells A and B are summed $(0.45 + 0.12)$ to equal the marginal proportion for this row (0.57). Multiply the marginal proportions of the outermost row and column of the table $[(0.57)(0.53)$, in this case] and add to the product of the marginal proportions of the innermost row and column $[(0.43)(0.47)$, in this case]. In the example in Fig. 7-5, $P_c = (0.57)(0.53) + (0.43)(0.47) = 0.3021 + 0.2021 = 0.5042$. Then,

$$k = \frac{0.80 - 0.5042}{1 - 0.5042} = \frac{0.2958}{0.4958} = 0.597$$

Not surprisingly, when chance is taken into account, the size of the proportion of agreement decreases.

Interpretation of the reliability coefficient

Since the proportion of agreement, P, can be affected by chance allocations, values of P below 0.50 are unacceptable. Thus, the *interpretable range* of P is 0.50 to 1.00. In other words, a P of 0.50 is interpreted as a P of 0.00. Although values of k can range from -1.00 to $+1.00$, the interpretable range of k is 0.00 to 1.00. Negative values of k have no meaning in the context of reliability, since test information either contributes positively to the consistency of classification or it does not.

When the group being tested consists of a large proportion of masters or nonmasters, P tends to be high. This is an expected characteristic of P, since it will be easier to classify people when they display low or high skill levels because their scores will be far below or above the cutoff point. Students who fall in between are more difficult to classify. When the test group consists primarily of this category of examinees, P typically drops, reflecting the difficulty of classifying people consistently as their scores approach the cutoff score.

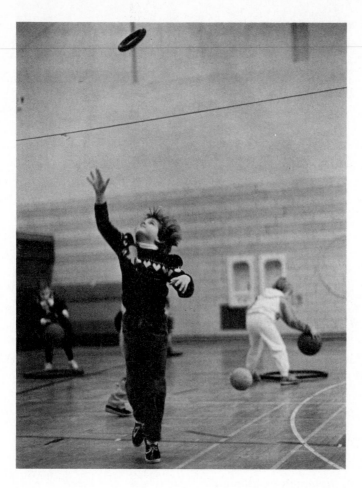

SUMMARY

The criterion-referenced test offers an excellent option to norm-referenced testing when the identification of masters and nonmasters based on test performance is of interest. On the other hand, the concept of criterion-referenced measurement is often not fully understood, leading to oversimplified tests of mastery. Although a cutoff score can be determined with relative ease if set arbitrarily, this score, and thus the test, lacks validity unless the score can be interpreted in light of a criterion behavior. The validity and reliability of criterion-referenced tests are defined differently than the definitions of these concepts in a norm-referenced context. The validity of a mastery test is defined as the accuracy of classifications; reliability is the consistency of classifications.

LEARNING EXPERIENCES

1. This exercise is designed to give you some practical experience with criterion-referenced testing. Collect 15 pennies and a plastic container. Ask 10 people to try to toss the pennies in the container one at a time. Tell them that mastery on this task is successfully tossing 10 of the 15 pennies into the container. (Try it first yourself, so that the distance of the toss is realistic.) Record the number of successes out of 15 trials. Then ask each person to repeat the test, beginning again with all 15 pennies. After recording these successes, calculate P, the proportion of agreement. How reliable is this data set? Evaluate the size of this coefficient and indicate ways it might be increased.

2. An exercise specialist wishes to check the validity of a sit-ups test as a measure of abdominal strength. He compares the sit-ups test with a criterion test, electromyographic (EMG) readings of the activity of the abdominal muscles. Both tests are used in a criterion-referenced framework. On the EMG test a cutoff score of 27 or above reflects substantial activity in the abdominal muscles. The exercise specialist decides to try using a cutoff score of 55 or above on the sit-ups test to check the criterion-referenced test validity. He obtains the following test scores.

Subject	Sit-ups test	EMG test
1	73	32
2	42	20
3	51	19
4	63	25
5	59	27
6	39	18
7	57	33
8	70	36
9	65	29
10	69	28
11	46	19
12	51	21
13	52	30
14	56	31
15	64	27
16	71	17
17	42	19
18	50	25
19	50	23
20	60	29

a. Develop a contingency table for these scores.
b. Calculate C, the validity coefficient.
c. Is the sit-ups test valid? Explain.

ANSWERS TO LEARNING EXPERIENCES

2a. Hint: To develop the contingency table, each of the scores must be converted to a 0 or 1 score. See Fig. 7-6 for the answer to this problem.

b. $C = 0.45 + 0.40 = 0.85$

c. A C of 0.85 indicates a high degree of accuracy of classification; thus, the validity of the sit-ups test is acceptable.

*Number of people

†Proportion of people (number in cell divided by total number; in this case, N = 20)

FIG. 7-6. Contingency table; answer to Learning Experience 2a.

REFERENCES

Nitko, A.J. 1984. Defining "criterion-referenced test." In R.A. Berk, editor. A guide to criterion-referenced test construction. Baltimore: The Johns Hopkins University Press.

Popham, W.J. 1978. Criterion-referenced measurement. Englewood Cliffs, N.J.: Prentice-Hall, Inc.

Popham, W.J. 1981. Modern educational measurement. Englewood Cliffs, N.J.: Prentice-Hall, Inc.

Safrit, M.J. 1981. Evaluation in physical education. Englewood Cliffs, N.J.: Prentice-Hall, Inc.

Swaminathan, H., Hambleton, R.K., and Algina, J.A. 1974. Reliability of criterion-referenced tests: a decision-theoretic formulation. Journal of Educational Measurement 11:263-268.

ANNOTATED READINGS

Educational Testing Service. 1982. Passing scores. Princeton, N.J.: Educational Testing Service.

Focuses on setting standards of performance on tests; describes in clear, nontechnical language various methods of making decisions related to passing scores; provides advice for making fair and impartial decisions.

Glass, G.V. 1978. Standards and criteria. Journal of Educational Measurement **15**: 237-271.

An excellent treatise of the current procedures used to set standards along with a critique of their shortcomings; suggests that the arbitrariness of standard-setting is predominant, and other alternatives to determining mastery may be more viable.

Guskey, T.R. 1985. Implementing mastery learning. Belmont, Calif.: Wadsworth Publishing Co.

Written specifically for teachers; describes the system of mastery learning and how to implement it in the schools; includes examples of teacher-made lesson plans based on mastery learning; demonstrates and explains formative and summative evaluation.

Linn, R.L. 1982. Two weak spots in the practice of criterion-referenced measurement. Educational Measurement **1**(1):12-13, 25.

Discusses the terminology associated with criterion-referenced measurement; describes several of the problems associated with setting standards.

Nitko, A.J. 1984. Defining "criterion-referenced test." In R.A. Berk, editor. A guide to criterion-referenced test construction. Baltimore: The Johns Hopkins University Press.

Differentiates between norm-referenced and criterion-referenced tests; reviews various definitions of criterion-referenced tests; proposes two categories for classifying criterion-referenced tests; provides guidelines for practitioners.

Safrit, M.J., Baumgartner, T.A., Jackson, A.S., and Stamm, C.L. 1980. Issues in setting motor performance standards. Quest **32**(2):152-162.

Discusses issues in setting standards in physical education; a brief review of procedures for standard-setting; an examination of gender differences in motor performance and the impact of these differences on standard setting.

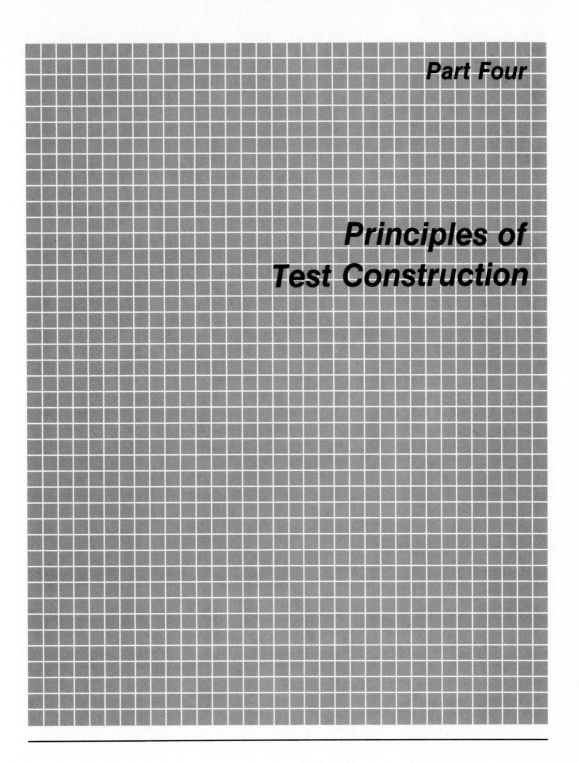

Part Four

**Principles of
Test Construction**

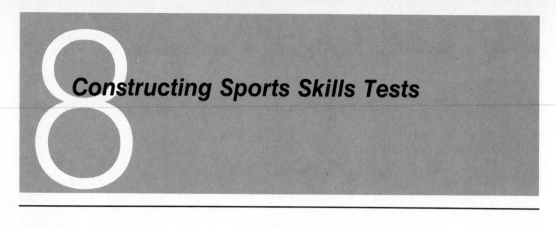

8 Constructing Sports Skills Tests

Whenever you as a teacher need a test in physical education or exercise science, try to find an appropriate one from the many already available. Test development is a time-consuming process that must be handled with carefulness and thoroughness. There is nothing magical about the process, but full-time teachers and exercise specialists often do not have sufficient time for this purpose. If you work in a fitness club, you will already have at your fingertips a number of tests you can administer to your clients. In a school setting you may not always be able to find the type of test you need, partially because of the variety of physical activities taught. Consider the number of sports alone that are included in many physical education curricula. In each of these sports, many skills must be learned and, theoretically, tested; however, administering a great number of tests would not be very practical. Therefore a decision on what to test must be made, taking into consideration the most important skills, and which will receive the greatest emphasis.

The first step is to review the available tests of the skills that will be given the most emphasis. Looking through a variety of textbooks in measurement and evaluation is a cumbersome and time-consuming process. However, two available sources should provide a comprehensive overview of sports skills tests: a book by Collins and Hodges (1978), which is devoted to descriptions of sports skills tests, and a series of manuals, published by AAHPERD, each dealing with skills tests for a specific sport. These test manuals are currently being revised, with greatly improved tests (see Chapter 10).

Developing a clear idea of the most appropriate type of test saves a lot of time when reviewing test literature. A test can be designed to measure a specific skill, a combination of skills, or playing ability. It may be developed as part of a **battery** of tests. For example, assume that a dribbling skill has been emphasized in a basketball class and that Mr. Masters, the teacher, is going to test the students on this skill. He finds a test that measures a combination of dribbling and shooting. This seems to be a legitimate basketball test, since the dribbling-shooting combination of skills occurs all the time in basketball. However, Mr. Masters reasons that a test measuring only dribbling would be more desirable. Using a test of dribbling alleviates any questions about interpreting the test score. It will reflect only dribbling ability. A test measuring both dribbling and shooting might yield a score that could have several interpretations. In another situation, the dribbling-shooting combination test might be most appropriate. The test's appropriateness depends on the reason for using the test.

Perhaps after you have looked through the literature and have been unable to find a good, suitable test, you decide to develop your own test. The remainder of this chapter provides guidance in developing a test.

STEPS IN DEVELOPING A SPORTS SKILLS TEST

Be forewarned that test development is a lengthy process. Developing a good test takes, at best, several months. The following test construction procedures are for a test of a sport skill such as the volleyball serve, baseball throw, or badminton short serve. Seven steps should be followed in developing this type of test:

1. Write the test objective.
2. Review the test literature.
3. Design the test.
4. Standardize test directions.
5. Administer test on a pilot basis.
6. Determine validity and reliability.
7. Develop norms.

Obviously, following this process is not recommended, unless important decisions will be made on the basis of the test score and the test will be used on a regular basis. For simple testing during a class session (similar to a drill) where the test is used only in a practice setting and no major decision is made using the test score, strictly following these steps is not necessary. A quick-and-easy test can be developed for this purpose.

Test objective

The first step in constructing a skill test is to write the objective of the test. This process is not difficult, but it does require careful thought. Which **components of the skill** have been emphasized? The test should be designed to measure these components. Note, for example, the Brumbach Volleyball Serve Test (1967) described in Chapter 10. The test objective is to measure the ability to serve the volleyball low and deep into the opponent's backcourt. Obviously, Brumbach felt that two components of skill in serving the volleyball were important—hitting the ball low (close to the net) and deep (close to the baseline). Do not try to incorporate too many components of the skill in your objective. Remember that the test is supposed to measure each of these components. As the number of components increases, so does the complexity of the test. You may finish with a test that is not practical for a school setting. A compromise is in order. Select only the most important components to be measured.

Review of literature

After writing the test objective, review the test literature for the sport. Presumably you have already done this for the specific skill, since you would not develop a new test if a suitable one were already available. Familiarize yourself with *tests of other skills* used in the same sport, which may provide useful ideas in developing your own test. Review books and pamphlets on the sport written by experts, including successful teachers, coaches, and outstanding players. Their assessment of the important components of the skill you wish to test might be useful in designing the test.

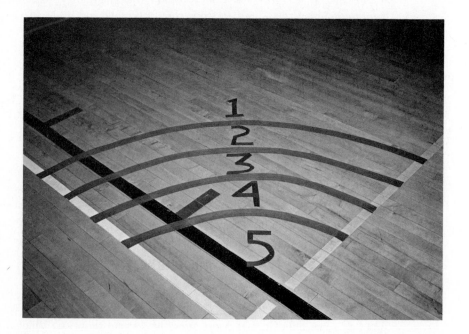

Design of test

Now you are ready to design the test. Each component of skill mentioned in the test objective should be measured in the test. For example, in the Brumbach Volleyball Serve Test a rope is strung above the volleyball net to determine whether the ball is hit low over the net. Then a target is placed on the floor of the court opposite the server, with higher point values closer to the baseline, to assess the depth of the serve. The test was designed so that both components of volleyball serve skill—ball hit low over the net and deep into the backcourt—were measured. Specific dimensions of the test layout should be determined at this time. How high should the rope be placed above the net? What are the dimensions of the target? Determine ways of marking the gymnasium floor that will not damage the floor or the permanent markings, such as special tape or water colors. Set up the test and ask one or two students to try it. Their performance will help you decide if the test is too difficult or too easy. Make the necessary modifications before proceeding to the next step.

Standardization of directions

Before administering the test, even on a trial basis, think through the instructions for administration of the test. These should be written as precisely as possible. Consistency in test administration is essential. Where should the examinee stand? How many practice trials are allowed? How many test trials does the test include? What faults can occur during testing? How are the faults scored? The entire scoring process should be clearly delineated.

Administration of test

Try the test out first in a pilot study. Use your own students, if you wish, or a group that is similar to ones you will be testing in the future. The larger the number of students you can test, the better. If possible, administer the test to the same group of students on 2 different days (especially if your test consists of only one trial). This will allow you to estimate the test-retest reliability of the test. Be sure to follow the test instructions closely.

Validity and reliability

The next step in test development is to establish the validity and reliability of the test. (All of the procedures recommended in this section are described in detail in Chapters 6 and 7. Refer to these chapters for additional information and examples.)

If the test is designed so that it measures each component of skill in the test objective, *logical validity* can be claimed for the test. However, this does not mean that your test objective cannot be questioned by others. Maybe an important component of the skill in the test objective was omitted. What if Brumbach had mentioned only one component of the volleyball serve—that it be hit deep into the opponent's backcourt. All his test would require is a target measuring the landing point of the ball. However, many volleyball teachers might question this objective, noting that a great difference exists between a serve that passes close to the net and one that loops high over the net. Yet both could receive the same score. Your test objective, then, must not only lead to a practical test but also should include the components that others would agree are essential. Since you are developing this test for the objectives of your school system only, you may think this does not matter. However, the basic essentials of a skill ought to be taught, and the objective should be rewritten to ensure that this actually happens. Establishing evidence of logical validity is essential in developing a test, either norm-referenced or criterion-referenced.

Establishing *concurrent validity* as well as logical validity is useful if you are developing a norm-referenced test. (See Chapter 6. Types of statistical validity for a criterion-referenced test are described in Chapter 7.) Remember that to establish concurrent validity, a *criterion test* must be administered to the group in your pilot study. The criterion test might be *subjective* ratings of the ability to use the skill in a game setting. This may sound simple and straightforward, but it requires the development of a rating scale, which is discussed later in this chapter. Once a rating scale has been developed, raters must be trained to use it. You can see why good test development cannot be accomplished in a short period of time! To determine concurrent validity, the test scores are correlated with the ratings of skill. Sometimes a measure of playing ability (e.g., ratings in game setting or tournament rankings) is used as the criterion test for a test of skill. However, measures of playing ability reflect an individual's ability using many skills as well as using game strategies, and your test is designed to measure a single skill. Thus this is not a desirable criterion measure. Not surprisingly, the validity coefficients that result from this method of test development are often low.

Evidence of statistical validity is determined by correlating scores on the test being developed with criterion test scores. The higher the validity coefficient, the greater the validity of the test. The familiar *Pearson product-moment correlation* procedure is used to calculate the validity coefficient. The establishment of concurrent validity, while not always essential, is highly desirable since it provides strong supportive evidence of test validity.

Next, the reliability of the test should be established. If you were able to administer the test twice, a test-retest reliability coefficient can be calculated (see Chapter 6). In brief, two approaches to estimating test-retest reliability were described. One was the interclass reliability coefficient ($r_{xx'}$), which is also calculated using the Pearson product-moment correlation method. The other was the intraclass correlation coefficient ($R_{xx'}$), which is estimated using a statistical technique known as analysis of variance. (An example of the interclass method is presented in Chapter 6.) If you only administered the test once and your test consists of more than one trial, the reliability of the single test administration can be calculated. One such approach is described in Chapter 6 as the split-half method for estimating reliability. Essentially, the test is split into two equal sets of trials, and the averages of these trials are correlated. Then, the reliability coefficient must be "stepped up" using the *Spearman-Brown Prophecy formula.* (An example is provided in Chapter 6; one of the learning experiences at the end of this chapter also focuses on this process.)

Development of norms

If the test is to be used as a norm-referenced measure, developing a table of norms is desirable. (The calculation of both percentiles and T-scores is described in Chapters 4 and 5.) A simple method for developing a table of T-scores is the constant-value method, which is exemplified in Chapter 5. Test scores for several hundred students are needed for each table. That amount of test data may not be available from your pilot testing, but test scores for a year or two can be accumulated, if necessary. Developing separate norms for boys and girls may be necessary, depending on the nature of the particular skill. A federal law mandates that, when appropriate, separate performance standards must be set for boys and for girls. This is discussed in greater detail later in this textbook.

DEVELOPMENT OF A BATTERY OF SKILLS TESTS

Often a battery of skills tests is developed to measure the most important skills in a sport. A good example of this type of test battery is the basketball skills test series (Hopkins, Shick, and Plack, 1984) published by AAHPERD. (See Chapter 10. See also the hypothetical softball test battery described by Mood, 1980, and the battery of defensive softball skills tests by Shick, 1970.) Developing the individual tests in a battery is no different than the method described in the previous section. However, the validity and reliability of the total battery should also be determined. The validity is determined, in part, on logical grounds. A good, strong rationale should be presented for the inclusion of a specific set of skills in the battery. This logical appraisal can be substantiated using a statistical procedure known as factor analysis. Statistical validity can also be determined by comparing the combined tests with a criterion test of playing ability. This is beyond the scope of this book, since a multiple correlation coefficient must be calculated to estimate validity. The reliability of the test battery should also be estimated, but the appropriate procedures are also beyond the scope of this book since they require knowledge of multivariate statistics.

DEVELOPMENT OF RATING SCALES

Ratings scales are frequently used in the physical education field to measure skills that are difficult to measure in the more traditional manner. Since these scales are usually associated with subjective measurement, they must be carefully developed so that the examinee clearly understands the basis of the ratings. For instance, suppose Ms. Miller, a physical education teacher, decides to measure her students' playing ability in badminton. She observes each of them as they play games and uses the following scale to rate them:

5 Excellent
4 Good
3 Average
2 Fair
1 Poor

The problem with this scale is that no one except Ms. Miller knows what she means by *Excellent, Good,* and so forth, and perhaps Ms. Miller does not have a clear distinction between ratings. If John received a *4* and Mary a *5,* in what ways was John's performance inferior to Mary's? In an educational setting test scores should have meaning to students as well as teachers. Granted, expecting a rating scale to incorporate every aspect of the ability being rated is unreasonable, but general descriptors should certainly be written for each category.

Review a rating scale for the badminton short serve, as shown in the boxed material. A rating of *5,* which could still be viewed as *Excellent,* now has specific meaning to the player. A student receiving a rating of *4* knows that his or her ability to place the serve needs more work. Sometimes it is not possible to be this specific in rating more general abilities, since a combination of factors must be considered. However, if a rater is able to judge the examinee's ability by taking these factors into account, it should be possible to write descriptors for each rating used in the scale.

Rating scale for badminton short serve

5 No faults*; serve close to net; serve close to short service line; placement appropriate for opponent's weaknesses or position.
4 No faults*; serve close to short service line; no evidence of placement.
3 No faults*; serve either close to net or close to short service line; no apparent placement.†
2 No faults*; serve neither close to net nor close to short service line; no apparent placement.†
1 One or more faults; serve neither close to net nor close to short service line; no apparent placement.†

*If one or more faults occur, lower the score by 1 point.
†If placement is considered satisfactory, raise the score by 1 point.

Rating scales do not necessarily have to be complex and elaborate. In beginning badminton a teacher may have few expectations of the student in a game setting, especially if the unit of instruction is short. However, the teacher has every right to expect the students to meet these expectations; thus, a rating scale could be devised to measure the aspects of playing ability deemed important. These aspects might include the following abilities: to hit the shuttle away from one's opponent, to use a variety of basic skills in the game, and to maintain good court position during the game. This type of rating scale would be fairly simple to develop and use, and the players would know what is expected of them.

Of course, a rating scale, no matter how well developed, must be used by one or more raters. This introduces an element of subjectivity into the measurement process. However, subjectivity can be reduced by practicing the use of a rating scale before using it in an actual testing setting. If more than one rater is used, the ratings should be compared in a practice setting before actual testing. In Chapter 6 some of the problems associated with the process of rating skills and abilities in diving and gymnastics are discussed, along with procedures for determining the objectivity of raters.

Rating scales constitute an important approach to measurement in the physical education field, especially when the form used in executing a skill is of primary concern. This is probably the most abused testing procedure in physical education because it can be misused so easily. If the scale is too subjective, the rating might be influenced by factors totally unrelated to the examinee's skill. For example, teachers have been known to be influenced in their ratings by students' personalities. Judges at Olympic events may modify their ratings depending on the nationality of the performer. However, rating scales should not be avoided; a properly developed and carefully used scale can be a valuable measurement tool.

OTHER APPROACHES TO MEASURING SKILL

Sometimes tournament rankings are used as an indicator of specific skills or playing ability in a sport. This is a much weaker measure than a well-developed rating scale. Tournament play incorporates not only skills and abilities but also elements of competition and chance factors that may not be of greatest concern in an educational setting. Notice that the suggestions for a rating scale of playing ability in badminton described in the previous section did not take into account who won the game. Of primary interest was the student's ability to employ some basic game strategy, even if this resulted in losing the game. At more advanced levels of skill, a rating scale may incorporate a won-loss component, but this would not be recommended as the sole indicator of playing ability. Tournaments in an educational setting should be educational, not simulations of a competitive circuit. **Game statistics** can also be used to supplement the rating of playing ability. If desired, this can be done at a very simplistic level. With the increasing popularity of microcomputers a student or teacher who is a computer buff could easily computerize a system for recording and summarizing data during a game that would make this type of data gathering much more feasible for the average physical educator. Much more sophisticated systems are being developed for the coach. In addition to gathering game statistics, microcomputer programs are being written to assist coaches in making decisions by calculating the probability of success of a play after a specified sequence of events has occurred.

SUMMARY

Test development is a time-consuming process. Whenever possible, a test should be selected from the existing test literature. If an appropriate test cannot be found, use the seven-step approach to develop the desired test. These steps include identifying the test objective, reviewing the test literature, designing the test, standardizing directions, administering the test on a pilot basis, determining test validity and reliability, and developing norms. This process should also be used in developing rating scales and test batteries. Several excellent sources of tests are available.

LEARNING EXPERIENCES

1. Select your favorite sport. Choose one skill in this sport and review the literature to examine tests of this skill. Write an analysis of *one* of these tests. Is the test objective acceptable? Is the test valid? Reliable? Discuss ways in which the test could be improved.
2. Identify a sport skill for which *no* test is available. Carry out steps *1* through *4* of the process recommended for the development of a skill test. Also, discuss how validity and reliability could be determined. This can be done either as an individual or a group project. If a group project is chosen, *all* members of the group should review the test literature.
3. Draw three targets that could be used to measure the accuracy of a volleyball serve. The first target should be drawn so that a beginner, at the end of a course, could hit it and obtain a high score. Do not oversimplify, however. The second target should be of medium difficulty and the third, very difficult (but not so difficult that even highly skilled volleyball players could not obtain a high score). Include the dimensions of each target in feet and inches. Describe the elements of targets *2* and *3*, and discuss how these elements increase the difficulty level of the targets. Explain when you would use each of these three targets. Describe each situation specifically.

REFERENCES

Collins, D.R., and Hodges, P.B. 1978. A comprehensive guide to sports skills tests and measurement. Springfield, Ill.: Charles C Thomas, Publisher.

Hopkins, D.R., Shick, J., and Plack, J.J. 1984. Basketball for boys and girls: skills test manual. Reston, Va.: American Alliance for Health, Physical Education, Recreation, and Dance. (NOTE: This is a recent revision of one of the AAHPERD skills test series. Test manuals are also available for other sports.)

Mood, D.P. 1980. Numbers in motion. Palo Alto, Calif.: Mayfield Publishing Co.

Shick, J. 1970. Battery of defensive softball skills tests for college women. Research Quarterly **41**(1):82-87.

ANNOTATED READINGS

Bobo, M. 1978. Skill testing—a positive step toward interpreting secondary school physical education. Journal of Physical Education and Recreation 49:45.

Discusses students' need for meaningful feedback from skills testing; stresses the importance of using valid and reliable skills tests to develop a positive attitude among students toward physical education; lists steps that can be taken by a teacher to provide functional, reliable, and enjoyable skills tests; recommends use of individual school norms for these tests.

Brown, E.W. 1982. Visual evaluation techniques for skill analysis. Journal of Physical Education, Recreation and Dance 53(1):21-26, 29.

Describes visual evaluation techniques for observing physical skills; techniques grouped into five categories: vantage point, movement simplification, balance and stability, movement relationships, and range of movement; provides examples of the technique applied to the tennis serve, a wrestling takedown, batting, soccer instep kick, and other skills.

Davis, M.W., and Hopkins, V.L. 1979. Improving evaluation of physical fitness and sport skill performance. Journal of Physical Education and Recreation 50:76-78.

Describes problems of evaluating student performance in physical education; stresses importance of improving performance in a variety of sports skills and physical fitness; recommends using profiles for feedback to students and parents; includes graphical example of a tennis student's profile representing performance on tests of skill in tennis.

Hensley, L.D. 1983. Biomechanical analysis. Journal of Physical Education, Recreation and Dance 54(8):21-23.

Demonstrates how a rating scale can be developed through a biomechanical analysis; uses basic process evaluation techniques to identify the underlying components of a movement; presents an example of a kinesiogram, a biomechanical profile analysis.

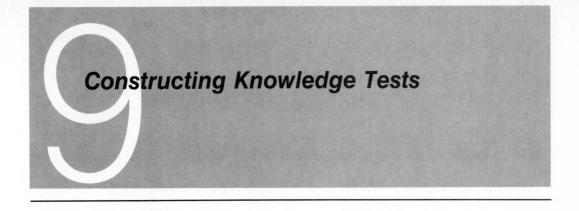

9 Constructing Knowledge Tests

KEY WORDS *Watch for these words as you read the following chapter:*

correction for guessing	item analysis	multiple choice item
essay item	item difficulty	short-answer item
halo effect	item function	table of specifications
index of discrimination	matching item	true-false item

Since the motor performance of an individual is of primary concern to physical educators and exercise scientists, the major portion of this textbook is devoted to the measurement of various forms of sport and physical activity. However, educators also teach people the principles underlying the efficient use of their bodies as well as a knowledge of the relationship of physical activity to health and well-being. Educators teach rules that must be learned to participate in a sport, steps to be followed in carrying out life-saving skills, and game strategies. Students are expected to learn these knowledges. It is hoped that clients in fitness clubs do more than participate in physical activity—that they learn more about the short-term and long-term effects of exercise and the scientific principles on which an exercise prescription is based. In private sport clubs members should be taught principles of conditioning for a specific sport as well as skills and rules. Thus, there is a need to develop and use knowledge tests as well as skills tests. In a school setting teachers usually grade knowledge tests. If knowledge tests are administered in a private club, they are often used in a self-testing capacity. However, in either setting, a knowledge test is a good way to reinforce learning.

In this chapter the development of various types of written test items is described. Items may be generated for norm-referenced or criterion-referenced tests (Roid, 1984). Most likely, you will have taken tests exemplifying all of these types of items, so you will be familiar with them. As you might recall from the discussion of content validity in Chapter 6, developing a knowledge test must be

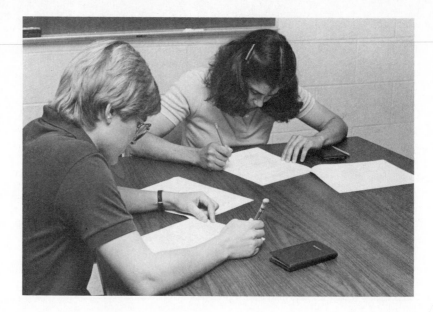

undertaken in as careful a manner as any other type of test. A list of sources of physical education written tests can be found in Mood (1980).

TABLE OF SPECIFICATIONS

The first step in devising any type of knowledge test is to develop a **table of specifications,** in which the basic categories of knowledge are identified and a decision is made on the relative importance of each. Without this plan the efforts of the test writer tend to be haphazard. Deciding how many items should test memorization of facts and application of facts is also a good idea. The table of specifications is then set up as described in Chapter 6. The relative importance of each category is reflected in its weighting, which dictates the number of items to be written for the category. For example, in an exercise class the scientific principles of exercise might be viewed as twice as important as the knowledge of basic exercise prescriptions. If so, twice as many items should be written on principles. In a basketball class rules may be more important or less important than knowledge of game strategies; the number of items should be adjusted accordingly.

Of course, other factors affect the length of the test. For example, an examinee should be able to answer the total number of items in the time available for testing. As a general rule of thumb, allow 45 seconds for each multiple choice item and 30 seconds for each true-false item. However, practical experience with the test provides more definitive feedback on test length.

TEST ADMINISTRATION

The directions for test administration should be clearly stated. The most desirable method of presenting test directions is to print them on the test itself, which enables the test taker to read and reread them. At the beginning of the testing period, these directions should be read aloud by the administrator since it is well known that some examinees do not read directions carefully. The following example of directions might be used for a written test:

Directions: Read the following directions carefully before beginning the test. This is a six-page test consisting of 35 multiple choice items. Be sure your test contains six pages and that all pages are in correct sequence. Circle the response that represents the *best* answer to the question or lead statement. Only one answer is correct for each item. Each item counts 2 points. Write your name at the top of this page and begin the test.

The administrator should also inform the examinee if a correction for guessing will be used. (The concept of correcting for guessing is explained later in this chapter.) The student should be notified if guessing will be penalized.

The test taker's attention should be called to anything else that will help the individual to interpret the test. For example, how much time will be allowed for the test? At periodic intervals the examinee should be informed of the amount of time remaining. Are there multiple pages of the test? If so, the group should be asked to count the number of pages to be sure no page is missing or blank. Are certain sections of the test weighted more heavily than others? If so, note this at the beginning of the test period so the examinee can allocate time wisely. The number of points allocated to each section should also be printed on the test.

Because of the availability of microcomputers, developing tests is easier using a test writer program. A number of these types of programs can now be purchased. Items are entered into the computer and then printed. Modification of test items is then a simple matter. Sometimes a test user might not realize an item is poor until it has been used once; thus, the item must be either revised or discarded. This can be done by changing the particular item on the computer without retyping the whole test. Sometimes an educator does not teach every concept covered in the previous year's unit, so last year's test may be inadequate this year. The items not covered can be eliminated on the computer, and a new version of the test can be printed. Better yet, a bank of items can be entered, and specific items can be requested. A random sample of items can also be drawn from each category of items (with the number of items designated by the teacher) that is different for each student's test. In other words, if the test is being administered to 20 people, 20 different versions of the test could be randomly generated. This facilitates monitoring an examination in a school setting, since copying someone else's answers to a different examination makes no sense.

The administration of a test, then, requires careful consideration before the actual testing period. Educators are primarily interested in how well the test taker can deal with the *content* of the test and not in the trappings of the test.

TYPES OF TEST ITEMS

Five types of knowledge test items are commonly used: true-false, multiple choice, matching, short answer, and essay. Generally, the multiple choice items are the hardest to write, since a number of choices must be prepared for each item. However, they are easy to score. The essay item, on the other hand, is often considered to be easy to write, yet it is difficult to grade because of the subjective nature of the test response. A review of each type follows.

True-false

Since the **true-false item** consists of a single statement, it seems relatively easy to write. It is a familiar type of test item and is widely used. Although there are several variations of the true-false item, none is appreciably different from the standard true-false version. Examples of several of these versions are presented in the boxed material. The *correction* variety, last in the box, requires the test taker to correct the statement, with the correction limited to the underlined word(s).

Samples of true-false items

The true-false variety.
The mean is a measure of central tendency.   *T*   F

The right-wrong variety.
When aiming in field archery, the correct anchor point for the
hand is directly under the chin.   R   *W*

The yes-no variety.
Is "dunking" the ball legal in college basketball?   *Y*   N

The cluster variety.
A badminton serve that lands in the proper court is legal when
the shuttlecock is hit:
T   F   1. by the frame of the racket
T   *F*   2. above the racket hand
T   F   3. below the waist
T   *F*   4. while on one foot

The correction variety.
The skill with which a tennis serve is executed can be measured by determining the *accuracy* of the serve.   *(accuracy and force)*

The true-false item has been criticized in the past for several reasons. First, some teachers have developed true-false tests by merely taking complete sentences out of a textbook, either leaving them as they are or changing one or two words. This, of course, encourages students to study for these types of test by memorizing portions of the textbook, causing some to think that the true-false test has become associated with the lowest level of cognitive behavior. However, well-written test items can tap higher levels of cognitive behavior. (Refer to Chapter 2 for more information on levels of cognitive behavior.) Second, the true-false item is often ambiguous since, with no standard of comparison, it must be judged in isolation. It must be *clearly* true or *clearly* false, rather than subject to multiple interpretations. A carefully written item leaves little or no room for ambiguity. A third objection to the true-false item is that it is less reliable than the multiple choice item. This is true if we compare a 20-item true-false test with a 20-item multiple choice test. However, more true-false items than multiple choice items can be answered during a given time period. By increasing the number of true-false items, the reliability of the total test is improved.

Critics of the true-false item test often note that an examinee could receive a good score merely by guessing the answer. By guessing on every item, there is a 50-50 chance of answering each item correctly. However, it is not likely that many test takers actually guess blindly on all questions. Think of your own test taking behavior. You may not be certain you know the correct answer, but you may have an educated guess. Based on your overall knowledge of the test content, you may make a plausible response although you are not sure it is correct. Thus, the probability of answering correctly is no longer 50-50. Although a correction for guessing can be applied, as you will see later, it may not be desirable.

SUGGESTIONS FOR WRITING TRUE-FALSE ITEMS. As noted earlier, the process of writing a true-false item can seem deceptively simple. In reality, it is one of the more difficult items to write *well*. The following list summarizes a number of suggestions for writing good true-false items:

1. Avoid trivial items. Write items that measure meaningful content and that require application of concepts. Consider, for example, the following item from a volleyball test written for beginning volleyball players at the high school level:

   T   F The dimensions of a volleyball court are 20 feet by 50 feet. (F)

   How important is this content for a beginning volleyball player in a high school physical education class? It is questionable whether a student at this level of skill needs to know this information at all. Of far greater value would be items dealing with skill execution and rules of the game, along with simple game strategies.

2. Avoid using sentences from textbooks or stereotyped phrases as items.

3. Avoid ambiguity.

4. Include an equal number of true and false items, or include more false items than true. (The tendency in constructing true-false tests is to include more true items than false, yet evidence shows that an examinee tends to mark an item true when uncertain of the correct answer. False items discriminate better than true ones.)

5. Reorder the test items randomly after completing all of them. Otherwise, you might generate a pattern of responses that can be detected by the test-wise student.

6. Express only a single idea in each item statement. Examine, as an example, the following item from a badminton test:

   T   F A serve is illegal if the shuttlecock touches the net before landing in the proper court or if the server steps over the service line.

   This item refers to two rules affecting service. The first hypothesis is false and the second is true. How should the test taker respond? This item should be divided into two separate items, so that a clear-cut, correct response is possible for each one.

7. Avoid negative statements. If an occasional item lends itself to the negative form, underline the negative term(s) in the statement. Consider the following example:

   T   F The Kraus-Weber Test is *no longer* viewed as a valid test of the physical fitness of school children. (T)

   In this case the negative form is justifiable because it accurately reflects a change in the way the test has been interpreted over the past 30 years. It was accepted (although erroneously) as a valid test of fitness for children, but now the test is correctly interpreted as a test of minimum strength.

8. Avoid the use of words such as *sometimes, usually,* or *often* in true statements, or *always, never,* or *impossible* in false statements.

9. Make false statements plausible.

10. Make true statements clearly true.

Multiple choice

The **multiple choice item** contains a **stem**—an introductory question or incomplete statement—and a set of **alternatives**—or suggested options, sometimes referred to as *foils*. The correct alternative is referred to as the *answer;* the incorrect alternatives are called *distractors*. Several varieties of the multiple choice item are shown in the boxed material. In the *correct-answer* variety only one alternative is correct. More than one answer is correct, but one answer is better than the other in the *best-answer* variety. In the *multiple-answer* variety more than one answer may be correct.

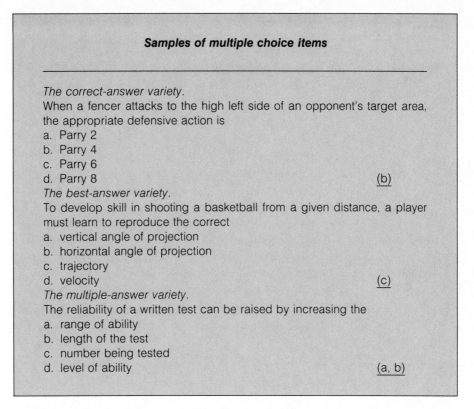

The correct-answer variety.
When a fencer attacks to the high left side of an opponent's target area, the appropriate defensive action is
a. Parry 2
b. Parry 4
c. Parry 6
d. Parry 8   (b)

The best-answer variety.
To develop skill in shooting a basketball from a given distance, a player must learn to reproduce the correct
a. vertical angle of projection
b. horizontal angle of projection
c. trajectory
d. velocity   (c)

The multiple-answer variety.
The reliability of a written test can be raised by increasing the
a. range of ability
b. length of the test
c. number being tested
d. level of ability   (a, b)

THE STEM. The stem is written either as a direct question or as an incomplete sentence. Usually the incomplete sentence consists of fewer words than the direct question and thus is more economical. However, the direct question is often easier to use effectively. When the stem is an incomplete sentence, each alternative must be written to conform satisfactorily to the stem. When the stem is a direct question, the task is simplified somewhat because the alternatives are written only to conform with each other.

The stem should present the problem clearly and briefly. Be aware that if the stem is too long, the test taker may forget what he or she has read by the time the alternatives are reached. On the other hand, do not be so brief that no message is conveyed, as in the following:

Conscious relaxation is . . .

An exact, more meaningful statement follows:

The major characteristic of conscious relaxation is . . .

As is true with true-false statements, stereotyped phrases should be avoided. Generally, the stem should be written in the positive, not the negative, form.

THE ALTERNATIVES. Usually between three and five alternatives are written for a multiple choice question. Using the same number of alternatives with all items is not absolutely necessary. Writing five alternatives might be easy for one test item but difficult for another. Developing fewer, well-written alternatives is better than adding one or two poorly written ones for the sake of generating a predetermined number of alternatives. There is an advantage, however, to preparing five alternatives for each item. As the number of alternatives increases, the reliability of the test increases and the chance level for getting an answer correct is reduced. Regardless of the number of alternatives used, plan to spend considerable time writing good ones.

Some test users find the distractors harder to write than the correct answer. It is only logical that the distractors should seem plausible to the test taker. One way of generating ideas about possible distractors is to administer a set of open-ended questions to a group similar to those who will be tested. There will, of course, be a number of correct answers, but there will also be a variety of incorrect responses. These can be used as a basis for developing good distractors.

The distractors should be parallel in grammatical form and of the same approximate length. Note the length of the alternatives in the following item from an archery knowledge test:

How many arrows are shot in a Columbia Round? (b)
    a. 12   c. 36
    b. 24 at 50, 40, and 30 yards   d. 48

The difference in the length of *b* compared with the other three alternatives suggests that it might be the correct answer, which it is. The general format of all four alternatives should conform. Furthermore, the smallest and largest number of arrows in *a* and *d* do not appear to be as plausible as *b* and *c* are. A better version of this item follows:

How many arrows are shot in a Columbia Round? (b)
    a. 24 at 40, 30, and 20 yards   c. 36 at 40, 30, and 20 yards
    b. 24 at 50, 40, and 30 yards   d. 36 at 50, 40, and 30 yards

As is true with true-false items, words such as *always* and *never* should be avoided. *None of the above* and *All of the above* should be used sparingly as distractors and not used as substitutes for the alternative that is difficult to write.

Be sure that no pattern to the correct responses exists. Sometimes a patterning occurs even though the test writer is unaware of it. An easy way to prevent this occurrence is to order the alternatives randomly. If an item has four alternatives, drop slips of paper numbered *1* through *4* into a container, and draw them out one by one. This represents the random ordering of the alternatives.

Multiple choice items, like any other type of item, can easily be written in an ambiguous way. The only way ambiguity can be reduced is by writing and rewriting the item until there is general agreement on the interpretation of the item and the feasibility of the alternatives.

Matching

A **matching item** consists of two columns of words or phrases, with the column on the right containing the alternatives. The examinee is instructed to select one alternative from the right column to correspond with each item in the left column. Two examples of matching questions are given in the boxed material.

Sample matching items*

Directions: Place the *letter* of the appropriate organization in the space.

___ 1. Organization governing amateur sports in America
___ 2. Organization governing college athletics in America
___ 3. National professional physical education association
___ 4. Governed women's collegiate athletics
___ 5. Rules governing body for golf

(a) AAHPERD
(b) AAU
(c) AIAW
(d) NCAA
(e) USGA
(f) USLTA

Directions: Place the *letter* of the appropriate person in the space provided to the left of each statement.

___ 1. Grandfather of physical education
___ 2. First president of physical education professional organization
___ 3. Thought aim of education was happiness
___ 4. Instrumental in growth of measurement in physical education
___ 5. Developed athletic achievement tests with YMCA
___ 6. Founded interpretive dancing
___ 7. Gave first "modern dance" concert
___ 8. Day's order of exercises in public schools

(a) Aristotle
(b) Catherine Beecher
(c) Isadora Duncan
(d) Martha Graham
(e) Luther Gulick
(f) Guts Muth
(g) Margaret H'Doubler
(h) Edward Hitchcock
(i) Dio Lewis
(j) Dudley Sargent
(k) Jesse F. Williams

---

*From Haskins, M.J.

It is desirable to include a larger number of alternatives in the second column than the number of items in the first column, as depicted in the example in the boxed material above. If the number of alternatives is equal to the number of items, answering the last one or two items merely through the process of elimination may be possible. Between 5 and 15 items per test section are recommended.

Many variations of the matching item exist. A popular version in physical education is the use of a small number of alternatives, each of which can be used more than once. See the boxed material below for two examples of this variation.

Samples of variation of matching question

Volleyball

Directions: Indicate the official's decision in the following situations, using the key letters for your answers. There is only one best answer. Assume that no conditions exist other than those stated.

P—point	L—legal, or play continues
SO—side out	R—re-serve, or serve over

_____1. Server steps on the end line as the ball leaves her hand.

_____2. On the service, the ball touches the top of the net and lands on the boundary line of the receiving team's court.

_____3. A player on the receiving team spikes the ball before it crosses to her side of the net. She does not touch the net.

_____4. A front line player on the serving team, in spiking the ball, returns to the floor across the center line. On the same play, a front line player of the receiving team who attempts to block the ball steps on the center line.

_____5. As a player on the serving team attempts to contact the ball, it touches her upper arm.

Soccer

Directions: Place the appropriate letter in the space provided.

A—Free kick for opposing team	E—Free kick on penalty circle
B—Kick-in for opposing team	F—Penalty kick
C—Roll in	G—No penalty
D—Corner kick	H—Score

_____1. On a kick-in player A dribbles the ball rather than kicking it.

_____2. A team "B" player, taking a kick-in, sends the ball between the goal posts.

_____3. "A" is tackling "B" who has the ball; it goes out of bounds off both players.

_____4. During play the ball is lofted into the air, and the left inner bounces it off his knee through the goal posts.

From Haskins, M.J.

Short-answer

The **short-answer item** is undoubtedly the easiest of all items to construct; however, there are drawbacks. More than one response may be correct. The test taker often has the difficult task of trying to think of the answer the *test developer* has in mind. Several words or phrases may be appropriate. Furthermore, this type of item often measures simple recall. Examples of three versions of short-answer items are shown in the boxed material: the *question* variety, consisting of a direct question; the *completion* variety, written as an incomplete statement; and the *identification* or *association* variety, containing a list of words or phrases that the examinee must identify in the designated way.

Samples of short-answer items

The question variety.
If a bowler gets a strike in the first frame and six pins in the second frame, what is his second frame score?
                         (22)

The completion variety.
The extension of the foil arm in fencing is called the
                         (thrust)

The identification or association variety.
After each name write the sport in which he (or she) achieved fame.

Larry Bird	(Basketball)
Bobby Jones	(Golf)
Knute Rockne	(Football)
Billie Jean King	(Tennis)
Jane Blalock	(Golf)
Vida Blue	(Baseball)

Short-answer items should only be used when the desired answer is clear to experts and when the answer can be given in one or two words. These items are often used in tests of first aid and cardiopulmonary resuscitation (CPR), where the series of steps that should be followed in an emergency setting has been established by experts.

Essay Items

An essay test usually contains a small number of **essay items**, each one requiring the examinee to construct a response at least several sentences long. Often an interpretation of facts is expected; therefore, no one response is correct, and a variety of responses might be acceptable.

One of the major limitations of an essay item is the lack of consistency that may occur in evaluating the answer. Various raters might assess the same response differently, and one rater might judge a response differently on two separate occasions. The lack of objectivity on the part of raters exists for several reasons. First, some raters are more severe than others and will always assign lower ratings. Second, some raters tend to give "middle-of-the-road" ratings, and others use the full range of ratings. If a rater predominantly uses the "middle-of-the-road" range, the best responses are penalized and the poorest ones are unduly rewarded. Third, raters may differ in the relative values they assign to different responses because each rater uses a separate criterion. One rater may emphasize writing form and style; another looks primarily for content.

Other factors also affect the consistency of ratings of essay items. The **halo effect,** where the rater is affected by the examinee's previous performance, can lower objectivity. For example, a good essay written by a usually poor student may receive a lower rating than a paper of the same quality written by a generally good student. One way of controlling this source of error is to ask that the examinee's name be placed only on the first page of the test. Then this page can be folded back out of sight until all examinations have been graded. Extraneous factors such as handwriting, spelling, and organization can contribute to less objective ratings. Carefully describe the degree to which these factors will be taken into account when the test is scored. Otherwise, the examinee may assume only content is being evaluated.

Since including a large number of items on an essay examination is not possible, the reliability of the test may be low. Because of time limitations, sampling a wide range of content on an essay examination is usually not feasible. For this reason, students sometimes feel penalized by the particular set of questions included on an essay test. (Do you recall an occasion where you felt you would have gotten a higher score on a test if the test had included *any* other set of questions?)

CONSTRUCTION OF ESSAY ITEMS. At first glance, the essay test seems much easier to develop than an objective test. It is tempting to put together a few items in the shortest possible amount of time, but this often leads to a vague test that does not tap the desired knowledges. To avoid this, the objectives of the test should be carefully defined, and the items should be formulated based on these objectives. General questions, such as the following, should be avoided.

Discuss the mechanical principles of swimming.

There is no reasonable focus to this question; thus, it might be answered in a broad, surface manner. The question should be delimited, perhaps in the following way:

Discuss the principle of buoyancy as it applies to the breast stroke. Include the following points:

1. Definition of principle of bouyancy
2. Application with regard to coordination of body parts
3. Application with regard to position of body parts

Including from 10 to 15 questions that require relatively short answers is preferable to asking two or three questions needing longer responses. The greater the number of questions, the better the sampling of content will be.

After the items have been written, but before the test is administered, a model answer should be constructed for each item. The model answer can be prepared in outline form, including all major points the student would be expected to make. These responses should be prepared in less than the amount of time the examinees will have to complete the test, since the student will have to compose an answer rather than merely formulate an outline. If problems arise in writing the model answer, perhaps the items need revision.

Sometimes the test taker is allowed to choose a number of items out of the total number available. If the test is tailormade for a specific individual, this is not unreasonable. However, if the test is being administered to a group, allowing a choice might not be as fair as it seems. When examinees select different sets of items, each with different difficulty levels, comparing performances on the test is difficult. This is a problem especially when the tests are to be graded in a school setting.

SCORING ESSAY ITEMS. Ebel (1972) has described six deficiencies that commonly occur in the response to an essay item:

1. Incorrect statements were included in the answer.
2. Important ideas necessary to an adequate answer were omitted.
3. Correct statements having little or no relation to the question were included.
4. Unsound conclusions were reached, either because of mistakes in reasoning or because of misapplication of principles.
5. Bad writing obscured the development and exposition of the student's ideas.
6. A number of errors occurred in spelling and the mechanics of correct writing.

For maximum objectivity in scoring, evaluate one question for all examinees before moving to the next question. As discussed earlier, do not look at the examinee's name until the scoring of all tests is completed. Sometimes the rater's standards will change after scoring the first few items. Occasionally turning back and rechecking the first item on the tests initially scored is wise to be sure consistent standards have been applied. An even better approach is to skim through all answers to an item before scoring it to arrive at a feeling for the range of responses; this can lead to greater consistency in grading from the outset.

WEIGHTING TEST COMPONENTS

Earlier in this chapter the relationship of the number of items to the importance of the content area was discussed. In general, if more items are included on a given topic than any other one, this topic is automatically weighted more heavily. Although this may seem obvious, sometimes test developers neglect to examine the proportion of items per topic on a test.

Other factors also affect the weighting of test components. If a test item is answered correctly by all examinees, then it is essentially weighted 0. The item does not discriminate among examinees. The same effect occurs if *no* examinee can answer an item correctly. The weighting of test components, then, is affected not only by the number of items per component but also by the ability of the items to discriminate.

CORRECTION FOR GUESSING

When an objective knowledge test is used, it is possible to apply a **correction for guessing.** For the true-false test Formula 9-1 is used.

$$S = R - W \qquad\qquad \text{Formula 9-1}$$

where S = corrected *score*
R = number of *right* answers
W = number of *wrong* answers

Clearly, when using this formula, one assumes that wrong answers are a function of guessing. This, of course, may not be true.

For multiple choice tests, Formula 9-2 is used to correct for guessing.

$$S = R - \frac{W}{n - 1} \qquad\qquad \text{Formula 9-2}$$

where *n* = *number* of alternatives per items

Note that Formula 9-1 is a special case of Formula 9-2 when $n = 2$.

When an objective knowledge test is developed so that all examinees should be able to finish in a given time period, a correction for guessing formula is not necessary. This covers the majority of tests used in physical education and exercise science. However, when speed is an important part of the test, a correction formula should be used. Certain types of tests include so many items that the typical examinee is not expected to complete the test in the designated time period. In the physical education field these tests might be used in perceptual-motor learning test batteries and sport psychology test batteries. Here the use of a correction formula is recommended.

ITEM ANALYSIS

An **item analysis** is a procedure for determining the usefulness of each individual item as a part of the total test. It is applied after the test has been administered to a group of examinees. Overall, the results of an item analysis provide information on the effectiveness of the total test. It is a good idea to accumulate test scores for approximately 100 students before undertaking an item analysis. However, an informal analysis can be used with smaller numbers, especially if a rough indicator of how the items are working is needed. Two aspects of an item analysis are described—item difficulty and item discrimination.

Item difficulty

How difficult was a particular item? **Item difficulty** can be determined quite easily by calculating the proportion of examinees answering the item correctly.

$$p = \frac{\#R}{N}$$ Formula 9-3

where p = item *difficulty*
#R = *number* answering correctly
N = total *number* in group

Overall the item should not be too easy or too difficult, because both extremes do not provide very much information on the achievement of the examinees. A general range of .30-.70 is recommended (Ebel, 1972).

Knowing something about the level of difficulty of the item does not relate anything about the people who answered correctly. Did people who answered the item correctly also receive higher scores on the test, and vice versa? This is unknown, based on p alone. The next step is to calculate D, the index of discrimination.

Item discrimination

If an item discriminates well, more high scorers answer the item correctly than low scorers. If the reverse occurs (i.e., more low scorers answer the item correctly), the item is poorly constructed. The statistic used to determine item discrimination is known as the **index of discrimination.** The index of discrimination, D, compares the proportion of high scorers and low scorers who answer an item correctly.

The following steps are used to calculate the index of discrimination:
1. Separate two subgroups of test papers, an upper group (approximately 27% of the total group) who received highest scores on the test and a lower group (same percentage of total group) who received the lowest scores.
2. Count the number of times the correct response to each item was chosen on the papers of the upper group, then do the same for the lower group.
3. Tally these response counts on a copy of the test.
4. Subtract the lower group count of correct responses from the upper group count of correct responses. Divide this difference by the maximum possi-

ble difference, that is, the total number of people in the upper (or lower) group. This is essentially Formula 9-4.

$$D = \frac{R_u - R_l}{N_u}$$

Formula 9-4

where D = index of *discrimination*
R_u = number of correct *responses* in *upper* group
R_l = number of correct *responses* in *lower* group
N_u = total *number* in *upper* group

Although taking 27% of the upper and lower extremes is often recommended to maximize the differences between the extremes, any percentage between 25% and 33% is acceptable (Ebel, 1972). If the total group size is small, the top 9% and bottom 9% may be counted twice.

Theoretically, the index of discrimination can be as high as 1.00. In reality, an index this high is never obtained. If $D \geq 0.40$, the item discriminates well. Refer to Table 9-1 for an evaluation of the size of the index of discrimination.

TABLE 9-1. *Evaluation of the size of the index of discrimination**

Index of discrimination	Item evaluation
0.40 and up	Very good items
0.30-0.39	Reasonably good but possibly subject to improvement
0.20-0.29	Marginal items, usually needing and being subject to improvement
Below 0.19	Poor items, to be rejected or improved by revision

From Ebel, R.L.

OTHER ITEM DISCRIMINATION METHODS. In a classroom setting there is a simpler way of obtaining the numbers of high and low scorers answering an item correctly. The teacher can identify the test score that represents the cutoff score for the high group and the cutoff score identifying the low group. Then, for each item, the teacher asks those in the high group who answered the item correctly to raise their hands. The number is counted and recorded, and the same request is made of the low group. The groups can be labeled *A* and *B* instead of high and low, to avoid possible embarrassment of the low scorers. The middle group could even be asked for a show of hands on each item to allow total class participation, although this information would not actually be used. The number of students in the low group who answered the item correctly should be subtracted from the number in the high group answering correctly and divided by the total number in either group, as shown in Formula 9-4.

A computer can provide much more technical information, however. Many computer programs have been written to conduct an item analysis on a set of test scores. Although the results may be in more technical form, they nonetheless consist of item difficulty, item discrimination, and total test reliability.

Also of interest is the degree to which each alternative functions, referred to as **item function.** This is determined by the percentage of examinees choosing a given alternative. Tally the number of students who responded to each alternative. Each alternative should be plausible enough to be selected by 2% to 3% of the examinees. If not, it should be revised.

SUMMARY

Knowledge tests should be carefully constructed to ensure content validity. Before the test items are written, a table of specifications is prepared to provide the guidelines for test development. Test items are written according to this plan. The usefulness of individual items can be checked by conducting an item analysis. Additional validation techniques, as well as reliability estimation procedures, are described in Chapter 6.

LEARNING EXPERIENCES

1. Write 10 multiple choice items dealing with knowledge about a sport or principles of exercise. Exchange items with one of your classmates, and carefully analyze his or her items. Note ambiguous items that need rewriting. Revise

your items according to his or her suggestions and give them to your instructor to be evaluated.

2. Use the 10-item test you developed in 1. Another revision may be necessary once the instructor has evaluated your items. Administer the test to 30 students on your campus. Group administration is not necessary; the test may be taken by one, two, or more students at a time. However, each student should have *some* knowledge of the sport or exercise principle measured by the test. When 30 students have completed the test, determine the score for each test and conduct an item analysis. Use the 10 top scores for the upper group and the 10 lowest scores for the lower group. Prepare a list of results, as shown below.

Item number	Item difficulty	Item discrimination	Item function
1			
2			
3			
4			
5			
6			
7			
8			
9			
10			

Discuss any items that do not discriminate well. How might they be improved? Keep in mind, however, that a group of 30 people is too small for a definitive item analysis. Therefore, results should be interpreted somewhat tentatively.

REFERENCES

Ebel, R.L. 1972. Essentials of educational measurement. Englewood Cliffs, N.J.: Prentice-Hall, Inc.

Haskins, M.J. 1971. Evaluation in physical education. Dubuque, Iowa: Wm C Brown Group.

Mood, D.P. 1980. Numbers in motion. Palo Alto, Calif.: Mayfield Publishing Co.

Roid, G.H. 1984. Generating the test items. In R.A. Berk, editor. A guide to criterion-referenced test construction. Baltimore: The Johns Hopkins University Press.

ANNOTATED READINGS

Hambleton, R.K. 1984. Using microcomputers to develop tests. Educational Measurement 3(2):10-14.

Discusses the advantages of item banking, a collection of test items uniquely coded for easy retrieval; describes an item banking and test assembly system for microcomputers; points to the need to identify situations where computer testing enhances the quality of testing in appropriate and cost-effective ways.

Hopkins, K.D., and Stanley, J.C. 1981. Educational and psychological measurement and evaluation, ed. 6, Englewood Cliffs, N.J.: Prentice-Hall, Inc.

Describes Blooms's taxonomy of educational objectives for the cognitive domain in simple, straightforward language; provides many practical suggestions for preparing a test, including the readability (reading difficulty) of the test; excellent illustrations of test items.

Millman, J. 1984. Individualizing test construction and administration by computer. In R.A. Berk, editor. A guide to criterion-referenced test construction. Baltimore: The Johns Hopkins University Press.

Addresses computer-assisted testing (CAT); compares various approaches to individualized testing; includes guidelines for practitioners.

Popham, W.J. 1981. Modern educational measurement. Englewood Cliffs, N.J.: Prentice-Hall, Inc.

Includes an excellent section on developing educational tests, chapters on test specifications, construction of test items, improvement of test items, observations and ratings, and creation of affective measures; differentiates between norm-referenced and criterion-referenced test items.

Shick, J. 1981. Written tests in activity classes. Journal of Physical Education, Recreation and Dance 52(4):21-22, 83.

Presents examples of various types of test items, including true-false, multiple choice, multiple response, rearrangement, and multiple choice with constant alternatives; sample items are provided for bowling, golf, archery, badminton, and fencing.

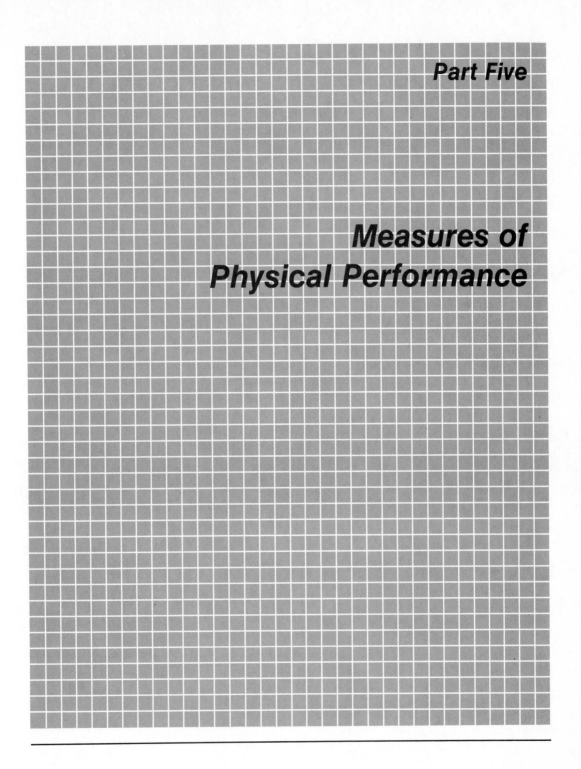

Part Five

Measures of
Physical Performance

10

Tests of Sports Skills

Many examples of sports skills tests can be found in the literature. Collins and Hodges (1978) provide an excellent overview of a variety of these tests. The entire book is devoted to tests of skill in a variety of sports. A sampling of sports skills tests is included here to exemplify the types of tests that have been developed in the field of physical education. Describing all tests in each sport is unrealistic in a measurement and evaluation textbook. (See Chapter 17 for examples of skills tests for elementary school children. For information on other tests, refer to the Collins and Hodges text and the AAHPERD skills test series, which is undergoing revision.)

Although key words have been included at the beginning of all other chapters in this book, they are omitted here since the primary purpose of this material is to provide examples of sports skills tests for 13 sports: archery, badminton, baseball, basketball, field hockey, football, golf, racquetball, soccer, softball, swimming, tennis, and volleyball.

One precaution should be kept in mind when reviewing the test set-ups. Many tests of sports skills require the use of a target on the floor or the wall of the gymnasium. The use of masking tape and fiber tape should be avoided, since they can pull the seal off the floor. Special tape can be purchased that does not damage the floor. Water paints can also be used on some floors.

EXAMPLES OF TESTS
Archery tests

AAHPER ARCHERY TEST (AAHPER, 1967)

Test objective. To measure skill in archery.

Description. No more than four archers should be placed at each target. Two ends of six arrows each are shot at distances of 10, 20, and 30 yards for boys and 10 and 20 yards for girls. The test is started at the 10-yard distance. When all archers have completed two ends, the group moves back to the 20-yard line, and so forth. Any examinee not scoring at least 10 points at one distance is not permitted to shoot at the next distance.

Test area. Archery range adequate to test a group of archers at distances of 10, 20, and 30 yards or a standard-size gymnasium with proper backstops.

Equipment. Standard 48-inch target faces; bows ranging from 15 to 40 pounds in pull; matched arrows 24 to 28 inches in length.

Scoring. Standard target scoring is used, with gold = 9, red = 7, blue = 5, black = 3, and white = 1. Arrows falling outside the white area are scored 0. Arrows bouncing off the target or passing completely through are awarded 7 points. The total test score is the sum of the total points at each distance.

Validity. Face validity (a test that appears to be valid but has not been formally validated).

Reliability. No reliability estimate given in test manual; manual includes statement that no test in the battery has a reliability less than .70, the AAHPER minimum standard.

Comments. Abbreviated tables of norms for this test are included in Tables 10-1 and 10-2. Full-length tables are available in the manual. Four practice arrows are permitted at each distance. Generally, two class periods are required to administer the test to girls, and three periods for the boys.

TABLE 10-1. *Percentile ranks for AAHPER Archery Test; 20 yards—12 arrows; girls**

	Age				
Percentile	12-13	14	15	16	17-18
95	40	47	55	58	71
75	17	28	34	36	42
50	9	18	23	22	26
25	0	8	13	12	16
5	0	0	0	0	0

*Abbreviated form of Table 6 of AAHPER.

TABLE 10-2. *Percentile ranks for AAHPER Archery Test; 20 yards—12 arrows; boys**

	Age				
Percentile	12-13	14	15	16	17-18
95	53	61	77	78	78
75	31	38	58	59	59
50	22	26	39	46	43
25	12	16	24	33	29
5	3	6	9	14	11

*Abbreviated form of Table 2 of AAHPER.

CRITERION-REFERENCED ARCHERY TEST (SHIFFLETT AND SHUMAN, 1982)

Test objective. To measure ability in archery using the criterion-referenced testing approach.

Description. Examinees stand at a target line 20 yards from the target. Two ends (12 arrows) are shot at a 48-inch target face.

Test area. Indoor or outdoor archery range.

Equipment. Bows (variety of weights), arrows (variety of lengths), targets, target faces, tripods, and scorecards.

Scoring. Target scores of 1, 3, and 5 are converted to 0; scores of 7 and 9, to 1. The total test score is the sum of the converted scores for all 12 trials. A student with a test score of 5 or greater is classified as a *master* and with a test score of less than 5, a *nonmaster*.

Validity. The validity coefficient is .73, based on test scores of college men and women using the instructed/uninstructed approach to validation.

Reliability. $P = 0.87$, where P is the proportion of agreement between two administrations of the test; subjects—college women.

Comments. The same test standard is used for both males and females. The test developers suggest that this test could be used to exempt students from a beginning archery class or to grade students in physical education where a pass-fail grading system is used.

Badminton tests

POOLE LONG SERVE TEST (POOLE AND NELSON, 1970)

Test objective. To measure the ability to serve high and deep into the opponent's backcourt.

Description. The examinee stands behind the short service line, anywhere in the service court diagonally opposite the target area. Twelve consecutive trials are taken, in which the examinee attempts to serve the shuttle over the extended racket of an assistant standing in a square 11 feet from the net, as shown in Fig. 10-1.

Test area. Regulation-size badminton court.

Equipment. Badminton racquets, 12 shuttlecocks, floor tape, and scorecards.

Scoring. The scorer stands in the court adjacent to the target area. If the shuttlecock passes over the extended racket of the assistant, a check is recorded for height. The point value of the target area in which the shuttle lands is recorded for accuracy. If the shuttle does not pass over the racket, verified by the assistant calling "low," an X is recorded under "height" and one point is subtracted from the point value of the target area. The total test score is the sum of the best 10 of 12 trials.

FIG. 10-1. *Court markings for the Poole Long Serve Test.*
Redrawn from Johnson, B.L., and Nelson, J.K.

Validity. r_{xy} = 0.51, using the results of tournament play as a criterion measure.

Reliability. $R_{xx'}$ = 0.81, using the test-retest method; subjects—college men and women.

Comments. Although this test is simpler to set up than the Scott-Fox Test (Scott and French, 1959), it is not as objective because an assistant with an extended racket is substituted for a rope. Poole and Nelson believe the use of an assistant is more realistic, but they agree that a rope could also be used to judge the height of the serve. The test developers suggest that the height of the assistant is immaterial, except in extreme cases. The target area is more appropriate, compared with the Scott-Fox target, for examinees of average ability. Note that the target extends beyond the baseline by a few inches. Generally, a shuttle dropping into this area would be returned by the receiver. If this test cannot be used because of its length requirements, the authors recommend shortening it to the best 6 of 8 trials.

FRENCH SHORT SERVE TEST (SCOTT AND OTHERS, 1941)

Test objective. To measure the examinee's ability to serve accurately with a low and short placement.

Description. The examinee stands behind the short service line, anywhere in the right service area, and takes 20 short serves. Each serve that passes between the net and the rope and lands in the target area shown in Fig. 10-2 is scored.

FIG. 10-2. *Court markings for the French Short Serve Test.*
In Scott, M.G., and French, E.

The serve must be executed legally; for example, the examinee may not take a step while performing the serve.

Test area. Regulation-size badminton court.

Equipment. Badminton rackets, 25 shuttlecocks, rope to stretch above net, tape, and scorecards.

Scoring. A scorer stands in the court adjacent to the target area and records a check if the shuttle passes between the rope and net and an X if it does not. The target score (5, 4, 3, 2, or 1) is also recorded if the height was acceptable; otherwise, a 0 is recorded for the target score. If the shuttle lands on a target line, the score value of the higher area is given. If it hits the rope, the trial is retaken. The total test score is the sum of 20 trials.

Validity. $r_{xy} = 0.66$, using a criterion measure of ladder tournament rankings.

Reliability. $R_{xx'} = 0.51$ to 0.89; subjects—college women (physical education majors).

Comments. Two practice trials are permitted. Approximately 20 students can be tested in a 60-minute period at a single testing station. This test is also appropriate for junior high and high school students. A version of the test adopted by the University of Wisconsin uses the same rope height but an easier target. Instead of a fan-shaped target, the Wisconsin version is a series of lines parallel to the short service line, with the highest point value given to the area closest to the service line.

POOLE FOREHAND CLEAR TEST (POOLE AND NELSON, 1970)

Test objective. To measure the ability to hit a forehand clear from the back-court high and deep into the opponent's backcourt.

Description. The examinee stands with one foot in the square marked X as in Fig. 10-3. If the examinee is right-handed, the right foot should be in the square and vice versa. Place the shuttle with the feather end down on the fore-hand side of the racket. The shuttle is tossed into the air by the examinee, who then hits an overhead forehand clear so that the shuttle passes over the extended racket of an assistant standing at point 0 as in Fig. 10-3. The foot in contact with the square should remain so until the shuttle is hit; 12 trials are taken.

FIG. 10-3. *Court markings for the Poole Forehand Clear Test.*
Redrawn from Johnson, B.L., and Nelson, J.K.

Test area. Regulation-size badminton court.

Equipment. Badminton rackets, 12 shuttlecocks, floor tape, and scorecards.

Scoring. Same as Poole Long Serve Test.

Validity. $r_{xy} = 0.70$, using tournament play as a criterion measure.

Reliability. $R_{xx'} = 0.90$, using test-retest method; subjects—college men and women.

Comments. The test developers note that tossing the shuttle in the pre-scribed manner should be practiced on several occasions before actual testing. This test can also be used to measure the backhand clear, although it is not quite as valid and reliable as the forehand clear test. A shortened version of the test, consisting of the best 6 of 8 trials, can be used.

LOCKHART-MCPHERSON BADMINTON TEST (LOCKHART AND MCPHERSON, 1949)

Test objective. To measure badminton playing ability.

Description. The examinee assumes a service stance in back of the starting line on the floor 6½ feet from and parallel to the base of the wall. On the signal *Ready, Go!* the examinee serves the shuttle against the wall. The shuttle is then hit as many times as possible during a 30-second time period, as long as it is hit from behind the restraining line, which is 3 feet from and parallel to the base of the wall and above a 5-foot line on the wall. Three 30-second trials are taken. A 15-second practice session is permitted before testing.

Test area. Smooth wall at least 10 feet by 10 feet and floor space of equal dimensions.

Equipment. Racket, six shuttlecocks, stopwatch, tape measure, floor and wall tape, and scorecards.

Scoring. A point is scored each time the shuttle is hit from behind the restraining line and strikes the wall on or above the 5-foot wall line. If the shuttle falls to the floor during a trial, the examinee must pick it up and restart the wall volley with a legal serve. If, while taking consecutive hits, the examinee steps on or across the restraining line or strikes under the wall line, the trial continues but no points are scored. The total test score is the sum of the legal hits in three 30-second trials.

Validity. $r_{xy} = 0.71$ to 0.90, using criterion measures of judges' ratings and round robin tournament rankings.

Reliability. $R_{xx'} = 0.90$ (test-retest); subjects—college women.

Comments. This test is appropriate for both males and females as young as junior high school age. It is easy to administer, and several testing stations can often be used with ease. However, the volleys are sometimes executed with poor form. In these cases proper form should immediately be stressed.

The Miller Wall Volley Test (Miller, 1951) is another version of this test. The lines are set higher and farther from the wall so that the performer must use an overhead clear to perform well on the test. The restraining line is 10 feet from the wall, and the wall height is 7½ feet from the floor. Although any type of stroke can be used in the Miller test, a definitive advantage exists for the player who is able to hit repeated clears against the wall.

Baseball tests

KELSON BASEBALL CLASSIFICATION PLAN (KELSON, 1953)

Test objective. To classify boys for baseball participation at the elementary school and Little League levels.

Description. This is a simple baseball throw for distance. The testing takes place out-of-doors. The examinee, holding a baseball, either stands behind the restraining line or runs up to the line, as long as the line is not stepped on or over. Three trials are taken, with instructions to throw the ball as far as possible.

Test area. Level field 250 feet long and 50 feet wide; the throwing area is marked off from 50 to 200 feet with lines 5 feet apart.

Equipment. Baseballs, field marking materials, tape measure, and scorecards.

Scoring. The best of the three throws is the test score. Each of the three trial scores is recorded by the scorers. For the most effective scoring, it is recommended that scorers be positioned every 25 feet of the throwing area.

Validity. $r_{xy} = 0.85$, using a criterion measure of a composite of baseball skills including batting averages and judges' ratings of throwing, catching, and fielding.

Reliability. Not reported for this specific test.

Comments. The strength of this test is purported to be its ability to classify boys in baseball quickly and easily. Kelson developed a classification chart that can be obtained from the original source (Kelson, 1953).

Basketball tests

SPEED SHOT SHOOTING (HOPKINS, SHICK, AND PLACK, 1984)*

Test objective. "To measure skill in rapidly shooting from specific positions and, to a certain extent, agility and ball handling" (p. 9).

---

*The next four tests—speed shot, passing, control dribble, and defensive movement—are part of a battery of basketball skills tests published by AAHPERD (Hopkins, Shick, and Plack, 1984). Refer to the test manual for detailed information on this test battery. All four tests can be administered in two class periods.

Description. The player begins the test with one foot behind any one of five markers, as shown in Fig. 10-4. The 15-foot markers are appropriate for grades 10, 11, and 12 and college. For upper elementary grades 5 and 6, the markers are placed 9 feet from the target; for grades 7, 8, and 9, markers are placed 12 feet from the target. On the signal *Ready, Go!* the examinee takes the first of three 60-second trials. The ball is shot, retrieved, dribbled to the next marker, and shot again. At least one shot must be taken from each of the five markers. Although most shots must be taken from the marker, four lay-ups are permitted during the testing period, but no two may be taken in succession.

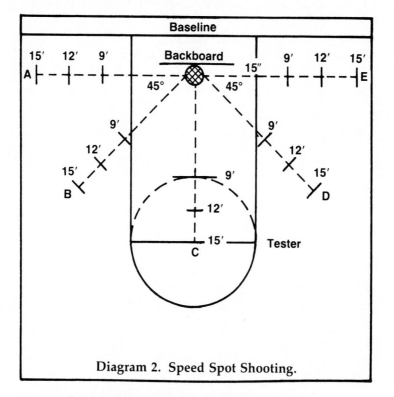

Diagram 2. Speed Spot Shooting.

FIG. 10-4. *Court markings for the Speed Spot Shooting Test.*
From Hopkins, D.R., Shick, J., and Plack, J.J.

Test area. Half of a regulation-size basketball court.

Equipment. Basketballs, stopwatch, floor tape, tape measure, and scorecards.

Scoring. The first trial is a practice trial; the next two are recorded. Two points are awarded for each shot made. One point is given for each unsuccessful shot that hits the rim. The total test score is the sum of scores for the two trials.

Validity. $r_{xy} = 0.37$ to 0.91 for all ages on individual test items, using a criterion measure of two subjective ratings of skill in shooting and game performance; $r_{xy} = 0.65$ to 0.95 for test battery as a whole.

Reliability. $R_{xx'} = 0.87$ to 0.95 for females (test-retest); $R_{xx'} = 0.84$ to 0.95 for males (test-retest).

Comments. Abbreviated tables of norms are shown in Tables 10-3 and 10-4. Full-length tables are provided in the test manual. The scoring is somewhat complicated since the scorer must record the following: whether the examinee took at least one shot from each of the five markers (A, B, C, D, E); the number of lay-ups the student took; and the point value for each legal shot. Refer to the test manual for assistance in setting up a scorecard.

TABLE 10-3. *Percentile norms—Speed Spot Shooting; males**

	Age							
Percentile	10	11	12	13	14	15	16-17	College
95	23	25	27	28	30	27	28	30
75	17	18	19	19	23	20	22	25
50	13	14	15	15	18	16	16	22
25	10	10	11	12	13	11	12	19
5	7	6	7	7	9	6	7	14

*Abbreviated form of Table 6, p. 18, from Hopkins, D.R., Shick, J., and Plack, J.J.

TABLE 10-4. *Percentile norms—Speed Spot Shooting; females**

	Age							
Percentile	10	11	12	13	14	15	16-17	College
95	18	19	22	22	25	23	23	35
75	11	11	13	13	15	15	14	21
50	8	8	10	10	11	11	11	17
25	5	5	7	8	9	8	7	13
5	2	2	3	4	4	4	3	8

*Abbreviated form of Table 5, p. 18, from Hopkins, D.R., Shick, J., and Plack, J.J.

No score is given when ball-handling infractions occur, more than four lay-ups are attempted, or a lay-up is taken immediately following another one. If the examinee does not take a shot from each of the five markers, the trial must be retaken. Each floor marker should be 2 feet long and 1 inch wide.

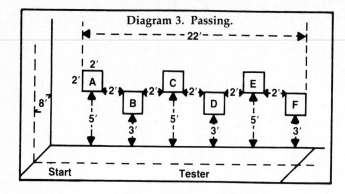

FIG. 10-5. *Wall markings for the Passing Test.*
From Hopkins, D.R., Shick, J., and Plack, J.J.

PASSING TEST*

Test objective. "To measure skill in passing and recovering the ball accurately while moving" (p. 11).

Description. The examinee, holding a basketball, assumes a ready position behind the restraining line opposite the *A* target, as shown in Fig. 10-5. On the signal *Ready, Go!* the ball is passed to the first target (*A*), rebounds, and is recovered while moving in line with the second target (*B*). This sequence continues until the last target (*F*) is reached. The ball is passed twice to target *F*, and the examinee moves back toward target *A*, attempting to hit each target in succession. The trial is terminated at the end of 30 seconds. Three trials are taken, with the first used as a practice trial. Only the chest pass may be used throughout this test.

Test area. Smooth wall surface of 30 feet.

Equipment. Basketballs, stopwatch, floor tape, wall tape or chalk, tape measure, and scorecards.

Scoring. Each pass landing within the target or on a target line scores 2 points. Each pass hitting the wall between targets scores 1 point. The total test score is the sum of scores for the two trials.

Validity. r_{xy} = 0.37 to 0.91, for individual tests and both sexes; r_{xy} = 0.65 to 0.95, for total test battery.

Reliability. $R_{xx'}$ = 0.82 to 0.91, for females (test-retest); $R_{xx'}$ = 0.88 to 0.96, for males (test-retest).

Comments. Each pass must be taken from behind the restraining line. It is recommended that a student assistant be used to call out foot faults. No points are awarded if the examinee's foot is on or over the line, a second pass is taken at the same target (except *A* and *F* when appropriate), or a chest pass is not used. Abbreviated norms tables for males and females are given in Tables 10-5 and 10-6. Refer to the test manual for full-length norms tables.

*The original source for this test is Johnson and Nelson, 1974.

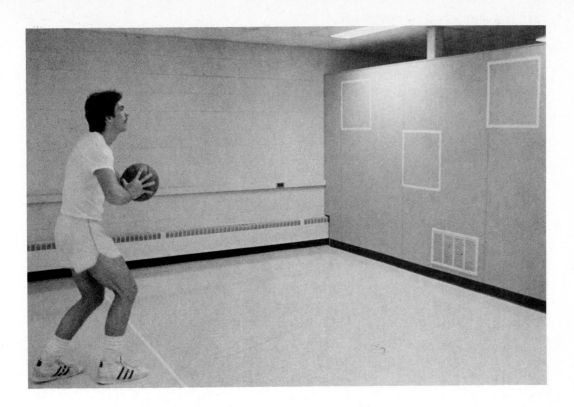

TABLE 10-5. *Percentile norms—passing; females**

Percentile	Age							
	10	11	12	13	14	15	16-17	College
95	36	38	43	44	46	47	48	54
75	30	31	35	37	39	40	39	47
50	25	27	31	32	34	35	34	42
25	21	23	26	29	29	28	24	37
5	7	13	20	23	24	19	18	21

*Abbreviated form of Table 7, p. 19, from Hopkins, D.R., Shick, J., and Plack, J.J.

TABLE 10-6. *Percentile norms—passing; males**

Percentile	Age							
	10	11	12	13	14	15	16-17	College
95	41	43	48	54	55	55	57	70
75	35	36	40	43	45	48	49	58
50	31	32	35	39	40	39	41	53
25	25	28	30	35	35	23	25	47
5	8	18	22	23	23	18	21	35

*Abbreviated form of Table 8, p. 19, from Hopkins, D.R., Shick, J., and Plack, J.J.

CONTROL DRIBBLE TEST

Test objective. "To measure skill in handling the ball while the body is moving" (p. 13).

Description. The player begins the test at cone A in Fig. 10-6. Use the upper diagram for right-handed examinees and the lower one for left-handed individuals. On the signal *Ready, Go!* the ball is dribbled with the nondominant hand to the nondominant side of cone B. Thereafter the preferred hand may be used to dribble, and hands may be changed whenever appropriate. The watch is stopped as the examinee crosses the finish line. One practice and two test trials are administered.

FIG. 10-6. *Court markings for the Control Dribble Test.* From Hopkins, D.R., Shick, J., and Plack, J.J.

Test area. Half of a regulation-size basketball court.

Equipment. Basketballs, six cones, stopwatch, and scorecards.

Scoring. The trial score is the time required to complete the course legally. Record each trial score to the nearest tenth of a second. The total test score is the sum of the times for two trials.

Validity. r_{xy} = 0.37 to 0.91, for individual tests and both sexes; r_{xy} = 0.65 to 0.95, for total test battery.

Reliability. $R_{xx'}$ = 0.93 to 0.97, for females (test-retest); $R_{xx'}$ = 0.88 to 0.95, for males (test-retest).

Comments. The trial must be retaken in the event of ball-handling infractions, failure to remain outside the cone (by either player or ball), and failure to continue the test from the proper spot when control has been lost. For abbreviated norms tables, see Tables 10-7 and 10-8. For the full-length tables, refer to the test manual.

TABLE 10-7. *Percentile norms—Control Dribble; males**

	Age							
Percentile	10	11	12	13	14	15	16-17	College
95	9.2	9.0	8.7	7.8	7.5	7.0	7.0	6.7
75	10.4	10.1	9.5	9.0	8.5	8.1	8.1	7.3
50	11.7	11.1	10.5	9.8	9.3	8.9	9.0	7.8
25	13.7	12.6	11.7	10.7	10.3	10.0	10.0	8.5
5	23.0	16.8	16.0	14.4	13.5	12.0	12.4	10.0

*Abbreviated form of Table 10, p. 20, from Hopkins, D.R., Shick, J., and Plack, J.J.

TABLE 10-8. *Percentile norms—Control Dribble; females**

	Age							
Percentile	10	11	12	13	14.	15	16-17	College
95	10.8	10.3	8.8	8.7	8.4	8.2	8.2	7.6
75	12.3	11.8	10.6	10.0	9.6	9.7	9.8	8.5
50	14.3	13.2	11.9	11.0	10.7	10.7	10.7	9.3
25	16.6	15.0	13.3	12.4	12.0	12.0	12.2	10.4
5	21.7	20.5	19.0	17.8	18.1	15.8	15.0	13.8

*Abbreviated form of Table 9, p. 20, from Hopkins, D.R., Shick, J., and Plack, J.J.

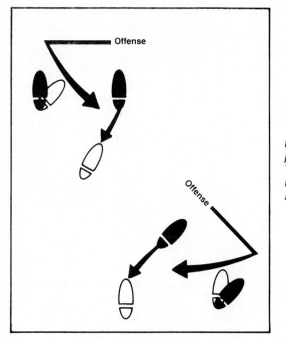

FIG. 10-7. *Court markings and foot positions for the Defensive Movement Test.*
From Hopkins, D.R., Shick, J., and Plack, J.J.

DEFENSIVE MOVEMENT TEST

Test objective. "To measure performance of basic defensive movements" (p. 15).

Description. Three trials are administered—one practice and two test. The test is begun at point *A*, as shown in Fig. 10-7. The examinee faces away from the basket, slides to the left without crossing over the left foot, reaches point *B*, and touches the floor outside the lane with the left hand. The examinee then executes a dropstep (see Fig. 10-7), slides to point *C*, and touches the floor outside the lane with the right hand. This continues until the course is completed back at point *A*. The stopwatch is started on the signal *Ready, Go!* and stopped as the examinee crosses the finish line *(A)* with both feet.

Test area. Half of a regulation-size basketball court.

Equipment. Basketballs, stopwatch, floor tape, tape measure, and scorecards.

Scoring. A trial score is the time required to complete the course, measured to the nearest tenth of a second. The total test score is the sum of two trials.

Validity. r_{xy} = 0.37 to 0.91, for individual tests, males and females; r_{xy} = 0.65 to 0.95, for total test battery, males and females.

Reliability. $R_{xx'}$ = 0.95 to 0.96, for females (test-retest); $R_{xx'}$ = 0.90 to 0.97, for males (test-retest).

Comments. The trial is retaken if the feet cross during the slide or turn, the examinee runs, or the dropstep occurs before the hand touches the floor. Abbreviated tables of norms are presented in Tables 10-9 and 10-10. Refer to the test manual for the full-length norms tables.

TABLE 10-9. *Percentile norms—defensive movement; females**

Percentile	Age							
	10	11	12	13	14	15	16-17	College
95	10.5	10.3	9.5	10.0	9.6	9.7	9.6	8.7
75	11.8	11.8	11.5	11.5	11.0	11.0	11.1	10.3
50	13.2	13.0	12.8	12.5	12.0	12.0	12.0	11.0
25	14.6	14.3	14.1	13.6	13.2	13.4	13.2	12.0
5	19.6	17.4	17.0	16.8	16.4	16.4	16.4	14.5

*Abbreviated form of Table 11, p. 21, from Hopkins, D.R., Shick, J., and Plack, J.J.

TABLE 10-10. *Percentile norms—defensive movement; males**

Percentile	Age							
	10	11	12	13	14	15	16-17	College
95	10.0	9.0	8.9	8.9	8.7	7.9	7.3	8.4
75	11.5	10.9	10.7	10.3	10.1	9.3	9.6	9.4
50	12.7	12.0	11.9	11.4	11.3	10.3	10.3	10.3
25	13.9	13.7	13.0	12.8	12.4	11.3	11.5	11.2
5	18.7	17.2	17.0	16.6	15.8	14.0	15.2	12.9

*Abbreviated form of Table 12, p. 21, from Hopkins, D.R., Shick, J., and Plack, J.J.

Field hockey tests

CHAPMAN BALL CONTROL TEST (Chapman, 1982)

Test objective. To measure "the subject's ability to combine quickness in wrist and hand movements needed to manipulate the stick with ability to control the force element when contacting the ball" (p. 239).

Description. The ball is placed just beyond the outer circle of the target. On the signal *Ready, Go!* the examinee taps the ball in and out of the center circle, with a hockey stick. Three 15-second trials are administered. The two lower examples in Fig. 10-8 depict legal hits. Before actual testing, the tester should demonstrate the procedures and the examinees should be allowed to practice.

Test area. Small indoor testing area; target on floor according to the dimensions shown in upper portion of Fig. 10-8; outer circle of target should be colored so that it contrasts with gymnasium floor (orange is suggested).

Equipment. Hockey sticks, several hockey balls, floor tape, stopwatch, and scorecards.

FIG. 10-8. *Target for the Chapman Ball Control Test.*
From Chapman, N.L.

Scoring. Score 1 point whenever the ball is tapped (not pushed) either into or through the center circle. A point may also be scored when the ball is tapped from the center of the circle to the outside of the target area, if it passes through a different segment from the one it entered (see the lower right side of Fig. 10-8). To score a point, the ball must be tapped from either within the center circle or outside the outer circle. No points are scored when the ball is tapped on the orange area or with the rounded side of the stick. The total test score is the sum of points made on the three 15-second trials.

Validity. Logical validity; construct validity, on the basis of significant differences between varsity and junior varsity team performances on the test; and concurrent validity (r_{xy} = 0.63 and 0.64), using a criterion measure of ratings of stickwork skills.

Reliability. $R_{xx'}$ = 0.89, single test administration.

Comments. The use of three targets is recommended—two practice and one test. While two examinees practice, a third person can be tested. If only one test administrator is available, the test can be timed using an audio tape of *Ready, Go!* and *Stop!* recorded at 15-second intervals.

Football tests

BALL CHANGING ZIGZAG RUN (AAHPER, 1966)

Test objective. To measure speed of execution of zigzag movement as the football is changed from arm to arm.

Description. Place five chairs in a line 10 feet apart. The first chair is 10 feet from the starting line. To begin the test, the player assumes a ready position behind the starting line, with a football under his right arm. On the signal *Go!* he runs to the right of the first chair, shifts the ball to his left arm as he passes to the left of the second chair, and continues in this manner, as shown in Fig.

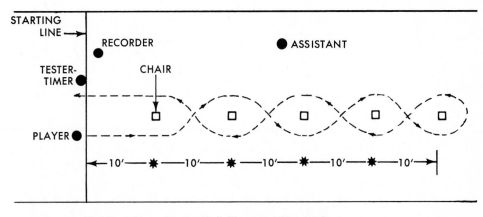

FIG. 10-9. *Field markings for the Ball Changing Zigzag Run.*
From AAHPER.

10-9. The ball must be under the outside arm each time a chair is passed, and the inside arm must be extended (as in a stiff arm in football) toward the chair being passed. Two trials are taken.

Test area. Football field or any grass field.

Equipment. Five chairs, footballs, stopwatch, and measuring tape.

Scoring. Each trial is timed to the nearest tenth of a second, starting with the signal *Go!* and stopping when the player crosses the starting line at the end of the run. The trial with the best time is the test score.

Validity. Not reported for this specific test.

Reliability. Not reported for this specific test.

Norms. An abbreviated table of norms is presented in Table 10-11. The full-length norms table can be found in the test manual.

TABLE 10-11. *Ball Changing Zigzag Run (test scores in seconds and tenths)**

Percentile	Age							
	10	11	12	13	14	15	16	17-18
95th	9.9	7.7	7.8	8.0	8.7	7.7	7.7	8.4
75th	10.7	9.3	8.8	9.0	9.5	8.6	8.7	9.0
50th	11.5	10.3	9.6	9.7	10.0	9.1	9.3	9.6
25th	12.5	11.3	10.5	10.3	10.7	9.9	10.1	10.3
5th	15.8	14.2	12.3	12.1	12.0	11.5	12.2	12.1

*From AAHPER.

Comments. One practice run is allowed before being tested. The prescribed position (ball under outside arm, inside arm extended) must be maintained when running to the side of a chair throughout the test. Touching a chair is illegal.

Golf tests

INDOOR GOLF SKILL TEST FOR JUNIOR HIGH SCHOOL BOYS (SHICK AND BERG, 1983)

Test objective. To measure golf skills, either indoors or outdoors, performed by junior high school boys.

Description. A target is placed on the floor of the testing area, as shown in Fig. 10-10. Colored markers are recommended to identify the scoring areas. A mat is placed at the front edge of the target, where the student stands. A driving mat is placed 1 foot from the target line. The student hits a plastic ball off the driving mat with a 5-iron as far as possible, aiming for an orange cone. Two practice and 20 test trials are taken.

Test area. Small gymnasium or multipurpose room.

Equipment. At least two 5-iron clubs, one right-handed and one left-handed; 25 plastic balls; orange cone; floor tape; tape measure; scorecards; mat for examinee; and driving mat.

Scoring. Each trial score is the landing point of the ball on the target. If a ball lands beyond the target but is in line with the farthermost target areas (see *4, 6, 4* of Fig. 10-10), the ball is assigned the point value of the closest area. In this case, assume the target lines are extended by imaginary lines. A topped ball that passes through the scoring area is given 1 point. A missed ball is given a score of 0. A ball landing on a target line is given the score of the highest adjacent target area. The total test score is the sum of the trial scores.

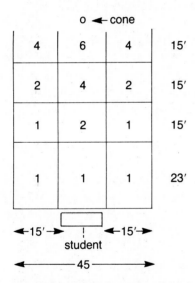

FIG. 10-10. *Target for Indoor Golf Skill Test for Junior High School Boys.*
From Shick, J., and Berg, N.G.

Validity. $r_{xy} = -0.84$, using a criterion measure of the best of three scores on a par-3, nine-hole golf course.

Reliability. $R_{xx'} = 0.97$, for single test administration; $R_{xx'} = 0.91$, for test-retest administration.

Comments. This is a modification of a test developed for older examinees (Cotten, Thomas, and Plaster, 1972). With two testing stations, 20 students can be tested in one 45-minute class period. Since test validity ($r_{xy} = -0.80$) and reliability ($R_{xx'} = 0.90$) were also acceptable for 10 trials administered on one day, using a shortened (10-trial) version of the test would be appropriate.

Racquetball tests
RACQUETBALL SKILLS TEST (HENSLEY, EAST, AND STILLWELL, 1979)

Test objective. To measure two fundamental components of racquetball— speed and power; although accuracy is not emphasized, a gross accuracy component is measured.

Description. Two measures are administered—a short wall volley test and a long wall volley test. In the short wall volley test, the examinee, holding two racquetballs, stands behind the short line, drops a ball, and volleys it against the front wall for 30 seconds. All strokes must occur from behind the short line. The ball may be hit in the air or after taking one or more bounces. If the ball does not return to the short line or if the examinee misses it, the ball may be retrieved or a new ball may be obtained from the scorer. The test consists of two 30-second trials, preceded by a 30-second practice period.

The testing procedures for the long wall volley test are essentially the same except that the ball is volleyed from behind a restraining line located 12 feet behind and parallel to the short line. In both tests any stroke may be used to keep the ball in play.

Test area. Regulation-size racquetball court.

Equipment. Racquets, four new racquetballs, colored floor tape, stopwatch, scorecards, and tape measure.

Scoring. The stopwatch should be started when the examinee releases the ball on the initial drop. The score in each test is the number of legal hits for two 30-second periods. In scoring the short wall volley test, it is recommended that the scorer stand inside the court; for the long wall volley test, standing outside the court, if possible, is recommended. No points are scored when the student steps on or over the restraining line or when the ball hits the floor or a side wall before reaching the front wall.

Validity. Content validity; concurrent validity: $r_{xy} = 0.79$ for the short test, and $r_{xy} = 0.86$ for the long test, using a criterion measure of instructor ratings of ability to sustain a rally.

Reliability. The following are test-retest coefficients:
$R_{xx'} = 0.82$ for the long test, college women;
$R_{xx'} = 0.85$ for the long test, college men;
$R_{xx'} = 0.86$ for the short test, college women; and
$R_{xx'} = 0.76$ for the short test, college men.

Comments. Refer to the original source for norms for college men and women. This test is easy to administer and requires about 3 minutes of testing time per student. Two extra balls should be available at all times during both tests. If the scorer is able to stand outside the court to score the long wall volley test, place the two extra balls in the crease at the back corner of the court.

Soccer tests

MCDONALD VOLLEYING SOCCER TEST (MCDONALD, 1951)

Test objective. To measure general soccer ability.

Description. The soccer ball is kicked against the wall as many times as possible in 30 seconds. Any type of kick may be used. Both ground balls and fly balls hitting the target count, if the ball is kicked from the ground behind the restraining line. Any part of the body, including the hands, may be used for retrieving a ball. If the player loses control of the ball, a spare ball may be used. This ball must be positioned behind the restraining line before being kicked. Four trials are taken.

Test area. Wall 30 feet wide and 11½ feet high, with a restraining line 9 feet from the wall and parallel to it.

Equipment. Three soccer balls (the two spares are placed 9 feet behind the restraining line in the center of the area), stopwatch, and tape measure.

Scoring. The score is the number of legal kicks in a 30-second period.

Validity. The test scores were correlated with coaches' ratings of playing ability.

r_{xy} = 0.94 varsity players;

r_{xy} = 0.63 junior varsity players;

r_{xy} = 0.76 freshman varsity players; and

r_{xy} = 0.85 combined group.

Reliability. Not reported for this specific test.

Comments. This test can be used with younger age groups by reducing the size of the target and moving the restraining line closer to the wall.

Softball tests

SHICK SOFTBALL TEST BATTERY (SHICK, 1970)

Test objective. To measure defensive softball skills in college women.

Description. Three tests are included in the test battery—repeated throws, fielding test, and target test. They can be used as a battery or as individual tests.

REPEATED THROWS. The examinee stands behind a restraining line placed on the floor 23 feet from the wall. On the signal *Ready, Go!* the examinee throws a softball at the wall and attempts to hit the wall above the 10 foot line, which is on the wall parallel to the floor. Either an overarm or a sidearm throw may be used. The rebounding ball may either be caught in the air or fielded from the floor. This is repeated as many times as possible in 30 seconds. Four trials are allowed. No penalty is given for a fumbled rebound, since this results in a loss of time. One practice throw is permitted before each trial.

The total test score is the sum of the number of times that the ball hit the wall in four trials. If the examinee steps on or over the restraining line or if the ball is thrown below the wall line, no hit is recorded. The validity of this test is $r_{xy} = 0.69$, using a criterion measure of judges' ratings of individual performance in game situations. Test reliability is $R_{xx'} = 0.86$.

FIELDING TEST. This test is similar to the repeated throws measure except that the primary objective is to field the ball on a bounce or from the floor rather than catching it in the air. The wall line is 4 feet from the floor, and the restraining line is 15 feet from the wall. Otherwise, the test is the same as the repeated throws measure in all respects but two: any type throw may be used, and the ball should be thrown so that it hits the wall below the wall line.

The total test score is the sum of the number of times the ball is legally thrown and hits the wall below the line in four trials. Test validity is 0.48, using the same criterion measure. Test reliability is 0.89.

TARGET TEST. Wall and floor targets must be set up as shown in Fig. 10-11. The wall target is 66 inches square with the center of the target 36 inches from the floor. The restraining line is 40 feet from the wall. It is recommended that the target areas be color-coded. The test consists of two trials of 10 throws each. The examinee stands behind the restraining line with a softball in hand. Two

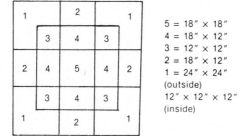

5 = 18″ × 18″
4 = 18″ × 12″
3 = 12″ × 12″
2 = 18″ × 12″
1 = 24″ × 24″
(outside)
12″ × 12″ × 12″
(inside)

Wall

FIG. 10-11. *Wall and floor targets for the Target Test. From Shick, J.*

practice throws are permitted. Two scores are given for each test throw: the point value of the wall target area in which the ball is hit and the section of the floor target where the ball lands on its first bounce. No points are given for hits outside the two target areas. The scores are then summed across target areas and trials. Test validity is 0.63, using the same criterion measure. Test reliability is 0.88.

Test area. Regulation-size gymnasium.

Equipment. Softballs, stopwatches, floor tape, tape measure, scorecards, and softball gloves.

Comments. For the total test battery, test validity is 0.75 and test reliability is 0.88. The entire battery can be administered in two 40-minute class periods.

Swimming tests

12-MINUTE SWIM TEST (JACKSON, JACKSON, AND FRANKIEWICZ, 1979)

Test objective. To provide a practical field test of swimming endurance using the crawl stroke.

Description. Each examinee is assigned to swim in an individual lane. The poolside should be marked in 5-yard distances. The swimmer is instructed to start in the water with a pushoff from the side and to swim the crawl stroke for 12 minutes, attempting to cover as much distance as possible. At the signal *Ready, Go!* the stopwatch is started and the swimmers push off. A partner assigned to each swimmer counts the number of laps. On the signal *Stop!* the partner records the yardage closest to the swimmer's hand and the number of full laps the swimmer completes. The swimmer should continue swimming at a leisurely pace for another 2 to 3 minutes to unwind from the all-out effort.

Test area. Pool of 25 yards or longer, with lane dividers.

Equipment. Stopwatch or other suitable timing device in pool and scorecards.

Validity. $r_{xy} = 0.898$, using criterion measure of tethered swim, where the heart rate reached at least 172 beats per minute (concurrent validity); significant difference in test scores of competitive swimmers and noncompetitors (construct validity).

Reliability. $R_{xx'}$ (alpha coefficient) $= 0.99$ for single administration of the test; subjects—college males; $R_{xx'} = 0.98$ for test-retest; subjects—college men and women (Fried, 1983).

Comments. Before taking the test, swimmers should take a 5- to 10-minute warm-up in the water. It is assumed that the swimmers have had previous instruction and practice in pacing and stroke efficiency. If the swimmers are below average in swimming skills, it might be desirable to remove the effect of swimming skill using the residual score method described in Jackson, Jackson, and Frankiewicz (1979).

Tennis tests

HEWITT TENNIS ACHIEVEMENT TEST (HEWITT, 1966)

Test objective. To measure three basic tennis skills—forehand drive, backhand drive, and service; the service placement test, speed of service test, and forehand/backhand drive tests are used.

Test area. Regulation-size tennis court.

Equipment. Tennis rackets, 25 tennis balls, and scorecards.

SERVICE PLACEMENT TEST. A 10-minute warm-up is permitted. The examinee stands behind the baseline and serves 10 balls into the marked service court, as shown in Fig. 10-12. The ball should pass between the net and the 7-foot-high rope. If this occurs, the trial score is the point value of the target area in which the ball lands. A ball traveling over the rope is scored 0.

FIG. 10-12. *Court markings for the Service Placement Test.*
From Hewitt, J.E.

The test score is the sum of 10 trials. The validity of test ranges from 0.625 to 0.93, using a criterion measure of round robin tournament rankings. Test-retest reliability is 0.94.

SPEED OF SERVICE TEST. The court is divided into zones, (see Fig. 10-13). The examinee serves the ball into the designated court, and the score is based on the zone in which the second bounce lands. The underlying assumption is that the distance the ball travels between the first and second bounce is a valid indicator of the speed of service. The zone number is the score for the trial.

The total test score is the sum of 10 trials. Test validity ranges from 0.723 to 0.89, using a criterion measure of round robin tournament rankings. Test-retest reliability is 0.84. This test can be given at the same time as the service placement test. Place both targets on the same side of the court; the placement score is the target value on the service court, and the speed score is the zone value.

FIG. 10-13. *Court markings for Speed of Service Test.*
From Hewitt, J.E.

FIG. 10-14. *Court markings for the Forehand and Backhand Drive Test.*
From Hewitt, J.E.

FOREHAND AND BACKHAND DRIVE TESTS. The examinee stands at the center of the baseline, as shown in Fig. 10-14. Five practice trials are allowed. The ball is hit to the examinee by the instructor or propelled by a ball machine and lands just beyond the service line. Using either a forehand or backhand drive, the examinee returns the ball. Then 20 test trials are administered in the same way.

Although 10 test trials are given for each drive, the examinee is allowed to choose which 10 balls to hit forehand and backhand.

The ball should travel between the rope and the net to maximize the target score. If the ball passes over the rope, half the value of the regular target is awarded. The validity estimates range from 0.57 to 0.67 for the forehand trials and 0.52 to 0.62 for the backhand trials, using a criterion measure of round robin tournament rankings. The test-retest reliability is 0.75 for the forehand drive and 0.78 for the backhand.

Comments. A ball machine should be used whenever possible to test the drive. No information is given on recommended settings for the machine. A composite score for the three test items is not recommended. Each test item is scored separately.

HEWITT REVISION OF THE DYER BACKBOARD TEST
(HEWITT, 1965)

Test objective. To classify students by measuring rallying and serving ability.

Description. With two new tennis balls in hand, the examinee serves the ball against the wall from a restraining line 20 feet from the wall. The stopwatch is started when the ball hits the wall. On the rebound the player begins a rally by hitting the ball continuously against the wall so that the ball hits on or above a wall line placed 3 feet above the testing surface. Three trials of 30 seconds each are taken.

Test area. Smooth gymnasium wall or indoor/outdoor backboard of 20 feet high and 20 feet wide and a 20 foot by 20 foot floor space.

Equipment. Tennis racket, two dozen balls, stopwatch (records to the nearest tenth of a second), tape measure, floor and wall tape, and scorecards.

Scoring. One point is scored each time the ball hits on or above the wall line. If the examinee steps on or over the restraining line, the rally is continued but no point is scored and the player should be warned. The total score is the sum of three trials.

Validity. $r_{xy} = 0.68$ to 0.73, for beginners;
$\qquad r_{xy} = 0.84$ to 0.89, for intermediates.

Reliability. $R_{xx'} = 0.82$, for beginners (test-retest);
$\qquad R_{xx'} = 0.93$, for intermediates (test-retest).

Comments. All lines should be 1 inch wide. Approximately 15 students can be tested at each station in 40 minutes. If the ball does not return to the examinee, another one can be taken from the basket and served against the wall to initiate the rally again. No points are scored on the serve. The count should begin again with the first wall hit after the serve.

TENNIS FOREHAND/BACKHAND DRIVE TEST (PURCELL, 1981)

Test objective. To measure the forehand and backhand drives in a setting that closely resembles the actual game situation; to evaluate depth, direction and speed of the drive by rewarding shots directed deep to the center of the court with sufficient speed.

Description. The test examinee stands within 3 to 6 feet of the baseline of the court, facing the target area, as shown in Fig. 10-15. A pneumatic ball-pitching machine is used to project the tennis ball to the examinee, who attempts to return the ball over the net and into the target area. Three practice and 10 test trials are administered for each drive, forehand and backhand. The ball flight is timed from the point of contact to the landing point.

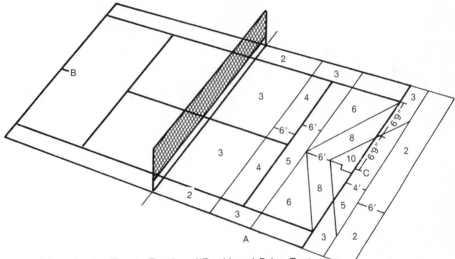

FIG. 10-15. *Court markings for the Tennis Forehand/Backhand Drive Test.*
From Purcell, K.

The speed and angle of the ball machine are set so that the ball will pass approximately 2½ feet above the center of the net, land on or close to the service line, and bounce to its highest point about 3 feet from the baseline. With these settings the maximum height of the bounce should be roughly 3 feet; the horizontal velocity should be approximately 59 feet per second. The time of flight of the machine-projected ball should be approximately 1.02 seconds.

Test area. Regulation-size tennis court, with target areas marked on the court using ordinary chalk.

Equipment. Ball machine, 40 balls, tennis racket, stopwatch, scorecards, and tape measure.

Scoring. The target values for each set of 10 trials are summed, as well as the times for 10 trials. To determine the correction factor for the total time score, see Table 10-12. The total target score is multiplied by the correction factor to yield the test score. This is done for both the forehand and backhand drives. When a ball is clearly deflected by the net, the trial should be retaken. A typical "let" ball is scored in the regular manner.

TABLE 10-12. *Correction factors for converting target value totals into skill test scores using time in flight (TF)**

TF for 10 trials	Correction factor
5 sec.	1.35
6	1.30
7	1.25
8	1.20
9	1.15
10	1.10
11	1.05
12	1.00
13	.95
14	.90
15	.85
16	.80
17	.75
18	.70

*From Purcell, K.

Validity. $r_{xy} = 0.83$, using a criterion measure of judges' ratings of the forehand and backhand stroke;

$r_{xy} = 0.70$, for forehand trials alone; and

$r_{xy} = 0.83$, for backhand trials alone.

Reliability. The following test-retest reliability coefficients were calculated for college women:

$R_{xx'} = 0.84$ total test;

$R_{xx'} = 0.86$ forehand trials alone; and

$R_{xx'} = 0.83$ backhand trials alone. For the criterion measure, the interjudge objectivity was $R_{j_1 j_2} = 0.87$.

Comments. Total testing time per examinee, including practice trials, is about 3½ minutes. Little time is lost between tests if the next examinee is ready to step up to the line as soon as the previous examinee has completed testing. For the group tested in the original study, the following descriptive statistics were reported for college women:

	Mean	Standard deviation
Forehand	30.3	9.4
Backhand	23.6	9.5
TOTAL	53.9	17.7

Once the target lines have been marked on the court, the test should be relatively easy to administer, assuming that a ball machine is available.

Volleyball tests

BRADY VOLLEYBALL TEST (BRADY, 1945)

Test objective. To measure general volleyball playing ability.

Description. No restraining line is used. The examinee begins the test by throwing the ball against the wall and attempting to hit the ball into the target area on the wall repeatedly (see Fig. 10-16). One 60-second trial is administered. Only legal hits are allowed. If the examinee catches the ball or loses control of the ball, the test must be restarted by throwing the ball against the wall.

FIG. 10-16. *Wall target for the Brady Volleyball Test. From Brady, G.F.*

Test area. Smooth wall space, 15 feet by 15 feet.

Equipment. Volleyballs, stopwatch, wall tape or chalk, tape measure, and scorecards.

Scoring. The test score is the number of legal hits in 1 minute. Thrown balls are not scored, but balls landing on the target line are scored.

Validity. $r_{xy} = 0.86$, using a criterion measure of subjective ratings of playing ability.

Reliability. $r_{xx'} = 0.93$ (test-retest).

Comments. Allow practice time before taking the test. Several students may be tested at the same time. Approximately 2 minutes per person is required to administer the test. This test is especially useful for making quick classifications of students in a class setting. The height of the target might be lowered for younger age groups, especially junior high or grade school students.

BRUMBACH VOLLEYBALL SERVICE TEST (BRUMBACH, 1967)

Test objective. To measure the ability to serve the volleyball low and deep into the opponent's court.

Description. The examinee stands behind the baseline and serves the ball, attempting to hit it between the net and the rope and deep into the backcourt on the opposite side (see Fig. 10-17). The test consists of 12 trials, in two sets of six.

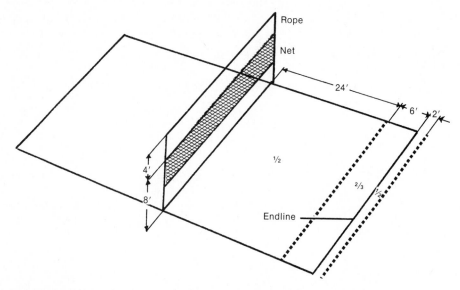

FIG. 10-17. *Court markings for the Brumbach Volleyball Service Test.*
From Brumbach, W.B.

Test area. Regulation-size volleyball court.

Equipment. Volleyballs, standard extensions, rope, floor tape or chalk, tape measure, and scorecards.

Scoring. A ball hit between the net and the rope and landing in the target area receives the higher of the two scores assigned to the target area. A ball passing over the rope and landing in the target area is given the lower of the two scores. The total test score is the sum of the 10 best trials. Foot faults, balls hitting the net, and balls landing outside the target area are scored 0.

Validity. Not reported for this specific test.

Reliability. Not reported for this specific test.

Comments. In one court 20 students can be tested in less than an hour. Only legal serves should be scored. Although this test may be viewed as logically valid, the validity and reliability should be systematically studied. It appears to be appropriate for junior high, high school, and college students.

SUMMARY

This chapter was designed to present a broad overview of the skills tests available in the physical education field. Other than the references already mentioned, the *Research Quarterly for Exercise and Sport* usually publishes the best of the recently developed tests.

LEARNING EXPERIENCES

1. This exercise will be most valuable for students who plan to teach physical education but will also be useful for those who may work in a private sports club. Select one of the tests described in this chapter and administer it to the other students in class. Prepare carefully and well ahead of time for the testing. Plan how you will organize the group during the test administration. Take care of any court markings or targets before the actual testing session. Develop a score sheet or scorecard for each examinee. Sometime after the testing has been completed, discuss the results with the examinees, telling them their scores and the summary data for the class.

2. Select one of the tests in this chapter in which a floor target is used. Determine two ways this target could be safely marked on a gymnasium floor. Experiment with both methods. Write a brief report of the two approaches, comparing them in terms of efficiency, cost, practicality, and so forth. Discuss your preference and give a rationale for your choice.

REFERENCES

American Association for Health, Physical Education and Recreation. 1967. Archery for boys and girls: skills test manual. Washington, D.C.: AAHPER.

American Association for Health, Physical Education and Recreation. 1966. Football: skills test manual. Washington, D.C.: AAHPER.

Brady, G.F. 1945. Preliminary investigations of volleyball playing ability. Research Quarterly **16**:14-17.

Brumbach, W. 1967. Beginning volleyball, a syllabus for teachers, revised edition. Eugene, Ore.: Wayne Baker Brumbach (Distributed by the University of Oregon).

Chapman, N.L. 1982. Chapman Ball Control Test—field hockey. Research Quarterly for Exercise and Sport **53**(3):239-242.

Collins, D.R., and Hodges, P.B. 1978. A comprehensive guide to sports skills tests and measurement. Springfield, Ill.: Charles C Thomas, Publisher.

Cotten, D., Thomas, J.R., and Plaster, T. A plastic ball test for golf iron skill, Unpublished study presented at the American Alliance for Health, Physical Education, Recreation and Dance National Convention, Houston, March 1972.

Fried, C.R. 1983. An examination of the test characteristics of the 12-Minute Swim Test, Unpublished Master's thesis. University of Wisconsin, Madison.

Hensley, L.D., East, W.B., and Stillwell, J.L. 1979. A racquetball skills test. Research Quarterly for Exercise and Sport **50**(1):114-118.

Hewitt, J.E. 1966. Hewitt's tennis achievement test. Research Quarterly **37**:231-237.

Hewitt, J.E. 1965. Revision of the Dyer Backboard Tennis Test. Research Quarterly **37**:231-240.

Hopkins, D.R., Shick, J., and Plack, J.J. 1984. Basketball for boys and girls: skills test manual. Reston, Va.: American Alliance for Health, Physical Education, Recreation and Dance.

Jackson, A., Jackson, A.S., and Frankiewicz, R.G. 1979. The construct and concurrent validity of a 12-minute crawl stroke swim as a field test of swimming endurance. Research Quarterly for Exercise and Sport **50**(4):641-648.

Johnson, B.L. and Nelson, J.K. 1979. Practical measurements for evaluation in physical education. Minneapolis: Burgess Publishing Co.

Kelson, R.E. 1953. Baseball classification plan for boys. Research Quarterly **24**:304-307.

Lockhart, A., and McPherson, F.A. 1949. The development of a test of badminton playing ability. Research Quarterly **20**:402-405.

McDonald, L.G. 1951. The construction of a kicking skill test as an index of general soccer ability, Unpublished Master's Thesis. Springfield College, Mass.

Miller F.A. 1951. A badminton wall volley test. Research Quarterly **22**:208-213.

Poole, J., and Nelson, J.K. 1970. Construction of a badminton skills test battery, Unpublished study. Louisiana State University, Baton Rouge.

Purcell, K. 1981. A tennis forehand-backhand drive skill test which measures ball control and stroke firmness. Research Quarterly for Exercise and Sport **52**(2):238-245.

Scott, M.G., and French, E. 1959. Measurement and evaluation in physical education. Dubuque, Iowa: Wm C Brown Group.

Scott, M.G., and others. 1941. Achievement examinations in badminton. Research Quarterly **12**:242-253.

Shick, J. 1970. Battery of defensive softball skills tests for college women. Research Quarterly **41**:82-87.

Shick, J., and Berg, N.G. 1983. Indoor golf skill test for junior high school boys. Research Quarterly for Exercise and Sport **54**(1):75-78.

Shifflett, B., and Schuman, B.J. 1982. A criterion-referenced test for archery. Research Quarterly for Exercise and Sport **53**(4):330-335.

ANNOTATED READINGS

American Association for Health, Physical Education, and Recreation. 1966-67. Skills test series. Washington, D.C.: AAHPER.

Separate manual of skills tests for a variety of sports, including archery, basketball, football, softball, and volleyball; revision now available for basketball skills tests, and underway for tennis and volleyball tests; although many tests are outdated, can be modified by the teacher to provide valuable learning experiences.

Avery, C.A., Richardson, P.A., and Jackson, A.W. 1979. A practical tennis serve test: measurement of a skill under simulated game conditions. Research Quarterly for Exercise and Sport **50**(4):554-564.

Good example of more complex type of test that can be used in a class setting; describes a tennis serve test with a high degree of logical as well as statistical validity; excellent test for intermediate and advanced players.

Collins, D.R., and Hodges, P.B. 1978. A comprehensive guide to sports skills tests and measurement. Springfield, Ill.: Charles C Thomas, Publisher.

A valuable reference for every physical education teacher; presents a wide variety of published and unpublished tests of sports skills; provides thorough descriptions of tests; includes more tests than can be found in any measurement and evaluation textbook in physical education.

Hopkins, D.R. 1979. Using the AAHPERD basketball skills test for women. Journal of Physical Education and Recreation **50**:72-73.

Describes use of test by coaches in selecting team members; evaluates 9-item test battery primarily designed for instructional purposes; presents descriptive statistics; lists resources for other skills tests.

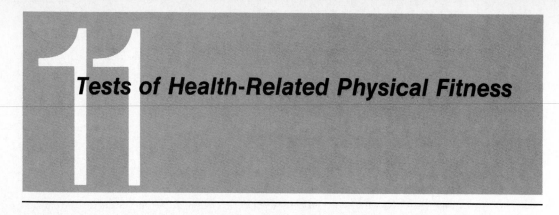

11

Tests of Health-Related Physical Fitness

KEY WORDS   *Watch for these words as you read the following chapter:*

AAHPERD Health-Related
Physical Fitness Test

AAHPER Youth Fitness
Test

body composition

field test

hydrostatic weighing

Kraus-Weber Test

physical fitness
(health-related)

skinfold caliper

step test

Although many physical fitness tests have been published in the United States, only a handful have been developed with an adequate concern for type of fitness, test validity, and test reliability. In addition to having these characteristics, a sound test should be accompanied by a table of norms that is useful on a national scale. Throughout most of the twentieth century, physical fitness has received its greatest emphasis during times of war. The focus on fitness was a result of the drafting of young men into the armed forces; inevitably a substantial number of men were not able to meet the physical requirements of the draft. Each time this occurred, government officials expressed dismay about the level of physical fitness of American citizens. After World War II, President Eisenhower became a strong advocate of the development of physical fitness throughout the United States. His support was largely because of the results of the **Kraus-Weber Test,** which was administered to elementary school children in the United States and Europe. President Eisenhower was distressed that American children fared poorly on the test in comparison with European children.

Although the presidential support of physical fitness generated by the poor results on the Kraus-Weber Test was beneficial, it is rather curious in one sense in that the Kraus-Weber Test was not designed as a measure of overall physical fitness. It was developed as a measure of minimal functioning of the low back area. Individuals who could pass the test were considered unlikely candidates for developing low back problems but were not judged to be physically fit in a broader context. A brief examination of two of the six test items will verify the actual purpose of this test, which is still used today in clinical settings.

One item consists of a sit-up test with the examinee in a supine position, hands behind the neck. The feet are held down by an examiner. The objective of the test is to perform one sit-up. Another item requires the examinee to lie prone with a pillow under the hips and lower abdomen. The hands are clasped behind the neck, and the feet are held down by the examiner. The examinee raises the chest, head, and shoulders and holds this position for 10 seconds. It is evident that these two tests are not high-powered indicators of strength and endurance, but this was not the intent of the test developers. Thus even though the test was inappropriately used as a measure of physical fitness, it generated a nationwide interest in fitness. Furthermore, it led to another positive outcome under the leadership of President Eisenhower—the initiation of a conference to consider ways of promoting physical fitness throughout the United States.

In the 1970s a surge of interest in physical fitness was observed throughout the United States, only this time the emphasis was more closely tied to personal health and well-being than to fitness for fighting wars. To what extent does physical fitness contribute to a healthy life-style? This question has been studied extensively in recent years by exercise scientists, including doctors, physical ed-

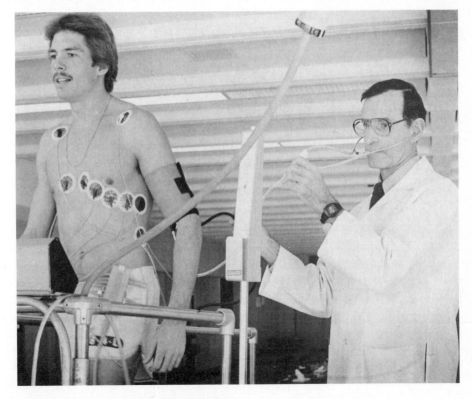

Administration of the Balke Treadmill Test.

ucators, exercise physiologists, health specialists, and others. The answer to this question is quite complex and not yet fully known. However, there is considerable evidence to support the value of maintaining an adequate state of physical fitness. How, then, can this state of fitness be assessed? The focus of this chapter is on tests developed to measure one or more components of health-related fitness. This type of fitness is related to one's positive health state rather than one's athletic ability, acknowledging that there is some overlap between the two.

In Appendix E a microcomputer program has been included to calculate estimates of percent body fat and ideal weight. The program is written for the Apple II computer but can easily be modified for other microcomputers.

DEFINITION OF HEALTH-RELATED PHYSICAL FITNESS

The American Alliance for Health, Physical Education, Recreation and Dance (AAHPERD) has gone on record in support of physical fitness tests and programs that emphasize the relationship between health and physical activity. According to AAHPERD, **health-related physical fitness** can be viewed thus:

Physical fitness is a multifaceted continuum extending from birth to death. Affected by physical activity, it ranges from optimal abilities in all aspects of life through high and low levels of different physical fitness, to severely limiting disease and dysfunction. (AAHPERD, 1980:3)

Most physical educators and exercise scientists are not medical doctors and thus are not qualified to work independently with the physical activity needs of the person in a disease state. Although exercise physiologists may be associated with cardiac rehabilitation programs, their work is under the supervision of a cardiologist. Generally, it is the job of the physical educator to work with the healthy person using physical activity as a medium for maintaining and improving that person's health state and preventing disease. This global statement must be qualified by noting that lack of physical activity is only one of the risk factors associated with certain diseases. Certainly other factors such as nutrition must be taken into account. At the same time, our unique function in physical education and exercise science is our training and background in sport and physical activity. Specialists in these areas should be qualified to provide exercise prescriptions for the healthy person.

To determine the level of physical fitness of an individual, a test that reflects an accurate definition of physical fitness should be used. In the context of health-related physical fitness, a test measuring short distance runs (e.g., 100 yards) would not be valid, since it is the longer distances that affect one's capacity to use oxygen. The remainder of this chapter is devoted to an overview of tests of physical fitness that are typically used in school and laboratory settings. (For fitness testing in a nonschool setting, see Chapter 3.)

MEASURING HEALTH-RELATED FITNESS

In a laboratory setting fairly precise measures of health-related fitness can be made. Usually students are exposed to some of these measures in an exercise physiology course. Since using laboratory tests in a practical setting is not feasible, **field tests** are used. A good field test does not require expensive equipment that can only be used by highly trained personnel in controlled settings. There must be evidence that the test is a valid measure of some aspect of physical fitness, perhaps not as valid as the laboratory test but with acceptable validity nonetheless. The majority of the field tests of health-related physical fitness can be used in a variety of settings, including schools, private clubs, YMCAs, YWCAs, and so forth. Although this section focuses on measures that are appropriate in a school setting, their applicability extends beyond the schools.

The AAHPERD Health-Related Physical Fitness Test

During the early 1950s the American Association (now Alliance) for Health, Physical Education, and Recreation began exploring tests that could be used to measure fitness on a broad scale in the public schools and that could be standardized, including tables of norms. The outcome of this exploration was the development of the **AAHPER Youth Fitness Test,** now sponsored by the AAHPERD. Although the developers of this test did not define physical fitness before developing the test, the latest version of the test manual (AAHPER, 1976) states that one criterion was that the test measure different components of fitness. The manual further noted that this test measures elements of strength, agility, and endurance as well as proficiency in running and jumping. This test has become very popular in the United States. The test items are reasonably familiar, require little or no equipment, can be administered to both boys and girls, can be administered to the entire range of grades 5 through 12, and allow self-testing by students (AAHPER, 1976:10). On the other hand, the test has been criticized as a test of health-related physical fitness because of the types of items included. These criticisms became pronounced in the early 1970s when physical educators and exercise scientists became more concerned about the health-related fitness of Americans. The AAHPER Youth Fitness Test was generally viewed as a measure of physical performance related primarily to athletic ability. Furthermore, the test did not convey a definition of fitness that would be appropriate across the life span. In other words, a test measuring health-related fitness should be appropriate for persons of any age whether young, middle-aged, or elderly. The Youth Fitness Test includes items such as the standing long jump and the 50-yard dash. Although these items are useful as measures of athletic performance–related fitness, they are not valid indicators of health-related fitness.

As a result of these concerns, the **AAHPERD Health-Related Physical Fitness Test (HRPFT)** was developed in 1980. Specific criteria were identified for choosing test items:

1. A physical fitness test should measure a range which extends from severely limiting dysfunction to high levels of functional capacity;
2. It should measure capacities that can be improved with appropriate physical activity; and
3. It should accurately reflect an individual's physical fitness status as well as changes in functional capacity by corresponding test scores and changes in these scores. (AAHPERD, 1980:4-5)

Three areas of physiological function appeared to be related to the above criteria: cardiorespiratory (CR) function, body composition (leanness/fatness), and abdominal and low back–hamstring musculoskeletal function. A test battery was designed to include measures of each of these components. Each of the test items is described in detail in the next section. A test manual (AAHPERD, 1980) and a technical manual (Falls and others, 1984) provide specific information about the test. The test manual includes a description of the tests, tables of norms, and criterion-referenced standards along with a section on scientific principles for developing physical fitness programs. In the technical manual scientific evidence supporting the selection of the test items is presented.

DISTANCE RUNS. Distance runs are included in the battery as measures of CR function. An individual who possesses a satisfactory level of CR function is able to engage in sports or other physical activities that require sustained effort. A number of physiological parameters reflect CR function; however, a person's maximal oxygen uptake is widely accepted as the best single indicator of this function. Maximal oxygen uptake (max $\dot{V}O_2$) is the maximal amount of oxygen an individual can transport and use during exercise (Astrand and Rodahl, 1970); (see also Chapter 3). When the exercise continues to become more difficult, yet the oxygen consumption fails to increase, this is referred to as *maximal oxygen uptake* or *maximal oxygen consumption*. "Maximal oxygen consumption is one of the most important factors that determine a person's capacity to sustain high-intensity exercise for longer than 4 to 5 minutes" (Katch and McArdle, 1983:56).

Test objective. The distance runs are used to measure maximal functional capacity and endurance of the CR system.

Description. The 1-mile run for time or the 9-minute run for distance may be administered, depending primarily on the teacher's personal preference. In addition, optional distance run tests may be used for students 13 years of age and older. These are the 1½-mile run for time or the 12-minute run for distance. The distance runs can be tested in a variety of settings. Examples of some of these are included in Fig. 11-1.

FIG. 11-1. *Schematic drawing of areas that can be used for distance run tests.*
From Health-Related Physical Fitness Test Manual.

Instructions. Regardless of whether the distance or the time of the run is fixed, students are instructed to run with maximal effort.

ONE-MILE RUN. Instruct the students to run as fast as possible, beginning on the signal *"Ready, Start!"* As the student crosses the finish line, call out the elapsed time, which should be recorded by the student or the student's partner. Walking, although permissible, should be discouraged since the purpose of the test is to measure maximal capacity. These instructions are also appropriate for the 1½-mile run.

NINE-MINUTE RUN. Instruct the students to run as far as possible, beginning on the signal *"Ready, Start!"* After 9 minutes, a whistle is blown and the student's partner records the distance run. These instructions are also appropriate for the 12-minute run test.

Test area. The distance run tests can be administered on a 440-yard or 400-meter track or on any other flat, measured surface. Examples of tests areas are displayed in Fig. 11-1.

Equipment. Stopwatch, scorecards, and pencils.

Scoring. The 1-mile and 1½-mile runs are scored to the nearest second. The 9-minute and 12-minute runs are scored to the nearest 10 yards or 10 meters.

Instructions on recording scores are included in Appendix A of the Test Manual (AAHPERD, 1980).

Validity. Generally, the validity of distance run tests has been established by correlating the test scores with max $\dot{V}O_2$ scores expressed in milliliters of oxygen per kilogram of body weight per minute (ml/kg min). This expression is used to adjust for individual variations in body size. Validity coefficients of 0.81 for elementary school boys and 0.71 for girls at the same grade levels have been reported by Jackson and Coleman (1976) for the 9-minute run test. For the 12-minute run test, validity coefficients range from 0.65 to 0.90. The lower sizes of some of the coefficients may be attributable to a lack of motivation in the performance of the distance runs, body fatness, or running efficiency. For example, if a student is not motivated to run as fast as possible, the distance run score will not be highly related to max $\dot{V}O_2$ scores calculated directly from a treadmill test.

Reliability. Performance on distance run tests is usually highly reliable, with the reliability coefficients ranging from 0.75 to 0.94. In most cases the reliability estimates fall at the high end of this range. Factors such as motivation, body fatness, and running efficiency can affect the reliability as well as the validity of distance runs.

Norms. Normative data are provided for each distance run test. Portions of the tables of norms are included in Tables 11-1 to 11-4.

Comments. Students should be taught to warm up with passive stretches and walking before participating in a distance run and to cool down in the same way afterward. Check to see that no medical reason exists to prevent a student from engaging in strenuous exercise of this nature. Prepare students in advance for the distance run by teaching them how to pace themselves throughout the run. Begin with shorter runs and gradually increase the distance of the run.

TABLE 11-1. *Percentile norms for girls for the 9-minute run (in yards)**

Percentile	Age											
	5	6	7	8	9	10	11	12	13	14	15	16	17+
95	1540	1700	1900	1860	2050	2067	2000	2175	2085	2123	2161	2199	2237
75	1300	1440	1540	1540	1650	1650	1723	1760	1785	1823	1861	1899	1937
50	1140	1208	1344	1358	1425	1460	1480	1590	1577	1615	1653	1691	1729
25	950	1017	1150	1225	1243	1250	1345	1356	1369	1407	1445	1483	1521
5	700	750	860	970	960	940	904	1000	1069	1107	1145	1183	1221

*Modified from Health-Related Physical Fitness Test Manual.

TABLE 11-2. *Percentile norms for boys for the 9-minute run (in yards)**

	Age												
Percentile	5	6	7	8	9	10	11	12	13	14	15	16	17+
95	1760	1750	2020	2200	2175	2250	2250	2400	2402	2473	2544	2615	2615
75	1320	1469	1683	1810	1835	1910	1925	1975	2096	2167	2238	2309	2380
50	1170	1280	1440	1595	1660	1690	1725	1760	1885	1956	2027	2098	2169
25	990	1090	1243	1380	1440	1487	1540	1500	1674	1745	1816	1887	1958
5	600	816	990	1053	1104	1110	1170	1000	1368	1439	1510	1581	1652

*Modified from Health-Related Physical Fitness Test Manual.

TABLE 11-3. *Percentile norms for girls for the 1-mile run (in minutes and seconds)**

	Age												
Percentile	5	6	7	8	9	10	11	12	13	14	15	16	17+
95	9:45	9:18	8:48	8:45	8:24	7:59	7:46	7:26	7:10	7:18	7:39	7:07	7:26
75	13:09	11:24	10:55	10:35	9:58	9:30	9:12	8:36	8:18	8:13	8:42	9:00	9:03
50	15:08	13:48	12:30	12:00	11:12	11:06	10:27	9:47	9:27	9:35	10:05	10:45	9:47
25	17:59	15:27	14:30	14:16	13:18	12:54	12:10	11:34	10:56	11:43	12:21	13:00	11:28
5	19:00	18:50	17:44	16:58	16:42	17:00	16:56	14:46	14:55	16:59	16:22	15:30	15:24

*Modified from Health-Related Physical Fitness Test Manual.

TABLE 11-4. *Percentile norms for boys for the 1-mile run (in minutes and seconds)**

	Age												
Percentile	5	6	7	8	9	10	11	12	13	14	15	16	17+
95	9:02	9:06	8:06	7:58	7:17	6:56	6:50	6:27	6:11	5:51	6:01	5:48	6:01
75	11:32	10:55	9:37	9:14	8:36	8:10	8:00	7:24	6:52	6:36	6:35	6:28	6:36
50	13:46	12:29	11:25	11:00	9:56	9:19	9:06	8:20	7:27	7:10	7:14	7:11	7:25
25	16:05	15:10	14:02	13:29	12:00	11:05	11:31	10:00	8:35	8:02	8:04	8:07	8:26
5	18:25	17:38	17:17	16:19	15:44	14:28	15:25	13:41	10:23	10:32	10:37	10:40	10:56

*Modified from Health-Related Physical Fitness Test Manual.

SUM OF SKINFOLD FAT. The body composition of a person consists of bone, muscle mass, and fatty tissue. Obesity is the result of an excess of fatty tissue and is associated with a number of disease states such as diabetes, hypertension, heart disease, and heat intolerance. Thus it is appropriate to include a measure of body composition in a health-related fitness battery.

Test objective. This test is used to assess **body composition,** or more specifically, the level of fatness in an individual.

Description. Two skinfold sites are used in this particular battery to measure body fatness—the specific spots on the triceps and the subscapular muscles. The subcutaneous adipose tissue can be lifted with the fingers to form a skinfold. A **skinfold caliper** is used to obtain the skinfold measure by measuring the thickness of a double layer of subcutaneous fat and skin at the designated site.

Instructions. To ensure accuracy and consistency across skinfold measures, the sites should be marked with a grease pencil. To obtain the triceps skinfold, mark the point halfway between the elbow and the acromial process of the scapula. The mark for the skinfold should be made parallel to the longitudinal axis of the upper arm. Mark the subscapular site 1 cm (½ inch) below the inferior angle of the scapula in line with the natural cleavage lines of the skin. Both measurements are taken on the right side of the body. (Refer to the figures for examples of properly marked sites.)

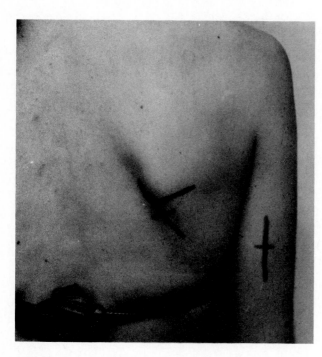

Markings of sites for subscapular and triceps skinfold measurement.
From Pollock, M.L., Schmidt, D.H., and Jackson, A.S.

Measurement of triceps skinfold.
From Pollock, M.L., Schmidt, D.H., and Jackson, A.S.

Measurement of subscapular skinfold.
From Pollock, M.L., Schmidt, D.H., and Jackson A.S.

Various devices for measuring body fatness—the Lange caliper is shown in the upper
right portion of the photograph, the Harpenden caliper is shown in lower right.
From Pollock, M.L., Schmidt, D.H., and Jackson, A.S.

The AAHPERD Test Manual (1980, p. 13) recommends the following procedure for obtaining a skinfold measure:

1. Firmly grasp the skinfold between the thumb and forefinger and lift up.
2. Place the contact surface of the caliper 1 cm (½ inch) above or below the finger.
3. Slowly release the grip on the caliper enabling them (the jaws of the caliper) to exert
   their full tension on the skinfold.
4. Read skinfold to nearest 0.5 millimeter after needle stops (1 to 2 seconds after releas-
   ing grip on caliper).

Test area. A private testing area should be available for administering this test, so that students will not suffer any embarrassment resulting from the test.

Equipment. The AAHPERD Test Manual (1980) recommends either Harpenden or Lange skinfold calipers for this test. (See photograph on p. 236.) These calipers are expensive, but they provide a constant pressure of 10 gm/mm^2 throughout the range of skinfold thicknesses. Other less expensive calipers are now on the market and may be suitable for testing in a school setting. However, the pressure may not be constant throughout the lower portion of the range, thus yielding inaccurate measures.

Scoring. Three measures are taken at each site, and the median of each set of three measures is recorded to the nearest 0.5 mm. The median scores for the two sites are then summed, as in the following example:

Triceps—10, 7, 8   Median = 8
Subscapular—6, 5, 7   Median = 6
TOTAL SCORE   14

Validity. The validity of the sum of skinfold fat is usually determined by correlating this sum with body fatness measured through **hydrostatic weighing,** where the percent body fat and lean body mass are determined by submerging the individual underwater. The validity coefficients range from 0.70 to 0.90 in both children and adults (Baumgartner and Jackson, 1982).

Reliability. The test-retest reliability of skinfold measures is high, over 0.95 when experienced testers are used.

Norms. The AAHPERD Test Manual (1980) includes percentile norms for 12,000 children from 6 to 17 years of age. Representative norms are presented in Tables 11-5 and 11-6. The desired degree of fatness for children is a skinfold sum between the 50th percentile and the 90th percentile.

TABLE 11-5. *Percentile norms for boys for sum of triceps plus subscapular skinfolds (in millimeters)**

	Age											
Percentile	6	7	8	9	10	11	12	13	14	15	16	17+
95	8	9	9	9	9	9	9	9	9	9	9	9
75	11	11	11	11	12	12	11	12	11	12	12	12
50	12	12	13	14	14	16	15	15	14	14	14	15
25	14	15	17	18	19	22	21	22	20	20	20	21
5	20	24	28	34	33	38	44	46	37	40	37	38

*Modified from Health-Related Physical Fitness Test Manual.

TABLE 11-6. *Percentile norms for girls for sum of triceps plus subscapular skinfolds (in millimeters)**

Percentile	Age											
	6	7	8	9	10	11	12	13	14	15	16	17+
95	9	10	10	10	10	11	11	12	13	14	14	15
75	12	12	13	14	14	15	15	16	18	20	20	20
50	14	15	16	17	18	19	19	20	24	25	25	27
25	17	19	21	24	25	25	27	30	32	34	34	36
5	26	28	36	40	41	42	48	51	52	56	57	58

*Modified from Health-Related Physical Fitness Test Manual.

Comments. Be careful to place the caliper properly. The correct location is midway between the crest and base of the skinfold, not *at* the base. Teachers who are inexperienced in using the caliper should practice measuring skinfolds with students as subjects. Measure each site a number of times and try to obtain the same reading within 1 or 2 mm.

Much is still unknown about the relationship of skinfold fat to body fatness in children, since changes occur with gender and with age. A specific skinfold thickness, then, does not represent the same amount of body fat in a young child as it does in an older child.

Skinfold measures can be used to estimate percent body fat and ideal weight. A simple program for calculating these estimates on the Apple II microcomputer is included in Appendix E. Three skinfold sites must be measured to use this program—chest, abdomen, and thigh for men; and triceps, thigh, and suprailium for women.

MODIFIED SIT-UPS. The remaining two test items are included in the HRPFT battery as measures of musculoskeletal function in the abdominal and low back area. The Modified Sit-ups Test is characterized by a 1-minute time limit and a positioning of the arms in front of the chest.

Many Americans are affected by low back pain. This dysfunction can lead to a state of extreme discomfort, causing the sufferer to lose work days and preventing him or her from leading a normal life. In a functional health context this syndrome is associated with weak abdominal muscles and excessively contracted muscles in the lower back. Many doctors recommend exercise to reduce low back pain.

Test objective. The Modified Sit-ups Test is used to measure abdominal strength and endurance.

Description. The starting position of the test is a back-lying position with knees flexed, feet on floor, and heels between 12 and 18 inches from the buttocks. The arms are crossed on the chest with the hands on opposite shoulders. A partner holds the examinee's feet to keep them in contact with the testing surface. The examinee curls to a sitting position, maintaining arm contact with the chest. The chin should be tucked on the chest and should remain in this position until the completion of the sit-up. When the elbows touch the thighs, the sit-up is completed. The examinee curls back down to the floor until the midback contacts the testing surface. Another sit-up may then be attempted. (See photographs below)

Starting position for the Modified Sit-Ups Test.

Up position for the Modified Sit-Ups Test.

Instructions. The examinee begins executing consecutive sit-ups on the word *"Go!"*, using the signal *"Ready, Go!"* At the end of 60 seconds, the test is ended with the word *"Stop!"* The score is the number of sit-ups executed correctly during this time. Pausing between sit-ups is permissible.

Test area. Any area with sufficient floor space may be used.

Equipment. Mats are recommended for safety and comfort and a stopwatch.

Scoring. The score is the number of sit-ups executed correctly during 60 seconds. Incorrect execution includes failure to curl up, pulling the arms away from the chest, failure to touch the thighs with the elbows, and failure to touch the midback to the testing surface in the down position.

Validity. The validity of the sit-ups test has not been clearly established. Electromyographic studies of sit-ups have shown that the abdominal muscles are active during the execution of a sit-up, yet no evidence exists that a specified number of sit-ups reflects a desirable amount of abdominal strength. Thus, the Modified Sit-ups Test is validated on the basis of logical validity.

Reliability. The reliability of this test is generally satisfactory. The range of

TABLE 11-7. *Percentile norms for boys for sit-ups (number)**

	Age												
Percentile	5	6	7	8	9	10	11	12	13	14	15	16	17+
95	30	36	42	48	47	50	51	56	58	59	59	61	62
75	23	26	33	37	38	40	41	46	48	49	49	51	52
50	18	20	26	30	32	34	37	39	41	42	44	45	46
25	11	15	19	25	25	27	30	31	35	36	38	38	38
5	2	6	10	15	15	15	17	19	25	27	28	28	25

*Modified from Health-Related Physical Fitness Test Manual.

TABLE 11-8. *Percentile norms for girls for sit-ups (number)**

	Age												
Percentile	5	6	7	8	9	10	11	12	13	14	15	16	17+
95	28	35	40	44	44	47	50	52	51	51	56	54	54
75	24	28	31	35	35	39	40	41	41	42	43	42	44
50	19	22	25	29	29	32	34	36	35	35	37	33	37
25	12	14	20	22	23	25	28	30	29	30	30	29	31
5	2	6	10	12	14	15	19	19	18	20	20	20	19

*Modified from Health-Related Physical Fitness Test Manual.

test-retest reliability coefficients is 0.68 to 0.94; the lower coefficients are probably attributable to inconsistency in the level of motivation.

Norms. Normative data are provided in the Test Manual (1980) based on 12,000 school children in 13 states. Portions of these tables are presented in Tables 11-7 and 11-8.

Comments. The position assumed by the examinee should be carefully checked before and during the execution of the sit-up. The distance between the heels and the buttocks (12 to 18 inches) should be monitored continuously, measuring if necessary. The use of partners to count and record scores is permissible; however, the execution of the sit-ups must be observed by the tester to be sure the partners are counting only correctly executed sit-ups. For example, as an examinee begins to fatigue, sit-ups are often executed with a straight back rather than a curl up. Partners should be instructed not to count the straight-back sit-ups.

SIT-AND-REACH TEST. The Sit-and-Reach Test is the second of the two tests included as measures of abdominal and low back-hamstring musculoskeletal function. The abdominal area is tested by the Modified Sit-ups Test, and the Sit-and-Reach Test is used to measure the low back-hamstring area.

Test objective. The Sit-and-Reach Test is designed to evaluate the flexibility of the low back and posterior thigh.

Description. The examinees must remove their shoes to be tested. To begin the test, the examinee sits in front of the test apparatus with feet flat against the end board. The knees should be fully extended and the feet, shoulder-width apart. To perform the test, the examinee extends the arms forward with one hand placed on top of the other.

Instructions. In the actual test the examinee reaches forward, palms down, along the measuring scale of the testing apparatus. (See Figs. 11-2 and 11-3 for drawings of the initial and final test positions.) The reach is repeated three consecutive times and, on the fourth trial, the maximum reach is held for 1 second. The distance of the maximum reach is recorded as the test score.

Test area. Any small testing area with adequate floor space would be suitable.

Equipment. The test apparatus is a specially constructed box with a measuring scale in which 23 cm is set at the level of the feet. A drawing of one version of the box is presented in Fig. 11-4. Refer to the Test Manual (AAHPERD, 1980) for detailed instructions on constructing this version of the apparatus.

Scoring. The score, measured to the nearest centimeter, is the most distant point reached on the fourth trial. The fingertips of both hands should reach this point. If the reach of the two hands is uneven, the test should be readministered.

FIG. 11-2. *Initial test position for the Sit-and-Reach Test.*

FIG. 11-3. *Final test position for the Sit-and-Reach Test.*

Validity. The Sit-and-Reach Test has been validated by comparing it with several other types of flexibility tests, with validity coefficients ranging between 0.80 and 0.90. Logical validity has also been claimed for the test, since higher scores reflect better extensibility in the low back, hip, and posterior thigh.

Reliability. This test has acceptable reliability, with reliability coefficients of 0.70 or higher.

Norms. Normative data are provided in the Test Manual (1980) based on scores for 12,000 school-age children in 13 states. Portions of the tables of norms are presented in Tables 11-9 and 11-10.

FIG. 11-4. Apparatus for measuring the Sit-and-Reach Test.

TABLE 11-9. Percentile norms for girls for Sit-and-Reach Test (in centimeters)*

Percentile	Age												
	5	6	7	8	9	10	11	12	13	14	15	16	17+
95	34	34	34	36	35	35	37	40	43	44	46	46	44
75	30	30	31	31	31	31	32	34	36	38	41	39	40
50	27	27	27	28	28	28	29	30	31	33	36	34	35
25	23	23	24	23	23	24	24	25	24	28	31	30	31
5	18	18	16	17	17	16	16	15	17	18	19	14	22

*Modified from Health-Related Physical Fitness Test Manual.

TABLE 11-10. Percentile norms for boys for Sit-and-Reach Test (in centimeters)*

Percentile	Age												
	5	6	7	8	9	10	11	12	13	14	15	16	17+
95	32	34	33	34	34	33	34	35	36	39	41	42	45
75	29	29	28	29	29	28	29	29	30	33	34	36	40
50	25	26	25	25	25	25	25	26	26	28	30	30	34
25	22	22	22	22	22	20	21	21	20	23	24	25	28
5	17	16	16	16	16	12	12	13	12	15	13	11	15

*Modified from Health-Related Physical Fitness Test Manual.

Comments. The test must be repeated if the knees are flexed during the reach. To ensure that the knees remain extended, the tester should place one hand lightly across the knees. As with all measures of physical fitness, the accuracy and consistency of test scores are increased by adequately warming up before testing. In this case warmups should include passive stretching of the low back–hamstring area. If the recommended test apparatus cannot be secured, a bench with a metric ruler attached may be substituted. When preadolescent boys and girls as well as those in their adolescent growth spurt are tested, it is normal for many of them to be unable to reach 23. During this growth period the legs become proportionally longer than the trunk.

OVERVIEW OF THE AAHPERD HEALTH-RELATED PHYSICAL FITNESS TEST. The AAHPERD Health-Related Physical Fitness Test is now recommended by the Alliance as a test of health-related fitness; however, the test is not without criticism. Questions have been raised about the validity of distance run tests as indicators of CR capacity.

Cureton (1982) discusses several factors other than CR capacity that might reflect individual differences in distance running performance—body fatness, running skill or efficiency, motivation, and use of proper pace. Cureton notes that distance run tests have usually been validated by using max $\dot{V}O_2$ expressed as milliliters per kilogram of body weight per minute (ml/kgBW/min) as a criterion measure. However, both variables (distance run score and max $\dot{V}O_2$ as previously expressed) are negatively affected by the percentage of body fat. In other words, as percent fat increases, both distance run performance and max $\dot{V}O_2$ decrease. Because of this fact, Cureton suggests that max $\dot{V}O_2$ would be more appropriately expressed by milliliters per kilogram of fat-free weight per minute (ml/kgFFW/min). He then demonstrates the accuracy of his analysis using data from a number of studies of adults and a single study of children. For example, he refers to a 1977 study (Cureton and others, 1977), which showed the following relationships for boys and girls ages 8 to 12.

Distance	$\dot{V}O_2$ max (BW)	$\dot{V}O_2$ max (FFW)
600 yards	− .62	− .32
1 mile	− .66	− .40

In short, between 35% and 45% of the variance in distance runs can be accounted for by $\dot{V}O_2$ max when total body weight is used to adjust the expression, but the percentage of variance accounted for drops to between 9% and 15% when fat-free weight is used. Thus variability in body fatness accounts for almost half of the relationship between max $\dot{V}O_2$ and distance runs. For this reason, it is inappropriate to suggest that distance run tests measure only one physiological variable.

Cureton also notes that changes in distance run performance in children are often not paralleled by similar changes in max $\dot{V}O_2$. Changes are more likely to occur in running efficiency as well as percent fat and anaerobic capacity. Nonetheless, he supports the use of distance run tests in the assessment of physical fitness in children. Such tests evaluate a unique physical ability not tapped in most other tests of physical performance. They reflect "the level of energy expenditure that a person can sustain over an extended period of time, or the physical work capacity in weight-bearing exercise" (Cureton, 1982:66).

Problems in measuring the skinfold thicknesses of young children have been summarized by Lohman (1982). In laboratory settings investigators assume children are chemically mature with regard to such elements as potassium and water content. Under these assumptions, a mean fat content of 20% is usually found. In a field setting a different value for body fat is estimated using a regression equation. However, equations for predicting percent body fat of adults are not appropriate for children. Furthermore, the relationship between anthropometric measures and body density varies between ages 8 and 15. For these reasons it is both logical and defensible to use the sum of skinfolds to measure body composition in elementary school-age children rather than applying invalid prediction equations in an effort to estimate percent body fat.

The expense of the skinfold caliper required to measure body composition has been viewed as problematic by some. The major criterion for a skinfold caliper is that it exert a constant force of 10 gm/mm^2 at the skinfold site, regardless of the thickness of the skinfold. Large errors in skinfold measures occur at low pressures, that is, lower than 10 gm/mm^2. In a study conducted by Lohman and Pollock (1981), three types of calipers were compared. A plastic caliper with neither spring nor tension required the tester to apply the appropriate amount of tension. A plastic caliper with a spring depended on the spring for the tension exerted. The third instrument was metal with a uniform tension independent of skinfold thickness. Both experienced and inexperienced testers measured a group of children at the triceps and subscapular sites. Differences between the scores of experienced and inexperienced testers occurred except when the expensive metal caliper was used. When the inexperienced testers were trained, the scores obtained using both pairs of calipers were more similar. The less expensive calipers may prove to be suitable for use in a field test setting, providing that the tester is well trained. Several inexpensive skinfold calipers are shown in Fig. 11-5.

Lohman and Pollock make several suggestions regarding the training of testers. At the very least, inexperienced testers should be trained above and beyond the required reading of the test manual. To attain proficiency in measuring skinfold thicknesses, testers should practice measuring between 50 and 100 people. Initially the sites should be marked with a grease pencil on the skin of the individual being tested. Testers within the same fitness club or school system should train together.

FIG. 11-5. *Variety of inexpensive skinfold calipers.*

Several articles on the Health-Related Physical Fitness Test, which should be useful for the practitioner, have been published in recent years. For the physical education teacher, Pate and Corbin (1981) propose implications for curriculum. Program ideas are presented, including those with cognitive and affective outcomes as well as psychomotor. The article includes excellent suggestions for teachers, which an innovative reader could apply in a nonschool setting as well. Their taxonomy of physical fitness objectives is shown in Table 11-11. The levels of the taxonomy range from the acquisition of a physical fitness vocabulary to the development of physical fitness problem-solving ability. Another excellent article for teachers and exercise specialists is written by Pollock and Blair (1981). An overview of the state of the art of exercise prescription is presented, beginning with a discussion of the physiological and behavioral components of exercise prescription. This is followed by a review of the principles of overload, specificity, warm-up, initial levels of fitness, progressions, and individual differences. Finally, the effect of exercise on CR function is discussed, in particular, frequency, intensity, duration, and mode of exercise. A number of articles of this nature have appeared in the Journal of Physical Education, Recreation and Dance, published by the AAHPERD.

TABLE 11-11. *Physical fitness objectives**

Level	Objective
1	Physical fitness vocabulary (fitness components; distinction between health-related and skill-related components)
2	Exercising (teacher interacts and encourages students to exercise)
3	Achieving physical fitness (help children experience the satisfaction of being fit)
4	Establishing regular exercise patterns (objectives become learner-oriented rather than teacher-oriented)
5	Physical fitness evaluation
6	Physical fitness problem solving (interpret data and modify own exercise program)

*From Pate, R., and Corbin, C.

National Children and Youth Fitness Study

The most recent study of youth fitness, the National Children and Youth Fitness Study (NCYFS), was published in 1985 by the Department of Health and Human Services (Ross and Gilbert, 1985). The purposes of the study were to describe the current fitness status of children and youth of the United States and the patterns of participation in physical activity and to evaluate the relationship among physical activity patterns and measured fitness. The HRPFT and a chin-ups test were used to measure health-related fitness. The means and standard deviations for the national sample on the five test items are shown in Tables 11-12 and 11-13.

The test was administered to 8800 boys and girls ages 10 through 17 across the country. Excellent sampling techniques were used in that these children and youths were selected on a probability basis guaranteeing that they were representative of all American boys and girls in the 10 to 17 age group. The fitness norms developed from the data of this national sample represent the most recent norms available for the HRPFT. They are probably the most accurate norms as well, since the sampling procedures used in the NCYFS were superior to the initial study used to develop norms, as reported in the HRPFT test manual. The sex/age norms for the HRPFT, along with norms for the chin-ups test, are included in Appendix F.

In general, the NCYFS data reveals that boys and girls showed continual improvement in most of the fitness test items as they advanced in age from 10

TABLE 11-12. *Average scores for boys by age on the NCYFS Fitness Test**

Test	Measures	10	11	12	13	14	15	16	17	18
Sum of triceps and subscapular skinfolds (mm)	Body fatness	20.90	21.20	21.60	20.10	20.10	20.10	19.40	20.10	20.20
Sit-and-reach (inches)	Flexibility	13.10	13.10	12.70	12.90	13.30	14.10	14.80	15.10	15.10
Bent-knee sit-ups (number in 60 seconds)	Abdominal strength	34.40	35.30	37.90	39.60	41.00	42.00	43.50	43.50	42.70
Chin-ups (number completed)	Upper body strength	2.70	2.90	3.40	4.60	5.70	7.20	8.60	9.00	9.70
Mile walk/run (minutes and seconds)	Cardiorespiratory endurance	10:20	9:50	9:24	8:41	8:40	8:00	7:44	8:20	8:10

*From the National Children and Youth Fitness Study.

TABLE 11-13. *Average scores for girls by age on the NCYFS Fitness Test**

Test	Measures	10	11	12	13	14	15	16	17	18
Sum of triceps and subscapular skinfolds (mm)	Body fatness	22.60	24.80	25.30	26.80	27.90	30.00	28.70	30.20	28.90
Sit-and-reach (inches)	Flexibility	14.10	14.80	15.50	16.10	16.40	17.00	17.50	17.20	17.10
Bent-knee sit-ups (number in 60 seconds)	Abdominal strength	31.40	31.60	33.70	33.60	34.80	34.60	35.10	35.10	35.40
Chin-ups (number completed)	Upper body strength	.90	.80	.80	.60	.80	.60	.90	.70	.60
Mile walk/run (minutes and seconds)	Cardiorespiratory endurance	11:38	11:52	11:32	11:05	10:42	11:14	11:03	11:00	11:20

*From the National Children and Youth Fitness Study.

to 17. However, the sum of skinfold data demonstrated a tendency for all age groups to be fatter than comparable groups in the 1960s. Other results of the study pertained to the activity patterns of boys and girls. Over 80% of the students in this study were enrolled in physical education classes, which met an average of 3.6 times a week. Competitive sports were stressed for the older students; relays and informal games were emphasized for the younger students.

This points to a deficiency in meeting one of the major national goals recently advocated for the public school—that of developing physical skills needed for an active life-style throughout adulthood. Almost half of these students failed to engage in an adequate amount of vigorous physical activity to maintain a healthy cardiovascular system. The NCYFS is a landmark investigation of youth fitness in the 1980s.

President's Council on Physical Fitness and Sports

The President's Council on Physical Fitness and Sports is an organization based in Washington, D.C. The primary mission of the Council is to promote physical fitness and sports throughout the United States. This group recommends the Youth Fitness Test (AAHPER, 1976) as the most effective physical fitness test battery for public schools. The Youth Fitness Test, which includes health-related and athletic performance-related fitness items, is described in detail in the next chapter.

A series of awards may be purchased to recognize students who achieve outstanding levels of fitness, based on test results. Winners of the Presidential Physical Fitness Award, the highest given, receive a certificate suitable for framing, a decal, and an emblem (AAHPERD, 1976:91). Information on the entire awards structure can be obtained from the American Alliance for Health, Physical Education, Recreation, and Dance, 1900 Association Drive, Reston, VA 22091.

FITNESSGRAM

The National Youth Fitness Program is sponsored by the AAHPERD, Campbell Soup Company, Institute for Aerobics Research, and President's Council on Physical Fitness. The FITNESSGRAM is a part of this program (Institute for Aerobics Research, 1983). FITNESSGRAM is a program designed to measure and contribute to the improvement of youth fitness. Either the Health-Related Physical Fitness Test or the Youth Fitness Test may be used for public school students as a part of this program. The FITNESSGRAM program is a computerized system for scoring and reporting physical fitness test results. Based on student performance on the fitness test, the physical fitness report card provides parents with a fitness profile for their child. Each FITNESSGRAM features the student's scores on the test items, the student's rank against a national norm, an overall fitness score and its rank against national norms, and the student's height and weight. A sample of a FITNESSGRAM is included in Fig. 11-6.

The national program model includes program delivery at three levels: direct service, in which the Institute for Aerobics Research produces the fitness report cards for the school district; development of microcomputer software for use by a school district to produce FITNESSGRAMS locally; and availability of consultants to help selected districts program large computer systems to produce the cards and do statistical analyses locally (Institute for Aerobics Research, 1983).

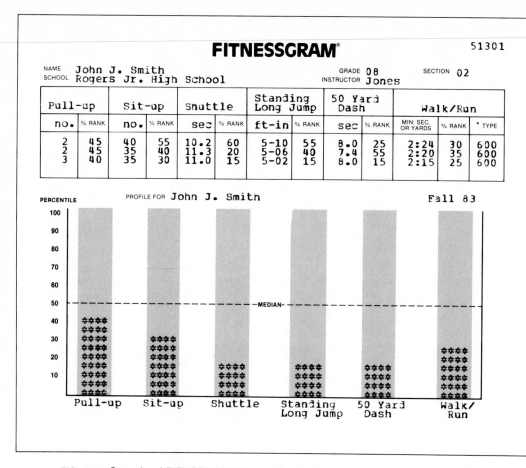

FIG. 11-6. *Sample of FITNESSGRAM used in the National Youth Fitness Program. By permission of the Institute of Aerobics Research.*

Step tests

Distance run tests, already described as measures of CR function, can be used as a part of the AAHPERD Health-Related Physical Fitness Test or can be administered separately by physical education teachers and exercise specialists. Another practical test of CR function that can be used in a field setting is the step test. In this section the Harvard Step Test, the first of the step tests, is described, followed by a description of several modifications of the Harvard test.

THE HARVARD STEP TEST. The Harvard Step Test was developed at the Harvard Fatigue Laboratory in 1943. A landmark test in its day, it is no longer widely used because of its strenuousness. However, it still provides the standard for all step tests developed since that time and thus merits a thorough overview.

TOTAL PHYSICAL FITNESS SCORE	
EXCELLENT	352 +
ABOVE AVERAGE	316-351
AVERAGE	287-315
BELOW AVERAGE	251-286
WELL BELOW AVERAGE	0-250

DATE	HEIGHT	WEIGHT	TOTAL FITNESS SCORE
SEM - YR	FT - IN	LBS	
Fa 82	5-02	157	295
Sp 83	5-03	160	283
Fa 83	5-04	163	259

These activities are recommended:

To improve your cardiorespiratory endurance: jogging, swimming, rope jumping, walking, and cycling.

To improve your abdominal strength: bent knee sit-ups and leg lifts.

* WALK/RUN TYPE
600 = 600 YARD (MIN:SEC)
1 mi = 1 MILE (MIN:SEC)
1.5 = 1.5 MILE (MIN:SEC)
9 = 9 MINUTE (YARDS)
12 = 12 MINUTE (YARDS)

Dear Parent:
We are pleased to send you this FITNESSGRAM to provide information on your child's level of physical fitness as indicated by his/her performance in the AAHPERD Youth Fitness Test recently administered in our school. This test was developed by the American Alliance for Health, Physical Education, Recreation and Dance.

Your child participates in the test in the fall and spring. The FITNESSGRAM will show you any progress in his/her growth and development over the school years.

The FITNESSGRAM provides the following information:

1. A total physical fitness score for your child based on assessments of
   - upper body strength and endurance--measured by flexed-arm hang or pull-up test;
   - abdominal strength and endurance--1 minute sit-up test;
   - speed with change of direction--shuttle run;
   - explosive power--standing long jump test;
   - speed--50 yard dash;
   - cardiovascular fitness--600 yard, 1-mile, 1.5-mile, 9-minute, or 12-minute walk/run.

2. A percentile rank (% RANK) for each test item is computed based on a national norm developed over the last 20 years. You can see both your child's score and the national average (50%) of students of his/her age who have taken the test.

3. An exciting feature of the FITNESSGRAM is the recommendation for activities which can help improve your child's individual scores.

4. The FITNESSGRAM reflects past performances which will allow the monitoring of improvement from test date to test date!

We hope you will find the FITNESSGRAM a useful tool to assess your child's fitness level, height and weight development--and to encourage your entire family to enjoy the benefits of an active lifestyle.

Mr. Jerry G. Jones
Physical Education Instructor
Rogers Elementary

Test objective. The Harvard Step Test was designed to measure the CR function of adult males.

Description. The examinee exercises on a 20-inch bench for as long a period as possible up to 5 minutes.

Instructions. The stepping pattern is up with the left foot, up with the right foot, down with the left foot, and down with the right foot. Both of the examinee's legs should be straight when standing on the bench. The steps should be taken at a cadence of 30 steps per minute. The cadence can be most easily established using a metronome, although a stopwatch can also be used. The test ends after the 5-minute period has elapsed, although examinees may stop at any time before the 5-minute limit.

Whenever the examinee stops exercising, a pulse count is taken during three recovery periods—from 1 to 1½ minutes, 2 to 2½ minutes, and 3 to 3½ minutes after exercise ceases. Two scores are recorded: the number of seconds the examinee exercised and the sum of the pulse counts in the three recovery periods.

Test area. One of the desirable features of a step test is that it can be administered in small areas.

Equipment. Metronome or stopwatch and 20-inch bench.

Scoring. Formula 11-1 is used to determine the index of physical efficiency.

$$\text{Index} = \frac{\text{Duration of exercise in seconds} \times 100}{2 \times \text{sum of 3 recovery pulse counts}} \qquad \text{Formula 11-1}$$

Suppose an examinee stops exercising at the end of 4 minutes (240 seconds) and his recovery pulse rates are 80, 60, and 50, respectively. Using Formula 11-1, determine his index of physical efficiency.

$$\text{Index} = \frac{240 \times 100}{2(80 + 60 + 50)} = 63.2$$

What does a score of 63.2 mean? Is it a good or poor score? Mathews (1978:269) at Ohio State developed a set of standards for adult males based on a large data set accumulated over a period of several years.

Harvard Step Test Standards

Above 90	Excellent
80-89	Good
65-79	Average
55-64	Low Average
Below 55	Poor

In the hypothetical example the score of 63.2 is interpreted as a low average score.

Validity. The validity of the Harvard Step Test has been determined by correlating it with max $\dot{V}O_2$, a maximal stress test, as a criterion measure. Validity coefficients ranging from -0.35 to 0.77 have been reported, suggesting that this step test is not a very precise indicator of CR function. Negative validity coefficients were obtained because several investigators used a modified scoring system. High (or low) index scores are not necessarily associated with high (or low) max $\dot{V}O_2$ values.

Reliability. Reliability coefficients ranging from 0.65-0.95 have been obtained for the Harvard Step Test or the test in modified form. Most of these coefficients are higher than 0.80. The reproducibility or objectivity of the test, which is the ability to obtain the same heart rate using different testers, is high. Coefficients of 0.992 to 0.995 have been reported by Montoye (1978). Most of the reliability estimates are confounded (probably made lower) by the potential for error in obtaining the pulse rate. Sometimes the pulse rate is measured by a partner. On other occasions the same tester is not used for both testing sessions. Certainly, the lack of objectivity in obtaining a pulse rate is a problem, but the extent to which this problem affects the size of the reliability coefficient is unknown.

Comments. The Harvard Step Test has been modified for young women and for boys and girls. Montoye (1978) has recommended specific bench heights, rates of stepping, and maximum durations for various age groups and both sexes:

AGES 8 TO 10 (BOYS AND GIRLS). Use a bench height of 8 inches, a stepping rate of 24 (4 counting cycles per minute), and a maximum duration of 3 minutes.

AGES 10 TO 12 (BOYS AND GIRLS). Use a bench height of 12 inches, a stepping rate of 24, and a maximum duration of 3 minutes.

AGES 12 TO 14 (BOYS AND GIRLS). Use a bench height of 18 inches, a stepping rate of 24, and a maximum duration of 3 minutes.

AGES 15 TO 22 (GIRLS). Use a bench height of 18 inches, a stepping rate of 24, and a maximum duration of 3 minutes. (These test specifications can also be used for women, ages 23 to 34.)

AGES 15 TO 22 (BOYS). Use a bench height of 20 inches, a stepping rate of 30, and a maximum duration of 5 minutes. (These test specifications can also be used for men, ages 23 to 34.)

THE OHIO STATE UNIVERSITY STEP TEST. Because of the strenuous nature of the Harvard Step Test, a more practical and less taxing step test was developed at Ohio State University (OSU) in 1969. This test can easily be used in a field setting.

Test objective. The purpose of this test is to measure cardiorespiratory function for males and females.

Description. The OSU Step Test is divided into a series of 18 innings of exercise. Each inning of exercise is 30 seconds long and is followed by a 20-second rest period. Each 20-second rest period consists of 5 seconds to find the pulse, 10 seconds to count the pulse, and 5 seconds to prepare for the beginning of the next inning. Therefore a new inning of exercise begins every 50 seconds. The 18 innings are divided into 3 phases:

Phase I—6 innings at 24 steps/minute on the 15-inch bench
Phase II—6 innings at 30 steps/minute on the 15-inch bench
Phase III—6 innings at 30 steps/minute on the 20-inch bench

During the 10-second interval of each rest period, the pulse rate is counted. If the pulse rate is less than 25 beats per 10 seconds, the examinee continues with the next inning. The first rest interval in which the pulse rate reaches or exceeds 25 is the inning that terminates the test. The test can also be terminated by completing all 18 innings without attaining a pulse rate of 25.

Instructions. Before beginning the test, the examinee stands in front of the bench and grasps the handbar with both hands. The handbar should be level with the top of the examinee's head. The stepping pattern is initiated at the signal "Ready, Go!", and the examinee proceeds in cadence with the metronome. The up-up-down-down stepping pattern described for the Harvard Step Test is used, except either the left or the right foot can initiate the first step up. Again, the legs must be straight when both feet are on the bench, and the back should also be straight at this point. The examinee should be forewarned when the cadence changes at the beginning of a new phase.

Test area. A relatively small space is sufficient for administering the OSU Step Test.

Equipment. A split-level bench with an adjustable handbar (lower level of the bench is 15 inches high; higher level, 20 inches) and a metronome and stopwatch, unless the cadence and time units will be recorded on tape.

Scoring. The score is the number of innings the individual is able to complete before reaching a heart rate of 25 in 10 seconds. The examinee may be permitted to count his or her own pulse, if able to do so fairly accurately. The tester should make arrangements before administering a step test to have additional help available for those who have difficulty detecting their pulse. Several students in class might assist in this capacity. The entire group of examinees should be informed that this type of assistance is available.

Validity. The validity coefficient for the OSU Step Test when compared with a submaximal stress test is 0.94. Max $\dot{V}O_2$ values were estimated from the submaximal test. When the OSU Step Test scores were correlated with max $\dot{V}O_2$ values from a maximal stress test, the validity coefficients were considerably lower, ranging from 0.47 to 0.57. These latter coefficients correspond closely to those obtained for the Harvard Step Test.

Reliability. The OSU Step Test has acceptable reliability, with reliability coefficients ranging from 0.69 to 0.94.

Comments. The OSU Test has been modified for college women (Witten, 1973) and for elementary school boys (Callan, 1968).

COLLEGE WOMEN. A trilevel bench is used with heights of 14, 17, and 20 inches. Twenty innings, divided into four phases, are used. In innings 1 to 5, a cadence of 24 steps per minute is used with a bench height of 14 inches. In innings 6 to 10, the cadence is 30 steps per minute with a bench height of 14 inches. In innings of 11 to 15, the cadence is 30 steps per minute using a bench height of 17 inches. In the final innings, 16 to 20, the cadence is 30 steps per minute with a bench height of 20 inches. Otherwise the test is similar to the OSU Test for college males, except that the test is terminated when the pulse rate reaches 28 or higher.

ELEMENTARY SCHOOL BOYS. This is an adaptation for boys in grades 4 through 6. This test is identical to the test for college males, with two exceptions—the tester must count the heart rate using a stethoscope and the test is terminated when the heart rate reaches 29 beats during the 10-second period.

THE QUEENS COLLEGE STEP TEST. A simplified version of the step test, developed at Queens College (Katch and McArdle, 1983), is useful for the quick screening of the CR function of college students. A bench height of 16¼ inches is used. This is the height of a bleacher step at Queens, thus allowing for mass testing. A metronome is used to monitor the stepping cadence, which is 88 steps per minute (22 complete step-ups) for women and 96 steps per minute (24 complete step-ups) for men. After a 15-second practice period, all examinees begin the test and continue for 3 minutes. At the end of 3 minutes the examinees are stopped. They are allowed 5 seconds to detect their pulse at the carotid artery. After 5 seconds examinees count their pulse rate for 15 seconds and multiply the

TABLE 11-14. *Percentile rankings for recovery heart rate and predicted maximal oxygen consumption for male and female college students**

Percentile ranking	Recovery HR, female	Predicted max $\dot{V}O_2$ (ml/kg · min)	Recovery HR, male	Predicted max $\dot{V}O_2$ (ml/kg · min)
100	128	42.2	120	60.9
95	140	40.0	124	59.3
90	148	38.5	128	57.6
85	152	37.7	136	54.2
80	156	37.0	140	52.5
75	158	36.6	144	50.9
70	160	36.3	148	49.2
65	162	35.9	149	48.8
60	163	35.7	152	47.5
55	164	35.5	154	46.7
50	166	35.1	156	45.8
45	168	34.8	160	44.1
40	170	34.4	162	43.3
35	171	34.2	164	42.5
30	172	34.0	166	41.6
25	176	33.3	168	40.8
20	180	32.6	172	39.1
15	182	32.2	176	37.4
10	184	31.8	178	36.6
5	196	29.6	184	34.1

*From Nutrition, Weight Control, and Exercise. By Klatch, F.I. and McArdle, W.D., 1983. ed. 2. By permission of Lea and Febiger.

FIG. 11-7. *Palpation of carotid artery to determine heart rate.*

value by 4. A table of percentile ranks and predicted maximal oxygen consumption for male and female students is shown in Table 11-14.

To determine test validity, scores on the Queens College Test were correlated with measures of max $\dot{V}O_2$ obtained during treadmill testing. Validity coefficients are $-.75$ for college women and $-.72$ for college men. These coefficients are negative since lower heart rates are associated with higher max $\dot{V}O_2$ values. The test is highly reliable, with coefficients of 0.92 reported for women and 0.89 for men.

A number of fitness tests require the determination of heart rate through palpation of the carotid artery in the neck. The correct positioning of the fingers is shown in Fig. 11-7. The pressure on the artery should be firm but light. Excessive pressure will distort the heart rate.

MEASURING HEALTH-RELATED FITNESS IN A LABORATORY SETTING
Cardiorespiratory function

The most desirable approach to determining cardiorespiratory function is to measure it *during* exercise. With this approach, changes in physiological parameters can be measured throughout the exercise cycle.

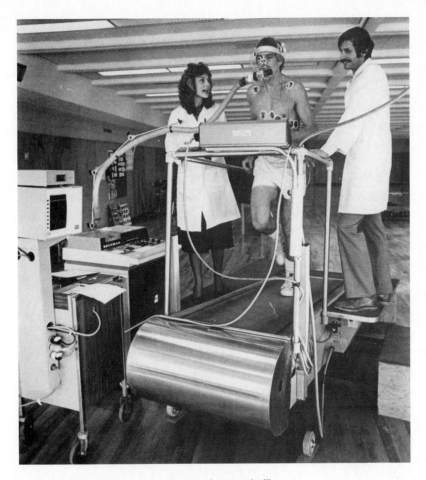

FIG. 11-8. *Maximal stress testing on the treadmill.*

MAXIMAL STRESS TESTING. To assess max $\dot{V}O_2$ directly, an individual's expired air is measured during exhaustive physical work. Typically, the examinee exercises on a bicycle ergometer or a motor-driven treadmill, as depicted in Fig. 11-8, although a stepping bench can also be used. The workload is gradually increased. On the treadmill this is accomplished by increasing the speed, raising the slope, or both. On the bicycle ergometer the workload is increased by increasing the friction on the flywheel. As the workload increases, oxygen consumption also increases. Throughout the test period exhaled air is collected using a portable spirometer, Douglas bags, or computerized instrumentation. When the examinee can no longer continue, the test is stopped. Maximal oxygen uptake is obtained when the increased workload is no longer accompanied by an increase in oxygen uptake.

Measuring time on the treadmill (between the initiation of the test to the point of exhaustion) can also be used to determine maximal stress. The time score is then used to predict oxygen uptake.

SUBMAXIMAL STRESS TESTING. Indirect methods of measuring CR function are frequently used in a laboratory setting. Since heart rate and oxygen uptake increase linearly with increases in workload, heart rate can be used to *predict* oxygen uptake. While these tests are not as accurate as a direct measure, they do not require the examinee to exercise to exhaustion.

BALKE TREADMILL TEST. Balke (1952) devised a submaximal test that measures the duration of exercise required to produce a heart rate of 180 beats per minute. The examinee walks on the treadmill at a constant speed, approximately 3.5 mph. At the end of each minute, the heart rate is taken and the slope of the treadmill is increased. Blood pressure is also usually recorded, as shown in Fig. 11-9. After the first minute and each succeeding minute of exercise, the slope is increased by a 1% grade. The equipment required to administer the test is a

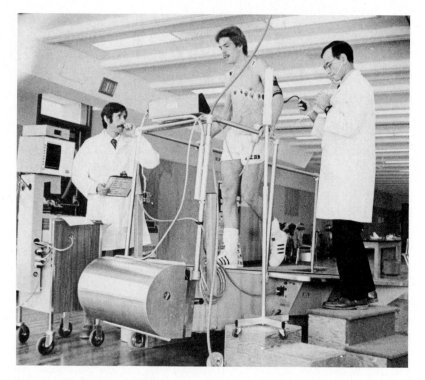

FIG. 11-9. Balke Treadmill Test.

treadmill, stopwatch, and electrocardiograph. The test score is the number of minutes required to attain a heart rate of 180. The test is highly reliable and valid, although an individual's performance can be affected by several possible sources of error, such as time of most recent meal, time of day, temperature, and emotional state. One of the notable advantages of the Balke test is its safety. Since the work is increased at a gradual pace, the subject's physiological changes can be monitored on a continual basis and the test can be stopped when appropriate for an individual subject.

A classification scale has been devised to interpret test scores of adult men:

Minutes to HR of 180	Classification
22-above	Excellent
20-21	Very good
18-19	Good
17	Average
15-16	Fair
13-14	Poor
12-below	Very poor

ASTRAND AND RYHMING TEST. A submaximal stress test on the bicycle ergometer was developed by Astrand and Ryhming (1954). The examinee pedals for 6 or more minutes at a set cadence, with a heart rate between 125 and 170 beats per minute. Baumgartner and Jackson (1982) recommend workloads of 600 kpm/min for college women and 800 kpm/min for college men. The test score must be corrected for subjects 30 years of age and older. Validity coefficients ranging from 0.33 to 0.872 have been reported. In both cases the test scores were compared with a direct measure of CR function.

A maximal stress test can also be conducted on the bicycle ergometer. This procedure, with expired gas collected in Douglas bags, is shown in Fig. 11-10.

PWC$_{170}$ TEST. The PWC$_{170}$ Test is administered on a bicycle ergometer, with 4 to 10 minutes of exercise at each workload. The subject's work capacity is the workload maintained up to a heart rate of 170. Heart rate is measured at each workload. Since PWC$_{170}$ is correlated with body size, a correction of the test score is necessary. The validity coefficients range from 0.57 to 0.88, when PWC$_{170}$ scores are correlated with max $\dot{V}O_2$ values. This test is often recommended for testing the physical work capacity of children.

Recommendations. For purposes of mass screening, Montoye (1978) recommends administering some form of a step test to individuals between the ages of 8 and 22. A step test may also be used to test healthy subjects ages 22 to 34, although a progressive test such as the Balke Test is preferred. For individuals over 35 years of age, Montoye notes the potential medical risks and recommends that a physician be present when fitness tests are administered.

FIG. 11-10. Maximal stress testing on the bicycle ergometer.

Measuring heart rate and collecting expired gas during maximal stress test on the bicycle ergometer.

Body composition

A direct measure of body composition can be made by chemical analysis. Until recently, making this analysis required a human cadaver. However, a new method of determining body composition using electrical waves passing through the wrists and ankles has now been developed. The most frequently used indirect measure in a laboratory setting is hydrostatic weighing.

HYDROSTATIC WEIGHING. Generally, the assessment of body composition involves determining the relative percentage of fat and muscle. Specific gravity, which reflects body density, is a better indicator of body composition than weight alone. Specific gravity equals the ratio of the density of a body to that of an equal volume of water. The specific gravity of human beings is usually estimated by weighing the body in water. The subject is immersed up to the neck in a specially built tank of water warmed to a comfortable temperature. The subject is instructed to hold his or her breath for 5 seconds, lower the head underwater, and expire the air forcefully, as depicted in Fig. 11-11. At this point the underwater weight of the subject is recorded. To ensure accurate results, 10 to 12 repeated weighings are recommended.

FIG. 11-11. *Assessment of body composition through underwater weighing.*
From Pollock, M.L., Schmidt, D.H., and Jackson A.S.

After the forceful expiration of air, some air remains in the lungs. This residual lung volume is measured before the underwater weighing; it must be used in calculating body density.

SUMMARY

The emphasis on health-related physical fitness is pervasive in both school and nonschool settings. A distinction must be made between measures of health-related fitness and measures of athletic performance. Although tests of athletic performance are often referred to as fitness measures, this label is a misnomer. The 50-yard dash, for example, does not measure health-related physical fitness; rather, it measures a certain fitness for athletic performance, in this case, speed. However, the term *fitness* is used loosely in this context. Health-related physical fitness can be measured in both laboratory and field settings with an acceptable degree of validity and reliability.

LEARNING EXPERIENCES

1. Practice marking the site for triceps skinfold measurement. Use a grease pencil to mark the site. Measure the site a number of times using a skinfold caliper. Try to obtain the same reading within 1 or 2 mm.
2. Visit a health club or fitness center in your community. Ask the manager or one of the instructors about the tests (if any) they administer to new clients. Request a copy of the form used to record test results to take back to your measurement class. Evaluate the testing program in light of desirable physical fitness objectives.
3. Practice checking your heart rate by palpating the carotid artery in your neck. Then practice on another person, both before and after exercise.
4. Administer the Health-Related Fitness Test to several of your fellow students. Study the instructions for test administration carefully before beginning. After you have completed the testing, write a short paper on the problems you encountered in administering the test and how you would alleviate these problems in future administrations of the test.

REFERENCES

American Alliance for Health, Physical Education, Recreation and Dance, 1980. AAHPERD Health-Related Physical Fitness Test Manual. Reston, Va.: AAHPERD.

American Association for Health, Physical Education, and Recreation. 1976. AAHPER Youth Fitness Test Manual. Washington, D.C.: AAHPERD.

Astrand, P.O., and Ryhming, I. 1954. A nomograph for calculation of aerobic capacity (physical fitness) from pulse rate during submaximal work. Journal of Applied Physiology 7:218-235.

Balke, B. 1952. Correlation of static and physical endurance. I. A test of physical performance based on the cardiovascular and respiratory response to gradually increased work. Air University, USAF School of Aviation Medicine, Project No. 21-32-004, Report No. 1, April.

Baumgartner, T.A., and Jackson, A.S. 1982. Measurement for Evaluation in Physical Education, ed. 2, Dubuque, Iowa: Wm C Brown Group.

Cureton, K.J. 1982. Distance running performance tests in children—what do they mean? Journal of Physical Education, Recreation and Dance 53(7):64-66.

Cureton, K.J., Boileau, R.A., Lohman, T.G., and Misner, J.E. 1977. Determinants of distance running performance in children: analysis of a path model. Research Quarterly 48:270-279.

Institute for Aerobics Research. 1983. FITNESSGRAM: Instructor Certification Manual. Reston, Va. and Dallas: AAHPERD and the Institute for Aerobics Research.

Katch, F.I., and McArdle, W.D. 1983. Nutrition, Weight Control, and Exercise, ed. 2, Philadelphia: Lea & Febiger.

Lohman, T.J. 1982. Measurement of body composition in children. Journal of Physical Education, Recreation and Dance 53(7):67-70.

Lohman, T.G., and Pollock, M.L. 1981. Which caliper? How much training? Journal of Physical Education, Recreation and Dance 52(1):27-29.

Montoye, H.J. 1978. An Introduction to Measurement in Physical Education. Boston: Allyn & Bacon, Inc.

Pate, R., and Corbin, C. 1981. Implications for curriculum. Journal of Physical Education, Recreation and Dance 52(1):36-38.

Pollock, M.L., and Blair, S.N. 1981. Exercise prescription. Journal of Physical Education, Recreation and Dance 52(1):30-35, 81.

Ross, J.G., and Gilbert, G.G. 1985. A summary of findings. Journal of Physical Education, Recreation and Dance 56(1):45-50.

ANNOTATED READINGS

Cooter, G.R. 1976. Who wants to be normal? Journal of Physical Education and Recreation 47:50.

Cites misuse of norms by doctors, physical educators, and weight-conscious people; notes that norms represent average characteristics; in the health-related professions, desirable standards rather than normative standards should be stressed; gives examples of misuse of norms in measuring physical fitness, weight, cholesterol, percent body fat, blood pressure, and other physical parameters.

Lacy, E., and Marshall, B. 1984. FITNESSGRAM: an answer to physical fitness improvement for school children. Journal of Physical Education, Recreation and Dance 55(1):18-19.

Describes the pilot program of FITNESSGRAM in Tulsa, Oklahoma; discusses the unique aspects of the FITNESSGRAM program in promoting physical fitness in the community.

Pate, R.R. 1978. Fitness testing with a realistic purpose. Journal of Physical Education and Recreation 49:47.

Notes that fitness testing may be popular for the wrong reasons when teachers fail to consider the purposes of these tests; suggests reassessing current beliefs in the proper role of fitness testing; discusses contributions of fitness testing and five objectives dealing with fitness testing.

Pate, R.R., Ross, J.G., Dotson, C.O., and Gilbert, G.G. 1985. The new norms: a comparison with the 1980 AAHPERD norms. Journal of Physical Education, Recreation and Dance 56(1):70-72.

A comparison of the norms developed from the National Children and Youth Fitness Study data with the 1980 norms developed for the AAHPERD Health-Related Physical Fitness Test; discussion of sampling approaches used in both studies.

Ross, J.G., Dotson, C.O., Gilbert, G.G., and Katz, S.J. 1985. Maturation and fitness test performance. Journal of Physical Education, Recreation and Dance **56**(1):67-69.

Provides a new perspective of developmental trends in fitness by examining test performance on five different dimensions of fitness; the common beliefs about the effects of age on fitness test performance were not verified by the data from the National Children and Youth Fitness Study.

Ross, J.G., Dotson, C.O., Gilbert, G.G., and Katz, S.J. 1985. New standards for fitness measurement. Journal of Physical Education, Recreation and Dance **56**(1):62-66.

Discusses the development of fitness norms (included in Appendix F) based on data from the National Children and Youth Fitness Study; includes tables of percentiles by age and sex for five fitness tests, consisting of the Health-Related Physical Fitness Test and a chin-ups test.

12

Tests of Athletic Performance-Related Physical Fitness

KEY WORDS   *Watch for these words as you read the following chapter:*

AAHPER Youth Fitness Test

athletic performance–related physical fitness

Flexed-Arm Hang Test

Fifty-Yard Dash Test

individually based norms

percentile norms

Pull-Ups Test

Sit-Ups Test

Shuttle Run Test

Standing Long Jump Test

systematic decrease in scores

systematic increase in scores

600-Yard Run

Every physical education teacher and exercise scientist knows that the physical fitness necessary to engage in sports and other forms of physical activity encompasses something more than health-related physical fitness. (For a discussion of the distinction between health-related physical fitness and athletic performance–related physical fitness, see Chapter 11.) Other aspects of fitness may be related to a specific sport or to a general factor found in a cluster of activities, referred to as **athletic performance–related physical fitness.** One example of this type of fitness is arm and shoulder girdle strength. There are many instances in which physical education teachers recognize the need to increase the arm and shoulder girdle strength of students. An optimal amount of strength may be needed so that each student can effectively handle his or her body weight in a gymnastics unit. Strength is highly specific to a body part; thus, there is no valid measure of overall strength. However, strength is not a component of health-related physical fitness, since it does not meet the criteria (see Chapter 11). A one-to-one relationship between arm and shoulder girdle strength, for example, and a positive health state does not exist. Nonetheless, a task-specific measure of strength might be used in a school or nonschool setting as a measure of athletic performance–related physical fitness. A person might also be motivated to develop strength in a generic sense, for example, general conditioning or body building. (For a discussion of the measurement of strength and endurance in greater detail, see Chapter 13.)

Soccer Test.

The standardized tests described in this chapter incorporate both health-related and athletic performance–related items and have been used on a large-scale basis for many years in the physical education field. As long as the reader understands the distinction between the two types of fitness, the inclusion of both types of items should not be confusing.

It bears repeating that the examinee's medical record should be checked before administering any type of fitness test. In a school setting these checks are usually routinely made before participation in physical education classes. Because of this procedure, little risk exists in administering a fitness test to a school-age child. In a nonschool setting care must be taken to see that the appropriate medical information is obtained for each client. If the client is over 35 years of age, a physician's permission should be obtained before the client is allowed to participate in vigorous physical activity. However, general medical information should be secured from a client of *any* age who joins a health or fitness club.

AAHPER YOUTH FITNESS TEST

The **AAHPER Youth Fitness Test** consists of six items, four of which measure athletic performance–related physical fitness: pull-ups (boys) or flexed-arm hang (girls), standing long jump, 50-yard dash, and shuttle run. The remaining two items—sit-ups and the options to the 600-yard run-walk and the 9-minute (or 1-mile) or 12-minute (or 1½ mile) run—measure health-related physical fitness. The 600-yard walk-run taps some unknown combination of both types of fitness. The Youth Fitness Test is now published by the American Alliance for Health, Physical Education, Recreation and Dance (AAHPERD), which is the national organization for our field of study. The most recent version of the test manual (AAHPER, 1976) contains test instructions, national norms for each item, and information on the award system for the test.

The first version of the Youth Fitness Test was published in 1958. Seven test items were included in the original battery, with each test judged to be a valid component of fitness. In 1963 Ponthieux and Barker studied the validity of the total battery by using a procedure known as factor analysis to determine the relationships between the seven test items. If the items clustered together under one factor, they would be considered measures of the same dimension of youth fitness. If each item were associated with a different factor, it would be interpreted as measuring seven different dimensions of youth fitness. Their analysis yielded three factors, which they labeled circulorespiratory endurance, gross body coordination, and muscular explosiveness. Three items clustered under the circulorespiratory endurance factor: pull-ups, sit-ups, and 600-yard run-walk. The shuttle run, standing long jump, and 50-yard dash clustered under the muscular explosiveness factor. The softball throw appeared alone under the gross body coordination factor. These results indicated that fewer than seven dimensions of youth fitness were being measured by the AAHPER Test.

Both the age and classification norms were revised (Hunsicker and Reiff, 1966) and published in the 1965 revision of the test manual. The classification norms were based on a combination of age, height, and weight. The normative data in the 1965 manual showed considerable improvement on most test items for boys and girls at almost every age level.

In 1975 the battery was revised:

1. The sit-up was changed from a straight-leg to a bent-knee position to provide a more accurate measure of strength of the abdominal muscles.
2. The softball throw was eliminated because it measured a specific skill to a large extent, whereas the primary purpose of the battery was to measure fitness.
3. The 600-yard walk-run was modified to include two optional runs: the 1-mile or 9-minute run for ages 10 to 12 or the 1½-mile or 12-minute run for children age 13 or older. The optional runs were recommended as valid substitutes in schools where extensive running is a regular part of the physical education program.

In 1976 a revised set of age norms was published, and the use of classification norms was dropped. The organization of the test battery and the development of national norms represent a significant contribution to the physical education field. The test is popular in many parts of the United States for a variety of reasons—the items are motivating to students and the award system enables the student to receive national recognition for his or her performance on the test. Furthermore, many value the measurement of a combination of health-related and athletic performance–related fitness. However, the test does not reflect a definition of health-related fitness that applies to all individuals, as does the Health-Related Physical Fitness Test. The Youth Fitness Test is not a test that would appeal in its entirety to older age groups in general. Questions have also been raised about the measurement characteristics of the test, in particular, the validity and reliability. In the test manual no validation procedures are described for the individual test items, except for a general statement of expert opinion regarding the important components of fitness. Reliability estimates for the various age groups on the battery items are not reported in the manual. However, studies of the Youth Fitness Test have been published in a variety of journals, and an effort has been made to incorporate this information into the test descriptions presented in the next section. Generally, these studies have reported that the items in the Youth Fitness Test have satisfactory reliability.

As described in Chapter 11, the Youth Fitness Test is endorsed by the President's Council on Physical Fitness and is a part of the FITNESSGRAM program. Either this test or the Health-Related Physical Fitness Test can be used with the FITNESSGRAM program. (See Chapter 11 for more information on this program.)

PULL-UPS (BOYS) AND FLEXED-ARM HANG (GIRLS)
(AAHPER Youth Fitness Test, 1976)

Test objective. To measure arm and shoulder girdle strength.

Description. To perform the **Pull-Ups Test,** the student begins by hanging from the bar using an overhand (palms outward) grip (see Figs. 12-1 and 12-2) with his legs and arms fully extended. The feet should not contact the floor. From the hanging position, the student raises his body using his arms until his chin is positioned over the bar. He then lowers his body to a full hang, the starting position. This task is repeated as many times as possible. One trial is allowed.

In the **Flexed-Arm Hang Test** two spotters should assist in administering the test, one in front and one in back of the girl. The height of the bar should be adjusted so that it is approximately equal to the standing height of the examinee. The correct position of the hands is depicted in Fig. 12-3 and 12-4. With the assistance of both spotters, the examinee lifts the girl's body off the floor until her chin is positioned above the bar, elbows flexed, and chest close to the bar. This position should be held as long as possible. One trial is allowed.

FIG. 12-1. *Equipment options for Pull-ups Test.*
From Youth Fitness Test Manual.

FIG. 12-2. *Starting position for Pull-ups Test.*
From Youth Fitness Test Manual.

FIG. 12-3. *Starting position for Flexed-Arm Hang Test.*
From Youth Fitness Test Manual.

FIG. 12-4. *Flexed-arm hang.*
From Youth Fitness Test Manual.

Test area. For the Pull-Ups Test the manual suggests that only space adequate for the equipment is needed. A doorway, a small area for an inclined ladder, or a separate bar unit would suffice. The Flexed-Arm Hang Test can be administered in the same space.

Equipment. Metal or wooden bar roughly 1½ inches in diameter (alternatives are a doorway gym bar, a piece of pipe, or an inclined ladder).

Scoring. The score for the Pull-Ups Test is the number of completed pull-ups to the nearest whole number. For the Flexed-Arm Hang Test, the score is the number of seconds to the nearest second the student holds the hanging position. There is no criterion time after which the test should be terminated. The student should maintain the position as long as possible.

Validity. No evidence of validity for either the Pull-Ups Test or the Flexed-Arm Hang Test is reported in the manual. Several educators and therapists have suggested that pull-ups might not be an adequate measure of arm strength. Berger and Medlin (1969) noted that using chin-ups as a measure of absolute strength is not valid because body weight is inversely related to the number of chin-ups performed. Thus, body weight must be taken into account. Kendall (1965) questioned the adequacy of pull-ups as a test because the test yields too many 0 scores. When many students receive scores of 0, the measure does not discriminate.

Considine (1973) analyzed selected upper body performance tasks as measures of strength. The criterion measure was an isokinetic dynamometer pull, designed to determine the amount of force exerted in foot-pounds at any given point throughout the range of motion. The correlations between this measure and both the flexed-arm hang and pull-ups were low, as were the relationships between the latter two measures and lean body mass. The isokinetic measure, however, was related to lean body mass. This analysis demonstrated the inability of pull-ups and the flexed-arm hang to provide an indicator of the full range of arm and shoulder girdle strength. It also suggested that body fatness, not total body weight, affected performance on both of these test items.

The muscular strength and endurance of the arms and shoulder girdle involve the ability to move or support one's body weight with the arms. Both strength and endurance are needed to execute the flexed-arm hang/pull-ups, but in varying degrees for different people. Performance on these tests is negatively correlated with body weight, presumably because of the relationship between the tests and body fatness. Verifying that *either* test measures strength and endurance is difficult. When the endurance tests dips and bench press were used to evaluate performance in body conditioning courses at the University of Houston, the correlation between the two tests was low, only 0.32. This indicates that the two tests measure different abilities. When a repetition bench press test was correlated with the maximum weight a student could lift (strength), the correlation was over 0.90 (Jackson and Smith, 1974).

MODIFIED PULL-UPS TEST. Baumgartner (1978) devised a *Modified Pull-Ups Test* for all ages and both sexes. This test appears to resolve many of the difficulties associated with other measures of arm and shoulder girdle strength-endurance, such as pull-ups and the flexed-arm hang. A special piece of equipment now available commercially is used. Baumgartner suggests that the parts required to construct the equipment can be purchased for approximately $50.

In the modified test the examinee performs pull-ups on an inclined board. An overhand grip is used, with hands placed shoulder width apart. Otherwise, the test is performed like the regular pull-ups test. All examinees, including elementary school girls and college women, were able to execute at least one pull-up; most performed four or more. Logical validity was claimed for the test. Only the data set for college women was substantial enough to estimate reliability and calculate norms. The intraclass correlation coefficient for one trial over 2 days was 0.91, reflecting highly acceptable test reliability.

Starting position for the Modified Pull-ups Test.

Up position for the Modified Pull-ups Test.

The equipment for the Modified Pull-Ups Test has recently been improved to make it safer (Baumgartner and others, 1984). Additional norms have also been developed for the test. For example, the 50th percentile for college males is 30 modified pull-ups; for college females, 11 modified pull-ups. Scores below 2 and above 60 are rare.

FLEXED-ARM HANG. Cotten and Marwitz (1969) studied the validity of the flexed-arm hang for girls by comparing performance on the AAHPER Youth Fitness Test with a pull-ups test and a modified flexed-arm hang test. Pull-ups were measured using the overhand grip and partial scores were given, up to 1 (0.25, 0.50, 0.75). The reliability of the pull-ups test was 0.89. The correlation between

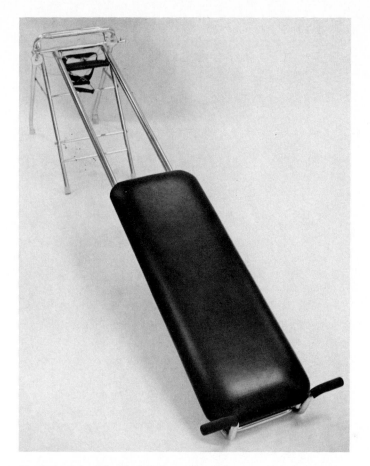

Equipment for Modified Pull-ups Test.

this test and the AAHPER Flexed-Arm Hang was 0.72. In the modified Flexed-Arm Hang Test developed by Cotten and Marwitz, the hanging position was identical to the AAHPER Test, but the stopwatch was allowed to run until the angle at the elbow became greater than 90 degrees. The reliability for the modified test was 0.83. The correlation between the modified hang and the pull-ups was 0.93. The results of this study indicate that the modified flexed-arm hang may be a better measure of the kind of arm strength measured by pull-ups than the standard flexed-arm hang test. However, this conclusion must be viewed with caution since the results were based on test scores of only 14 college women.

Reliability. Reliability estimates ranging from 0.74 to 0.89 have been reported for the two tests. A summary of the reliabilities of AAHPER Youth Fitness items is presented in Table 12-1.

TABLE 12-1. *Reliabilities for AAHPER Youth Fitness Test Items*

Item	Source	Sample	Trials (t) and Days (d)		Reliability coefficient
Pull-ups	Klesius (1968)	150 tenth-grade males	1t	2d	0.89, 0.82
Flexed-arm hang	Cotten and Marwitz (1969)	14 female P.E. majors	2t	1d	0.74
Standing long jump	Klesius (1968)	150 tenth-grade males	2t	1d	0.94, 0.93
	Fleishman (1964)	Adult males	2t		0.90
	Kane and Meredith (1952)	100 males, age 7	12t[a], 1d		0.97
		100 females, age 7	12t[a], 1d		0.98
		100 males, age 8	12t[a], 1d		0.98
		100 females, age 8	12t[a], 1d		0.98
		100 males, age 9	12t[a], 1d		0.99
		100 females, age 9	12t[a], 1d		0.98
		75 males, age 7	12t	2d[b]	0.83
		75 females, age 7	12t	2d[b]	0.86
50-yard dash	Baumgartner and Jackson (1970)	76 male P.E. majors	2t	1d	0.949[c]
	Klesius (1968)	150 tenth-grade males	2t	1d	0.86, 0.83
Softball throw	Klesius (1968)	150 tenth-grade males	2t	1d	0.93, 0.90
	Fleishman (1964)	adult males	2t		0.93
600-yard run-walk	Klesius (1968)	150 tenth-grade males	1t	2d	0.80, 0.80
	Wilgoose and others (1961)	70 junior high males	1t	2d	0.92
		70 junior high females	1t	2d	0.92
	Askew (1966)	71 senior high males	1t	2d	0.762
		46 senior high females	1t	2d	0.653
	Doolittle and Bigbee (1968)	9 ninth-grade males			0.92
Sit-ups	Klesius (1968)	150 tenth-grade males	1t	2d	0.57, 0.68
Shuttle run	Klesius (1968)	150 tenth-grade males	1t	2d	0.68, 0.75

[a]Best of 12 correlated with second-best.
[b]Best of 12 on one day correlated with best of 12 on second day.
[c]Intraclass correlation coefficient.

Norms. Norms are published in the test manual for ages 9 through 17+ and both genders. An abbreviated form of the tables of norms is presented in Table 12-2 and 12-3.

Comments. When administering the Youth Fitness Test, carefully monitor the alignment and positioning of the student's body. When the youth performs the Pull-Ups Test, his body must not swing during the execution of the movement. If the student begins swinging, the tester should check this by extending the arm across the front of the thighs. The examinee's body should remain ver-

TABLE 12-2. *Percentile rank norms for girls on the AAHPER flexed-arm hang test (in seconds)**

Percentile	Age							
	9-10	11	12	13	14	15	16	17+
95	42	39	33	34	35	36	31	34
75	18	20	18	16	21	18	15	17
50	9	10	9	8	9	9	7	8
25	3	3	3	3	3	4	3	3
5	0	0	0	0	0	0	0	0

*Modified from Youth Fitness Test Manual.

TABLE 12-3. *Percentile rank norms for boys on the AAHPER pull-ups test (number)**

Percentile	Age							
	9-10	11	12	13	14	15	16	17+
95	9	8	9	10	12	15	14	15
75	3	4	4	5	7	9	10	10
50	1	2	2	3	4	6	7	7
25	0	0	0	1	2	3	4	4
5	0	0	0	0	0	0	1	0

*Modified from Youth Fitness Test Manual.

tical during the pull-up. Neither raising the knees nor kicking the legs is permitted. In the Flexed-Arm Hang Test the stopwatch should be started as soon as the student is fully supporting herself in the hanging position. Stop the watch when her chin touches the bar, her head tilts backward to keep the chin above the bar, or her chin falls below the level of the bar.

Gabbard and his associates (1983) studied the effects of grip and forearm position on flexed-arm hang performance. Superior performance on the hang was obtained with the forearm supinated (palms turned inward) and the thumb over the bar. Their work demonstrates the need for standardizing both thumb and forearm positions in the flexed-arm hang test.

SIT-UPS (FLEXED LEG) (AAHPER Youth Fitness Test, 1976)

Test objectives. To measure abdominal strength.

Test description. In the **sit-ups test** the student assumes the starting position

FIG. 12-5. *Starting position for Flexed-leg Sit-up Test.*
From Youth Fitness Test Manual.

FIG. 12-6. *Flexed-leg sit-up.*
From Youth Fitness Test Manual.

lying on the back with knees bent, feet on the floor, and heels not more than 12 inches from the buttocks. The angle at the knees should be less than 90 degrees. The hands are clasped in back of the neck, with fingers intertwined, and the elbows are touching the test surface. A partner holds the feet, as shown in Figs. 12-5 and 12-6. On the signal *Ready, Go!* the student curls up to a sitting position, touching elbows to knees. This represents one sit-up. The student then curls down to the starting position with elbows touching the surface and continues executing as many sit-ups as possible in 60 seconds. At the signal *Stop!* the test ends. One trial is administered. Be precise in starting the stopwatch on the word *Go* and stopping it on the word *Stop*.

Test area. Any room with adequate space for testing students on the floor would be suitable. The test may also be administered out-of-doors.

Equipment. Stopwatch and floor mats.

Scoring. The score is the number of sit-ups correctly executed in 1 minute. An incorrect execution nullifies the count for that sit-up. No resting between sit-ups is permitted. The fingers must remain clasped behind the neck throughout the test. The elbows cannot be used to push the body off the floor. Both elbows should be brought forward as the sit-up is initiated. The elbows *must* touch the testing surface before beginning the next sit-up.

Validity. The validity of the Sit-ups Test has been discussed in Chapter 11. The position of the hands and arms in this version of the test has been criticized because students sometimes attempt to use the arms to thrust the body into a sitting position. In the Health-Related Physical Fitness Test the position of the arms and hands is modified so that the arms are crossed at the chest, with hands on opposite shoulders. This encourages maximum use of the abdominal muscles in initiating the curl up.

Reliability. Estimates of reliability, determined on a test-retest basis, range from 0.57 to 0.68. (See Table 12-1.)

Norms. Norms have been published for boys and girls ages 9 to 10 through 17+ in the AAHPER Youth Fitness Test Manual (AAHPER, 1976). An abbreviated form of the tables of norms is shown in Tables 12-4 and 12-5.

TABLE 12-4. *Percentile rank norms for boys on the AAHPER sit-ups test (number)**

Percentile	Age							
	9-10	11	12	13	14	15	16	17+
95	47	48	50	53	55	57	55	54
75	38	40	42	45	47	48	47	46
50	31	34	35	38	41	42	41	41
25	25	26	30	30	34	37	35	35
5	13	15	18	20	24	28	28	26

*Modified from Youth Fitness Test Manual.

TABLE 12-5. *Percentile rank norms for girls on the AAHPER sit-ups test (number)**

Percentile	Age							
	9-10	11	12	13	14	15	16	17+
95	45	43	44	45	45	45	43	45
75	34	35	36	36	37	36	35	35
50	27	29	29	30	30	31	30	30
25	21	22	24	23	24	25	24	25
5	10	9	13	15	16	15	15	14

*Modified from Youth Fitness Test Manual.

Comments. It is extremely important that the sit-up be performed properly. With knees bent, the curling motion should begin with the head, followed by the trunk. When returning to the starting position, the student should reverse the pattern. As a student fatigues, he or she may attempt to revert to a straight trunk sit-up. Partners should be instructed to observe the sit-up action closely, and stop the count when the curling pattern is no longer observed.

SHUTTLE RUN TEST (AAHPER Youth Fitness Test, 1976)

Test objective. To measure speed and change of direction.

Description. For the **shuttle run test** place two parallel lines on the floor 30 feet apart. Place two wooden blocks behind one of the lines, as shown in Fig. 12-7. The student starts from behind the other line. To start the test, use the signal *Ready, Go!* On the word *Go!* the student runs to the blocks, picks one up, runs back to the starting line, and places the block on the floor beyond the line. Then the student runs back, picks up the other block, and runs across the starting line as fast as possible. Start the stopwatch on the signal *Go* and stop it as the student crosses the starting line. Two trials are administered, with a rest in between.

FIG. 12-7. *Shuttle Run Test.*
From Youth Fitness Test Manual.

Test area. An area equivalent to the width of a volleyball court is suitable.

Equipment. Two blocks of wood, 2 inches by 2 inches by 4 inches, and a stopwatch. (If two stopwatches are available, or one with a split-second timer, two students can be tested at the same time.)

Scoring. The time of the better of two trials, recorded to the nearest tenth of a second, is the score.

Validity. No studies have been conducted on the validity of the shuttle run test; however, the nature of agility has been studied. Several investigators (Hilsendager, Strow, and Ackerman, 1969) attempted to improve agility by increasing speed and strength. They found that students who practiced specific agility items increased in agility more than those who practiced either speed or strength. Their study also showed that the so-called agility tests that have been published do not measure the same underlying ability. The test directions for the shuttle run test are more complex than those of other items in the battery. Furthermore, the test tends to be less familiar to students. If the student has not had sufficient practice on this test, the score may represent performance on a novel task rather than a test of agility.

Reliability. Reliability estimates, based on test-retest data, range from 0.68 to 0.75.

Norms. Normative data have been published for boys and girls ages 9 to 10 through 17+ in the AAHPER Youth Fitness Test Manual (AAHPER, 1976). An abbreviated form of the tables of norms is shown in Tables 12-6 and 12-7.

Comments. To eliminate the necessity of returning the blocks after each trial, start the trials alternatively, first from behind one line and then from behind the other. Students should wear sneakers or run barefooted. Marmis and colleagues (1969) studied the number of trials needed for a reliable test and concluded that three instead of two trials of the shuttle run test should be administered.

TABLE 12-6. *Percentile rank norms for girls on the shuttle run (in seconds and tenths)**

	Age							
Percentile	9-10	11	12	13	14	15	16	17+
95	10.2	10.0	9.9	9.9	9.7	9.9	10.0	9.6
75	11.1	10.8	10.8	10.5	10.3	10.4	10.6	10.4
50	11.8	11.5	11.4	11.2	11.0	11.0	11.2	11.1
25	12.5	12.1	12.0	12.0	12.0	11.8	12.0	12.0
5	14.3	14.0	13.3	13.2	13.1	13.3	13.7	14.0

*Modified from Youth Fitness Test Manual.

TABLE 12-7. *Percentile rank norms for boys on the shuttle run (in seconds and tenths)**

	Age							
Percentile	9-10	11	12	13	14	15	16	17+
95	10.0	9.7	9.6	9.3	8.9	8.9	8.6	8.6
75	10.6	10.4	10.2	10.0	9.6	9.4	9.3	9.2
50	11.2	10.9	10.7	10.4	10.1	9.9	9.9	9.8
25	12.0	11.5	11.4	11.0	10.7	10.4	10.5	10.4
5	13.1	12.9	12.4	12.4	11.9	11.7	11.9	11.7

*Modified from Youth Fitness Test Manual.

STANDING LONG JUMP (AAHPER Youth Fitness Test, 1976)

Test objective. To measure explosive leg power.

Description. In the **standing long jump test** the student stands behind the restraining line, with the feet several inches apart and the toes pointed straight ahead, as shown in Fig. 12-8. To get ready for the jump, the examinee should swing the arms backward and bend the knees. To execute the jump, the student should swing the arms forward, extend the knees, and jump forward as far as possible, attempting to land on the feet and to fall forward instead of backward if balance is lost. Three trials are taken.

Test area. The jump may be tested in an outdoor jumping pit or on a flat surface indoors or outdoors, with a 25 foot clearance.

Equipment. If testing takes place on a flat surface as opposed to a jumping pit, a mat is preferred; use a tape measure to determine the distance of the jump.

FIG. 12-8. *Standing Long Jump.*
From Youth Fitness Test Manual.

Scoring. Measure the distance from the restraining line to the heel or other part of the body that touched the floor closest to the restraining line. If the student falls backward and touches the testing surface with the hand, the distance is measured from the part of the hand closest to the restraining line to the line itself. Record the best of three trials in feet and inches to the nearest inch.

Validity. The standing long jump is generally accepted as an adequate measure of explosive power, although an element of timing exists in executing the jump that does not exist to the same extent for other measures of explosive power such as the vertical jump. The validity of this test might be improved by standardizing the directions for executing the jump.

Reliability. This item tends to be highly reliable, with reliability coefficients ranging from 0.83 to 0.99 reported in various studies.

Norms. National norms have been published for boys and girls, ages 9 to 10 through 17 + . An abbreviated form of the tables of norms is shown in Tables 12-8 and 12-9.

Comments. Be sure the student knows how to perform a jump off both feet, landing on both feet. Children who are not familiar with this procedure have been tested and their natural tendency is to jump off one foot. Of course, this invalidates the trial and valuable time must be spent in teaching the student how to execute the jump properly. If the test is administered indoors, tape the tape measure to the floor and stand to the side, noting the distance to the nearest inch after each jump. Marmis and colleagues (1969) studied the number of trials recommended by the test manual and concluded that only two trials of the standing long jump are needed.

TABLE 12-8. Percentile rank norms for boys on the standing long jump (in feet and inches)*

Percentile	Age							
	9-10	11	12	13	14	15	16	17+
95	6' 0"	6'2"	6' 6"	7'1"	7'6"	8'0"	8'2"	8'5"
75	5' 4"	5'7"	5'11"	6'3"	6'8"	7'2"	7'6"	7'9"
50	4'11"	5'2"	5' 5"	5'9"	6'2"	6'8"	7'0"	7'2"
25	4' 6"	4'8"	5' 0"	5'2"	5'6"	6'1"	6'6"	6'6"
5	3'10"	4'0"	4' 2"	4'4"	4'8"	5'2"	5'5"	5'3"

*Modified from Youth Fitness Test Manual.

TABLE 12-9. Percentile rank norms for girls on the standing long jump (in feet and inches)*

Percentile	Age							
	9-10	11	12	13	14	15	16	17+
95	5'10"	6' 0"	6' 2"	6'5"	6' 8"	6' 7"	6'6"	6' 9"
75	5' 2"	5' 4"	5' 6"	5'9"	5'11"	5'10"	5'9"	6' 0"
50	4' 8"	4'11"	5' 0"	5'3"	5' 4"	5' 5"	5'3"	5' 5"
25	4' 1"	4' 4"	4' 6"	4'9"	4'10"	4'11"	4'9"	4'11"
5	3' 5"	3' 8"	3'10"	4'0"	4' 0"	4' 2"	4'0"	4' 1"

*Modified from Youth Fitness Test Manual.

50-YARD DASH (AAHPER Youth Fitness Test, 1976)

Test objective. To measure speed.

Description. For the **50-yard dash test** the student assumes a standing start behind the restraining line. Use the commands "Are you ready?" and "Go!", timing the latter signal with a downward sweep of the arm. The student runs as fast as possible, without slowing down until he or she crosses the finish line. (See Fig. 12-9.) The stopwatch is started as the starter's arm reaches the downward position and is stopped as the finish line is crossed. Two trials are taken.

Test area. Usually administered outdoors, using any open area.

Equipment. One stopwatch is essential; using two watches or a split-second timer for simultaneous testing of two students is recommended.

Scoring. Record the time in seconds, to the nearest tenth of a second.

Validity. Performance on the 50-yard dash is a function of running efficiency as well as pure speed. The student must clearly understand that slowing down before reaching the finish line will invalidate the test.

FIG. 12-9. *50-Yard Dash.*
From Youth Fitness Test Manual.

Reliability. Reliability coefficients ranging from 0.83 to 0.95 have been reported. The 50-yard dash is a very reliable measure, but the greatest source of error occurs during the first 20 yards. The student requires time to build up to maximum speed. However, the test as a whole has satisfactory reliability. Only if finer discrimination is desired might the teacher consider timing only the last 30 yards of the dash as the student's score. Norms must then be developed for the modified test.

Norms. Norms have been published for boys and girls, ages 9 to 10 through 17+. An abbreviated form of the tables of norms is presented in Tables 12-10 and 12-11.

TABLE 12-10. *Percentile rank norms for girls on the 50-yard dash (in seconds and tenths of seconds)**

	Age							
Percentile	9-10	11	12	13	14	15	16	17+
95	7.4	7.3	7.0	6.9	6.8	6.9	7.0	6.8
75	8.0	7.9	7.6	7.4	7.3	7.4	7.5	7.4
50	8.6	8.3	8.1	8.0	7.8	7.8	7.9	7.9
25	9.1	9.0	8.7	8.5	8.3	8.2	8.3	8.4
5	10.3	10.0	10.0	10.0	9.6	9.2	9.3	9.5

*Modified from Youth Fitness Test Manual.

TABLE 12-11. *Percentile rank norms for boys on the 50-yard dash (in seconds and tenths of second)**

	Age							
Percentile	9-10	11	12	13	14	15	16	17+
95	7.3	7.1	6.8	6.5	6.2	6.0	6.0	5.9
75	7.8	7.6	7.4	7.0	6.8	6.5	6.5	6.3
50	8.2	8.0	7.8	7.5	7.2	6.9	6.7	6.6
25	8.9	8.6	8.3	8.0	7.7	7.3	7.0	7.0
5	9.9	9.5	9.5	9.0	8.8	8.0	7.7	7.9

*Modified from Youth Fitness Test Manual.

Comments. Require the students to practice starting the test with the maximal speed possible and continuing at the fastest pace possible until *past* the finish line. Motivation is always important in test administration but especially in tests of short duration.

600-YARD RUN (AAHPER Youth Fitness Test, 1976)

Test objective. To measure cardiorespiratory (CR) function.

Description. Instruct the student to use a standing start. Give the signal *Ready, Go!,* and start the stopwatch on the signal *Go!* The student begins running and continues running as fast as possible until he or she crosses the finish line. Although the examinee *may* walk during the test, it is not encouraged. One trial is taken.

Test area. A variety of open spaces is suitable. See the examples presented in Figs. 12-10 to 12-12.

FIG. 12-10. *Using football field for 600-Yard Run Test.*
From Youth Fitness Test Manual.

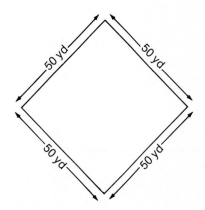

FIG. 12-11. *Using any open area for 600-Yard Run Test.*
From Youth Fitness Test Manual.

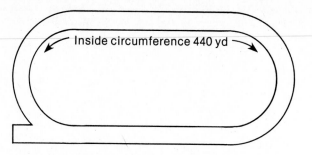

FIG. 12-12. *Using inside track for 600-Yard Run Test.*
From Youth Fitness Test Manual.

Equipment. A stopwatch.

Scoring. The time is recorded in minutes and seconds. A partner should be identified for each runner. As a runner crosses the finish line, the timer calls out the time. The partner either records the time or remembers it and reports it to the scorer.

Validity. When the 600-Yard Run has been correlated with a measure of max $\dot{V}O_2$, moderate correlations have resulted ranging from -0.27 to -0.71. This result means there is some relationship between the test and criterion measure, but the relationship is not substantial. As the walk-run scores improve (i.e., distance is run in a *shorter* time), the max $\dot{V}O_2$ scores also get better (i.e., scores are *higher*) for some subjects. However, this does not happen in all cases; thus the relationship is not very strong. The 600-yard run, then, may not be an adequate predictor of CR endurance. (See Chapter 11 for a more detailed treatment of this topic.) The options available for this test (1 mile or 9 minutes; 1½ mile or 12 minutes) have greater validity.

Reliability. Reliability coefficients ranging from 0.65 to 0.92 have been reported. In general, the estimates are high, suggesting that with proper motivation the test can be reliably administered.

Norms. Norms have been published for boys and girls, ages 9 to 10 through 17+. An abbreviated form of the tables of norms is shown in Tables 12-12 and 12-13.

Comments. Before administering any of the distance run tests, warm-up preparatory training is essential. The student should be instructed about proper pacing and running efficiency. A group of students may be tested at one time, each working with a partner. The student should not attempt to run as fast as possible but should run at a pace that can be maintained throughout the entire distance. However, this pace should be maintained at as fast a rate as possible during the test. As discussed previously, the 600-yard run is not the best field test of CR function. The optional tests, which consist of the longer distance runs,

TABLE 12-12. *Percentile rank norms for boys on the AAHPER 600-yard run (in minutes and seconds)**

	Age							
Percentile	9-10	11	12	13	14	15	16	17+
95	2:05	2:02	1:52	1:45	1:39	1:36	1:34	1:32
75	2:17	2:15	2:06	1:59	1:52	1:46	1:44	1:43
50	2:33	2:27	2:19	2:10	2:03	1:56	1:52	1:52
25	2:53	2:47	2:37	2:27	2:16	2:08	2:01	2:02
5	3:22	3:29	3:06	3:00	2:51	2:30	2:31	2:38

*Modified from Youth Fitness Test Manual.

TABLE 12-13. *Percentile rank norms for girls on the AAHPER 600-yard run (in minutes and seconds)**

	Age							
Percentile	9-10	11	12	13	14	15	16	17+
95	2:20	2:14	2:06	2:04	2:02	2:00	2:08	2:02
75	2:39	2:35	2:26	2:23	2:19	2:22	2:26	2:24
50	2:56	2:53	2:47	2:41	2:40	2:37	2:43	2:41
25	3:15	3:16	3:13	3:06	3:01	3:00	3:03	3:02
5	4:00	4:15	3:59	3:49	3:49	3:28	3:49	3:45

*Modified from Youth Fitness Test Manual.

are strongly recommended. Abbreviated forms of the tables of norms for longer distances are included in Chapter 11.

EXAMPLES OF OTHER TESTS

There are many versions of tests designed to measure physical fitness. In general, the older tests do not differentiate between health-related physical fitness and athletic performance–related physical fitness. Many of these tests include both types of items. As long as it is understood that both types of fitness are being measured, these tests can provide useful information on the fitness state of an individual.

Texas physical fitness–motor ability test

The Texas Test (1973) was one of the first to identify two types of fitness within one test battery. Recognizing the importance of health-related fitness, the Texas

Governor's Commission on Physical Fitness developed a test, usually classified as a motor fitness test, that includes two categories of motor performance—physical fitness and motor ability. Each category is further broken down into three components. An attractive feature of the test is that more than one measure is included for each component, allowing the tester to select the tests he or she wishes to administer. The ability to choose does not detract from the validity of the test, and it individualizes the process for the tester. However, if comparisons are to be made across classes or schools, the same tests must be used.

The six components and options for test selection follow:
1. Physical fitness components
    a. Muscular strength and endurance of arms and shoulder girdle
       Tests: Chin-ups, dips, 90-second flexed-arm hang
    b. Muscular strength and endurance of abdominal region
       Test: 2-minute bent-leg sit-ups
    c. CR endurance
       Tests: 12-minute run-walk, 9-minute run-walk (grades 4 through 6), 1½-mile run-walk, 1-mile run-walk (grades 4 through 6)
2. Motor ability components
    a. Running speed
       Tests: 50-yard timed sprint, 8-second run for distance
    b. Running agility
       Tests: Shuttle run for distance, zigzag run
    c. Explosive movement
       Tests: Vertical jump, standing long jump

Normative data are available for each test item. It is frequently desirable to administer this type of test at the beginning and end of the year. However, keep in mind that performance can change simply because the child has grown older. Also, the heavier child should not be penalized because of weight.

Manitoba Physical Fitness Performance Test

The province of Manitoba has taken leadership in Canada by developing the Manitoba Physical Fitness Performance Test (1977), which identifies desirable fitness and life-style objectives for Canadian schoolchildren and teachers. The test measures primarily the health-related fitness of youths ages 5 through 19. However, an agility item is included, which is a questionable measure of health-related fitness, according to the manual. Six items are included in the test battery:
1. One-Minute Speed Sit-Ups—to measure abdominal endurance
2. Sit and Reach—to measure flexibility
3. Flexed-Arm Hang—to measure upper body muscular endurance
4. Agility Run—to measure agility
5. Meter Run—to measure cardiovascular fitness

6. Skinfold Measurement—to measure subcutaneous body fat (biceps, triceps, subscapular, and suprailiac)

A fine test manual has been published for this battery. Although extensive technical material on reliability and validity is not included, the test descriptions are excellent. The manual also includes general guidelines for test administration, suggestions to improve performance, tables of percentile norms for students, and an excellent section on criterion-referenced standards for students, ages 5 through 19, and teachers, ages 20 to 60+! While the standards may be tentative and in need of further study, the Canadian test presents the first large-scale effort to identify performance standards in the fitness area for a large population of individuals.

ADMINISTRATION OF PHYSICAL FITNESS TESTS

Tests of motor performance are more complex to administer than most written tests. First, the examinee must understand the test instructions. Then he or she must be able to translate these instructions into the movements required by the test. Assume, for example, that John is taking a shuttle run test for the first time.

Test administrator.

On the first attempt he makes several errors. Perhaps he threw the block across the line instead of placing it on the floor, or maybe he forgot the number of times he should change directions. Did the errors occur because he did not understand the instructions or because he was unable to follow them? Before actual testing, John should see a demonstration of the test, first in slow motion and then at full speed. Then he should be allowed to move through the test slowly while the test administrator gives him cues on his movements. The test instructions can also be written on an index card and posted on a bulletin board in the gym. If a student has difficulty with the instructions, a review of the written instructions might be helpful. Finally, John should have the opportunity to practice the test at his maximum speed. *Now* John is ready to be tested. Remember that if John cannot perform the test properly, the trial must be thrown out and another taken. This is time-consuming and inefficient. The time taken in preparing examinees for the test is time well spent.

Preparation for testing

When fitness tests are administered, test users expect the student to perform at his or her maximum ability. If John had not received the preparation described previously, his agility would not be tested; rather, his ability to perform a *novel* task would be measured. This really is not the purpose of administering the shuttle run test. Although proper preparation for testing should be emphasized, it can be, on the other hand, carried to extremes. Requiring the student to practice the shuttle run test day after day as a part of the regular physical education program makes no sense. If practicing the shuttle run increases the student's agility, some practice is justifiable. However, other means of improving the student's agility are probably incorporated into the physical education program. This is an assumption since no valid measure of overall agility has been developed. Furthermore, it is more likely that agility is highly task-specific. This means that one's performance on the AAHPER Shuttle Run Test might not reflect how well (or poorly) one would perform on another agility test. Yet, it is still very popular in the physical education field to select a single test, such as the shuttle run, as a measure of a component of fitness (agility), assuming that this test measures one's "general" agility. This is not a fault of the test but rather of the test user who is making an erroneous assumption about the test.

Many practical matters should be considered in preparing examinees for a test. One such matter is the clothing worn for testing. In junior and senior high school where students are expected to bring appropriate clothes for their physical education class, this is not a problem. In the elementary school where special gym wear may not be required, the clothes worn on the day that fitness tests are to be administered can create problems. A wide variety of clothing is satisfactory, however, if the student is able to move freely. Tennis shoes should always be worn, whether testing takes place indoors or outdoors. Without them, it is unlikely that maximum performance can be achieved. No matter how hard one may try, running as fast as possible in leather-soled shoes is difficult, if not impossible. Although wearing various types of sports shoes is now quite common for students, these should not be worn in a gymnasium because of the dirt collected on the soles. Even for outdoor testing, the sports shoe worn on a daily basis may not be preferred, especially if the shoes are in poor condition. Removing the shoes during testing does not solve the problem; it merely creates a new one. For example, if a shuttle run is performed indoors with bare feet, the quick shift of directions can create enough friction between the floor and the bottoms of the feet to be painful and cause blisters. Simply be firm about having students bring proper shoes, instructing them well in advance of the testing day.

Because fitness testing is usually conducted on a mass testing basis, assistants are often needed. Students, teachers, parents, or other members of the community can be recruited as assistants. They should be thoroughly familiarized with the tests they will administer, which will not occur if they are simply given the test instructions to read. The following is a good rule of thumb to follow: *Preparing properly for testing always takes longer than you think it will!* Do not assume *anything*. Bring the assistants together for a practice session. Review and demonstrate the tests, giving each assistant experience in administering the tests or performing the assigned administrative task. Even when a test is administered year after year in a school, a brief review of procedures is essential. This is equally important in a nonschool setting where new clients are continually coming into the program and the same tests are administered frequently. A periodic check of testing procedures should take place. Provide all materials needed to administer and score the test, and be sure the assistants know how to use them.

In addition to training assistants, frequently equipment must be gathered or lines and targets must be placed for testing. Adequate time must be allowed for setting up the test, which can be very time-consuming. In fact, the amount of time required to set up a test is often the primary factor in deciding whether to use the test. This factor alone has prevented teachers from using some well-designed tests in physical education classes. If tape will be used for the lines or the target, take care of the taping ahead of time. If good quality tape is used, it will not damage the gymnasium floor and is durable enough that it will remain on the floor for several weeks. If a wall target is to be formed with tape, be sure the texture of the wall will support the tape. In preparing for a test session at the University of Wisconsin, two other teachers and I had to place tape high on the gymnasium wall to form targets for a wall volley test. This required climbing a 15-foot ladder, measuring the target dimensions, and placing the tape accordingly. Realizing this task needed to be completed before the testing session began, we went to the gymnasium between classes and put up the targets, placing them high on the wall according to the test instructions. For many years we had used a type of tape that adheres well to a variety of surfaces, so we used this tape to make the targets. When we returned later for the testing session, the tapes had lost their adhesiveness and were hanging in strips from the wall. Of course, it was not feasible to put up new targets; the testing session could not be completed on that day. The tape we used was excellent for the gymnasium floor, but totally inappropriate for the walls, which consisted of a different texture. It was, in reality, a different brand of tape than we had used in the past! Little problems like the adhesiveness of tape can ruin an entire testing session. Plan carefully for the testing session, and have an alternate strategy ready to put into operation for each possible problem.

Data processing of physical fitness test results

The process of administering fitness tests to a large group of people is itself an enormous task. Once the test scores have been recorded, the test user is faced with the job of analyzing them. There is no point in administering the tests if you do not use the results. Many school districts own a mainframe computer or a minicomputer or have access to one. Until recently, this provided the best mechanism for analyzing fitness data. It still is preferred when dealing with large data sets. For example, physical education teachers in Illinois have access to a computerized system for analyzing scores on the Health-Related Fitness Test. The results can be sent to Northern Illinois University, where the scores are fed into a computer and analyzed descriptively. The computer output containing the results of the analysis is then sent back to the school system. This procedure is also handled locally within a number of school systems around the country, generally when the system has access to a mainframe or minicomputer. Now the availability of the microcomputer opens up these services to virtually any professional in the country. In Chapter 22 a sample program to convert raw scores to T-scores is included. This is written more as an example for students than a program to be used by teachers, but it serves to exemplify the ease with which these types of programs can be made available to the teacher. Every teacher need not learn how to write programs; however, properly written programs can be easily used by any teacher. (See Chapters 21 and 22 for more information on microcomputers.)

Several microcomputer programs are available for summarizing data from fitness tests and for determining norms. The following programs can be purchased at modest prices:

To be used with the Youth Fitness Test:
President's Physical Fitness Program
Hartley Courseware, Inc.
Dimondale, MI 48821

To be used with the Health-Related Fitness Test for ages 7 through 12:
AAHPERD
1900 Association Drive
Reston, VA 22091
To be used with the Health-Related Fitness Test for ages 13 through 17+:
AAHPERD
1900 Association Drive
Reston, VA 22091

Number of trials

When a test is developed, information is always included on the number of trials to be administered. In this way the motor performance test differs significantly from the written test. The written test contains a number of test items, each different from the other. The motor performance test consists of one or more trials, each one exactly the same. There are reasons for this difference, of course. Repeating the same test item in a written test would make no sense. On the other hand, attempting to vary each trial on a motor performance test is non-sensical. Even though the examinee knows the next trial will be the same as the previous one, mental memory differs from motor memory in this context. This knowledge does not mean the trial will be performed the same way as the previous one, in spite of the examinee's effort to do so (or to change it if the previous performance was not satisfactory).

How, then, is the number of trials determined? The number is usually determined by finding out how many trials are needed for a *reliable* performance. Let's suppose that you are interested in developing a bowling test. You decide in advance that the test ought to have a reliability of at least 0.80. After compiling the test you decide to work with 10 trials as a starter. You administer the test to a group of students and determine that the reliability of the test is 0.92. This is above the target reliability, but you may decide to use the 10-trial test. However, maybe you could use fewer trials and still reach your target reliability. This has a significant practical advantage in that the test would require less time to administer. After experimenting with different numbers of trials, which can be done with a formula (see the discussion of the Spearman-Brown Prophecy formula in Chapter 6), you find that a five-trial test yields a reliability of 0.82. The test has been reduced by half, and it still has acceptable reliability! The main point is that the number of trials of a test is not determined arbitrarily. One cannot casually decide to use a different number of trials than the number recommended by the test developer. Let's say you are interested in a batting test for elementary school children. You find a test you like, but it requires 20 trials. You decide there is not sufficient time to administer a 20-trial test in class, but a 10-trial test could be administered. *Stop right here!* You cannot simply drop 10 trials from a test because you have no idea whether a 10-trial test is reliable. Unless you have time to determine the reliability of the shorter version of the test, you should not use it.

A lot of time and effort goes into determining the number of trials to include in a test. Surprisingly, many test users record the best trial out of the total number for the examinee's score. This practice is acceptable in a competitive situation or when the individual's best performance is of primary interest. In most physical education classes test users are interested in the student's true ability rather than the student's day-to-day fluctuations. In other words, teachers would like to assume there is some stability (or reliability) to the student's level of ability. Except for a few tests measuring maximum performance, one trial of a test is usually not adequate to reflect reliable performance.

To obtain a stable representation of performance, the effects of practice, learning, and fatigue must be eliminated. One way practice and learning are eliminated is to prepare the examinee properly, as described in the previous section. Practice trials are usually administered before the actual test for this reason. A good test developer will also plot the trial scores and examine them closely. If the trial scores systematically increase or decrease, obviously a reliable performance has not been obtained. Note the example presented in Fig. 12-13. Six trials of a test were plotted in this figure. Notice that the scores increase from Trials 1 to 2, 2 to 3, and 3 to 4; then the performance stabilizes. If this test were administered to a student, the test developer might recommend that six trials actually be administered but the average of only the last three trials be used for the student's score.

Baumgartner and Jackson (1970) computed reliabilities for tests having **systematic increases** or **systematic decreases** in trial scores. The trials causing the systematic changes were then dropped and reliabilities were estimated for the remaining trials. The standing long jump was one of the tests they studied. When six trials were administered to junior high school boys, their performance was stable on the first three trials, but dropped off systematically over the last three trials. Presumably, the boys in this age group began to fatigue after the third trial, as depicted in Fig. 12-14. Baumgartner and Jackson recommend that the test score be represented by the average of the first three trials. In this case only three trials must be administered. The reliability of the test under these conditions was reported as 0.96. When six trials of the same test were administered to high school boys, the scores increased systematically up to Trial 4 (as in Fig. 12-13) and then leveled off. Apparently a practice effect caused the change in scores. In this case administration of a six-trial test was recommended, using the average of the last three trials as the test score. The reliability of the three-trial test was 0.97. Of course, it would be best if enough practice trials could be administered before the test to obtain stable test trials. At the very least, when

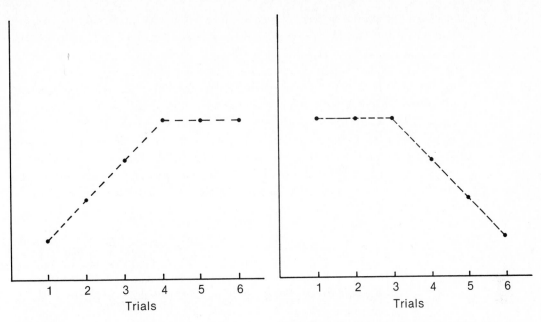

FIG. 12-13. *Systematic increase in the scores of trials 1 to 4.*

FIG. 12-14. *Systematic decrease in the scores of trials 4 to 6.*

administering a test with more than one trial, plot the trials on a piece of paper. Examine the plot for systematic changes. If they exist, you will have some evidence that performance is being affected by practice, learning, or fatigue. Nothing can be done about the score values at that point, but the test user may decide not to place much weight on the test results.

Use of norms

It is very helpful if norms have been published for the test you have administered, especially if you wish to determine the effectiveness of your program. To be used properly, norms should be available for the same age and gender as the individuals tested. Then any score can be compared with the same score in the table of **individually based norms.** For example, the AAHPER Youth Fitness Test Manual includes tables of **percentile norms.** A test score can be matched with the same score in the appropriate norms table, and the percentile corresponding with this score can be read from the table.

The norms should be used to determine the percentiles for scores of *individual students* only. Using tables of norms to interpret *group* data, although intuitively appealing, is not appropriate. For example, assume a physical educator has administered the Youth Fitness Test to a group of students. A mean and standard deviation is calculated for each test. The teacher refers to the tables of norms and then matches each mean with a score in the appropriate table. The percentile for each mean is then read from the table. The teacher would like to be able to say, for example, that performance on the long jump for this group of students falls at the 70th (or some other) percentile. This procedure is incorrect! The norms tables were developed on the basis of *individually based* norms. As Spray (1977) demonstrates, a group mean should not be compared with individually based norms since the variability of individual norms differs from the variability of group means. Thus, as shown in Fig. 12-15, the norm for the group mean is an *underestimate* if the class is above average and an *overestimate* if the class is below the average. The same situation occurs when the median is used.

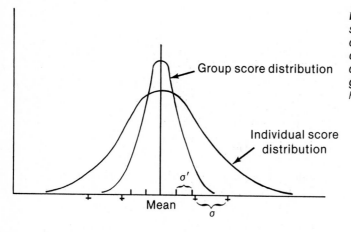

FIG. 12-15. *Distribution of individual scores versus mean scores (σ = one standard deviation unit for individual score distribution; σ' = one standard deviation unit for group score distribution). From Spray, J.A.*

Spray (1977) describes several ways of interpreting group averages when only individually based norms tables are available. In one approach the percentage of students receiving scores above the 50th percentile for the national norm group is identified for each test item. (For an example of this method, see Table 12-14.) This information could be very useful in evaluating a physical education program. Data for boys in all classes at each grade level were used in determining the percentages for the Waunakee group. Find the percentage of seventh grade boys scoring at or above the 50th percentile on the Sit-ups Test in Table 12-14. Since 85% of the boys performed more than 38 sit-ups, the number representing the 50th percentile for the national norm group, one could conclude that they have above-average abdominal and leg flexor strength. On the other hand, only 33.9% performed above the 50th percentile on the 50-yard dash, suggesting a need for modifications in the physical education instructional program.

TABLE 12-14. *Seventh- and Eighth-Grade Boys' AAHPER Fitness Test Results**

	Percent of students above the national 50th percentile
Eighth grade	
Shuttle run	88.6
600-yard run	77.5
Standing broad jump	72.3
Pull-ups	66.3
Sit-ups	65.2
50-yard dash	50.0
Seventh grade	
Shuttle run	87.6
Sit-ups	85.0
600-yard run	80.9
Standing broad jump	62.4
Pull-ups	58.0
50-yard dash	33.9

*From Table 1 in Spray, J.A.

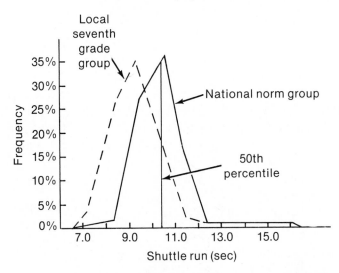

FIG. 12-16. *Thirteen-year-old boys national norm group versus seventh grade boys (Waunakee Jr. High School): shuttle run. The distributions appear to be positively skewed since a lower time implies a better performance on the shuttle run.*

From Spray, J.A.

A second alternative is to compare the distribution for the national norm group to the distribution of scores for a class. In Fig. 12-16, the distribution of scores on the Shuttle Run Test for all seventh-grade boys in a junior high school is compared with the distribution for the national norm group. A large portion of the distribution for the local group falls above the 50th percentile for the national group. In this case lower times on the shuttle run reflect better performance; therefore, the higher percentiles are located to the left of the 50th percentile. The same information is shown in Table 12-14 in tabular form.

TESTS OF PHYSICAL FITNESS KNOWLEDGE

Few tests of physical fitness knowledge are available to the physical education teacher. Mood (1971) prepared an extensively developed written test; two forms of this 60-item test are available. Ten content areas, including the physiological aspects of physical fitness, physical fitness programs, and nutritional aspects of fitness, are identified to describe the universe of content associated with physical fitness knowledge. Each area is weighted according to its degree of importance in the body of knowledge. In addition to describing the content validity of the test, Mood provides evidence of validity by examining the physical education grade-point averages of high and low scorers on the fitness test. High scorers tended to have higher grades in physical education courses. Furthermore, physical education majors obtained higher scores on the knowledge test than non-majors, and students with a background in physiology of exercise tended to be higher than those with no background. Test reliabilities ranged from 0.74 to 0.77. Since the test was developed over 10 years ago, a revision and update of the items would be appropriate.

SUMMARY

In this chapter tests of athletic performance-related physical fitness are discussed and differentiated from tests of health-related physical fitness, which are described in Chapter 11. A certain type of fitness unrelated to the performer's positive health state is required for participation in athletic events. This does not mean health-related fitness is unimportant to the athlete but rather that another type of fitness is required as well. However, while health-related fitness applies to the entire population of healthy individuals, athletic performance–related fitness is relevant primarily to persons performing in athletic events, including recreational participation as well as organized teams.

LEARNING EXPERIENCES

1. Administer the Youth Fitness Test in your class or to a class of children in a neighborhood school. Average the scores for each test. (If you are a female, use the test scores for the females in class. If you are a male, use only the male test scores. Do not combine the male and female data.) Since you cannot convert the class averages to percentiles using the tables of norms (Why can't you do this?) that have been published, how can you use the information in the tables to interpret your results? Interpret the results for all six tests.

2. Using one of the above data sets, calculate the z-score and T-score for each raw score in the group. If you need to review the formulas, see Chapter 5.

3. Write a short paper on the problems you encountered in administering the Youth Fitness Test. How could these problems be avoided in the future?

REFERENCES

American Alliance for Health, Physical Education and Recreation. 1976. Youth Fitness Test Manual. Washington, D.C.: AAHPER.

Askew, N.R. 1966. Reliability of the 600-yard run-walk at the secondary school level. Research Quarterly 37:451-454.

Baumgartner, T.A. 1978. Modified pull-up test. Research Quarterly 49:80-84.

Baumgartner, T.A., and others. 1984. Equipment improvements and additional norms for the modified pull-up test. Research Quarterly for Exercise and Sport 55(1):64-68.

Baumgartner, T.A., and Jackson, A.S. 1970. Measurement schedules for tests of motor performance. Research Quarterly 41:10-14.

Berger, R.A., and Medlin, R.L. 1969. Evaluation of Berger's 1-RM chin test for junior high males. Research Quarterly 40:460-463.

Burke, E.J. 1976. Validity of selected laboratory and field tests of physical working capacity. Research Quarterly 47:95-104.

Considine, W.J. 1973. An analysis of selected upper body tasks as measures of strength (abstract). AAHPER Research Section.

Cotten, D.J., and Marwitz, B. 1971. Relationship between two flexed-arm hangs and pull-ups for college women. Research Quarterly 40:415-416.

Doolittle, T.L., and Bigbee, R. 1968. The twelve-minute run-walk: a test of cardiorespiratory fitness of adolescent boys. Research Quarterly 39:491-495.

Falls, H.B., Ismail, A.H., and McLeod, D.F. 1966. Estimation of maximum oxygen uptake in adults from AAHPER Youth Fitness Test items. Research Quarterly 37:192-201.

Fleishman, E.A. 1964. The structure and measurement of physical fitness. Englewood Cliffs, N.J.: Prentice-Hall, Inc.

Gabbard, C., Gibbons, E., and Elledge, J. 1983. Effects of grip and forearm position on flexed arm hang performance. Research Quarterly for Exercise and Sport 54(2):198-199.

Hilsendager, D.R., Strow, M.H., and Ackerman, K.J. 1969. Comparison of speed, strength, and agility exercises in the development of agility. Research Quarterly 37:71-75.

Hunsicker, P., and Reiff, G. 1966. A survey and comparison of youth fitness 1958-1965. Journal of Health, Physical Education, and Recreation 37:22-25.

Jackson, A.S., and Baumgartner, T.A. 1969. Measurement schedules of sprint running. Research Quarterly 40:708-711.

Jackson, A.S., and Smith, L. March, 1974. The validation of an evaluation system for weight training, Unpublished study presented at the AAHPER Convention, Anaheim, Calif.

Kendall, F.P. 1965. A criticism of current tests and exercises for physical fitness. Journal of the American Physical Therapy Association 45:187-197.

Klesius, S.E. 1968. Reliability of the AAHPER Youth Fitness items and relative efficiency of the performance measures. Research Quarterly 39:801-811.

Manitoba Department of Education. 1977. Manitoba Physical Fitness Performance Test and fitness objectives. Manitoba: Department of Education.

Marmis, C., and others. 1969. Reliability of the multi-trial items of the AAHPER Youth Fitness Test. Research Quarterly 40:240-245.

Metz, K.F., and Alexander, J.F. 1970. An investigation of the relationship between maximum aerobic work capacity and physical fitness in twelve-to-fifteen year-old boys. Research Quarterly 41:75-81.

Mood, D. 1971. Test of physical fitness knowledge: construction, administration, and norms. Research Quarterly **42**:423-430.

Olree, H., and others. 1965. Evaluation of the AAHPER Youth Fitness Test. Journal of Sports Medicine and Physical Fitness **5**:67-71.

Ponthieux, N.A., and Barker, D.G. 1963. An analysis of the AAHPER Youth Fitness Test. Research Quarterly **34**:525-526.

Safrit, M.J. 1969. The physical performance of inner city children in Milwaukee, Wisconsin, Tech. Report. May 1969, University of Wisconsin, Milwaukee, Department of Physical Education.

Sigerseth, P.O. 1978. Flexibility. In H.J. Montoye, editor. An introduction to measurement in physical education. Boston: Allyn & Bacon, Inc.

Spray, J.A. 1977. Interpreting group or class performances using AAHPER Youth Fitness Test norms. Journal of Physical Education and Recreation **48**:56-57.

Texas Governor's Commission on Physical Fitness. 1973. Physical Fitness-Motor Ability Test. Austin, Texas: The Commission.

Wilgoose, C.E., Askew, N.R., and Askew, M.P. 1961. Reliability of the 600-yard run-walk at the junior high school level. Research Quarterly **32**:264-266.

ANNOTATED READINGS

Fragione, F.J. 1977. Integrating the "why" in measurement and evaluation. Journal of Physical Education and Recreation **48**:56.

Stresses the need for physical education teachers to emphasize the "why" of physical activity in their classes; demonstrates the point using an agility test, a step test, and a height-weight chart; adheres to belief that students must understand the reason for participating in various forms of activity to become physically educated.

Hunsicker, P., and Reiff, G. 1977. Youth fitness report: 1958-1965-1975. Journal of Physical Education and Recreation **48**:31-33.

Describes the large-scale studies of physical fitness using the Youth Fitness Test; reveals that little or no improvement took place from 1965 to 1975; compares both boys and girls in grades 5 through 12; samples selected from homerooms rather than from physical education classes.

Plowman, S.A., and Falls, H.B. 1978. AAHPER Youth Fitness Test revision. Journal of Physical Education and Recreation **49**:22-24.

Analyzes the Youth Fitness Test; discusses the rationale for revising the test; recommends a test that includes three components of health-related fitness—cardiorespiratory function, body composition, and musculoskeletal function.

Smith, C.D. 1972. Fitness testing: questions about how, why, and with what. Journal of Health, Physical Education, and Recreation **43**:37-38.

Suggests ways to approach physical fitness testing; stresses the importance of being open to evolving new ideas about fitness testing; includes an analysis of AAHPER Youth Fitness Test and what it measures; discusses the value of each test item.

Vincent, W.J., and Britten, S.D. 1980. Evaluation of the curl up. Journal of Physical Education and Recreation **51**(2):74-75.

Discusses the inappropriateness of the straight leg sit-up based on scientific evidence; suggests that the bent knee sit-up is also unacceptable and provides a rationale for this conclusion; recommends the curl up as an acceptable substitute; reports low reliabilities for the curl up test and notes several possible reasons for this unreliability.

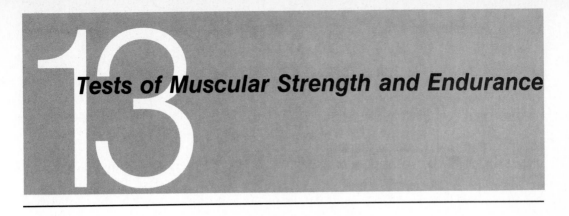

Tests of Muscular Strength and Endurance

KEY WORDS *Watch for these words as you read the following chapter:*

cable tensiometer	muscular endurance	static strength
dynamic strength	muscular strength	vertical jump
dynamometer	power	weight-training machine
electromechanical instrument		

Muscular strength and endurance can be measured in many ways, ranging from practical tests requiring little or no equipment to expensive machines. Practical tests can be used in settings that have neither the space nor the money for gym machines. On the other hand, an isokinetic machine such as the Cybex is expensive but provides the most accurate information about the strength of a particular muscle group. In this chapter the most expensive alternatives are dealt with only briefly. Examples of tests requiring use of weight-training machines such as Nautilus or Universal Gym equipment are included, as well as tests requiring the use of free weights or gymnastics equipment available in many schools.

Muscular strength is defined as "the maximum force or tension level that can be produced by the muscle group"; **muscular endurance** is "the ability of the muscle to maintain submaximum force levels for extended periods" (Heyward, 1984:4-5). Tests requiring continuous repetitions of a movement measure endurance, not strength. A true measure of strength determines the maximum amount of weight that can be moved in a single effort. However, a high relationship does exist between strength and endurance measures. Correlations of 0.90 and higher have been reported between one maximum effort and the number of submaximum repetitions (Baumgartner and Jackson, 1982). In this chapter examples of both strength and endurance tests are presented. Since the same tests are included under both topics in several cases, keep in mind the distinguishing factor between strength and endurance tests. When the test is used as a measure of strength, one repetition to maximum is executed. When it is used to measure endurance, a number of submaximum repetitions is performed.

There is no individual test of overall body strength or endurance. Both strength and endurance are specific to a muscle group. Thus a person may have strong legs and weak arms or strong abdominal muscles and a weak grip. Since muscle groups must be tested separately, choices about the most important muscle groups to be tested in a given setting must be made.

Body weight is often a factor in strength and endurance testing. When an examinee must move (lift or lower) his or her body in executing a strength or endurance test, standards are often varied according to weight. For instance, a higher score would be given to a lighter person who executes a given number of repetitions than to a heavier person executing the same number.

Several practical tests of strength and endurance can be found in Chapters 11 and 12. For example, the Sit-ups Test is a test of endurance of the abdominal muscles; the Pull-ups Test measures endurance of the arm and shoulder girdle muscles; and the Standing Long Jump Test is a measure of explosive leg power.

TECHNIQUES FOR MEASURING MUSCULAR STRENGTH AND ENDURANCE

When special equipment is required for strength and endurance testing, it is usually one of four types—dynamometers, cable tensiometers, weight-training machines, and electromechanical instruments. Many colleges and universities have all four types, but some public school systems do not have any. Weight-training machines are becoming common, however, in health and fitness clubs.

DYNAMOMETERS. A **dynamometer** is used to measure static strength and endurance. Strength and endurance may be referred to as static or dynamic. **Static strength** is the force exerted against an immovable resistance; **dynamic strength** is force exerted by a muscle group as a body part moves through space. Static strength is often called *isometric* strength; dynamic strength, *isotonic* strength.

Two types of dynamometers are available, one for handgrip and one for back and leg strength. The most common type is the hand or grip dynamometer shown in Fig. 13-1.

To use the hand dynamometer, adjust the handgrip size to fit the examinee's hand. The subject should stand, holding the dynamometer parallel to the side with the dial facing away from the body. To measure grip strength, the dynamometer should be squeezed as hard as possible without moving the arm. Three trials are recommended with a 1-minute rest between trials (Heyward, 1984).

When measuring grip endurance, the examinee should squeeze as hard as possible and continue squeezing for 60 seconds. Record the force in kilograms (kg) every 10 seconds. Relative endurance can be determined by dividing the final force by the initial force times 100. Instead of an all-out force, a submaximal force can be used, such as 50% of maximum. This is scored by the amount of time the submaximal force can be maintained.

CABLE TENSIOMETER. A **cable tensiometer** is used to assess static strength. This technique, which was developed and refined by Harrison Clarke (1966) at the University of Oregon, can be used to test 38 different muscle groups. A goniometer is used to position the cable at the proper angle. The tensiometer yields a score in pounds, with possible scores ranging from 0 to 400. An example of the use of the cable tensiometer is shown in Fig. 13-2.

WEIGHT-TRAINING MACHINES. Weight-training machines are designed to measure dynamic muscle strength and endurance. The most useful of these machines offers both constant and variable resistance. The force varies through the movement, which is better for overall strength and endurance. Many tests of dynamic strength measure maximum strength only at one point during the motion. A variable resistance machine can adjust the load so that maximum strength is being measured during several phases of the movement; however, measuring maximum contraction throughout the movement on these machines is not possible.

FIG. 13-1. *Hand dynamometer.*

FIG. 13-2. *Cable tensiometer.*

FIG. 13-3. Cybex II.

ELECTROMECHANICAL INSTRUMENTS. Electromechanical instruments measure static and dynamic strength, endurance, and power. A well-known example is the Cybex II, depicted in Fig. 13-3. When this machine is used, the maximum contraction of a muscle group is measured at a constant speed throughout the entire range of the movement.

EXAMPLES OF STRENGTH TESTS

When strength measurement is being discussed, the term *1-RM* is often used, meaning *one repetition maximum.* This method, used to test a variety of muscle groups, such as those used in the bench press, standing press, arm curl, and leg press, is described first, followed by other techniques requiring less expensive equipment.

THE 1-RM TEST

Test objective. To measure dynamic strength; to measure the maximum weight lifted in 1-RM.

Description. Determine the 1-RM value by trial and error. Start with a weight the examinee can lift. After a successful trial, allow the examinee to rest for 2 to 3 minutes. Increase the weight by 5 to 10 pounds, and take another trial.

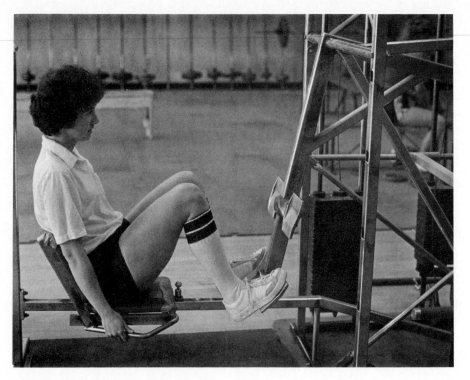

FIG. 13-4. *Leg press with knees flexed.*

Allow for resting, then continue with the same pattern until the examinee can no longer execute a successful trial.

   As an example, to test the leg extensors, seat the subject with hips and knees flexed, holding onto the chair rung with the hands. (See Figs. 13-4 and 13-5.) Adjust the seat to standardize the knee angle at approximately 120 degrees. The weights are lifted by fully extending the legs. To determine the maximum weight, refer to the previous paragraph.

   Test area. A small, multipurpose room.

   Equipment. A weight-training machine and scorecards.

   Scoring. A direct relationship exists between body weight and weight lifted. All other factors being equal, heavier people can lift heavier weights. Thus the test score—the maximum weight that can be lifted—should be interpreted considering the person's weight.

   Validity. Logical validity.

   Reliability. Can be expected to be very high, since an all-out effort is being measured.

   Norms. See Table 13-1 for norms based on gender and body weight.

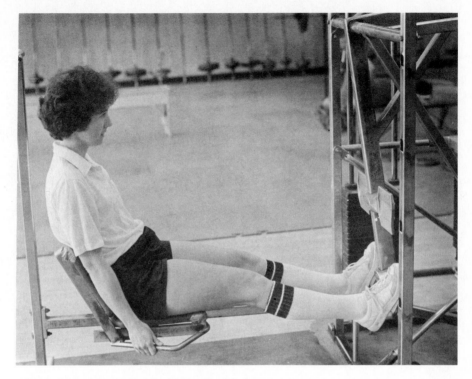

FIG. 13-5. *Leg press with legs fully extended.*

TABLE 13-1. *Optimal strength values for various body weights (based on the 1-RM Test)*†‡*

Body weight	Bench press		Standing press		Curl		Leg press	
	Men	Women	Men	Women	Men	Women	Men	Women
80	80	56	53	37	40	28	160	112
100	100	70	67	47	50	35	200	140
120	120	84	80	56	60	42	240	168
140	140	98	93	65	70	49	280	196
160	160	112	107	75	80	56	320	224
180	180	126	120	84	90	63	360	252
200	200	140	133	93	100	70	400	280
220	220	154	147	103	110	77	440	308
240	240	168	160	112	120	84	480	336

*From Pollock, M.L., and others.
†Data collected on Universal Gym apparatus. Information collected on other apparatus could modify results.
‡Data expressed in pounds.

FIG. 13-6. *Bench press with arms flexed.*

FIG. 13-7. *Bench press with arms extended.*

TABLE 13-2. *Strength-to-body weight ratios for selected dynamic strength tests*†*

			Men			
Bench press	Arm curl	Lateral pull-down	Leg press	Leg extension	Leg curl	Points
1.50	0.70	1.20	3.00	0.80	0.70	10
1.40	0.65	1.15	2.80	0.75	0.65	9
1.30	0.60	1.10	2.60	0.70	0.60	8
1.20	0.55	1.05	2.40	0.65	0.55	7
1.10	0.50	1.00	2.20	0.60	0.50	6
1.00	0.45	0.95	2.00	0.55	0.45	5
0.90	0.40	0.90	1.80	0.50	0.40	4
0.80	0.35	0.85	1.60	0.45	0.35	3
0.70	0.30	0.80	1.40	0.40	0.30	2
0.60	0.25	0.75	1.20	0.35	0.25	1
			Women			
0.90	0.50	0.85	2.70	0.70	0.60	10
0.85	0.45	0.80	2.50	0.65	0.55	9
0.80	0.42	0.75	2.30	0.60	0.52	8
0.70	0.38	0.73	2.10	0.55	0.50	7
0.65	0.35	0.70	2.00	0.52	0.45	6
0.60	0.32	0.65	1.80	0.50	0.40	5
0.55	0.28	0.63	1.60	0.45	0.35	4
0.50	0.25	0.60	1.40	0.40	0.30	3
0.45	0.21	0.55	1.20	0.35	0.25	2
0.35	0.18	0.50	1.00	0.30	0.20	1

Total points	Strength fitness category†
48-60	Excellent
37-47	Good
25-36	Average
13-24	Fair
0-12	Poor

*From Heyward, V.H.
†Based on data compiled by author for 250 college-age men and women.

Comments. Another way of evaluating dynamic strength is to express 1-RM as a percentage of body weight. Table 13-2 is used to determine the score. For example, a 140-pound woman who bench presses 100 pounds has a strength-to-body weight ratio of 0.71. (See Figs. 13-6 and 13-7.) Referring to the closest ratio (0.70) in Table 13-2, the score on the bench press test is 7.

If no weight-training machine is available, free weights can be used. (See Figs. 13-8 and 13-9.) Select a 5- to 6-foot–long weight bar and a variety of weight plates. A test-retest reliability coefficient of 0.93 was reported for the free weight version of the test (Johnson, 1966).

FIG. 13-8. Bench press using free weights, with arms flexed.

FIG. 13-9. Bench press using free weights, with arms extended.

BENCH SQUAT TEST (Johnson, 1966)

Test objective. To measure leg and back strength.

Description. Use two assistants to handle the weight bar. The examinee should sit near the edge of the chair or bench. The assistants should place the bar on the shoulders and behind the neck of the subject. With feet a comfortable distance apart, the examinee should grasp the bar firmly and lower the body to a sitting position on the chair or bench. Using a smooth movement, the examinee stands again. Two trials may be taken. The weight can be adjusted before the second trial.

Test area. A small, multipurpose room.

Equipment. Bench or chair, 15 to 17 inches in height; weight bar 5 to 6 feet long; sufficient assortment of weight plates; and a thick towel to provide padding at the base of the neck where the bar will be placed.

Scoring. Total weight of the barbell lifted in the maximum repetition divided by body weight.

Validity. Face validity.

FIG. 13-10 *Squat test—bar lifted off pins.*

FIG. 13-11. Squat test—body lowered.

Reliability. $r_{xx'} = 0.95$, test-retest.

Norms. Norms have been developed for college men (see Johnson and Nelson, 1974).

Comments. This test can be used with females as well as males. Careful spotting is required by the two assistants, in case the examinee loses control of the bar or begins to fall. Be sure the examinee sits on the edge of the chair or bench rather than farther back. Adjusting the height of the bench or chair may improve the testing conditions.

Although strength and endurance are highly correlated, the use of continuous repetitions of a leg movement is not recommended (Baumgartner and Jackson, 1982). Some subjects can continue indefinitely; thus, the development of a valid table of norms is a problem.

Because of the potential danger to the spine in executing a squat test requiring the examinee to sit down on a bench, use of the standard equipment shown in Figs. 13-10 and 13-11 is recommended. The subject lifts the bar off the pins in the support poles, rests the bar on the shoulders, and lowers the body in the squat position until the tape adhered to the support poles is broken. The lower pins are a safety feature, in case the subject drops the bar.

PULL-UPS TEST

The Pull-ups Test (see Figs. 13-12 and 13-13) is used to measure arm and shoulder girdle endurance. (See Chapter 12.) It is recommended for males age 10 and older. Although it is often referred to as a strength test, it is more accurately classified as an endurance test.

Johnson (1966) developed a version of the pull-ups test measuring maximum effort on one repetition. In addition to the usual equipment, weight plates of 2½, 5, 10, and 25 pounds must be available. A rope or strap should be used to secure the weight to the waist of the subject. Actually, the weight can hang in back of the subject, secured to a strap around the waist.

FIG. 13-12. *Pull-ups Test—body extended.*

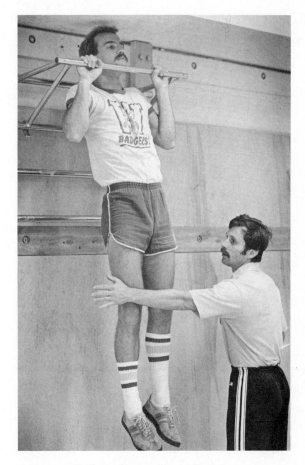

FIG. 13-13. *Pull-ups Test—elbows flexed.*

The examinee stands on a chair and grasps the chinning bar. The chair is removed, and the subject assumes a straight-arm hang. One pull-up is performed; the chair is replaced and he lowers himself to the chair. A second trial is taken, if desired. The weight may be adjusted before the second trial. The score is the amount of extra weight lifted in the best of two trials divided by body weight. A score of 0 is given to any subject who cannot complete the pull-up with more than his own body weight.

A reliability coefficient of 0.99 was reported (Johnson, 1966); otherwise, the test description is similar to that in Chapter 12.

SIT-UPS TEST

This test is almost identical to a repeated sit-ups test, except only one repetition is executed. A weight plate should be held behind the neck. A dumbbell or barbell can also be used. The score is the maximum number of pounds lifted in a single repetition.

EXAMPLES OF ENDURANCE TESTS
LATERAL PULL-DOWN (Jackson and Smith, 1974)

Test objective. To measure arm strength; to execute repeated lifts using arm flexors.

Description. Select a weight that can be pulled down at least once by everyone in the group. The examinee assumes a kneeling position on the floor, grasping the bar on the handle grips, as shown in Fig. 13-14. For one repetition, the examinee pulls the bar down behind the head until it touches the upper back at shoulder level. (See Fig. 13-15.) The weight is then returned to the starting position, avoiding jerky movements. The knees and lower legs must remain on the floor during the return movements. Use a 3-second cadence for each repetition. Note the way in which a spotter is used in this test. The examinee can be asked to touch the spotter's hands with the bar to complete the pull-down. The use of a spotter is especially important if a 1-RM test is being administered.

Test area and equipment. Identical to those described in the Bench Press Test.

Scoring, validity, reliability, and norms. Identical to those described in the Bench Press Test.

The bar can also be pulled down to the front of the body, as shown in Figs. 13-16 and 13-17. Note that the hands are placed much closer together on the bar. A different muscle group is used in this pull-down action.

Comments. Instead of using the same weight for everyone, the test can be individualized by using a weight that requires a percentage of maximum strength

FIG. 13-14. *Lateral pull-down—bar properly grasped.*

FIG. 13-15. *Lateral pull-down—bar touching upper back.*

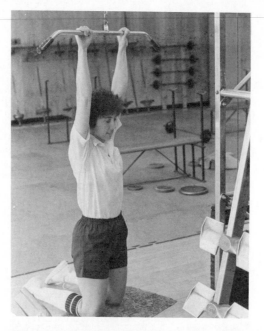

FIG. 13-16. *Alternate pull-down—bar properly grasped.*

FIG. 13-17. *Alternate pull-down—bar pulled in front of body.*

to be lifted. Pollock and associates (1978) recommend using a weight that is 70% of the 1-RM value for each exercise.

BENCH PRESS (Jackson and Smith, 1974)

Test objective. To measure arm strength by lifting a constant weight load repeatedly until exhausted.

Description. The weight load is constant for everyone in the group. The examinee assumes a back-lying position on the bench, similar to the position shown in Figs. 13-6 and 13-7, except that the feet must be flat on the floor. Use a weight load that can be lifted at least once by all examinees in the group. For example, a weight load of 110 pounds is recommended for male college freshmen.

The back should rest flat on the bench. The handles are grasped with both hands, placed farther apart than the shoulders. The weight is lifted upward until the arms are fully extended, then lowered until the weights touch the weights beneath them. The weights should not be dropped or slammed. If free weights are used, the bar should be lowered to the chest.

Continue with repetitions of the same movement on a 3-second cadence. The examinee should not be allowed to begin a new repetition until the beginning of a new 3-second interval.

Test area. A small, multipurpose room.

Equipment. A weight-training machine or free weights, metronome or tape with recording of cadence, and scorecards.

Scoring. The score is the number of repetitions completed. The test is ended when an examinee can no longer execute a repetition correctly or maintain the proper cadence.

Validity. Logical, as an endurance measure; concurrent, as a strength measure—high correlation with the maximum weight lifted with one repetition $(r_{xy} > 0.90)$.

Reliability. Not reported, but can be expected to be high if examinees are motivated to maximum performance.

Norms. Available for college men in original source.

Comments. Although this is a measure of muscular endurance, the authors believe the test can be used as a measure of strength since it is highly correlated with 1-RM.

ARM CURL (Jackson and Smith, 1974)

Test objective. To measure arm strength; to execute repeated curls using arm flexors.

Description. Before beginning the test, the examinee must first be stabilized by standing with head, shoulders, and buttocks against a wall. The feet, placed

FIG. 13-18. *Arm curl with arms extended.*

12 to 15 inches from the wall, are used to brace the back. To ensure that this position is maintained during exercise, the test developers recommend placing a sheet of paper behind the buttocks. The paper must remain pinned against the wall throughout the test. When the paper falls, the test is terminated.

To administer this test as described, the weight-training unit must be positioned close to a wall. Obviously, this may not be possible in many settings. If it is not possible, the standard curl shown in Figs. 13-18 and 13-19 may be used. If the hips are thrust forward during the repetitions, the test should be terminated. Only the arms should move during this test.

The examinee should begin with arms fully extended. In this position the

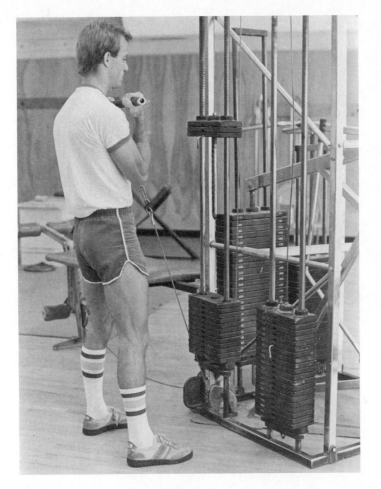

FIG. 13-19. Arm curl with arms flexed.

exercise weight should be suspended slightly above the remaining weights. The examinee should flex the arms fully, touch the bar to the chin, and fully extend the arms again. A 3-second cadence for each repetition is used.

This test can also be administered using free weights, as shown in Figs. 13-20 and 13-21. Note the equipment used to stabilize the examinee. This prevents any other body part from being used to assist in executing the curl.

Test area and equipment. Identical to those described in the Bench Press Test.

Scoring, validity, reliability, and norms. Identical to those described in the Bench Press Test.

FIG. 13-20. *Arm curl using free weights, arms extended.*

FIG. 13-21. *Arm curl using free weights, arms flexed.*

SQUAT THRUST TEST (Burpee, R.H.)

Test objective. To measure the general muscular endurance of the body.

Description. The examinee stands erect, with arms hanging at the side. At the signal *Ready, Go!* a squat position is assumed with hands on the floor. Then the body is extended fully, as shown in Fig. 13-22. The examinee returns to the squat position and then to the standing position. The procedure is repeated as rapidly as possible for 10 seconds. On the signal *Stop!* the test ends. Three trials are taken.

Test area. Small room with smooth floor surface.

FIG. 13-22. *Squat thrust.*

Equipment. Stopwatch and scorecards.

Scoring. Score 1 point for each completed squat thrust. Each quarter movement is given $\frac{1}{4}$ point. The test score is the best of three trials.

Validity. $r_{xy} = 0.55$, reported by C.H. McCloy.

Reliability. $r_{xx'} = 0.92$, reported by C.H. McCloy.

Comments. A large group of examinees can be tested at the same time. Each examinee should work with a partner, who counts the number of squat thrusts. Careful attention should be paid to the positions assumed during the squat thrust. In particular, be sure the body is fully extended at position No. 2. Instruct examinees on the correct procedure for executing this movement before the actual test.

OTHER APPROACHES TO ENDURANCE TESTING. A number of other practical approaches to endurance testing have been reported in the literature. Among the more popular items are push-ups, used to measure arm and shoulder girdle endurance. (See Figs. 13-23 and 13-24.) The problem with this test is that, like pull-ups, some examinees will not be able to execute even one. Thus it is not a discriminating measure for some groups.

Modified push-ups may be used as an alternative test for female examinees. These push-ups are performed with the knees touching the floor instead of the feet, as in the full-length push-up. This test is depicted in Figs. 13-25 and 13-26.

If gymnastics equipment is available, the parallel bars can be used to test repeated executions of the dip. The parallel bars on a weight-training machine can also be used for this test. (See Figs. 13-27 and 13-28.) The dip is performed by lowering the body until the elbow forms a 90-degree angle. A simpler version of endurance testing using the dip is a modified test using a single bar. The lower bar of the uneven bars can be used for this purpose. The body and arms are fully extended on the bar. The dip is performed by lowering the body on the bar until the elbows are at right angles. Then full extension again takes place.

POWER TESTING

Power is the ability to generate maximum force in a minimum amount of time. Several practical tests of explosive power are quite popular in the physical education field. Two examples are the standing long jump, described in Chapter 12, and the Vertical Jump Test, described below.

VERTICAL JUMP TEST (Sargent, 1921)

Test objective. To measure the explosive power of the leg extensors.

Description. For the **vertical jump** the examinee stands with the dominant arm extended, as shown in Fig. 13-29, holding a piece of chalk to mark the wall. The feet are flat on the floor. The examinee should reach as high as possible,

Text continued on p. 325.

FIG. 13-23. Push-up with arms flexed.

FIG. 13-24. Push-up with arms extended.

FIG. 13-25. *Modified push-up with arms flexed.*

FIG. 13-26. *Modified push-up with arms extended.*

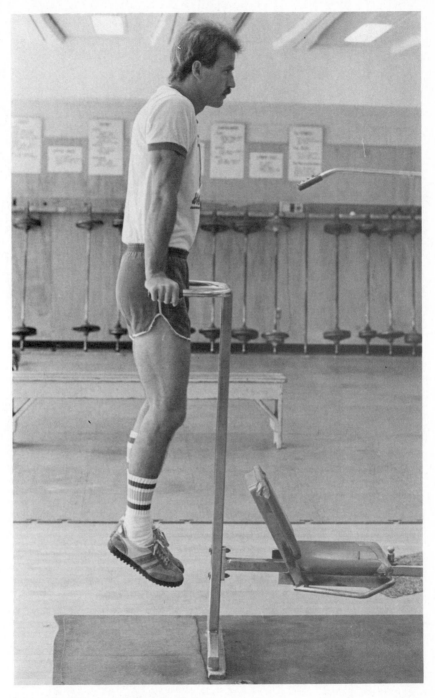

FIG. 13-27. *Dip—arms fully extended.*

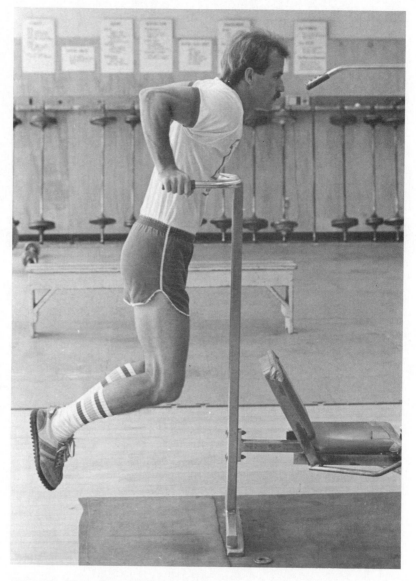

FIG. 13-28. *Dip—elbow at 90-degree angle.*

FIG. 13-29. Vertical jump.

making a chalk mark on the measuring board. Then a preparatory position should be taken for the jump, which is a squat position with feet still flat on the floor. The subject should jump as high as possible, touching the board again with the chalk at the height of the jump. Three trials are taken.

Test area. Small room with sufficient wall space.

Equipment. Measuring board (self-constructed or purchased commercially), marked in half-inches, attached to the wall (if possible, the board should be attached 6 inches out from the wall so the examinee does not scrape the arm or side of the body while jumping), chalk and damp cloth (or eraser), yardstick, and scorecards.

Scoring. For each trial the score is the distance between the two chalk marks, measured to the nearest half-inch. The test score is the best trial score.

Validity. $r_{xy} = 0.78$, using a criterion test of four power events in track and field.

Reliability. $r_{xx'} = 0.93$; objectivity coefficients $>.90$ have been reported.

Norms. Norms for the vertical jump test are included in Table 13-3.

TABLE 13-3. Vertical Jump scoring table*†

	100	90	80	70	60	50	40	30	20	10	0
Boys and girls 9-10-11	16	15	14	12	11	10	9	7	4	2	0
Boys 12-13-14	20	18	17	16	14	13	11	9	5	2	0
Girls 12-13-14	16	15	14	13	12	11	10	8	4	2	0
Boys 15-17	25	24	23	21	19	16	12	8	5	2	0
Girls 15-17	17	16	15	14	13	11	8	6	3	2	0
Men 18-34	26	25	24	23	19	16	13	9	8	2	0
Women 18-34	14	13	13	12	10	8	6	4	2	1	0

*From Friermood, H.T.
†Raw scores are located in the chart in accordance with age and sex, and percentile scores are located across the top.

Comments. The following are four of the many versions of this test:

1. Instead of using a piece of chalk, magnesium chalk can be placed on the fingertips of the hand on the wall side; or the fingertips can be dipped in water; or, a stepladder can be placed adjacent to the measuring board, and an assistant can measure the height from this position. If chalk is used, the chalk marks must be removed, preferably with a damp cloth, after each trial.
2. Instead of facing the wall to take the initial measurement, the subject can stand with one side to the wall with toes touching the wall.
3. Instead of standing flat-footed to take the initial measurement, the subject stands on tip-toes. This procedure takes foot length into account in the execution of the jump.
4. The measurement is taken to the nearest quarter of an inch instead of the nearest half-inch.

This test can be administered to 30 students in 45 minutes. If desired, the score can be adjusted so that body weight is taken into account.

SUMMARY

The measurement of muscular strength and endurance requires careful attention to the position of the examinee and the execution of the movement. Serious injuries can occur if the proper protocol is not followed. The spotters must be thoroughly trained and remain attentive throughout the testing. The safety of the examinee must receive top priority. Test selection depends on the type of equipment available. Several strength and endurance tests require little or no equipment. Although tests using sophisticated and expensive equipment may be more valid, the practical versions are satisfactory for field testing.

LEARNING EXPERIENCES

1. To understand strength and endurance testing more fully, enroll in a weight-training class. This will familiarize you with the proper positions, the safety considerations, and the use of appropriate equipment. If it is not possible to enroll in such a course, observe a class two or three times at your campus or a private fitness club. Write a short paper on the safety rules that were or should have been followed during these sessions.

2. Ask a *qualified* classmate to administer an arm press and a leg press test to you. Be sure this person is thoroughly familiar with the protocol. Compare your scores to the norms in this chapter.

3. Administer the Vertical Jump Test to everyone in your class. Obtain the weight of each classmate as well. Correlate vertical jump scores with weight. Is there a substantial enough relationship to warrant using body weight to adjust vertical jump scores? How might this sort of adjustment be made?

REFERENCES

Baumgartner, T.A., and Jackson, A.S. 1982. Measurement for evaluation in physical education. Dubuque, Iowa: Wm C Brown Group.

Clarke, H.H. 1966. Muscular strength and endurance in man. Englewood Cliffs, N.J.: Prentice-Hall, Inc.

Clarke, H.H. 1976. Application of measurement to health and physical education. Englewood Cliffs, N.J.: Prentice-Hall, Inc.

Heyward, V.H. 1984. Designs for fitness. Minneapolis: Burgess Publishing Co.

Jackson, A.S., and Smith, L. 1974. The validation of an evaluation system for weight training, Unpublished study presented at the AAHPER Convention, March, 1977, Anaheim, Calif.

Johnson, B.L. 1966. Isometric strength tests. Northeast Louisiana University, Monroe.

Johnson, B.L., and Nelson, J.K. 1974. Practical measurements for evaluation in physical education. Minneapolis: Burgess Publishing Co.

Pollock, M.L., Wilmore, J.H., and Fox, S.M. 1978. Health and fitness through physical activity. New York: John Wiley & Sons.

Sargent, D.A. 1921. Physical test of a man. American Physical Education Review **26**(4):188-194.

ANNOTATED READINGS

Heyward, V.H. 1984. Assessment of muscular strength and endurance. In designs for fitness. Minneapolis: Burgess Publishing Co.

Describes devices for measuring strength and muscular endurance; discusses problems associated with the assessment of static and dynamic muscle strength and endurance; analyzes calisthenic-type strength and endurance tests.

Katch, F.I., and McArdle, W.D. 1983. Conditioning for muscular strength. In Nutrition, weight control, and exercise, ed. 2, Philadelphia: Lea & Febiger.

Describes three exercise systems for developing muscular strength—weight training, isometric training, and isokinetic training; includes sections on muscular adaptations with strength training, strength training for women, and circuit weight training; presents step-by-step procedure for planning a workout; provides instruction on selecting proper weights.

Leighton, J.R. 1983. Fitness, body development, and sports conditioning through weight training. Springfield, Ill.: Charles C Thomas, Publisher.

Provides beginning and advanced exercise programs for both men and women using free weights, multistation exercise machines, and variable resistance equipment; discusses conditioning for a variety of activities, such as running, golf, racquet sports, and soccer.

Sharkey, B.J. 1984. Physiology of fitness, ed. 2, Champaign, Ill.: Human Kinetics Publishers, Inc.

Includes section on muscular fitness training; presents tests for fitness, training programs, and exercises in the appendix; covers latest information on fitness.

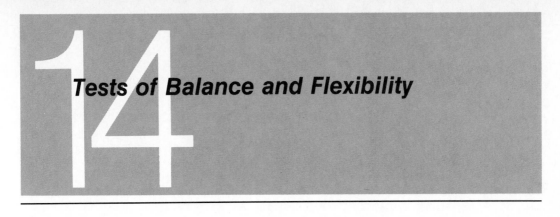

Tests of Balance and Flexibility

KEY WORDS *Watch for these words as you read the following chapter:*

balance	flexibility	posture
dynamic balance	flexometer	static balance
elgon	goniometer	task specificity

Performance of any motor skill is dependent, to some extent, on one's balance and flexibility. Years ago physical educators thought that people possessed a general ability to balance and another general ability reflecting overall flexibility. In other words, if a person could balance well on one body part, it was assumed that he or she could balance well on any body part. Based on this rationale, the development of practical tests of balance was quite straightforward. Only one balance test, for example, was needed to measure overall balance ability. Over the last two decades, however, research on both balance and flexibility has not substantiated the concept of general abilities. Rather, each of these abilities tends to be specific to a body part. This means that a person who is flexible at the hip joint is not necessarily flexible in the shoulder joint. Yet, we have all seen gymnasts who are flexible in all joints. Does this not point to a general ability? Probably not. More likely, it reflects **task specificity,** a high level of flexibility in many specific abilities. Task specificity suggests that not only is the ability specific to a particular body part but also to a particular task.

These research results complicate the measurement of balance and flexibility considerably, unless one's interest lies only with measurement at a specific site. Yet many tests of these two attributes have been developed in the physical education field. While none is valid as a test of general balance or flexibility, some are useful in more specific settings. Although precise measures of both attributes are available, these are not emphasized in this textbook since they are impractical for the typical school and private club setting. Several that might be useful in a nonschool setting are briefly described.

MEASURING BALANCE

Balance is the ability to maintain equilibrium. Even before a great deal of research was conducted on the nature of balance, it was deduced that two types of balance exist—**static balance,** the ability to maintain equilibrium in a stationary position, and **dynamic balance,** the ability to maintain equilibrium while in motion. Several tests are described for each type of balance.

Examples of tests of static balance

BASS STICK TEST (Lengthwise) (Bass, 1939)

Test objective. To measure the ability to balance in a stationary, upright position using a small base of support.

Description. The examinee places the dominant foot lengthwise on a special stick, as shown in Fig. 14-1. Both the ball of the foot and the heel should rest on the stick. The opposite foot is lifted from the floor and held in this position as long as possible. The stopwatch is started when the opposite foot leaves the floor and stopped when it touches the floor again, or when any part of the supporting foot touches the floor. Three trials are taken on each foot.

Test area. Smooth, flat floor.

Equipment. Stick 1 inch wide, 1 inch high, and 12 inches long; stopwatch; and tape (to hold stick to floor).

Scoring. The test score is the time for the best of three trials.

Validity. Face validity.

Reliability. $r_{xx'} = 0.90$.

Norms. Not reported for this specific test.

Comments. If an examinee loses balance during the first 3 seconds of a trial, the trial may be restarted. This is a popular test in the field and is usually motivating to the examinee, although it measures only a very specific type of balance.

BASS STICK TEST (Crosswise) (Bass, 1939)

Same as the Bass Stick Test (Lengthwise), except that the foot is placed crosswise on the stick and the examinee balances on the ball of the foot. (See Fig. 14-2.)

STORK STAND

Test objective. To measure the ability to balance in a stationary, upright position using a small base of support.

Description. The examinee stands on the dominant foot, flat on the floor. The other foot is held so that it touches the inside of the supporting knee, as shown in Fig. 14-3. The hands are placed on the hips. As soon as the proper position has been established, the stopwatch is started. The examinee holds the position as long as possible. When the nondominant foot is moved away from the knee, stop the watch. This constitutes one trial; three trials are taken.

FIG. 14-1. Bass Stick Test (Lengthwise).

FIG. 14-2. Bass Stick Test (Crosswise).

FIG. 14-3. Stork Stand Test.

Test area. Smooth, flat floor.

Equipment. Stopwatch.

Scoring. The best of three trials is the test score.

Validity. Face validity.

Reliability. $r_{xx'} = 0.85$, test-retest (as reported by Jensen and Hirst, 1980); $r_{xx'} = 0.87$, test-retest (as reported by Johnson and Nelson, 1979).

Norms. Available for college men and women in Johnson and Nelson (1979) for a slightly different version of the test in which the examinee balances on the ball of the foot.

Comments. The lack of a time limit is a drawback in administering this test. An examinee who can balance well in this position can hold the position for a lengthy period. If a group of students is being tested, this test could be too time-consuming.

Examples of tests of dynamic balance

JOHNSON MODIFICATION OF THE BASS TEST OF DYNAMIC BALANCE
(Johnson and Leach, 1968)

Test objective. To measure dynamic balance.

Description. Using the floor plan shown in Fig. 14-4, the examinee begins with the right foot on the starting mark and leaps to the first tape mark, landing on the left foot and balancing on the ball of the foot as long as possible, up to 5 seconds. The examinee leaps to the next square, lands on the right foot, and tries to maintain balance for 5 seconds. This procedure is continued to the end of the floor pattern.

Test area. Smooth floor surface, 50 inches by 180 inches.

Equipment. Stopwatch, tape measure, and floor tape.

Scoring. For each successful landing on the tape mark, 5 points are scored; 1 point is scored for each second the examinee remains balanced on the mark, up to 5 seconds. It is possible to score 10 points at each tape mark and 100 points on the total test. The examinee is penalized 5 points for any of the follow-

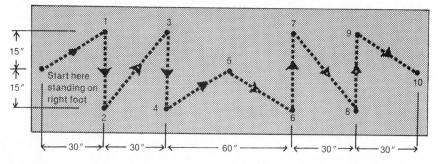

FIG. 14-4. *Floor markings for the Johnson Modification of the Bass Test of Dynamic Balance.*

ing landing errors: not stopping after landing on the tape mark, touching the floor with any body part other than the supporting foot, and not covering the tape mark with the ball of the foot. If the examinee makes a landing error, the correct position can be resumed for the 5-second balance.

An additional 1-point penalty is given for each of the following errors *during the 5-second balance*: touching the floor with the heel of the hand or any other body part other than the supporting foot and not holding the foot steady in the balance position. If balance is lost, the examinee should return to the proper mark before leaping to the next mark.

Validity. Face validity; r_{xy} = 0.46, using criterion of original Bass Test of Dynamic Balance (as reported by Kirkendall, Gruber, and Johnson, 1980).

Reliability. $r_{xx'}$ = 0.75, test-retest.

Norms. Norms are available for college women in Johnson and Nelson (1979).

Comments. While this is an interesting test, it is not a direct measure of dynamic balance. Usually, dynamic balance refers to balancing *while* the body (or body part) is moving. In this test, as in other tests of dynamic balance, the examinee moves but then stops and maintains a static balance.

MODIFIED SIDEWARD LEAP (Scott and French, 1959)

Test objective. To measure dynamic balance.

Description. The examinee begins on spot X, as shown in Fig. 14-5, and places a small object on spots B and C. The starting position is assumed by

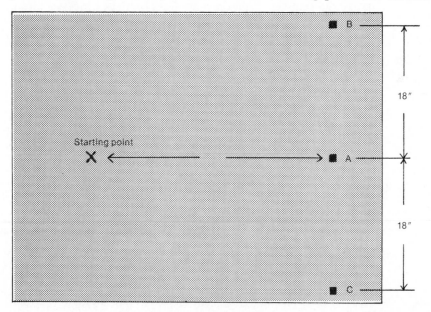

FIG. 14-5. *Floor markings for the Modified Sideward Leap Test. Spot A is the landing point; spots B and C mark the placement of a small object.*

standing on the left foot, with the right side toward spot A. The examinee takes a sideward leap to spot A, landing on the ball of the right foot, leans to spot B, and brushes the object off, using one hand. Balance on the ball of the foot should then be maintained for 5 seconds. Four trials are taken, two to each side.

Test area. Smooth floor surface, 50 inches by 50 inches.

Equipment. Stopwatch; tape measure; floor tape; and a small, light object, such as a badminton shuttlecock.

Scoring. The maximum number of points for each trial is 20:

1. 5 points for landing correctly on spot A
2. 1 point for each second balance is held on spot A, up to 5 seconds
3. 5 points for leaning and pushing object off spot B or C
4. 1 point for each second balance is held on spot B or C, up to 5 seconds

Validity. Face validity.

Reliability. $r_{xx'} = 0.66$ to 0.88.

Norms. Not reported for this specific test.

Comments. Like the original version, this modification measures the ability to balance while performing other movements.

BALANCE BEAM WALK (Jensen and Hirst, 1980*)

Test objective. To measure dynamic balance.

Description. The examinee should stand on one end of the balance beam, slowly walk the full length of the beam (see Fig. 14-6), pause for 5 seconds, turn around, and return to the starting position. Three trials are taken.

Test area. Smooth floor surface, 5 feet by 15 feet.

Equipment. Balance beam and stopwatch.

Scoring. Pass-fail.

Validity. Face validity.

Reliability. Not reported for this specific test.

Norms. Not reported for this specific test.

Comments. There should be a time limit for this test; otherwise, the examinee could move at an excessively slow pace, consuming an unreasonable amount of time. Also, penalties should be identified for errors that occur throughout the test.

MEASURING FLEXIBILITY

Flexibility is the range of movement in a joint, specifically from a position of extension to flexion or the opposite movement. As noted previously, there is ample evidence that flexibility is specific to a given joint. In this chapter both precise and practical measures of flexibility are discussed.

---

*Although this test is described in Jensen and Hirst (1980), various versions of it have been in use for many years.

FIG. 14-6. *Balance Beam Walk Test.*

Precise measures of flexibility

Three devices are often mentioned when a precise measure of flexibility is desired. The **goniometer,** a 180-degree protractor with extended arms, provides the least precision of the three but is inexpensive and relatively easy to use. The **flexometer** is an instrument with a weighted 360-degree dial and a weighted pointer (Leighton, 1942). Both dial and pointer move independently and are affected by gravity. The flexometer is not affected by the length of the segments and can be used to measure all body segments. Standard directions for measuring 30 segments are provided by Leighton (1955). The reliability of the flexometer has ranged from 0.901 to 0.983. The most sophisticated of the three, the **elgon,** is a goniometer with a potentiometer substituted for the protractor. Also known as an electrogoniometer, it records changes in degrees continuously throughout the movement. All three devices measure the movement of bodily segments in degrees. For more details, refer to Sigerseth's chapter in Montoye (1978).

Practical tests of flexibility

Because of the specific nature of flexibility tests, not many of the practical tests have a high degree of validity as measures of general flexibility, but some have a certain usefulness as measures of the flexibility of specific segments. However, caution must be used in the selection of flexibility tests, since certain measures require positioning the body in ways that might cause physical injury to some examinees.

SIT-AND-REACH TEST

The Sit-and-Reach Test, described in detail in Chapter 12, is designed to measure flexibility of the low back and posterior thigh muscles. Although this is a reasonably practical test, it is not without problems. Flexibility is measured in centimeters (or, more recently, inches) rather than degrees. Performance on the test is somewhat dependent on the ratio of trunk length to lower body length. However, the test does provide comparative measurements. Furthermore, it requires little equipment, is inexpensive and easy to administer, and requires little time to administer. Students can learn to administer the test to each other. (See Chapter 12 for more information on this test, including abbreviated tables of norms.)

KRAUS-WEBER FLOOR-TOUCH TEST (Kraus and Hirschland, 1954*)

Test objective. To measure trunk flexibility or length of the back and hamstring muscles.

Description. The examinee should assume an erect standing position in bare or stocking feet, with feet together. The arms should hang by the sides. With no prior warm-up bounces, the examinee should slowly lean downward, attempting to touch the floor with the fingertips (see Fig. 14-7), and hold the floor-touch position for 3 seconds. The knees must be straight throughout the test.

Test area. A small room.

Equipment. Stopwatch.

Scoring. As the test battery was originally devised, all test items were scored on a pass-fail basis. Using this procedure, if the floor-touch position is held for 3 seconds, the examinee *passes* the test. Otherwise, the examinee receives a *fail*. This system of scoring appears to be the most frequently used. Another scoring option uses numerical scores ranging from 0 to 10. If the floor-touch position is held for 3 seconds, the examinee receives a score of 10. If the floor is not touched, 1 point is subtracted for every inch between the floor and the fingertips. If this distance is 10 inches or more, the score is 0.

---

*This test is a part of the Kraus-Weber Tests of Minimum Muscular Fitness described in Chapter 12. The test battery includes six items.

FIG. 14-7. *Kraus-Weber Floor-Touch Test.*

Validity. The validity of the Kraus-Weber Tests of Minimum Muscular Fitness is based on clinical evidence that patients with low back pain were unable to pass one or more of the Kraus-Weber test items. As their back conditions improved, their test results also improved.

Reliability. Not reported for this specific test.

Norms. Since the scoring is usually pass-fail, the use of norms is not relevant.

Comments. The test administrator might wish to hold the knees of the examinee being tested to ensure that they remain straight throughout the test.

TRUNK EXTENSION (Cureton, 1941)

Test objective. To measure the ability to hyperextend the trunk.

Description. To assume the starting position of this test, the examinee should lie in a prone position on a mat. Both hands are placed on the lower back. A partner should hold the hips against the mat, as shown in Fig. 14-8. The examinee should raise the trunk from the mat. Using a tape measure, determine the distance from the mat to the suprasternal notch, the pronounced depression at the upper end of the sternum, at the base of the neck. Measure to the nearest quarter inch.

FIG. 14-8. *Trunk Extension Test.*

Test area. A small room.

Equipment. Mat and tape measure.

Scoring. To determine the test score, a *standard* measure of trunk length must first be taken. The examinee should sit with his or her back against the wall. Using a tape measure, determine the distance between the suprasternal notch and the floor or bench where the examinee is seated. Measure to the nearest quarter inch. Then, multiply the *test* measurement by 100 and divide by the *standard* measurement of trunk length to determine the test score (Jensen and Hirst, 1980).

Norms. No national norms have been reported. In a local setting the 50th percentile for college men was a score of 40; the 50th percentile for college women, a score of 38 (Johnson and Nelson, 1979).

Comments. This test can be administered to an entire class of students within one class period.

FORWARD BEND OF TRUNK (Jensen and Hirst, 1980)

Test objective. To measure the flexion of the trunk and hips.

Description. This test can be administered either on the floor or on a table. The examinee assumes a sitting position with feet against the wall, hip-width apart. The knees must remain straight throughout the test. The hands are placed palms down on the mat, next to the upper thighs. The examinee should lean forward and downward as far as possible, reaching toward the heels of the feet.

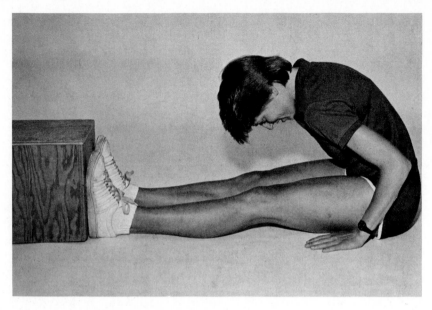

FIG. 14-9. *Forward Bend of Trunk Test.*

(See Fig. 14-9.) Measure the vertical distance from the suprasternal notch to the floor, and record the distance to the nearest quarter inch.

    Test area. A small room with a smooth wall surface.

    Equipment. Mat (preferred) and tape measure.

    Scoring. The test score is the distance measured to the nearest quarter inch.

    Validity. Not reported for this specific test.

    Reliability. Not reported for this specific test.

    Norms. None available. Setting up a table of norms for one's own students is advisable.

    Comments. Keep in mind that lower scores (shorter distances) represent greater flexibility.

MEASURING POSTURE

Although the measurement of posture is not a measure of balance or flexibility, these aspects certainly affect one's posture. **Posture** is defined as the alignment of the body and its segments.

NEW YORK STATE POSTURE RATING TEST (New York State Education Department, 1966)

    Test objective. To evaluate the posture of public school students grades 4 through 12.

    Description. The posture rating chart in Fig. 14-10 is used to assess 13 areas

FIG. 14-10. *Posture Chart.*

By permission of the State Education Department, State University of New York, Albany.

GRADE | 4 | 5 | 6 | 7 | 8 | 9 | 10 | 11 | 12

RATER'S INITIALS

DATE OF TEST

5	3	1
Head erect gravity line passes directly through center	Head twisted or turned to one side slightly	Head twisted or turned to one side markedly
Shoulders level (horizontally)	One shoulder slightly higher than other	One shoulder markedly higher than other
Spine straight	Spine slightly curved laterally	Spine markedly curved laterally
Hips level (horizontally)	One hip slightly higher	One hip markedly higher
Feet pointed straight ahead	Feet pointed out	Feet pointed out markedly, ankles sag in (pronation)
Arches high	Arches lower, feet slightly flat	Arches low, feet markedly flat

TOTAL PAGE ONE

GRADE | 4 | 5 | 6 | 7 | 8 | 9 | 10 | 11 | 12

TOTAL PAGE ONE

5 — Neck erect, chin in, head in balance directly above shoulders
3 — Neck slightly forward, chin slightly out
1 — Neck markedly forward, chin markedly out

5 — Chest elevated, breastbone furthest forward part of body
3 — Chest slightly depressed
1 — Chest markedly depressed (flat)

5 — Shoulders centered
3 — Shoulders slightly forward
1 — Shoulders markedly forward (shoulder blades protruding in rear)

5 — Upper back normally rounded
3 — Upper back slightly more rounded
1 — Upper back markedly rounded

5 — Trunk erect
3 — Trunk inclined to rear slightly
1 — Trunk inclined to rear markedly

5 — Abdomen flat
3 — Abdomen protruding
1 — Abdomen protruding and sagging

5 — Lower back normally curved
3 — Lower back slightly hollow
1 — Lower back markedly hollow

TOTAL RAW SCORE

To obtain total raw score:

1. Determine the score for each of the above 13 items as follows:
   5 points if description in left-hand column applies
   3 points if description in middle column applies
   1 point if description in right-hand column applies
2. Enter score for each item under proper grade in the scoring column
3. Add all 13 scores and place total in appropriate space

of the body. Three profiles are shown for each area: the correct position, a slight deviation, and a pronounced deviation from the correct position. The examinee stands on a line in front of a screen. A plumb line is suspended just in front of the line. Another line is placed at right angles to the first line, extending 10 feet in front of the screen and perpendicular to it. The total distance from the screen to the end of the line is 13 feet. The 13-foot point marks the location of the examiner.

The first six areas of the body are rated while the examinee stands facing the screen, with the plumb line bisecting the back of the head, the spine, and the legs and feet. The remaining seven areas are rated with the examinee's left side to the screen. The plumb line should fall along the ear, shoulder, hip, knee, and ankle.

Test area. Area 15 feet by 10 feet.

Equipment. Screen, rating chart, and plumb line.

Scoring. For the correct position, 5 points are scored; for a slight deviation, 3 points are scored; and for a pronounced deviation, 1 point is scored. The total point value is the student's score. Space to record the student's posture ratings in grades 4 through 12 is provided on the chart.

Validity. Logical validity.

Reliability. 0.93 to 0.98, for boys and girls at various grade levels.

Norms. Norms are reported by sex and grade in the original source.

Comments. This test has been in use in the physical education field for many years. It is fairly easy to administer, although prior training in using the chart is necessary. If a teacher administers the test, it can be quite time-consuming, since individual testing is necessary. For a rough screening of students' posture, older students can be trained to use the chart. Having students test each other is an effective way of making them aware of the elements of good posture.

SUMMARY

Although it is evident that balance and flexibility are important attributes in the performance of a motor skill, the task-specific nature of each prohibits the use of one measure for each attribute. Since an individual may be flexible in one joint and not another, each joint must be measured separately to determine flexibility. The most valid measures are those requiring expensive equipment, trained personnel, and individual testing that is frequently time-consuming. Practical tests of balance or flexibility have several drawbacks, but some of them can be useful to measure a specific segment of the body if carefully selected.

LEARNING EXPERIENCES

1. Administer the Stork Stand Test to at least 10 people. This can be done outside of class, as long as you have a stopwatch or a watch with a second hand. Plot the trials for each person. Does each person improve as the number of trials increases? Analyze this test in terms of logical validity.

2. Take the Sit-and-Reach Test in your class or laboratory session. Summarize the data for males and females separately, including the means and standard deviations or medians and interpercentile ranges. Plot a frequency distribution for each gender.

3. Select a partner and review the posture chart in Fig. 14-10. Use the chart to evaluate the posture of at least two other people. Ask each one to assume his or her *normal* posture first, then his or her *best* posture. Rate both postures independently. Discuss the ratings with your partner *after* the assessment has been completed. Where discrepancies exist between ratings, discuss the differences. If there are major differences between ratings, rate the same examinees again.

REFERENCES

Bass, R.I. 1939. An analysis of the components of tests of semi-circular canal function and of static and dynamic balance. Research Quarterly 10:33-42.

Cureton, T.K. 1941. Flexibility as an aspect of physical fitness. Research Quarterly Supplement 12:388-389.

Jensen, C.R., and Hirst, C.C. 1980. Measurement in physical education and athletics. New York: Macmillan Publishing Co., Inc.

Johnson, B.L., and Leach, J. 1968. A modification of the Bass Test of Dynamic Balance, Unpublished study, Commerce: East Texas State University.

Johnson, B.L., and Nelson, J.K. 1979. Practical measurements for evaluation in physical education. Minneapolis: Burgess Publishing Co.

Kirkendall, D.R., Gruber, J.J., and Johnson, R.E. 1980. Measurement and evaluation for physical educators. Dubuque, Iowa: Wm C Brown Group.

Kraus, H., and Hirschland, R.P. 1954. Minimum muscular fitness tests in school children. Research Quarterly 25:177-188.

Leighton, J.R. 1942. A simple objective and reliable measure of flexibility. Research Quarterly 13:205-216.

Leighton, J.R. 1955. An instrument and technic for the measurement of range of joint motion. Archives of Physical Medicine and Rehabilitation 36:571-578.

New York State Education Department. 1966. New York State Physical Fitness Test for Boys and Girls Grades 4-12. New York: New York State Education Department.

Scott, M.G., and French, E. 1959. Measurement and evaluation in physical education. Dubuque, Iowa: Wm C Brown Group.

Sigerseth, P.O. 1978. Flexibility. In Montoye, H.J., editor. An introduction to measurement in physical education and exercise science. Boston: Allyn & Bacon, Inc.

ANNOTATED READINGS

American Alliance for Health, Physical Education, Recreation and Dance. 1980. Health-Related Physical Fitness Test manual. Reston, Va.: AAHPERD.

Reviews exercises for improving the flexibility of the low back region; presents exercises in terms of progressive difficulty; can be used as an aid to diagnose, as well as a basis for development; provides excellent photographs of starting and exercise positions.

Corbin, C.B., and Noble, L. 1985. Flexibility—a major component of physical fitness. In Cundiff, D.E., editor. Implementation of health fitness exercise programs. Reston, Va.: American Alliance for Health, Physical Education, Recreation and Dance.

Defines static and dynamic flexibility; discusses the joint specificity of flexibility; reviews measurement techniques; analyzes the relationship between flexibility and good health and flexibility and performance in sport; recommends techniques for improving flexibility.

Sigerseth, P.O. 1978. Flexibility. In Montoye, H.J., editor. An introduction to measurement in physical education. Boston: Allyn & Bacon, Inc.

Required reading for physical educators interested in precise measures of flexibility at each joint; describes the use of the Leighton flexometer to measure 30 joint movements at the neck, trunk, shoulder joint, elbow joint, radial-ulnar, wrist joint, hip joint, knee, and ankle joint; recommends exercises for improving flexibility.

Simri, U. 1974. Assessment procedures for human performance. In Larson, L.A., editor. Fitness, health, and work capacity: international standards for assessment. New York: Macmillan Publishing Co., Inc.

Presents international standards for measuring flexibility; recommends a test of forward flexion of the trunk (for a practical setting), since this movement is one of greatest importance in human movement; in a clinical setting Simri recommends that the flexibility of each joint should be tested separately.

Tests of Motor Ability

KEY WORDS   *Watch for these words as you read the following chapter:*

motor ability   motor educability   trait

motor capacity   task specificity

During the early part of the twentieth century, a number of educators and psychologists explored the measurement of intelligence. Intelligence was viewed as an innate ability that could be measured by using intelligence tests and deriving an intelligent quotient (IQ). At the same time physical educators drew a parallel to motor behavior and surmised that there must be an innate ability to perform motor tasks. This was commonly referred to as motor ability. A few of the more prominent motor ability tests in the physical education field are described here. This chapter is an expanded version of a paper by M.J. Safrit and T.M. Wood entitled "The Use of Motor Ability Tests to Achieve Sex Fair Ability Groupings."

To understand motor ability tests better, the concepts on which they were based are reviewed first. Motor ability, motor educability, and motor capacity, while somewhat related in meaning, are distinct terms which, to the confusion of the practitioner, have often been used interchangeably in the motor ability literature. **Motor ability** is defined as "a present aptitude for physical skills" (Alden, Horton, and Caldwell, 1932), which includes strength and coordination as they appear in everyday motor habits (Howe, 1930). Similarly, McCloy (1934) distinguishes between general motor ability—motor capability at a given time—and general motor capacity—one's potential motor capability. Humiston (1937), taking a different approach, describes motor ability as the "ability to get around in situations demanding the use of big muscles—the ability to shift the body from one place to another" (p. 182). Scott and French (1959) link motor ability and motor educability in describing motor ability as "achievement in basic motor skills, or it may be interpreted as a more general term combining the concepts of motor educability and achievement" (p. 343). **Motor educability** is defined as the ease with which one learns motor skills (Singer, 1975).

When this information is synthesized, it appears that *motor capacity* refers to an individual's potential ability to perform motor skills, *motor ability* reflects an individual's present ability to perform motor skills, and *motor educability* deals with an individual's ability to learn new motor skills. Singer (1975) and Kirkendall, Gruber, and Johnson (1980) present other descriptions of motor ability. Singer (1975) describes motor ability as indicating present athletic ability and as denoting "the immediate state of the individual to perform in a wide range of motor skills" (p. 107). Kirkendall and associates suggest that motor ability is "a general quality that can facilitate more specific performances" (p. 213).

The extent to which motor ability is innate is unknown. Certainly a person is born with certain genetic features that affect the ability to perform motor skills. However, environment also plays an important role in the ability to execute motor tasks. Ability can be improved through learning. These issues continue to intrigue and baffle scientists. If the true nature—and indeed the existence—of something called motor ability is not clearly understood, how can it be measured? This confusion about the concept of motor ability did not exist to the same extent when the classic tests of motor ability were developed. Lacking scientific evidence to the contrary, the developers of these tests used a logical analysis as the basis for test construction.

Perhaps the most difficult challenge in constructing a test of motor ability was the determination of motor ability elements. Clarke (1976) lists nine elements frequently considered in constructing tests of motor ability: arm-eye coordination, muscular power, agility, muscular strength, muscular endurance, circulorespiratory endurance, flexibility, speed, and foot-eye coordination. Other lists have been generated over the years, but the benefits of examining lists of this type are limited since each test developer identifies a different set of elements representing motor ability. This paradox has never been resolved, although it is obviously contradictory to discuss "general" motor ability and then to describe the components of motor ability in a magnitude of different ways. Generally, however, several common elements were in the various sets of components.

The development of motor ability tests has come to a complete halt the last two decades for several reasons. First, many exercise scientists and physical educators have questioned the existence of a general motor ability. This is a result of the research evidence indicating that ability may be task specific. Second, the construct validity of these test batteries has never been established. Third, legitimate questions can be raised about the extent to which this ability, if it exists, is affected by genetics in contrast to environment.

Although there are many questions concerning the use of motor ability tests, they are discussed in this text because they have played an important historic role in the exercise science profession. Students should be familiar with one or two of the most widely used motor ability tests. Although no final answer on the value of motor ability tests has been attained and their use is now questionable, the elimination of the concept entirely is not a foregone conclusion. Examples of several motor ability tests are included in the next section. Because of their careful development and widespread use, these tests are often viewed as classics in the field. (See Chapter 17 for information on motor ability tests for children.)

EXAMPLES OF MOTOR ABILITY TESTS

The concept of *motor ability* implies an enduring trait that indicates one's present ability for most athletic activities. Therefore, researchers in the first half of this century have attempted to develop tests that measure this trait for the purposes of classifying individuals for instruction and of predicting future athletic success. The development of separate motor ability tests for male and female students beyond elementary school age has been a generally consistent trend. Only the Scott Motor Ability Test and the Barrow Motor Ability Test are described in detail here. A third test, developed by McCloy, is mentioned briefly because of its historic value.

McCloy's General Motor Ability Test (McCloy, 1934)

In recognition of Charles H. McCloy's contributions as a pioneer in measurement in the exercise science field, it is appropriate to place McCloy's General Motor Ability Test first. During his lifetime McCloy exerted a major influence on test development by using scientific measurement in his own work. He constructed tests of motor capacity, motor educability, and motor ability, along with a variety of measures in other areas. The significant influence of this distinguished physical educator is now legendary. McCloy developed two motor ability test batteries, one for boys and one for girls.

BOYS' BATTERY. (Events vary according to age and experience of group)
1. Pull-ups or chinning
2. Sprint (50 to 100 yards)
3. Long jump (running or standing)
4. Running high jump
5. Weight throwing (shot put, basketball throw, or baseball throw)

General Motor Ability Score
$$= 0.1022 \text{ (track and field score)} - 0.3928 \text{ (chinning strength)}$$

To determine the track and field score, test items 2 through 5 are scored using McCloy's scoring tables and then summed. Chinning strength is calculated using Formula 15-1.

$$\text{Chinning strength} = (\text{No. of pull-ups}) \left(\frac{W}{10} + H - 60 \right) \quad \text{Formula 15-1}$$

where W = weight in pounds
H = height in inches

GIRLS' BATTERY

1. Modified pull-ups
2. Sprint
3. Long jump
4. Throw

General Motor Ability Score = 0.42 (track and field score) + 9.6 (number of pull-ups)

To determine the track and field score test items 2 through 4 are scored using McCloy's tables and then summed.

Scott Motor Ability Test (Scott, 1943)

The Scott Motor Ability Test was developed to measure the motor ability of college women and high school girls. Two test batteries were formed, one containing four items and a shorter version with three items. The shorter battery is presented in this chapter since it is almost as valid as the longer battery and is easier to administer. Both batteries can be administered indoors.

TEST 1—BASKETBALL THROW

Test objective. To measure arm and shoulder girdle strength and coordination.

Description. The examinee stands behind the restraining line and throws the basketball as far as possible. Any type of throw may be used. Three trials are taken. If an examinee steps on or over the restraining line during or after the throw, the trial is not scored. The trial score is the distance recorded to the nearest foot. The test score is the best of three trials.

Test area. Floor area 80 feet by 20 feet.

Equipment. Several regulation basketballs, tape measure, floor tape, and scorecards.

Validity. Test validity is 0.79, with the McCloy General Motor Ability Test used as the criterion measure; 0.78, when correlated with a composite criterion and subjective ratings.

Reliability. The within-day reliability estimate is 0.89.

Comments. No demonstration of the basketball throw is permitted. Examinees should be allowed to warm up, although the number of practice trials is not specified in the test directions. This should be standardized, if practice trials are to be taken.

TEST 2—BROAD JUMP

The Broad Jump Test is the same as the Standing Long Jump described in Chapter 12. By using the criteria specified in the previous section, validity coefficients of 0.79 and 0.78 were calculated. Reliability coefficients of 0.79 for college women and 0.91 for high school girls were reported.

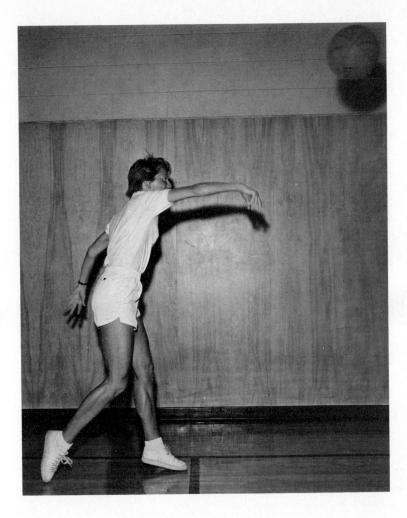

TEST 3—OBSTACLE RACE

Test objective. To measure speed, agility, and general body coordination. The course used for this test is shown in Fig. 15-1.

Description. The examinee assumes a back-lying position with the heels just behind the starting line. On the signal *Ready, Go!* she gets up quickly and begins moving through the obstacle course. She runs to the first square (see Fig. 15-1) and steps on the square with both feet. The same protocol is followed with the next two squares. She then runs to the jump standard, circles it twice, and races to the crossbar. She passes under the crossbar, attempting not to touch it, gets up, and runs to the end line as quickly as possible, touching this line with her hand. She runs back to line *F*, to the end line again, and to line *F* again, each time touching the line with her hand. Then she races across the end line

FIG. 15-1. Floor markings for the Scott Obstacle Race.

to complete the test. One trial is administered. The score is the time required
to complete the course.

Test area. Floor area 60 feet by 30 feet.

Equipment. Stopwatch, jump standard, 6-foot crossbar and support poles,
floor tape, and scorecards.

Validity. By using the criteria described under the Basketball Throw for Distance, validity coefficients of 0.65 and 0.58 were calculated for a longer version
of the test.

Reliability. Test-retest reliability of 0.91 was reported.

Comments. Although examinees should be instructed not to touch the crossbar, a foul is not constituted even if the bar is dislodged. It is assumed that the
time will be slower as a result. The jump standard, however, cannot be touched.
If it is, a foul is declared and the trial must be retaken. The test should be
demonstrated and examinees should be allowed to walk through the course before being tested. An assistant should be stationed between line *F* and the endline. When the examinee reaches line *F*, she should be reminded of each reverse
turn and encouraged to run with maximum effort across the endline after the
last turn. Otherwise, far too many examinees will not remember the correct
sequence, thus invalidating the test. Also, examinees have a tendency to slow
down as they approach the endline for the last time. The examinee should be
reminded to run as fast as possible *across* the endline. Be sure individuals being
tested are wearing proper shoes.

Test norms for college women and high school girls are shown in Tables
15-1 and 15-2. These norms have not been updated in recent years but can be
used as rough guidelines of performance expectations.

Barrow Motor Ability Test (Barrow, 1954)

The Barrow Motor Ability Test is designed to measure the motor ability of college men and junior and senior high school boys. Two test batteries, one consisting of six items and a shorter version with three items, were developed. Only
the shorter battery is included in this chapter, since it has high validity (r_{xy} =
0.92 when correlated with a composite of 29 test items measuring eight different
components of motor ability). The shorter version can easily be administered
indoors.

TEST 1—STANDING BROAD JUMP

The Standing Broad Jump (SBJ) Test, used as a measure of explosive leg power,
is described in Chapter 12. (See Standing Long Jump.) The test-retest reliability
is 0.895, and the objectivity (comparing two scorers) is 0.996. The validity, based
on a comparison with the composite of 29 tests, is 0.759.

TABLE 15-1. *T-Scores for college women on Scott Motor Ability Test**

T-score	Basketball throw (feet)	Broad jump (inches)	Obstacle race (seconds)	T-score	Basketball throw (feet)	Broad jump (inches)	Obstacle race (seconds)
85	75	86	17.5-17.9	48		60	
84				47	34	59	25.0-25.4
83	71		18.0-18.4	46	33	58	
82				45	32	57	25.5-25.9
81		85		44	31		
80	70			43		56	26.0-26.4
79	69		18.5-18.9	42	30	55	
78	68	84		41		54	26.5-26.9
77	67	83		40	29	53	27.0-27.4
76	66			39	28	52	
75	65	82	19.0-19.4	38			27.5-27.9
74	64	81		37	27	51	28.0-28.4
73	62	80		36	26	50	
72	61	79	19.5-19.9	35		49	28.5-28.9
71	59			34	25	48	29.0-29.4
70	58	78	20.0-20.4	33		47	29.5-29.9
69	57	77		32		46	30.0-30.4
68	56	76		31		45	30.5-30.9
67	55	75	20.5-20.9	30	24	44	31.0-31.4
66	54	74		29		43	31.5-31.9
65	52			28	23	42	32.0-32.4
64	51	73	21.0-21.4	27	21	41	32.5-32.9
63	50	72		26		40	33.0-33.4
62	48	71	21.5-21.9	25	20	39	33.5-33.9
61	47			24		38	34.0-34.4
60	46	70		23		37	34.5-34.9
59	45	69	22.0-22.4	22		36	
58	44	68		21	19		35.0-35.4
57	43	67	22.5-22.9	20			
56	42			19		35	35.5-35.9
55	41	66	23.0-23.4	18			
54	40	65		17	18		
53	39	64	23.5-23.9	16			
52	38	63		15			
51	37		24.0-24.4	14			43.5-43.9
50	36	62		13		30	45.5-45.9
49	35	61	24.5-24.9				

*Reprinted by permission of Dr. M. Gladys Scott.

TABLE 15-2. *T-Scores for high school girls on Scott Motor Ability Test**

T-score	Basketball throw (feet) (310)†	Broad jump (inches) (287)†	Obstacle race (seconds) (374)†	T-score	Basketball throw (feet) (310)†	Broad jump (inches) (387)†	Obstacle race (seconds) (374)†
80	71			49	35	70	
79		96		48		68	23.0-23.4
78				47	34	66	
77	68	94		46	33		23.5-23.9
76	66		18.5-18.9	45	32	64	
75	65			44	31		24.0-24.4
74	64	92		43		62	
73	63			43	30		24.5-24.9
72	61			41	29	60	
71	59	90		40	28		
70	55	88	19.0-19.4	39		58	25.0-25.4
69	54			38	27	56	
68	52	86		37		54	25.5-25.9
67	51		19.5-19.9	36	26		26.0-26.4
66	50			35		52	26.5-26.9
65	49			34	25	50	27.0-27.4
64	48	84	20.0-20.4	33			
63	47			32	24	47	27.5-27.9
62	46	82	20.5-20.9	31	23		
61		80		30		44	28.0-28.4
60	45			29	22		28.5-28.9
59	44	78	21.0-21.4	28			29.0-29.4
58	43			27	21		29.5-29.9
57	42	76	21.5-21.9	26		40	30.0-30.4
56	41			25	20		
55	40	74		24			30.5-31.4
54			22.0-22.4	23	19	36	31.5-32.4
53	39			22			32.5-34.9
52		72		21	16		
51	37		22.5-22.9	20			35.0-36.0
50	36						

*Reprinted by permission of Dr. M. Gladys Scott.
†Size of normative group.

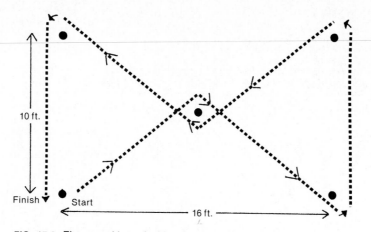

FIG. 15-2. *Floor markings for the Barrow Zigzag Run.*

TEST 2—ZIGZAG RUN

Test objective. To measure agility. The course for the Zigzag Run (ZR) is shown in Fig. 15-2.

Description. The examinee assumes a ready position (standing) at the starting point. On the signal *Ready, Go!*, he runs the course in the designated manner as fast as possible. The cones should not be touched throughout the run. The examinee continues to run the course for a total of three times. As the finish line is crossed at the end of the third circuit, the timer stops the stopwatch. The score is the time recorded to the nearest tenth of a second. If the cones are moved during the run, the trial is retaken.

Test area. Floor area 30 feet by 50 feet.

Equipment. Stopwatch, five traffic cones, floor tape, and scorecards.

Validity. Test validity is 0.736, based on a comparison of the test with a composite of 29 tests measuring eight different components of motor ability.

Reliability. Test-retest reliability is 0.795. Test objectivity, comparing two timers, is 0.996.

Comments. Before test day the run should be demonstrated and the examinees should be allowed to walk or jog through the course. An assistant should be stationed near the finish line to remind the test taker to run the course three times and not to slow down until he has crossed the finish line. Proper shoes should be required.

TEST 3—MEDICINE BALL PUT

Test objective. To measure arm and shoulder girdle strength. The examinee is required to put a 6-pound medicine ball as far as possible.

Description. For the Medicine Ball Put (MBP), the examinee stands between two restraining lines 15 feet apart. The medicine ball is held in one hand, close to the point where the shoulder joins the neck. The ball is thrust outward as far as possible. If a boy steps on or over the restraining line during or after the put, the trial is not scored. Three trials are taken. The score is the best of three throws, recorded to the nearest foot.

Test area. Floor area 90 feet by 25 feet.

Equipment. Two or three 6-pound medicine balls, tape measure, floor tape, and scorecards.

Validity. The validity of the test is 0.736, based on a comparison of the test with a composite of 29 tests measuring eight different components of motor ability.

Reliability. The test-retest reliability is 0.893, and the objectivity for two scorers is 0.997.

Comments. The regression equation for the General Motor Ability Score (GMAS) is 2.2(SBJ) + 1.6(ZR) + 1.2(MBP). Use Table 15-3 to interpret the GMAS.

Each throw must be measured directly from the landing point to the middle of the closest restraining line. Scoring may be facilitated by stretching out a tape measure and leaving it there to measure each throw. The tape must be moved for each put, however. It is possible to use floor tapes, but they must be laid out in arcs so that the proper distance will be measured no matter where the ball lands. Norms for all three tests are included in Tables 15-4 (college men) and 15-5 through 15-7 (junior and senior high school boys).

TABLE 15-3. *GMAS categories for college men (three-item test)**

Category	P.E. majors	Nonmajors
Excellent	197-higher	185-higher
Good	180-196	163-184
Average	161-179	138-162
Poor	143-160	116-137
Inferior	142-lower	115-lower

*Reprinted by permission of Dr. H.M. Barrow.

TABLE 15-4. *T-Scores for college men**

T-score	Standing broad jump (inches)	Zigzag run (seconds)	Medicine ball put (feet)	T-score
80	113 Up	20.8 Up	58 Up	80
75	109-112	21.6-20.9	55-57	75
70	105-108	22.4-21.7	52-54	70
65	101-104	23.1-22.5	48-51	65
60	97-100	23.9-23.2	45-47	60
55	93-96	24.7-24.0	42-44	55
50	89-92	25.5-24.8	39-41	50
45	85-88	26.3-25.6	35-38	45
40	81-84	27.1-26.4	32-34	40
35	77-80	27.8-27.2	29-31	35
30	73-76	28.6-27.9	26-28	30
25	69-72	29.4-28.7	23-25	25
20	68 Down	29.5 Up	22 Down	20

*Reprinted by permission of Dr. H.M. Barrow.

TABLE 15-5. *Standing Broad Jump T-scores for high school and junior high school boys**

Grade	7	8	9	10	11	
T-score						T-score
80	90 Up	97 Up	103 Up	105 Up	112 Up	80
75	86-89	92-96	98-102	101-104	107-111	75
70	82-85	88-91	93-97	97-100	103-106	70
65	77-81	83-87	88-92	92-96	97-102	65
60	73-76	78-82	83-87	88-91	93-96	60
55	69-72	73-77	79-82	83-87	88-92	55
50	65-68	69-72	74-78	79-82	83-87	50
45	61-64	64-68	69-73	75-78	78-82	45
40	56-60	59-63	64-68	71-74	74-77	40
35	52-55	54-58	59-63	66-70	69-73	35
30	48-51	50-53	54-58	62-65	64-68	30
25	44-47	45-49	49-53	58-61	59-63	25
20	43 Down	44 Down	48 Down	57 Down	58 Down	20

*Reprinted by permission of Dr. H.M. Barrow.

TABLE 15-6. *Zigzag Run T-scores for high school and junior high school boys**

Grade	7	8	9	10	11	
T-score						T-score
80	20.1 Down	17.8 Down	20.2 Down	21.6 Down	21.5 Down	80
75	21.4-20.2	19.5-17.9	21.3-20.3	22.7-21.7	22.6-21.6	75
70	22.7-21.5	21.2-19.6	22.4-21.4	23.8-22.8	23.7-22.7	70
65	24.0-22.8	22.8-21.3	23.5-22.5	24.8-23.9	24.7-23.8	65
60	25.2-24.1	24.5-22.9	24.6-23.6	25.8-24.9	25.8-24.8	60
55	26.5-25.3	26.2-24.6	25.7-24.7	26.9-25.9	26.8-25.9	55
50	27.8-26.6	27.8-26.3	26.8-25.8	27.9-27.0	27.8-26.9	50
45	29.0-27.9	29.5-27.9	27.9-26.9	28.9-28.0	28.9-27.9	45
40	30.3-29.1	31.2-29.6	29.0-28.0	29.9-29.0	29.9-29.0	40
35	31.6-30.4	32.8-31.3	30.1-29.1	31.0-30.0	31.0-30.0	35
30	32.8-31.7	34.5-32.9	31.2-30.2	32.1-31.1	32.0-31.1	30
25	34.1-32.9	36.2-34.6	32.3-31.3	33.1-32.2	33.0-32.1	25
20	34.2 Up	36.3 Up	32.4 Up	33.2 Up	33.1 Up	20

*Reprinted by permission of Dr. H.M. Barrow.

TABLE 15-7. *Medicine Ball Put T-scores for high school and junior high school boys**

Grade	7	8	9	10	11	
T-score						T-score
80	43 Up	45 Up	49 Up	50 Up	54 Up	80
75	38-42	43-44	46-48	47-49	51-53	75
70	35-37	40-42	44-45	44-46	48-50	70
65	33-34	37-39	41-43	42-43	46-47	65
60	30-32	34-36	38-40	39-41	43-45	60
55	27-29	31-33	35-37	37-38	40-42	55
50	25-26	28-30	32-34	34-36	37-39	50
45	22-24	25-27	29-31	32-33	34-36	45
40	19-21	23-24	27-28	29-31	31-33	40
35	17-18	20-22	24-26	27-28	28-30	35
30	14-16	17-19	21-23	24-26	25-27	30
25	12-13	14-16	18-20	22-23	22-24	25
20	11 Down	13 Down	17 Down	21 Down	21 Down	20

*Reprinted by permission of Dr. H.M. Barrow.

CRITIQUE OF MOTOR ABILITY TESTS

The underlying assumption of the existence of a trait called *motor ability* has never been substantiated through a rigorously developed network of scientific evidence. Moreover, the use of the label **trait** in describing motor ability suggests that this ability is an enduring and unchanging dimension of motor behavior. Yet it is evident that the items included in motor ability tests can be improved with practice; thus, these items cannot measure innate motor ability. Of course, the same problems face researchers in the areas of intelligence testing and affective measurement. Barrow and McGee (1980) observe that, even though motor ability improves with training, experience, and maturity, individual differences in students tend to remain the same throughout the school years. However, no documentation is provided in support of this observation.

At the height of popularity of motor ability test usage, the procedure used to validate motor ability tests was fairly standard. Basically, it involved administering a large number of tests thought to represent various components of motor ability. A much smaller group of test items was extracted from this larger set, usually on the basis of two factors: It could be administered to a large group in a reasonable amount of time; and it correlated highly with the large test set, suggesting that it measured the same thing. Although this approach to validation was considered sound at the time, it was not without problems. There was no evidence that the large test set actually measured motor ability and simply no way of knowing whether it did or not.

Thus, although some motor ability tests were carefully developed, legitimate questions can be raised about the validity of these batteries. Unless new evidence is uncovered regarding a general motor ability component, motor ability tests will continue to be neglected in the future.

SHOULD MOTOR ABILITY TESTS BE USED FOR ABILITY GROUPING?

Unfortunately the validity of motor ability batteries is questionable, since many physical educators intuitively feel these types of tests would be useful to group individuals for participation in a physical activity program. Clarke (1976) is a strong proponent of ability grouping by general abilities in a physical education program, "where activities may vary either within a single class period or from day to day, or where the same activity does not continue on consecutive days for more than a week or two at most" (p. 229). Methodological problems aside, what is the practical usefulness of motor ability tests for classifying students?

If people are to be grouped on the basis of performance, what type of test should be used? Regrettably, several factors work against the use of motor ability tests for classification purposes. As early as 1934, researchers began questioning the concept of general motor ability in favor of **task specificity,** a concept of ability being specific to a given task rather than general across tasks. Ragsdale and Breckenfield (1934) in an investigation of junior high school boys conclude that "it is probably incorrect to speak of general motor ability in the same sense that we speak of general intelligence. In this study we [Ragsdale and Breckenfield] have distinguished two general factors which we have called strength and speed in running" (p. 54). In a study of motor ability of college men, Hoskins (1934) reported low correlations between motor ability as measured by the McCloy Test and subjective ratings of athletic skill in several activities. In direct contrast, McCloy (1934) reported correlations of 0.92 between his track and field items and subjective ratings of basketball skill and 0.84 between these items and subjective ratings of soccer skill. A year later Jones (1935) obtained low correlations between several motor ability tests, while Seashore (1942) distinguished between fine and gross motor abilities. In the late 1950s the task specificity concept gained impetus with the work of Franklin Henry. Henry (1958) argued:

The theory of specific motor abilities implies that some individuals are gifted with many specific abilities and others with only a few; it follows that there will inevitably be significant correlations between total test battery scores when tests involving many abilities are lumped together. The general motor factor which thus makes its appearance is a sample, fundamentally, of how many specifics the individual has, and general motor ability does exist in this sense (p. 127).

Support for Henry's argument came swiftly. Lotter (1961) found that the neuro-motor specificity of speed of movement ability of arms and legs was extremely high. Lotter stated that "task specificity . . . implies that it is largely a matter of chance whether an individual who has relatively high (or low) ability in one motor task will have a high or low ability in another motor task unless the two tasks are so similar as to be practically identical" (p. 57).

Further evidence for task specificity can be found in studies that reveal that general motor ability test scores do not correlate highly with various sports skills. Singer (1975) prepared an excellent review of this literature. One example of such research is a study by Burdeshaw, Spagens, and Weis (1970), who used the Scott Motor Ability Test to classify 106 women as a low motor ability group. This group was subdivided into three groups: Group 1 received a basic skills course; Group 2, a sport course other than badminton; and Group 3, no special treatment. All groups were subsequently enrolled in a badminton course. Testing at the midpoint and end of the badminton course revealed no difference among groups. The authors concluded that the "results supported the theory of specificity in motor skills and did not support the worth of basic skills courses in facilitating subsequent performance in the specific skills of badminton" (p. 472). Current motor learning textbooks summarize the same literature and draw similar conclusions about motor ability. (See the References at the end of this chapter.)

Not only do motor ability tests appear to be inappropriate for ability grouping in general, they also do not resolve the problem of determining sex-fair ability groups. For many years the separation of males and females in physical education programs in the United States was a common practice, especially in junior and senior high schools and colleges. During the early part of the twentieth century, several affluent communities even provided separate gymnasiums and swimming pools for males and females. When the Title IX legislation was adopted, many schools complied with this law by offering a substantial number of coeducational classes. This is a desirable practice, of course, for appropriate activities. However, Title IX does not specify that *all* physical education units must be coeducational. In fact, the law allows "separation by sex within physical education during competition in wrestling, boxing, ice hockey, football, basketball and other sports, the purpose or major activity of which involves bodily contact" (Federal Register, 1977:24132). On the other hand, the more general and pervasive policy dictates the use of ability grouping in physical education with the understanding that *group membership is determined on the basis of individual performance rather than sex.* The important point is that a male or female should not be assigned to a group in physical education merely on the basis of his or her sex but rather on the basis of ability to perform the activity being taught.

Safrit and others (1980) presented an overview of the research on three gender differences in motor performance—physical performance differences, body structure and composition differences, and differences in cardiorespiratory function. Thus true gender differences exist for many forms of motor behavior. How are these considered when dealing with motor ability tests as a means of grouping?

Even if the use of motor ability tests for sex-fair ability grouping could be justified, physical educators would face the practical problem of developing valid motor ability tests for both sexes. When separate programs existed for males and females in the past, apparently developing separate motor ability instruments, one for each sex, seemed reasonable. Thus, although a number of motor ability tests have been developed, none of these was designed to be administered to both sexes. Certainly ability grouping will not be sex-fair unless the same test is used to classify all students. The Illinois State Board of Education (1982) published a booklet containing practical tips on ability grouping and performance evaluation in physical education. The board recommends that motor ability tests not be used to group students by ability.

SUMMARY

The issues associated with the concept of motor ability and its measurement were once a major focus in the physical education field. This emphasis has been diminished by the experimental findings that ability seemed to be specific to a given motor task rather than general across tasks. Nonetheless, at the time motor ability tests were being constructed, the measurement techniques were quite sophisticated and served as models for subsequent test development in other aspects of physical education and exercise science. Currently, the tests have limited usefulness, either as measures of general motor ability or as a means of ability grouping.

LEARNING EXPERIENCES

1. From the library select one of the older textbooks in measurement and evaluation in physical education (published before 1950). Review the sections on the measurement of motor ability, motor capacity, and motor educability. Examine the test items in each type of test. In what ways are the three types of tests different? Write a report on your analysis.
2. Set up the Scott Obstacle Race and the Barrow Zigzag Run Test in a laboratory or gymnasium setting. The women in your class should take the Scott test; the men should take the Barrow test. Calculate the mean, standard deviation, and T-scores for each gender, and compare these values with the norms in Table 15-1 (Scott test) and Table 15-4 (Barrow test).

REFERENCES

Alden, F.D., Horton, M.O., and Caldwell, G.M. 1932. A motor ability test for university women for the classification of entering students into homogeneous groups. Research Quarterly 3(1):85-120.

Barrow, H.M. 1954. Test of motor ability for college men. Research Quarterly **25**(3): 253-260.

Barrow, H.M., and McGee, R. 1980. A practical approach to measurement in physical education. Philadelphia: Lea & Febiger.

Burdeshaw, D., Spagens, J.E., and Weis, P.A. 1970. Evaluation of general versus specific instruction of badminton skills to women of low motor ability. Research Quarterly **41**(4):472-477.

Clarke, H.H. 1976. Application of measurement to health and physical education. Englewood Cliffs, N.J.: Prentice-Hall, Inc.

Henry, F.M. 1958. Specificity versus generality in learning motor skills. Proceedings of the College Physical Education Association **61**:127.

Hoskins, R.N. 1934. The relationship of measurements of general motor capacity to the learning of specific psychomotor skills. Research Quarterly **5**(1):63-72.

Howe, E.C. 1930. The precision and validation of physical fitness. Research Quarterly **1**(2):90-96.

Humiston, D. 1937. A measurement of motor ability in college women. Research Quarterly **8**(2):181-185.

Illinois State Board of Education. 1982. Tips and techniques: ability grouping and performance evaluation in physical education. Springfield, Ill.: Illinois State Board of Education.

Jones, L.M. 1935. A factorial analysis of ability in fundamental motor skills. In Contributions to education. New York: Teachers College, Columbia University.

Kirkendall, D.R., Gruber, J.J., and Johnson, R.E. 1980. Measurement and evaluation for physical educators. Dubuque, Iowa: Wm C Brown Group.

Lotter, W.S. 1961. Specificity or generality of speed of systematically related movements. Research Quarterly **32**(1):55-62.

McCloy, C.H. 1934. The measurement of general motor capacity and general motor ability. Research Quarterly, March Suppl.: 46-61.

Ragsdale, C.E., and Breckenfield, I.J. 1934. The organization of physical and motor traits in junior high school boys. Research Quarterly **5**(3):47-55.

Safrit, M.J., and others. 1980. Issues in setting motor performance standards. Quest **32**(2):152-162.

Scott, M.G. 1939. The assessment of motor abilities of college women through objective tests. Research Quarterly **10**(3):63-83.

Scott, M.G., and French, E. 1959. Measurement and evaluation in physical education. Dubuque, Iowa: Wm C Brown Group.

Seashore, H.G. 1942. Some relationships of fine and gross motor abilities. Research Quarterly **13**(3):259-274.

Singer, R.N. 1975. Motor learning and performance: an application to physical education skills. London: Collier Macmillan Ltd.

United States Department of Health, Education, and Welfare, 1977. Federal Register **40**(108), June 4.

ANNOTATED READINGS

Keogh, J., and Sugden, D. 1985. Movement skill development. New York: Macmillan Publishing Co., pp. 182-194.

Includes chapter on movement abilities; attempts to identify children's movement abilities; views ability not as a general trait but rather as represented as components of ability, including factors such as balance, general flexibility, speed, and strength.

Magill, R.A. 1985. Motor learning: concepts and applications, ed. 2, Dubuque, Iowa: Wm C Brown Group, pp. 252-281.

Includes chapter on individual differences; notes that individual differences research does not support the notion of a "general motor ability"; points out that this research has identified various motor abilities that characterize individuals; describes a task analysis process to identify abilities underlying a motor skill; uses the tennis serve as an example.

Oxendine, J.B. 1984. Psychology of motor learning, ed. 2, Englewood Cliffs, N.J.: Prentice-Hall, Inc., pp. 315-332.

Includes chapter on the dimensions of human differences; discusses the lack of support for the view of motor ability as a general trait; notes that general motor ability tests have proved to have little validity in determining one's overall capacity or potential in motor skills.

Sage, G.E. 1984. Motor learning and control. Dubuque, Iowa: Wm C Brown Group, pp. 273-283.

Includes chapter on motor abilities and motor behavior; discusses the notion of a general motor ability as one of the most persistent bits of folklore in physical education and coaching; reviews the development of motor ability tests and the reasons they are not valid indicators of an underlying trait thought to be general motor ability; recommends a classification system of motor abilities.

Schmidt, R.A. 1982. Motor control and learning. Champaign, Ill.: Human Kinetics Publishers, Inc., pp. 379-433.

Includes chapter on individual differences and capabilities; discusses the concept of general motor ability and notes that considerable doubt can be cast on the general motor ability hypothesis; demonstrates that research has not supported this hypothesis; reinforces the view that motor abilities are specific to a particular task.

Singer, R.N. 1975. Motor learning and human performance, ed. 2, New York: Macmillan Publishing Co., pp. 213-306.

Refers to tests of motor capacity, motor fitness, and motor ability; notes that a strong relationship between motor ability and athletic ability has not been demonstrated; suggests that if general motor ability really exists, it must be verified in future research.

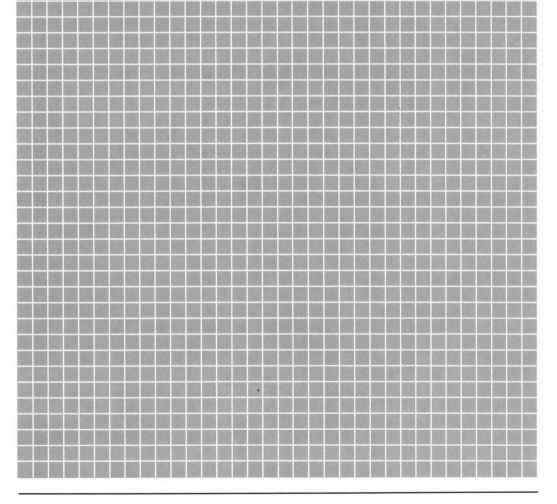

Part Six

Measures of Related Abilities

16

Tests of Affective Behavior

An **affect** is a sociological or psychological characteristic manifested in a feeling or behavior. Affective behaviors of interest to the physical educator and exercise scientist include attitudes, interests, values, psychological traits, and emotional states of the individual. Physical educators have tended to be most interested in the development of inventories to measure the attitudes of individuals toward physical education or physical activity. Other inventories have been constructed to assess the psychological characteristics of individuals in a sport or physical activity; however, the majority of these instruments have been employed by researchers rather than by physical education teachers and exercise specialists.

An **attitude** is a feeling one has about a specific attitude object, such as a situation, a person, an activity, and so forth. The interest in the measurement of attitudes toward physical education or physical activity is not surprising, since it is often assumed that an individual with a positive attitude toward physical education will be more inclined to participate in physical activity. Although this line of reasoning is intuitively appealing, it has been shown repeatedly that attitudes do not reflect behavior. When people are asked about their attitude toward physical activity in general, most will express a positive view; yet many of these individuals have sedentary life-styles.

In private fitness clubs as well as physical education classes, the belief that unfavorable attitudes toward physical activity can be altered with a good instructional program has provided a rationale for the measurement of attitudes. In view of the favorable attitudes generally expressed toward physical activity, this rationale loses much of its impact, and the practical significance of changing an individual's attitude from favorable to more favorable is minimal.

Another affective behavior frequently measured in the physical education field is **interests,** which reflect one's likes and dislikes about various forms of physical activity, programming, scheduling, and so forth. In a school setting **sportsmanship** is often stressed. In fact, some teachers grade each student on sportsmanship, although they may not measure this characteristic in a systematic, objective manner. (This is discussed in more detail later in the chapter.) Several instruments have been developed to measure **social behavior,** which encompasses the relationships among peers, in a physical education setting. Of long-standing interest in the field are the measures of psychological characteristics, such as stress, anxiety, and a variety of elements of personality, which should be tested by a person trained in psychology.

Several shortcomings are associated with the use of affective inventories. When changes in affective behavior are of interest, the second administration of the inventory might be affected by a **reactive effect** from the first testing session. For instance, examinees may remember how they responded to the items during the first administration, or their affective behavior might change because of the first test session. For example, some may have given little thought to their feelings about physical activity, especially in a broad context. Once they are exposed to new ideas, they may begin to examine their feelings carefully, leading to a solidification of attitudes. The next time the inventory is administered, they may change their responses to the items. In these cases the score would reflect a change in attitude when, in reality, no change has taken place.

A second deficiency of many instruments measuring affective behavior is the possibility of **response distortion.** For example examinees may not always respond with total honesty to these measures, faking good or bad responses, answering in a socially desirable way, or distorting responses in other ways. The more sophisticated inventories measuring affective behavior frequently include items designed to detect the tendency of examinees to distort items.

TYPES OF MEASURES

To construct a measure of affective behavior, the type of affect must be carefully defined and the subcategories of behavior identified so that a table of specifications can be developed, as described in Chapter 9. The number of items for each category is decided on the basis of the importance of each. (Remember that the number of items represents the weighting of each category.) At this stage a decision must be made on the type of item to use—generally, rating scales, forced-choice inventories, and questionnaires.

Likert scale

The **Likert scale** requires an expression of the individual's degree of agreement or disagreement with a series of affective statements. Kenyon's Attitude Toward

Physical Activity Inventory uses a Likert scale. One of the items on this inventory is the statement, "I would gladly put in the necessary years of daily hard training for the chance to try out for the U.S. Olympic team." Response choices are the following: Very strongly agree, Strongly agree, Agree, Undecided, Disagree, Strongly disagree, and Very strongly disagree. The examinee responds by circling the desired response on the answer sheet. A five-step version of a Likert scale is shown below:

1	2	3	4	5
Strongly disagree	Disagree	Undecided	Agree	Strongly agree

Likert scales typically include five or seven steps. However, a two-step format (agree-disagree) may also be encountered, as well as scales including 10 or more steps. Increasing the number of scale steps increases the reliability of the item, up to a point. Most raters are not humanly capable of using a large number of steps; therefore, it is probably best not to exceed seven categories.

Semantic differential scale

The **semantic differential scale** involves the rating of concepts using bipolar adjectives with scales anchored at the extremes. *Bipolar adjectives* represent opposite meanings, such as good-bad, strong-weak, and active-passive. An example of the semantic differential scale used to assess one's attitude toward physical activity is shown in the boxed material. (Later in the chapter the Children's Attitude Toward Physical Activity Scale, which uses the semantic differential scale, is described.)

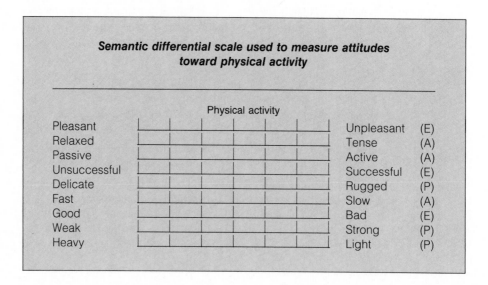

Semantic differential scale used to measure attitudes toward physical activity

Physical activity

Pleasant	Unpleasant	(E)
Relaxed	Tense	(A)
Passive	Active	(A)
Unsuccessful	Successful	(E)
Delicate	Rugged	(P)
Fast	Slow	(A)
Good	Bad	(E)
Weak	Strong	(P)
Heavy	Light	(P)

The bipolar adjectives can readily be adapted to evaluate numerous concepts, and individuals can easily evaluate several different concepts using the same rating form. The examinee is asked to mark one of the seven points best reflecting his or her feelings about the concept. The score for each item ranges from 1 to 7 if the positive adjective in the pair is listed to the right, and from 7 to 1 if the positive adjective is placed to the left.

Note that a letter—E, A, or P—appears to the right of each item, representing the three dimensions of a concept that can be measured with the semantic differential. The Evaluation dimension is best described by the good-bad adjective pair; the Activity dimension, by the fast-slow pair; and the Potency dimension by the strong-weak pair. At least three items should be included for each dimension. (These letters are displayed in the boxed material for illustrative purposes only.) Although the test user should know the correct dimension for each item, this information does not have to be included on the test form.

Other types of scales

When the Likert scale or the semantic differential scale is used, the respondent indicates agreement or disagreement with a statement or preference for specific meanings of a particular concept. Statements that must be answered either true or false provide another example of agree-disagree scales. The Physical Estimation and Attraction Scale, described later in this chapter, uses true-false responses. This scale is similar in style to the **forced-choice item.** With scales of forced-choice items the examinee is required to choose among two or more alternatives that appear equally favorable or unfavorable. Discrimination and preference values of the items are determined, and the alternatives are combined in such a manner as to equalize these values.

Rating scales such as the type described in Chapter 8 are also used to measure affective behavior. For example, a five-point scale could be used to measure sportsmanship, with a descriptor specifically dealing with sportsmanship listed under each point. The desired elements of sportsmanship would be included under point 5, and the undesirable elements, under point 1. The points in-between would reflect various stages of sportsmanship.

Another method for measuring affective behavior is a *questionnaire.* Typically, the examinee responds to questions by selecting a response out of a set of options. An example of this type of instrument is the Health-Related Physical Fitness Opinionnaire (Safrit and Wood, 1983). Users and nonusers of the AAHPERD Health-Related Physical Fitness Test are asked about their opinions of the test and how it compares with the Youth Fitness Test.

Another type of scale used in exercise science is the **perceived exertion scale** (Borg, 1973), which assesses the examinee's perception of his or her physical exertion during exercise. It is described later in this chapter.

Weak measures

Recall that a **weak measure** is a measure with inadequate evidence of validity and reliability. When a measure is used to make a short-term decision about an examinee that could readily be modified, a weak measure can be quite useful in the absence of a more valid indicator. For example, a physical education program may include a goal of developing physical fitness. Time may be allotted for daily participation in jogging to meet an objective for cardiorespiratory function. Formative evaluation procedures may be used to monitor progress toward the predetermined standard. Since many teachers identify concomitant concerns associated with each major objective, testing *attitudes* toward this form of physical activity on a regular basis may be desirable. Although positive attitudes do not ensure participation in vigorous physical activity, a negative attitude would cause some concern since it might reflect an unwillingness to engage in aerobic activities in the future.

A simple rating scale could be devised to obtain feedback on the students' attitudinal dispositions, as shown in the following boxed material. Although this is a *weak* measure, it can be justified if used on a continuing basis to provide a rough estimate of attitude. Students could be *forced* to run for 12 minutes during every class period; if they dislike this activity, however, they might develop negative attitudes toward physical fitness—even toward physical education—which may be retained.

Weak measure of student attitude toward jogging

How did you feel about jogging today?

Awful   1   2   3   4   5   6   7   Great

Students would be asked to circle the number that best represents their feelings. Little time is required to obtain this information, since students can record a response as they leave class. They are asked not to mark the form in any other way, thus assuring anonymity. One word of caution here: one should avoid collecting this type of data only on one day of the week. If the data were always collected on Fridays, for example, the students' perceptions might be affected by the forthcoming weekend or by fatigue from the previous school week. A random selection of days is preferable. The averages of the responses for all students can be calculated every week and plotted, as in Fig. 16-1.

Since a rating of 4 represents the neutral point on the scale, it is desirable if the average falls above that point. If more students feel *awful* about jogging than

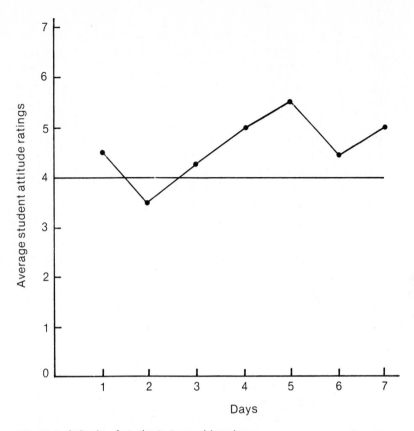

FIG. 16-1. *Attitude of students toward jogging.*

great, some type of intervention is necessary. Initially, the physical education staff might talk to them to find out why they have negative feelings.

USES OF AFFECTIVE MEASURES

Measures of affective behavior within the realm of sport and physical activity have been used in at least three ways: to assess the affective behavior of individual students in physical education classes, to assess the level of affective behavior for a class, and to control or manipulate some aspect of affective behavior in conducting a research study.

Considering the affective behavior of an individual student first, educators most frequently express concerns about attitudes toward physical education, sportsmanship, and self-concept. Many physical education teachers feel that a student's *attitude* should be an important component of his or her grade. Usually the teacher is most interested in the student's attitude toward participation in physical education classes, that is, the behavior of the student in class. Sometimes attitude is judged on the basis of the answers to these questions: Is the appropriate uniform worn? Does the student "try" in class? Does the student shower at the end of class? (See Chapter 19 for a discussion of whether factors such as these should be considered in determining a student's grade.)

Very few well-developed instruments are available to assess the affective behavior of an *individual student* in a physical education setting. Although a number of tests have been developed in the field, they were constructed years ago when the standards for test development were not as rigorous as today's. Several affective measures used in the exercise science field are included at the end of this chapter to provide examples of this test market.

Most of the affective inventories in the field should be used only to examine *group* behavior. It would be appropriate to administer an attitude inventory to a physical education class, calculate the mean and standard deviation of the class data, and use this information as part of the evaluation of the physical education program in the school. If, on the average, the class attitude is negative, the physical education teacher could attempt to create a more positive environment. On the other hand, it would be inappropriate to use an individual's score on the inventory to determine his or her grade on attitude toward physical education.

EXAMPLES OF AFFECTIVE MEASURES

While many instruments have been developed to measure the affective behavior of interest to the physical educator and exercise scientist, few have been developed according to the rigorous standards set for the construction of educational and psychological tests (American Psychological Association, 1984). In most cases, while reliabilities have been acceptable, content validity has been minimal and construct validity has been inadequate and frequently overlooked. Examples of four types of instruments are included in this section: stress and anxiety, social behavior, attitudes, and sportsmanship and leadership.

Stress and anxiety

STRESS INVENTORY (Miller and Allen, 1982)

Test objective. To measure an individual's level of stress.

Test description. The inventory is presented in the boxed material.

Comments. This inventory provides information on a variety of stress indicators and, in this respect, would have logical validity. Obviously the examinee who marks "Yes" by many items would be viewed as having a high level of stress. A low-stress individual would respond "No" to most of the items. It would be unusual for an individual to mark "No" by *all* items, since everyone functions with a certain level of stress. For information on other aspects of this inventory, including reliability, validity, and scoring, refer to the original source.*

---

*For more information, write to Fitness: A Lifetime Commitment, D.K. Miller and T.E. Allen, Burgess Publishing Company, 7108 Ohms Lane, Minneapolis, MN 55435.

Stress inventory*

Answer yes or no to each of the following questions:

Yes	No	
_____	_____	1. Do you often experience headaches or backaches?
_____	_____	2. When sitting in a chair and talking to someone, do you continually move in the chair to seek a comfortable position?
_____	_____	3. When retiring for the night, are you unable to fall asleep immediately?
_____	_____	4. Do you often grind your teeth when you are confronted with an unpleasant experience?
_____	_____	5. Do you easily become angry or frustrated when you are faced with a problem for which there is no immediate solution?
_____	_____	6. Do you often complain of being tired?
_____	_____	7. Does your face often hold expressions of intense concentration?
_____	_____	8. Do you often drum your fingers aimlessly or forcibly to express irritation?
_____	_____	9. Does your posture appear stiff when you sit or walk?
_____	_____	10. Are you unable to concentrate on one problem at a time?
_____	_____	11. Are you unable to relax voluntarily?
_____	_____	12. Do you often experience nervousness and uneasy feelings?
_____	_____	13. Do you become upset when your plans are interrupted or must be changed?
_____	_____	14. Are you highly competitive in sports, in your test grades, in your daily responsibilities?
_____	_____	15. Are you time-conscious?
_____	_____	16. Do you experience extreme dissatisfaction and anxiety when you fail to achieve success in your endeavors?
_____	_____	17. Are you an aggressive person?
_____	_____	18. Are you often too busy to allow time for physical activity?
_____	_____	19. Do you plan your day's activities and often budget your time?
_____	_____	20. Are you critical of yourself when you make a mistake?
_____	_____	21. Do you feel "uptight" at the end of the day?
_____	_____	22. Are you impatient when others are late for an appointment with you?
_____	_____	23. Do you often set high goals or levels of achievement for yourself?
_____	_____	24. Do you experience bad moods often?
_____	_____	25. Are you unyielding when others disagree with your beliefs or convictions?

*From Miller, D.K., and Allen, T.E.

SPORT COMPETITION ANXIETY TEST (Martens, 1977)

Test objective. To measure individual differences in the construct of *competitive sport anxiety;* to measure competitive A (anxiety) trait, which is defined as "a construct that describes individual differences in the tendency to perceive competitive situations as threatening and to respond to these situations with A (anxiety)-state reactions of varying intensity" (Martens, 1977: 36).

Description. The Sport Competition Anxiety Test for Children (SCAT-C) is presented in Table 16-1.

Materials. Test forms and pencils.

Scoring. Items 2, 3, 5, 8, 9, 12, 14, and 15 are scored using the following key:

1 = Hardly ever   2 = Sometimes   3 = Often

Items 6 and 11 are scored using the following key:

1 = Often   2 = Sometimes   3 = Hardly ever

Items 1, 4, 7, 10, and 13, the remaining items, are not scored; they are included in the inventory as spurious items, to direct attention to elements of competition other than anxiety.

TABLE 16-1. *Sport Competition Anxiety Test for Children**

Illinois competition questionnaire
Form C

Directions: We want to know how you feel about *competition*. You know what competition is. We all compete. We try to do better than our brother or sister or friend at something. We try to score more points in a game. We try to get the best grade in class or win a prize that we want. We all compete in sports and games. Below are some sentences about how boys and girls feel when they compete in sports and games. Read each statement below and decide if *you* HARDLY EVER, or SOMETIMES, or OFTEN feel this way when you compete in sports and games. Mark A if your choice is HARDLY EVER, mark B if you choose SOMETIMES, and mark C if you choose OFTEN. There are no right or wrong answers. Do not spend too much time on any one statement. *Remember:* choose the word that describes how you *usually* feel when competing in *sports and games.*

	Hardly ever	Sometimes	Often
1. Competing against others is fun.	A ☐	B ☐	C ☐
2. Before I compete I feel uneasy.	A ☐	B ☐	C ☐
3. Before I compete I worry about not performing well.	A ☐	B ☐	C ☐
4. I am a good sportsman when I compete.	A ☐	B ☐	C ☐
5. When I compete I worry about making mistakes.	A ☐	B ☐	C ☐
6. Before I compete I am calm.	A ☐	B ☐	C ☐
7. Setting a goal is important when competing.	A ☐	B ☐	C ☐
8. Before I compete I get a funny feeling in my stomach.	A ☐	B ☐	C ☐
9. Just before competing I notice my heart beats faster than usual.	A ☐	B ☐	C ☐
10. I like rough games.	A ☐	B ☐	C ☐
11. Before I compete I feel relaxed.	A ☐	B ☐	C ☐
12. Before I compete I am nervous.	A ☐	B ☐	C ☐
13. Team sports are more exciting than individual sports.	A ☐	B ☐	C ☐
14. I get nervous wanting to start the game.	A ☐	B ☐	C ☐
15. Before I compete I usually get uptight.	A ☐	B ☐	C ☐

*From Martens, R.

Validity. Content validity was claimed on the basis of the assessment by six judges of the content validity and grammatical clarity of the items. Extensive evidence of construct validity is presented in Martens' monograph. The details of these studies are beyond the scope of this book; however, the general approaches to construct validity included studies of group differences. High scorers on the SCAT-C were expected to manifest higher A states in stressful competitive situations than low scorers on the SCAT-C.

Reliability. Test-retest reliability was determined for both sexes of grades 5 and 6, and 8 and 9. Within-day reliability coefficients ranged from 0.85 to 0.93. Test-retest reliabilities ranged from 0.61 to 0.87. When $R_{xx'}$ was calculated to estimate reliability, the range of the coefficients was 0.68 to 0.89.

Norms. Both standard scores and percentile norms for normal children, grades 4 to 6 and grades 7 to 9, are presented in Table 16-2.

Comments. This test is easy to administer in a group setting. However, the Martens monograph should be reviewed before using SCAT so that the theoretical framework generating this instrument is understood.

Social behavior
COWELL SOCIAL ADJUSTMENT INDEX (Cowell, 1958)

Test objective. To measure the extent of students' social adjustment, both positive and negative, within their social group.

Description. Forms A and B of the scale are shown in Table 16-3. Each student is rated by the teacher. A mark is placed in the cell that best reflects the degree to which the behavior is judged to be displayed.

Materials. Test forms and pencils.

Scoring. The total index score is the sum of the points for the 10 items in Form A minus the sum of the points for the 10 items in Form B.

Validity. $r_{xy} = 0.63$, using the Pupil Who's Who Ratings as a criterion measure; $r_{xy} = 0.50$, using the Pupil Personal Distance Ballot.

Reliability. $r_{xx'} = 0.82$.

Norms. Norms are available for junior high school boys in the original source.

Comments. This index was developed by Charles Cowell, a well-known physical educator and long-time faculty member at Purdue University. It can be used with boys and girls, ages 12 to 17.

BLANCHARD BEHAVIOR RATING SCALE (Blanchard, 1936)

Test objective. To measure the character and personality of students.

Description. The scale shown in Table 16-4 is used by the teacher to evaluate students in classes. For each item the teacher circles the number that best reflects his or her judgment of the student's behavior. A form is used for each student.

TABLE 16-2. *Normative data for Sport Competition Anxiety Test**

SCAT-C Norms for normal children, grades 4-6

Raw score	Male Standard score	Percentile	Female Standard score	Percentile
30	744	99	734	99
29	722	99	711	99
28	700	99	688	98
27	678	97	666	97
26	656	95	643	92
25	634	90	620	88
24	612	87	597	85
23	590	84	575	80
22	568	77	552	74
21	546	71	529	67
20	524	63	507	56
19	502	56	484	48
18	480	46	461	39
17	458	41	438	31
16	436	33	416	24
15	415	28	393	16
14	393	21	370	14
13	371	13	347	10
12	349	9	325	6
11	327	2	302	2
10	305	1	279	1

SCAT-C Norms for normal children, grades 7-9

Raw score	Male Standard score	Percentile	Female Standard score	Percentile
30	730	99	688	99
29	709	99	669	97
28	687	99	649	96
27	665	97	630	91
26	644	93	610	88
25	622	90	591	84
24	601	85	571	76
23	579	79	552	70
22	558	73	532	63
21	536	66	513	53
20	515	59	493	49
19	493	51	473	42
18	472	43	454	35
17	450	37	434	30
16	429	30	415	26
15	407	24	395	19
14	386	18	376	17
13	364	12	356	12
12	342	8	337	9
11	321	4	317	5
10	299	2	298	2

*From Martens, R.

TABLE 16-3. Cowell Social Adjustment Index*

Form A

Instructions: Think carefully of the student's behavior in group situations; check each behavior trend according to its degree of descriptiveness.

Behavior trends	Descriptive of student			
	Markedly (+3)	Somewhat (+2)	Only slightly (+1)	Not at all (0)
1. Enters heartily and with enjoyment into the spirit of social intercourse.				
2. Frank, talkative and sociable, does not stand on ceremony.				
3. Self-confident and self-reliant, tends to take success for granted, strong initiative, prefers to lead.				
4. Quick and decisive in movement, pronounced or excessive energy output.				
5. Prefers group activities, work or play, not easily satisfied with individual projects.				
6. Adaptable to new situations, makes adjustments readily, welcomes change.				
7. Is self-composed, seldom shows signs of embarrassment.				
8. Tends to elation of spirits, seldom gloomy or moody.				
9. Seeks a broad range of friendships, not selective or exclusive in games and the like.				
10. Hearty and cordial, even to strangers, forms acquaintanceships very easily.				

Form B

Instructions: Think carefully of the student's behavior in group situations; check each behavior trend according to its degree of descriptiveness.

Behavior trends	Descriptive of student			
	Markedly (−3)	Somewhat (−2)	Only slightly (−1)	Not at all (0)
1. Somewhat prudish, awkward, easily embarrassed in his social contacts.				
2. Secretive, seclusive, not inclined to talk unless spoken to.				
3. Lacking in self-confidence and initiative, a follower.				
4. Slow in movement, deliberative, or perhaps indecisive. Energy output moderate or deficient.				
5. Prefers to work and play alone, tends to avoid group activities.				
6. Shrinks from making new adjustments, prefers the habitual to the stress of reorganization required by the new.				
7. Is self-conscious, easily embarrassed, timid, or "bashful."				
8. Tends to depression, frequently gloomy or moody.				
9. Shows preference for a narrow range of intimate friends and tends to exclude others from his association.				
10. Reserved and distant except to intimate friends, does not form acquaintanceships readily.				

*From Cowell, C.C.

TABLE 16-4. *Blanchard Behavior Frequency Rating Scale**

Personal information	No opportunity to observe	Never	Seldom	Fairly often	Frequently	Extremely often	Score
Leadership							
1. He is popular with classmates		1	2	3	4	5	
2. He seeks responsibility in the classroom		1	2	3	4	5	
3. He shows intellectual leadership in the classroom		1	2	3	4	5	
Positive active qualities							
4. He quits on tasks requiring perseverance.		5	4	3	2	1	
5. He exhibits aggressiveness in his relationship with others. . .		1	2	3	4	5	
6. He shows initiative in assuming responsibility in unfamiliar situations.		1	2	3	4	5	
7. He is alert to new opportunities		1	2	3	4	5	
Positive mental qualities							
8. He shows keenness of mind.		1	2	3	4	5	
9. He volunteers ideas		1	2	3	4	5	
Self-control							
10. He grumbles over decisions of classmates		5	4	3	2	1	
11. He takes a justified criticism by teacher or classmate without showing anger or pouting		1	2	3	4	5	
Cooperation							
12. He is loyal to his group		1	2	3	4	5	
13. He discharges his group responsibilities well		1	2	3	4	5	
14. He is cooperative in his attitude toward the teacher		1	2	3	4	5	
Social action standards							
15. He makes loud-mouthed criticisms and comments.		5	4	3	2	1	
16. He respects the rights of others		1	2	3	4	5	
Ethical social qualities							
17. He cheats.		5	4	3	2	1	
18. He is truthful.		1	2	3	4	5	
Qualities of efficiency							
19. He seems satisifed to "get by" with tasks assigned		5	4	3	2	1	
20. He is dependable and trustworthy		1	2	3	4	5	
21. He has good study habits.		1	2	3	4	5	
Sociability							
22. He is liked by others		1	2	3	4	5	
23. He makes a friendly approach to others in the group.		1	2	3	4	5	
24. He is friendly		1	2	3	4	5	

*From Blanchard, B.E.

Materials. Test forms and pencils.

Scoring. The total score is the sum of the numbers that have been circled for all 24 items. The maximum number of points attainable is 120.

Validity. $r_{xy} = 0.93$, using a criterion of the average of the correlations of each item with the remainder of the items measuring the same trait.

Reliability. $r_{xx'} = 0.71$; this coefficient actually represents the correlation between the scores of teacher and student raters (interrater agreement).

Norms. No norms were reported. Local norms can easily be calculated for several classes, a school, or a school district. Norms developed at the local level are often the most useful, since the tests are more likely to measure the curricular goals of the school system.

Comments. This scale can be used with both boys and girls, ages 12 to 17. The form in Table 16-7 can be adapted by changing the "he" to "she." The general nature of some of the items may lead to considerable bias in the ratings. For example, note item *24:* "He is friendly." What behaviors would a teacher expect to observe for a rating of 5? A rating of 2? Would another teacher make identical judgments of the same student?

Attitudes

ATTITUDE TOWARD PHYSICAL ACTIVITY INVENTORY
(Kenyon, 1968a,b)

Test objective. To measure six dimensions of the attitude construct of active and passive involvement in physical activity.

Description. The test items in the Health and Fitness Scale, one of the six dimensions of involvement in physical activity, are shown in Table 16-5. Both the men's and women's versions of the Attitude Toward Physical Activity (ATPA) Inventory, can be obtained by writing to Dr. Kenyon at the address on p.382.

Materials. Test forms, scoring key, and pencils.

Scoring. Each scale of the ATPA Inventory is scored separately. Thus, each examinee will receive six scores, one for each scale. The six scores should not be summed in an attempt to obtain a single indicator of attitude toward physical activity. Since the profile of six scores most accurately describes the examinee's attitude, a total of the scores is difficult to interpret.

A response to an item can range from *Very Strongly Disagree* to *Very Strongly Agree*, using a 7-point scale. The maximum number of points that can be scored for each dimension is presented in Table 16-6.

Keep in mind that the scoring must be reversed on several items before summing the dimension score. Note, for example, one of the Health and Fitness Scale items: "Being strong and highly fit is *not* the most important thing in my life." An examinee who strongly agrees with this statement would record a score

TABLE 16-5. *Health and Fitness Scale Items**

VSA	SA	A	U	D	SD	VSD	Of all physical activities, those whose purpose is primarily to develop physical fitness would *not* be my first choice.
VSA	SA	A	U	D	SD	VSD	I would usually choose strenuous physical activity over light physical activity, if given the choice.
VSA	SA	A	U	D	SD	VSD	A large part of our daily lives must be committed to vigorous exercise.
VSA	SA	A	U	D	SD	VSD	Being strong and highly fit is *not* the most important thing in my life.
VSA	SA	A	U	D	SD	VSD	The time spent doing daily calisthenics could probably be used more profitably in other ways.
VSA	SA	A	U	D	SD	VSD	Strength and physical stamina are the most important prerequisites to a full life.
VSA	SA	A	U	D	SD	VSD	I believe calisthenics are among the less desirable forms of physical activity.
VSA	SA	A	U	D	SD	VSD	People should spend 20 to 30 minutes a day doing vigorous calisthenics.
VSA	SA	A	U	D	SD	VSD	Of all physical activities, my first choice would be those whose purpose is primarily to develop and maintain physical fitness.
VSA	SA	A	U	D	SD	VSD	Vigorous daily exercises are absolutely necessary to maintain one's general health.

*Reprinted by permission of Kenyon, G.S., University of Lethbridge, Lethbridge, Alberta, Canada.

TABLE 16-6. *Maximum scores for ATPA dimensions*

	Men	Women
Social	70 (10 items)	56 (8 items)
Health and fitness	70 (10 items)	77 (11 items)
Vertigo	70 (10 items)	63 (9 items)
Aesthetic	70 (10 items)	63 (9 items)
Catharsis	63 (9 items)	63 (9 items)
Ascetic	70 (10 items)	56 (8 items)

of 7 on the item. However, since the statement is worded negatively, his or her score should be converted to a score of 1, to convey the expression of a negative attitude toward physical fitness. Adhere closely to the scoring key when scoring this instrument.

Validity. The six dimensions of attitude toward physical activity as hypothesized by Kenyon were verified using factor analytic procedures. Expert opinion also confirmed that the six dimensions adequately represented attitude toward active and passive involvement in physical activity. Several studies of construct validity have been conducted, using the group differences approach. Generally, athletes and nonathletes differed on the scales, as did males and females.

Reliability. The within-day reliability coefficients for males and females on all six dimensions are given in Table 16-7.

Norms. Although means and standard deviations have been reported in studies, too numerous to report in this textbook, no norms have been developed. However, an annotated bibliography by Kenyon and Andrews includes most of

TABLE 16-7. *Within-day reliability coefficients for ATPA**

	Male	Female	N
Social			
United States	0.782	0.794	120
England	0.783	0.790	120
Health and fitness			
United States	0.866	0.883	120
England	0.782	0.840	120
Pursuit of vertigo			
United States	0.910	0.883	120
England	0.867	0.806	120
Aesthetic			
United States	0.865	0.915	120
England	0.851	0.839	120
Catharsis			
United States	0.859	0.873	120
England	0.884	0.868	120
Ascetic			
United States	0.874	0.892	120
England	0.780	0.789	120

*From Pooley, J.C.

these studies up to 1981. References that became available after 1981 are included in the System of Information Retrieval for Leisure and Sport (SIRLS),* a retrieval system at the University of Waterloo.

Comments. This is an excellent inventory, developed by an outstanding sport sociologist in the field. It can be used in a practical as well as a research setting and is appropriate for males and females of high school through college age.

CHILDREN'S ATTITUDE TOWARD PHYSICAL ACTIVITY INVENTORY
(Simon and Smoll, 1974)

Test objective. To measure children's attitude toward vigorous physical activity.

Description. The Children's Attitude Toward Physical Activity (CATPA) was modeled after the ATPA, described in the previous section. A semantic differential scale was used, with each dimension evaluated on the basis of eight pairs of bipolar adjectives, which are used to assess the value of each domain. The items for the social dimension of CATPA are shown on p. 383.

Materials. Test forms and pencils.

Scoring. Each of the six CATPA scales is scored separately. The bipolar adjectives of each pair are separated by a 7-point continuum, and the numerical values assigned to each of the eight adjective pairs are summed for the score on a single dimension. The maximum score for each domain is 56.

Validity. It was assumed that the six ATPA dimensions were equally representative for young children. Except for the ascetic dimension, dimension names on the CATPA are the same as those used for the ATPA. The wording of the dimension descriptions was changed to be more appropriate for young children. In a study of construct validity, children's scores on the CATPA were significantly related to active involvement in physical activity but had no relationship to motor skill proficiency.

Reliability. $R_{xx'} = 0.80 - 0.89$, within-day estimates; $R_{xx'} = 0.44 - 0.62$, test-retest estimates.

Norms. Not reported for this specific test.

Comments. This inventory is useful for program evaluation in the elementary and junior high schools.

PHYSICAL ESTIMATION AND ATTRACTION SCALE (Sonstroem, 1974)

Test objective. To measure the motivational properties of physical self-esteem (Estimation) and interest in vigorous physical activity (Attraction).

---

*The bibliography and more information on references available after 1981 can be obtained by writing to G.S. Kenyon, University of Lethbridge, Lethbridge, Alberta, Canada T1K 3M4.

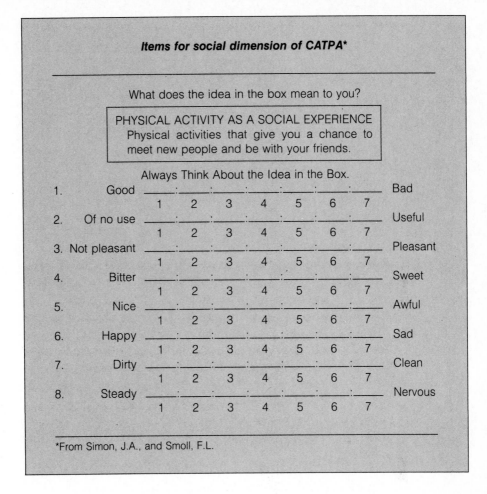

Items for social dimension of CATPA*

What does the idea in the box mean to you?

> PHYSICAL ACTIVITY AS A SOCIAL EXPERIENCE
> Physical activities that give you a chance to
> meet new people and be with your friends.

Always Think About the Idea in the Box.

		1	2	3	4	5	6	7	
1.	Good								Bad
2.	Of no use								Useful
3.	Not pleasant								Pleasant
4.	Bitter								Sweet
5.	Nice								Awful
6.	Happy								Sad
7.	Dirty								Clean
8.	Steady								Nervous

*From Simon, J.A., and Smoll, F.L.

Description. The Physical Estimation and Attraction (PEAS) consists of a random ordering of 11 neutral items, 50 Attraction items, and 33 Estimation items. Sample items are presented on p. 384, and the full-length test along with the scoring key can be obtained from Dr. Sonstroem at the University of Rhode Island. There are two response choices: *true,* if the examinee agrees with the statement, and *false,* if not. Many of the items are of the forced-choice type, requiring the examinee to choose one activity over another.

Materials. Test forms, pencils, and scoring key.

Scoring. For each correct response, 1 point is scored.

Sample Items from PEAS

Estimation Items

Item 6. My body is strong and muscular compared to other boys my age.

Item 26. I am better coordinated than most people I know.

Item 33. I am a good deal stronger than most of my friends.

Attraction Items

Item 4. I would much rather play softball than go for a ride in a car.

Item 17. I like to be in sports that don't require a great amount of running.

Item 34. I would rather play poker than softball.

*From Sonstroem, R.J. Reprinted by permission of the author, University of Rhode Island, Kingston.

Validity. A number of studies of construct validity have been conducted (Sonstroem, 1978). High- and low-fit boys differed significantly in their scores on both the Estimation and Attraction dimensions of the PEAS. Moderate relationships were reported between Estimation scores and a fitness index and between Estimation scores and self-esteem. (Remember that the Estimation dimension taps one's *physical* self-esteem.)

Reliability. $r_{xx'} = 0.87$, Attraction scale, within-day estimate; $r_{xx'} = 0.87$, Estimation scale, within-day estimate; and $r_{xx'} = 0.90$, total scale, test-retest estimate.

Norms. No norms were reported. Summary data from Sonstroem's studies are given in Table 16-8.

Comments. Although the scale has been used with male and female adults and adolescent boys, validity has been determined primarily for the latter sample. Since responses to PEAS items can be distorted and the scores influenced by response sets, the use of a distortion scale is advisable. Response distortion, one of the key words in this chapter, was described in the introductory section.

TABLE 16-8. Summary statistics for PEAS

Group	Scale	N	Mean	Standard deviation
Boys, grades 9-12	Estimation	187	20.40	6.60
	Attraction	187	35.52	8.99
Boys, high school	Estimation	106	22.2	5.75
Boys, junior high school	Estimation	112	21.96	6.29

WEAR ATTITUDE SCALE (Wear, 1955)

Test objective. To measure attitudes toward physical education.

Description. Two forms of the scale, A and B, were developed. Form A is shown in the boxed material on pp. 386 and 387. The students are instructed to respond to the scale according to their perceptions of physical education as an activity course taught during a regular class period. The five possible responses are *Strongly agree, Agree, Undecided, Disagree,* and *Strongly disagree.* Students should answer anonymously, or they should be informed that their responses will not affect their physical education grades.

Materials. Test forms and pencils.

Scoring. The total score is the sum of the scores of the 30 items. Positively worded items are scored 5-4-3-2-1, and negatively worded items are scored 1-2-3-4-5. High scores reflect positive attitudes toward physical education.

Validity. Face validity.

Reliability. $r_{xx'} = 0.94$, Form A; and $r_{xx'} = 0.96$, Form B.

Comments. The Wear Attitude Scale, one of the classic scales of attitude toward physical education, has been widely cited and used. Although the psychometric properties could be strengthened by today's standards, the scale stood for many years as one of the best affective measures in physical education.

Sportsmanship and leadership
LAKIE ATTITUDE TOWARD ATHLETIC COMPETITION SCALE
(Lakie, 1964)

Test objective. To measure players' attitudes toward competition.

Description. Lakie's scale is shown in the boxed material on pp. 388-389. Examinees are instructed to read each item carefully and circle the number of the response best reflecting their judgment of the action described.

Materials. Test forms and pencils.

Scoring. Total the scores for each item. Use the reverse order (5-4-3-2-1) to score negative items. The higher the score, the more competitive the player. A high score reflects a desire to win at any cost. The scale includes 22 items; thus, the highest possible score is 110 points.

Validity. Face validity.

Reliability. $r_{xx'} = 0.81$.

Norms. Not reported for this specific test.

Comments. The Lakie Attitude Scale is similar in type to a number of other measures, mostly unpublished, that have been developed in the field. Attitudes about competition have changed over the years, and some actions that are more acceptable today were viewed as poor sportsmanship many years ago. It is difficult to develop this type of instrument without including items that seem to have quite obvious answers.

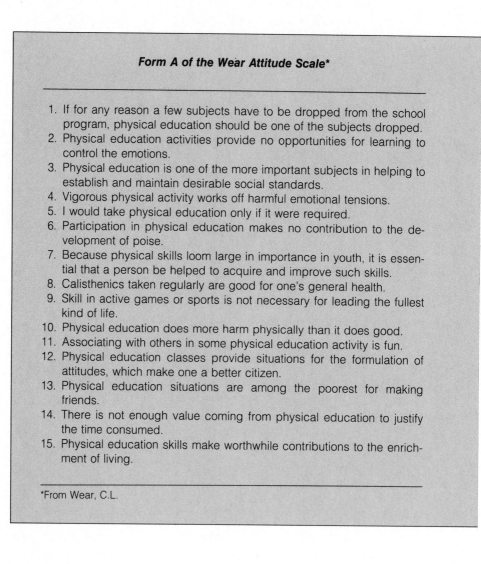

Form A of the Wear Attitude Scale*

1. If for any reason a few subjects have to be dropped from the school program, physical education should be one of the subjects dropped.
2. Physical education activities provide no opportunities for learning to control the emotions.
3. Physical education is one of the more important subjects in helping to establish and maintain desirable social standards.
4. Vigorous physical activity works off harmful emotional tensions.
5. I would take physical education only if it were required.
6. Participation in physical education makes no contribution to the development of poise.
7. Because physical skills loom large in importance in youth, it is essential that a person be helped to acquire and improve such skills.
8. Calisthenics taken regularly are good for one's general health.
9. Skill in active games or sports is not necessary for leading the fullest kind of life.
10. Physical education does more harm physically than it does good.
11. Associating with others in some physical education activity is fun.
12. Physical education classes provide situations for the formulation of attitudes, which make one a better citizen.
13. Physical education situations are among the poorest for making friends.
14. There is not enough value coming from physical education to justify the time consumed.
15. Physical education skills make worthwhile contributions to the enrichment of living.

*From Wear, C.L.

16. People get all the physical exercise they need in just taking care of their daily work.
17. All who are physically able will profit from an hour of physical education each day.
18. Physical education makes a valuable contribution toward building up an adequate reserve of strength and endurance for everyday living.
19. Physical education tears down sociability by encouraging people to attempt to surpass each other in many of the activities.
20. Participation in physical education activities makes for a more wholesome outlook on life.
21. Physical education adds nothing to the improvement of social behavior.
22. Physical education class activities will help to relieve and relax physical tensions.
23. Participation in physical education activities helps a person to maintain a healthful emotional life.
24. Physical education is one of the more important subjects in the school program.
25. There is little value in physical education as far as physical well-being is concerned.
26. Physical education should be included in the program of every school.
27. Skills learned in physical education class do not benefit a person.
28. Physical education provides situations for developing character qualities.
29. Physical education makes for more enjoyable living.
30. Physical education has no place in modern education.

Lakie Attitude Toward Athletic Competition Scale*

The following situations describe behavior demonstrated in sports. Circle the category that indicates your feeling toward the behavior described in each of the situations.

1. Strongly approve 2. Approve 3. Undecided 4. Disapprove 5. Strongly disapprove

1 2 3 4 5   1. During a football game team A has the ball on its own 45-yard line, fourth down and 1 yard to go for a first down. The coach of team A signals to the quarterback the play that he wants the team to run.

1 2 3 4 5   2. Team A is the visiting basketball team; and each time a member of the team is given a free shot, the home crowd sets up a continual din of noise until the shot has been taken.

1 2 3 4 5   3. Tennis player A frequently calls out, throws up his arms, or otherwise tries to indicate that his opponent's serve is out of bounds when it is questionable.

1 2 3 4 5   4. In a track meet, team A enters a man in the mile run who is to set a fast pace for the first half of the race and then drop out.

1 2 3 4 5   5. In a football game, team B's quarterback was tackled repeatedly after handing off and after he was out of the play.

1 2 3 4 5   6. Sam, playing golf with his friends, hit a drive into the rough. He accidentally moved the ball with his foot; although not improving his position, he added a penalty stroke to his score.

1 2 3 4 5   7. A basketball player was caught out of position on defense; and rather than allow his opponent to attempt a field goal, he fouled him.

1 2 3 4 5   8. Player A during a golf match made quick noises and movements when player B was getting ready to make a shot.

1 2 3 4 5   9. School A has a powerful but quite slow football team. The night before playing a smaller but faster team, they allowed the field sprinkling system to remain on, causing the field to be heavy and slow.

1 2 3 4 5 10. A basketball team used player A to draw the opponent's high scorer into fouling situations.

*From Lakie, W.L.

1 2 3 4 5 11. The alumni of College A pressured the Board of Trustees to lower the admission and eligibility requirements for athletes.

1 2 3 4 5 12. Team A, by use of fake injuries, was able to stop the clock long enough to get off the play that resulted in the winning touchdown.

1 2 3 4 5 13. A tennis player was given the advantage of a bad call in a close match. He then "evened up" the call by intentionally hitting the ball out of bounds.

1 2 3 4 5 14. The coach of basketball team A removed his team from the floor in protest of an official's decision.

1 2 3 4 5 15. Between seasons a coach moved from College A to College B, and he then persuaded three of College A's athletes to transfer to College B.

1 2 3 4 5 16. After losing a close football game, the coach of the losing team publicly accused the game officials of favoritism when the game movies showed the the winning touchdown had been scored by using an illegal maneuver.

1 2 3 4 5 17. College C lowered the admission requirements for boys awarded athletic scholarships.

1 2 3 4 5 18. Team A's safety man returned a punt for a touchdown. Unseen by the officials, he had stepped out of bounds in front of his team's bench. His coach notified the officials of this fact.

1 2 3 4 5 19. A college with very few athletic scholarships to offer gives athletes preference on all types of campus jobs.

1 2 3 4 5 20. Several wealthy alumni of College C make a monthly gift to several athletes who are in need of financial assistance.

1 2 3 4 5 21. College K has a policy of not allowing any member of a varsity squad to associate with the visiting team until the contest or meet is completed.

1 2 3 4 5 22. The Board of Trustees of College C fired the football coach and gave as the reason for his dismissal his failure to win a conference championship during the past five years.

Nelson Sports Leadership Questionnaire (Coaches)*

The same names can be used any number of times, and in all cases give you first and second choice for each question.

1. Who are the most popular men on your squad?
   1. _____   2. _____
2. Which players on the team know the most basketball, in terms of strategy, team play, etc.?
   1. _____   2. _____
3. Of all the players on your team, who exhibits the most poise on the floor during the crucial parts of the game?
   1. _____   2. _____
4. Who are the "take charge" men on your squad?
   1. _____   2. _____
5. Who are the most consistent ball handlers on your squad?
   1. _____   2. _____
6. Who are the most consistent shooters on your squad?
   1. _____   2. _____
7. Who are the most valuable players on your squad?
   1. _____   2. _____
8. Who are the two players who play "most for the team"?
   1. _____   2. _____
9. Which players have the most overall ability on the squad?
   1. _____   2. _____
10. Who are the most likable players on the squad?
    1. _____   2. _____
11. Which players do you think would make the best coaches?
    1. _____   2. _____
12. If you were not present for practice, which players would you place in charge of the practice?
    1. _____   2. _____
13. Who are the players endowed with leadership qualities?
    1. _____   2. _____
14. Who are the players least endowed with leadership ability?
    1. _____   2. _____

*From Nelson, D.O.

NELSON SPORTS LEADERSHIP QUESTIONNAIRE (Nelson, 1966)

Test objective. To measure leadership in athletic settings.

Description. Two questionnaires were designed, one for coaches and one for members of athletic teams. (See both sections of the boxed material on p. 390 and below.) The coaches' questionnaire has 14 items; the players', 20 items. On the team members' forms the examinee must list a first choice (under No. 1) and a second choice (under No. 2) of team members, excluding his or her own name. A team member's name can be used any number of times. Examinees are asked *not* to sign the questionnaire.

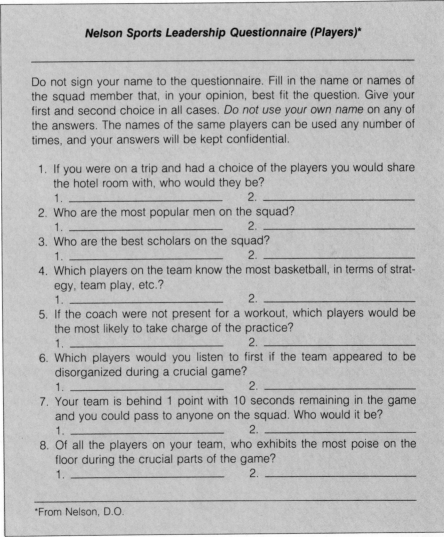

Nelson Sports Leadership Questionnaire (Players)*

Do not sign your name to the questionnaire. Fill in the name or names of the squad member that, in your opinion, best fit the question. Give your first and second choice in all cases. *Do not use your own name* on any of the answers. The names of the same players can be used any number of times, and your answers will be kept confidential.

1. If you were on a trip and had a choice of the players you would share the hotel room with, who would they be?
   1. _____ 2. _____
2. Who are the most popular men on the squad?
   1. _____ 2. _____
3. Who are the best scholars on the squad?
   1. _____ 2. _____
4. Which players on the team know the most basketball, in terms of strategy, team play, etc.?
   1. _____ 2. _____
5. If the coach were not present for a workout, which players would be the most likely to take charge of the practice?
   1. _____ 2. _____
6. Which players would you listen to first if the team appeared to be disorganized during a crucial game?
   1. _____ 2. _____
7. Your team is behind 1 point with 10 seconds remaining in the game and you could pass to anyone on the squad. Who would it be?
   1. _____ 2. _____
8. Of all the players on your team, who exhibits the most poise on the floor during the crucial parts of the game?
   1. _____ 2. _____

**From Nelson, D.O.

Continued.

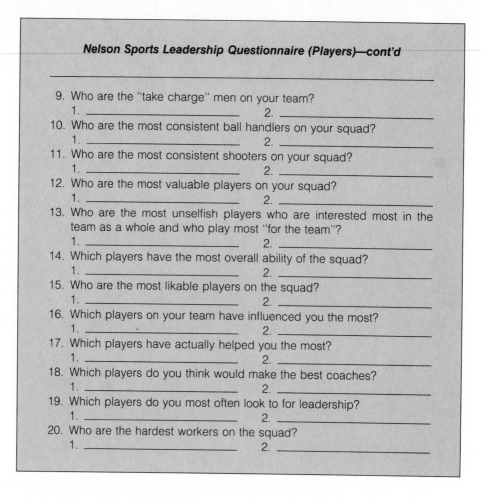

Nelson Sports Leadership Questionnaire (Players)—cont'd

9. Who are the "take charge" men on your team?
   1. _____ 2. _____
10. Who are the most consistent ball handlers on your squad?
    1. _____ 2. _____
11. Who are the most consistent shooters on your squad?
    1. _____ 2. _____
12. Who are the most valuable players on your squad?
    1. _____ 2. _____
13. Who are the most unselfish players who are interested most in the team as a whole and who play most "for the team"?
    1. _____ 2. _____
14. Which players have the most overall ability of the squad?
    1. _____ 2. _____
15. Who are the most likable players on the squad?
    1. _____ 2. _____
16. Which players on your team have influenced you the most?
    1. _____ 2. _____
17. Which players have actually helped you the most?
    1. _____ 2. _____
18. Which players do you think would make the best coaches?
    1. _____ 2. _____
19. Which players do you most often look to for leadership?
    1. _____ 2. _____
20. Who are the hardest workers on the squad?
    1. _____ 2. _____

Materials. Test forms and pencils.

Scoring. List the names of team members appearing on a questionnaire. Allocate 5 points to a name appearing under No. 1 and 3 points to a name under No. 2. Add the number of points for each player. These points can then be summed by players, across all questionnaires. Players can then be ranked according to total points or average number of points.

Validity. Face validity; construct validity, by comparing leaders and nonleaders.

Reliability. $r_{xx'} = 0.96$, 9th grade football players; $r_{xx'} = 0.78$, varsity college basketball players.

Both of the above estimates were reported in Johnson and Nelson (1974).

Norms. Not reported for this specific test.

Comments. Test directions should be typed onto the questionnaire. It can be used for males and females, junior high school through college level. A modified version of the players' questionnaire is presented in Johnson and Nelson (1974, p. 396). In this version the terms are not restricted to a specific sport; thus, it has more widespread applicability.

Other measures

PERCEIVED EXERTION (Borg, 1973)

Test objective. To assess one's perception of his or her physical exertion during exercise.

Description. The scale is shown in the boxed material below. At regular intervals during exercise the examinee is asked to select a rating that reflects his or her perception of physical exertion. At some point the activity may be terminated when a certain rating is reached; this is dependent on the protocol being used. Typically, other data are also considered before terminating exercise. The photograph preceding the test description shows the perceived exertion scale being used in conjunction with a stress test on the treadmill.

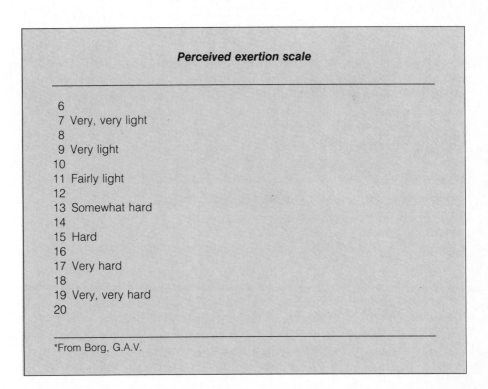

Perceived exertion scale

6
7 Very, very light
8
9 Very light
10
11 Fairly light
12
13 Somewhat hard
14
15 Hard
16
17 Very hard
18
19 Very, very hard
20

*From Borg, G.A.V.

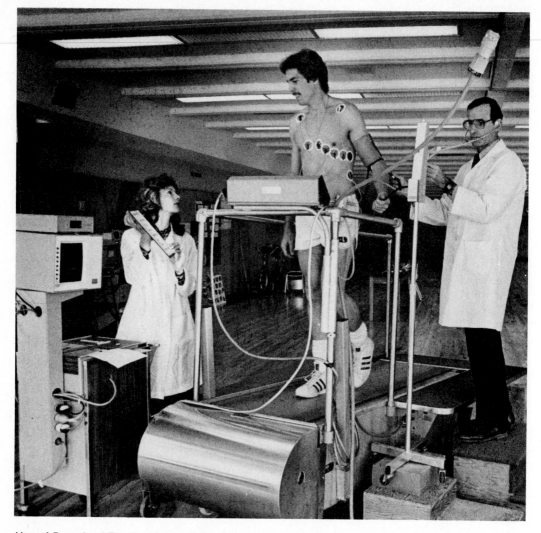

Use of Perceived Exertion Scale during stress test on treadmill.

Comments. Borg has developed a new version of the perceived exertion scale that has ratio properties (Borg, 1982). In a review of the study and application of perceived exertion, Pandolf (1983) discusses the new scale and recommends that its usage be limited to research. "Although this new scale may be more advantageous for studies requiring ratio scaling methods, Borg concluded that his old 15-point scale is still the best for applied studies" (Pandolf, 1983:129).

SUMMARY

Measures of affective behavior are designed to measure attitudes, interests, values, psychological traits, social behavior, and emotional states of the individual. Many types of affective behavior are of interest to the physical educator, coach, and exercise specialist. Although a number of instruments have been developed to measure affective behavior in the field, many of these measures do not have strong psychometric underpinnings. However, they may have some usefulness if used as an indicator of a characteristic of a group of examinees rather than of an individual person. They might also be useful in a formative evaluation context. Few instruments are available that would be suitable in a research setting.

LEARNING EXPERIENCES

1. Analyze the Lakie Attitude Toward Athletic Competition Scale. First, take the test and determine your score. Identify the aspects of competition that are measured by this scale by naming each aspect of competition and listing the items falling under each. Are some aspects of competition overemphasized in this scale? If so, which ones? Are some aspects underemphasized? If so, which ones? Do you think this scale is useful in today's competitive settings? Give a thorough rationale for your answer.

2. Develop a rating scale to measure attitudes toward an official in a game. Use a 5-4-3-2-1 rating scale, and write a descriptor for each point value. Each descriptor should reflect behaviors rather than a general phrase such as 5 = excellent attitude, 4 = good attitude, and so forth. What behaviors would you expect to see in a person who is given a rating of 5? A rating of 1? This means you must write several short phrases for each descriptor.

REFERENCES

American Psychological Association. 1984. Standards for educational and psychological tests. Washington, D.C.: APA.

Blanchard, B.E. 1936. A behavior frequency rating scale for the measurement of character and personality traits in a physical education classroom situation. Research Quarterly 7:56-66.

Borg, G.A.V. 1973. Perceived exertion: a note on "history" and methods. Medicine and Science in Sports 5:90-93.

Borg, G.A.V. 1982. Psychophysical bases of perceived exertion. Medicine and Science in Sports and Exercise 14:377-381.

Cowell, C.C. 1958. Validating an index of social adjustment for high school use. Research Quarterly 29:7-18.

Johnson, B.L., and Nelson, J.K. 1974. Practical measurements for evaluation in physical education. Minneapolis: Burgess Publishing Co.

Kenyon, G.S. 1968a. A conceptual model for characterizing physical activity. Research Quarterly 39:96-195.

Kenyon, G.S. 1968b. Six scales for assessing attitude toward physical activity. Research Quarterly 39:566-574.

Lakie, W.L. 1964. Expressed attitudes of various groups of athletes toward athletic competition. Research Quarterly 35:497-503.

Martens, R. 1977. Sport Competition Anxiety Test. Champaign, Ill.: Human Kinetics Publishers.

Miller, D.K., and Allen, T.E. 1982. Fitness: a lifetime commitment, ed. 2. Minneapolis: Burgess Publishing Co.

Nelson, D.O. 1966. Nelson Sports Leadership Questionnaire. Research Quarterly 37:268-275.

Pandolf, K.B. 1983. Advances in the study and application of perceived exertion. In Terjung, R.L., editor: Exercise and sport science reviews. Philadelphia: The Franklin Institute Press.

Pooley, J.C. 1971. The professionalism of physical education in the United States and England, Unpublished doctoral dissertation, Madison, University of Wisconsin.

Safrit, M.J., and Wood, T.M. 1983. The Health-Related Fitness Opinnionnaire: a pilot survey. Research Quarterly for Exercise and Sport 54:204-207.

Simon, J.A., and Smoll, F.L. 1974. An instrument for assessing children's attitude toward physical activity. Research Quarterly 45:21-27.

Sonstroem, R.J. 1974. Attitude testing: examining certain psychological correlates of physical activity. Research Quarterly 45:93-103.

Sonstroem, R.J. 1978. Physical estimation and attraction scales: rationale and research. Medicine and Science in Sports 10:97-102.

Wear, C.L. 1955. Construction of equivalent forms of an attitude scale. Research Quarterly 26:113-119.

ANNOTATED READINGS

Jones, J.G. 1975. An affective evaluation of an outdoor education experience. Journal of Physical Education and Recreation 46:54-55.

Describes the construction of two test forms to evaluate ten outdoor activities in terms of student enjoyment, desire to continue the activity, and perceived learning; presents descriptive statistics for both forms of the test; concludes that the outdoor experience primarily emphasizes skill development and improved attitudes toward outdoor living.

Frye, P.A. 1983. Measurement of psychosocial aspects of physical education. Journal of Physical Education, Recreation and Dance 54(8):26-27.

Discusses the principles and practices of measurement and evaluation as applied to psychosocial characteristics; suggests using available tests to draw inferences about group rather than individual behavior.

McGee, R. 1977. Measuring affective behavior in physical education. Journal of Physical Education and Recreation 48:29-30.

Notes that the affective domain deserves special attention by physical educators; recommends that affective measures such as self-concept, attitude, and social adjustment not be used for grading; should provide student with opportunity to know one's self better; discusses four instruments and their current usage in the field.

Weise, C.E., and Schick, J., editors. 1982. Affective measurement in physical education: doing well and feeling good. Journal of Physical Education, Recreation and Dance 53(2):15-25, 86.

Offers a series of articles on measuring affective behavior in physical education; presents discussion of the pros and cons of evaluation in the affective domain; includes uses and abuses of affective measurement.

Part Seven

Unique Measurement Concerns

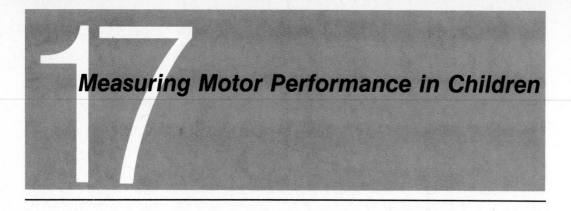

17 Measuring Motor Performance in Children

KEY WORDS *Watch for these words as you read the following chapter:*

basic movement patterns

component model of
intratask development

face validity

intratask analysis

motor ability

Several surveys in recent years have verified that less testing in physical education occurs at the elementary school level than at any other level. Why is this true? One reason advanced by some is that the limited number of days and short class hours scheduled for physical education in most elementary schools is prohibitive for teaching as well as testing. Furthermore, physical education classes in the elementary schools are not always taught by trained specialists in physical education. In many schools the regular classroom teacher may not be as knowl-

FIG. 17-1. *Child taking batting test.*

edgeable about testing motor behavior as he or she is about testing cognitive skills. Another reason for the infrequent use of tests is that test development for this age group has been limited in the past. The existing tests may not be the most useful ones for the elementary school setting. For instance, the teacher may be interested in the measurement of basic movement patterns, such as running, throwing, and jumping. Some may stress the outcome of the movement—how fast the child can run, how far the child can throw the ball, and so forth. Others may emphasize the execution of the movement—the form displayed in running, throwing, or jumping, for example. Regardless of the approach used, the measuring instruments available to the teacher are limited. Thus teachers often resort to subjective evaluation of performance based on a cursory judgment of the child's skills.

A third reason for not using tests is the notion that testing must be formal, with time set aside from instruction for this purpose. This point of view, discussed in Chapter 1, suggests that testing automatically takes time away from instruction. Implicit in this way of thinking is the assumption that testing is not desirable because it interferes with teaching. This, of course, does not have to be true. Rather than considering testing and teaching as separate activities, testing should be viewed as an integral part of teaching. In this context testing is an ongoing activity. This is the concept of *formative evaluation*, previously described in Chapter 1. When this approach is used, children can take some of the responsibility for their own learning. They can keep records of their performance using charts posted on bulletin boards in the gymnasium. They can work independently on a task and then check with the teacher when ready to be evaluated. In other words, self-assessment can become an important part of the learning process.

In this chapter examples of the types of tests that can be used in an elementary physical education program are discussed. This assumes that a well-rounded program is implemented, including the following aspects of motor behavior: basic movement patterns, basic skills and games, physical fitness, perceptual-motor behavior, and athletic competition. Affective tests for children are described in Chapter 16, and cognitive test development is discussed in Chapter 9.

ASSESSING BASIC MOVEMENT PATTERNS

The area of motor development in the physical education field has encompassed the study of the development of basic movement patterns in children. **Basic movement patterns** are types of movement that emerge developmentally, usually at a young age, such as running, jumping, and throwing. In general, two theories have been espoused to describe how children develop motorically. See-feldt, Reuschlein, and Vogel (1972) advocate one approach; Roberton (Roberton and Halverson, 1984), the other. The assessment of movement patterns usually involves the use of a checklist. It must be carefully validated and have satisfactory reliability and objectivity just like any other test. Objectivity is extremely important when developing a checklist, since a highly valid instrument might be too complex for an observer to use. All too often, the development of a checklist is handled in a casual, offhanded manner. This criticism also applies to the development of rating scales, perhaps because these measures seem to be so easy to compile. The checklist may be short and easy to use, but it should also include all appropriate test characteristics.

Intratask analysis

The **intratask analysis** of a basic movement pattern is based on the identification of stages of the development of a task from the time it is first attempted to the time it is performed at a mature or adult level. Seefeldt and associates (1972) identify the stages of development of a number of motor tasks, based on the work of Wild (1938). An example of their description of stages is shown in the boxed material. The task is the overarm throw, and five developmental stages have been identified (Seefeldt and Haubenstricker, 1982). The child is observed throwing a ball and then is placed in one of the five following categories.

Stages in overarm throwing*

Stage 1

The throwing motion is essentially posterior-anterior in direction.

The feet usually remain stationary during the throw.

There is little or no trunk rotation in the most rudimentary pattern at this stage, but those at the point of transition between Stages 1 and 2 may evoke a slight trunk rotation in preparation for the throw and extensive hip and trunk rotation in the follow-through.

The force of projection of the ball comes primarily from hip flexion, shoulder protraction, and elbow extension.

Stage 2

The distinctive feature of this stage is the rotation of the body about an imaginary vertical axis, with the hips, spine, and shoulders rotating as one unit.

The performer may step forward with either an ipsilateral or contralateral pattern, but the arm is brought forward in a transverse plane.

The motion may resemble a sling rather than a throw because of the extended arm position during the course of the throw.

---

*From Seefeldt, V., and Haubenstricker, J.

Stages in overarm throwing—cont'd

Stage 3

The distinctive characteristic is the ipsilateral arm-leg action.

The ball is placed into a throwing position above the shoulder by a vertical and posterior motion of the arm at the time that the ipsilateral leg is moving forward.

There is little or no rotation of the spine and hips in preparation for the throw.

The follow-through phase includes flexion at the hip joint and some trunk rotation toward the side opposite the throwing hand.

Stage 4

The movement is contralateral, with the leg opposite the throwing arm striding forward as the throwing arm is moved in a vertical and posterior direction during the 'wind-up' phase. Thus, the motion of the trunk and arm closely resembles those of Stages 1 and 3.

The stride forward with the contralateral leg provides for a wide base of support and greater stability during the force production phase.

Stage 5

The shift of weight is entirely to the rear leg, as it pivots in response to the rotating joints above it.

The throwing hand moves in a downward arc and then backward as the opposite leg moves forward.

Concurrently, the hip and spine rotate into position for forceful de-rotation.

As the contralateral foot strikes the surface, the hips, spine, and shoulder begin to de-rotate in sequence.

The contralateral leg begins to extend at the knee as the shoulder protracts, the humerus rotates, and the elbow extends, thus providing an equal and opposite reaction to the throwing arm.

The opposite arm also moves forcefully toward the body to assist in the equal and opposite reaction to the throwing arm.

The throwing pattern should be observed several times on one or more days. On a given day observing more than one stage in a child's performance is possible. If this happens, the stage represented most frequently should be used to classify the child. Also, the type of throw should be standardized for all children. Force should be emphasized, with accuracy viewed as secondary. If the child throws at a target, with the only force requirement being to project the ball to the target, a different movement pattern is elicited. Once the child is throwing at the level of Stage 5, skills tests can be used to measure the force and accuracy.

Component analysis of intratask development

The **component model of intratask development** is based on the identification of developmental characteristics of *body parts* within a task. This approach evolved from the work of Roberton (Roberton and Halverson, 1984), whose innovative thinking about motor development led to the idea that changes in one body part in executing a task are not always associated with specified changes in another body part. For example, one child may display the trunk action of one stage and the arm action of another. Thus Roberton proposed analyzing the development of body parts as separate *components*. Her model can be used to generate checklists, as exemplified in the boxed material below. This checklist was developed to assess the child's level of ability in hopping.

Observation checklist for hopping*

Child: *Jones, Randy*   Classroom: *S. Johnson*
Motor task: *Hopping*

Movement component:	Level observed		
leg action	Jan. 4		
Step 1. Momentary flight			
Step 2: Fall and catch; swing leg inactive	(		
Step 3: Projected takeoff; swing leg assists	✓		
Step 4. Projection delay; swing leg leads			
Movement component: arm action			
Step 1. Bilateral inactive			
Step 2. Bilateral reactive			
Step 3. Bilateral assist			
Step 4. Semiopposition			
Step 5. Opposing assist	✓		
Overall movement profile Legs	3		
Arms	5		
Movement situation Teacher selected			
Child selected	✓		
Observation type Direct	✓		
Videotape			
Film			
Comments:			

*From Roberton, M.A., and Halverson, L.E.

Note that two different movement components have been identified for hopping—leg action and arm action. Under leg action four steps (somewhat like stages within a component) were delineated. In the example the child being observed was placed in Step 3 of the leg action. However, he was classified in Step 5 of the arm action, which includes five steps altogether. The movement profile recorded on the checklist is illustrated in Fig. 17-2. Two other pieces of information are also recorded—movement situation, which indicates whether the child or the teacher selected the movement to be observed, and observation type, which determines whether the child was observed directly or on film or videotape. The hopping components and their associated steps have been partially validated, and the checklist is reliable and objective. For information on checklists to be used with other movement patterns, refer to Roberton and Halverson (1984).

FIG. 17-2. *Hopping: Leg action, Step 3; Arm action, Step 5.*
Redrawn from Roberton, M.A., and Halverson, L.E.

TESTS OF SPORTS SKILLS

Few tests of sports skills have been developed specifically for children, especially in recent years. Although a great deal of informal skills testing may take place in the elementary schools, much of this work has not been published. Examples of tests of sports skills in this chapter are limited to those with published evidence of reliability and validity. Although they were developed many years ago, they represent the small number of sports skills tests for elementary school children that are available. The reliability and validity of these tests are not always acceptable; however, this information is the basis on which a test user makes a decision on whether or not to use a test. Although portions of some of these tests may be outdated, they serve as a useful framework for revising the tests in light of the skills as they are used today.

FIG. 17-3. *Test layout for the Basketball Wall Pass Test.*
Reprinted by permission of the American Alliance for Health, Physical Education, Recreation and Dance.

BASKETBALL WALL PASS TEST (Latchaw, 1954)

Test objective. To measure passing skills of fourth, fifth, and sixth grade students.

Description. The test layout is shown in Fig. 17-3. The student stands behind the restraining line. On the signal *Ready, Go!* the ball is thrown at the target as many times as possible in 15 seconds. If a student loses control of the ball, he or she is responsible for recovering it. A 10-second practice period is allowed, followed by two 15-second trials.

Test area. Floor area 8 feet by 4 feet; wall area 7 feet by 8 feet.

Equipment. Stopwatch, regulation basketballs, tape measure, floor tape, and scorecards.

Scoring. The trial score is the number of correct hits in the 15-second period. The test score is the best of the two trials. Balls touching the target line do not count. If the student steps on or over the restraining line, the pass does not count.

Validity. **Face validity.** (A test with face validity is one that appears to be valid but has not been formally validated.)

Reliability. Boys $r_{xx'}$ = 0.91 4th grade

$\qquad r_{xx'}$ = 0.84 5th grade

$\qquad r_{xx'}$ = 0.78 6th grade

$$\text{Girls } r_{xx'} = 0.94 \text{ 4th grade}$$
$$r_{xx'} = 0.89 \text{ 5th grade}$$
$$r_{xx'} = 0.83 \text{ 6th grade}$$

Norms. Norms are presented in Table 17-1.

Comments. Use two assistants at each testing station, if possible. One should count the hits and the other, the faults. The ball must land *inside* the target, not on the line, to score a point.

TABLE 17-1. *Achievement scales: Basketball Wall Pass Test**

T-Score	Girls Grade IV	Grade V	Grade VI	Boys Grade IV	Grade V	Grade VI	Percentile
77				24	27		99
76	19						99
75			22	23	26	30	99
74					25		99
73		20		22	24		98
72	18				23	29	98
71				21	22	28	98
70						27	97
69						26	97
68	17		21		21	25	96
67		19				24	95
66				20			94
65						23	93
64		18	20				92
63	16	17		19	20		90
62						22	88
61				18			86
60	15		19		19		84
59		16		17			81
58						21	78
57			18		18		75
56	14	15		16			72
55							69
54			17			20	65
53					17		61
52	13	14					57
51			16			19	53
50	12				16		50
49						18	46
48			15	14			42
47	11	13			15		38
46						17	34

*From Scott, M.G., and French, E.

Continued.

TABLE 17-1. *Achievement scales: Basketball Wall Pass Test—cont'd*

	Girls			Boys			
T-Score	Grade IV	Grade V	Grade VI	Grade IV	Grade V	Grade VI	Percentile
45	10		14				30
44		12		13	14		27
43	9						24
42			13			16	21
41		11		12	13		18
40	8						15
39		10			12	15	13
38			12				11
37				11	11		9
36	7	9				14	8
35			11				6
34		8		10	10		5
33			10				4
32	6	7				13	3
31				9	9		3
30			9				2
29					8		2
28		6			7		2
27				8			1
26	5						1
25			8		6	12	1

VOLLEYBALL WALL VOLLEY TEST (Latchaw, 1954)

Test objective. To measure the ability of fourth, fifth, and sixth grade students to strike objects.

Description. Use the test set-up for the Basketball Wall Pass Test, shown in Fig. 17-3. The student stands behind the restraining line. On the signal *Ready, Go!* the ball is thrown against the wall. As it bounces off the wall, the student attempts to hit the ball repeatedly against the target. Any type of hit may be used. Allow one 10-second practice trial and four 15-second test trials.

Test area. Same as Basketball Wall Pass Test.

Equipment. Volleyballs, stopwatch, tape measure, floor tape, and scorecards.

Scoring. The trial score is the number of correct hits in the 15-second period. The test score is the best of four trials. The initial throw against the wall is not scored. Only balls that are hit count. If a student throws or carries the ball, it is not scored. If control of the ball is lost, it is the responsibility of the student to recover it. Then the ball must again be put into play with a throw against the target.

Validity. Face validity.

Reliability. Boys $r_{xx'}$ = 0.89 4th grade

$r_{xx'}$ = 0.89 5th grade

$r_{xx'}$ = 0.89 6th grade

Girls $r_{xx'}$ = 0.84 4th grade

$r_{xx'}$ = 0.85 5th grade

$r_{xx'}$ = 0.79 6th grade

Norms. Norms are presented in Table 17-2.

Comments. Balls must land *inside* the target, not touching the line, to be scored.

TABLE 17-2. *Achievement scales: Volleyball Wall Volley Test**

	Girls			Boys			
T-Score	Grade IV	Grade V	Grade VI	Grade IV	Grade V	Grade VI	Percentile
77			21			29	99
76		18					99
75						28	99
74	13	17				27	99
73		15	20	20		26	98
72	12	14			20		98
71	11	13	19	18		25	98
70				16		24	97
69	10		18	15			97
68		12		14	19		96
67			17	13		23	95
66	9			12	18	22	94
65		11		11	17	21	93
64			16		16		92
63	8	10	15		15	20	90
62			14	10		19	88
61		9			14	18	86
60			13				84
59	7					17	81
58		8	12		13		78
57			11		12	16	75
56	6	7		8	11		72
55			10				69
54					10	15	65
53	5		9	7			61
52		6			9	14	57
51							53

*From Scott, M.G., and French, E.

Continued.

TABLE 17-2. *Achievement scales: Volleyball Wall Volley Test—cont'd*

	Girls			Boys			
T-Score	Grade IV	Grade V	Grade VI	Grade IV	Grade V	Grade VI	Percentile
50	4		8	6	8	13	50
49							46
48		5			7	12	42
47						11	38
46	3		7	5			34
45						10	30
44					6		27
43		4				9	24
42			6	4		8	21
41					5		18
40	2						15
39		3				7	13
38							11
37				3			9
36			5		4	6	8
35						5	6
34		2		2			5
33							4
32	1				3	4	3
31							3
30			3			3	2
29		1					2
28							2
27				1		2	1
26							1
25							1
24					2	1	1
23			2				0

SOCCER WALL VOLLEY TEST (Latchaw, 1954)

Test objective. To measure the ability of fourth, fifth, and sixth grade students to kick the ball.

Description. Use the target layout shown in Fig. 17-4. The student stands behind the restraining line. Place the ball anywhere in back of the line. On the signal *Ready, Go!* the student attempts to kick the ball into the target area on the wall as many times as possible in 15 seconds. If the student loses control of the ball, he or she must recover it. If the ball is within the 4 feet by 2½ feet floor area, the hands cannot be used for retrieval. If the ball is outside of this area, the hands may be used. Allow one 15-second practice period and four test trials.

FIG. 17-4. *Test layout for the Soccer Wall Volley Test.*
Reprinted by permission of the American Alliance for Health, Physical Education, Recreation and Dance.

Test area. Wall area 4 feet by 2½ feet; floor area 4 feet by 2½ feet, with a 6 foot restraining line.

Equipment. Soccer balls, stopwatch, tape measure, floor tape, and scorecards.

Scoring. The trial score is the number of correct hits in 15 seconds. The test score is the best of four trials. Deduct a 1-point penalty whenever the ball is touched with the hands within the rectangular floor area.

Validity. Face validity.

Reliability. Boys $r_{xx'} = 0.82$ 4th grade

$r_{xx'} = 0.89$ 5th grade

$r_{xx'} = 0.88$ 6th grade

Girls $r_{xx'} = 0.77$ 4th grade

$r_{xx'} = 0.83$ 5th grade

$r_{xx'} = 0.77$ 6th grade

Norms. Norms are presented in Table 17-3.

Comments. The ball can be kicked from within the rectangular area, but the kick is not scored; however, this can be followed by a kick (from behind the restraining line), which is legal.

TABLE 17-3. *Achievement scales: Soccer Wall Volley Test**

	Girls			Boys			
T-Score	Grade IV	Grade V	Grade VI	Grade IV	Grade V	Grade VI	Percentile
76		15		14	16		99
74	13					18	99
73		14			15		98
71				13		17	98
70		13	13				97
69	12					16	97
68					14		96
67						15	95
66	11	12	12				94
65				12			93
64		11			13	14	92
63	10						90
61			11		12		86
60		10		11		13	84
59	9						81
57			10		11		75
56		9		10		12	72
54	8						65
53			9	9	10	11	61
52		8					57
49	7					10	46
48			8	8	9		42
46		7				9	34
44	6						27
43			7	7	8		24
40		6				8	15
39					7		13
38			6	6			11
37	5						9
35						7	6
34		5					5
32			5				3
29	4					6	2
27		4		4			1
26			4				1
24			3	3	5	5	0

*From Scott, M.G., and French, E.

SOFTBALL REPEATED THROWS TEST (Latchaw, 1954)

Test objective. To measure the ball-throwing ability of fourth, fifth, and sixth grade students.

Description. The layout for this test is shown in Fig. 17-5. The student stands anywhere within the 5½ foot square throwing area. On the signal *Ready, Go!* the ball is thrown at the target using an overarm throw. The rebound is caught, either in the air or on the bounce, and the student continues throwing as many times as possible in 15 seconds. A 10-second practice trial is allowed, followed by two 15-second test trials.

FIG. 17-5. *Test layout for the Softball Repeated Throws Test.*
Reprinted by permission of the American Alliance for Health, Physical Education, Recreation and Dance.

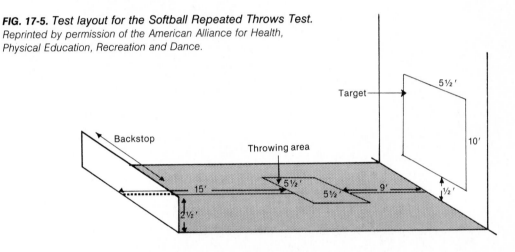

Test area. Floor area 6 feet by 30 feet; wall area 5½ feet by 10½ feet.

Equipment. Softballs, stopwatch, tape measure, floor tape, and scorecards.

Scoring. The trial score is the number of correct hits in 15 seconds. The test score is the best of two trials. A hit is not scored if the examinee steps on or over any one of the lines of the throwing area or the ball lands on or outside one of the target lines.

Validity. Face validity.

Reliability. Boys $r_{xx'}$ = 0.82 4th grade
$\qquad\qquad r_{xx'}$ = 0.81 5th grade
$\qquad\qquad r_{xx'}$ = 0.85 6th grade
$\qquad$ Girls $r_{xx'}$ = 0.80 4th grade
$\qquad\qquad r_{xx'}$ = 0.82 5th grade
$\qquad\qquad r_{xx'}$ = 0.85 6th grade

Norms. Norms are presented in Table 17-4.

Comments. If the student loses control of the ball, he or she is responsible for retrieving it. It is desirable to have on hand a dozen or more balls, since the

TABLE 17-4. *Achievement scales: Softball Repeated Throws Test**

	Girls			Boys			
T-Score	Grade IV	Grade V	Grade VI	Grade IV	Grade V	Grade VI	Percentile
78	9	10					99
76				12			99
74			12			15	99
73				11	14		98
72	8	9					98
68					13	14	96
66			11				94
65				10			93
64					12		92
63	7					13	90
61			10				86
60					11		84
58				9		12	78
55		8	9		10		69
54						11	65
51				8	9		53
49			8			10	46
48		7					42
47	6						38
46					8		34
45			7	7			30
44						9	27
41	5						18
40		6			7		15
39				6		8	13
38			6				11
35	4						6
33				5		7	4
32		5			6		3
29			5				2
28	3	4				6	2
27				4			1
24		3	4		5	5	1

*From Scott, M.G., and French, E.

impact of a ball hitting the wall can affect the shape of the ball. If construction of a backstop is not feasible, a rolled mat may be used.

KICKING TEST (Johnson, 1962)

Test objective. To measure the kicking skills (accuracy) of children in grades 1 through 6.

FIG 17-6. *Test layout for the Kicking Test.*
Reprinted by permission of the American Alliance for Health, Physical Education, Recreation and Dance.

Description. Use the test setup depicted in Fig. 17-6. Begin the test by placing a soccer ball behind the first 10 foot line. The student kicks the ball against the wall, trying to hit the center of the target. Two practice kicks and three trials are taken. The same procedure is followed from behind the 20 foot and 30 foot lines.

Test area. Wall area 5 feet by 10 feet; floor area 30 feet by 10 feet.

Equipment. Soccer balls, floor and wall tape, tape measure, and scorecards.

Scoring. The score for each kick is the number of the target area the ball hits. Add the total of the nine trials to obtain the total test score. A ball landing on a line between two target areas receives the higher point value of the two areas.

Validity. Concurrent validity, using a criterion measure of teachers' ratings of kicking performance.

Grade	Boys*	Girls*
1	0.29	0.41
2	0.66	0.43
3	0.34	0.13
4	0.38	0.51
5	0.04	0.12
6	0.17	0.49

*Correlation coefficients.

Reliability. Test-retest coefficients.

Grade	Boys*	Girls*
1	0.38	0.82
2	0.86	0.88
3	0.83	0.80
4	0.78	0.78
5	0.49	0.67
6	0.84	0.82

*Correlation coefficients.

TABLE 17-5. Percentiles for Kicking Test (points)*

Percentile	Grades											
	1		2		3		4		5		6	
	B†	G‡	B	G	B	G	B	G	B	G	B	G
100	34	30	36	35	40	36	42	39	43	40	44	42
95	28	27	33	33	37	34	38	37	40	38	41	40
90	27	26	31	31	36	32	37	35	39	36	40	38
85	26	25	30	30	34	31	36	34	38	35	39	36
80			28	29	33	30	35	33	37	34	37	35
75	25	24		28				32	36	33		34
70			27	27	32	29	34	31	35		36	
65	24	23		26	31	28				32	35	33
60		22	26		30	27	33	30	34	31		
55	23			25		26						32
50			25	24	29	25	32	29	33		34	
45						24	31			30		31
40	22	21	24	23	28				32		33	
35			23	22	27	23	30	28		29	32	30
30	21		21	20		22	29	27	31	28		
	20	20										
25		19	20		26	21		26		27	31	29
20	19	18	19	19	25	20	28	25	30	26	30	28
15	18	16	18	18	23	19	27	24	29	25	29	27
10	17	14	17	16	22	18	25	22	28	23	28	25
5	14	10	14	14	20	17	23	20	26	20	26	20
0	12	8	10	12	16	16	19	16	23	14	23	15

*From Johnson, R.D.
†Boys.
‡Girls.

Norms. A table of percentiles is presented in Table 17-5.

Comments. If the examinee steps on or over the restraining line, the trial is retaken.

THROW-AND-CATCH TEST (Johnson, 1962)

Test objective. To measure the ability of first through sixth grade students to throw and catch.

Description. Use the test setup shown in Fig. 17-7. To begin the test the student stands in the first square and throws the ball at the wall target, using an underhand throw. Two practice trials and three test trials are taken. The same sequence is repeated from each of the remaining four squares.

FIG. 17-7. *Test layout for the Throw-and-Catch Test.*
Reprinted by permission of the American Alliance for Health, Physical Education, Recreation and Dance.

Test area. Wall area 7 feet by 4 feet; floor area 20 feet by 3 feet.

Equipment. Playground balls (8½ inches in diameter) for first through third grades; volleyballs for fourth through sixth grades.

Scoring. The total test score is the sum of 15 trials. The following scoring system is used:

1. Score 2 points for hitting the inner wall target.
2. Score 2 points for catching the rebound in the air while standing in the proper floor square.
3. Score 1 point for hitting the outer section of the wall target.
4. Score 1 point for catching the rebound in the air while standing on the line or outside the proper floor square.

Validity. Concurrent validity, using a criterior measure of teachers' ratings of throwing and catching performance.

Grade	Girls*	Boys*
1	0.54	0.47
2	0.33	0.54
3	0.33	0.54
4	0.50	0.45
5	0.15	0.38
6	0.30	0.47

*Correlation coefficients.

Reliability. Test-retest coefficients.

Grade	Girls*	Boys*
1	0.94	0.89
2	0.79	0.92
3	0.90	0.84
4	0.78	0.81
5	0.65	0.84
6	0.93	0.91

*Correlation coefficients.

TABLE 17-6. *Percentiles for Throw-and-Catch Test (points)**

	Grades											
	1		2		3		4		5		6	
Percentile	B†	G‡	B	G	B	G	B	G	B	G	B	G
100	34	29	39	35	41	38	50	43	57	53	59	55
95	26	23	38	31	40	34	47	40	54	50	56	51
90	24	21	34	28	39	33	45	39	52	45	54	49
85	23	20	32	27	38	32	43	38	50	44	53	47
80	22	19	31	26	37	30	42	37	48	43	52	46
75	21	18	30	25	36	29	41	36	47	42	51	45
70	20	17	29	24	35	28	40	35	46	41	50	44
65	19		28	23	34			34	45	40	49	43
60	18	16	27	22	33	27	39		44		48	
55		15	26	21		26	38	33		39	47	42
50	17		25		32	25		32	43	38	46	41
45		14	24	20	31		37		42	37		40
40	16	13		19	30	24	36		41		45	
35	15	12	23	18		23	35	30	40	36	44	39
30	14	11	22	17	29	22	34	29	39	35	43	38
25	13	10	21	16		21	33	28	38	34	42	37
20	12		20	15	28	20	32	27	37	33	41	36
15	11	9	19	14	27	19	31	26	36	32	40	35
10	10	8	17	12	25	18	30	24	34	31	39	33
5	9	5	13	10	21	16	27	21	33	29	37	31
0	6	3	8	7	17	13	23	16	29	24	34	28

*From Johnson, R.D.
†Boys.
‡Girls.

Norms. A table of percentiles is presented in Table 17-6.

Comments. The trial is retaken if the student steps out of the square while throwing.

TESTS OF PHYSICAL FITNESS AND MOTOR ABILITY

Tests focusing on other aspects of physical education for the elementary school child can be found in the testing literature. Two of these aspects are physical fitness and motor ability.

Physical fitness

A well-rounded curriculum for elementary school physical education should include physical fitness. Two types of fitness might be emphasized: one is the type needed for athletic performance; the other is tied to the individual's health state, focusing on the relationship between physical activity and a positive health state. Standardized tests available for each type of fitness are described in the following section.

AAHPER YOUTH FITNESS TEST. The AAHPER Youth Fitness Test (1976), described in detail in Chapter 12, includes six items—Pull-ups Test (or Flexed-

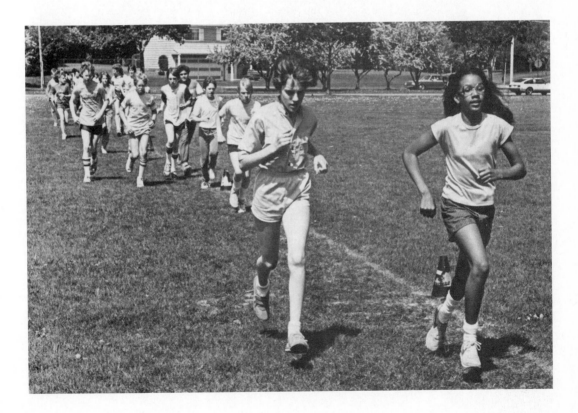

Arm Hang), Sit-ups Test, Standing Long Jump, 50-yard Dash, Shuttle Run Test, and 600-yard Run. Recommended for use with examinees ages 9 through 17 and those of college age, this test measures primarily the type of fitness needed for athletic performance.

AAHPERD HEALTH-RELATED PHYSICAL FITNESS TEST. The AAHPERD Health-Related Physical Fitness Test (1980) is described in detail in Chapter 11. Four items are included in this test—Distance Run, Sit-ups Test, Sit-and-Reach Test, and Skinfold Measures. Each item measures a component of health-related physical fitness that is affected by vigorous physical activity. This test is appropriate for any school-age child, including ages 5 through 17 and those of college age.

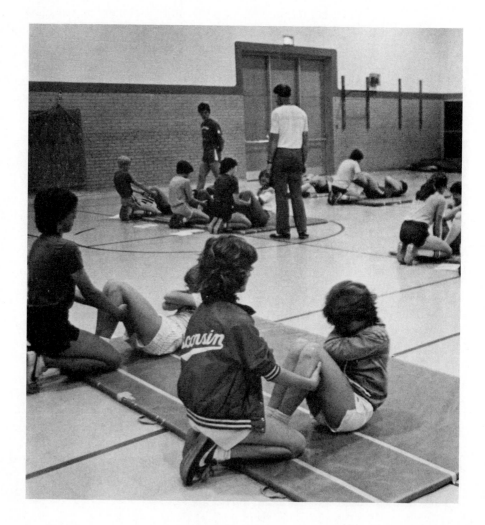

Motor ability

The difficulties in defining and measuring something called motor ability are discussed in detail in Chapter 15. Research evidence has shown that general motor ability may not exist; rather, there appears to be a number of abilities, each specific to a given task. However, efforts to develop test batteries measuring some sort of general ability in children have occurred, although not in recent years. Two of these batteries, which include sports skill–related items, are briefly described here.

LATCHAW MOTOR ACHIEVEMENT TEST. The Latchaw Motor Achievement Test (1954) was designed to measure general motor achievement in fourth, fifth, and sixth grade students. The Basketball Wall Pass Test, Volleyball Wall Volley Test, Soccer Wall Volley Test, and Softball Repeated Throws Test, described earlier in this chapter, are four tests designed to measure basic sports skills (or basic movement patterns, as some might interpret it). Three other tests are part of the battery—Vertical Jump (Chapter 12), Standing Broad Jump (Chapter 13), and Shuttle Run. The Shuttle Run Test is similar to the Youth Fitness Test version in Chapter 12, except that no blocks are used. Instead, the examinee merely has to touch the lines with his or her foot. Although T-score tables for each test are presented in Scott and French (1959), they should be updated.

JOHNSON TEST OF ACHIEVEMENT IN FUNDAMENTAL SKILLS. The Johnson Test of Achievement in Fundamental Skills (1962) was developed to measure the achievement of elementary school children (grades 1 through 6) in selected fundamental skills. Five tests are included in this battery—Throw-and-Catch Test, Jump-and-Reach Test, Zigzag Run Test, Kicking Test, and Batting Test. The Throw-and-Catch Test and Kicking Test are described in detail as measures of sports skills on pp. 412-417. The Batting Test is not described since it requires a special batting kit that must be ordered from a distributor. The Jump-and-Reach Test is similar to the Vertical Jump, described in Chapter 13, and the Zigzag Run Test is fairly typical of the agility tests used in the physical education field. It uses four chairs placed 6 feet apart between a starting line and an "X" placed on the gymnasium wall. As usual, the run is timed to the nearest tenth of a second. Percentile tables are included in the original source, but these should be updated.

TESTS OF PERCEPTUAL MOTOR BEHAVIOR

Educators and clinicians working with preschool and early elementary age children are frequently interested in their perceptual-motor behavior. A number of well-known tests of this type are described in Chapter 18. Most of these tests are appropriate for children with or without handicaps, although many are used to screen children to identify those with perceptual-motor deficiencies.

FIG. 17-8. *Physical Growth NCHS Percentile Chart for Girls.*

FIG. 17-9. *Physical Growth NCHS Percentile Chart for Boys.*

EXAMPLES OF GROWTH CHARTS

A number of procedures may be used to monitor the physical growth and development of children, but two of the most widely used growth charts are available from the American Medical Association (AMA) (discussed below) and Ross Laboratories (see Figs. 17-8 and 17-9).

AMA GROWTH CHARTS (AMA, 1978)

Test objective. To plot the growth curves of children 4 to 18 years of age.

Description. Two charts are available, one for boys and one for girls. The most recent version of the charts (AMA, 1978) was developed by H.V. Meredith and J.H. Spurgeon for the Joint Committee on Health Problems in Education of the National Education Association (NEA) and the AMA. To ensure accuracy in assessing students' weight, students should remove their shoes and wear minimal or lightweight clothing. Record weight to the nearest ½ pound and height to the nearest ¼ inch. Then find the age of the child on the appropriate chart. Plot and record the height and weight measurements in the respective portions of the chart. Repeat the assessment on an annual basis and connect the points within each portion (height and weight) of the chart. Both portions contain channels representing tall, heavy (upper 10%), average (next 20% and middle 40%), and short, light (next 20% and lower 10%). The child's growth is generally considered satisfactory if the plotted points remain within a channel.

Supplies. Growth charts can be ordered from the American Medical Association, Order Department OP-311, 535 N. Dearborn Street, Chicago, IL 60610.

Validity. The growth charts were developed after extensive study of the growth records of children at various age levels. They were based on height and weight measurements collected between 1960 and 1975 on boys and girls attending public schools in Iowa and South Carolina. The height and weight channels were obtained by subdividing height and weight distributions at different ages.

Reliability. None reported for this specific test.

Comments. When the child's growth curve moves from one channel to another, the underlying cause of this change should be determined and appropriate measures taken.

SUMMARY

Although informal testing may take place in elementary school physical education programs, few standardized tests of sport and physical activity were developed for this age group in the past. Now, however, the picture is changing. Since youth sports has become a viable area of study, a need has been generated for a wide variety of tests to measure different aspects of the sports environment. To test physical fitness, the AAHPERD Health-Related Physical Fitness Test can be used in the lower as well as upper elementary grades. Some of the more recently developed checklists used to assess basic movement patterns are based on sound theory rather than arm-chair judgment. More tests with substantiated validity and reliability are needed that can be administered in a short period of time. The development of criterion-referenced tests for elementary school physical education would make a valuable contribution to a testing program for young children. Finally, any type of testing program is unlikely to be used with success in the elementary schools unless it is integrated into the instructional program in physical education.

LEARNING EXPERIENCES

1. Form a group with three other students in class. Study the checklist presented in the boxed material on p. 402. Take turns demonstrating each level (step) of arm action and leg action in hopping. Then attempt to use the checklist by evaluating the children in Figs. 17-10 and 17-11. Use the detailed description of leg and arm action in the two sections of boxed material on p. 424. The correct classifications are included on p. 426.

FIG. 17-10. *Arm and leg action in hopping.*
Redrawn from Roberton, M.A., and Halverson, L.E.

FIG. 17-11. *Arm and leg action in hopping.*
Redrawn from Roberton, M.A., and Halverson, L.E.

Developmental sequence for leg action in hopping*

Step 1. Momentary flight. The support knee and hip quickly flex, pulling (instead of projecting) the foot from the floor. The flight is momentary. Only one or two hops can be achieved. The swing leg is lifted high and held in an inactive position to the side or in front of the body.

Step 2. Fall and catch; swing leg inactive. Body leaning forward allows the minimal knee and ankle extension to help the body "fall" forward of the support foot and, then, quickly catch itself again. The swing leg is inactive. Repeat hops are now possible.

Step 3. Projected takeoff; swing leg assists. Perceptible pretakeoff extension occurs in the hip, knee, and ankle in the support leg. There is little or no delay in changing from knee and ankle flexion on landing to extension prior to takeoff. The swing leg now pumps up and down to assist in projection. The range of the swing is insufficient to carry it behind the support leg when viewed from the side.

Step 4. Projection delay; swing leg leads. The weight of the child on landing is now smoothly transferred along the foot to the ball before the knee and ankle extend to takeoff. The support leg nearly reaches full extension on the takeoff. The swing leg now leads the upward-forward movement of the takeoff phase, while the support leg is still rotating over the ball of the foot. The range of the pumping action in the swing leg increases so that it passes behind the support leg when viewed from the side.

*From Roberton, M.A. and Halverson, L.E.

Developmental sequence for arm action in hopping*

Step 1. Bilateral inactive. The arms are held bilaterally, usually high and out to the side, although other positions behind or in front of the body may occur. Any arm action is usually slight and not consistent.

Step 2. Bilateral reactive. Arms swing upward briefly, then are medially rotated at the shoulder in a winging movement prior to takeoff. It appears that this movement is in reaction to loss of balance.

Step 3. Bilateral assist. The arms pump up and down together, usually in front of the line of the trunk. Any downward and backward motion of the arms occurs *after* takeoff. The arms may move parallel to each other or be held at different levels as they move up and down.

Step 4. Semiopposition. The arm on the side opposite the swing leg swings forward with that leg and back as the leg moves down. The position of the other arm is variable, often staying in front of the body or to the side.

Step 5. Opposing-assist. The arm opposite the swing leg moves forward and upward in synchrony with the forward and upward movement of that leg. The other arm moves in the direction opposite to the action of the swing leg. The range of movement in the arm action may be minimal unless the task requires speed or distance.

*From Roberton, M.A., and Halverson, L.E.

Finally, observe at least two children performing a hop and attempt to classify them, using the checklist. Check with the other members of the group to determine how closely you agreed on your classifications. If there is considerable disagreement, observe the children again and attempt to uncover the sources of disagreement.

2. Observe a group of elementary age children being tested on some aspect of their motor performance. Write a short paper on the problems that can be encountered in administering a test to young children. Suggest ways of avoiding these problems.

REFERENCES

American Alliance for Health, Physical Education, Recreation and Dance. 1980. Health-related Physical Fitness Test Manual. Reston, Va.: AAHPERD.

American Medical Association. 1978. Height-weight interpretation folder for boys. Chicago: AMA Medicine/Education Committee.

American Medical Association. 1978. Height-weight interpretation folder for girls. Chicago: AMA Medicine/Education Committee.

Johnson, R.D. 1962. Measurements of achievement in fundamental skills. Research Quarterly 33:94-103.

Latchaw, M. 1954. Measuring selected motor skills in fourth, fifth, and sixth grades. Research Quarterly 25:439-449.

Roberton, M.A. 1978. Stages in motor development. In Ridenour, M., editor. Motor development: issues and applications. Princeton, N.J.: Princeton Book Co., Publishers.

Roberton, M.A., and Halverson, L.E. 1984. Developing children—their changing movement. Philadelphia: Lea & Febiger.

Scott, M.G., and French, E. 1959. Measurement and evaluation in physical education. Dubuque, Iowa: Wm C Brown Group.

Seefeldt, V., and Haubenstricker, J. 1982. Patterns, phases, or stages: an analytical model for the study of developmental movement. In Kelso, J.A.S., and Clark, J.E., editors. The development of movement control and co-ordination. London: John Wiley & Sons, Ltd.

Seefeldt, V., Reuschlein, S., and Vogel, P. 1972. Sequencing motor skills within the physical education curriculum, Paper presented at the American Association for Health, Physical Education, and Recreation National Convention, Houston, March 27, 1972.

Thomas, J.R. 1983. Motor development during childhood and adolescence. Minneapolis: Burgess Publishing Co.

Wild, M.R. 1938. The behavior pattern of throwing and some observations concerning its course of development in children. Research Quarterly 9:20-24.

ANNOTATED READINGS

Hardin, D.H., and Garcia, M.J. 1982. Diagnostic performance tests for elementary school children (Grades 1-4). Journal of Physical Education, Recreation and Dance 53(2): 48-49.

Recommends the use of four performance tests measuring running, jumping, throwing, and ball-handling in elementary school physical education; norms are presented for children ages 6 through 9.

Melville, S. 1985. Teaching and evaluating cognitive skills in elementary physical education. Journal of Physical Education, Recreation and Dance **56**(2):26-28.

Describes the development of a written examination on cognitive skill acquisition for third and fourth graders; discusses the benefits of using written examinations in elementary physical education.

Seefeldt, V. 1984. Physical fitness in preschool elementary and elementary school-aged children. Journal of Physical Education, Recreation and Dance **55**(9):33-37, 40.

Documents the importance of enhancing children's physical fitness during their early years; discusses the relationship between fundamental motor skills and fitness in preschool years.

Thomas, J.R., and Thomas, K.T. 1983. Strange kids and strange numbers: assessing children's motor development. Journal of Physical Education, Recreation and Dance **54**(8):19-20.

Identifies important motor behaviors and characteristics to be measured in children; discusses the selection of appropriate tests of the movement performance of preschool and elementary school-age children; reviews the circumstances under which assessments should be made.

ANSWERS TO LEARNING EXPERIENCES. Figure 17-10 represents Leg action, Step 2; Arm action, Step 2. Figure 17-11 represents Leg action, Step 4; Arm action, Step 5.

18

Adapting Tests and Measurements for Special Populations

KEY WORDS *Watch for these words as you read the following chapter:*

anomaly	hard of hearing	orthopedically impaired
cerebral palsy	impaired	paraplegia
congenital	Individualized Education Program (IEP)	reflexes
deaf		seriously emotionally disturbed
disabled	mentally retarded	
educable	motor ability	specific learning disability
handicapped	multihandicapped	
	needs assessment	speech impairment
		visually handicapped

Measurement and evaluation techniques of the **impaired** are frequently used for purposes similar to those used for testing in regular physical education classes. For example, tests may be used to motivate students, to classify them, and for many other reasons (see Chapter 1). However, when students have physical, emotional, or mental impairments that lead to physical **disabilities,** initial testing assumes special significance.

Before initiating a program of physical activity for an individual, a teacher must determine his or her level of physical functioning. Because of the wide variety of handicaps that exist, testing must often take place on an individualized basis. The physical education teacher, working with the appropriate specialists, tests the student to determine the level of psychomotor functioning. This information is used to plan a physical education program based on objectives developed specifically for the individual. The student is then evaluated in light of these objectives. In essence, before a student with impairments is allowed to participate in any form of physical activity in an educational setting, a two-stage approach to testing should take place. A therapist often handles the first stage— *determining the extent of the disability.* Ideally, a specialist in adapted physical education assists the therapist in this assessment. The results are used to prepare individualized objectives, and the adequacy of these objectives is then checked. Are they written at the appropriate level for the child? Are some objectives too easy? Too difficult? This analysis represents the second stage of planning, essentially a **needs assessment**—*determining the extent to which the student is capable of meeting the individualized objectives.* If the child can already meet an objective, it should be modified or rewritten. By this process the objectives are fine-tuned. After these assessments are completed, a program of physical activity can be initiated. The long-range goal of the program is to enhance performance in the nonimpaired areas and to reduce the level of impairment as much as possible. Many textbooks on adapted physical education stress the importance of using *formative evaluation* to provide continuous monitoring of performance so that adjustments can be made in a program when necessary (Sherrill, 1981; Seaman and DePauw, 1982; Fait and Dunn, 1984). Although norm-referenced approaches to measurement are sometimes advocated, primary emphasis is placed on *criterion-referenced testing.*

As you might expect, there is no universal agreement on the factors related to motor performance that should be measured in this special population. Kirkendall, Gruber, and Johnson (1980) proposed testing 10 physical factors.

Basic areas
1. Strength
2. Endurance (muscular and cardiovascular)
3. Range of motion
4. Balance

Intermediate areas
5. Body awareness
6. Body sides awareness
7. Space awareness
8. Timing awareness

Advanced areas
9. Coordination
10. Agility

Seaman and DePauw (1982) refer to four broad levels of assessment, ranging from the basic to the complex:
1. Reflex behavior
2. Sensory systems
3. Motor patterns
4. Movement skills

Examples of tests fitting several of these categories are presented later in this chapter. Several of these tests are also appropriate for preschool and elementary school children without handicaps in a physical education setting. For example, it is not unusual to find the Denver Developmental Screening Test described in

Warm-up for bicycle ergometer test.

textbooks on elementary physical education, motor development, and adapted physical education. However, whether the child is with or without **handicaps,** many of these tests must be administered on an individualized basis, with, of course, certain exceptions. For example, when the handicapping condition is mild, such as mild mental retardation, group testing is possible. When the AAHPERD Motor Fitness Test for the Moderately Mentally Retarded is used, it can be administered to students as a group. As the extent of retardation becomes more severe, individualized testing is more effective. Most of the tests used to screen students for classification purposes require one-on-one testing, regardless of the extent of the handicap.

LEGAL MANDATES AFFECTING EVALUATION

Although it is assumed that good instruction incorporates sound measurement and evaluation practices, the individual with impairments has special needs and thus has been given unique protection by legal action. In effect since 1975, the Education for All Handicapped Children Act (Public Law 94-142) has precise implications for evaluation in physical education. Although many aspects of education are affected by the law, the focus in this chapter is directed to measurement and evaluation in the physical education field.

Public Law 94-142 mandates an **Individualized Education Program** (IEP) for each disabled or handicapped child receiving special education services. The IEP must include documentation about evaluation of the child's educational program. It must be approved by a committee whose membership, which must include at least one parent, is determined under the law. Assessments must be completed within 30 days of the date of parental permission. Complete assessments are required by law every 3 years, and the results of the assessment must be reported in a formal meeting. Although several adapted physical education textbooks have thorough discussions of this law, the portions of the law affecting evaluation are especially well presented in Fait and Dunn (1984). A summary of part of their review follows.

Due process

If the child is judged to have impairments requiring a special testing program, the school is required to inform the parents and the child of their rights with the provision to challenge educational decisions they feel are unfair. This requirement includes five components:

1. *Permission before assessment.* The parents must give written permission to have their child evaluated.
2. *Results of the assessment.* The results must be interpreted in a meeting with the parents.
3. *Outside evaluation.* The parent may request that an independent evaluation be conducted outside the school. The parent must pay for these expenses unless the results differ from those reported by the school, in which case the school district must cover them.
4. *Hearings.* If the parents and the school system cannot agree on the evaluation findings, a special hearing must be held.
5. *Confidentiality of records.* Records of all evaluations must be kept confidential.

Standards for evaluation

Public Law 94-142 also specifies standards for evaluation, including test selection, test administration, and test examiners.

1. *Test selection.* The school system must use tests to measure the *achievement level* rather than the *impairment* of the child. More than one test procedure must be used. All tests cannot be subjective (such as observational scales), nor can all be objective (like performance tests).
2. *Test administration.* Tests must be administered to test the student's *ability* rather than his or her *communication skills*. This is particularly critical

for those with sensory impairments. If the child's native language is not English, the test instructions should be given in the native language, if necessary. If the child is **deaf,** sign language can be used.

3. *Test examiners.* A multidisciplinary team is required for the testing. Ideally, this team includes a specialist in adapted physical education. All testers must be trained and qualified to administer the measures.

The rest of this chapter contains examples of measures that are frequently recommended by specialists in the field. As you review each test, consider the feasibility of using it in a kindergarten or elementary physical education setting with children who have no handicapping conditions.

OBSERVATIONAL TECHNIQUES

Checklists for assessing the child with impairments are available in adapted physical education textbooks, such as Sherrill (1981), Seaman and DePauw (1982), and Fait and Dunn (1984). Some of these observational techniques were developed by physical educators who have had years of experience working with students having a variety of handicapping conditions, including those with a **specific learning disability** and those who are **seriously emotionally disturbed.** However, most of these observational tools are weak measures of the student's physical ability because they lack evidence of validity and reliability. Although logical validity may be self-evident to a certain extent, it does not substitute for the proper establishment of test characteristics. If the techniques are used as quick-screening devices before more thorough assessment, their use is more defensible. If the results of a weak measure are used to make temporary decisions that can be modified in the near future, the consequences of assessment are not as severe as those used to make decisions with long-term implications for the child.

PERFORMANCE TESTS
Reflex testing

Generally, adapted physical education specialists are not expected to test **reflexes** (inborn, involuntary behaviors), although the physical education teacher working in an adaptive setting needs to know the results of reflex testing to analyze the movement deficiencies of the student. This information should be a part of the student's records and is usually obtained by a therapist.

Sensorimotor testing

Sensorimotor or perceptual-motor testing samples the function of the underlying sensory system through observable motor performance (Seaman and DePauw, 1982). A description of one test in this category, the Purdue Perceptual Motor Survey, follows. (Sources for obtaining two other tests, the Quick Neurological Screening Test and the Frostig Developmental Test of Visual Perception, are included at the end of this chapter.)

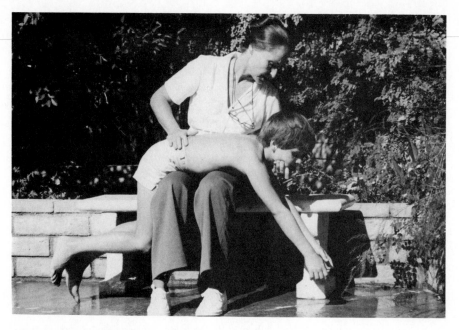

Test of the tonic labyrinthine reflex.
Courtesy Janet A. Seaman.

PURDUE PERCEPTUAL MOTOR SURVEY (Roach and Kephart, 1966)

Test objective. To sample the functions of the sensory systems as they support or contribute to efficient movement.

Description. The survey consists of 12 test items:

A. Balance and posture
    Test No. 1: Walking board
    Test No. 2: Hopping and jumping

B. Body image and right-left (R-L) discrimination
    Test No. 3: Identification of body parts
    Test No. 4: Imitation of movement
    Test No. 5: Obstacle course
    Test No. 6: Kraus-Weber Test
    Test No. 7: Angels-in-the-snow

C. Perceptual-motor match
    Test No. 8: Chalkboard activities
    Test No. 9: Rhythmic writing

D. Test No. 10: Ocular control
    Test No. 11: Ocular pursuits

E. Test No. 12: Form reproduction (drawing simple geometric figures on blank paper)

Test area. A multipurpose room or gymnasium is needed for several of the items; otherwise, a classroom can be used.

Equipment. Chalkboard, chalk, penlight, yardstick or dowel, and visual achievement forms.

Scoring. A 4-point rating scale is used.

Validity. A validity coefficient of 0.65 was reported between the survey and teacher ratings.

Reliability. The test-retest reliability was 0.95, with 1 week intervening between test administrations.

Norms. Norms have been published for grades 1 through 4, based on the scores of 200 children with 50 randomly selected from each grade.

Comments. The Test Manual should be purchased and reviewed before administering the survey. The survey can be administered to an individual in 45 minutes.

Motor development profiles

Many qualitative measures of the development of movement patterns have been published. These scales typically assess changes in whole body configurations as the child grows and develops. The Denver Developmental Screening Test (Frankenburg and Dodds, 1967; Frankenburg, Dodds, and Fandel, 1973) follows.

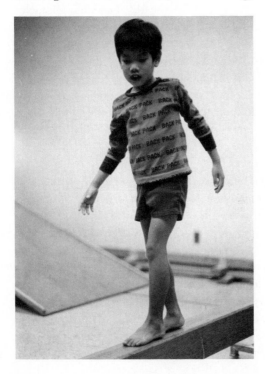

Assessment of asymmetrical tonic neck reflex in an upright position.
Courtesy Janet A. Seaman.

(Sources for obtaining two other tests, the California State University Motor Development Checklist and the Bayley Scales of Motor Development, are presented at the end of this chapter.)

DENVER DEVELOPMENTAL SCREENING TEST (Frankenberg and Dodds, 1967)

Test objective. To evaluate children up to age 6 in fine motor, gross motor, social, and language skills.

Description. There are 105 tasks selected to identify developmental delays in the above four categories. The tester uses an instruction sheet of 28 items to elicit responses from the examinee. The tester also records behavioral observations (e.g., how the child feels at the time of the test, relation to tester).

Test area. A small room provides sufficient space.

Equipment. Small toy, rattle, piece of yarn, paper and pencil, box of raisins, eight small cubes, small bottle, pictures of familiar objects, and small ball.

Scoring. Each item is scored in one of four ways—*pass, fail, refusal,* or *no opportunity for child to respond.*

Validity. A validity coefficient of 0.97 was reported, based on a comparison of the Denver Test with the Yale Developmental Examination, a lengthier, more complex test.

Reliability. Reliability coefficient estimates calculated for each of the four categories (fine motor, gross motor, social, and language skills) ranged from 0.66 to 0.93.

Norms. Charts have been developed showing the age level at which 10%, 25%, 50%, 75%, and 90% of the children can perform specific tasks. Data from 1043 children through age 6 were used to determine these standards.

Comments. Administration time varies, depending on the age and maturity of the child. Test items must be administered individually.

Motor ability tests

Motor ability, a rather nebulous term, was originally used to represent one's innate ability to perform motor tasks. However, it was impossible to separate innate ability from learned skills. Motor ability has also been referred to as a predictor of athletic ability. Gradually the term took on a new meaning and is now thought to reflect motor educability, one's ability to learn motor skills. Although it seems intuitively reasonable that individuals possess an innate motor ability, there is no scientific evidence that the tests available at the present time tap this trait. This does not mean these tests are not at all useful in an educational setting, but rather that labeling these tests as measures of motor ability is questionable. The Bruininks-Oseretsky Motor Development Scale, classified by Seaman and DePauw (1982) as a motor ability test often used with disabled stu-

Assessment of quality of running form. Item from Adapted Physical Education Assessment Scale.
Courtesy Janet A. Seaman.

dents, follows. (Sources for obtaining two other motor ability tests, the Six Category Gross Motor Test and the Basic Motor Ability Test—Revised, are included at the end of this chapter.)

THE BRUININKS-OSERETSKY TEST OF MOTOR PROFICIENCY
(Bruininks, 1978)

Test objective. This is an individually administered test that assesses the motor functioning of children from 4½ to 14½ years of age.

Description. Both a Complete Battery and a Short Form are available. The Complete Battery includes eight subtests, four to measure gross motor skills, three to measure fine motor skills, and one for both fine and gross motor skills:

Subtest No. 1: Running speed and agility (one item)
Subtest No. 2: Balance (eight items)
Subtest No. 3: Bilateral coordination (eight items)
Subtest No. 4: Strength (three items)
Subtest No. 5: Upper-limb coordination (nine items)

Subtest No. 6: Response speed (one item)

Subtest No. 7: Visual-motor control (eight items)

Subtest No. 8: Upper limb speed and dexterity (eight items)

The Short Form, consisting of 14 items from the Complete Battery, follows, along with the respective subtest numbers.

Subtest No. 1. *Item 1:* Running speed and agility

Subtest No. 2. *Item 2:* Standing on preferred leg while making circles with fingers

Item 7: Walking forward heel-to-toe on balance beam

Subtest No. 3. *Item 1:* Tapping feet alternatively while making circles with fingers

Item 6: Jumping up and clapping hands

Subtest No. 4. *Item 1:* Standing broad jump

Subtest No. 5. *Item 3:* Catching a tossed ball with both hands

Item 5: Throwing a ball at a target with preferred hand

Subtest No. 6. *Item 1:* Response speed

Subtest No. 7. *Item 3:* Drawing a line through a straight path with preferred hand

Item 5: Copying a circle on paper with preferred hand

Item 8: Copying overlapping pencils with preferred hand

Subtest No. 8. *Item 3:* Sorting shape cards with preferred hand

Item 7: Drawing dots in circles with preferred hand

Test area. Room of any size, as long as space can be cleared for testing.

Equipment. All equipment needed for administration of the scale: ball, mazes, scissors, balance rod, matchbook, coins, small boxes, thread, playing cards, matchsticks, ballpoint pen, and paper. The kit can be purchased in a specially designed metal carrying case. In addition to the equipment, the kit includes an Examiner's Manual, individual record forms for the Complete Battery and the Short Form, and a package of 25 student booklets (for test items that require cutting or paper-and-pencil responses).

Scoring. Scale items are scored on a pass/fail basis. For the Complete Battery, there is a gross motor composite (Subtest Nos. 1 through 4) and a fine motor composite (Subtest Nos. 6 through 8). For the Short Form a single score provides an index of motor proficiency.

Validity. Evidence of validity is primarily construct validity.

1. The relationship of test content to research findings in motor development was established.

2. A number of statistical properties of the test were reported: relationship of test scores to chronological age, internal consistency of subtest, and factor analysis of subtest items.

3. Comparisons were made between contrast groups: mildly retarded with

normal subjects, moderately to severely retarded with normal subjects, and learning disabled with normal subjects. The interrelationships between subtests were low to moderate, meaning that the subtests tapped different abilities.

Reliability. The test-retest reliability was high for composite scores (ranging from 0.68 to 0.86, with only the 0.68 estimate falling on the low side). The coefficients were lower for some of the subtests, where reliability estimates as low as 0.29 were reported; however, the range of estimates was from 0.29 to 0.89. Interrater reliability was generally quite satisfactory, ranging from 0.77 to 0.97. This type of reliability is quite important since much of the scoring is subjective. The standard error of measurement was also reported for all age groups on each subtest.

Norms. Percentile norms were reported for males and females ranging from 6 to 14 years of age.

Comments. The Lincoln-Oseretsky version of this test is described in detail in Sloan (1955). The scale has undergone several revisions, with the latest being the Bruininks-Oseretsky Test of Motor Proficiency (1978).* Approximately 45 minutes is required to administer the Complete Battery and 15 to 20 minutes to administer the Short Form. The Bruininks' revision was very well developed. Evidence of an item analysis and standardization of the test is included. Differences between individual standard scores are also reported.

Physical fitness tests

Sherrill (1981) notes that, although many children with impairments have low levels of physical fitness, programs to improve their fitness are often neglected. One must remember the definition of health-related physical fitness (See Chapter 11) and its emphasis of universal application. Sherrill recommends administering the AAHPERD Health-Related Physical Fitness Test to students with impairments. Adjustments in the test may be necessary, depending on the extent and type of the disability. For example, if a student has severe cognitive disorders, a buddy system might be used effectively in administering distance run tests. If necessary, the distance run can be reduced to 600 or even 300 yards. At these shorter distances the test is no longer a valid measure of cardiorespiratory (CR) function, but it nonetheless taps other physiological parameters. The AAHPERD Motor Fitness Test for the Moderately Mentally Retarded is presented here in detail even though it is similar to the AAHPER Youth Fitness Test described in Chapter 12. The test for mentally retarded youth parallels two other tests for impaired youth published by AAHPERD, the AAHPER Youth Fitness Test Adaptation for the Blind and the Special Fitness Test for the Men-

---

*The Bruininks-Oseretsky Test of Motor Proficiency can be ordered from American Guidance Services, Circle Pines, MN 55014.

Warm-up for the treadmill test.

tally Retarded. The second test—the Project UNIQUE Physical Fitness Test—
is presented in less detail but is nevertheless an important contribution to the
fitness test area because of its exceptionally sound psychometric underpinnings.

AAHPERD MOTOR FITNESS TEST FOR THE MODERATELY MENTALLY RETARDED (Johnson and Londeree, 1976)

The AAHPERD Motor Fitness Test for the Moderately Mentally Retarded is a
modification of the AAHPER Youth Fitness Test for **educable** (capable of learning) mentally retarded children. Individuals with this level of retardation have
IQs ranging from 50 to 70. Included in the Test Manual are 13 items—flexed-
arm hang, sit-ups, standing long jump, softball throw for distance, 50-yard dash,
300-yard run-walk, height, weight, sitting bob-and-reach, skipping, tumbling
progression, and target throw. The first six items are recommended as sufficient
for testing the motor fitness of the moderately mentally retarded, with the other
items usable in local situations. In the Test Manual norms are published for boys
and girls, ages 6 through 20, although the norms are based on small sample sizes
in many cases. An award system is also available for these age groups.

FLEXED-ARM HANG

Test objective. Although the objective is not stated in the Test Manual, the Flexed-Arm Hang is usually included in a fitness test battery as a measure of arm and shoulder girdle strength and endurance.

Description. Adjust the bar to approximately standing height. Instruct the student to grasp the bar with an overhand grip (palms away from body). The student jumps (and is simultaneously lifted by a tester) to the flexed-arm position, with the chin above the bar and parallel to the floor. The elbows are held close to the sides and the chin is just above the bar. Once the student is in motionless, hanging position and is no longer assisted by the tester, the stopwatch is started. Stop the watch when "the chin touches the bar, the head tilts back to keep the chin above the bar, or the chin drops below the bar" (Johnson and Londeree, 1976: 16). One trial is administered. Do not allow the student to kick or swing the legs or lift the knees.

Test area. Small indoor area, even a doorway, is adequate.

Equipment. In the Test Manual a metal or wooden bar 1½ inches in diameter is recommended. However, a doorway gym bar or an angled or horizontal ladder would also be suitable. A stopwatch is used to time the test.

Scoring. The score is the amount of time, to the nearest tenth of a second, the proper position is held.

Validity. Although the manual includes a brief discussion of the validity of the total test battery, there is no reference to the validity of this specific test.

Reliability. Test-retest reliability coefficients of 0.90 were reported, with 6 months intervening between test administrations.

Norms. Norms are available for moderately mentally retarded boys and girls, ages 6 through 20. However, the norms are based on small sample sizes and should be used only as rough guidelines.

Comments. Evidence of validity and reliability for the population of educable mentally retarded youth needs to be obtained for future revisions of the manual. Reliability should be estimated with no more than 2 weeks elapsing between test periods. The most critical issue related to the Flexed-Arm Hang Test is whether it can adequately measure differences in strength across all ages and both genders. In the tables of norms for this test, more than 50% of the male samples could not maintain the proper position for any recorded time. At least 50% of the girls were unable to obtain any score at all, regardless of age. The manual stated that children in this group had very low arm and shoulder strength and endurance. Yet, the test results suggest that many have *no* strength in this area, which cannot be true. Stating that the test is not discriminating well is probably more accurate. It lacks a basic characteristic of measurement—that as ability changes, the test score changes correspondingly. Even in a normal population, too many 0 scores are obtained on the flexed-arm hang. Other techniques for measuring arm and shoulder girdle strength, such as Baumgartner's Modified Pull-Ups Test, might be considered as substitutes. In cases of more severe impairments, a straight-arm hang has been suggested as a reasonable substitute.

SIT-UPS IN 30 SECONDS

Test objective. Although no objective is stated in the manual, this test is usually used to measure abdominal strength and endurance.

Description. The starting position is a back-lying position with knees flexed to less than 90 degrees, feet on the mat, and heels 12 inches from the buttocks. The hands are clasped behind the neck with fingers interlaced, and the elbows are resting on the mat. The feet are held in contact with the mat throughout the test by a partner. To begin the test use the command *"Go!"* The student curls to a sitting position and touches one elbow to the opposite knee, curls back to the starting position, and curls up again, touching the other elbow and knee. This sequence is continued until a 30-second time period has elapsed.

Test area. For group testing a gymnasium or multipurpose room can be used; for individual testing a very small area will suffice.

Equipment. Tumbling mat and stopwatch.

Scoring. The number of sit-ups correctly executed in 30 seconds is the score. The sit-up is not counted if the student does not begin it from the starting position or if the elbow is not touched to the opposite knee. Also, the fingers must remain clasped behind the neck throughout the sit-up. One trial is administered.

Validity. There is no reference to the validity of this specific test.

Reliability. The Test Manual reports reliability estimates of 0.80 and above for a group of test items, presumably including the sit-ups test.

Norms. Norms are available for moderately mentally retarded boys and girls, ages 6 through 20. However, the norms are based on small sample sizes and should be used only as rough guidelines.

Comments. The position of the arms and hands should be altered to reflect currently recommended procedures. Therapists have noted that when hands are clasped behind the neck, a tendency to use the arms in sitting up occurs. Furthermore, this position seems to encourage straight-back sit-ups. For these reasons the Health-Related Physical Fitness Test uses a modified position with the arms crossed at chest level and hands placed on opposite shoulders.

STANDING LONG JUMP

Test objective. Although the objective of the Standing Long Jump Test is not stated in the Test Manual, it is usually used as a measure of explosive leg power.

Description. In the starting position the student stands behind the restraining line. The toes must not touch the line, and the feet are several inches apart. Although any preliminary motions may be made as long as the feet are not moved, usually the examinee dips the body several times swinging the arms backward with one dip and forward with the next. On the actual jump the arms swing forward and the body leans in a forward direction. Both feet must leave the floor at the same time and land at the same time. The object of the test is to jump as far as possible.

Test area. The test can be administered on a floor or a paved, outdoor surface. The manual recommends marking an open area with a restraining line and lines parallel to this line every inch, starting at 12 inches. A testing area of 120 inches is suggested, although this can be modified, if necessary. Each line should be 30 inches long, with the distance clearly marked. Another alternative is to tape a tape measure on the floor perpendicular to the restraining line.

Equipment. Tape measure, if the alternate setup is used, and a yardstick to line up the distance on the tape with the student's heels.

Scoring. Record the best of three trials to the nearest inch. "Measure the perpendicular distance from the restraining line to the heel or other body part that touches the floor nearest the takeoff line. Be sure to note carefully the point where the heels first contact the floor because there is a tendency for the feet to slide forward" (Johnson and Londeree, 1976: 19).

Validity. There is no reference in the Test Manual to the validity of this specific test.

Reliability. The Test Manual reports reliability estimates of 0.80 or higher for a group of test items, presumably including the Standing Long Jump.

Norms. Norms are published for moderately mentally retarded boys and girls, ages 6 through 20. However, the sample sizes are small; thus the norms should be interpreted with caution.

Comments. The test developers note that the best jump is often not attained in three trials. They recommend that the youngsters build up to a point where they can perform 20 to 25 jumps with all-out effort. The tester should chart the students' performance over a number of days and determine when the best jump is made. On the actual testing day the student should be given as many practice trials as needed, as determined in previous weeks. The number of test trials remains the same for all students, although the number of practice trials may vary. If one student achieved his maximum distance on trial 12, he should be given 10 practice trials before testing.

SOFTBALL THROW FOR DISTANCE

Test objective. Although there is no statement in the Test Manual on the objective of the Softball Throw for Distance Test, it is usually used to measure coordination.

Description. The student throws overhand as far as possible, three times in succession. Mark the distance of the first throw. If the next throw is longer, remove the marking of the first throw and mark the better one. If not, leave the marking at the landing point of the first throw. Handle the third throw the same way. Use two or more students to retrieve balls after they hit the ground. Any type of approach may be used as long as the student does not cross the restraining line. The throw must be overhand. Students should warm up by playing catch.

Test area. An open field is recommended for administration of this test, with a width of 50 feet and a length of 250 feet. Use agricultural lime to mark the field. Mark the restraining line first, then start 15 feet from the restraining line and mark lines at 5 foot intervals, up to 225 feet. This distance may be adjusted for different groups.

Equipment. A minimum of three softballs (12-inch) in good condition is needed.

Scoring. The test score is the best of three trials. The score is the perpendicular distance from the restraining line to the landing point. Record the distance to the nearest foot.

Validity. There is no reference in the Test Manual to the validity of this specific test.

Reliability. The test manual reports reliability estimates of 0.80 or higher for a group of test items, presumably including the Softball Throw for Distance Test.

Norms. Norms are published for moderately mentally retarded boys and girls, ages 6 through 20. Because of the small sample sizes of the norm groups, the norms should be used only as rough guidelines.

Comments. This test was eliminated from the AAHPER Youth Fitness Test in the 1976 manual, because there was no evidence that coordination could be measured by a single item of this type. The softball throw seems to measure a specific skill rather than a general motor fitness trait. Whether it should be retained in this test battery is questionable. Other adapted physical education specialists (Winnick and Short, 1985) have suggested that the Softball Throw for Distance might be used as a substitute for a strength item in special cases. The test item probably measures a specific type of fitness required to perform a softball skill. It is unlikely that this ability generalizes to other sport skills.

The most reliable indicator of the student's ability to throw the softball is the average of three trials rather than the best of three. This is a proven fact in measurement theory. Therefore, the scoring procedure for this test should be reexamined.

50-YARD DASH

Test objective. Although there is no statement in the Test Manual on the objective of the 50-Yard Dash, this test is usually used as a measure of speed.

Description. The manual recommends testing two students at the same time.

The students take starting positions behind the starting line. The test administrator (at the finish line) raises both arms sideways to indicate the *Set* position. The *Go* signal is given by rapidly lowering the arms to the side. The administrator has a stopwatch in each hand, and both watches are started when the arms reach the side of the body. The two students run as fast as possible across the finish line. The watch for a designated runner is stopped when the student's body (not head or arms) crosses the finish line. One trial is taken.

Test area. An outdoor space is usually preferred, although any smooth, solid surface of the appropriate distance may be used.

Equipment. The Test Manual recommends using two stopwatches if students are to be tested in pairs. If only one watch is available, the students could be tested individually; however, they could still run in pairs for motivational purposes.

Scoring. The score is the time between the *Go* signal and the moment the student's body crosses the finish line. The time is recorded to the nearest tenth of a second.

Validity. There is no reference to the validity of this specific test.

Reliability. The Test Manual reports reliability coefficients of 0.80 or higher for a group of tests, presumably including the 50-Yard Dash Test.

Norms. Norms are published for moderately mentally retarded boys and girls, ages 6 through 20. These norms should be used with caution because of small sample sizes.

Comments. Does the visual signal provide a more accurate start than a verbal signal? Obviously, a visual signal requires the examinee to watch the examiner closely. This may lead to a slower start. Further study of these starts would be useful. The advantage of a visual start is that only one tester is needed to administer the test.

300 YARD RUN-WALK

Test objective. Although no statement of the objective of the 300 Yard Run-Walk was given in the Test Manual, it is usually used as a measure of CR function.

Description. The manual suggests testing five to ten students at a time. Examinees should stand in a single row behind the starting line, using a standing start. On the signal *Ready, Go!* the students begin running. The 300-yard distance should be run as fast as possible. Walking is permitted but should not be encouraged. As the runner crosses the finish line, the timer calls out the time to the scorer.

Test area. A track is ideal for testing the 300 Yard Run-Walk; however, any paved area or smooth, solid surface, either indoors or outdoors, can be used.

Equipment. Stopwatch.

Scoring. The score should be recorded in seconds.

Validity. No evidence of the validity of this specific test is included in the Test Manual.

Reliability. No reliability estimates were reported for the 300 Yard Run-Walk.

Norms. Norms are published for moderately mentally retarded boys and girls, ages 6 through 20. These norms should be used as rough guidelines because of small sample sizes.

Comments. An abundance of scientific evidence now indicates that distances under 1 mile are not effective measures of CR function. Certainly a distance of 300 yards would not tap this parameter. Since CR function is such an important aspect of health-related fitness, strong consideration should be given to increasing the test distance to 1 mile for handicapped students who have been properly trained to run this distance.

Summary of test battery

The previous six items were presented in detail as an example of the type of fitness tests available for children with impairments. For additional information on the test battery and award system, refer to the AAHPERD Motor Fitness Testing Manual for the Moderately Mentally Retarded (Johnson and Londeree, 1976). In general, the test items in this battery measure fitness associated with athletic ability rather than health-related physical fitness. The objectives for using this test should be clearly in mind when it is used in a school setting. The normative data were collected during the spring of 1973. The norms should be updated using substantial sample sizes from a cross section of the United States rather than a single state. Finally, the test items should be revised in light of sound measurement principles and scientific evidence on the measurement of physiological parameters. This fine contribution to the testing literature for children with impairments should be continually modified so that it remains useful for teachers in school settings.

PROJECT UNIQUE PHYSICAL FITNESS TEST (Winnick and Short, 1985)

In an excellent study of the physical fitness of sensory and orthopedically impaired youth, Winnick and Short (1985) noted that the *components* of fitness are essentially the same for normal and sensory or orthopedically impaired children, but the *performance* of the **impaired** individual generally falls below that of the normal individual. Age, gender, educational setting, and type and severity of handicapping condition must be considered in interpreting the results of physical fitness tests.

Based on a sound psychometric approach, the test battery identifies seven test items. Since all of the items are described elsewhere in this text, only a summary of the battery follows.

Warm-up for arm ergometer test.

Test objective. The battery is designed to measure body composition, flexibility, CR endurance, and muscular strength and endurance.

Description. The test battery consists of seven items:

Item 1: Skinfold measures (triceps, subscapular, and sum of triceps and subscapular)

Item 2: Grip strength (see Fig. 18-2)

Item 3: 50 yard/meter dash (see Fig. 18-1)

Item 4: Sit-ups (number in 60 seconds)

Item 5: Softball throw (distance)

Item 6: Sit-and-reach

Item 7: Long distance run (1-mile/9-minute run or 1½-mile/12-minute run)

Test area, equipment, and scoring. See Chapters 11 and 12 on fitness testing.

Validity. This test is exceptionally well validated. First, the logical validity of each test item is demonstrated. Second, evidence of criterion-related and construct validity is presented. In particular, the factorial validity of the instrument is stressed, forming the basis of this impressive study. Finally, scientific evidence supporting the validity of the test items is included where appropriate.

Reliability. A number of reliability coefficients are presented for each test item. These estimates range from 0.49 to .975, although most coefficients are very high—in the 0.90s. Reliability data are presented for **visually handicapped, hard of hearing,** and **orthopedically impaired,** as well as **mentally retarded,**

FIG. 18-1. *The 50-year/meter dash.*
From Winnick, J.P., and Short, F.X.

Start

50
yards

50
meters
(55 yards)

FIG 18-2. *Measurement of grip strength.*
From Winnick, J.P., and Short, F.X.

Adjust hand grip dynamometer
to fit subject's grip

individuals. Anyone using these test items should refer to the Project UNIQUE report (Winnick and Short, 1985), which includes one of the best and most thorough tables of reliability estimates for fitness tests.

Norms. Means and standard deviations are presented for each age and sex within each subject category. Four major categories of subjects were identified: normal (nonimpaired), visually impaired, auditory impaired, and orthopedically impaired. The sample sizes were too small to convert the data to norms.

Comments. Since it is not possible for individuals with certain impairments to take some of the test items, Winnick and Short have recommended substitutions for specific situations. Although a rationale is not presented for the selection of these substitutions, it is apparent that the test developers do not necessarily view the substitute tests as measures of equivalent fitness parameters when compared to the original measures. Rather, a testable area of fitness is selected, depending on the nature and extent of the handicapping condition. Consider the following examples of substitute tests:

1. For boys with **cerebral palsy,** use an arm hang test instead of grip strength (see Fig. 18-3).

Overhand grip

FIG. 18-3. *Measurement of flexed-arm hang.*
From Winnick, J.P., and Short, F.X.

2. For boys with **paraplegic** wheelchair spinal neuromuscular disorder, use an arm hang test instead of grip strength.
3. For boys classified as **congenital anomaly**/amputee, use an arm hang test instead of grip strength.
4. For boys and girls classified as paraplegic wheelchair spinal neuromuscular, the softball throw for distance can be used instead of grip strength (see Fig. 18-4).

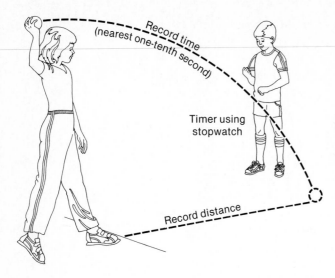

FIG. 18-4. *Softball throw for distance.*
By permission of Joseph P. Winnick.

Record time
(nearest one-tenth second)

Timer using
stopwatch

Record distance

5. For some boys and girls classified as congenital anomaly/amputee, the softball throw for distance may be substituted for sit-ups.
6. For boys and girls who have visual and auditory impairments, the broad jump may be substituted for grip strength.

Summary of test battery

The soundness of the development of the Project UNIQUE Physical Fitness Test gives it an edge over other physical fitness tests for children with impairments. The test administrator should keep in mind, however, that the items in the battery measure different types of fitness. Several of the items test health-related physical fitness, and a few measure fitness in an athletic performance context. All in all, the physical fitness test batteries for impaired children do not differ markedly from those developed for the nonimpaired child. There is no need for the items to be different, except when a type of impairment prevents performance of an item. Of course, certain modifications of items may be necessary, and norms should be developed for different types of impairments.

MOTOR PERFORMANCE TESTING

Many strategies have been developed to provide initial screening of students in a physical education setting. This screening must be followed by a formal testing program. The Los Angeles Unified School District has developed a scale that can be used to determine appropriate placement of students in physical education. An overview of the Adaptive Physical Education Assessment Scale*, follows.

---

*For more information on the scale, test manual, or norms, write to Adapted Physical Education Consultant, Los Angeles Unified School District, 450 North Grand Avenue—Building G, Los Angeles, Calif.

Self-testing of weight-pulling by guadraplegic.
Courtesy Janet A. Seaman.

THE ADAPTIVE PHYSICAL EDUCATION ASSESSMENT SCALE (IN SEAMAN AND DEPAUW, 1982)

Test objective. To place students appropriately in physical education. It measures five areas of motor performance: motor development, motor achievement, perceptual-motor function, posture, and physical fitness.

Description. The scale includes 18 items measuring motor performance:

1. Agility run	10. Vertical jump
2. Throwing accuracy	11. Jumping form
3. Hand preference	12. Ocular control
4. Kick stationary ball	13. Bent-knee curl up
5. Foot preference	14. Imitation of postures
6. Catching	15. Standing balance
7. Kicking rolling ball	16. Alternate hopping
8. Running	17. Arhythmical hopping
9. Posture	18. Endurance

A brief description of each of these items can be found in Seaman and DePauw (1982).

Standing balance item from the Adapted Physical Education Assessment Scale.
Courtesy Janet A. Seaman.

Test area. The first eight items should be measured outdoors during a single testing session. The remaining items may be administered either indoors or outdoors during another testing session. The outdoor space requirements are a 4 foot by 18 foot wall target with at least 15 feet by 16 feet of free space in front for throwing, running, and kicking; and a 50-yard rectangular running course.

Equipment. In addition to the test manual and scoring materials, equipment needs include an 8½ inch rubber ball, 18 inch ruler, five bean bags 6 inches by 6 inches, stopwatch, and chalk.

Scoring. Eight items are scored using ratios representing distance or repetitions, eight incorporate ratings, and two items yield categorical data. The objectivity of these scoring procedures ranges from 0.39 to 0.96.

Validity. The validity as reported in Seaman and DePauw (1982) is "face with literature" (p. 211). Evidence of factorial validity has also been presented by the Los Angeles Unified School District, as well as predictive validity based on a discriminant analysis showing that the scale correctly classifies students 89% of the time.

Alternate hopping item from the Adapted Physical Education Assessment Scale.
Courtesy Janet A. Seaman.

Reliability. Ten of the 18 items have reliability estimates of 0.70 or greater on a test-retest basis (Seaman and DePauw, 1982).

Norms. Norms are based on scores for 2100 children, ages 5 through 18, from the Los Angeles area, including 1% trainably mentally retarded and 1% severe language-delayed children. Percentile ranks are available at 6-month intervals for 5 through 7.11 years and 1-year intervals for 8 through 18 years. These norms were generated during the 1980 revision of the scale.

Comments. Testing time per student is approximately 20 minutes. The primary usefulness of this battery lies in its ability to place students in physical education with what appears to be an impressive degree of accuracy. Of course, the validity is defensible only for the Los Angeles area, but it would be a relatively straightforward matter to validate the procedure in other areas. Reducing the length of the test is highly desirable. If the test is to be used primarily for placement, are 18 items necessary? In spite of several low reliability and objectivity estimates, the scale has many positive dimensions. Certainly it provides a useful model for placement in adaptive physical education.

SUMMARY

It is not feasible to present all of the motor performance tests developed for children with impairments in a measurement and evaluation textbook. Observational techniques are most frequently used on a daily basis in a field setting. Unless these instruments have acceptable reliability and validity, they should not be used in a more formal situation, as when the child's ability is assessed before developing an individualized education program. Other types of tests, particularly performance measures, have been standardized and can be used with greater confidence in their validity. Some examples of these types are motor proficiency scales, developmental scales, and physical fitness tests. Few tests are available to measure performance on a variety of sport skills. Excellent resources on this topic can be found in Seaman and DePauw (1982). Part II of their book is devoted to assessment, and Chapter 8 provides descriptions of many tests. Furthermore, a quick reference to tests on the market is included in Appendix D. The student interested in adaptive physical education is urged to review other sources of tests in this area.

LEARNING EXPERIENCES

1. Under the direction of your instructor, observe the administration of one or more motor performance tests to children with some type of impairment. What aspects of test administration differ from testing in a physical education setting for the nonimpaired child? Record these considerations and note how the tester handled them.

2. Assume you are working with a paraplegic confined to a wheelchair. How would you test this individual on cardiorespiratory function, body fatness, and low back/abdominal flexibility? First of all, are these important objectives for this person? If so, why? If not, what factors would you test? Why? How would the tests you select differ from those you would administer to a nonimpaired individual?

REFERENCES

Bruininks, R.H. 1978. The Bruininks-Oseretsky Test of Motor Proficiency. Circle Pines, Minn.: American Guidance Service.

Fait, H.F., and Dunn, J.M. 1984. Special physical education. ed. 5, Chicago: W.B. Saunders Publishing Co.

Frankenberg, W.K., and Dodds, J.B. 1967. The Denver Developmental Screening Test. Journal of Pediatrics 71:181-191.

Frankenberg, W.K., Dodds, J.B., and Fandel, A.W. 1973. Denver Developmental Screening Test manual/workbook for nursing and paramedical personnel. University of Colorado Medical Center, Denver.

Johnson, L., and Londeree, B. 1976. Motor fitness testing manual for the moderately mentally retarded. Reston, Va.: The American Alliance for Health, Physical Education, Recreation and Dance.

Kirkendall, D.R., Gruber, J.J., and Johnson, R.E. 1980. Measurement and evaluation for physical educators. Dubuque, Iowa: Wm C Brown Group.

Roach, E.G., and Kephart, N.C. 1966. The Purdue Perceptual-Motor Survey. Columbus, Ohio: Charles E Merrill Publishing Co.

Seaman, J.A., and DePauw, K.P. 1982. The new adapted physical education: a developmental approach. Palo Alto, Calif.: Mayfield Publishing Co.

Sherrill, C. 1981. Adapted physical education and recreation. ed. 2, Dubuque, Iowa: Wm C Brown Group.

Sloan, W. 1955. The Lincoln-Oseretsky Motor Development Scale. Chicago: C.H. Stoelting Co.

Winnick, J.P., and Short, F.X. 1985. Physical fitness testing of the disabled: Project UNIQUE. Champaign, Ill.: Human Kinetics Publishers, Inc.

ANNOTATED READINGS

American Alliance for Health, Physical Education, Recreation and Dance. 1985. Testing for impaired, disabled, and handicapped individuals. Reston, Va.: AAHPERD.

Begins with a general introduction to a philosophy of and rationale for testing; presents background information to aid in selecting tests; includes brief summaries of physical fitness tests, psychomotor (perceptual-motor) scales, and developmental profiles; does not include information about sports skills tests, since the purpose of the publication is to assist others in selecting instruments for diagnostic and prescriptive purposes.

Auxter, D., and Pyfer, J. 1985. Principles and methods of adapted physical education and recreation. St Louis: The C.V. Mosby Co.

Includes chapter on types and purposes of assessment; describes purpose and appropriate usage of each test type; presents examples; also includes chapter on integrating evaluation and programming; provides chart of selected motor tests, including source, population, motor components, and norms.

Brunt, D., and Dearmond, D.A. 1981. Evaluating motor profiles of the hearing impaired. Journal of Physical Education, Recreation, and Health 52(9):50-53.

Describes project in which the motor ability of approximately 150 upper elementary children with hearing impairments was assessed using the Bruininks-Oseretsky Test of Motor Proficiency; provides a brief overview of the Bruininks-Oseretsky Test, including a description of the eight subtests designed for children with severe or profound hearing loss.

Seaman, J.A., and Baumgartner, T.A. 1983. Measurement implications of PL 94-142. In Hensley, L., and East, W., editors. Measurement and evaluation symposium proceedings. Cedar Falls: University of Northern Iowa.

Summarizes the evaluation requirements mandated by Public Law 94-142; discusses efforts to develop a physical fitness test for special populations.

Ulrich, D.A. 1984. The reliability of classification decisions made with the Objectives-Based Motor Skill Assessment Instrument. Adapted Physical Education Quarterly 1(1):52-60.

Examines the reliability of classification decisions made with the Objectives-Based Motor Skill Assessment Instrument based on two different cut-off scores using a mentally retarded group and a nonhandicapped group; concludes that the instrument consistently assigned examinees to the same mastery state in the fundamental motor skill domain for both mastery levels.

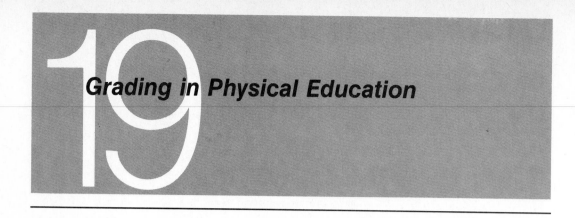

Grading in Physical Education

19

If you plan to teach physical education, you must be prepared to establish some
sort of grading system as soon as you assume your first teaching position. This is
not an easy task. In fact, even seasoned teachers often express dissatisfaction
with the grading system they use. A **grade** is a permanent record of a student's
achievement. It remains on record during and even after the lifetime of the
student. Thus it is quite reasonable to expect teachers to think carefully about
their approach to grading, making every effort to use the fairest and most objective system possible. Most prospective teachers would welcome straightforward
recommendations from experienced teachers, administrators, and measurement
specialists on the best grading system to use. Unfortunately, with all of the advances in education, no one has developed a foolproof system of grading.

In this chapter several approaches to grading are examined, but no specific

© 1984 United Feature Syndicate, Inc.

system is recommended. Each system has advantages and disadvantages that must be taken into account. Sometimes a teacher's choice of a grading system depends on his or her general philosophy about how students learn. It would be ideal if every teacher determined a grading system in this manner, but all too often an armchair approach is taken to grading.

Why does grading present such a problem? Averaging a set of unit grades to determine a final grade certainly is not difficult. It is the decision-making aspect of grading that presents the problem. What does the grade mean? Does it reflect achievement? improvement? attitude? How is a letter grade assigned? Is a normative approach to grading used or an approach involving mastery of a set of standards? If these questions are not carefully analyzed, inappropriate grading systems often result. Grades can vary from class to class and teacher to teacher; for example, an *A* in one course may be equivalent to a *C* in another course of the same type. Furthermore, the grades may not be based on objective evidence. The halo effect often operates in the determination of grades. Good grades may be used as a reward and poor grades as a punishment. Teachers are human beings and can succumb to a tendency to allow a student's personality to influence his or her grade. However, this is less likely to happen if the system is formulated as objectively as possible.

An unfortunate tie has been made between grades and testing. Testing is perceived to take place for the sole purpose of determining grades. This is one of the reasons for testing but certainly not the only one. In several other chapters measurement as an integral part of learning is discussed. Even if there were no grades, testing would be worthwhile as a means of improving performance.

The student should be informed at the beginning of a unit how the unit grade is to be determined. For older students a handout describing the grading system is helpful. If some tests are to be weighted more heavily than others, this should be noted. At the end of the unit, the student should receive no surprises regarding the prearranged grading system.

One final point should be emphasized: grades should *always* reflect the objectives of the course. Physical education teachers should be aware of the relationship between the initial objectives of a unit and the degree to which these objectives have been met in determining a grade. Otherwise, the basis for determining grades might be quite arbitrary. This is one of the most important concepts to remember about grading. In fact, it is one of the basic tenets of good teaching.

USE OF GRADES

Grades have many uses in the school system. They are used to inform the student of his or her status; inform parents, teachers, and administrators of the student's status; provide information for the student's permanent record; and motivate students. Even though many people dislike grades, they are a part of the American school system. Grading, although an imperfect aspect of education, can be acceptable if the system is carefully developed and refined.

Inform students of status

In a physical education class where the teaching/learning process is operating efficiently, students will continually receive feedback on performance. However, at the end of a unit, most students would probably benefit from some type of summary information of his or her achievement. A unit grade can provide this kind of information.

Inform parents of student's status

Although a student may receive feedback from day to day in a physical education class, the student's grade is the major method of communication between the school and the parents. As much information as possible should be given along with the grade. For example, the major objectives of the unit might be listed along with an indication of the student's progress toward meeting them. An excellent example of a well-developed procedure for informing parents of their children's fitness status is the FITNESSGRAM program. The FITNESSGRAM, described in Chapter 11, includes a student's fitness test scores and the corresponding norms, along with a brief exercise prescription for areas needing improvement. This information is printed from a computer and mailed to the child's parents.

Inform teachers of student's status

Although all good teachers have a fairly concise view of the level of ability of each student, an overview of the ability of all students in the class may not be as clear. The class grades can be useful for providing this overview. They can be used to aid in the evaluation of teaching effectiveness, course content, and the curriculum. A most valuable outcome of grading is to help the teacher gain a better overall understanding of the students' achievement. Information on grades can be valuable in providing future instruction to each individual in the class as well as the class as a whole.

When a teacher begins a new year with a new group of students, grades from the previous year can be used in classifying the students into groups. Previous grades can also be used in planning units of instruction. However, teachers should avoid placing total reliance on previous grades, since there will always be a margin for error in grading.

Inform administrators of student's status

The student's grades are used in many ways within a school system. They provide evidence that students are either meeting or not meeting stated objectives. Grades are also used for purposes of promotion, graduation, honors, athletic eligibility, and college entrance.

Add to student's permanent record

Grades are routinely added to a student's permanent record in the administrative office and retained indefinitely, often beyond the student's lifetime. This suggests that each grade has considerable importance to the student. Teachers must understand that a casually determined grade is not only unfair to the student at the time it is given, but that it can also have a long-term negative impact.

Motivate students

Grades are motivational devices for most students. Whether teachers like it or not, students' motivation is often to do whatever is needed to receive a satisfactory grade. If the process of grading improves learning in the desired direction, deriving motivation from grades is not necessarily bad. In this context working for a grade may not be undesirable.

DETERMINING A FINAL UNIT GRADE

Measurement specialists in physical education agree that one important basis for determining a grade is achievement in one or more aspects of motor performance. These can include sports skills, playing ability, and physical fitness. Specialists also generally agree that the achievement of cognitive skills (including knowledges and understanding of the principles and mechanics of movement, rules, safety, conditioning, history, and so forth) should be graded, although perhaps to a lesser extent. The predominant area of disagreement is whether a physical education grade should be based, in part, on the student's affective behavior (including social behaviors such as effort, attitude, sportsmanship, and citizenship). Whether all three areas—motor, cognitive, and affective—should be considered in determining a grade is largely a matter of philosophy. Whether all three areas can be measured with sufficient objectivity to justify contributing to the determination of a grade is another matter.

Achievement in motor skills as a basis for grading

Many physical educators believe that the achievement of skill and ability in physical education should receive the greatest emphasis in grading. The type of achievement expected depends on the objectives of the unit. In a beginning class emphasis may be placed on skill development, whereas in an intermediate class skill development and playing ability may be equally stressed.

One of the objectives of many physical education programs is the development of physical fitness. If so, assessment of the student's level of fitness should be incorporated into the final grade. It might be informative to separate the fitness grade from the unit grades that are given throughout the year. Hanson (1967) suggests using several criteria rather than a single standard of fitness, because of individual differences in body build. These differences may be partially taken into account by using tables of norms based on age or weight.

Improvement in motor skills as a basis for grading

When a student's performance improves over a given period of time, we assume that learning has taken place, although performance and learning are not synonymous. Intuitively, it seems highly desirable to use improvement as one means of determining a student's grade. After all, a teacher may reason, isn't the fact that improvement took place more important than the final level of achievement? This seems plausible to many physical education teachers. Obviously students hope to improve, and teachers want them to do so. The problem lies in attempting to use improvement as a basis for grading.

In the first place, how is improvement usually determined? Usually a test is administered at the beginning and the end of a unit. The pretest score is subtracted from the posttest score to yield an improvement score. Unfortunately, an improvement score calculated this way has been shown repeatedly to be notably unreliable. There is a degree of unreliability associated with both the pretest and the posttest scores. The measurement error associated with each of these tests is compounded in the improvement score.

Furthermore, the amount of improvement a student can attain depends on his or her initial level of skill. The highly skilled person cannot be expected to improve as much as the poorly skilled, because there is less room for improvement at higher levels of performance. In addition, a child's performance on a test of physical performance may improve simply because he or she has grown older and become more mature physically during the time period between the pretest and the posttest. For example, as a child grows taller and heavier, throwing a ball farther or jumping a longer distance is possible as a result of the maturation factor. In other words, little or no actual improvement because of learning might have taken place.

Another problem associated with grading on improvement is commonly known as "sandbagging." If it is common knowledge that final grades are to be based on improvement, some students will deliberately perform at a low level of skill on the pretest when they are capable of obtaining higher test scores. By obtaining a low pretest score, greater improvement will be reflected in the pretest-posttest score comparison at the end of the unit.

Hanson (1967) notes that if improvement is to occur, adequate time must be allowed for it. Some students need to practice over long periods to improve. Since instructional units in physical education are often scheduled for 6 weeks or less, there may not be adequate time for improvement to occur. For example, expecting students to hit 8 out of 10 free throws successfully after only a 6-week basketball unit may be unrealistic.

Finally, emphasizing the student's improvement score does not conceal the true achievement level. If a student's performance is poor compared to others in class, it will be obvious. Grading on improvement, although desirable, should probably be minimized until more appropriate ways are developed to handle improvement scores. A procedure for obtaining more valid improvement scores is described in Chapter 20.

Development of cognitive skills as a basis for grading

There is general agreement that knowledge of the course content of the instructional unit in physical education should be part of the final grade. Understanding the principles and mechanics of movement, along with the application of these principles to specific activities, is among the most important cognitive skills. Lower level cognitive skills such as knowledge of rules and strategies of a sport can also be used in determining grades. Other cognitive skills that might be measured are safety factors, history of the sport, and principles of conditioning.

Development of affective skills as a basis for grading

Grades based on affective skills are determined by such factors as attitude, attendance, sportsmanship, effort, dress, and, in some instances, whether or not the student showers after participating in a physical education class. Unfortunately, these factors constitute the major part of the grade in some physical education classes, even though their assessment is generally unreliable and frequently punitive in nature. They are often considered a reflection of attitude; that is, if a student's attitude is good, he or she will attend class, be a good sport, try hard, wear the proper clothes, and shower after class. The measurement of some of these factors is highly subjective, often bringing into play the halo effect. Moreover, an overemphasis on affective behavior often leads to the neglect of cognitive and motor skills. Furthermore, the presence of desired affective skills in no way guarantees achievement in motor skills or understanding of movement. On the other hand, we must recognize that some physical education teachers use these factors in determining grades in an attempt to deal with student apathy or disciplinary problems. Although these are genuine concerns and must be dealt with in some way, grades may not be the best way. Of greater importance is that grades based only on these factors are not valid. Let's examine more closely a few of the affective skills that are often used in determining a grade.

ATTENDANCE. According to a report by Mathews (1958), in 80% of the schools to which 50 student teachers were assigned, grades were based solely on students being present and in uniform daily. Generally, the factors on which a grade is based depends on the course objectives. Is regular attendance a course objective, or is it a matter of school policy? Attendance is usually governed by school policy, and deviant behavior related to attendance is dealt with by the principal or other designated authorities.

The practice of grading on attendance has sometimes been justified by the view that a student cannot learn when not in class. If, however, the student is able to meet course objectives satisfactorily, his or her grade should not be reduced because of poor attendance. Certainly disciplinary action should be taken against a student who is in school but does not attend class. Whether this action comes from the principal or the teacher, however, punishment should never take the form of reducing a grade.

EFFORT. Effort is extremely difficult to evaluate. Does a student who performs well with seemingly little effort work less than the student with less skill who obviously works hard? Can a teacher judge the amount of effort displayed by an individual based on facial expression or how tired he or she looks? If part of the grade is based on effort, it must be evaluated with a reasonable degree of objectivity. A physical education teacher may genuinely feel effort can be judged adequately using subjective judgment, but personal values will probably interfere.

Usually we assume that effort is reflected in achievement. However, if the achievement level is unchanged, is the effort meaningful? If effort is so important that it is part of a course objective, a procedure should be developed to objectively, systematically measure this affective skill.

DRESS AND SHOWERS. The need for gym clothes appropriate for physical education classes is obvious; however, the practice of grading on uniforms is questionable. In fact, fewer schools in the United States now require specific uniforms for physical education. However, most students are expected to change into clothing suitable for participation in physical activity. If the student has dirty gym clothes or no gym clothes at all, a penalty is appropriate, although not in the form of lowering an achievement grade.

No longer do a majority of physical education programs require students to take a shower at the end of class. In settings where this is still a practice, the requirement should be controlled by departmental policy. What represents a satisfactory shower? a wet body? wetness on some part of the body? Some teachers think showering is an important enough health habit to be graded. Some believe that it reflects a positive attitude. Explaining the importance of showers to students and encouraging them to take showers regularly is not unreasonable, yet grading the student on showers is no assurance that the value will become ingrained. Whether showers are mandatory or not, grades should not be based on them.

SPORTSMANSHIP. Every physical education teacher hopes to implant values associated with good sportsmanship in students. The development and encouragement of habits reflecting good sportsmanship are basic to all physical education programs, yet this is a difficult affective trait to measure. The measurement of sportsmanship is often haphazard and unreliable. If this affective skill is to be graded, the teacher should systematically record incidents of behavior for each student that reflect varying degrees of sportsmanship in a class situation. Although this process may be unrealistic because of the time involved, this is the only way to reduce the effect of the teacher's personal values on such judgments. (For more details, see Chapter 16.)

COMMENTS. In a 1982 study of the use of evaluation by physical education teachers, many teachers still used a subjective assessment of effort, sportsmanship, class attendance, and assessment of behavior to determine grades (Imwold, Rider, and Johnson, 1982). The subjective approach was used most frequently by elementary physical education teachers, the group most likely to use no tests at all. While it might be desirable to include this type of information on the report form, an assessment of achievement should not be ignored. In fact, achievement of skills and abilities should be the primary focus of a report form.

NORM-REFERENCED APPROACH TO GRADING

In general, a norm-referenced test (see Chapter 1) is used to detect individual differences among examinees. Grades can also be determined in a norm-referenced context by considering a student's performance relative to others in class. This system is based on the normal probability curve. If letter grades of A, B, C, D, and F are used, the curve is divided into five sections with each section representing a letter grade. As you know from reading the statistics chapters in this book, the entire area under the curve equals 100%. If the curve is divided into sections, the area in each section represents a certain percentage of the whole and the sum of the percentages across all sections would equal 100%. When you use a norm-referenced system of grading, your primary task is to identify the areas under the curve that will represent each grade and their corresponding percentages.

In the following section two methods of norm-referenced grading are described—the **standard deviation method** and the **percentage method.** Although all of the examples use five grade categories (representing A, B, C, D, and F), any number of grade categories could be used in the same way. Note that this type of grading is sometimes referred to as "grading on the curve" and criticized as being unfair to students. This criticism need not be true if the grade categories are properly determined. They should, for example, be based on a large number of students, not merely one or two classes. This issue is examined in the next section.

Standard deviation method

You have just given a test to a group of students and now you wish to assign a grade to each test score. The standard deviation method is based on the standard deviation of the distribution of scores. Thus the first step to take is to calculate the mean and standard deviation of the set of scores, then divide the distribution into five sections using standard deviation values. For example, in Table 19-1 note the area of the curve that is 1.5 standard deviations above the mean or higher. All scores falling in this area would receive a grade of *A*. Let's assume a test has a mean of 60 and a standard deviation of 8. Using Table 19-1, a score of 72 (mean plus 1.5 standard deviations = 60 + 12 = 72) or higher would receive an *A*. Scores ranging from 71 to 64 (mean plus .5 standard deviation = 60 + 4 = 64) would be assigned a *B*, and so forth.

TABLE 19-1. *Example of the standard deviation method of grading*

Grade	Standard(s) deviation range	Percent
A	1.5s or more above mean	7
B	Between +0.5s and +1.5s	24
C	Between +0.5s and −0.5s	38
D	Between −0.5s and −1.5s	24
F	1.5s or more below the mean	7

Note that we calculated the mean and standard deviation for a group of students in the above example. However, the group might consist of only 30 or 40 people. Because the number is so small, the distribution of scores might be badly distorted. Thus, it is best to accumulate scores from several classes, even if it takes a year or more to do so. The grade categories can be determined from this larger data set, since we have more faith in a distribution of this size. In subsequent classes you only need to convert scores to letter grades using something like the example in Table 19-1. Don't be concerned if the percentage of students in each category turns out differently from the percentages in the table. Remember that Table 19-1 is meant to be applied to a large sample. Your small sample may fluctuate because of the small numbers, but nothing at all is wrong with this.

This method is also known as the **standard score method.** In this approach the standard deviation is converted to a standard score; overwise, the procedure is identical to the one described in this section. Actually the example in Table 19-1 can be viewed as the standard score method. Under the category for A, for example, the number 1.5 preceding s is actually a *z-score*.

An advantage of this system is that scores for all tests are transformed to a common scale. For example, assume two tests are administered in a basketball unit. One test measures dribbling skill and is scored in seconds. The other is a shooting test, scored according to the number of successful shots in a given time period. By using standard deviation units, the same grading standard can be used for each test even though their actual score units are different. For each test a score falling at or above +1.5 standard deviation would receive an A, following the example shown in Table 19-1. In this way scores can be directly compared from test to test, then the grades can be averaged to determine a final grade.

A disadvantage of the system is that students set the standard. Not all classes are typical, yet some students in each class will receive As and some will receive Fs. This problem is reduced by using a large data set to determine the scale. This is the most reliable of any grading system. The standard deviation method can be used in physical education classes for grading cognitive skills (Weber and Paul, 1971), as well as sports skills and other forms of physical activity (Barrow and McGee, 1980; Broer, 1959).

When this approach to grading is used, the test with the greatest variability will automatically be weighted the most. For example, a test that is twice as variable as another is weighted twice as much. The variability of each test, then, must be taken into account when developing a system of weights.

Percentage method

In the *percentage method* of grading, grade categories are assigned by designating the percentage of students who are to receive each grade. For instance, a teacher might decide to give As to the top 10% of the students, as shown in Example 2 in Table 19-2. If the percentages in the examples in this table are based on a large sample of students, this method is no different than the standard deviation method. The percentages in Example 2 will divide distributions of test scores at the same (or very close to) standard deviation points (z-scores), as shown in Table 19-1. If the method is used with sets of test scores from one small class, comparing the grades of different tests may not be feasible because of fluctuations that can occur with small samples. Only three varieties of the percentage method of grading are presented in Table 19-2, although many other varieties are possible.

TABLE 19-2. *Examples of the percentage method of grading*

Grade	Example 1	Example 2	Example 3
A	7	10	15
B	24	20	20
C	38	40	30
D	24	20	20
F	7	10	15

Which method to use?

Which method of norm-referenced grading is preferred—the standard deviation method or the percentage method? If the grade categories are determined using a large sample of students, either approach will lead to similar results. They merely approach the same problem from different directions. When the categories are used with small classes, the percentages of students in each category are not necessarily identical to those in Tables 19-1 or 19-2. This is not a problem since we expect it to occur with small sample fluctuations. The major decision to be made is whether to use a norm-referenced or criterion-referenced approach to grading. Sometimes this is a policy dictated by the school, rather than a decision to be made by individual teachers.

CRITERION-REFERENCED APPROACH TO GRADING

How is a criterion-referenced approach to grading applied? First of all, recall that a criterion-referenced measure is a type of measure in which a standard of performance is identified that is referenced to a criterion behavior. This is a seemingly simple definition, but it defines a decidedly complex process. Once the performance standard is set, students scoring at or above the standard are given a grade (let's use Pass as a starter) and those scoring below the standard are given another grade (Fail). However, as discussed earlier, school systems use a five-point grading scale. Using the criterion-referenced approach, this means we have to identify four cutoff points or performance standards to obtain five grade categories.

Percentage-correct method

In the section on norm-referenced grading, the determination of grade categories based on the *percentage of students* in a given category is discussed. Here, we will review a method where the percentage of items or trials successfully completed (**percentage-correct method**) is used to determine grade categories. (See Table 19-3.) To receive an *A* on a test, the student would have to success-

---

TABLE 19-3. *Example of percentage-correct method of grading*

Grade	Percentage-correct score
A	90-100
B	80-89
C	70-79
D	60-69
F	Below 60

---

fully complete 90% of the trials. In other words, 9 out of 10 trials (or 18 out of 20) must be properly executed. In a written test 90 out of 100 items would have to be answered correctly.

It may be necessary to use a point system rather than percentages to designate grade categories, especially when there is no maximum score. For example, in a softball throw for distance, the maximum score for a given age group is unknown. In this case a distance of x feet or greater could be set for the category for a grade of A. However, grades cannot be directly compared across tests, since the level of difficulty of each test will vary. This is readily apparent in testing muscular endurance, where different levels of endurance may be observed across muscle groups.

Setting performance standards for grading

How are performance standards set? Let's go back to the definition of criterion-referenced measurement. It specifies that the performance standard must be referenced to a criterion behavior. In Chapter 7 the meaning of a cutoff score of 42 sit-ups was discussed in terms of a criterion behavior. Does the ability to perform 42 sit-ups mean that a 14- or 15-year-old girl has adequate abdominal strength? Of course there is no evidence to support such a statement. We know that only 25% of the girls in this age group can perform *more* than 42 sit-ups in 1 minute, but this is a norm-referenced rather than a criterion-referenced standard. As you can see, proper standard-setting is very difficult.

With this seemingly insoluble problem in determining a cutoff score, why discuss the criterion-referenced approach to grading? Primarily because teachers who use the mastery learning model of instruction feel it is a more appropriate method for establishing grades than the norm-referenced approach. In the mastery learning model there are no constraints on the number of students who can satisfactorily meet an objective. Thus there are no limits on the number of students who receive As, Bs, and so forth. This means the grade distribution for a class is not determined in advance. This is not true when the normal distribution is used in determining norm-referenced grades. Regardless of the ability level of the students, some will receive *A*s, *B*s, and so forth, according to a predetermined categorization of the distribution. Of course, as noted on p. 463 the grade distribution in an ordinary class is not necessarily the same as the distribution for the large sample used to determine the categories. Nonetheless, this approach is designed to reflect individual differences in ability, and it should be expected that the entire grade range will be represented in any class.

In a mastery learning setting the teacher typically expects to have nonmasters in class at the beginning of the year. When students are measured on an objective at this point, the distribution of scores should be skewed in a positive direction since most of the students would receive low scores and only a small percentage would receive high scores. At the end of the unit of instruction, the majority of the students are expected to master the skill. Now the students' scores on this objective are distributed negatively, since only a few students receive low scores. It is possible that many students would receive *A*s and *B*s. Once a letter grade has been determined for each test administered during the unit, the unit grade is calculated in the usual manner. Each letter grade is converted to a numerical value, weighted according to its importance, and the weighted grades are then averaged to yield a unit grade.

Another advantage of the criterion-referenced approach to grading is that repeated testing of the student in a formative evaluation context is encouraged. The disadvantages of criterion-referenced grading are associated with setting standards. First of all, it is an arbitrary process. However, this does not sanction careless standard-setting. Every effort must be made to reduce the degree of subjectivity in setting standards. Several solutions to this problem were discussed in Chapter 7. The second disadvantage of criterion-referenced grading is the problem of misclassifications. In classifying students in different grade categories, it is evident that sometimes we will be wrong. Sometimes a student will be given a *C* and should have been given a *B*, and vice versa. This is a measurement problem that may never be fully resolved, yet the probability of misclassifications can be reduced as the validity of the cutoff score is increased. (See Chapter 7 for more information on procedures for determining validity.)

CALCULATING FINAL GRADES

Once letter grades have been assigned to each test, they must be converted to numbers to calculate the final grade. The conversion table given in Table 19-4 exemplifies the finest breakdown a teacher could possibly need for grade conversion. If desired, the scale can easily be reduced to a smaller size. Some teachers prefer to use a point system whereby test scores are not assigned a letter grade. The total points for each test are accumulated and weighted accordingly; grade categories are then developed and a letter grade assigned to each. To use

TABLE 19-4. *Table for converting letter grades to numbers*

Grade	Number	Grade	Number
A+	12	C	5
A	11	C−	4
A−	10	D+	3
B+	9	D	2
B	8	D−	1
B−	7	F	0
C+	6		

this approach, the test scales must be compatible. For example, it would be inappropriate to add time scores (in seconds) and distance scores (in inches). This is a valid way to determine a final grade and does not require a series of conversions from test score to letter grade to letter grade conversion, and so forth. Furthermore, averaging letter grades may result in a loss of precision compared with averaging raw test scores.

USE OF WEIGHTS IN CALCULATING GRADES

Since some tests will be of greater importance than others in a given unit, many teachers use a system of **weighting** the tests. If the scores of each test are averaged using a tranformation and the tests are similar in difficulty level, each test automatically receives the same weight. A teacher assigns higher weights to tests of greater importance. If one test is twice as important as another, a 2:1 ratio of weights might be used, as shown in Table 19-5. Note that skill development in

TABLE 19-5. *Use of weights in determining grades*

Badminton Unit for Beginners			
Test	Weight	Grade	Total
Skill development Short serve Long serve Overhead clear	3	B−	$3 \times 7 = 21$
Development of knowledges Knowledge of rules Knowledge of principles	2	C	$2 \times 5 = 10$
Playing ability	$\frac{1}{6}$	B+	$\frac{1 \times 9 = \quad 9}{40}$

Grade $= 40/6 = 6.67 = $ B−

badminton is weighted more heavily than any other ability. This was appropriate since skill development received the greatest emphasis in the instructional unit.

Three letter grades are shown in Table 19-5. Using the conversion table in Table 19-4, we can determine the numerical value for each letter grade. For example, the numerical value for the skills grade of $B-$ is 7. The weight for skill development (3) is multiplied by the numerical value for $B-$ (7), yielding a total of 21. Follow this procedure for each component to be used in determining the final grade, then add the total points for the components (40) and divide by the sum of the weights (6). In this case the average numerical grade is 6.67, which should be rounded off to 7. Referring again to Table 19-4, notice that the letter grade for a numerical grade of 7 is $B-$.

USING THE MICROCOMPUTER TO CALCULATE FINAL GRADES

A program to calculate final grades has been written for the Apple IIe computer; however, it can easily be modified for other brands of microcomputers. This program is described in Chapter 22 and included in its entirety in Appendix E (2). It can be used with or without a printer, although the availability of a printer allows a printed copy of each student's name, individual grades, and final grade to be obtained.

OTHER SYSTEMS OF GRADING

Educators have used many other systems of grading, including pass-fail grading and a checklist of objectives.

Pass-fail method

Physical educators often recommend the use of a two-grade category, such as **pass-fail** or mastery-nonmastery, so that students' attempts to achieve for the sake of a grade will be reduced. In addition, this method is thought to reduce the error that occurs when attempting to classify students into a five-grade category. According to the literature, two-grade categories are less reliable than their five-grade category counterparts. This may be true if a norm-referenced approach is used to estimate reliability. However, when a criterion-referenced reliability estimate is computed, a two-category grade system can be quite reliable. On the other hand, the larger the number of grade categories, the more information available about the students in a class. A two-category system is simply not as discriminatory as a more elaborate system, although a more elaborate system will yield a larger number of misclassifications. When a misclassification occurs, it is more serious in the two-category case. In other words, giving a student a grade of C when the grade should have been a B is a serious matter, but not nearly as severe as giving the student a *Fail* when he or she should have received a *Pass*.

Checklist of objectives

A grading system commonly used at the elementary school level is a set of symbols that can be used with a list of the major objectives of the program (**checklist of objectives**). The following symbols might be used to rate each objective:

O (Outstanding)
S (Satisfactory)
N (Needs improvement)

The appropriate symbol is placed next to each objective on the list. This system of marking is exemplified in Table 19-6.

TABLE 19-6. *Sample checklist of objectives for elementary school physical education*

Symbol	Objective
S	Ability to move at different speeds, using different levels.
S	Ability to handle various sizes of balls in a variety of ways.
N	Ability to use a variety of locomotor patterns.

The student's report card will probably not have adequate space to list the major objectives for each class; therefore, the physical education teacher may wish to send a letter containing more detailed information to the parents of each child or develop a special report card for physical education. An example of a complete report card used in elementary physical education in Madison, Wisconsin, is shown in Fig. 19-1. This report includes an evaluation of specific objectives as well as an overall assessment of the child's performance.

An excellent way of reporting the student's fitness status is the use of the newly developed FITNESSGRAM, depicted in Chapter 11. If it is used in conjunction with the Health-Related Physical Fitness Test, a report can be prepared for students 5 through 17+ years of age. If the Youth Fitness Test is administered, the applicable age range is 10 through 17+ years.

USE OF INSTITUTIONAL GRADES

Measurement specialists unanimously recommend the use of a common grading system throughout a school. When a common grading system is used, the grades will form similar distributions regardless of the area of instruction. In addition, the reliability of the grading system is somewhat increased. The same kind of information is provided for students in all areas of the curriculum. Special areas, such as physical education, should use grades to discriminate to the same degree as other parts of the curriculum so that excellence in performance is recognized in all areas.

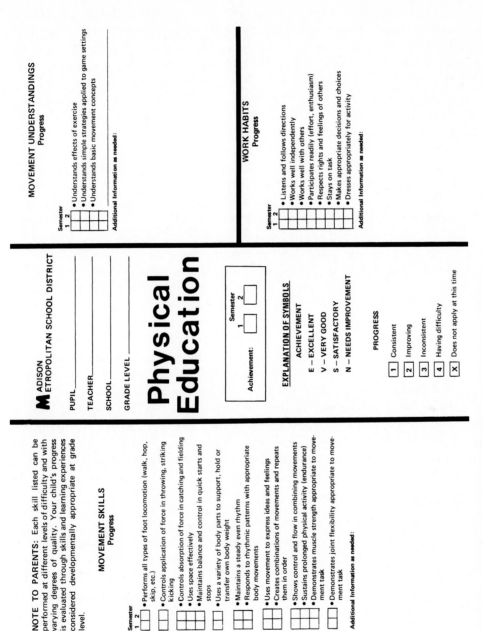

FIG. 19-1. *Sample report form for elementary physical education.*

REPORTING MULTIPLE GRADES

A procedure for reporting more than one grade for each curricular area is often recommended so that one of the grades can be based purely on achievement. Frequently a second grade is classified as a "citizenship" grade. In physical education separating motor skill grades from cognitive and affective grades would also provide useful information for all concerned. Although such a separation is somewhat artificial, the use of multiple grades will have more meaning than a single grade.

SUMMARY

Grades in physical education should represent the degree to which students have attained the objectives of the curricular units. These often include the development of motor, cognitive, and affective skills within the physical education program. There is general agreement that the achievement of sports skills and other forms of physical activity should be given major emphasis in determining a physical education grade. Cognitive skills may be given less weight but nonetheless represent an important component of the grade. Although grading the affective behavior of students is intuitively appealing, it is difficult to measure these skills objectively and systematically.

Two systems of grading for physical education students are the norm-referenced method and the criterion-referenced method. The normal distribution is the basis for determining grade categories in the norm-referenced approach. Of primary interest is the student's performance relative to others in class. The criterion-referenced method of grading designates grade categories based on predetermined performance standards. This method is tied to the mastery learning instructional method, where many students are expected to meet minimal standards at the end of a unit. Either system can be used effectively in a school setting. The choice of a grading system is dependent on the philosophy of teaching/learning adopted by the instructional staff.

LEARNING EXPERIENCES

1. A test was administered to five beginning badminton classes. The mean for the set of test scores is 32 and the standard deviation is 4. Using Table 19-1, develop a table showing the range of test scores for each grade category. Then, calculate the grades for the following five students:

Student	Test score
A	40
B	30
C	25
D	33
E	36

2. Using the information given below, calculate the final grades for five students.

Test	Weight
No. 1	1
No. 2	2
No. 3	1.5
No. 4	2.5

Student	Test No. 1	Test No. 2	Test No. 3	Test No. 4
A	A	C	B	D+
B	C	B	B−	C+
C	B	A	A−	A
D	B	D	C+	B+
E	B−	C	D	C

REFERENCES

Barrow, H.M., and McGee, R. 1980. A practical approach to measurement in physical education, ed. 3, Philadelphia: Lea & Febiger.

Broer, M.R. 1959. Are physical education grades fair? Journal of Health, Physical Education, and Recreation 30:27, 83.

Hanson, D.L. 1967. Grading in physical education. Journal of Health, Physical Education, and Recreation 38:34-39.

Imwold, C.H., Rider, R.A., and Johnson, D.J. 1982. The use of evaluation in public school physical education. Journal of Teaching in Physical Education 2:13-18.

Mathews, D.K. 1958. Measurement in physical education. Philadelphia: W.B. Saunders Co.

Shea, J.B. 1971. The pass-fail option in physical education. Journal of Health, Physical Education, and Recreation 42:19-20.

Weber, L.J., and Paul, T.L. 1971. Approaches to grading in physical education. The Physical Educator 28:59-62.

ANNOTATED READINGS

Cotten, D.J., and Cotten, M.B. 1985. Grading: the ultimate weapon? Journal of Physical Education, Recreation and Dance 56(2):52-53.

Emphasizes the importance of basing grades on objectives; identifies issues that should be considered when formulating a grading strategy; discusses the grading of group assignments.

Davis, M.W. 1983. Let's talk about Johnny's 'C' in P.E.! In Hensley, L., and East, W., editors. Measurement and evaluation symposium proceedings. Cedar Falls, Iowa: University of Northern Iowa.

Discusses the need for meaningful and effective evaluation in physical education; proposes a sports skill and physical fitness profile as the most desirable approach to an individualized evaluation summary; describes and illustrates the phases of profile development.

Shea, J.B. 1971. The pass-fail option and physical education. Journal of Health, Physical Education, and Recreation 42:19-20.

Recommends the pass-fail option as the most practical approach to grading in physical education since it does not require changes in the basic requirements in physical education; lists advantages of the pass-fail option; provides suggested guidelines for structuring a pass-fail grading system.

Turner, E.T. 1975. A creative evaluation experiment. Journal of Physical Education and Recreation **46**:24-25.

Points to increased effort to reform grading practices; discusses a recently adopted practice by many schools to use a pass-fail system of grading; this system has led to lack of incentive among students; believes that pass-fail systems provide little information about the student's capabilities and achievement; describes student evaluation profile as a more viable approach to grading.

ANSWERS TO LEARNING EXPERIENCES

1. The following table was developed showing the range of test scores for each grade category by using Table 19-1:

Grade	Range of test scores
A	38 and above
B	34-37
C	30-33
D	26-29
F	25 and below

A grade was determined for each of the students listed below:

Student	Test score	Grade
A	40	A
B	30	C
C	25	F
D	33	C
F	36	B

2. Table 19-4 was used to convert letter grades to numbers. The individual test grades (now numbers) were multiplied by the weighting for the respective test. These values were summed across all four tests and are shown below in column 2:

Student	Sum of grade by weight	Average of column 2	Grade
A	40.5	5.78	C+
B	46.5	6.64	B−
C	72.5	10.36	A−
D	43.5	6.21	C+
F	32.5	4.64	C

In the third column the sums in the second column were divided by the sum of the weights for the four tests, in this case, 7. Then, Table 19-4 was used to convert the numerical value in column 3 to a composite letter grade, shown in the fourth column.

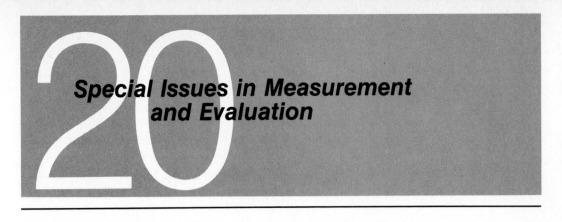

Special Issues in Measurement and Evaluation

KEY WORDS *Watch for these words as you read the following chapter:*

improvement   program evaluation

Measurement and evaluation do not occur in isolation. Scores must be interpreted in some meaningful way, and three major interpretive issues are examined in this chapter. The first issue focuses on measuring improvement. The second issue encompasses several evaluation topics, including objective assessments of instructional effectiveness, programs, and curricula. In the third section sex differences in motor performance and their impact on standard-setting are discussed.

MEASURING IMPROVEMENT

Many physical educators strongly support the concept of measuring **improvement,** and it appears to be an inherently fair way of grading students. Unfortunately several problems are associated with the measurement of improvement—inequality of scale units, unreliability of improvement scores, and difficulty in motivating students during the initial testing session. Because a practical solution has been developed for the first problem, the solution is described in detail. The other two problems do not have satisfactory resolutions; therefore, they will not be emphasized.

The first problem, inequality of scale units, occurs because performers with low scores have more room for improvement than performers with high initial scores. For example, an improvement of 4 seconds on the 1-mile run has a different meaning for a world-class runner than it does for a novice runner, even though the numerical value of the improvement score (4 seconds) is the same for each performer. If the world-class runner's time improved from 4:11 to 4:07, it would probably represent a significant improvement. On the other hand, a change in the novice runner's time from 8:11 to 8:07 might have little or no practical significance. Decreasing one's running time by 4 seconds is easy if the time is initially slow.

One procedure developed for measuring improvement in physical education does show promise. Hale and Hale (1972) used a mathematical procedure to transform test scores so that improvement at a low level of performance is not weighted as heavily as the same amount of improvement at a higher level of performance. This procedure requires that the initial and final test scores be standardized by converting them to T-scores. In some cases tables of T-scores are published for skills tests; otherwise, the teacher can easily develop such a table, as described in Chapter 5. Once the raw scores have been transformed to T-scores, a conversion table (see Table 20-1) is used to determine each student's progression score. The progression score representing the initial test score is subtracted from the progression score for the final test score.

TABLE 20-1. *Conversion of T-scores to progression scores**

T-score	Progression score	T-score	Progression score	T-score	Progression score
20	2.52	40	6.34	60	15.94
21	2.64	41	6.65	61	16.70
22	2.76	42	6.95	62	17.48
23	2.89	43	7.27	63	18.31
24	3.03	44	7.62	64	19.16
25	3.17	45	7.98	65	20.09
26	3.32	46	8.35	66	21.03
27	3.48	47	8.75	67	22.02
28	3.64	48	9.16	68	23.07
29	3.81	49	9.60	69	24.14
30	3.99	50	10.05	70	25.29
31	4.18	51	10.52	71	26.46
32	4.38	52	11.03	72	27.72
33	4.59	53	11.54	73	29.09
34	4.80	54	12.09	74	30.42
35	5.03	55	12.66	75	31.86
36	5.26	56	13.25	76	33.37
37	5.51	57	13.87	77	34.92
38	5.77	58	14.53	78	36.58
39	6.05	59	15.23	79	38.31
				80	40.13

*From Hale, P.W., and Hale, R.M.

As an example, consider the pretest and the posttest scores of two students in a bowling class, as shown in Table 20-2. Student A bowled an average of 90 during the testing period at the beginning of the unit and an average of 120 during the posttest period. These scores were converted to T-scores of 30 and 50, respectively. Using these T-scores and referring to the conversion table in Table 20-1, subtract the progression score for a T-score of 30 (3.99) from the progression score for a T-score of 50 (10.05). The improvement score for Student A is 6.06. Note that the raw gain was 30 points, the T-score gain was 20 units, and the actual improvement score was 6.06.

TABLE 20-2. *Example of Hale and Hale (1972) method*

Student	Pretest score	T-score	Posttest score	T-score	Progression score
A	90	30	120	50	6.06
B	170	70	180	75	6.57

Student B, on the other hand, bowled an average of 170 during initial testing and 180 during final testing. In this case the raw gain was 10 points and the T-score gain (70-75) was 5 units. If these students were being graded on their raw gain scores, Student A would receive a higher grade than Student B; yet in terms of actual performance, B's improvement may be equal to or better than A's. When the conversion table is used to calculate B's improvement score, the score is 6.57, slightly higher than A's score.

Even though the application of this procedure yields more valid improvement scores than the use of raw improvement scores, the well-known problems of the unreliability of improvement scores and the lack of student motivation on the pretest (sandbagging) remain. In addition, the mathematical procedure used to generate the conversion table is not infallible.

PROGRAM CHANGE, a refinement of this procedure, was programmed for the Apple IIe by East (1985) and is included in Appendix E.

EVALUATION TOPICS

As you recall from Chapter 1, *measurement* involves the administration of a test and *evaluation* pertains to the interpretation of the test scores. A test has many purposes, including assessment of the effectiveness of a course, teacher, curriculum, or program.

The *formative evaluation* approach is emphasized in this chapter. When courses or programs dealing with sport or physical activity are evaluated, the traditional approach is to evaluate at the end of some designated period. If weaknesses are detected, plans are usually made to correct these weaknesses during the coming year. However, the next time the evaluation takes place the same weaknesses may exist; thus, an entire year has been consumed in applying ineffective solutions. If the evaluation had been of the formative type, determining that the proposed solutions were ineffective and in need of modification or replacement would have been possible early in the school year. Keep in mind that the purpose of evaluation is to improve the course or program, not to judge it. Of course, evaluation techniques must be used to make judgments sometimes, but in most cases passing judgment should not be the primary reason for evaluation.

Accepting the premise that the use of formative evaluation is an appropriate method for improving effectiveness, what techniques can be used to obtain data over time? Essentially the evaluator must ask three basic questions:

1. Is the program, teacher, student, or administrator functioning successfully?
2. If not, how should one intervene?
3. Is the intervention successful?

Course and instructor evaluation

In the 1970s the emphasis on evaluating the effectiveness of courses and instructors increased a great deal, particularly in colleges and universities. Many institutions of higher learning required or strongly encouraged faculty members to obtain periodic evaluations of their courses and teaching. Much effort has been expended in the development of instruments that can be used for this purpose; the most popular type is an evaluation form using a Likert-type scale. Usually administered at the end of a unit or a year of instruction, this instrument represents the summative approach to evaluation. Although certain items on the scale would apply to any course, the evaluation forms are generally not applicable to activity courses in sport and physical activity. Efforts to develop a form for activity courses usable nationwide have not been successful, probably because institutions have different missions and course objectives.

In the following sections a formative approach to course and instructor evaluation able to be used in elementary and secondary schools, private clubs, colleges, and universities is demonstrated. The underlying goal is to provide evidence of the effectiveness of a course or an instructor by monitoring behavior on a regular basis. When satisfactory progress is not being made, an intervention should take place. Three examples are used to illustrate this approach.

EXAMPLE 1—VOLLEYBALL UNIT. A physical education teacher establishes a goal for her students in learning the bump. The goal is to execute 10 consecutive, legal bumps within a given height range and area by the middle of the volleyball unit. Achievement of the goal would indicate that the students have developed adequate control and are ready for more refined work on the skill. Fig. 20-1 shows the results obtained in a beginning class. The solid line is the criterion line, indicating a hypothetical line of improvement from 0 to 10 consec-

FIG. 20-1. Performance on the volleyball bump.

utive hits. The criterion line is used only as a guide since the performance curve would not necessarily be expected to be linear. The solid line connecting dots is the actual performance curve for the class. Note that the performance line drops below the criterion line on day 5 and falls further away on days 6 and 7. Since we do not know the learning curve for students on this skill (perhaps research will show this drop is to be expected), we must assume that the students are not going to reach the criterion unless the teacher intervenes in some way. The mark at day 7 represents a planned intervention, which might consist of additional instruction by the teacher, close supervision by a partner, use of instructional materials, or varying teaching methodology. In this case the performance line begins to move toward the criterion line again, revealing the intervention as successful. By monitoring progress daily the course itself or one aspect of it is evaluated on an ongoing basis.

EXAMPLE 2—CLASS MANAGEMENT. A physical education teacher senses that he spends too much time in class talking to his students (e.g., giving directions and discussing mechanical principles). Although he feels the information he provides is important, he would like to impart it more efficiently, that is, in less time. He would also like to increase the amount of active learning time his students have in class. First, he needs to know how much time he actually spends in class on verbal presentations. This information may be obtained in several ways—by audiotaping his classes or by having someone, perhaps a stu-

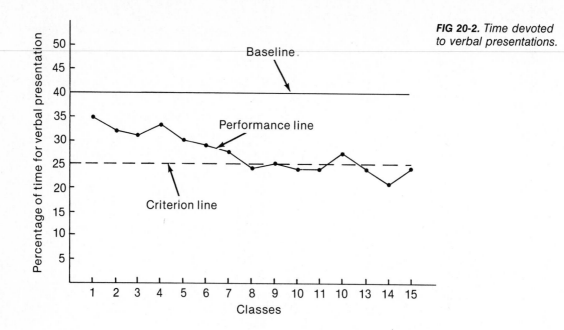

FIG 20-2. *Time devoted to verbal presentations.*

dent from study hall, monitor the amount of time he spends talking in class for a week. These results would provide him with a baseline from which to work. In this case the teacher spent an average of 40% of the total class time talking. This is shown in Fig. 20-2 as the baseline. The teacher decides that 25% of class time should be adequate for class discussion. This is represented in Fig. 20-2 as the dashed line, the criterion line set by the teacher. How can this designated criterion be met? Perhaps some of the material could be presented by preparing handouts for students and by using loopfilms on an individualized basis. If his talk time decreases to 25% and remains there, he has achieved his goal. If the percentage of time increases again, another method of intervening should be used. In Fig. 20-2 the solid line connecting dots represents the teacher's performance. Since talk time is being decreased in the desired direction and reaches the criterion line during class 8, no intervention is necessary. The performance curve remains around the 25% level for the next seven sessions; therefore, the teacher has some assurance that he will be able to maintain this amount of talk time. Using this approach, a teacher may monitor any aspect of instructional effectiveness on a continual basis. Problems can be identified and corrected before the end of the unit, course, or year, when modifying the teacher's behavior would essentially be ineffectual.

EXAMPLE 3—INSTRUCTOR EVALUATION. A college instructor in a theory class administers a course evaluation form at the end of each semester and finds that the students consistently rate the clarity of her instruction from average to below average. If the material is not being presented clearly, the students cannot be expected to understand and apply it. The instructor does not wish to wait until the end of the next semester to find out whether her presentations are improving in clarity. An evaluation procedure consisting of a rating scale (see Fig. 20-3) is devised. The student picks up the rating form at the end of each class, circles the number best reflecting the perceived degree of clarity of instruction, and turns in the form to another student who collects and returns them to the instructor. This process assures the student of an anonymous response.

<table>
<tr><td colspan="4">Clarity of instructor's presentation</td></tr>
<tr><td>Date ————</td><td></td><td></td><td></td></tr>
<tr><td>Not at all
clear</td><td>1 2 3 4 5 6 7 8 9</td><td>Very
clear</td></tr>
</table>

FIG. 20-3. *Rating scale to monitor clarity of instruction.*

The ratings are averaged each day and plotted, as in Fig. 20-4. The solid line represents the baseline, the average end-of-semester rating the instructor has been receiving. She decides to strive for an average daily rating of 6 or higher,

FIG. 20-4. *Ratings of clarity of instruction.*

represented by the criterion (dashed) line. The solid line connecting dots is the teacher's performance curve, measured by the daily rating of students. By organizing the structure of the classes more carefully, the instructor is able to maintain clarity ratings at a satisfactory level. If the performance curve had fallen below 6 for two or more consecutive classes, possibilities for intervention would have to be explored. One approach might be to ask the students why the presentation did not seem clear. Another approach would be to prepare at least two examples of each concept presented in class and discuss these examples. A low clarity rating might simply indicate that the instructor needs to present the same material again during the next class session. Unless experimental evidence on the best method of intervening is available, the instructor must intervene on the basis of a logical analysis.

Although the evaluation procedures described in the previous examples are useful, the measures used in all three examples are weak measures. For instance, a student rating of clarity of instruction may reflect something other than clarity, such as the instructor's personality. This effect can be controlled to some extent by obtaining two different measures of the same attribute. Student ratings of the clarity of instruction might be accompanied by an observer's rating of the clarity of instruction or a rating of tape recordings of class sessions. Unobtrusive measures such as content analysis of lesson plans or instructional materials might also be used. This approach lacks the controls necessary in an experimental study. No control groups are used, only one teacher is involved, and factors other than the planned intervention might account for the desired performance.

Even with the foregoing limitations, if this informal approach assists a teacher or exercise scientist in achieving personal goals, it seems to be a worthwhile evaluation tool. It forces one to identify problems, work actively to alter behavior in the desired direction, and increase awareness of strengths and opportunities for improvement. It enables the professional to perform and somewhat control his or her self-evaluation in a nonthreatening environment.

Program evaluation

The **evaluation of programs** dealing with sport and physical activity incorporates the same techniques used to evaluate any program. Two examples of evaluating program goals in the school setting are provided to emphasize important aspects of program evaluation and to describe approaches to the use of formative evaluation techniques. The first example was developed for a high school physical education program, and the second, for a middle school physical education program.

A basic assumption is that all physical education teachers have a list of program goals stated in some fashion. If program goals are stated in general rather than behavioral terms, the evaluation of their effectiveness may be imprecise. For example, a high school program goal might be stated as follows:

Goal 1 (general): To develop and maintain an optimal level of physical fitness needed to function in everyday life.

To evaluate this goal, more specific information is needed. What is an optimal level of physical fitness? Also, what type of physical fitness is of concern? Let's assume that cardiorespiratory (CR) endurance was identified as the most important type of fitness. A more explicit statement of this goal follows:

Goal 1 (specific): All high school students will develop an above-average level of CR endurance by the end of the school year. An "above-average" level is defined as Cooper's category labeled "Good" for 12-minute run performance; 80% of the students are expected to achieve this goal.

When the program goal is stated in behavioral terms, the procedure for evaluating the goal is precisely described.

Of course it seems logical to assume that the students cannot meet this goal already, or it would not be identified this way initially. Sometimes test users are not sure, however. A *needs assessment* can then be conducted, in which the actual status of the students is compared with the desired status. If no discrepancy exists, the goal should be rewritten. In this example the 12-minute run test would be administered to all students. Their performance represents their *actual status* on CR endurance, and the teacher's standard represents the *desired status*. Since Cooper identified separate standards for males and females, the actual

TABLE 20-3. *Discrepancy between actual and desired status on 12-minute run (percent)*

12-minute run categories	Actual status		Desired status	
	Boys	Girls	Boys	Girls
Excellent (V)	6	7		
Good (IV)	10	15	80	80
Average (III)	27	33		
Fair (II)	33	25		
Poor (I)	24	20	20	20

status of boys and girls is recorded in Table 20-3 and compared to the desired status.

According to this comparison, the students' performance level is far from the desired status. Only 16% of the boys and 22% of the girls perform well enough to be classified in the *Good* or *Excellent* categories. Using a formative evaluation approach, one can assess the students' average monthly performance on the 12-minute run and plot the results, as shown in Fig. 20-5.

FIG. 20-5. *Monthly performance on 12-minute run test.*

Now we can determine the monthly progress being made toward the desired status. If the average performance levels off in 2 or more months and it becomes clear that the desired status will not be reached at the present rate of improvement, the physical education teacher must intervene. Intervention may take the following forms: increasing the class time devoted to improving CR endurance, determining how the presently allocated time for improving CR endurance is being used, or using different ways to motivate students.

Once a program goal has been stated in behavioral terms, actual status can be determined and ways to monitor progress toward the desired status can be developed. However, the physical education teacher may also wish to identify concomitant concerns that should not be sacrificed for the sake of achieving the goal. For example, it is reasonable to ask what kind of conditioning program is necessary to effectively improve CR endurance. Certainly the students must exercise regularly, at least three or four times a week. If the activity is jogging, the amount of distance run should be gradually increased within a given time limit. Thus the physical education teacher must commit a part of every class period to this goal, since the typical activity in class (even basketball and football) will not contribute to a CR endurance goal to any great extent. Is the teacher willing to spend the time necessary to develop CR endurance? How much class time is presently devoted to improving CR endurance? Plotting the way class time is allocated in physical education is possible. A student aide could easily record this information. After reviewing this chart, the teacher may decide that a goal involving improvement of CR endurance in class is not realistic because the achievement of this goal would require too much class time. The goal might be rewritten so that students are expected to understand the need for developing and maintaining CR endurance and be aware of ways of achieving an optimal level of endurance. On the other hand, the teacher may decide that this goal is so important that it warrants using whatever class time is necessary.

A second example of setting goals in a school setting deals with lifetime sports. This goal for middle school physical education students might be stated as follows:

Goal 2 (general): To develop skills in lifetime sports.

Again, more information is needed. How many lifetime sports? What level of skill is expected? How many students are expected to meet the standard? A better statement of the goal follows:

Goal 2 (specific): All middle school students will demonstrate skill attainment in at least one lifetime sport each year by achieving either a beginning or an intermediate competency level for four of the five subunits for that sport; 75% of the students are expected to achieve this goal.

To write the specific goal in this way, the teacher would have to establish beginning and intermediate standards for each sport; however, this is not unrealistic. For example, Memorial High School in Madison, Wisconsin, has established competency levels for *all* activities—not just lifetime sports. To monitor student progress toward this goal, daily performance could be plotted. The teacher might wish to review individual charts weekly or perhaps monthly.

Here again there may be concomitant factors the teacher wishes not to forgo in achieving a goal. These factors should be noted in writing by the teacher. Some of these goals follow:

1. The student must have a positive attitude toward and feel satisfied about achieving the goal.
2. The teacher must have a positive attitude toward and feel satisfied about achieving the goal.
3. Opportunities should be provided for using varied instructional approaches in classes.
4. Classes should be balanced, with some time devoted to learning skills and some devoted to using skills and strategies in a game setting.
5. The teacher should provide each student with some individual attention at least every other class period.

Formative evaluation procedures could be developed for each of these factors to monitor them throughout the year.

If there is more than one physical education teacher in a school, all must agree on the most important program goals. Usually this can be resolved informally. However, if citywide consensus is expected, more formal techniques can be adopted to aid the group in reaching an agreement. In the Delphi technique each staff member ranks goals individually. These rankings are then summed for each goal and averaged. Each member is given the average rankings, and all members rank the goals again. If one member of the group ranks a goal very differently from the group ranking, a written rationale is submitted for retaining it. This process is continued until consensus is achieved. A second and perhaps more efficient technique in a school setting is the nominal group method. Using this method, the staff members form a group but work independently within that group. In other words, the individuals do not interact with one another in the early stages, even though they are physically together in a group. Again, feedback is given to the group and gradually group interaction increases. Once a list of program goals has been generated, the group works toward agreeing on priorities. Although these techniques may be more effective if conducted by someone not on the physical education staff, good results can be obtained using a staff member who has had some experience in working with small groups.

By planning in advance how progress toward the achievement of program goals can be monitored, the chances of actually achieving the goals are greatly enhanced. Teachers evaluate to detect weaknesses and determine ways of correcting those weaknesses. Evaluation, then, becomes an integral part of the educational process.

Curriculum evaluation

Although evaluating many aspects of the physical education curriculum is possible, this section discusses the evaluation of the *overall merit of the curriculum*. (The more familiar process of evaluating specific objectives within the curriculum receives extensive examination on pp. 27-29) Let's assume that a staff of physical education teachers has decided to use the Purpose-Process Curriculum Framework (PPCF) as a guide for making curricular decisions (Jewett and others, 1971). One approach to implementing this framework might be to use the grid shown in Table 20-4. Only one of the major categories of purposes for moving is included in Table 20-4 to exemplify this evaluative procedure. The first task of the physical education staff would be to select combinations of purposes and processes that are to receive emphasis in their physical education program. (The purposes for moving are represented across the top of the grid; the movement processes, along the side.) These purpose/process combinations can be viewed jointly by marking the appropriate cells in the grid. For example, in Table 20-4 an X has been placed in the cell representing a combination of circulorespiratory endurance (purpose) and patterning (process). When all purpose/process combinations of interest have been recorded on the grid, the overall framework of the physical education curriculum has been identified.

However, the selections within the PPCF should be justifiable in the eyes of physical educators who are qualified to make such judgments. Otherwise, curric-

TABLE 20-4. *Portion of grid for evaluating Purpose/Process Curriculum Framework*

Process	Man master of himself						
	Physiological efficiency				Psychic equilibrium		
	C-R efficiency	Mechanical efficiency	N-M efficiency	Joy	Self-knowledge	Catharsis	Challenge
Perceiving							
Patterning	X						
Adapting							
Refining							
Varying							
Improvising							
Composing							

ular choices may be merely a reflection of the personal biases of the physical education staff. If, for example, a curriculum is considered too broad or too narrow by physical education curriculum experts, the staff has not established sufficiently the *merit* of the curriculum.

How can physical education teachers evaluate the merit of a curriculum? First, a written rationale should be set forth for the choices made within the PPCF. This step provides the outside observer with the staff's philosophical orientation toward physical education. It also helps to ensure that curricular choices are made on a logical basis. This rationale would provide input to the curriculum evaluator. One might disagree with the philosophical approach but at the same time judge the curricular choices to be appropriate.

Bringing in outside evaluators to assess a physical education curriculum is not always possible. A team of teachers and administrators within a school system might be asked to review the rationale and subsequent curricular choices. A needs assessment might be conducted to determine whether these choices meet the needs of students, parents, other community members, teachers, and administrators. It cannot be overemphasized that these curricular choices are not arbitrary; they must be fully justifiable.

Once the purpose/process combinations have been selected, the activities that will contribute to these combinations must be identified. Presumably different approaches could be taken at this stage. A variety of activities might be used to meet a given purpose at an identified process level. For example, if the purpose for moving is object projection, the student might experience throwing, striking, and kicking a variety of objects in a structured environment. As an alternative approach, a single sport might be selected as a means of emphasizing a purpose. Softball might be an appropriate sport for providing many opportunities for a variety of object projection tasks. Regardless of the approach to selecting activities, these activities must be justified as bona fide contributors to the designated purpose/process combinations.

The first step in justifying the selection of activities is to review the literature to obtain supporting evidence from research studies. Consider circulorespiratory endurance as a purpose of interest. Evidence supports the selection of running as an activity that contributes to circulorespiratory endurance, assuming the run takes place over a reasonably long distance. If the distance is too short (½ mile, for instance), running would no longer be an appropriate activity for this purpose. The literature review may not be fruitful in many cases, since experimental studies have been conducted only on a small number of purposes. If this is the case, the next best source to use in justifying the selection of activities is the content specialist in physical education. If the purpose is psychological in nature (e.g., catharsis), the sport psychologist would be the appropriate content specialist to contact. The biomechanics specialist would be called on to deal with purposes such as object projection. If research evidence does not exist, at least the best possible logical judgment can be made.

In a curriculum evaluation the merit of the total curriculum as well as the worthiness of specific goals must be examined. Only then is it appropriate to assess the extent to which curricular goals are being attained. However, even this assessment cannot be conducted in isolation but must be considered in conjunction with other factors the physical education staff views as important.

SEX DIFFERENCES IN MOTOR PERFORMANCE

That sex differences exist in motor performance cannot be denied. However, to what extent are these differences culturally induced or genuinely physiological? This question has been widely discussed for many years and remains controversial in the exercise science field.

Research has shown that, in general, boys have more strength, height, weight, and CR endurance than girls. In addition, they tend to have a smaller percentage of body fat. The gender gap may be narrowing for some aspects of strength. While there is a clear sex difference in arm and shoulder girdle

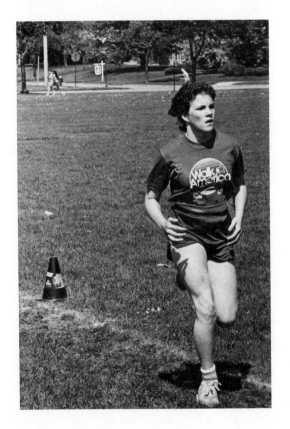

strength, performance on leg strength measures demonstrates considerable over-lap. Even so, the strongest individuals are usually male and the weakest, female. Girls generally possess greater flexibility, rhythmic ability, and buoyancy. However, there are certainly exceptions to this delineation of sex differences, in particular among upper elementary school-age boys and girls and highly skilled versus poorly skilled performers.

Sex differences have also been reported in sports skills. For example, Stamm (1979) noted differences in the test scores of college men and women in tennis and bowling classes. This suggests the need to consider separate performance standards for men and women. However, separate standards are not necessarily appropriate for all activities. At the U.S. Air Force Academy (1978) the same performance standards were used for both male and female cadets in swimming classes. In this situation men and women were equally capable. Drawing conclusions about sex differences in motor performance is difficult without a substantial, recent data base for all ages, girls and boys.

Implications for ability grouping

Ability grouping is neither required nor prohibited by the Title IX regulation. However, if it is used, group membership cannot be determined on the basis of sex. On the other hand, the assignment of an equal number of boys and girls to a group does not necessarily yield a sex-fair grouping. Group membership must be determined objectively. During the practice or competition of contact sports, students may be separated by sex. However, this grouping may not be permissible during the instructional portion of the class.

What are the implications for ability grouping? In a report prepared by the State of Illinois, the use of sports skills tests was recommended for ability grouping when these skills were incorporated into the unit objectives. If the objective involves physical fitness, a number of fitness tests are available to be used in grouping. Motor ability tests are *not* recommended to ability group students. "There is no evidence that a phenomenon such as motor ability is measurable or that the phenomenon even exists" (Illinois State Board of Education, 1982:5). Random assignment to groups is recommended when the objective is to help students learn to appreciate the skill level of others.

When students of similar ability compete, the same standard should be used for ability grouping. When excellence in performance is the primary goal, separate standards should be used, in particular for fitness and sports skill objectives. With traditional mass instruction, a single standard is recommended. With an individualized approach, separate standards are recommended.

Implications for performance evaluation

The Illinois report also makes recommendations on sex-fair performance evaluation. Separate (higher) standards are proposed for boys when performance is based on strength, endurance, height, weight, or lean body mass. Separate (higher) standards for girls are recommended when performance is based on flexibility, bouyancy or rhythm.

When an accuracy test is administered, where strength and power are not factors, a single standard should be used. A single standard is also proposed for wall volley tests not dependent on strength or power and for the assessment of form and game strategy.

SUMMARY

To interpret scores on motor behavior tests, several factors should be taken into account, including course and program objectives and gender differences. Actual status of student ability as well as desired status must be considered in determining objectives. Typically, desired status is reflected in the course and program objectives. Gender differences, in particular ones that are physiological in nature, may lead to a different interpretation of scores for males and females. In general, the process of interpreting test scores should be handled as conscientiously as the process of selecting and administering the test.

LEARNING EXPERIENCES

1. Assume one of the goals for female members of your fitness club is to increase arm and shoulder girdle strength. Your club owns a Universal gym machine (or something similar). Write a *specific* objective for this goal, including a performance standard. Note how you could monitor progress in achieving the objective on an ongoing basis. If a client does not progress as expected, what type of intervention would you propose? Draw a hypothetical graph of your formative evaluation.

2. Assume you are a physical education teacher working with high school boys. Lately you have observed some problems with sportsmanship in your classes. You would like to monitor this behavior on an *ongoing* basis to determine its severity. Describe a *simple* procedure you might use to monitor sportsmanship on a daily basis. Propose several methods of intervening if the behavior problems become severe. Draw a hypothetical graph of this evaluation. Be *specific* in stating your evaluation objective, including a standard of performance for the class as a whole.

REFERENCES

East, W. 1985. PROGRAM CHANGE. Cedar Falls, Iowa: Department of Physical Education, University of Northern Iowa.

Hale, P.W., and Hale, R.M. 1972. Comparison of student improvement by exponential modification of test-retest scores. Research Quarterly 43:113-20.

Jewett, A.E., and others. 1971. Educational change through a taxonomy for writing physical education objectives. Quest **15**:32-38.

Illinois State Board of Education. 1982. Tips and techniques: ability grouping and performance evaluation in physical education. Springfield, Ill.: Illinois State Board of Education.

Stamm, C.L. 1979. The evaluation of co-educational physical education activity classes. Journal of Health, Physical Education, and Recreation **50**:68-69.

United States Air Force Academy. 1978. Women's integration research project-phase III. Department of Athletics, April 10.

United States Department of Health, Education, and Welfare. 1975. Federal Register **40**(108), June 4.

ANNOTATED READINGS

Finke, C.W. 1972. Use evaluation positively. Journal of Health, Physical Education, and Recreation **43**:16.

Suggests that too many testing procedures in physical education produce anxiety; believes evaluation should build the learner's self-reliance and increase the desire and ability to move; supports the concept of continuous evaluation, using both teacher evaluations and self-evaluations.

Kneer, M.E. 1982. Ability grouping in physical education. Journal of Physical Education, Recreation, and Dance **53**(9):10-13, 68.

Discusses the identification of performance standards to be used in grouping students in physical education on the basis of their ability; prescribes curricular and instructional approaches to accommodating these abilities.

Kosekoff, J., and Fink, A. 1982. Evaluation basics: a practitioners manual. Beverly Hills, Calif.: Sage Publications, Inc.

Provides a thorough introduction and overview of the techniques needed for a do-it-yourself evaluation; offers guidelines, checklists, and key points to watch at every step of the evaluation process; uses almost 100 examples to illustrate its practical advice; invaluable to anyone who needs to know the basics of evaluating programs.

McDonald, D., and Yeates, M.E. 1979. Measuring improvement in physical education. Journal of Physical Education and Recreation **50**:79-80.

Discusses problems encountered in measuring improvement; reviews the Hale and Hale method for adjusting raw improvement scores so that the inequality of scale units is taken into account; presents a simplified procedure, in tabular form, for calculating the improvement score.

Potter, G., and Wandzilak, T. 1981. Youth sports: a program evaluation. Journal of Physical Education and Recreation **52**(3):67-68.

Describes the evaluation of a basketball program for seventh and eighth grade boys; use of preseason and postseason questionnaires to determine whether program objectives were met; includes discussion of results.

Stringfellow, M.E. 1976. Competency-based instruction in measurement and evaluation. Journal of Physical Education and Recreation **47**:50-51.

Describes the use of a competency-based approach to teaching a traditional undergraduate course in measurement and evaluation at the university level; prepares students to become critical test analyzers; includes samples of course outlines, general objectives, behavioral objectives, and grade criteria.

Zakrajsek, D.B. 1979. Student evaluations of teaching performance. Journal of Physical Education and Recreation **49**:64-65.

Presents a method of collecting objective evidence to evaluate instruction; discusses the validity of student ratings; measures students' perceptions of effective instruction using an opinionnaire; presents a 20-item example of student opinionnaire.

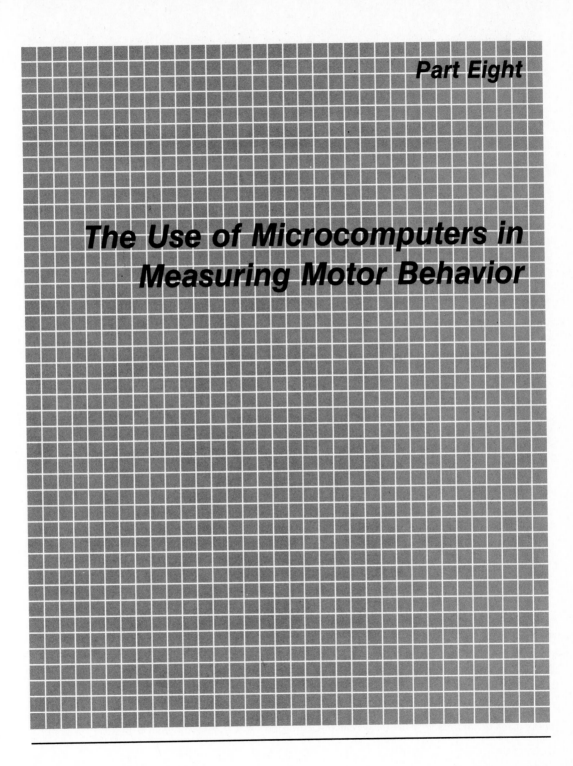

Part Eight

The Use of Microcomputers in Measuring Motor Behavior

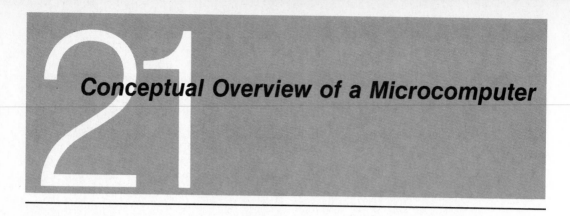

Conceptual Overview of a Microcomputer

KEY WORDS *Watch for these words as you read the following chapter:*

bit	display	modem
booting	gates	monitor
byte	hardware	peripheral
Central Processing Unit (CPU)	keyboard	Random Access Memory (RAM)
computer literacy	kilobyte (k)	Read Only Memory (ROM)
disk drive	microchip	software
Disk Operating System (DOS)		

The use of microcomputers in measurement and evaluation has unlimited potential. They can be used to administer, score, and develop tests; summarize, analyze, and transform scores; and compare scores with norms. Data banks consisting of test scores can be established and expanded using the microcomputer. The objective of this chapter is to familiarize the novice with the microcomputer. For the student with some expertise on a microcomputer, this chapter serves as a cursory overview. For the student who is a rank beginner, even this chapter may seem overwhelming at first. Do not be discouraged if the material initially seems confusing, since this is true for most people who have had no experience with computers. Learning to use a microcomputer requires a considerable amount of patience. Rereading various sections of this chapter now and returning to review this chapter after completing Chapter 22, which covers some applications in the field, will help the material to fall into place.

Keep in mind, however, that entire books have been written on using microcomputers, even a specific microcomputer brand, and other texts are devoted entirely to a programming language. Although covering a great amount of information in a textbook on measurement and evaluation is not feasible, a general

IBM-PC microcomputer

overview is essential. Microcomputers are here to stay. They will be a part of your life, both personally and professionally. If you plan to teach, your students will probably be receiving constant exposure to microcomputers. A general understanding of these machines is therefore essential for every teacher in the public schools, even those who do not teach microcomputer skills. For those who intend to be exercise specialists, a knowledge of computers is valuable for more efficient recordkeeping as well as a means of providing information to clients on their health and fitness status. In some corporate fitness centers a bank of microcomputers is installed in a central location. As employees enter the center, they slip an identification card into a slot in one of the microcomputers, and data on their exercise prescription and physiological state are printed on the screen. On completion of the exercise period, the employee enters information on the type, duration, and intensity of the exercise, along with his or her exercise heart rate. This information is added to the employee's records on the computer and is used to modify, if necessary, the exercise prescription. Since all employees participating in the fitness program use a microcomputer to record their fitness data, a summary of these data may be obtained for the total corporation to use in evaluating the program.

A BRIEF HISTORY

The first large-scale electronic computer was built at the University of Pennsylvania in 1946. This huge machine required a room 30 feet by 50 feet for its storage. It used 18,000 vacuum tubes and miles of wiring to operate. In the 1960s the **microchip,** a silicon board the size of a fingernail, was developed, resulting in a tremendous impact on our society. By 1981 the equivalent of 750,000 vacuum tubes could be etched on a single microchip.

A microchip contains many microscopic switches known as **gates.** An electrical charge opens some gates and closes others, creating a pattern simulating human logic. The chips in a microcomputer contain thousands of electronic circuits. One kind of microchip executes instructions; the other stores information in memory. The development of the microchip made manufacturing small desktop computers at affordable prices possible. Since the 1970s the microcomputer boom has become so widespread it is inconceivable that anyone in our society would be unaware of its existence.

How has our society responded to this technology? Astronomical numbers of microcomputers are being sold every month. How they are being used is another matter. Should every school have at least one microcomputer? Of course, many schools already have microcomputer laboratories. What kind of instruction takes place in these labs? Issues of this type are being hotly debated across the country, often under the label of **computer literacy.** An unresolved question among educators and scientists is how computer literacy should be defined. Some believe it should reflect a knowledge of programming and programming skills. Others describe it as a knowledge of computer systems and what they can do. A loose definition of computer literacy is "a threshold of knowledge that qualifies an individual for participation in the computer age" (Benderson, 1983). The Educational Testing Service (1985, p. 10) prepared a more precise definition: "Computer literacy may be defined as whatever a person needs to know and do with computers to function competently in our information-based society. It involves three kinds of competence—the ability to use and instruct computers to aid in learning, solving problems, and managing information; the knowledge of functions, applications, capabilities, limitations, and social implications of computers and related technology; and the understanding needed to learn and evaluate new applications and social issues as they arise." Although a limited discussion of the BASIC (Beginners All-Purpose Symbolic Instruction Code) programming language is presented in Chapter 22, the primary objective of these two chapters is to help you develop a small amount of computer literacy.

THE MAKEUP OF A MICROCOMPUTER

Microcomputers are often referred to as *personal* computers, which indicates that only one person can use the computer at a time. These single-user computers process information more slowly than the larger versions and are generally affordable to the average person. Microcomputers are sometimes used exclusively for entertainment purposes. Two other types of computers, minicomputers and mainframe computers, have been available for many years. A *minicomputer* can process information faster than a microcomputer and accommodate several users at once. Of course, it is also costlier than the microcomputer. The grandfather of all computers, the *mainframe* computer, is a large multiuser machine, which is even faster and more expensive than the minicomputer.

If you went to a computer store and asked about purchasing a microcomputer, you would be shown a bewildering array of equipment. The physical components of the computer and its peripherals are referred to as **hardware.** A **peripheral** is a device that can send information to the computer as well as receive information from it. At the very least, the hardware you would probably need includes the computer itself (a case housing the central processing unit), a keyboard, a monitor, and a disk drive or a tape recorder. The **keyboard** is similar to the keyboard on a typewriter and is used to transmit information to the computer. A **monitor** is like a television set; in fact, a television set can easily be used for this purpose. A monitor purchased specifically to use with a computer consists of a screen and a cathode ray tube (CRT). A **display** appears on the screen, either in color or monochrome. A **disk drive** is a storage device that can store data and retrieve it. A dual disk drive is shown in the photograph.

Dual disk drive

The basic features are shown in the following photograph of the Apple IIe microcomputer. This brand of microcomputer is used to exemplify microcomputers and their operation in both this chapter and Chapter 22. The Apple IIe was chosen since many are available in the public schools. However, this does not mean the Apple brand is the best of the microcomputers. Many other fine brands of microcomputers have been manufactured, such as the IBM-PC (the photograph at the beginning of the chapter), Commodore (the photograph at the end of this chapter), Corona, TRS (Radio Shack), Atari, Compaq, and Epson.

Apple IIe microcomputer, keyboard, monitor, two disk drives

Computer memory

Computer hardware must use a machine language that is compatible with the **central processing unit** (CPU). The CPU of a microcomputer may be a single microchip or a portion of a microchip. This unit controls peripherals and memory. Remember that there are two kinds of microchips, one to execute commands and one to store information. Some of the microchips contain information permanently stored in the computer. These form the **Read Only Memory,** or ROM section, of the computer. ROM is the control system for the whole computer, including the program that allows the use of BASIC, a machine language. It is impossible to put any information into ROM. Recall that electric charges open and close gates on a microchip. In ROM the gates are permanently fixed in either the open or closed position. Other microchips can read and store information temporarily. This section of the computer is called **Random Access Memory,** or RAM. When you turn on a computer and begin using it, you are working in the RAM section. When you turn the computer off, you lose all of the information in RAM.

Data storage

Even though information can be stored temporarily in RAM, this information is lost once the computer is turned off. Thus a more permanent means of storage is needed. Information can be stored on tape cassettes, hard disks, floppy disks (see photograph this page), and video disks. Only the use of the floppy disk (also known as a diskette) is described here. The disk is inserted into the disk drive, or storage device. There must be a means of communicating between the disk in the disk drive and the central processor. The Disk Operating System (DOS) is a program written to establish this communication. The program must be loaded into the computer's memory (RAM) from a disk. This process is often referred to as **booting** a disk.

Floppy disk

Computer languages

Computer languages use the two-digit system of binary mathematics. It is based on Boolean algebra, a system of logic devised in the nineteenth century for solving complex problems through a series of binary (yes or no) choices. A discussion of how it works using a language such as BASIC follows. Each letter, number, and punctuation mark is represented by a **byte.** Each byte contains eight **bits** (or two nibbles), which are the yes-no choices represented by open and closed gates. Each byte, then, has eight *gates.* If all this is not confusing enough, there are also 16-bit processors such as the IBM Personal Computer (IBM-PC). This simply means that each byte in the IBM contains 16 bits and is approximately twice as fast as the 8-bit processors such as the Apple. The more recent IBM-PC AT uses a 32-bit processor and is four times as fast as the microcomputers with 8-bit processors.

The amount of memory in a computer is determined by the number of bytes in the system. For convenience, computer memory is usually reported in **kilobytes,** or k, with 1k equal to 1024 bytes. If an advertisement indicates that a microcomputer has 48k memory, it usually means there is 48k memory capacity in RAM.

Software

Previously DOS was described as a *program;* thus, it is not hardware. A computer program is referred to as software. Specifically, **software** refers to a set of instructions that makes the computer function in some desired way, such as word processing or statistical calculations. Many programs can be purchased through computer stores or companies advertising in computer magazines. It is not necessary to have any programming skills to use these programs. However, the software must be compatible with your computer. Furthermore, your computer must have the memory capacity required to use the program.

Peripherals

Other hardware may also be added to the basic components described above. A printer is useful for obtaining a paper copy of a computer program, the data you entered into the computer, and the results of running a program. When the information is printed on paper, this is referred to as a *hard copy.*

To communicate with other microcomputers, mainframe computers, and information services, a **modem** is needed. A *modem* is a device allowing a computer to communicate over telephone lines and other communication media. The term is actually a contraction of *modulator-demodulator.* Modems transmit information at different speeds, measured in a unit called a baud. A 300-baud modem will send or receive about 30 characters a second. There are two types of modems: acoustic and direct-connect. The acoustic modem consists of two

Printer

Modem

cups in which the telephone's handset fits. To use this modem, the telephone number of another computer is dialed, and the handset is placed in the modem's cups to allow communication. A direct-connect modem clips into a jack attached to your telephone line.

SUMMARY

The refinement of computer technology has been nothing short of phenomenal. The invention of the microchip has made relatively efficient desktop computers available to the masses. Both teachers of physical education and exercise specialists in nonschool settings will find many uses for these machines, not only to handle sets of test scores but also to provide computer-aided instruction. Imagine using the computer to teach students the rules of a sport or to instruct clients on nutritional factors related to physical fitness. Once basic computing skills have been mastered, the possibilities for applications in physical education and exercise science are unlimited.

Commadore microcomputer

LEARNING EXPERIENCES

1. Visit a computer store and try a demonstration disk that describes ways in which a microcomputer can be used. Select the type of computer available to you on your campus, and ask for the demonstration disk for this type. Try it on a microcomputer on display in the store. Do not hesitate to ask the salesman questions.

2. Visit a computer store and ask the salesman to demonstrate a commercially developed program dealing with statistical analyses. Actually try a portion of the demonstration disk that comes with the program, using one of the microcomputers on display in the store.

REFERENCES

Benderson, A. 1983. Computer literacy. Focus 11:1-32.

Educational Testing Service. 1985. A unique joint effort to create a computer literacy pool. Examiner. Princeton, N.J.: Educational Testing Service.

ANNOTATED READINGS

Bork, A. 1985. Personal computers for education. New York: Harper & Row, Publishers Inc.

Discusses the use of computers in education and the profound effects they will have in the future; focuses on computer literacy and programming; examines the computer as an intellectual tool and as an instructional device; surveys the role of the computer in the management of learning; proves to be a practical book for teachers, parents, and administrators.

Farrell, P. 1984. Computer literacy: what does it mean? Journal of Physical Education, Recreation, and Dance 55(4):54-55.

Advocates the use of computers at all levels of learning; defines and discusses computer literacy.

Hiscox, M.D. 1985. Computer-based testing systems. Educational Measurement 4(1):27-28.

Discusses the use of computers in item banking and test construction; analyzes the problems faced in attempting to develop a new micro-based testing system to be used on a widespread basis; suggests that the method of developing the system is more important than the product.

Kanter, H.M. 1985. Computer applications of educational measurement concepts. New York: Macmillan Publishing Co.

Provides a brief, hands-on introduction to the microcomputer system and BASIC; reinforces measurement and descriptive statistical concepts; incorporates computer literacy into coursework; contains a variety of examples and illustrations in each unit.

Poole, L. 1983. Apple II user's guide. Berkeley, Calif.: Osborne/McGraw-Hill, Inc.

First three chapters especially useful to the first time computer user; describes hardware and software; explains how to use the computer system; describes disk commands needed to run existing programs.

Microcomputer Applications

KEY WORDS   *Watch for these words as you read the following chapter:*

BASIC language	enter key	LOAD (program)
CATALOG	formatting a disk	NEW
compatibles	HOME	RUN (program)
DELETE (program)	initializing a disk	SAVE (program)
disk (floppy)	LIST	

The technology explosion elicited by the microcomputer has already influenced society a great deal and will continue to do so in the future, just as the Sputnik flight influenced curricular offerings in the public school systems by increasing the emphasis on sciences. The widespread availability of microcomputers has already spawned studies of users and potential users. Some of these studies have shown that many people suffer from computer phobia, a general anxiety or apprehension about using computers. Although the computer user actually controls the computer, this sometimes does not appear to be true. It helps to remember that microcomputers are virtually indestructible during the normal course of operating them. Children often play aimlessly with a home computer and no damage is done. Of course, programs can be accidentally erased, but it is extremely unlikely that the hardware would be damaged.

Microcomputers are being used in many aspects of physical education and exercise science. At least one test writing program has been developed by a physical educator and is being sold commercially (Cicciarella, 1983).* This program produces equivalent-form examinations of 100 questions or less on any topic from a pool of questions the user has originated. A microcomputer can control cardiovascular fitness testing. In one laboratory a microcomputer controls the speed and grade of the treadmill according to any protocol, turns on an electrocardiograph (ECG) at any predetermined time or on demand, converts

---

*For more information on this program, known as Test Writer, write to Charles F. Cicciarella, Persimmon Software, Greensboro, NC 20406.

the ECG signal for computer storage, and generates data, summaries, and individualized programs based on test results (Donnelly, 1983). At the University of Delaware computer-aided instruction is provided in fitness, sports such as volleyball and racquetball, biomechanics, nutrition, basic mathematics, and social dance (Barlow and Bayalis, 1983). A microcomputer can be used for data management (Mayhew and Rankin, 1983) and dance notation (Sealy, 1983).

In Chapter 21 microcomputers are described in a general context; this chapter provides a few practical experiences with a microcomputer. If you have not had an opportunity to use one, perhaps this exposure will convince you that a computer can easily be used in many ways in a measurement setting. Anytime a set of test scores is obtained, certain summary information should be calculated. If the appropriate program has been written for the microcomputer, this information can be obtained in minutes. However, the process should not be oversimplified. Learning to use a microcomputer takes time and patience, even if you are using available software rather than writing your own programs. However, your efforts will be well rewarded, both by making your job easier and by enhancing your understanding of a significant phenomenon in our society.

VARIATIONS IN MICROCOMPUTERS

Even though you may not have shopped for a microcomputer of your own, you are undoubtedly aware of the wide array of machines available on the market. In fact, because of the extensive advertising campaigns by certain companies, names such as Apple, IBM, Commodore, Radio Shack, and Texas Instruments are probably very familiar. Each of these machines has a different operating system. If you bought a program written for the Apple, it could not be used on the IBM unless an interpreter program was used to translate the Apple program. Many features of the computer differ across brands. For example, even keys on the keyboard are dissimilar in number, type, and layout. Of course, the prices can be notably different for various brands of microcomputers!

Richards and Engelhorn (1983) prepared a brief overview of microcomputer systems. Even though this type of information is rapidly outdated, many of the precautions they noted remain timely. A rank beginner with desktop computers would be wise to become familiar with one type of computer and to use it exclusively. Experienced users having some programming background will find it relatively easy to switch back and forth between certain brands of microcomputers once they are aware of the computers' basic differences. One final point—when a microcomputer appears on the market and becomes a best seller, other companies try to build a machine that is referred to as **compatible** with the first one. If the machine is truly compatible, it can use software written for the well-known microcomputer, and vice versa. However, the primary feature of the compatibles is usually that they are less expensive than the best seller and yet can perform most, if not all, of the same operations.

By permission of Johnny Hart and Field Enterprises, Inc.

COMPUTER LANGUAGES

To communicate with the computer a special language must be used. Language options can range from straightforward BASIC, the *Beginners All-Purpose Symbolic Instruction Code*, to more structured languages such as COBOL, FORTRAN, and PASCAL. Most microcomputers are set up to use BASIC. To use other languages with these computers, a special board must be inserted in a slot in the computer's central processing unit or a disk containing the program must be inserted into the disk drive and stored in RAM. The BASIC language is used in the examples in this text. Generally, microcomputer manufacturers install BASIC in the machine at the factory; then if you use a disk drive, a disk operating system must also be used. This may include a version of BASIC that is compatible with the operating system. Many brands use a version of Microsoft BASIC to achieve this compatibility. Although versions of Microsoft BASIC differ across brands, they are quite similar. This means that programming in BASIC is markedly similar, no matter what machine is used. Even so, these versions are not identical. For purposes of simplicity, Microsoft BASIC for the Apple computer is used in the examples in this textbook. Not only are Apple computers widely available in the public schools, but many colleges and universities are also developing microcomputer laboratories that include a number of Apple computers. These programs will usually work on other brands but sometimes require minor revisions. In most cases the commands differ across machines, but the actual program does not differ. In fact, the programs included in this chapter were written on an IBM microcomputer and then modified for the Apple. The modifications consisted of a few minor program alterations and changing some of the commands.

PREPARING THE DISK

This section should be covered only if you wish to store your work on file using a disk. You can go through every example in this chapter using the screen on your monitor, but you will lose the program and the results of running the program when you turn off the machine. If you do not want to type a program on the screen each time you wish to try it, you will want to file the program on a disk.

With the Apple computer you will need a **floppy disk,** a round sheet of plastic coated with iron oxide and inserted in a protective, black jacket. The disk should never be removed from its jacket. A disk 5¼ inches in diameter is needed; both single-sided and double-sided disks are available. You might start with a single-sided, single-density disk, which holds about 125,000 letters and numbers. Before a new disk can be used, it must be prepared in a special way known as **formatting.** Formatting magnetically imprints tracks, sectors, and other information onto the disk exactly where the computer's memory system needs them. Once the disk has been formatted, it is ready to store files.

On the Apple the process of formatting the disk is referred to as **initializing** the disk. First, the disk operating system (DOS) must be loaded into the computer. Then, the new disk is inserted in the disk drive. The program for initializing can be called any term, but it is usually referred to as the HELLO program. Follow these steps to initialize a disk:

1. Load the DOS. (This system is on a disk that comes with the Apple. If you are working in a microcomputer laboratory, your instructor will probably provide the disk with the operating system.)
2. Insert the new disk in the disk drive.
3. Press the Caps Lock key to the down position.
4. Use the keyboard to type the following information:

NEW
10 TEXT:HOME:?"MY FIRST DISK"
RUN
INIT HELLO

Now the new disk is initialized and ready to use. To check, shut off the machine, then turn it back on again. The words MY FIRST DISK should be on the screen.

ELEMENTARY COMPUTER COMMANDS

Before discussing a few simple computer programs usable with a set of test scores, a review of several commands used in the operation of the Apple is provided. Although an occasional point is made about programming in BASIC, keep in mind that the purpose of this chapter is not to teach you to program in BASIC but rather to illustrate how a simple program operates.

Commercial software

An enormous amount of commercial software is available through computer stores, magazines, and catalogs. For example, a number of word processing programs have been developed for a wide variety of computers. Screenwriter is a popular program written for the Apple; Volkswriter has been well received by IBM users. Statistical program packages are also available, allowing the user to calculate both descriptive and inferential statistics with ease. One of the best-selling pieces of software has been Visicalc, a spreadsheet for accounting. Many other versions of spreadsheets are also available. Another category of software packages includes the data base programs. These programs handle filing and data management problems. A good software program is written so that it can be used by a computer novice. Any computer commands that are needed should be presented to the user within the program itself. A tutorial, a file that helps the user learn to use the program, is included. A well-developed software program can be most valuable to the user; however, these programs can be expensive, so be certain your purchase is worthwhile. Do not buy a program until you have used the demonstration disk. Keep in mind that a lot of poor software is on the market, too.

User-developed software

Perhaps your instructor has several programs that have been written for the Apple for use in your class. A few simple programs written in BASIC are provided in the next section. Although these programs are quite easy to use, they are not as "user friendly" as commercial programs. In other words, you will need to know how to use a few simple commands on the Apple to use these programs. Let's review a few of these commands before trying out the programs. Note that each of these commands must be **entered** by pressing the Return key on the right side of the keyboard before the computer will respond to them.

NEW: The **NEW** command erases everything stored in random access memory (RAM), although it does not erase the screen. You were asked to type NEW when you initialized your disk to tell the computer that a new program was being initiated and that it should not confuse this program with anything else previously stored in RAM; therefore, the NEW command instructs the computer to erase any information in RAM. Remember to press the Return key after you have typed NEW.

HOME: The **HOME** command clears the screen, but it does not tamper with any information now in RAM. As long as you do not turn off your machine, nothing currently in RAM memory is destroyed.

CATALOG: If you have a disk in your disk drive, the CATALOG command lets you know what is on the disk. The computer will list the files on the disk. If you initialized a disk according to the instructions in the previous section, put this disk in the disk drive and type **CATALOG.** You should see the HELLO file listed. If nothing happens, it may be because you put the disk in after the computer had been turned on. The computer should not be turned on until the disk is in the disk drive. Turn the computer off, put the disk in, and turn the computer back on. Since the disk has been initialized, it contains the disk operating system, which must be loaded before the disk can be used.

RUN (program): The command (RUN) in capital letters and another word (program) in small letters and in parentheses means that you should type in the RUN command and the name of the program or file you wish to run. You must use capital letters for all of your entries, including the name you give to the program. Let's say you are interested in calculating the mean of a set of scores, and a program named MEAN is on the disk in the disk drive. You should type RUN (MEAN) and enter the command. The computer will load the program from the disk to RAM and run it. If you are not using a disk, you can type a program directly on the screen and instruct the computer to run it. Then you do not have to type in the program name since the program is already in RAM memory. (Although it is redundant to use the term "memory" after RAM, this is done on occasion to remind you of the various memories associated with a microcomputer.) Thus the computer knows which program you are referring to when you type RUN. Sometimes you might wish to do something with the program before you run it. If so, the program can be loaded (see next command description) into RAM initially. If you load the program, only RUN is needed to operate it. Again, once the program is in RAM memory, the computer does not have to be given the program name.

LOAD (program): The **LOAD (program)** command instructs the computer to take a program, for which you have provided the name, and put it into RAM. Remember that the program is automatically loaded if you type RUN and then the program name. On the other hand, once you have loaded the program, only the *RUN* command is necessary to execute it. Typing in the program name is not necessary.

LIST: The LIST command instructs the computer to list each line of the program. One reason the LIST command is used is to enable the user to see how the program is listed. A programmer may list a program to revise it in some way. All but one of the programs in this chapter are short and can be seen in their entirety on the fixed screen. Many programs are longer than the screen length; the command LIST causes the computer to scroll the lines of the program. The listing begins at the top of the screen. When the screen is filled, the top lines begin "scrolling" off the top of the screen and new lines appear at the bottom.

SAVE (**program**): The SAVE (**program**) command takes the program out of RAM and puts it onto the disk. If the program is a new one, you must give it a name. If it is already on your disk with a specified name and you wish to continue using this name, do so. If the program was revised while in RAM, the revised form will take the place of the previous version on the disk.

DELETE (**program**): The DELETE (**program**) command is used to erase a program from a disk. Be sure you will no longer need the program before deleting it. These commands should enable you to use the following simple programs.

EXAMPLES OF PROGRAMS

Four simple programs are included in this section to illustrate calculation of the mean, z-scores, T-scores, and grades. All of the programs are written in BASIC language. Each line is preceded by a line number. Without these line numbers the computer would carry out the operations immediately and the program lines would not be stored. The lines allow storage of the program and its operations until the RUN command is given. Be sure the Caps Lock key is down.

Program MEAN

Program MEAN was written to calculate the mean of a set of scores. To familiarize yourself with the program, enter it in your computer's memory using the keyboard. If you plan to save the program on a disk, be sure the disk has been initialized. (The disk should have been inserted in the disk drive before the computer was turned on.) This program is so short that typing it on the screen whenever you want to use it will not be difficult. On the other hand, disk storage saves time and prevents errors that can occur when retyping.

Enter the commands and program as presented below. Do not forget to enter each line after you have typed it by pressing return.

```
NEW
10   INPUT "How many scores are in the data set?   ";N
20   FOR S = 1 to N
30   INPUT "SCORE   ";X
40   SUM = SUM + X
```

```
50   NEXT S
60   MEAN = SUM/N
70   PRINT "MEAN =    ";MEAN
80   END
```

The number at the beginning of each line is used to identify the line. The first line is 10; the next line is 20. Using 11 rather than 20 is permissible; however, if the program required an addition between lines 10 and 11, it would have to be renumbered. Renumbering would not be a problem if the addition were to be made between lines 10 and 20, because a new line, given a number from 11 to 19, could be entered. Experiment with the program. The program is in RAM. Enter HOME. Notice that the screen has been cleared, but the program has not been lost. To take another look at the program, enter LIST. Now run the program using the following data:

$$N = 5$$
$$\text{Scores} = 30, 48, 37, 52, 29$$

Enter RUN. The computer will ask you how many scores are in the data set. Type in 5 and press the Return key. The computer will then ask you to enter each score. Remember to press the Return key after typing each score. Since the computer knows that five scores are in the data set, it will not ask you for any more scores after the fifth one. After it receives the fifth score, the computer will automatically calculate the mean. In this case, the mean equals 39.2.

Clear the screen by typing HOME, then list the program again by entering LIST. Since this is such a short, simple program, following the instructions given to the computer in BASIC is easy. Spend a few minutes studying the program. Of course, you can also study the printed version in this book! If your computer is hooked up to a printer, you could also print a copy of the program. Let's assume you do not have a printer available, but you would like to save the MEAN program on your disk. Enter SAVE MEAN. Now check to see if the program has been filed on your disk by entering CATALOG. If your disk only included the HELLO program before, the list should now show both the HELLO and MEAN programs. Experiment with this program using several other data sets.

Program Z-SCORE

Program Z-SCORE was written to convert raw scores to z-scores. (see Chapter 5). Assume you have administered a test and obtained a set of scores. You would like to compare these scores with the scores on another test. Unless the two tests have the same score range, mean and standard deviation, the raw scores cannot be directly compared. However, by converting the raw scores to z-scores, even different score units can be compared.

Type the z-score program onto the screen. Remember to press the Return key after each program line.

```
    NEW
     10  INPUT "How many scores do you want to convert to z-scores?   ";N
     20  INPUT "What is the mean?   ";M
     30  INPUT "What is the standard deviation?   ";S
     40  FOR A = 1 to N
     50  INPUT "What is the score?   ";X
     60  PRINT
     70  PRINT "The z-score equals   ";(X − M)/S
     80  PRINT
     90  NEXT A
    100  END
```

You can now type HOME, clear the screen, then run the program by typing RUN, or you can run the program without clearing the screen. Notice that this program asks for the mean and standard deviation before the test scores are input. However, this information needs to be provided only once for each data set. Then the program moves to a "loop" where a score is input and its z-score calculated. The next score is input, and so on, until N scores have been input; the program then ends. Use the following data to run the program:

$$\overline{X} = 50$$
$$s = 2$$
$$\text{Scores: } 56, 51, 48, 49, 45, 50$$
$$N = 6$$

The z-scores for the above raw scores are 3, .5, −1, −.5, −2.5, and 0. After you have typed in the sixth score, the program should end. The program is still in RAM and can be used repeatedly as long as you do not turn off the machine or accidentally erase it (by typing NEW, for example). If you want to keep the program on a disk, be sure your disk is in the disk drive. Then type SAVE Z-SCORE. As soon as the whirring sound has stopped, type CATALOG. Don't forget to press the Return key after each of these commands. The list of programs on your disk should now be on the screen. It should include HELLO, MEAN, and Z-SCORE, if you saved the MEAN program. Now you can turn off your machine or type NEW and go on to another program.

Since this program is short and simple, review the program line by line and see if it makes sense to you. If PROGRAM Z-SCORE is no longer in RAM but was stored on a disk, reload it into your machine memory by typing LOAD Z-SCORE. Then type LIST. Now examine the program closely. The calculation is straightforward since the mean and standard deviation are provided as input. A more complex program could be written in which the mean and standard deviation were calculated as a part of the program. In line 50 the computer is instructed to print a statement "The z-score equals " and then print the results of the calculation $(X − M)/S$. Several spaces were inserted after the word "equals" purely for cosmetic purposes to separate the answer from the statement and make it easier to read. When you have completed your examination of the program, type SAVE Z-SCORE if you wish to save the program on your disk.

Program T-SCORE

When test scores are transformed, the z-score transformation is often used. However, because z-scores can be negative and represented as decimals, it is not uncommon to transform these scores so that they can be more easily interpreted. A transformation commonly used in measures of motor performance is the T-score. In the next program T-scores are calculated. The required input consists of the mean and standard deviation of the set of scores, along with the raw scores. In this program the z-score is also calculated, but it is not printed since the T-score is of primary interest. First, type in the program as it is listed below. (An asterick [*] is the multiplication symbol, and a slash [/] is the division symbol.)

```
NEW
10   INPUT "How many scores do you want to convert to T-scores?   ";N
20   INPUT "What is the mean?   ";M
30   INPUT "What is the standard deviation?   ";S
40   FOR A = 1 to N
50   INPUT "What is the score?   ";X
60   PRINT
70   PRINT "The T-score equals   ";50 + ((X−M)/S)*10
80   PRINT
90   NEXT A
100  END
```

As an example, use the six test scores given in the previous section on Program Z-SCORE. Type RUN and then go through the program. The correct answers for the T-score calculations are 80, 55, 40, 45, 25, and 50.

Now list the program and examine it. Find the line in which the z-score is calculated, and note how the z-score is modified to obtain the T-score. You should be looking at line 70 now. If you would like to keep this program, save it on your disk.

A more elaborate T-score program is included in Appendix E. This program accepts a larger number of test scores and provides an option for printing a hard copy of the results.

Program GRADES

The following program can be used to determine the final grades for students in physical education classes. Although it is a little longer than the previous ones, it runs just as easily. The input needed to operate this program includes the individual test grades for each student and the weight given to each test by the teacher. Since the same weights will apply to all grades, they need only be input once. If each grade is of equal importance, simply input a 1 for each weight. If one skill test is twice as important as another, you might assign it a weight of 2 and the second test, a weight of 1.

First, enter the program into RAM memory.

```
10    HOME
20    INPUT "How many students?  ";S
30    INPUT "How many grades for each student?   ";N
40    PRINT
100   DIM GD(N,3),GD$(N)
120   FOR X = 1 to N
130   INPUT "Weight?   ";GD(X,2)
135   ADD = ADD + GD(X,2)
140   NEXT X
150   FOR Y = 1 to S
155   PRINT
200   FOR X = 1 to N
210   INPUT "GRADE?   ";GD$(X)
211   IF GD$(X) = "A+" THEN GD(X,1)  = 12
212   IF GD$(X) = "A" THEN GD(X,1)    = 11
213   IF GD$(X) = "A−" THEN GD(X,1)  = 10
214   IF GD$(X) = "B+" THEN GD(X,1)  = 9
215   IF GD$(X) = "B" THEN GD(X,1)    = 8
216   IF GD$(X) = "B−" THEN GD(X,1)  = 7
217   IF GD$(X) = "C+" THEN GD(X,1)  = 6
218   IF GD$(X) = "C" THEN GD(X,1)    = 5
219   IF GD$(X) = "C−" THEN GD(X,1)  = 4
220   IF GD$(X) = "D+" THEN GD(X,1)  = 3
221   IF GD$(X) = "D" THEN GD(X,1)    = 2
222   IF GD$(X) = "D−" THEN GD(X,1)  = 1
223   IF GD$(X) = "F" THEN GD(X,1)    = 0
310   GD(X,3) = GD(X,1)*GD(X,2)
320   NEXT X
330   LET SUM = 0
340   FOR X = 1 to N
350   SUM = SUM + GD(X,3)
360   NEXT X
370   PRINT
375   T = SUM/ADD
380   PRINT "AVERAGE GRADE =   ";T
381   IF T < 12.1 THEN T$ = "A+"
382   IF T < 11.5 THEN T$ = "A"
```

```
383   IF T <  10.5 THEN T$ = "A – "
384   IF T <   9.5 THEN T$ = "B + "
385   IF T <   8.5 THEN T$ = "B"
386   IF T <   7.5 THEN T$ = "B – "
387   IF T <   6.5 THEN T$ = "C + "
388   IF T <   5.5 THEN T$ = "C"
389   IF T <   4.5 THEN T$ = "C – "
390   IF T <   3.5 THEN T$ = "D + "
391   IF T <   2.5 THEN T$ = "D"
392   IF T <   1.5 THEN T$ = "D – "
393   IF T <    .5 THEN T$ = "F"
398   PRINT "AVERAGE LETTER GRADE =    "; T$
399   PRINT
400   PRINT
410   NEXT Y
420   END
```

Now that you have typed in the program, perhaps you should check it line by line. If you enter LIST, you will find that this program is too long to be displayed on the screen in its entirety. The computer will execute your command, but the first lines will scroll off the screen fairly quickly. You can instruct the computer to list specific lines you wish to see. If you are interested in the first 150 lines, enter LIST 1-150. If you have checked each line for accuracy, try to run the program.

For purposes of simplicity in an example, the final grades for two students will be calculated. Three tests were administered to each student during the unit of instruction. The computer will ask for the following information for the entire class: the number of students in class, the number of grades for each student, and the weights for each grade. Once this information has been entered, the program is completed by entering the numerical value of the grades for each student. Let's use the following information in our example:

> Number of students = 2
> Number of grades per student = 3
> Weights for the three grades = 1.5, 3, 2.5
> Grades for first student = C, B +, C +
> Grades for second student = A, B, C

When this program is run, the screen will automatically clear and the following question will appear: How many students? The output from the program will be displayed on your screen as follows, as long as you enter the appropriate information at the correct time. (The notes are used to clarify the example and will not appear on the screen.)

How many students? 2
How many grades for each student? 3

Weight? 1.5   Note: This information is input only once for each group of students, since
Weight? 3   the weights are the same for all students.
Weight? 2.5

Grade? C   Note: The program now asks you to input the grades for each student,
Grade? B+   beginning with the first one on your roster.
Grade? C+

AVERAGE GRADE = 7.071429
AVERAGE LETTER GRADE = B−

Note: The computer provides both the numerical average grade and the average letter grade. The grade should be recorded for each student whenever it appears on the screen.
Grade? A   Note: Now the program asks for the grades of the next student.
Grade? B
Grade? C
AVERAGE GRADE = 7.571429
AVERAGE LETTER GRADE = B

The program will automatically terminate at this point since we had indicated previously that grades for only two students would be input. This program can calculate a small number of final grades in a short period. The teacher's only task is to enter each student's grades and record the final grade, once the information for the entire class (number of students, number of grades per student, and weights for the grades) has been entered. An expanded version of this program is listed in Appendix E. It can handle grades for a large number of students and provides the option for obtaining a hard copy of the students' names and grades.

List the program again and examine the program lines closely. In the first 130 lines, data for the entire class are entered. In the remainder of the program, four loops are included—one to add the weights, one to average the grades numerically, one to convert the numerical average to a letter grade, and one to repeat the process for each student until the number of students (S) has been reached. Now run the program again either using hypothetical data or data provided by your instructor. If you want to save the program, enter SAVE GRADES.

SUMMARY

Some of the mystique of the computer is eliminated once you have completed a few simple, practical tasks. The programs included in this chapter provide a few examples of how computers can be used to facilitate measurement and evaluation, yet these examples only scratch the surface of their innumerable possibilities. New programs for physical educators and exercise scientists will become available every year, and these programs should be increasingly easy to use.

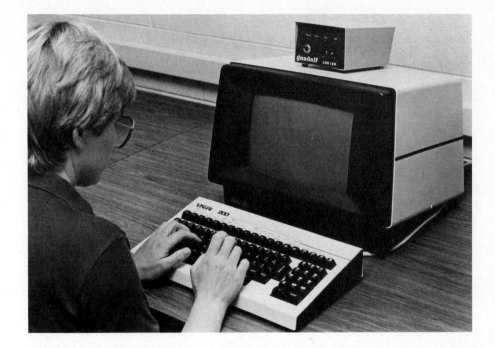

LEARNING EXPERIENCES

1. Read the article by Mayhew and Rankin (1983) included in the References. Try out at least one of the simple programs listed in their article. Your instructor may have a data set you can use. If not, make up a few numbers and use them to execute the program.

2. Use the Z-SCORE and T-SCORE programs to solve Problem 3 at the end of Chapter 5.

REFERENCES

Barlow, D.A., and Bayalis, P.A. 1983. Computer facilitated learning. Journal of Physical Education, Recreation and Dance **54**(9):27-29.

Cicciarella, C.F. 1983. The computer in physical education. Journal of Physical Education, Recreation and Dance **54**(9):18, 32.

Donnelly, J.E. 1983. Physiology and fitness testing. Journal of Physical Education, Recreation and Dance **54**(9):24-26.

Mayhew, J.L., and Rankin, B.A. 1983. Data management. Journal of Physical Education, Recreation and Dance **54**(9):22-23.

Richard, J.G., and Engelhorn, R. 1983. Selecting a microcomputer. Journal of Physical Education, Recreation and Dance **54**(9):19-21.

Sealy, D. 1983. Computer programs for dance notation. Journal of Physical Education, Recreation and Dance **54**(9):36-37.

ANNOTATED READINGS

Baun, M., and Baun, W.B. 1984. A corporate health and fitness program: motivation and management by computers. Journal of Physical Education, Recreation and Dance **55**(4):42-45.

Describes the computer system used in Tenneco's health and fitness program in Houston, Texas; incorporates a unique exercise logging function; program produces feedback to participants and health and fitness staff.

Brownell, B.A. 1985. Using microcomputers: a guidebook for writers, teachers, and researchers. Beverly Hills, Calif.: Sage Publications, Inc.

Written for people who have a limited understanding of the many ways in which microcomputers can enhance their professional lives; includes specific illustrations of computer applications, such as the creation and maintenance of bibliographies and references and the production of instructional materials; describes the most popular microcomputers and their operating systems; examines a variety of software.

Graham, G.P., and Wooldridge, W. 1983. Computer measurement of skinfolds. Journal of Physical Education, Recreation and Dance **54**(7):68-69.

Presents a microcomputer program for the Apple II to estimate the percentage of body fat for men (using chest, abdomen, and thigh) and women (using triceps and suprailiac) from skinfold measurements.

Marley, W.P. 1972. The computer in measurement and evaluation class. Journal of Health, Physical Education, and Recreation **43**:39.

Demonstrates the usefulness of computers in testing and evaluation in physical education; stresses the practical applications that are possible; emphasizes developing an understanding of the ways a computer can be used; deemphasizes the need for teachers to learn programming skills.

Mood, D.P. 1978. The undergraduate physical education major and the computer. Journal of Physical Education and Recreation **49**:66-67.

Provides rationale for using computers for statistics, calculating velocities and limb length, and movement analysis; also valuable for individualized instruction; enhances recordkeeping procedures in physical education courses; provides examples of ways computers can be used in physical education.

Vockell, E.L., and Rivers, R.H. 1984. Instructional computing for today's teachers. New York: Macmillan Publishing Co.

Assumes user has no prior knowledge of computers; gives an overview of Computer-Aided Instruction (CAI); provides guidelines for the selection of microcomputers and software; teaches readers to program using BASIC by modifying existing instructional programs; contains program modules for improving user-friendliness, information on the use of sequential data files, and a comprehensive list of software.

Glossary

AAHPER Youth Fitness Test: Battery of six test items measuring primarily athletic performance-related physical fitness, although two of the items are measures of health-related fitness (p. 266)

AAHPERD Health-Related Physical Fitness Test: Four-item test battery designed to measure physical performance, particularly health-related physical fitness (p. 229)

accountability: Provision of evidence that predetermined goals and objectives have been met (p. 24)

achievement: Ability level of an examinee at a designated point (p. 6)

affect: Sociological or psychological characteristic manifested in a feeling or behavior, such as attitude, interest, and sportsmanship (p. 367)

affective domain: Levels of emotional behavior, including attitudes, interests, and various personality characteristics (p. 32)

alternatives: Set of responses in a multiple choice item; correct alternative is the *answer*; incorrect alternatives are *distractors* (p. 176)

anomaly: Unusual; irregular; contrary to general rule (p. 447)

athletic performance–related physical fitness: Type of physical fitness that enhances performance in sports and other forms of physical activity; different from health-related physical fitness, although health-related fitness may also benefit performance (p. 265)

attitude: Feeling one has about a specific attitude object, such as a situation, a person, or an activity (p. 366)

balance: Ability to maintain equilibrium (p. 330)

BASIC language: Beginners All-Purpose Symbolic Instruction Code; a computer language (p. 496)

basic movement patterns: Types of movement that emerge developmentally, usually at a young age, such as running, jumping, and throwing (p. 399)

behavioral objective: Objective stated in terms of the behavior the student will exhibit when the objective is successfully attained (p. 22)

bicycle ergometer: Stationary bicycle that can be operated at a variety of workloads; used to measure physical work capacity (p. 46)

bit: Smallest amount of information that can be identified by a computer; can specify either of two alternatives, one or zero (p. 500)

body composition: Combination of bone, muscle mass, and fatty tissue (p. 245)

booting: Loading a program into the computer's memory (p. 499)

byte: Equals one character, which is a letter, number, or punctuation mark; made up of eight bits or two nibbles (p. 500)

cable tensiometer: Device used to measure static strength; cable tension is determined "from the force needed to create offset on a riser in a cable stretched between two points" (Clarke, 1976:124) (p. 301)

---

*The definitions of words marked with an asterisk (*) are taken from the Rules and Regulations for PL 94-192 published in the Federal Register,

†The definitions of words marked with a dagger are taken from the American Alliance For Health, Physical Education, Recreation and Dance, 1980.

carotid artery: Artery in the neck, along the side of the "Adam's apple"; often used to measure pulse rate (p. 46)

CATALOG: BASIC command to list the files on a disk (p. 509)

central processing unit: A microchip or portion of a microchip that controls peripherals and memory (p. 499)

central tendency: Center of distribution of test scores (p. 86)

cerebral palsy: Neuromuscular disability resulting from brain damage (p. 447)

checklist of objectives: Set of symbols to rate major objectives; often used in elementary schools (p. 470)

circumference measure: Measure of the outer surface of a body part, such as the upper arm; sometimes used to estimate body fatness (p. 46)

cognitive domain: Intellectual behavior ranging from a low level (memorization of facts) to a higher level (application of these facts) in some way (p. 31)

compatibles: Computer hardware that uses software written for another, often more expensive, computer (p. 505)

competency-based evaluation: Approach to evaluation in which a desired level of competency is identified, and examinees designated as competent must be able to meet or exceed this level (p. 15)

component model of intratask development: Identification of developmental characteristics of body parts in performing a task (p. 402)

components of skill: Elements of the skill that are essential to its correct execution (p. 161)

computer literacy: Possession of sufficient knowledge about computers to deal adequately with the computer age (p. 496)

concurrent validity: Degree to which a predictor test correlates with a criterion test (p. 126)

condition (in an objective): Situation in which behavior is expected to occur (p. 29)

congenital: Condition present at birth (p. 447)

construct validity: Degree to which a test measures an attribute or a trait that cannot be directly measured (p. 129)

content (in an objective): Material or skill the student is expected to learn (p. 28)

content validity: Degree to which the sample of test items, tasks, or questions on a test are representative of some defined universe or "domain" of content (American Psychological Association, 1984) (p. 121)

contingency coefficient: Method of determining the validity of a mastery test (p. 151)

contingency table: Table with numbers in each cell determined by jointly considering the two joint categories (p. 128)

contrasting groups method: Determination of valid cutoff point by comparing students expected to master an objective with those not expected to master it (p. 149)

correction for guessing: Alteration of test score based on number of items answered incorrectly (p. 184)

correlation: Relationship between two variables (p. 102)

correlation coefficient: Statistical procedure for estimating the relationship between two variables, X and Y (p. 102)

criterion: Standard of behavior (p. 126)

criterion-referenced test: Test with a predetermined standard of performance that is tied to a specified domain of behavior (p. 143)

criterion-related validity: Extent to which a test measures the true or criterion behavior of examinees, usually determined by correlational procedures (p. 126)

criterion test: Highly valid test of the attribute to be measured; cannot be used in a practical setting because of its complexity, expense, and need for specially trained testers; standard against which a practical test is compared (p. 164)

cumulative frequency (cf): Column in frequency distribution table obtained by summing the frequencies from the bottom to the top of the column; the number at the top of the column equals *N*, the number of scores; represents the number of examinees scoring at or below a given interval (p. 71)

cumulative percent (c%): Column in frequency distribution table obtained by dividing the cumulative frequency by *N* and multiplying by 100; represents the percentage of examinees scoring at or below a given interval (p. 71)

curriculum objective: Translation of long-term objective into specific behavior expected after exposure to a curriculum (p. 25)

deaf: Severe hearing loss (p. 447)

decision validity: Accuracy of classification of masters and nonmasters (p. 148)

DELETE (program): BASIC command to erase a file from a disk (p. 510)

descriptive statistics: Statistics used to describe a set of data (p. 66)

disabled: Because of an impairment, the individual is limited or restricted in executing some skills, performing specific jobs or tasks, or participating in certain activities (American Alliance for Health, Physical Education, Recreation and Dance) (p. 447)

disk (floppy): Round sheet of plastic coated with iron oxide and inserted in a protective, black jacket; a means of storing data (p. 507)

disk drive: Device for storing data; means of communication between disk and central processor (p. 497)

disk operating system (DOS): Means of communicating between the disk in disk drive and the central processor (p. 499)

display: Information appearing on screen of monitor (p. 497)

domain: Range of all possible criterion behaviors (p. 146)

domain-referenced validity: Extent to which the tasks sampled by the test adequately represent the total domain of tasks (p. 146)

dynamic balance: Ability to maintain equilibrium while in motion (p. 330)

dynamic strength: Force exerted by a muscle group as a body part moves through space (p. 301)

dynamometer: Device used to measure static strength and endurance (p. 301)

educable: Capable of learning or being educated, as in educable mentally retarded (p. 438)

electromechanical instrument: Device (such as Cybex II) used to measure static and dynamic strength, endurance, and power (p. 303)

elgon: Goniometer with a potentiometer substituted for the protractor; also known as electrogoniometer; used to measure flexibility (p. 335)

enter key: Key on the keyboard used to enter commands into the computer (p. 508)

essay item: Item requiring examinee to construct a response at least several sentences long (p. 181)

evaluation: Interpretation of a test score (p. 5)

evaluation objective: Short-term objective reflecting a change in behavior that has occurred over a short period (p. 25)

face validity: Having the appearance of validity, but not formally validated (p. 404)

field test: Practical but valid substitute for a more complex laboratory test (p. 229)

Flexed-Arm Hang Test: Measures arm and shoulder girdle strength; usually designated for girls (p. 268) *flexibility:* Range of movement about a joint, from a position of extension to flexion or the opposite movement (p. 329)

flexometer: Instrument with a weighted 360-degree dial and a weighted pointer, used to measure flexibility; both the dial and the pointer move independently as affected by gravity (p. 335)

forced-choice item: Item requiring examinee to choose among two or more alternatives that appear equally favorable or unfavorable (p. 369)

formative evaluation: Evaluation that occurs throughout a training period or instructional unit (p. 10)

formatting a disk: Preparing a disk for use; must be applied to new disks before using (p. 507)

frequency (f): Number of scores in an interval; sum of tallies in an interval (p. 70)

frequency distribution: Method of organizing test scores into mutually exclusive intervals (p. 69)

frequency polygon: Line graph of the frequency distribution, which score limits on the horizontal axis and frequency of cases on the vertical axis (p. 74)

game statistics: Record of events occurring during a game, such as number of shots attempted, percentage of successful shots, and so forth (p. 168)

gates: Pictorial representation of bits; open gate represents a "yes" choice; closed gate represents a "no" choice (p. 496)

goniometer: Protractor of 180 degrees with extended arms; used to measure flexibility (p. 301)

grade: Mark assigned to a student based on his or her performance on one or more tests (p. 454)

halo effect: Rater bias that may can occur when the rater is unduly influenced by previous performances of the examinee (p. 182)

handicapped†: Because of an impairment of disability, the individual is adversely affected psychologically, emotionally, or socially (p. 429)

hardware: Physical components of the computer, such as keyboard and monitor (p. 497)

health-related physical fitness: See Physical fitness (health-related) (p. 226)

histogram: Bar graph of the frequency distribution, with score limits on the horizontal axis and frequency of cases on the vertical axis (p. 74)

HOME: BASIC command to clear the screen (p. 509)

hydrostatic weighing: Assessment of body composition by weighing a person underwater (p. 261)

impaired†: Individual who has an identifiable organic or functional condition; some part of the body or a portion of an anatomical structure is actually missing; one or more parts of the body do not function properly; may be temporary or permanent (p. 427)

improvement: Change in behavior occurring between an initial and a final testing period (p. 475)

index of discrimination: Ratio of high to low scorers on the total test who answer a given item correctly (p. 185)

Individualized Education Program (IEP): Written plan of instruction, including evaluation procedures, developed for each student receiving special education (p. 430)

individually based norms: Norms based on the distribution of scores of individual examinees; type of norms used in the AAHPER Youth Fitness Test (p. 293)

initializing a disk: Preparing a disk for use, specifically on an Apple computer (p. 507) *instructed/uninstructed approach:* Determination of valid cutoff point by comparing an instructed group with an uninstructed group (p. 148)

interclass reliability coefficient: Method of estimating reliability ($r_{xx'}$) using correlation procedures (p. 131)

interests: Affect reflecting one's likes and dislikes about various matters, such as physical activity, programming, and scheduling (p. 367)

interjudge objectivity: Consistency in scoring between two or more independent judgments of the same performance (p. 139)

interpercentile range: Measure of variability used in conjunction with the median; can be represented by a variety of ranges as long as equal portions of each end of the distribution are eliminated (p. 89)

interval (i): Range of scores identified to form categories of a frequency distribution (p. 68)

intraclass reliability coefficient: Method of estimating reliability ($R_{xx'}$) using analysis of variance (p. 131)

intrajudge objectivity: Consistency in scoring when one person scores the same test two or more times (p. 138)

intratask analysis: Identification of stages of development of a task from the time the task is first attempted to the time it is performed at a mature or an adult level (p. 17-6)

item analysis: Method for determining the usefulness of each individual item as a part of the total test (p. 184)

item difficulty: Proportion of examinees answering the item correctly (p. 185)

item function: Percentage of examinees selecting an alternative as the correct response, whether it is correct or not (p. 187)

kappa coefficient (k): Method of determining the reliability of a mastery test where change is taken into account (p. 153)

keyboard: Used to transmit information to computer; similar to keyboard of typewriter (p. 497)

kilobyte (k): 1024 bytes (p. 500)

Kraus-Weber Test: Test of minimal functioning of the low back area (p. 336)

level of behavior: Level of the process (cognitive, affective, or psychomotor) the learner uses in attaining an objective (p. 31)

Likert scale: Scale measuring degree of agreement or disagreement with a series of affective statements (p. 367)

LIST: BASIC command to list each line of the program in RAM (p. 510)

LOAD (program): A BASIC command to take a specified program from the disk and put it into RAM (p. 509)

logical validity: Extent to which a test measures the most important components of skill required to perform the motor task adequately (p. 124)

long-range goals: Long-term global goals that describe the end product of a complete education (p. 25)

mastery learning: Model of instruction whereby frequent feedback is given to the learner and a large percentage of learners can attain at least minimal success in a unit of instruction (p. 144)

mastery test: Type of criterion-referenced test in which examinees are classified as masters or nonmasters (p. 9)

matching item: Item containing two columns of words or phrases, with the right-hand column used as alternatives to match with the material in the left-hand column (p. 179)

maximal oxygen uptake: Maximal amount of oxygen an individual can transport and use during exercise. Max Vo_2: Symbol for maximal oxygen uptake; often expressed as ml/kg/min, or milliliters per kilogram of body weight per minute (p. 50)

mean: Arithmetic average of a set of scores; a measure of central tendency (p. 86)

measure: When used as a noun, refers to an instrument or technique used to obtain information (usually a score) about an attribute of a person or an object; when used as a verb, refers to the process of obtaining the score (p. 5)

measurement: Process of assigning a number to an attribute of a person or an object; the process of obtaining test scores (p. 4)

median: Score dividing the distribution such that 50% of the scores fall above that point and 50% fall below; the 50th percentile (p. 75)

mentally retarded*: Significantly subaverage, general intellectual functioning existing concurrently with deficits in adaptive behavior and manifested in the developmental period, which adversely affects a child's education performance (p. 429)

MET: Energy value; a multiple of the resting metabolism; one MET equals average energy expenditure at rest (p. 50)

microchip: Tiny silicon chip containing many microscopic switches or gates; an electrical charge opens some switches and closes others, creating a pattern simulating human logic (p. 496)

mode: Most frequently occurring score in the distribution; a measure of central tendency (p. 86)

modem: Device allowing a computer to communicate over telephone lines and other communication media (p. 500)

monitor: Television set, often specially manufactured to be connected to a computer (p. 497)

motor ability: Originally, the innate ability to perform motor skills; more commonly, the ability to perform motor skills (p. 345)

motor capacity: Individual's capacity to perform motor skills (p. 345)

motor educability: Individual's ability to learn new motor skills (p. 345)

multiple choice item: Test item that is answered using one of three or more alternatives (p. 176)

muscular endurance: "The ability of the muscle to maintain submaximum force levels for extended periods" (Heyward, 1984:5)(p. 299)

muscular strength: "The maximum force or tension that can be produced by the muscle group" (Heyward, 1984:4)(p. 299)

needs assessment: Comparison of actual status of target group with desired status on some attribute to determine program needs (p. 428)

NEW: BASIC command to erase everything stored in RAM (p. 509)

normal curve: Bell-shaped curve with known properties (p. 93)

norm-referenced test: Test used to compare an examinee's score with the scores of other similar examinees (p. 9)

objective test: Test with highly precise scoring system, yielding little error (p. 138)

objectivity: Precision with which test is scored (p. 118)

orthopedically impaired*: Severe orthopedic impairment that adversely affects a child's educational performance; includes impairments caused by a congenital anomaly (e.g., clubfoot, absence of some member), impairments caused by disease (e.g., poliomyelitis), and impairments from other causes (e.g., cerebral palsy, leukemia) (p. 444) *paraplegia:* Paralysis of the legs and lower part of the body (p. 447)

pass-fail method: Method of grading using two grade categories (p. 469)

Pearson product-moment correlation coefficient: Statistical technique used to determine the relationship between two sets of measures of the same individuals (p. 102)

perceived exertion scale: Scale used to assess the examinee's perception of his or her physical exertion during exercise (p. 369)

percentage method: Method of grading based on the assignment of a percentage to each grade category; a norm-referenced approach to grading (p. 464)

percentage-correct method: Method of grading based on the percentage of test items or trials successfully completed; a criterion-referenced approach to grading (p. 465)

percentile: Score value for a specified percentage of cases in a distribution of scores (p. 67)

percentile norms: Norms calculated by converting raw scores to percentiles (p. 293)

percentile rank: Percentage of cases falling at or below a specified score in a distribution (p. 81)

peripheral: Device that can send information to the computer as well as receive information from it (p. 497)

physical fitness (health-related)†: Multifaceted continuum extending from birth to death; affected by physical activity; ranges from optimal abilities in all aspects of life to severely limiting disease and dysfunction (p. 228)

posture: Alignment of the body and its segments (p. 339)

power: Ability to generate maximum force in a minimum amount of time (p. 320)

predictive validity: Appropriateness of a test as a predictor of behavior (p. 127)

predictor: Test or variable that predicts a criterion behavior (p. 127)

program evaluation: Assessment of the extent to which a program has met predetermined objectives (p. 482)

proportion of agreement (P): Method of determining the reliability of a criterion-referenced test (p. 152)

psychomotor domain: Motor behavior ranging from a low level, reproducing a skill, to higher levels in which the skill is used creatively in a game setting (p. 34)

Pull-Ups Test: Measures arm and shoulder girdle strength; usually designated for boys (p. 268)

pulse rate: Estimation of heart rate; often made by placing the tips of two or three fingers on the skin above an artery and counting the beats (p. 46)

qualitative measurement: Predominantly judgmental approach to measurement (p. 4)

quantitative measurement: Objective approach to measurement in which a number is assigned to the attribute of interest (p. 4)

range: Spread of scores; in a distribution, the bottom score subtracted from the top score plus 1 (p. 71)

random access memory (RAM): Primary memory of a computer; information can be stored in RAM as well as retrieved and modified (p. 499)

rank difference correlation coefficient: Statistical technique used to calculate the correlation coefficient when the scores are ranked (p. 104)

rating scale: Scale used to subjectively assess performance (p. 165)

raw score: Score obtained by an examinee on a test (p. 88)

reactive effect: Change in affect resulting from heightened awareness because of the experience of taking an inventory measuring the affective behavior (p. 367)

read only memory (ROM): Computer memory in which information is stored once, usually by the manufacturer; cannot be changed (p. 499) *real limits:* Upper and lower limits of intervals in a frequency distribution representing the entire area between intervals; do not represent score units actually obtained on the test (p. 77)

reflexes: Inborn, genetically endowed, involuntary behaviors (p. 431)

reliability: Dependability of scores, their relative freedom from error; the consistency of an individual's performance on a test (p. 131)

reliability (criterion-referenced): Consistency of classification of masters and nonmasters (p. 151)

response distortion: Invalid response because of failure to respond to an item, usually an affective measure, with total honesty (p. 367)

RUN (program): BASIC command to execute a specified program (p. 509)

SAVE (program): BASIC command to take a specified program out of RAM and put it onto the disk for storage (p. 510)

score limits: Upper and lower limits of intervals in a frequency distribution represented in raw score units, that is, the actual scores obtained on the test (p. 77)

semantic differential scale: Rating of concepts with scales anchored at the extremes with bipolar adjectives (p. 368)

short-answer item: Test item including a statement with one or more blank spaces to be filled in by the examinee (p. 181)

Shuttle Run Test: Measures speed and change of direction (p. 277)

Sit-Ups Test: Measures abdominal strength (p. 268)

skewness: Shape of the curve when the majority of the scores falls at one end of the distribution, with the remainder of the scores tapering off as reflected in the long tail of the distribution (p. 95)

skinfold caliper: Device for measuring skinfold thickness (p. 234)

skinfold thickness: Thickness of a fold of skin when lifted away from the muscle; used to estimate body fatness (p. 46)

social behavior: Behavior displayed in dealing with others, such as relationships among peers (p. 364)

software: Set of instructions that makes the computer function in some desired way (p. 500)

speech impairment*: Communication disorder, such as stuttering, impaired articulation, language impairment, or voice impairment, which adversely affects a child's educational performance (p. 447)

split-half reliability estimate: Reliability estimate determined by dividing the test into halves and correlating scores on the two half-tests (p. 133)

sportsmanship: Behaviors considered appropriate for sports participants and spectators; for example, fair play, following rules, and showing respect for officials (p. 385)

standard deviation: Square root of the average of the squared deviations of scores from the mean; a measure of variability (p. 90) *standard deviation method:* Method of grading based on the standard deviation of the distribution of scores; a norm-referenced approach to grading (p. 463)

standard error of measurement: Estimate of the absolute error of an individual's score (p. 135)

standard of performance: Degree to which the student is expected to meet the objective (p. 29)

standard score: Score standardized by taking the deviation of the score from the mean and dividing it by the standard deviation (p. 96)

standard score method: Same as the standard deviation method of grading; use of z-scores (p. 464)

Standing Long Jump Test: Measures explosive leg power (p. 279)

static balance: Ability to maintain equilibrium in a stationary position (p. 330)

static strength: Force exerted against an immovable resistance (p. 301)

statistics: Methodology for analyzing a set of test scores (p. 66)

stem: Introductory question or statement in a multiple choice item (p. 176)

step test: Field test of cardiorespiratory function in which the examinee steps up and down on a bench until a predetermined heart rate is reached (p. 250)

subjective test: Test with imprecise scoring system, usually because of differences in the judgment of scorers (p. 138)

subjectivity: Use of individual judgment in evaluating motor performance (p. 168)

summative evaluation: Evaluation that takes place at the end of a training period or instructional unit (p. 10)

systematic decrease in scores: Gradual decrease in test scores from trial to trial, often because of fatigue or loss of motivation (p. 292)

systematic increase in scores: Gradual increase in test scores from trial to trial, often because of practice or learning (p. 292

table of specifications: Table of the categories of cognitive behavior (knowledge) to be tested; categories are weighed according to their importance (p. 172)

tally: Mark placed adjacent to an interval in a frequency distribution representing a score in the interval (p. 70)

task specificity: Concept that ability to perform a task is specific to the task (p. 14-17)

taxonomy: Classification scheme (p. 31)

terminal behavior: Behavior a student is expected to display upon successful attainment of the objective (p. 28)

test: Instrument or technique used to obtain information (usually a score) about an attribute of a person or object (p. 2)

test battery: Group of tests designed to measure complex abilities in sport and physical activity (p. 165)

test user: Individual who selects and/or administers the test (p. 4)

Title IX: Legislation providing for equality by gender in many areas, including physical education programs (p. 16)

trait: Enduring and unchanging characteristic (p. 358)

true-false item: Test item that is answered using one of two alternatives (p. 174)

T-scores: Distribution of standard scores with a mean of 50 and a standard deviation of 10; a conversion of the z-score distribution (p. 99)

validity: Soundness of the interpretation of a test; the extent to which a test measures what it is supposed to measure (p. 118)

validity coefficient: Correlation coefficient representing the relationship between a test and a criterion measure (p. 126) *variability:* Spread of scores in a distribution (p. 86)

variance: Squared deviations of scores from the mean; indicator of the variability or spread of a set of scores (p. 90)

vertical jump: Jump executed as high as possible in a vertical direction; reflects explosive power of leg extensor muscles (p. 320)

visually handicapped*: Visual impairment which, even with correction, adversely affects a child's educational performance; includes both partially seeing and blind children (p. 445)

weak measure: Measure lacking adequate evidence of validity and reliability (p. 370)

weight (of grade): Number designating the importance of a grade; higher number reflects greater importance (p. 464)

weight-training machine: Device used to measure muscular strength and endurance (p. 301)

50-Yard Dash Test: Measures speed (p. 281)

600-Yard Run: Measures cardiorespiratory function (p. 283)

z-scores: Most basic of standard score distributions, with a mean of 0 and a standard deviation of 1; used as the basis for many other standard score transformations (p. 97)

Appendices

A Critical values of the correlation coefficient

B Units of measure

C The F distribution

D Sources for selected sports skills tests

E Programs for Apple IIe Computer

   1 SFCALC program
   2 GRADES program
   3 DIRECTIONS program
   4 PERCENTILE program
   5 CHANGE program

F NCYFS norms

G Sources of tests and skinfold calipers

Critical values of the correlation coefficient*

df = n-2	α = .10	.05	.02	.01
1	.988	.997	.9995	.9999
2	.900	.950	.980	.990
3	.805	.878	.934	.959
4	.729	.811	.882	.917
5	.669	.754	.833	.874
6	.622	.707	.789	.834
7	.582	.666	.750	.798
8	.549	.632	.716	.765
9	.521	.602	.685	.735
10	.497	.576	.658	.708
11	.476	.553	.634	.684
12	.458	.532	.612	.661
13	.441	.514	.592	.641
14	.426	.497	.574	.623
15	.412	.482	.558	.606
16	.400	.468	.542	.590
17	.389	.456	.528	.575
18	.378	.444	.516	.561
19	.369	.433	.503	.549
20	.360	.423	.492	.537
21	.352	.413	.482	.526
22	.344	.404	.472	.515
23	.337	.396	.462	.505
24	.330	.388	.453	.496
25	.323	.381	.445	.487
26	.317	.374	.437	.479
27	.311	.367	.430	.471
28	.306	.361	.423	.463
29	.301	.355	.416	.456
30	.296	.349	.409	.449
35	.275	.325	.381	.418
40	.257	.304	.358	.393
45	.243	.288	.338	.372
50	.231	.273	.322	.354
60	.211	.250	.295	.325
70	.195	.232	.274	.302
80	.183	.217	.256	.283
90	.173	.205	.242	.267
100	.164	.195	.230	.254

*Appendix A is taken from Table V.A. of Fisher and Yates, Statistical methods for research workers, published by Oliver & Boyd, Edinburgh. By permission of the authors and publishers.

Appendix B

Units of measure

<table>
<tr><td colspan="2" align="center">Distance</td></tr>
<tr><td>1 inch</td><td>= 2.54 centimeters (cm) = 25.4 millimeters (mm) = 0.0254 meters (m)</td></tr>
<tr><td>1 foot</td><td>= 30.48 cm = 304.8 mm = 0.304 m</td></tr>
<tr><td>1 yard</td><td>= 91.44 cm = 914.4 mm = 0.914 m</td></tr>
<tr><td>1 mile</td><td>= 5280 ft = 1760 yd = 1609.35 m = 1.61 kilometers (km)</td></tr>
<tr><td>1 cm</td><td>= 0.3937 in</td></tr>
<tr><td>1 m</td><td>= 39.37 in = 3.28 ft = 1.09 yd = 100 cm = 1000 mm</td></tr>
<tr><td>1 km</td><td>= 0.62 mi = 1000 m</td></tr>
<tr><td colspan="2" align="center">Weights</td></tr>
<tr><td>1 ounce (oz)</td><td>= 0.0625 lb = 28.35 grams (g) = 0.028 kg</td></tr>
<tr><td>1 pound (lb)</td><td>= 16 oz = 454 g = 0.454 kg</td></tr>
<tr><td>1 g</td><td>= 0.035 oz = 0.0022 lb = 0.001 kg</td></tr>
<tr><td>1 kg</td><td>= 35.27 oz = 2.2 lb = 1000 g</td></tr>
</table>

Appendix C

The F distribution*

alpha = .05

V_1 = d.f. of numerator V_2 = d.f. of denominator

V_2 \ V_1	1	2	3	4	5	6	7	8	9	10
1	161.4	199.5	215.7	224.6	230.2	234.0	236.8	238.9	240.5	241.9
2	18.51	19.00	19.16	19.25	19.30	19.33	19.35	19.37	19.38	19.40
3	10.13	9.55	9.28	9.12	9.01	8.94	8.89	8.85	8.81	8.79
4	7.71	6.94	6.59	6.39	6.26	6.16	6.09	6.04	6.00	5.96
5	6.61	5.79	5.41	5.19	5.05	4.95	4.88	4.82	4.77	4.74
6	5.99	5.14	4.76	4.53	4.39	4.28	4.21	4.15	4.10	4.06
7	5.59	4.74	4.35	4.12	3.97	3.87	3.79	3.73	3.68	3.64
8	5.32	4.46	4.07	3.84	3.69	3.58	3.50	3.44	3.39	3.35
9	5.12	4.26	3.86	3.63	3.48	3.37	3.29	3.23	3.18	3.14
10	4.96	4.10	3.71	3.48	3.33	3.22	3.14	3.07	3.20	2.98
11	4.84	3.98	3.59	3.36	3.20	3.09	3.01	2.95	2.90	2.85
12	4.75	3.89	3.49	3.26	3.11	3.00	2.91	2.85	2.80	2.75
13	4.67	3.81	3.41	3.18	3.03	2.92	2.83	2.77	2.71	2.67
14	4.60	3.74	3.34	3.11	2.96	2.85	2.76	2.70	2.65	2.60
15	4.54	3.68	3.29	3.06	2.90	2.79	2.71	2.64	2.59	2.54
16	4.49	3.63	3.24	3.01	2.85	2.74	2.66	2.59	2.54	2.49
17	4.45	3.59	3.20	2.96	2.81	2.70	2.61	2.55	2.49	2.45
18	4.41	3.55	3.16	2.93	2.77	2.66	2.58	2.51	2.46	2.41
19	4.38	3.52	3.13	2.90	2.74	2.63	2.54	2.48	2.42	2.38
20	4.35	3.49	3.10	2.87	2.71	2.60	2.51	2.45	2.39	2.35
21	4.32	3.47	3.07	2.84	2.68	2.57	2.49	2.42	2.37	2.32
22	4.30	3.44	3.05	2.82	2.66	2.55	2.46	2.40	2.34	2.30
23	4.28	3.42	3.03	2.80	2.64	2.53	2.44	2.37	2.32	2.27
24	4.26	3.40	3.01	2.78	2.62	2.51	2.42	2.36	2.30	2.25
25	4.24	3.39	2.99	2.76	2.60	2.49	2.40	2.34	2.28	2.24
26	4.23	3.37	2.98	2.74	2.59	2.47	2.39	2.32	2.27	2.22
27	4.21	3.35	2.96	2.73	2.57	2.46	2.37	2.31	2.25	2.20
28	4.20	3.34	2.95	2.71	2.56	2.45	2.36	2.29	2.24	2.19
29	4.18	3.33	2.93	2.70	2.55	2.43	2.35	2.28	2.22	2.18
30	4.17	3.32	2.92	2.69	2.53	2.42	2.33	2.27	2.21	2.16
40	4.08	3.23	2.84	2.61	2.45	2.34	2.25	2.18	2.12	2.08
60	4.00	3.15	2.76	2.53	2.37	2.25	2.17	2.10	2.04	1.99
120	3.92	3.07	2.68	2.45	2.29	2.17	2.09	2.02	1.96	1.91
∞	3.84	3.00	2.60	2.37	2.21	2.10	2.01	1.94	1.88	1.83

*E.S. Pearson and H.O. Hartley. Biometrika tables for statisticians. New York: Cambridge University Press, 1966. Vol. I. By permission of the authors and publisher.

alpha = .05

V_1 V_2	12	15	20	24	30	40	60	120	∞
1	243.9	245.9	248.0	249.1	250.1	251.1	252.2	253.3	254.3
2	19.41	19.43	19.45	19.45	19.46	19.47	19.48	19.49	19.50
3	8.74	8.70	8.66	8.64	8.62	8.59	8.57	8.55	8.53
4	5.91	5.86	5.80	5.77	5.75	5.72	5.69	5.66	5.63
5	4.68	4.62	4.56	4.53	4.50	4.46	4.43	4.40	4.36
6	4.00	3.94	3.87	3.84	3.81	3.77	3.74	3.70	3.67
7	3.57	3.51	3.44	3.41	3.38	3.34	3.30	3.27	3.23
8	3.28	3.22	3.15	3.12	3.08	3.04	3.01	2.97	2.93
9	3.07	3.01	2.94	2.90	2.86	2.83	2.79	2.75	2.71
10	2.91	2.85	2.77	2.74	2.70	2.66	2.62	2.58	2.54
11	2.79	2.72	2.65	2.61	2.57	2.53	2.49	2.45	2.40
12	2.69	2.62	2.54	2.51	2.47	2.43	2.38	2.34	2.30
13	2.60	2.53	2.46	2.42	2.38	2.34	2.30	2.25	2.21
14	2.53	2.46	2.39	2.35	2.31	2.27	2.22	2.18	2.13
15	2.48	2.40	2.33	2.29	2.25	2.20	2.16	2.11	2.07
16	2.42	2.35	2.28	2.24	2.19	2.15	2.11	2.06	2.01
17	2.38	2.31	2.23	2.19	2.15	2.10	2.06	2.01	1.96
18	2.34	2.27	2.19	2.15	2.11	2.06	2.02	1.97	1.92
19	2.31	2.23	2.16	2.11	2.07	2.03	1.98	1.93	1.88
20	2.28	2.20	2.12	2.08	2.04	1.99	1.95	1.90	1.84
21	2.25	2.18	2.10	2.05	2.01	1.96	1.92	1.87	1.81
22	2.23	2.15	2.07	2.03	1.98	1.94	1.89	1.84	1.78
23	2.20	2.13	2.05	2.01	1.96	1.91	1.86	1.81	1.76
24	2.18	2.11	2.03	1.98	1.94	1.89	1.84	1.79	1.73
25	2.16	2.09	2.01	1.96	1.92	1.87	1.82	1.77	1.71
26	2.15	2.07	1.99	1.95	1.90	1.85	1.80	1.75	1.69
27	2.13	2.06	1.97	1.93	1.88	1.84	1.79	1.73	1.67
28	2.12	2.04	1.96	1.91	1.87	1.82	1.77	1.71	1.65
29	2.10	2.03	1.94	1.90	1.85	1.81	1.75	1.70	1.64
30	2.09	2.01	1.93	1.89	1.84	1.79	1.74	1.68	1.62
40	2.00	1.92	1.84	1.79	1.74	1.69	1.64	1.58	1.51
60	1.92	1.84	1.75	1.70	1.65	1.59	1.53	1.47	1.39
120	1.83	1.75	1.66	1.61	1.55	1.50	1.43	1.35	1.25
∞	1.75	1.67	1.57	1.52	1.46	1.39	1.32	1.22	1.00

alpha = .01

V_1 V_2	1	2	3	4	5	6	7	8	9	10
1	4052	4999.5	5403	5652	5764	5859	5928	5981	6022	6056
2	98.50	99.00	99.17	99.25	99.30	99.33	99.36	99.37	99.39	99.40
3	34.12	30.82	29.46	28.71	28.24	27.91	27.67	27.49	27.35	27.23
4	21.20	18.00	16.69	15.98	15.52	15.21	14.98	14.80	14.66	14.55
5	16.26	13.27	12.06	11.39	10.97	10.67	10.46	10.29	10.16	10.05
6	13.75	10.92	9.78	9.15	8.75	8.47	8.26	8.10	7.98	7.87
7	12.25	9.55	8.45	7.85	7.46	7.19	6.99	6.84	6.72	6.62
8	11.26	8.65	7.59	7.01	6.63	6.37	6.18	6.03	5.91	5.81
9	10.56	8.02	6.99	6.42	6.06	5.80	5.61	5.47	5.35	5.26
10	10.04	7.56	6.55	5.99	5.64	5.39	5.20	5.06	4.94	4.85
11	9.65	7.21	6.22	5.67	5.32	5.07	4.89	4.74	4.63	4.54
12	9.33	6.93	5.95	5.41	5.06	4.82	4.64	4.50	4.39	4.30
13	9.07	6.70	5.74	5.21	4.86	4.62	4.44	4.30	4.19	4.10
14	8.86	6.51	5.56	5.04	4.69	4.46	4.28	4.14	4.03	3.94
15	8.68	6.36	5.42	4.89	4.56	4.32	4.14	4.00	3.89	3.80
16	8.53	6.23	5.29	4.77	4.44	4.20	4.03	3.89	3.78	3.69
17	8.40	6.11	5.18	4.67	4.34	4.10	3.93	3.79	3.68	3.59
18	8.29	6.01	5.09	4.58	4.25	4.01	3.84	3.71	3.60	3.51
19	8.18	5.93	5.01	4.50	4.17	3.94	3.77	3.63	3.52	3.43
20	8.10	5.85	4.94	4.43	4.10	3.87	3.70	3.56	3.46	3.37
21	8.02	5.78	4.87	4.37	4.04	3.81	3.64	3.51	3.40	3.31
22	7.95	5.72	4.82	4.31	3.99	3.76	3.59	3.45	3.35	3.26
23	7.88	5.66	4.76	4.26	3.94	3.71	3.54	3.41	3.30	3.21
24	7.82	5.61	4.72	4.22	3.90	3.67	3.50	3.36	3.26	3.17
25	7.77	5.57	4.68	4.18	3.85	3.63	3.46	3.32	3.22	3.13
26	7.72	5.53	4.64	4.14	3.82	3.59	3.42	3.29	3.18	3.09
27	7.68	5.49	4.60	4.11	3.78	3.56	3.39	3.26	3.15	3.06
28	7.64	5.45	4.57	4.07	3.75	3.53	3.36	3.23	3.12	3.03
29	7.60	5.42	4.54	4.04	3.73	3.50	3.33	3.20	3.09	3.00
30	7.56	5.39	4.51	4.02	3.70	3.47	3.30	3.17	3.07	2.98
40	7.31	5.18	4.31	3.83	3.51	3.29	3.12	2.99	2.89	2.80
60	7.08	4.98	4.13	3.65	3.34	3.12	2.95	2.82	2.72	2.63
120	6.85	4.79	3.95	3.48	3.17	2.96	2.79	2.66	2.56	2.47
∞	6.63	4.61	3.78	3.32	3.02	2.80	2.64	2.51	2.41	2.32

alpha = .01

V_1 V_2	12	15	20	24	30	40	60	120	∞
1	6106	6157	6209	6235	6261	6287	6313	6339	6366
2	99.42	99.43	99.45	99.46	99.47	99.47	99.48	99.49	99.50
3	27.05	26.87	26.69	26.60	26.50	26.41	26.32	26.22	26.13
4	14.37	14.20	14.02	13.93	13.84	13.75	13.65	13.56	13.46
5	9.89	9.72	9.55	9.47	9.38	9.29	9.20	9.11	9.02
6	7.72	7.56	7.40	7.31	7.23	7.14	7.06	6.97	6.88
7	6.47	6.31	6.16	6.07	5.99	5.91	5.82	5.74	5.65
8	5.67	5.52	5.36	5.28	5.20	5.12	5.03	4.95	4.86
9	5.11	4.96	4.81	4.73	4.65	4.57	4.48	4.40	4.31
10	4.71	4.56	4.41	4.33	4.25	4.17	4.08	4.00	3.91
11	4.40	4.25	4.10	4.02	3.94	3.86	3.78	3.69	3.60
12	4.16	4.01	3.86	3.78	3.70	3.62	3.54	3.45	3.36
13	3.96	3.82	3.66	3.59	3.51	3.43	3.34	3.25	3.17
14	3.80	3.66	3.51	3.43	3.35	3.27	3.18	3.09	3.00
15	3.67	3.52	3.37	3.29	3.21	3.13	3.05	2.96	2.87
16	3.55	3.41	3.26	3.18	3.10	3.02	2.93	2.84	2.75
17	3.46	3.31	3.16	3.08	3.00	2.92	2.83	2.75	2.65
18	3.37	3.23	3.08	3.00	2.92	2.84	2.75	2.66	2.57
19	3.30	3.15	3.00	2.92	2.84	2.76	2.67	2.58	2.49
20	3.23	3.09	2.94	2.86	2.78	2.69	2.61	2.52	2.42
21	3.17	3.03	2.88	2.80	2.72	2.64	2.55	2.46	2.36
22	3.12	2.98	2.83	2.75	2.67	2.58	2.50	2.40	2.31
23	3.07	2.93	2.78	2.70	2.62	2.54	2.45	2.35	2.26
24	3.03	2.89	2.74	2.66	2.58	2.49	2.40	2.31	2.21
25	2.99	2.85	2.70	2.62	2.54	2.45	2.36	2.27	2.17
26	2.96	2.81	2.66	2.58	2.50	2.42	2.33	2.23	2.13
27	2.93	2.78	2.63	2.55	2.47	2.38	2.29	2.20	2.10
28	2.90	2.75	2.60	2.52	2.44	2.35	2.26	2.17	2.06
29	2.87	2.73	2.57	2.49	2.41	2.33	2.23	2.14	2.03
30	2.84	2.70	2.55	2.47	2.39	2.30	2.21	2.11	2.01
40	2.66	2.52	2.37	2.29	2.20	2.11	2.02	1.92	1.80
60	2.50	2.35	2.20	2.12	2.03	1.94	1.84	1.73	1.60
120	2.34	2.19	2.03	1.95	1.86	1.76	1.66	1.53	1.38
∞	2.18	2.04	1.88	1.79	1.70	1.59	1.47	1.32	1.00

Appendix D

Sources for selected sports skills tests

ARCHERY

American Association for Health, Physical Education and Recreation. 1967. Archery skills test manual. Washington, D.C.: AAHPER.

Bohn, R.W. 1962. An achievement test in archery, Unpublished master's thesis, The University of Wisconsin, Madison.

Hyde, E.I. 1937. An achievement scale in archery. Research Quarterly 8:109-116.

Shifflet, B., and Schuman, B. 1982. A criterion-referenced test for archery. Research Quarterly for Exercise and Sport 53:330-335.

Zabick, R.M., and Jackson, A.S. 1969. Reliability of archery achievement. Research Quarterly 40:254-255.

BADMINTON

French, E., and Stalter, E. 1949. Study of skill tests in badminton for college women. Research Quarterly 20:257-272.

Greiner, M.R. 1964. Construction of a short serve test for beginning badminton players. Master's thesis, The University of Wisconsin, Madison. (Microcard PE 670, University of Oregon, Eugene.)

Hale, P.A. 1970. Construction of a long serve test for beginning badminton players (singles). Master's thesis, The University of Wisconsin, Madison. (Microcard PE 1133, University of Oregon, Eugene.)

Hicks, J.V. 1967. The construction and evaluation of a battery of five badminton skill tests, Unpublished doctoral dissertation, Texas Women's University, Denton, Tex.

Johnson, B.L., and Nelson, J.K. 1979. Badminton smash test. In Practical measurements for evaluation in physical education. Minneapolis: Burgess Publishing Co.

Lockhart, A., and McPherson, F.A. 1949. The development of a test of badminton playing ability. Research Quarterly 20:402-405.

McDonald, E.D. 1968. The development of a skill test for the badminton high clear. Master's thesis, Southern Illinois University, Carbondale, Ill. (Microcard PE 1083, University of Oregon, Eugene.)

Miller, F.A. 1951. A badminton wall volley test. Research Quarterly 22:208-213.

Poole, J., and Nelson, J. 1970. Construction of a badminton skills test battery, Unpublished manuscript, Louisiana State University, Baton Rouge.

Scott, M.G. 1941. Achievement examinations in badminton. Research Quarterly 12:242-253.

Scott, M.G., and Fox, M. 1959. Long serve test. In Measurement and evaluation in physical education. Dubuque, Iowa: Wm C Brown Group.

Thorpe, J., and West, C. 1969. A test of game sense in badminton. Perceptual and Motor Skills 28:159-169.

BASEBALL

Kelson, R.E. 1953. Baseball classification plan for boys. Research Quarterly 24:304-309.

Rodgers, E.G., and Heath, M.L. 1931. An experiment in the use of knowledge and skill tests in playground baseball. Research Quarterly 2:113-131.

BASKETBALL

American Association for Health, Physical Education and Recreation. 1966. Basketball skills test manual for boys. Washington, D.C.: AAHPER.

American Association for Health, Physical Education and Recreation. 1966. Basketball skills test manual for girls. Washington, D.C.: AAHPER.

Barrow, H.M. 1959. Basketball skill test. The Physical Educator 16:26.

Dyer, J.T., Schurig, J.C., and Apgar, S.L. 1939. A basketball motor ability test for college women and secondary school girls. Research Quarterly 10:128-147.

Edgren, H.D. 1932. An experiment in the testing of ability and progress in basketball. Research Quarterly 3:159-171.

Glassow, R.B., Colvin, V., and Schwartz, M.M. 1938. Studies measuring basketball playing ability of college women. Research Quarterly 9:60-68.

Hopkins, D.R. 1977. Factor analysis of selected basketball skill test. Research Quarterly 48:535-540.

Hopkins, D.R., Shick, J. and Plack, J.J. 1984. Basketball for boys and girls: skills test manual. Reston, Va.: American Alliance for Health, Physical Education, Recreation and Dance.

Johnson, L.W. 1976. Objective tests in basketball for high school boys. In Clarke, H.H. Application of measurement to health and physical education. Englewood Cliffs, N.J.: Prentice-Hall, Inc.

Kay, H.K. 1966. A statistical analysis of the profile technique for the evaluation of competitive basketball performance, Unpublished master's thesis, University of Alberta, Edmonton, Canada.

Knox, R.K. 1947. Basketball ability tests. Scholastic Coach 17:45.

Lambert, A.T. 1969. A basketball skill test for college women, Unpublished master's thesis, University of North Carolina, Greensboro.

Latchaw, M. 1954. Measuring selected motor skills in fourth, fifth, and sixth grades. Research Quarterly 25:439-499.

Lehsten, N. 1948. A measure of basketball skills in high school boys. The Physical Educator 4:103-106.

Leilich, A. 1980. Leilich basketball test. In Barrow, H.M., and R., McGee. A practical approach to measurement in physical education, ed. 3, Philadelphia: Lea & Febiger.

Miller, W.K. 1954. Achievement levels in basketball skills for women physical education majors. Research Quarterly 25:450-455.

Schwartz, H. 1937. Knowledge and achievement tests in girls' basketball on the senior high school level. Research Quarterly 8:152-156.

Stroup, F. 1955. Game results as a criterion for validating basketball skill tests. Research Quarterly 26:353-357.

Thornes, M.B. 1963. An analysis of a basketball shooting test and its relation to other basketball skill tests. Master's thesis, The University of Wisconsin, Madison. (Microcard PE 694, University of Oregon, Eugene.)

Young, G., and Moser, H. 1934. A short battery of tests to measure playing ability in women's basketball. Research Quarterly 5:3-23.

BOWLING

Martin, J.L. 1960. Bowling norms for college men and women. Research Quarterly 31:113-116.

Martin, J., and Keogh, J. 1964. Bowling norms for college students in elective physical education classes. Research Quarterly **35**:325-327.

Olson, J.K., and Liba, M.R. 1967. A device for evaluating spot bowling ability. Research Quarterly **38**:193-210.

Phillips, M., and Summers, D. 1950. Bowling norms and learning curves for college women. Research Quarterly **21**:377-385.

Schunk, C. 1969. Test questions for bowling. Philadelphia: W.B. Saunders Co.

FENCING

Bowar, M.G. 1961. A test of general fencing ability, Unpublished master's thesis, University of Southern California, Los Angeles.

Cooper, C.K. 1968. The development of a fencing skill test for measuring achievement of beginning collegiate women fencers in using the advance, beat, and lunge. Unpublished master's thesis, Western Illinois University, Macomb.

Fein, J.T. 1964. Construction of skill tests for beginning collegiate women fencers, Unpublished master's thesis, University of Iowa, Iowa City.

Safrit, M.J. 1962. Construction of a skill test for beginning fencers, Unpublished master's thesis, The University of Wisconsin, Madison.

Schutz, J.K. 1940. Construction of an achievement scale in fencing for women, Unpublished master's thesis, University of Washington, Seattle.

Wyrick, W. 1958. A comparison of the effectiveness of two methods of teaching beginning fencing to college women, Unpublished master's thesis, The Woman's College of the University of North Carolina, Greensboro.

FIELD HOCKEY

Chapman, N.L. 1982. Chapman ball control test-field hockey. Research Quarterly for Exercise and Sport **53**:239-242.

Friedel, J.W. 1956. The development of a field hockey skill test for high school girls. Master's thesis, Illinois State University, Normal. (Microcard PE 289, University of Oregon, Eugene.)

Illner, J.A. 1968. The construction and validation of a skill test for the drive in field hockey. Master's thesis, Southern Illinois University, Carbondale. (Microcard PE 1075, University of Oregon, Eugene.)

Perry, E.L. 1969. An investigation of field hockey skills tests for college women, Unpublished master's thesis, Pennsylvania State University, University Park.

Schmithals, M., and French, E. 1940. Achievement tests in field hockey for college women. Research Quarterly **11**:84-92.

Strait, C.J. 1960. The construction and evaluation of a field hockey skills test, Unpublished master's thesis, Smith College, Northampton, Mass.

FOOTBALL

American Association for Health, Physical Education and Recreation. 1960. Football skills test manual. Washington, D.C.: AAHPER.

Borleske, S.E. 1937. Achievement of college men in touch football. In F.W. Cozens, editor. Ninth annual report of the committee on curriculum research of the college physical education association. Research Quarterly **8**:73-78.

McElroy, H.N 1938. A report on some experimentation with a skill test. Research Quarterly **9**:83-88.

GOLF

Brown, H.S. 1969. A test battery for evaluating golf skills. Texas Association for Health, Physical Education and Recreation Journal, pp. 4-5, 28-29.

Clevett, M.A. 1931. An experiment in teaching methods of golf. Research Quarterly 2:104-112.

Cochrane, J.F. 1960. The construction of indoor golf skills test as a measure of golfing ability, Unpublished master's thesis, University of Minnesota, Minneapolis.

Cotten, D., Thomas, J.R., and Plaster, T. 1972. A plastic ball test for golf iron skill, Unpublished study presented at the American Association for Health, Physical Education and Recreation Convention Houston, March 1972.

McKee, M.E. 1950. A test for the full swinging shot in golf. Research Quarterly 21:40-46.

Nelson, J.K. 1979. An achievement test in golf. In Johnson, B.L., and Nelson, J.K. Practical measurements for evaluation in physical education. Minneapolis: Burgess Publishing Co.

Shick, J., and Berg, N. 1983. Indoor golf skill test for junior high school boys. Research Quarterly for Exercise and Sport 54:75-78.

Vanderhoof, E.R. 1956. Beginning golf achievement tests. Master's thesis, State University of Iowa, Iowa City. (Microcard PE 306, University of Oregon, Eugene.)

Watts, H. 1942. Construction and evaluation of a target on testing the approach shot in golf. Unpublished master's thesis, The University of Wisconsin, Madison.

West, C., and Thorpe, J. 1968. Construction and validation of an eight-iron approach test. Research Quarterly 39:1115-1120.

GYMNASTICS

Bowers, C.O. 1965. Gymnastics skill test for beginning to low intermediate girls and women. Master's thesis, The Ohio State University, Columbus. (Microcard PE 734, University of Oregon, Eugene.)

Faulkner, J., and Loken, N. 1962. Objectivity of judging at the national collegiate athletic association gymnastic meet: a ten-year follow-up study. Research Quarterly 33:485-486.

HANDBALL

Cornish, C. 1949. A study of measurement of ability in handball. Research Quarterly 20:215-222.

Griffith, M.A. 1960. An objective method of evaluating ability in handball singles, Unpublished master's thesis, The Ohio State University, Columbus.

Montoye, H.J., and Brotzmann, J. 1951. An investigation of the validity of using the results of a doubles tournament as a measure of handball ability. Research Quarterly 22:214-218.

Pennington, G.G., and others. (1967). A measure of handball ability. Research Quarterly 38:247-253.

ICE HOCKEY

Merrifield, H.H., and Walford, G.A. 1969. Battery of ice hockey skill tests. Research Quarterly 40:146-152.

ICE SKATING

Carriere, D.L. 1969. An objective figure skating test for use in beginning classes, Unpublished master's thesis, University of Illinois, Urbana.

Leaming, T.W. 1959. A measure of endurance of young speed skaters, Unpublished master's thesis, University of Illinois, Urbana.

Recknagel, D. 1945. A test for beginners in figure skating. Journal of Health and Physical Education 26:91-92.

LACROSSE

Hodges, C.V. 1967. Construction of an objective knowledge test and skill tests in lacrosse for college women. Master's thesis, University of North Carolina, Greensboro. (Microcard PE 1074, University of Oregon, Eugene.)

Lutze, M.C. 1963. Achievement tests in beginning lacrosse for women, Unpublished master's thesis, State University of Iowa, Iowa City.

Wilke, B.J. 1967. Achievement tests for selected lacrosse skills of college women, Unpublished master's thesis, University of North Carolina, Greensboro.

RACQUETBALL

Hensley, L.D., East, W.B. and Stillwell, J.L. 1979. A racquetball skills test. Research Quarterly 50:114-118.

Karpman, M., and Isaacs, L.D. 1979. An improved racquetball skills test. Research Quarterly 50:526-527.

SKIING

Rogers, H.M. 1960. Construction of objectively scored skill tests for beginning skiers, Unpublished master's thesis, University of Colorado, Boulder.

Wolfe, J.E., and Merrifield, H.H. Predictability of beginning skiing success from basic skill tests in college age females, Paper presented at the National American Association for Health, Physical Education and Recreation Convention in Detroit, April, 1971.

SOCCER

Bailey, C.I., and Teller, F.L. 1969. Test questions for soccer. Philadelphia: W.B. Saunders Co.

Bontz, J. 1942. An experiment in the construction of a test for measuring ability in some of the fundamental skills used by fifth and sixth grade children in soccer, Unpublished master's thesis, State University of Iowa, Iowa City.

Heath, M.L., and Rodgers, E.G. 1932. A study in the use of knowledge and skill tests in soccer. Research Quarterly 3:33-43.

Johnson, J.R. 1963. The development of a single-item test as a measure of soccer skill. Microcarded master's thesis, University of British Columbia, Vancouver.

McDonald, L.G. 1951. The construction of a kicking skill test as an index of general soccer ability, Unpublished master's thesis, Springfield College, Springfield, Mass.

McElroy, H.N. 1938. A report on some experimentation with a skill test. Research Quarterly 9:82-88.

Mitchell, J.R. 1980. Mitchell modification of the McDonald soccer skill test. In Barrow, H.M., and McGee, R. A practical approach to measurement in physical education, ed. 3, Philadelphia: Lea & Febiger.

Schaufele, E.F. 1980. Schaufele soccer volleying test. In Barrow, H.M., and McGee, R. A practical approach to measurement in physical education, ed. 3, Philadelphia: Lea & Febiger.

Tomlinson, R. 1964. Soccer skill test. Soccer-speedball guide—July 1964-July 1966. Washington, D.C.: Division of Girls and Women's Sports, American Association for Health, Physical Education and Recreation.

Warner, G.F.H. 1950. Warner soccer test. Newsletter of the National Soccer Coaches Association of America **6**:13-22.

Whitney, A.H., and Chapin, H. 1946. Soccer skill testing for girls. Soccer-speedball guide—July 1946-July 1948. Washington, D.C.: National Section on Women's Athletics, American Association for Health, Physical Education and Recreation.

SOFTBALL

American Association for Health, Physical Education and Recreation. 1967. Softball skills test manual for boys. Washington, D.C.: AAHPER.

American Association for Health, Physical Education and Recreation. 1967. Softball skills test manual for girls. Washington, D.C.: AAHPER.

Broer, M.R. 1958. Reliability of certain skill tests for junior high school girls. Research Quarterly **29**:139-143.

Davis, R. 1959. The development of an objective softball batting test for college women. In Scott, M.G., and French, E. Measurement and evaluation in physical education. Dubuque, Iowa: Wm C Brown Group.

Dexter, G. 1957. Checklist for rating softball batting skills. Teachers guide to physical education for girls in high school. Sacramento, Calif.: California State Department of Education.

Elrod, J.M. 1969. Construction of a softball skill test battery for high school boys, Unpublished master's thesis, Louisiana State University, Baton Rouge.

Fox, M.G., and Young, O.G. 1954. A test of softball batting ability. Research Quarterly **25**:26-27.

Fringer, M.N. 1980. Fringer softball battery. In Barrow H.M., and McGee, R. A practical approach to measurement in physical education, ed. 2, Philadelphia: Lea & Febiger.

Kehtel, C.H. 1958. The development of a test to measure the ability of a softball player to field a ground ball and successfully throw it at a target, Unpublished master's thesis, University of Colorado, Boulder.

O'Donnell, D.J. 1960. Validation of softball skill tests for high school girls, Unpublished master's thesis, Indiana University, Bloomington.

Research Committee, Central Association for Physical Education of College Women. 1959. Fielding test. In Scott, M.G., and French, E. Measurement and evaluation in physical education. Dubuque, Iowa: Wm C Brown Group.

Safrit, M.J. 1974. Wisconsin softball pitching test: summative evaluation. Softball guide: January, 1974-January, 1976. Washington D.C.: Division of Girls' and Women's Sports, American Association for Health, Physical Education and Recreation.

Safrit, M.J., and Pavis, A. 1969. Overarm throw skill testing. In Felshin, J., and O'Brien, C., editors. Selected softball articles. Washington, D.C.: Division of Girls' and Women's Sports, American Association for Health, Physical Education and Recreation.

Scott, M.G., and French, E. 1959. Softball repeated throws test. In Scott, M.G., and French, E. Measurement and evaluation in physical education. Dubuque, Iowa: Wm C Brown Group.

Shick, J. 1970. Battery of defensive softball skills tests for college women. Research Quarterly **41**:82-87.

Sopa, A. 1967. Construction of an indoor batting skills test for junior high school girls, Unpublished master's thesis, The University of Wisconsin, Madison.

Thomas, J. 1947. Skill tests. In Softball-volleyball guide—July 1947-July 1949. Washington, D.C.: National Section on Women's Athletics, American Association for Health, Physical Education and Recreation.

SPEEDBALL

Buchanan, R.E. 1942. A study of achievement tests in speedball for high school girls, Unpublished master's thesis, State University of Iowa, Iowa City.

Smith, G. 1980. Speedball skills tests for college women. In Barrow, H.M., McGee, R. A practical approach to measurement in physical education, ed. 3, Philadelphia: Lea & Febiger.

STUNTS AND TUMBLING

Cotteral, B., and Cotteral, D. 1936. Scale for judging quality of performance in stunts and tumbling. The teaching of stunts and tumbling. New York: The Ronald Press Co.

Edwards, V.M. 1969. Test questions for tumbling. Philadelphia: W.B. Saunders Co.

SWIMMING AND DIVING

Bennett, L.M. 1942. A test of diving for use in beginning classes. Research Quarterly **13**:109-115.

Chapman, P.A. 1965. A comparison of three methods of measuring swimming stroke proficiency. Master's thesis, The University of Wisconsin, Madison. (Microcard PE 738, University of Oregon, Eugene.)

Fox, M.G. 1957. Swimming power test. Research Quarterly **28**:233-237.

Fried, C.R. 1983. An examination of the test characteristics of the 12-minute aerobic swim test, Unpublished master's thesis, University of Wisconsin, Madison.

Hewitt, J.E. 1948. Swimming achievement scales for college men. Research Quarterly **19**:282-289.

Hewitt, J.E. 1949. Swimming achievement scale scores for high school swimming. Research Quarterly **20**:170-179.

Jackson, A., Jackson, A.S., and Frankiewiez, R.G. 1979. The construct and concurrent validity of a 12-minute crawl stroke swim as a field test of swimming endurance. Research Quarterly for Exercise and Sport **50**:641-648.

Jackson, A.S., and Pettinger, J. 1969. The development and discriminant analysis of swimming profiles of college men. Proceedings of the 72nd annual meeting, National College Physical Education Association for Men.

Munt, M.R. 1964. Development of an objective test to measure the efficiency of the front crawl for college women, Unpublished master's thesis, The University of Michigan, Ann Arbor.

Rosentswieg, J.A. 1968. A revision of the power swimming test. Research Quarterly **39**:818-819.

Wilson, C.T. 1934. Coordination tests in swimming. Research Quarterly **5**:81-88.

Wilson, M.R. 1971. Wilson achievement test for intermediate swimming. In Barrow, H.M., and McGee, R., editors. A practical approach to measurement in physical education, ed. 2, Philadelphia: Lea & Febiger.

TABLE TENNIS

Mott, J.A., and Lockhart, A. 1946. Table tennis backboard test. Journal of Health and Physical Education **17:**550-552.

TENNIS

Avery, C.A., Richardson, P.A., and Jackson, A.W. 1979. A practical tennis serve test: measurement of skill under simulated game conditions. Research Quarterly for Exercise and Sport **50:**554-564.

Avery, C., Richardson, P., and Jackson, A. 1981. Response to McGhee's discussion. Research Quarterly for Exercise and Sport **52:**296-297.

Benton, R. 1963. Teaching tennis by testing. In Davis, D., editor. Selected tennis and badminton articles. Washington, D.C.: Division of Girls' and Women's Sports, American Association for Health, Physical Education and Recreation.

Broer, M.R., and Miller, D.M. 1950. Achievement tests for beginning and intermediate tennis. Research Quarterly **21:**301-313.

Cobane, E. 1962. Test for the service. In Tennis and badminton guide—June 1962-June 1964. Washington, D.C.: Division of Girls' and Women's Sports, American Association for Health, Physical Education and Recreation.

DiGennaro, J. 1969. Construction of forehand drive, backhand drive, and service tennis tests. Research Quarterly **40:**496-501.

Dyer, J.T. 1938. Revision of the backboard test of tennis ability. Research Quarterly **9:**25-31.

Edwards, J. 1965. A study of three measures of the tennis serve. Master's thesis, The University of Wisconsin, Madison. (Microcard PE 746, University of Oregon, Eugene.)

Felshin, J., and Spencer, E. 1963. Evaluation procedures for tennis. In Davis, D., editor. Selected tennis and badminton articles. Washington, D.C.: Division of Girls' and Women's Sports, American Association for Health, Physical Education and Recreation.

Fox, K. 1953. A study of the validity of the Dyer backboard test and the Miller forehand-backhand test for beginning tennis players. Research Quarterly **24:**1-8.

Hewitt, J.E. 1965. Revision of the Dyer backboard tennis test. Research Quarterly **36:**153-157.

Hewitt, J.E. 1966. Hewitt's tennis achievement test. Research Quarterly **37:**231-236.

Hewitt, J.E. 1968. Classification tests in tennis. Research Quarterly **39:**552-555.

Hubbell, N.C. 1960. A battery of tennis skill tests for college women, Unpublished master's thesis, Texas Women's University, Denton.

Hulac, G.M. 1971. Hulac rating scale for the tennis serve. In Barrow, H.M., and McGhee, R., editors. A practical approach to measurement in physical education, ed. 2, Philadelphia: Lea & Febiger.

Hulbert, B.A. 1966. A study of tests for the forehand drive in tennis. Master's thesis, The University of Wisconsin, Madison. (Microcard PE 818, University of Oregon, Eugene.)

Johnson, J. 1957. Tennis serve of advanced women players. Research Quarterly **28:**123-131.

Johnson, J. 1963. Tennis knowledge test. In Davis, D., editor. Selected tennis and badminton articles. Washington, D.C.: Division of Girls' and Women's Sports, American Association for Health, Physical Education and Recreation.

Kemp, J., and Vincent, M.F. 1968. Kemp-Vincent rally test of tennis skill. Research Quarterly **39:**1000-1004.

Malinak, N.R. 1961. The construction of an objective measure of accuracy in the performance of the tennis serve, Unpublished master's thesis, University of Illinois, Urbana.

McGhee, R. 1981. Discussion of "A practical tennis serve test: measurement of skill under simulated game conditions." Research Quarterly for Exercise and Sport **52**:294-295.

Purcell, K. 1981. A tennis forehand-backhand drive skill test which measures ball control and stroke firmness. Research Quarterly for Exercise and Sport **52**:238-245.

Ronning, H.E. 1959. Wall tests for evaluating tennis ability. Master's thesis, Washington State University, Pullman. (Microcard PE 441, University of Oregon, Eugene.)

Scott, M.G. 1941. Achievement examinations for elementary and intermediate tennis classes. Research Quarterly **7**:40-49.

Scott, M.G. and French, E. 1959. Scott-French revision of the Dyer wallboard test. In Scott, M.G., and French, E. Measurement and evaluation in physical education. Dubuque, Iowa: Wm C Brown Group.

Shepard, G.J. 1972. The tennis drive skills test. Tennis-badminton-squash guide. Washington, D.C.: Division of Girls' and Women's Sports, American Association for Health, Physical Education and Recreation.

VOLLEYBALL

American Association for Health, Physical Education and Recreation. 1967. Volleyball skills test manual. Washington, D.C.: American Association for Health, Physical Education and Recreation.

Bassett, G., Glassow, R.B., and Locke, M. 1937. Studies in testing volleyball skills. Research Quarterly **8**:60-72.

Blackman, C.J. 1968. The development of a volleyball test for the spike, Unpublished master's thesis, Southern Illinois University, Carbondale.

Brady, C.F. 1945. Preliminary investigation of volleyball playing ability. Research Quarterly **16**:14-17.

Broer, M.A. 1958. Reliability of certain skill tests for junior high school girls. Research Quarterly **29**:139-145.

Brumbach, W.B. 1979. Brumbach service test. In Johnson, B.L. and Nelson, J.K. Practical measurements for evaluation in physical education. Minneapolis: Burgess Publishing Co.

Clifton, M. 1962. Single hit volley test for women's volleyball. Research Quarterly **33**:208-211.

Crogan, C. 1943. A simple volleyball classification test for high school girls. The Physical Educator **4**:34-37.

Cunningham, P., and Garrison, J. 1968. High wall volley test for women. Research Quarterly **39**:486-490.

French, E.L., and Cooper, B.I. 1937. Achievement tests in volleyball for high school girls. Research Quarterly **8**:150-157.

Helmen, R.M. 1971. Development of power volleyball skill tests for college women. Paper presented at the Research Section of the 1971 American Association for Health, Physical Education and Recreation National Convention, Detroit.

Jackson, P.L. 1966. A rating scale for discriminating relative playing performance of skilled female volleyball players. Master's thesis, University of Alberta, Edmonton, Canada. (Microcard PE 931. University of Oregon, Eugene.)

Kessler, A. 1968. The validity and reliability of the Sandefur volleyball spiking test, Unpublished master's thesis, California State College, Long Beach.

Kronqvist, R.A., and Brumbach, W.B. 1968. A modification of the Brady volleyball skill test for high school boys. Research Quarterly **39**:116-120.

Latchaw, M. 1954. Measuring selected motor skills in fourth, fifth, and sixth grades. Research Quarterly **25**:439-449.

Liba, M.R., and Stauff, M.R. 1963. A test for the volleyball pass. Research Quarterly **34**:56-63.

Londeree, B.R., and Eicholtz, E.C. 1970. Reliabilities of selected volleyball skill tests. Paper presented at the Research Section of the 1970 American Association for Health, Physical Education Recreation National Convention, Seattle.

Lopez, D. 1957. Serve test. In Volleyball guide—July 1957-July 1959. Washington, D.C.: Division of Girls' and Women's Sport, American Association for Health, Physical Education and Recreation.

Mohr, D.R., and Haverstick, M.J. 1955. Repeated volleys tests for women's volleyball. Research Quarterly **26**:179-184.

Russell, N., and Lange, E. 1940. Achievement tests in volleyball for junior high school girls. Research Quarterly **11**:33-41.

Ryan, M.F. 1969. A study of tests for the volleyball serve. Master's thesis, The University of Wisconsin, Madison. (Microcard PE 1040, University of Oregon, Eugene.)

Slaymaker, T., and Brown, V.H. 1969. Test questions for power volleyball. Philadelphia: W.B. Saunders Co.

Snavely, M. 1960. Volleyball skill tests for girls. In Lockhart, A. editor. Selected volleyball articles. Washington, D.C.: Division of Girls' and Women's Sports, American Association for Health, Physical Education and Recreation.

Thorpe, J., and West, C. 1967. A volleyball skills chart with attainment levels for selected skills. Volleyball guide—July 1967-July 1969. Washington, D.C.: Division of Girls' and Women's Sports, American Association for Health, Physical Education and Recreation.

Watkins, A. 1960. Skill testing for large groups. In Lockhart, A., editor. Selected volleyball articles. Washington, D.C.: Division of Girls' and Women's Sports, American Association for Health, Physical Education and Recreation.

West, C. 1957. A comparative study between height and wall volley test scores as related to volleyball playing ability of girls and women, Unpublished master's thesis, The Women's College of the University of North Carolina, Greensboro.

WRESTLING

Sickels, W.L. 1980. Sickels amateur wrestling ability rating form. In Barrow, H.M., and McGee, R. A practical approach to measurement in physical education, ed. 3, Philadelphia: Lea & Febiger.

Yetter, H. 1963. A test of wrestling aptitude: a preliminary explanation, Unpublished master's thesis, University of Wisconsin, Madison.

Appendix E—Programs for Apple IIe Computer

(1) SFCALC PROGRAM*

Input data: Name, age, weight, and three skinfold measures
        Males: chest, abdomen, and thigh
        Females: triceps, thigh, and suprailium
Output data: Percent body fat and ideal weight
    LIST

```
10   REM PROGRAM "SFCALC"
20   REM
30   REM PROGRAMMED BY TERRY M. WOOD
40   REM
50   REM DEPARTMENT OF PHYSICAL EDUCATION
60   REM UNIVERSITY OF WISCONSIN, MADISON
70   REM
80   REM COPYRIGHT 1982
85   REM
86   REM THIS PROGRAM ASSUMES A PRINTER IN SLOT #1
87   REM
90   HOME
100  VTAB (6)
110  PRINT TAB( 8)"SKINFOLD-CALC: A PROGRAM"
120  VTAB (8)
130  PRINT TAB( 5)"TO CALCULATE PERCENT BODY FAT"
140  VTAB (10)
150  PRINT TAB( 10)"AND IDEAL BODY WEIGHT"
160  VTAB (13)
170  PRINT TAB( 13) "COPYRIGHT, 1982"
180  VTAB (15)
190  PRINT TAB( 4)"TERRY WOOD, DEPT. OF P.E. AND DANCE"
200  VTAB (17)
210  PRINT TAB( 5)"UNIVERSITY OF WISCONSIN-MADISON"
220  VTAB (20)
230  INPUT "DO YOU WISH TO CONTINUE? 1=YES 2=NO ";CTN
240  IF CTN = 1 THEN GOTO 290
250  IF CTN = 2 THEN GOTO 1740
260  PRINT
270  PRINT "THAT WAS NOT A 1 OR A 2!"
280  GOTO 230
290  HOME
```

---

*The SFCALC program is reproduced by permission of Terry M. Wood, Ph.D., Department of Physical Education, Oregon State University, Corvallis.

```
300   VTAB (4)
310   PRINT "SKINFOLD-CALC IS AN INTERACTIVE PROGRAM."
320   PRINT "WHEN THE PROGRAM ASKS YOU TO SUPPLY"
330   PRINT "INFORMATION, TYPE IN THE APPROPRIATE"
340   PRINT "RESPONSE AND THEN PRESS 'RETURN'."
350   VTAB (11)
360   INPUT "DO YOU WISH TO CONTINUE? 1=YES 2=NO ";CTN
370   IF CTN = 1 THEN GOTO 420
380   IF CTN = 2 THEN GOTO 1740
390   PRINT
400   PRINT "THAT WAS NOT A 1 OR A 2!"
410   GOTO 360
420   HOME
430   VTAB (4)
440   INPUT "HOW MANY SUBJECTS ARE IN YOUR SAMPLE?  ";N
450   IF N > = 1 THEN GOTO 500
460   PRINT
470   PRINT "SINCE THERE ARE NO SUBJECTS, THIS RUN"
480   PRINT "IS TERMINATED!"
490   GOTO 1730
500   HOME
510   VTAB (4)
520   PRINT "DATA MUST BE FROM MALES OR FROM FEMALES,"
530   PRINT "BUT NOT FROM BOTH."
540   PRINT "ARE YOUR SUBJECTS MALES OR FEMALES?"
550   INPUT "1=MALES 2=FEMALES ";SEX
560   IF (SEX = 1) OR (SEX = 2) THEN GOTO 600
570   PRINT
580   PRINT "THAT WAS NOT A 1 OR A 2!"
590   GOTO 540
600   HOME
610   VTAB (4)
620   PRINT "WHEN CALCULATING IDEAL BODY WEIGHT WHAT"
630   PRINT "PERCENT BODY FAT WILL YOU CONSIDER"
640   PRINT "NORMAL FOR YOUR POPULATION? YOU MUST"
650   PRINT "TYPE A NUMBER GREATER THAN ZERO."
660   PRINT "FOR EXAMPLE, TYPE A 23 IF YOU WANT 23"
670   PRINT "PERCENT."
680   PRINT
690   INPUT "WHAT PERCENT DO YOU WANT?  ";PCF
700   IF PCF > 0 THEN GOTO 740
710   PRINT
720   PRINT "THE NUMBER MUST BE GREATER THAN ZERO!"
730   GOTO 690
740   HOME
750   VTAB (4)
```

```
760   PRINT "NEXT YOU MUST INPUT THE DATA FOR EACH"
770   PRINT "SUBJECT SEPARATELY. TO DO THIS TYPE IN"
780   PRINT "THE SUBJECT'S FULL NAME, AGE (YEARS),"
790   PRINT "WEIGHT (LBS.), AND THREE SKINFOLD"
800   PRINT "MEASURES ON SEPARATE LINES."
810   PRINT "PRESS 'RETURN' AFTER EACH LINE."
820   PRINT "SKINFOLD MEASURES MUST BE CHEST, ABDOMEN,"
830   PRINT "AND THIGH FOR MALES AND TRICEPS,"
840   PRINT "THIGH, AND SUPRAILIUM FOR FEMALES."
850   PRINT "THE COMPUTER WILL 'BEEP' TO LET YOU "
860   PRINT "KNOW WHEN TO START TYPING THE NEXT": PRINT "LINE
      OF DATA."
870   PRINT "PLEASE LIMIT THE NAME FOR EACH SUBJECT": PRINT "TO
      18 CHARACTERS INCLUDING SPACES."
880   PRINT
890   INPUT "TO START DATA INPUT TYPE A 1 AND PRESS 'RETURN' ";CTN
900   IF CTN = 1 GOTO 940
910   PRINT
920   PRINT "THAT WAS NOT A 1!"
930   GOTO 890
940   S = - 16336
950   PRINT
960   DIM NAME$(N) ,AGE(N) ,WT(N) ,ASF(N) ,BSF(N) ,CSF(N)
970   IF SEX = 2 GOTO 1190
980   FOR I = 1 TO N
990   GOSUB 1690
1000  PRINT "NAME FOR SUBJECT #";I
1010  INPUT NAME$(I): PRINT
1020  GOSUB 1690
1030  PRINT "AGE (YEARS) FOR SUBJECT #";I
1040  INPUT AGE(I): PRINT
1050  GOSUB 1690
1060  PRINT "WEIGHT (LBS.) FOR SUBJECT #";I
1070  INPUT WT(I): PRINT
1080  GOSUB 1690
1090  PRINT "CHEST SKINFOLD FOR SUBJECT #";I
1100  INPUT ASF(I): PRINT
1110  GOSUB 1690
1120  PRINT "ABDOMEN SKINFOLD FOR SUBJECT #";I
1130  INPUT BSF(I): PRINT
1140  GOSUB 1690
1150  PRINT "THIGH SKINFOLD FOR SUBJECT #";I
1160  INPUT CSF(I): PRINT
1170  NEXT I
1180  GOTO 1390
```

```
1190   FOR I = 1 TO N
1200   GOSUB 1690
1210   PRINT "NAME FOR SUBJECT #";I
1220   INPUT NAME$(I): PRINT
1230   GOSUB 1690
1240   PRINT "AGE (YEARS) FOR SUBJECT #";I
1250   INPUT AGE(I): PRINT
1260   GOSUB 1690
1270   PRINT "WEIGHT (LBS.) FOR SUBJECT #";I
1280   INPUT WT(I): PRINT
1290   GOSUB 1690
1300   PRINT "TRICEPS SKINFOLD FOR SUBJECT #";I
1310   INPUT ASF(I): PRINT
1320   GOSUB 1690
1330   PRINT "THIGH SKINFOLD FOR SUBJECT #";I
1340   INPUT BSF(I): PRINT
1350   GOSUB 1690
1360   PRINT "SUPRAILIUM SKINFOLD FOR SUBJECT #";I
1370   INPUT CSF(I): PRINT
1380   NEXT I
1390   HOME
1395   VTAB (4): PRINT "DON'T FORGET TO TURN YOUR PRINTER ON!":
       PRINT : PRINT "PRESS ANY KEY TO START PRINTING"
1396   GET CC$
1400   PR# 1
1405   PRINT CHR$ (9);"8ON"
1410   VTAB (4)
1415   PRINT : PRINT
1420   PRINT "HERE ARE THE RESULTS FOR YOUR SUBJECTS."
1430   PRINT : PRINT "THE DATA INPUT FOR EACH SUBJECT WERE: ":
       PRINT
1440   PRINT "NAME";: HTAB 30: PRINT "AGE";: POKE 36,40: PRINT
       "WEIGHT";: POKE 36,50: PRINT "SF1";: POKE 36,57: PRINT "SF2";:
       POKE 36,64: PRINT "SF3"
1450   PRINT
1460   FOR I = 1 TO N: PRINT NAME$(I);: HTAB 31: PRINT AGE(I);: POKE 36,4
       1: PRINT WT(I);: POKE 36,50: PRINT ASF (I);: POKE 36,57: PRINT BSF(I);:
       POKE 36,64: PRINT CSF(I)
1470   NEXT I
1480   PRINT : PRINT : PRINT "THE % BODY FAT AND IDEAL WEIGHT FOR
       EACH SUBJECT ARE:": PRINT
1490   PRINT "NAME";: HTAB 30: PRINT "% BODY FAT";: POKE 36,50: PRINT
       "IDEAL WT.": PRINT
1500   IF SEX = 2 GOTO 1600
1510   FOR J = 1 TO N
```

```
1520   SUM = 0
1530   SUM = ASF(J) + BSF(J) + CSF(J)
1540   BD = 1.10938 - 0.0008267 * SUM + 0.0000016 * SUM ^ 2 - 0.0002574 *
       AGE(J)
1550   FT = (4.95 / BD - 4.5) * 100
1560   WEIGHT = (WT(J) - (WT(J) * FT) / 100) / (1 - PCF / 100)
1570   PRINT NAME$(J);: HTAB 30: PRINT FT;: POKE 36,50: PRINT WEIGHT
1580   NEXT J
1590   GOTO 1730
1600   FOR K = 1 TO N
1610   SUM = 0
1620   SUM = ASF(K) + BSF(K) + CSF(K)
1630   BD = 1.0994921 - 0.0009929 * SUM + 0.0000023 * SUM ^ 2 - 0.0001392
       * AGE(K)
1640   FT = (4.95 / BD - 4.5) * 100
1650   WEIGHT = (WT(K) - (WT(K) * FT) / 100) / (1 - PCF / 100)
1660   PRINT NAME$(K);: HTAB 30: PRINT FT;: POKE 36,50: PRINT WEIGHT
1670   NEXT K
1680   GOTO 1730
1690   FOR SND = 1 TO 20
1700   SOUND = PEEK (S) - PEEK (S) + PEEK (S) - PEEK (S)
1710   NEXT SND
1720   RETURN
1730   CLEAR : PR# 0: HOME
1732   PRINT : PRINT "DO YOU WISH TO RESTART THE PROGRAM?": INPUT
       "1=YES 2=NO  ";CTN
1733   IF CTN = 1 THEN GOTO 420
1734   IF CTN = 2 THEN GOTO 1740
1735   PRINT : PRINT "THAT WAS NOT A 1 OR A 2!": GOTO 1732
1740   PRINT : PRINT : PRINT "GOODBYE!"
1750   END
```

(2) GRADES PROGRAM

This is an expanded version of the GRADES Program in Chapter 22. This program allows you to print the results for each student.

```
 1   HOME
 2   SPEED = 100
 9   HTAB 3: PRINT "THIS IS A PROGRAM TO CALCULATE FINAL"
10   HTAB 3: PRINT "GRADES FOR A UNIT OF INSTRUCTION."
11   HTAB 3: PRINT "YOU WILL BE ASKED TO PROVIDE THE"
12   HTAB 3: PRINT "FOLLOWING DATA FOR YOUR STUDENTS:"
13   HTAB 3: PRINT "NUMBER OF STUDENTS, NUMBER OF GRADES"
14   HTAB 3: PRINT "FOR EACH STUDENT, AND THE WEIGHTS FOR"
15   HTAB 3: PRINT "EACH GRADE.": PRINT : FOR N = 1 TO 5000: NEXT N
16   HTAB 3: PRINT "IF ALL OF THE GRADES ARE OF EQUAL"
17   HTAB 3: PRINT "WEIGHT, ASSIGN A WEIGHT OF 1 TO EACH"
18   HTAB 3: PRINT "ONE. THAT IS, IF EACH GRADE IS AS"
19   HTAB 3: PRINT "IMPORTANT AS ANY OTHER GRADE, THEY"
20   HTAB 3: PRINT "SHOULD BE WEIGHTED THE SAME.": PRINT : FOR N
     = 1 TO 5000: NEXT N
21   HTAB 3: PRINT "ONCE YOU HAVE ENTERED THE DATA"
22   HTAB 3: PRINT "APPLYING TO ALL STUDENTS (NUMBER OF"
23   HTAB 3: PRINT "STUDENTS, NUMBER OF GRADES, AND"
24   HTAB 3: PRINT "WEIGHTS), THE COMPUTER WILL ASK YOU"
25   HTAB 3: PRINT "FOR THE NAME AND LETTER GRADES"
26   HTAB 3: PRINT "FOR EACH STUDENT.": PRINT : FOR N = 1 TO 5000:
     NEXT N
27   HTAB 3: PRINT "YOU CAN USE PLUSSES AND MINUSES"
28   HTAB 3: PRINT "WITH ALL GRADES EXCEPT AN F.": PRINT : FOR N
     = 1 TO 5000: NEXT N
32   HTAB 3: PRINT "REMEMBER TO PRESS THE RETURN KEY"
33   HTAB 3: PRINT "EACH TIME YOU TYPE INFORMATION INTO"
34   HTAB 3: PRINT "THE COMPUTER." : PRINT
35   FOR N = 1 TO 5000: NEXT N
44   HOME
45   PRINT : PRINT : PRINT
46   SPEED = 225
47   INPUT "HOW MANY STUDENTS?  ";S
48   PRINT
50   INPUT "HOW MANY GRADES FOR EACH STUDENT?  ";N
60   PRINT
65   DIM N$(S),GD(N,3),LG$(S,N),AG$(S),AG(S),T(S),T$(S)
70   LET ADD = 0
120  FOR X = 1 TO N
130  PRINT "WEIGHT FOR TEST";X;: INPUT ": ";GD(X,2)
```

```
134    PRINT
135    ADD = ADD + GD(X,2)
140    NEXT X
150    FOR Y = 1 TO S
155    PRINT
156    PRINT Y;"–STUDENT NAME:";
158    INPUT N$(Y)
160    PRINT
200    FOR X = 1 TO N
210    INPUT "GRADE? ";GD$(X)
211    IF GD$(X) = "A+" THEN GD(X,1) = 12
212    IF GD$(X) = "A" THEN GD(X,1) = 11
213    IF GD$(X) = "A–" THEN GD(X,1) = 10
214    IF GD$(X) = "B+" THEN GD(X,1) = 9
215    IF GD$(X) = "B" THEN GD(X,1) = 8
216    IF GD$(X) = "B–" THEN GD(X,1) = 7
217    IF GD$(X) = "C+" THEN GD(X,1) = 6
218    IF GD$(X) = "C" THEN GD(X,1) = 5
219    IF GD$(X) = "C–" THEN GD(X,1) = 4
220    IF GD$(X) = "D+" THEN GD(X,1) = 3
221    IF GD$(X) = "D" THEN GD(X,1) = 2
222    IF GD$(X) = "D–" THEN GD(X,1) = 1
223    IF GD$(X) = "F" THEN GD(X,1) = 0
310    GD(X,3) = GD(X,1) * GD(X,2)
315    LG$(Y,X) = GD$(X)
319    NEXT X
320    PRINT
321    PRINT N$(Y);"'S GRADES ARE:";
322    FOR X = 1 TO N
323    PRINT " ";LG$(Y,X);
324    NEXT X
325    PRINT
326    PRINT
327    INPUT "DO YOU WANT TO CHANGE ANYTHING? YES/NO ";A$
328    IF A$ = "YES" THEN GOTO 155
329    PRINT
330    LET SUM = 0
340    FOR X = 1 TO N
350    SUM = SUM + GD(X,3)
360    NEXT X
370    PRINT
375    T = SUM / ADD
381    IF T < 12.1 THEN T$ = "A+"
382    IF T < 11.5 THEN T$ = "A"
383    IF T < 10.5 THEN T$ = "A–"
384    IF T < 9.5 THEN T$ = "B+"
```

```
385   IF T < 8.5 THEN T$ = "B"
386   IF T < 7.5 THEN T$ = "B-"
387   IF T < 6.5 THEN T$ = "C+"
388   IF T < 5.5 THEN T$ = "C"
389   IF T < 4.5 THEN T$ = "C-"
390   IF T < 3.5 THEN T$ = "D+"
391   IF T < 2.5 THEN T$ = "D"
392   IF T < 1.5 THEN T$ = "D-"
393   IF T < .5 THEN T$ = "F"
394   AG(Y) = T
395   AG$(Y) = T$
396   NEXT Y
397   INPUT "DO YOU WANT A COPY OF THE RESULTS? YES/NO ";B$
398   IF B$ = "NO" THEN GOTO 403
399   PRINT
400   INPUT "PLEASE TURN ON THE PRINTER AND PRESS RETURN. ";C$
401   INPUT "TEST NAME OR NUMBER: ";Z$
402   PR# 1: HOME
403   PRINT Z$: PRINT
404   FOR Y = 1 TO S
405   PRINT Y;" - STUDENT NAME:";N$(Y)
407   PRINT TAB( 4) "GRADES: ";
408   FOR X = 1 TO N
409   PRINT LG$(Y,X);
410   IF X < N THEN PRINT ",";
412   NEXT X
420   PRINT
430   PRINT TAB( 4)"AVERAGE GRADE:"AG(Y)
450   PRINT TAB( 4)"AVERAGE LETTER GRADE: ";AG$(Y)
480   PRINT
482   PR# 0
485   INPUT "PRESS RETURN TO CONTINUE ";R$: PRINT
486   IF B$ = "NO" OR B$ = "N" THEN GOTO 490
487   PR# 1
490   NEXT Y
495   PR# 0
496   PRINT "DO YOU WANT TO START THE"
497   PRINT
498   INPUT "PROGRAM AGAIN? YES/NO ";D$
500   IF D$ = "YES" OR D$ = "Y" THEN RUN 44
510   FLASH
515   PRINT : PRINT : PRINT : PRINT
520   PRINT "THE PROGRAM IS OVER."
530   NORMAL
540   END
550   RUN 44
```

(3) DIRECTIONS PROGRAM

(Directions to using TSCORES Program)

```
5    PRINT: PRINT
10   PRINT "DIRECTIONS FOR TSCORES";
12   PRINT: PRINT
15   PRINT "1. LIMITED TO 60 STUDENTS";
20   PRINT: PRINT
25   PRINT "2. AVERAGE UP TO 5 SCORES";
30   PRINT: PRINT
35   PRINT "3. LINES 1320 – 1360 ASSIGN LETTER GRADE TO TSCORES";
40   PRINT: PRINT
45   PRINT "4. YOU CAN CHANGE LETTER GRADES";
50   PRINT: PRINT
55   PRINT "5. AVERAGE TSCORES OPTION WILL CALCULATE MEAN
     AND STANDARD DEVIATION FOR ANY SET OF SCORES";
100  END
```

TSCORES PROGRAM*

```
10   REM DESIGNED TO CALCULATE T-SCORES OR AVERAGE T-SCORES
20   L = 1
30   DIM S1(60,10),T(60),NM$(60),S9(60),M(60),T9(60),G$(60)
40   REM PAINT SCREEN
50   S9 = 0:M = 0:D = 0:T1 = 0:T2 = 0
60   A = 0
70   HOME: VTAB 4: PRINT "********** MAIN MENU **********"
80   VTAB 8: PRINT TAB( 5);"1) AVERAGE A SET OF T-SCORES"
90   VTAB 10: PRINT TAB( 5); "2) CALCULATE RAW DATA INTO T-SCORES"
100  VTAB 12: PRINT TAB( 5); "3) END PROGRAM"
110  VTAB 20: PRINT "ENTER SELECTION ⟨1,2,3⟩": GET S
120  IF S < 1 OR S > 3 THEN GOTO 110
130  IF S = 1 THEN GOTO 160
140  IF S = 2 THEN GOTO 770
150  IF S = 3 THEN GOTO 1640
160  REM AVG SET OF T-SCORES
170  HOME: INPUT "NUMBER OF STUDENTS: ";X1
180  VTAB 4: INPUT "NUMBER OF SCORES PER STUDENT: ";X2
190  HOME: PRINT "ENTER NAME AND SCORES"
200  PRINT: PRINT
210  FOR I = 1 TO X1
220  PRINT "NAME";I;" ";
```

---

*The DIRECTIONS and TSCORES programs are reproduced by permission of Diane Ross, Ph.D., Department of Physical Education, California State University, Fullerton.

```
230   INPUT NM$(I)
240   FOR J = 1 TO X2
250   PRINT TAB( 3);"SCORE";J;" ";
260   INPUT S1(I,J)
270   NEXT J
280   X3 = 0
290   NEXT I
300   HOME: PRINT "WOULD YOU LIKE TO VIEW THESE SCORES"
310   INPUT "⟨Y/N⟩ ";Y$
320   IF Y$ = "N" THEN GOTO 420
330   FOR I = L TO X1
340   PRINT I;" ";NM$(I)
350   FOR J = 1 TO X2
360   PRINT TAB( 3);S1(I,J)
370   NEXT J
380   L1 = I
390   X3 = X3 + (X2 + 1)
400   IF X3 = 18 OR X3 = 20 THEN GOTO 420
410   NEXT I
420   INPUT "ARE THESE SCORES CORRECT ⟨Y/N⟩ ";Y$
430   IF Y$ = "Y" AND X3 = 0 THEN GOTO 500
440   IF Y$ = "Y" AND X3 ⟨ ⟩ 0 THEN GOTO 1650
450   INPUT "STUDENT'S NO. TO BE CHANGED (0 TO END) ";Z
460   IF Z = 0 AND X3 = 0 THEN GOTO 500
470   IF Z = 0 AND X3 ⟨ ⟩ 0 THEN GOTO 1650
480   GOSUB 950
490   GOTO 420
500   FOR I = 1 TO X1
510   FOR J = 1 TO X2
520   LET T(I) = S1(I,J) + T(I)
530   NEXT J
540   NEXT I
550   FOR I = 1 TO X1
560   LET M(I) = T(I) / X2
570   LET M(I) = INT (M(I) * 10 + .5) / 10
580   T9(I) = M(I):A = 1
590   GOTO 1320
600   NEXT I
610   HOME: INPUT "WOULD YOU LIKE A HARD COPY ⟨Y/N⟩";Y$
620   IF Y$ = "Y" THEN Q = 1
630   IF Y$ = "N" THEN Q = 0
640   HOME: PRINT CHR$ (4);"PR#";Q
650   S = 0
660   PRINT TAB( 5);"NAME"; TAB( 28);"MEAN"; TAB( 34);"GRADE"
670   PRINT TAB( 5);"= = = ="; TAB( 28);"= = = ="; TAB( 34);"= = = ="
```

```
680    FOR I = 1 TO X1
690    IF I = 20 OR I = 40 AND Q = 0 THEN INPUT "PRESS RETURN ";Y$
700    PRINT NM$(I); TAB( 28);M(I); TAB( 36);G$(I)
710    NEXT I
720    IF Q = 1 THEN PRINT CHR$ (4);"PR#0"
730    PRINT: IF Q = 0 THEN INPUT "PRESS RETURN";Q$
740    FOR I = 1 TO X1:T(I) = M(I) = 0: NEXT I
750    X1 = X2 = 0
760    GOTO 50
770    REM CALCULATE T-SCORES
780    M = 0:D = 0:T1 = 0:T2 = 0
790    HOME
800    INPUT "NUMBER OF STUDENTS: ";N
801    FOR I = 1 TO N:T9(I) = S9(I) = 0: NEXT I
820    PRINT: PRINT
830    FOR I = 1 TO N
840    PRINT "NAME";I;" ";
850    INPUT NM$(I)
860    PRINT SPC( 3);"SCORE:";
870    INPUT S9(I)
880    NEXT I
890    FOR I = 1 TO N
900    IF I = 20 OR I = 40 THEN GOSUB 1090
910    PRINT I;" ";NM$(I); TAB( 30);S9(I)
920    NEXT I
930    IF I 〈 〉 20 AND I 〈 〉 40 THEN GOSUB 1090
940    GOTO 1180
950    REM SUBROUTINE TO CORRECT SCORES FOR AVG.
960    HOME: VTAB 6
970    PRINT NM$(Z)
980    FOR K = 1 TO X2
990    PRINT TAB( 3);"SCORE";K;" = ";S1(Z,K)
1000   NEXT K
1010   PRINT: PRINT
1020   INPUT "INPUT SCORE # TO BE CHANGED (0 TO END)  ";N9
1030   IF N9 < 0 OR N9 > X2 THEN GOTO 1020
1040   IF N9 = 0 THEN GOTO 1080
1050   PRINT : PRINT "OLD SCORE = ";S1(Z,N9);" ";
1060   INPUT "NEW SCORE = ";S1(Z,N9)
1070   VTAB 20: PRINT "PRESS RETURN": GET Q$
1080   RETURN
1090   REM SUBROUTINE TO CORRECT SCORES FOR T-SCORES
1100   PRINT : PRINT "ARE THESE SCORES CORRECT <Y/N> ";
1110   INPUT Y$
1120   IF Y$ = "Y" THEN 1170
1130   INPUT "NO. TO CORRECT  ";N1
```

```
1140    PRINT "OLD: ";S9(N1); TAB( 15);
1150    INPUT "NEW:  ";S9(N1)
1160    GOTO 1100
1170    RETURN
1180    FOR I = 1 TO N
1190    LET T1 = T1 + S9(I)
1200    LET T2 = T2 + S9(I) ^ 2
1210    NEXT I
1220    M = T1 / N
1230    D = SQR (((T2 − ((T1 ^ 2) / N)) / N))
1250    FOR I = 1 TO N
1260    T9(I) = 50 + (10 / D) * (S9(I) − M)
1270    LET T9(I) = INT (T9(I) * 10 + .5) / 10
1280    NEXT I
1300    REM PUT GRADE TO T-SCORE
1310    FOR I = 1 TO N
1320    IF T9(I) > = 60 THEN G$(I) = "A"
1330    IF T9(I) > = 50 AND T9(I) < = 59.9 THEN G$(I) = "B"
1340    IF T9(I) > = 40 AND T9(I) < = 49.9 THEN G$(I) = "C"
1350    IF T9(I) > = 30 AND T9(I) < = 39.9 THEN G$(I) = "D"
1360    IF T9(I) < = 29.9 THEN G$(I) = "F"
1370    IF A = 1 THEN GOTO 600
1380    NEXT I
1390    HOME : INPUT "WOULD YOU LIKE A HARDCOPY <Y/N> ";Y$
1400    IF Y$ = "Y" THEN Q = 1
1410    IF Y$ = "N" THEN Q = 0
1420    PRINT CHR$ (4);"PR#";Q
1430    PRINT TAB( 3);"NAME"; TAB( 20);"SCORE"; TAB( 27);"T-SCORE";
        TAB( 36);"GRADE"
1440    PRINT TAB( 3);"= = = ="; TAB( 20);"= = = = ="; TAB
        ( 27);"= = = = = = ="; TAB( 36);"= = = = ="
1450    PRINT
1460    FOR I = 1 TO N
1470    PRINT NM$(I); TAB( 22);S9(I); TAB( 29);T9(I); TAB( 38);G$(I)
1480    IF Q = 0 AND I = 20 OR I = 40 THEN INPUT "PRESS RETURN ";Q$
1490    NEXT I
1495    PRINT
1496    FLASH
1500    INPUT "PRESS RETURN ";Q$
1505    NORMAL
1510    PRINT : PRINT "CLASS MEAN = "; INT (M * 10 + .5) / 10
1520    PRINT "CLASS STAN. DEV. = "; INT (D * 10 + .5) / 10
1530    PRINT CHR$ (4);"PR#0"
1540    PRINT : INPUT "NEW RAW SCORES <Y/N> ";Y$
1550    IF Y$ = "N" THEN GOTO 50
```

```
1560   T1 = 0:T2 = 0:D = 0:M = 0
1570   FOR I = 1 TO N:T9(I) = S9(I) = 0: NEXT I
1580   FOR I = 1 TO N
1590   PRINT NM$(I)
1600   PRINT TAB( 3);"SCORE ";: INPUT S9(I)
1610   NEXT I
1620   GOSUB 1100
1630   GOTO 1180
1640   HOME : END
1650   X3 = 0
1660   L = L1 + 1
1670   IF L > X1 THEN 500
1680   GOTO 330
```

(4) PERCENTILE PROGRAM*

(to form table of percentiles)
LIST

```
  5   HOME
 10   READ N
 20   FOR I = 1 TO N
 30   READ X
 40   X1 = X1 + X
 50   X2 = X2 + X ^ 2
 60   NEXT I
 70   M = X1 / N
 80   S = ((X2 − X1 ^ 2 / N) / (N − 1)) ^ .5
 81   D(1) = 3.00 * S:D(2) = 1.64 * S:D(3) = 1.38 * S:D(4) = 1.04 * S:D(5) = .84
      * S:D(6) = .67 * S:D(7) = .52 * S:D(8) = .39 * S:D(9) = .25 * S:D(10) = .13
      * S
 85   VTAB 4: PRINT "THE 99.9TH PERCENTILE IS ";M + D(1)
 90   P = 95
100   FOR I = 2 TO 10
110   PRINT : PRINT "THE ";P;"THE PERCENTILE IS ";M + D(I)
112   P = P − 5
115   NEXT I
120   PRINT : PRINT "THE 50TH PERCENTILE IS ";M
124   PRINT
125   VTAB 24: INPUT "PRESS RETURN ";A$
130   P = 45
135   HOME
140   FOR I = 10 TO 2 STEP − 1
150   PRINT : PRINT "THE ";P;"THE PERCENTILE IS ";M − D(I)
155   P = P − 5
160   NEXT I
170   PRINT : PRINT "THE 0.1TH PERCENTILE IS ";M − D(1)
180   PRINT : PRINT "MEAN: ";M
190   PRINT "SD : ";S;
200   DATA 10
210   DATA 20,30,35,32,31,25,26,28,19,24
```

---

*To see how this program works, enter RUN PERCENTILES. To insert a new set of scores, enter:
LIST

```
200   DATA (number of scores)
210   DATA (enter each score, followed by a comma)
      RUN
```

The results can be used to form a table of percentile ranks.

(5) CHANGE PROGRAM

(to calculate improvement scores)

```
1   HOME
3   PRINT
    "==========================================="
4   PRINT : PRINT : PRINT
5   PRINT "THIS PROGRAM IS DESIGNED TO CALCULATE IMPROVE-
    MENT SCORES FOR PAIRS OF INITIAL (PREINSTRUCTIONAL) AND
    FINAL (POST- INSTRUCTIONAL SCORES)."
6   PRINT : PRINT : PRINT : PRINT : PRINT "PRESS RETURN": GET A$
8   HOME : VTAB 4: PRINT "HOW MANY STUDENTS ARE IN THE CLASS?"
9   INPUT N
11  SUMX = 0:FLAG = 0
12  SUMY = 0
13  SX2 = 0
14  SY2 = 0
15  ADDXY = 0
16  SMAX = 30.
18  HOME : VTAB 8: PRINT "WHAT IS THE MAXIMUM PERFORMANCE
    SCORE----IF IT IS UNKNOWN ENTER A '0' "
19  INPUT RMAX
25  DIM X(100),Y(100)
30  HOME : VTAB 3
35  FOR I = 1 TO N
37  PRINT "SCORE 1 FOR SUBJECT "; I;" = ";
38  INPUT X(I)
39  PRINT "SCORE 2 FOR SUBJECT "; I;" = ";
40  INPUT Y(I)
70  XX = XX + X(I)
80  YY = YY + Y(I)
90  XSQ = X(I) ^ 2
100 YSQ = Y(I) ^ 2
110 SX2 = SX2 + XSQ
120 SY2 = SY2 + YSQ
130 CROSSXY = X(I) * Y(I)
140 ADDXY = ADDXY + CROSSXY
145 PRINT : PRINT
150 NEXT I
154 REM
```

Reproduced by permission of Whitfield B. East, Ph.D., Department of Physical Education, University of Northern Iowa, Cedar Falls, Iowa.

```
155   REM COMPUTE THE PEARSON CORRELATION COEFFICIENT
156   REM
160   NUM = (N * ADDXY) − (XX * YY)
170   DEM = SQR (((N * SX2) − (XX ^ 2)) * ((N * SY2) − (YY ^ 2)))
180   R = NUM / DEM
184   Z = 0
185   HOME : VTAB 8: PRINT "DO YOU WANT A PRINTED COPY OF YOUR
      RESULTS − Y/N"
188   GET A$: IF A$ = "Y" THEN Z = 1
190   IF A$ = "N" THEN Z = 0
199   REM
200   REM COMPUTE THE MEANS AND STANDARD DEVIATIONS FOR THE
      INITIAL AND FINAL SCORES
201   REM
205   MEANX = XX / N
210   MNY = YY/N
215   SDX = SQR (((N * SX2) − XX ^ 2) / (N * (N − 1)))
220   STDY = SQR (((N * SY2) − YY ^ 2) / (N * (N − 1)))
222   HOME : PR# Z
223   VTAB 4: PRINT " MEANS AND STANDARD DEVIATION": PRINT "_____"
224   PRINT : PRINT
225   PRINT "MEAN FOR INITIAL SCORES = ";MEANX
230   PRINT "MEAN FOR FINAL SCORES = ";MNY
232   PRINT : PRINT : PRINT
235   PRINT "STANDARD DEV FOR INITIAL = ";SDX
240   PRINT "STANDARD DEV FOR FINAL = ";STDY
243   GOSUB 700
245   BETA = (R * (STDY / SDX))
250   IF RMAX > 0 GOTO 260
255   RMAX = (MNY + (3 * STDY))
260   ALPH = (( LOG (SMAX + 1)) / RMAX)
298   REM
299   REM
300   REM COMPUTE EXPONENTIAL IMPROVEMENT SCORES
301   REM
302   REM
305   DIM IMPROV(100),YRES(100)
310   FOR I = 1 TO N
315   IMPROV(I) = (( LOG (( EXP (ALPH * BETA) * ( EXP (ALPH * X(I)) − EXP
      (ALPH * MEANX))) + EXP (ALPH * MNY))) / ALPH)
320   YRES (I) = ((Y(I) − X(I)) / (IMPROV(I) − X(I))) * 100.
325   NEXT I
350   HOME : PR# Z: PRINT : PRINT : PRINT : PRINT
355   PRINT " RAW SCORES PREDICTED PERCENT"
360   PRINT
```

```
365   PRINT "SUB INITIAL FINAL FINAL IMPROVEMENT"
370   PRINT
371   M = 0:FLAG = 1
375   Q = N / 10.:TTL = 10:Q% = N / 10.:LFT = N − (10 * Q%)
377   IF Q% < > Q THEN Q% = Q% + 1                .
378   FOR I = 1 to Q%: IF I = Q% THEN TTL = LFT
379   FOR J = 1 TO TTL:M = M + 1: PR# Z
380   W = LEN ( STR$ (M)): HTAB 1: PRINT SPC ( 3 − W);M;
381   W = LEN ( STR$ (X(M))): HTAB 4: PRINT SPC ( 6 − W + 1);X(M):
382   W = LEN ( STR$ (Y(M))): HTAB 11: PRINT SPC ( 6 − W + 1);Y(M):
383   IMPROV(M) = INT (IMPROV(M) * 100 + .5) / 100.
384   W = LEN (STR$ ( INT (IMPROV(M)))) + 3
385   HTAB 19: PRINT SPC (8 − W + 1); IMPROV(M);
386   YRES(M) = INT (YRES(M) * 100 + .5) / 100.
387   W = LEN ( STR$ ( INT (YRES(M)))) + 3
388   HTAB 28: PRINT SPC ( 9 − W + 1);YRES (M)
389   NEXT J
390   GOSUB 700: VTAB 8: CALL − 958: PRINT : PRINT : PR# Z: NEXT I
398   PR# Z
399   HOME : PRINT : PRINT : PRINT : PRINT : HOME : PR# Z
400   HOME : HTAB 10: PRINT "IMPROVEMENT SCORES": HTAB 8: PRINT"_"
410   FLAG = 3:CT = 0
415   FOR I = 1 TO N
417   PRINT : PRINT
418   CT = CT + 1
420   PRINT I;" INITIAL SCORE";: HTAB 27: PRINT X(I)
425   PRINT " FINAL SCORE";: HTAB 27: PRINT Y(I)
430   PRINT " PREDICTED FINAL SCORE";: HTAB 27: PRINT IMPROV(I)
435   PRINT " PERCENT IMPROVEMENT";: HTAB 27: PRINT YRES(I)
440   ON CT = FLAG GOSUB 750: PR# Z: NEXT I
600   GOTO 800
700   PR# 0: VTAB 23: PRINT "PRESS 'RETURN' TO CONTINUE"
710   GET A$: IF FLAG = 0 THEN GOTO 725
715   RETURN
725   HOME : PRINT : PRINT : PRINT : PRINT : HOME : RETURN
750   PR# 0: VTAB 23: PRINT "PRESS 'RETURN' TO CONTINUE"
755   GET Z$:CT = 0: HOME : RETURN
800   END
```

Appendix F

NCYFS norms

TABLE A-1. *NCYFS norms by age for the one-mile walk/run—boys (in minutes and seconds)**

Percentile	10	11	12	13	14	15	16	17	18
99	6:55	6:21	6:21	5:59	5:43	5:40	5:31	5:14	5:33
90	8:13	7:25	7:13	6:48	6:27	6:23	6:13	6:08	6:10
80	8:35	7:52	7:41	7:07	6:58	6:43	6:31	6:31	6:33
75	8:48	8:02	7:53	7:14	7:08	6:52	6:39	6:40	6:42
70	9:02	8:12	8:03	7:24	7:18	7:00	6:50	6:46	6:57
60	9:26	8:38	8:23	7:46	7:34	7:13	7:07	7:10	7:15
50	9:52	9:03	8:48	8:04	7:51	7:30	7:27	7:31	7:35
40	10:15	9:25	9:17	8:26	8:14	7:50	7:48	7:59	7:53
30	10:44	10:17	9:57	8:54	8:46	8:18	8:04	8:24	8:12
25	11:00	10:32	10:13	9:06	9:10	8:30	8:18	8:37	8:34
20	11:25	10:55	10:38	9:20	9:28	8:50	8:34	8:55	9:10
10	12:27	12:07	11:48	10:38	10:34	10:13	9:36	10:43	10:50

*From the National Children and Youth Fitness Study.

TABLE A-2. *NCYFS norms by age for the one-mile walk/run—girls (in minutes and seconds)**

Percentile	10	11	12	13	14	15	16	17	18
99	7:55	7:14	7:20	7:08	7:01	6:59	7:03	6:52	6:58
90	9:09	8:45	8:34	8:27	8:11	8:23	8:28	8:20	8:22
80	9:56	9:35	9:30	9:13	8:49	9:04	9:06	9:10	9:27
75	10:09	9:56	9:52	9:30	9:16	9:28	9:25	9:26	9:31
70	10:27	10:10	10:05	9:48	9:31	9:49	9:41	9:41	9:36
60	10:51	10:35	10:32	10:22	10:04	10:20	10:15	10:16	10:08
50	11:14	11:15	10:58	10:52	10:32	10:46	10:34	10:34	10:51
40	11:54	11:46	11:26	11:22	10:58	11:20	11:08	10:59	11:27
30	12:27	12:33	12:03	11:55	11:35	11:53	11:49	11:43	11:58
25	12:52	12:54	12:33	12:17	11:49	12:18	12:10	12:03	12:14
20	13:12	13:17	12:53	12:43	12:10	12:48	12:32	12:30	12:37
10	14:20	14:35	14:07	13:45	13:13	14:07	13:42	13:46	15:18

*From the National Children and Youth Fitness Study.

TABLE A-3. *NCYFS norms by age for the timed bent-knee sit-ups—boys (number in 60 seconds)**

Percentile	10	11	12	13	14	15	16	17	18
99	60	60	61	62	64	65	65	68	67
90	47	48	50	52	52	53	55	56	54
80	43	43	46	48	49	50	51	51	50
75	40	41	44	46	47	48	49	50	50
70	38	40	43	45	45	46	48	49	48
60	36	38	40	41	43	44	45	46	44
50	34	36	38	40	41	42	43	43	43
40	32	34	35	37	39	40	41	41	40
30	30	31	33	34	37	37	39	39	38
25	28	30	32	32	35	36	38	37	36
20	26	28	30	31	34	35	36	35	35
10	22	22	25	28	30	31	32	31	31

*From the National Children and Youth Fitness Study.

TABLE A-4. *NCYFS norms by age for the timed bent-knee sit-ups—girls (number in 60 seconds)**

Percentile	10	11	12	13	14	15	16	17	18
99	50	53	66	58	57	56	59	60	65
90	43	42	46	46	47	45	49	47	47
80	39	39	41	41	42	42	42	41	42
75	37	37	40	40	41	40	40	40	40
70	36	36	39	39	40	39	39	39	40
60	33	34	36	35	37	36	37	37	38
50	31	32	33	33	35	35	35	36	35
40	30	30	31	31	32	32	33	33	33
30	27	28	30	28	30	30	30	31	30
25	25	26	28	27	29	30	30	30	30
20	24	24	27	25	27	28	28	29	28
10	20	20	21	21	23	24	23	24	24

*From the National Children and Youth Fitness Study.

TABLE A-5. *NCYFS norms by age for the sit-and-reach—boys (in inches)**

Percentile	10	11	12	13	14	15	16	17	18
99	18.0	18.5	18.5	19.5	20.0	21.5	22.0	21.5	22.0
90	16.0	16.5	16.0	16.5	17.5	18.0	19.0	19.5	19.5
80	15.0	15.5	15.0	15.0	16.0	17.0	18.0	18.0	18.0
75	14.5	15.0	15.0	15.0	15.5	16.5	17.0	17.5	17.5
70	14.5	14.5	14.5	14.5	15.0	16.0	17.0	17.0	17.0
60	14.0	14.0	13.5	13.5	14.0	15.0	16.0	16.0	16.0
50	13.5	13.0	13.0	13.0	13.5	14.0	15.0	15.5	15.0
40	12.5	12.5	12.0	12.5	13.0	13.5	14.0	14.5	14.5
30	12.0	12.0	11.5	12.0	12.0	12.5	13.5	13.5	13.5
25	11.5	11.5	11.0	11.0	11.0	12.0	13.0	13.0	13.0
20	11.0	11.0	10.5	10.5	11.0	11.5	12.0	12.5	12.5
10	10.0	9.5	8.5	9.0	9.0	9.5	10.0	10.5	10.0

*The 1980 AAHPERD norms used a 0 point of 23 cm, but NCYFS used 12 inches. To adjust the 0 point and to change inches to centimeters, use the following formula: Score in centimeters = (Score in inches × 2.54) − 7.48. From the National Children and Youth Fitness Study.

TABLE A-6. *NCYFS norms by age for the sit-and-reach—girls (in inches)**

Percentile	10	11	12	13	14	15	16	17	18
99	20.5	20.5	21.0	22.0	22.0	23.0	23.0	23.0	22.5
90	17.5	18.0	19.0	20.0	19.5	20.0	20.5	20.5	20.5
80	16.5	17.0	18.0	19.0	19.0	19.0	19.5	19.5	19.5
75	16.5	16.5	17.0	18.0	18.5	19.0	19.0	19.0	19.0
70	16.0	16.5	17.0	17.5	18.0	18.5	19.0	19.0	18.5
60	15.0	15.5	16.0	17.0	17.5	18.0	18.0	18.0	18.0
50	14.5	15.0	15.5	16.0	17.0	17.0	17.5	18.0	17.5
40	14.0	14.0	15.0	15.5	16.0	17.0	17.0	17.0	17.0
30	13.0	13.5	14.5	14.5	15.0	16.0	16.5	16.0	16.0
25	13.0	13.0	14.0	14.0	15.0	15.5	16.0	15.5	15.5
20	12.0	13.0	13.5	13.5	14.0	15.0	15.5	15.0	15.0
10	10.5	11.5	12.0	12.0	12.5	13.5	14.0	13.5	13.0

*The 1980 AAHPERD norms used a 0 point of 23 cm, but NCYFS used 12 inches. To adjust the 0 point and to change inches to centimeters, use the following formula: Score in centimeters = (Score in inches × 2.54) − 7.48. From the National Children and Youth Fitness Study.

TABLE A-7. NCYFS norms by age for the triceps skinfold—boys (in millimeters)*

Percentile	10	11	12	13	14	15	16	17	18
99	5	4	4	4	4	4	4	4	4
90	7	7	6	6	5	5	5	5	5
80	8	7	8	7	6	6	6	6	6
75	8	8	8	7	7	7	6	6	6
70	9	9	9	8	7	7	7	7	7
60	10	10	10	9	8	8	7	7	8
50	11	11	11	10	9	9	8	8	8
40	13	12	12	11	10	10	9	9	10
30	14	14	14	13	11	11	11	11	11
25	15	15	15	14	12	12	11	12	12
20	16	16	17	15	13	13	12	13	13
10	20	20	21	20	18	18	16	15	16

*From the National Children and Youth Fitness Study.

TABLE A-8. NCYFS norms by age for the triceps skinfold—girls (in millimeters)*

Percentile	10	11	12	13	14	15	16	17	18
99	5	6	6	6	6	7	7	8	7
90	7	8	9	9	9	10	10	11	10
80	9	9	10	10	11	12	12	12	12
75	10	10	10	11	12	13	12	13	13
70	10	10	11	11	12	13	13	14	13
60	11	12	12	13	14	15	14	15	14
50	12	13	13	14	15	16	15	17	15
40	14	15	14	15	16	17	17	18	17
30	15	16	16	17	18	19	18	20	19
25	16	17	17	18	19	20	19	21	20
20	17	19	18	20	20	21	20	21	21
10	21	23	22	24	23	25	24	24	23

*From the National Children and Youth Fitness Study.

TABLE A-9. *NCYFS norms by age for the sum of triceps and subscapular skinfolds—boys (in millimeters)**

Percentile	10	11	12	13	14	15	16	17	18
99	9	9	9	9	9	10	10	10	11
90	12	12	12	11	12	12	12	13	13
80	13	13	13	13	13	13	13	14	14
75	14	14	14	13	13	14	14	14	15
70	15	15	15	14	14	14	14	15	15
60	16	16	16	15	15	15	15	16	17
50	17	18	17	17	17	17	17	17	18
40	20	20	20	19	18	18	18	19	19
30	22	23	22	21	21	20	20	21	22
25	24	25	24	23	22	22	22	22	24
20	25	26	28	25	25	24	23	24	25
10	35	36	38	34	33	32	30	30	30

*From the National Children and Youth Fitness Study.

TABLE A-10. *NCYFS norms by age for the sum of triceps and subscapular skinfold—girls (in millimeters)**

Percentile	10	11	12	13	14	15	16	17	18
99	10	11	11	12	12	13	13	16	14
90	13	14	15	15	17	19	19	20	19
80	15	16	17	18	19	21	21	22	21
75	16	17	18	19	20	23	22	23	22
70	17	18	18	20	21	24	23	24	23
60	18	19	21	22	24	26	24	26	25
50	20	21	22	24	26	28	26	28	27
40	22	24	24	26	28	30	28	31	28
30	25	28	27	29	31	33	32	34	32
25	27	30	29	31	33	34	33	36	34
20	29	33	31	34	35	37	35	37	36
10	36	40	40	43	40	43	42	42	42

*From the National Children and Youth Fitness Study.

TABLE A-11. NCYFS norms by age for the chin-up—boys (number completed)*

Percentile	10	11	12	13	14	15	16	17	18
99	13	12	13	17	18	18	20	20	21
90	8	8	8	10	12	14	14	15	16
80	5	5	6	8	9	11	12	13	14
75	4	5	5	7	8	10	12	12	13
70	4	4	5	7	8	10	11	12	12
60	2	3	4	5	6	8	10	10	11
50	1	2	3	4	5	7	9	9	10
40	1	1	2	3	4	6	8	8	9
30	0	0	1	1	3	5	6	6	7
25	0	0	0	1	2	4	6	5	6
20	0	0	0	0	1	3	5	4	5
10	0	0	0	0	0	1	2	2	3

*From the National Children and Youth Fitness Study.

TABLE A-12. NCYFS norms by age for the chin-up—girls (number completed)*

Percentile	10	11	12	13	14	15	16	17	18
99	8	8	8	5	8	6	8	7	6
90	3	3	2	2	2	2	2	2	2
80	2	1	1	1	1	1	1	1	1
75	1	1	1	1	1	1	1	1	1
70	1	1	1	0	1	1	1	1	1
60	0	0	0	0	0	0	0	0	0
50	0	0	0	0	0	0	0	0	0
40	0	0	0	0	0	0	0	0	0
30	0	0	0	0	0	0	0	0	0
25	0	0	0	0	0	0	0	0	0
20	0	0	0	0	0	0	0	0	0
10	0	0	0	0	0	0	0	0	0

*From the National Children and Youth Fitness Study.

Appendix G

Sources of tests and skinfold calipers

CHAPTER 17

The following references are excellent sources of additional tests of motor behavior for children. Each reference includes an analytical critique of selected tests to assist the teacher in identifying appropriate tests.

Haubenstricker, J.L. 1977. A critical review of selected perceptual-motor tests and scales currently used in the assessment of motor behavior. In Landers, D., and Christina, R., editors. Psychology of motor behavior and sport—1977. Champaign, Ill.: Human Kinetics Publishers, Inc.

Herkowitz, J. 1977. Instruments which assess the efficiency/maturity of children's fundamental motor pattern performance. In Landers, D., and Christina, R., editors. Psychology of motor behavior and sport—1977. Champaign, Ill. Human Kinetics Publishers, Inc.

Herkowitz, J. 1978. Assessing the motor development of children: presentation and critique of tests. In Ridenour, M., editor. Motor development: issues and applications. Princeton, N.J.: Princeton Book Co., Publishers.

McGee, R. 1984. Evaluation of processes and products. In Logsden, B., editor. Physical education for children: a focus on the teaching process. Philadelphia: Lea & Febiger.

CHAPTER 18

Sensorimotor tests
Quick Neurological Screening Test
Academic Therapy Publications
20 Commercial Boulevard
Novato, CA 94949

Frostig Developmental Test of Visual
  Perception
Consulting Psychologist Press, Inc.
577 College Avenue
Palo Alto, CA 94360

Motor development tests
California State University Motor
Development Checklist
Janet A. Seaman
California State University
5151 State University Drive
Los Angeles, CA 90032

Bayley Scales of Motor Development
Psychological Corporation
757 Third Avenue
New York, NY 10017

Motor ability tests
Six Category Gross Motor Test
B.J. Cratty
*Perceptual Motor Behavior and
  Educational Processes*
Springfield, Ill.:
Charles C Thomas, Publisher, 1969

Basic Motor Ability Test—Revised
D. Arnheim and A. Sinclair
The Clumsy Child
St. Louis: The C.V. Mosby Co., 1979

CHAPTER 11

FAT-O-METER: Health Education Services Corp., 7N015 York Road, Bensenville, IL 60106

SLIM GUIDE: Creative Health Products, 9135 General Ct., Plymouth, MI 48170

PHYSIQUE METER: Dr. H. Co., P.O. Box 266, Chesterfield, MO 63017

HARPENDEN: Quinton Instrument Co., 2121 Terry Avenue, Seattle, WA 98121

LANGE: J.A. Preston Corp., 71 Fifth Ave., New York, NY 10013

Credits and Acknowledgments

Chapter 2 Measurement in a School-Based Setting
P. 21—Courtesy Measurement Laboratory, Department of Physical Education and Dance, University of Wisconsin, Madison; 23—Modified from Imwold, C.H., Rider, R.A., and Johnson, D.J. 1982. Journal of Teaching in Physical Education, **2**:13-18; 35-36—From Jewett, A.E., and Mullan, M.R. Curriculum design: purposes and processes in physical education teaching-learning. (Washington, D.C.: American Alliance for Health, Physical Education and Recreation. 1977). Reprinted by permission of the American Alliance for Health, Physical Education, Recreation and Dance, 1900 Association Drive, Reston, VA 22091; 39—Courtesy Biodynamics Laboratory, Department of Physical Education and Dance, University of Wisconsin, Madison.

Chapter 3 Measurement in a Nonschool-Based Setting
P. 45, 50, 59—Courtesy Biodynamics Laboratory, Department of Physical Education and Dance, University of Wisconsin, Madison; 47-48—From Vic Tanny International of Wisconsin. By permission of Dr. Paul Ward, Dr. Frank I. Katch, and Mr. Bernard F. Palluck, Vice President and Area Director; procedures were formulated by Dr. Ward; percent fat regression equation was developed by Drs. Katch and McArdle; 49—From the Olympic Health and Racquet Club. By permission of Ray Fraley; 51—From the Exercise Resource Facility, CUNA Mutual Insurance Group, Madison, Wis. By permission of Katie Munns; 52, 54-57—Courtesy Sentry World Headquarters, Stevens Point, Wis.

Chapter 4 Summarizing a Set of Test Scores
P. 67—Courtesy Midvale Elementary School, Madison, Wis.; 80—Courtesy Measurement Laboratory, Department of Physical Education and Dance, University of Wisconsin, Madison.

Chapter 5 Describing a Distribution of Test Scores
P. 94—From Text Service Notebook 148, 1980. p. 1: The Psychological Corporation; 107—Courtesy Midvale Elementary School, Madison, Wis.

Chapter 6 Validity and Reliability of Norm-Referenced Tests
P. 118—Courtesy Measurement Laboratory, Department of Physical Education and Dance, University of Wisconsin, Madison; 120—From Handbook for AAHPER Cooperative Physical Education Tests. Copyright ©1971 by Educational Testing Service. All rights reserved. Reproduced by permission; 129—From Morgan, W.P., and Johnson, R.W. 1978. Personality characteristics of successful and unsuccessful oarsmen, International Journal of Sports Psychology **9**:119-133. By permission of the publisher.

Chapter 7 Validity and Reliability of Criterion-Referenced Tests
P. 145, 154—Courtesy Midvale Elementary School, Madison, Wis.

Chapter 8 Constructing Sports Skills Tests
P. 162, 167—Courtesy Measurement Laboratory, Department of Physical Education and Dance, University of Wisconsin, Madison.

Chapter 9 Constructing Knowledge Tests
P. 179, 180—From Haskins, M.J. 1971. Evaluation in physical education. Dubuque, Iowa. Wm C Brown Group. By permission of the author; 186—From Ebel, R.L. 1965. Measuring educational achievement. Englewood Cliffs, N.J.: Prentice-Hall, Inc. By permission of the publisher.

Chapter 10 Tests of Sports Skills
P. 193—From Archery for boys and girls: Skills test manual. 1967. Washington, D.C.: AAHPER. Reprinted by permission of the American Alliance for Health, Physical Education, Recreation and Dance, 1900 Association Drive, Reston, VA 22091; 195, 197—Redrawn from Johnson, B.L., and Nelson, J.K. 1979. Practical measurements for evaluation in physical education. Minneapolis: Burgess Publishing Co. By permission of Nelson, J.K., Ph.D.; 196—In Scott, M.G., and French, E. 1959. Measurement and evaluation in physical education. Dubuque, Iowa: Wm C Brown Group. By permission of Scott, M.G., Ph.D.; 200-207—From Hopkins, D.R., Shick, J., and Plack, J.J. 1984. Basketball for boys and girls: skills test manual. Reston, Va.: AAHPERD. Reprinted by permission of the American Alliance for Health, Physical Education, Recreation and Dance, 1900 Association Drive, Reston, VA 22091; 208—From Chapman, N.L. 1982. Chapman ball control test-field hockey. Research Quarterly for Exercise and Sport **53**(3):239-242. Reprinted by permission of the American Alliance for Health, Physical Education, Recreation and Dance, 1900 Association Drive, Reston VA 22091; 209, 210—From AAHPER. 1966. Football: skills test manual. Washington, D.C.: AAHPER. Reprinted by permission of the American Alliance for Health, Physical Education, Recreation and Dance, 1900 Association Drive, Reston, VA 22091; 211—From Shick, J., and Berg, N.G. 1983. Indoor golf skill test for junior high school boys. Research Quarterly for Exerice and Sport **54**(1):75-78. Reprinted by permission of the American Alliance for Health, Physical Education, Recreation and Dance, 1900 Association Drive, Reston, VA 22091; 214—From Shick, J. 1970. Battery of softball skills tests for college

women. Research Quarterly **42**:82-87. Reprinted by permission of the American Alliance for Health, Physical Education, Recreation and Dance, 1900 Association Drive, Reston, VA 22091; 216-217—From Hewitt, J.E. 1966. Hewitt's tennis achievement test. Research Quarterly **31**:231-237. Reprinted by permission of the American Alliance for Health, Physical Education, Recreation and Dance, 1900 Association Drive, Reston, VA 22091; 219, 220—From Purcell, K. 1981. A tennis forehand-backhand drive skill test which measures ball control and stroke firmness. Research Quarterly for Exercise and Sport **52**(2):238-245. Reprinted by permission of the American Alliance for Health, Physical Education, Recreation and Dance, 1900 Association Drive, Reston, VA 22091; 221—From Brady, G.F. 1945. Preliminary investigation of volleyball playing ability. Research Quarterly **16**:14-17. Reprinted by permission of the American Alliance for Health, Physical Education, Recreation and Dance, 1900 Association Drive, Reston, VA 22091; 222—From Brumbach, W.B. 1967. Beginning volleyball, a syllabus for teachers, revised edition. Eugene, Ore.: Wayne Baker Brumbach. By permission of the author.

Chapter 11 Tests of Health-Related Physical Fitness
P. 227, 225-260—Courtesy Biodynamics Laboratory, University of Wisconsin, Madison; 230, 242—From Health-Related Physical Fitness Test Manual. Reston, VA: AAHPERD, 1980. By permission of the AAHPERD; 232-233, 237—Modified from Health-Related Physical Fitness Test Manual. Reston, VA: AAHPERD, 1980. Reprinted by permission of the American Alliance for Health, Physical Education, Recreation and Dance, 1900 Association Drive, Reston, VA 22091; 234-235—From Pollock, M.L., Schmidt, D.H., and Jackson, A.S. 1980. Measurement of cardiorespiratory fitness and body composition in the clinical setting.

Comprehensive Therapy **6**(9):12-27. By permission of the Laux Co., Inc., Harvard, Massachusetts; 234—Courtesy Pollock, M.L., Ph.D., Mount Sinai Medical Center, Milwaukee; 240, 243—Courtesy Measurement Laboratory, Department of Physical Education and Dance, University of Wisconsin, Madison; 247—From Pate, R., and Corbin, C. 1981. A taxonomy of physical fitness objectives. Implications for curriculum. Journal of Physical Education and Recreation **52**(1):36. Reprinted by permission of the American Alliance for Health, Physical Education, Recreation and Dance, 1900 Association Drive, Reston, VA 22091; 248, 250, 251—From the National Children and Youth Fitness Study. 1985. Public Health Service, Office of Disease Prevention and Health Promotion, U.S. Department of Health and Human Services: Washington, D.C. 20201; 248-249—By permission of the Institute of Aerobics Research, 12200 Preston Road, Dallas, TX 75230; 255—From Nutrition Weight Control and Exercise, by Katch, F.I., and McArdle, W.D. 1983. ed. 2. By permission of Lea & Febiger; 260—Courtesy Pollock, M.L. and the W.B. Saunders Co. From Pollock, M.L., Wilmore, J.M., and Fox, S.M. 1984. Exercise in health and disease: evaluation and prescription for prevention and rehabilitation. Philadelphia, W.B. Saunders Co.

Chapter 12 Tests of Athletic Performance-Related Physical Fitness
P. 266, 271-273, 288—Courtesy Measurement Laboratory, Department of Physical Education and Dance, University of Wisconsin, Madison; 269, 275-285—From Youth Fitness Test Manual. Washington, D.C.: AAHPER, 1976. Used by permission; 274—Reprinted by permission of the American Alliance for Health Physical Education, Recreation and Dance, 1900 Association Drive, Reston, VA 22091; 275-285—Modified from Youth Fitness Test Manual. Wash-

ington, D.C.: AAHPERD, 1976. Reprinted by permission of the American Alliance for Health, Physical Education, Recreation and Dance, 1900 Association Drive, Reston, VA 22091; 294-295—From Spray, J.A. 1977. Interpreting group or class performances using AAHPER Youth Fitness Test Norms. Journal of Physical Education and Recreation **48**:56-57. By permission of the publisher; 295—From Table 1 in Spray, J.A. 1977. Interpreting group or class performances using AAHPER Youth Fitness Test Norms. Journal of Physical Education and Recreation. **48**:56-57. Reprinted by permission of the American Alliance for Health, Physical Education, Recreation and Dance, 1900 Association Drive, Reston, VA 22091.

Chapter 13 Tests of Muscular Strength and Endurance
P. 305—Pollock, M.L., and others. 1978. Health and fitness through physical activity. New York: John Wiley & Sons. By permission of the publisher; 307—Heyward, V.H. 1984. Designs for Fitness. Minneapolis: Burgess Publishing Co. By permission of the publisher; 326—Friermood, H.T. 1967. "Volleyball Skills Contest for Olympic Development," in United States Volleyball Association, Annual Official Volleyball Rules and Reference Guide of the U.S. Volleyball Association, Berne, Ind.: USVBA Printer, pp. 134-135. By permission of H.T. Friermood and the U.S. Volleyball Association. *Raw scores are located in the chart in accordance with age and sex, and percentile scores are located across the top.

Chapter 14 Tests of Balance and Flexibility
P. 339, 342—By permission of the State Education Department, State University of New York, Albany.

Chapter 15 Tests of Motor Ability
P. 252-253—Reprinted by permission of Dr. M. Gladys Scott, Emerita Professor, University of Iowa,

Iowa City; 350-354—Courtesy Measurement Laboratory, Department of Physical Education and Dance, University of Wisconsin, Madison; 356-358—Reprinted by permission of Dr. Harold M. Barrow, Emeritus Professor, Wake Forest University, North Carolina.

Chapter 16 Tests of Affective Behavior

P. 373—From Miller, D.K., and Allen, T.E. 1982. Fitness: a lifetime commitment, ed. 2. Minneapolis: Burgess Publishing Co. Reprinted by permission of the publisher; 374, 376—From Martens, R. 1977. Sport Competition Anxiety Test. Champaign, Ill.: Human Kinetics Publishers. By permission of the publisher; 377—From Cowell, C.C. 1958. Validity: an index of social adjustment for high school use. Research Quarterly **29**:7-18. Reprinted by permission of the American Alliance for Health, Physical Education, Recreation and Dance, 1900 Association Drive, Reston, VA 22091; 378—From Blanchard, B.E. 1936. A behavior frequency rating scale for the measurement of character and personality traits in physical education classroom situations. Research Quarterly **7**:56-66. Reprinted by permission of the American Alliance for Health, Physical Education, Recreation and Dance, 1900 Association Drive, Reston, VA 22091; 380—Reprinted by permission of Kenyon, G.S., University of Lethbridge, Lethbridge, Alberta, Canada; 381—From Pooley, J.C. 1971. The professional socialization of physical education students in the United States and England. Unpublished doctoral dissertation, The University of Wisconsin, Madison. By permission of the author; 383— From Simon, J.A., and Smoll, F.L. 1974. An instrument for assessing children's attitudes toward physical activity. Research Quarterly **45**:21-27. By permission of the authors; 384—From Sonstroem, R.J. 1974. Attitude testing: examining certain psychological correlates of physical activity. Research Quarterly **39**:566-574. Reprinted by permission of the author, University of Rhode Island, Kingston; 386-387—From Wear, C.L. 1955. Construction of equivalent forms of an attitude scale. Research Quarterly **26**:113-119. Reprinted by permission of the American Alliance for Health, Physical Education, Recreation and Dance, 1900 Association Drive, Reston, VA 22091; 388-389—From Lakie, W.L. 1964. Expressed attitudes of various groups of athletes toward athletic competition. Research Quarterly **35**:497-503. Reprinted by permission of the American Alliance for Health, Physical Education, Recreation and Dance, 1900 Association Drive, Reston, VA 22091; 390-392—From Nelson, D.O. 1966. Nelson Sports Leadership Questionnaire. Research Quarterly **37**:268-275. Reprinted by permission of the author; 394—Courtesy Biodynamics Laboratory, Department of Physical Education and Dance, University of Wisconsin, Madison; 393—From Borg, G.A.V. 1973. Perceived exertion: a note on "history" and methods. Medicine and Science in Sports **5**:90-93. Reproduced by permission of the publisher.

Chapter 17 Measuring Motor Performance in Children

P. 400-401—From Seefeldt, V., and Haubenstricker, J. 1982. Patterns, phases, or stages: an analytical model for the study of developmental movement. In Kelso, J.A.S., and Clark, J.E., editors. The development of movement control and coordination. London: John Wiley & Sons, Ltd. By permission of the publisher; 402, 414—From Roberton, M.A., and Halverson, L.E. 1984. Developing children—their changing movement. Philadelphia: Lea & Febiger. By permission of the publisher; 403, 413—Redrawn from Roberton, M.A., and Halverson, L.E. 1984. Courtesy Motor Development and Child Study Laboratory, University of Wisconsin, Madison; 404, 406, 408, 411—Reprinted by permission of the American Alliance for Health, Physical Education, Recreation and Dance, 1900 Association Drive, Reston, VA 22091; 405, 407, 410, 412—From Scott, M.G., and French, E. 1959. Measurement and evaluation in physical education. Dubuque, Iowa: Wm C Brown Group. By permission of Scott, M.G., Ph.D.; 412-416—From Johnson, R.D. 1962. Measurements of achievement in fundamental skills of elementary school children. Research Quarterly **33**:94-103. Reprinted by permission of the American Alliance for Health, Physical Education, Recreation and Dance, 1900 Association Drive, Reston, VA 22091; 418—Courtesy American Medical Association. Copyright © 1978; 420-421—Reprinted by permission of Ross Laboratories. Adapted from Hamill, P.V.V., Dri\u017ed, T.A., Johnson, C.L., et al.: Physical growth: National Center for Health Statistics percentiles. Am. J. Clin. Nurtr. **32**:607-629, 1979. Data from the National Center for Health Statistics (NCHS), Hyattsville, Md.

Chapter 18 Adapting Tests and Measurements for Special Populations

P. 429, 438, 445—Courtesy Measurement and Biodynamics Laboratories, Department of Physical Education and Dance, University of Wisconsin, Madison; 431-434, 449-451—Courtesy Janet A. Seaman, Professor, California State University, Los Angeles; 432—Courtesy Ben Esparza, ESCAPE Clinic, California State University, Los Angeles; 444-448—From Winnick, J.P., and Short, F.X. 1982. The Physical Fitness of Sensory and Orthopedically Impaired Youth. By permission of Joseph P. Winnick.

Chapter 19 Grading in Physical Education

P. 309—"Peanuts Cartoon"; 471—Reprinted by permission of Hofeman, D.A., Ph.D., Superintendent, Madison Metropolitan School District, Madison, Wisconsin.

Chapter 20 Special Issues in Measurement and Evaluation
P. 476—From Hale, P.W., and Hale, R.M. 1972. Comparison of student improvement by exponential modification of test-retest scores. Research Quarterly **43**:119. Reprinted by permission of the American Alliance for Health, Physical Education, Recreation and Dance, 1900 Association Drive, Reston, VA 22091.

Chapter 22 Microcomputer Applications
P. 506—By permission of Johnny Hart and Field Enterprises, Inc.

Index

A

AAHPER Cooperative Physical Education Test, 121
AAHPER Youth Fitness Test, 229, 267-268, 417-418
AAHPERD, 9, 20, 267
AAHPERD Health-Related Physical Fitness Test, 229-247, 418, 437
AAHPERD Motor Fitness Test for the Moderately Mentally Retarded, 437-438
AMA Growth Charts, 420-423
Abilities, related, measures of, 365-396
Ability grouping, 490
Ability, motor, tests of, 345-363, 417-419
Accountability
    health clubs and, 62
    importance of to teachers, 24, 28-29
Achievement, tests and, 6
Acoustic modem, 500, 502
Actual status, in program evaluation, 483-484
Adapting, as objective in motor domain, 36
Adaptive Physical Education Assessment Scale, 449-451
Administration
    of physical fitness tests; see Physical fitness tests, administration of
    test, 173-174
Affect, 367
Affective behavior, tests of, 366-396
Affective domain, 32-34
Affective skills, grading and, 460-461
Age norms, 109
Agreement, proportion of, 152
Alternative(s), as aspect of multiple-choice test, 178-179
American Alliance for Health, Physical Education, Recreation, and Dance, 9, 20, 267
Analysis
    intratask, of basic movement patterns, 400-401
    item, 184-186
Anomaly, congenital, 447
Anxiety
    as a construct, 129
    stress and, measurement of level of, 372-373
Archery tests, 192-194
Arm curl test, 315-318
Assessment, needs, conducting of, 37-38
Astrand and Ryhming Test, 259
Athletic Badge Tests, 12

Athletic performance-related physical fitness, tests of, 265-298
Attendance, as factor in grading, 461
Attitude, physical activity and, 366, 379-385
Attraction, physical, scale of, 382-384

B

BASIC, 496, 499, 506
Backhand drive test, 217-218, 219-221
Badminton tests, 194-195
Balance beam walk, 334
Balance, tests of, 329-344
Balke Treadmill Test, 12, 258-259
Ball changing zigzag run, 209-210
Barrow Motor Ability Test, 351
Baseball tests, 198-199
Basic movement patterns, 399-400
Basketball tests, 199-207
Basketball Throw Test, 348
Basketball Wall Pass Test, 404-406
Bass Stick Test, 330
Battery, test, 165
Baud, 500
Behavior
    affective, tests of, 366-396
    as attribute of behavioral objectives, 28-30
    motor
        overview of measurement and evaluation in, 1-63
        use of microcomputers to measure, 493-518
Behavioral objectives, 22-24
Bench press test, 315
Bench squat test, 309-310
Bicycle ergometer test, 46, 50
Bit, computer, 500
Blanchard Behavior Rating Scale, 375, 378-379
Blood Ptosis Test, 11
Body composition, 44, 244-245, 261-262
Body Fat Analysis, 45-46
Booting, 21, 499
Brace, David, 12
Brady volleyball test, 221-222
Broad jump test, 348
Bruininks-Osterosky Test of Motor Proficiency, 435-437
Brumbach Volleyball Serve Test, 162-163, 222
Byte, 500

C

CATALOG, 509
CATPA, 382-383

cf, 70
CPU, 499
CRT, 497
CUNA Mutual Insurance Group, Exercise Resource Facility of, 46, 50
Cable tensiometer, 301
Calculation of percentiles, 75-80
Caliper, skinfold, 234-236
Capability, motor, 345
Capacity, motor, 345-347
Cardiorespiratory function, measurement of, 256-260
Cathode ray tube, 497
Central Processing Unit, 499
Central tendency, measurement of, 86-89
Cerebral palsy, 447
Chapman ball control test, 208-209
Checklist of objectives, as grading method, 470
Children's Attitude Toward Physical Activity Inventory, 382-383
Child(ren), measuring motor performance in, 398-426
Circumferential measurement, 46
Clarke, Harrison, 12
Class management, evaluation of, 479-480
Classification, tests and, 8
Clubs, sports, measuring fitness in, 43-44
Coefficient
    contingency, 151
    correlation, 67
    of determination, 107-108
    reliability, 153
    validity, 130, 151
Cognitive domain, 31-32
Cognitive skills, grading and, 460
Compatibles, 505
Competency-based evaluation, 15
Component model of intratask development, 402-403
Components of skill, 161-162
Composing, as objective in motor domain, 36
Composition, body, 44, 244-245, 261-262
Computer literacy, 496
Computer memory, 499
Computer; see Microcomputer
Concurrent validity, 126
Condition, as attribute of behavioral objectives, 28-30
Consensus, in program evaluation, 486

Constant-value method of calculating scores, 100
Constraints, sport, changes in, 14-15
Construct validity, 129-130
Construction, test, principles of, 159-170
Content validity, 121-124
Content, as attribute of behavioral objectives, 28-30
Contingency coefficient, 151
Contingency table, 150-151
Continuous variable, 68-69
Contrasting groups method, 149-151
Control dribble test, 204-206
Correction for guessing, 184
Correlation, 102-108
Correlation coefficient, 67
 interpretation of, 107-108
 rank difference, 104-105
Course of study, evaluation of, 478
Cowell Social Adjustment Index, 375, 377
Crampton, C. Ward, 11
Criterion groups, 150
Criterion-referenced approach to grading, 465-467
Criterion-referenced archery tests, 194
Criterion-referenced measurement, 8-10
Criterion-referenced test(s)
 uses of, 146
 validity and reliability of, 143-157
Criterion-referenced validity, 126-129
Crosswise Bass Stick Test, 330
Cumulative frequency, 72
Cumulative percent, 72
Curriculum objectives, 25-27
Curriculum, evaluation of, 487-489
Curve
 use of in distribution of scores, 92-95
 use of in grading, 463
Cybex, 299

D

DELETE, 510
DDST, 428-429, 434
DOS, 499, 507
Data processing of physical fitness test results, 290-291
Data, storage of, 499
Deaf, physical fitness and, 447
Decision validity, 148-151
Defensive movement test, basketball, 206-207
Denver Developmental Screening Test, 428-429, 434
Derived scores, 108
Desired status, in program evaluation, 483-484
Deviation, standard of, 90-92
Diagnosis, tests and, 6-7

Difficulty, item, 185
Direct-connect modem, 500, 502
Directions, standardization of, 163
Disability(ies), physical, 427
Discrete variable, 68-69
Discrimination, index of, 185-186
Disk drive, computer, 497
Disk Operating System, 499, 507
Disk(s), computer, 499
 dual, 497
 floppy, 507
 preparing of, 506-507
Display, computer, 497
Distance run(s), tests for, 230-232
Distractor(s), 176
Distribution(s)
 frequency, 66, 69-73
 graphing, 73-74
 of test scores, describing, 86-116
Domain, 146
Domain-referenced validity, 146-148
Dress, as factor in grading, 461-462
Dribble, control, test, 204-206
Dual disk drive, 497
Due process, handicapped child and, 430
Dyer backhand test, Hewitt revision of, 218
Dynamic balance, 330
Dynamic strength, 301
Dynamometer(s), use of, 301

E

Educability, motor, 346-347
Educable, as level of mental retardation, 438
Education for all handicapped children act, 429-430
Education, Amendments of, 1972, 16
Educational objectives, 24-37
Effect, reactive, 367
Effort, as factor in grading, 461
Electrogoniometer, 335
Electromechanical instrument, 303
Elgon, 335
Endurance, muscular, tests of, 299-328
Enter key, 508
Equivalent formula, 92
Ergometer, bicycle, 46, 50
Essay item, 181-183
Essay test(s), 181-183
Estimate, split-half reliability, 133-134
Estimation, physical, 382-384
Evaluation objectives, 25-27
Evaluation
 formative, 10-11, 399, 477-478
 measurement and, motor behavior and, 1-63
 value of, 2-4
 special issues in, 475-492

Evaluation—cont'd
 standards for, for handicapped children, 430-431
 subjective, 24
 tests and, 7-8
Exercise prescription, tests and, 7
Exertion, perceived, 369, 393-394
Extension, trunk, test of, 337-338

F

FITNESSGRAM, 17, 249, 268, 457
Fat, skinfold, 234-236
Field hockey tests, 208-209
Field test(s), uses of, 229
Fielding test, as aspect of softball test, 214
Fifty-yard dash test, 281-283
 for physically impaired, 442-443
Fitness centers, measuring of fitness in, 44-62
Fitness
 measuring of in fitness centers, 44-62
 physical
  athletic-performance-related, 265-298
  tests of, 417-419
Flexed-arm hang test, 268-270, 272-275
 for physically impaired, 439-440
Flexed-leg sit-ups test, 275-277
Flexibility, tests of, 329-344
Flexometer, 335
Floor-Touch Test, Kraus-Weber, 336-337
Floppy disk(s), 507
Foil(s), 176
Football tests, 209-210
Forced-choice item, 369
Forehand drive test, 217-218, 219-221
Formative evaluation, 10-11, 399, 477-478
Formatting, 507
Formula, percentile, 77-78
Forward bend, trunk, test of, 338-339
French short serve test, 195-196
Frequency distribution, 66, 69-73
Frequency polygon, 74
Frequency, 70-71
 cumulative, 72

G

GRADES (program), 513-514
Game statistics, 168
Gates, 496
Glassow, Ruth, 12
Goals, long-range, 25-26
Golf tests, 210-211
Goniometer, 301, 335
Grade norm(s), 108-109
Grades, use of in schools, 455-457

Grading
 physical education and, 454-474
 tests and, 7
Graphing distributions, 73-74
Group differences method, 129
Grouping, ability, 490
Growth, child(ren)'s, measuring of,
 420-423
Guessing, correction for, 184

H

HOME, 509
HRFT, 230
Halo effect, 182
Handicapped, physical fitness and, 429
Hard copy, 500
Hard of hearing, 445
Hardware, computer, 497
Harvard Step Test, 11, 250-253
Health-Related Physical Fitness Test(s),
 226-264, 267-268, 418
Hewitt revision of Dyer backhand test,
 218
Hewitt tennis achievement test, 216-218
Histogram, 74
Hitchcock, Edward, 11
Hopping, testing for in children, 402,
 403
Hydrostatic weighing, 261-262

I

IEP, 430
Impaired evaluation techniques for, 427
Improvement
 measurement of, 475-477
 tests and, 6
Improving, as objective in motor
 domain, 36
Index of discrimination, 185-186
Individualized Education Program, 430
Indoor golf skill test for junior high
 school boys, 210-211
Initializing, 507
Institutional grades, use of, 470
Instructed/uninstructed approach,
 148-149
Instructor(s), evaluation of, 480-482
Instrument(s), electromechanical, 303
Interclass correlation coefficient, 133
Intercollegiate Strength Test, 11
Interests, as affective behavior, 367
Interjudge objectivity, 139
Interpercentile range, 89
Interpretation of correlation coefficient,
 107-108
Interquartile range, 89
Interval, 69, 71, 72, 79
Interval scale, 68
Intrajudge objectivity, 138-139

Intratask analysis of basic movement
 patterns, 400-401
Intratask development, component
 model of, 402-403
Isometric strength, 301
Isotonic strength, 301
Item analysis, 184-186
Item difficulty, 185
Item
 essay, 181-183
 matching, 179-180
 multiple-choice, 176
 short-answer, 181
 true-false, 174-176

J

Jewett Taxonomy of Motor Domain, 35
Johnson Modification of Bass Test of
 Dynamic Balance, 332-333
Johnson Test of Achievement in
 Fundamental Skills, 419
Jump, vertical, 320, 325-326

K

Kappa coefficient, 153
Kelson baseball classification plan,
 198-199
Kenyon's Attitude Toward Physical
 Activity Inventory, 129-130,
 367-368, 379, 381-382
Keyboard, computer, 497
Kicking test, 412-415
Kilobyte(s), 500
Knowledge, physical fitness, test of, 296
 construction of, 171-189
Kraus-Weber Floor-Touch Test, 336-337
Kraus-Weber Test of Minimum
 Strength, 12, 226

L

LIST, 510
LOAD, 509
Labyrinthine reflex, tonic, 432
Lakie Attitude Toward Athletic
 Competition Scale, 385, 388-389
Language(s), computer, 500
Latchaw Motor Achievement Test, 419
Lateral pull-down test, 312-315
Leadership, measurement of, 385,
 390-393
Leap, modified sideward, 333-334
Learning, mastery, 144-145
Lengthwise Bass Stick Test, 330
Level of ability, as influence on
 reliability, 137
Liba and Stauff Volleyball Pass Test,
 14-15
Likert Scale, 367-368
Literacy, computer, 496
Local norms, 111-112

Lockhart-McPherson badminton test,
 198
Logical validity, 124-126
Lower score/better performance method
 of calculating scores, 101-102

M

MEAN, 510-511
METS, 50
Machines, weight-training, 301
Mainframe computer, 497
Manitoba physical fitness performance
 test, 286-287
Master/nonmaster classification, 150
Mastery learning, 144-145
Mastery test, 9
Matching item, 179-180
Max VO₂, 50
Maximal oxygen uptake, 50
Maximal stress testing, 257-258
McCloy, Charles, 12
McCloy's General Motor Ability Test,
 347
McDonald volleying soccer test, 213
Mean, 86, 87
Measure(s) of physical performance,
 191-225
Measurement, 66, 67-68
 evaluation and, motor behavior and,
 1-63
 value of, 2-4
 of motor behavior, use of
  microcomputer(s) in, 493-518
 in a nonschool-based setting, 42-64
 in a school-based setting, 20-41
 special issues in, 475-492
Measurement practices, recent changes
 in, 13-17
Median, 66, 75-76, 86, 87
Medicine Ball Put Test, 354-356
Memory, computer, 499
Mentally retarded, 429
Microchips, 496-497
Microcomputer(s), 15-16
 use of in grading, 469
 use of in measuring motor behavior,
 493-518
Microsoft BASIC, 506
Minicomputer, 497
Minnesota Multiphasic Personality
 Inventory, 128
Mode, 86, 87
Modem, 500
Modified sideward leap, 333-334
Modification of sports, 14-15
Modified sit-ups, tests, 238-240
Monitor, computer, 497
Motivation, tests and, 5

Motor ability
  profiles of for handicapped, 433-435
  tests of, 345-363, 417-419
Motor behavior
  use of microcomputer(s) to measure,
    493-518
  overview of measurement and
    evaluation in, 1-63
Motor capacity, 345-347
Motor domain, 34-37
Motor educability, 346-347
Motor performance
  in children, measuring of, 398-426
  sex differences in, 489-491
Motor skills, grading and, 458-459
Movement patterns, basic, 399-400
Multiple choice item, 176
Multiple grades, use of, 472
Muscular strength and endurance, tests
    of, 299-328

N

NEW, computer program, 509
National Children and Youth Fitness
    Study, 247-249
National norms, 111-112
Nautilus, 299
Needs assessment
  conducting of, 37-38
  for disabled, 428
Nelson Sports Leadership Questionnaire,
    390-393
New York State Posture Rating Test,
    339-342
Nominal scale, 67-68
Nonmaster/master classification, 150
Normal distribution, 110
Norm(s)
  development of, as step in
    development of tests, 165
  individual based and percentile, use of
    in administration of physical
    fitness tests, 293-295
  use of, 108-112
Norm-referenced measurement, 8-10
Norm-referenced tests, validity and
    reliability of, 118-142
Normal curve, use of in distribution of
    scores, 92-95

O

Objective test, 138
Objective(s)
  behavioral, 22-24
  checklist of, as grading method, 470
  curriculum, 25-27
  educational, 24-37
  evaluation, 25-27
  private sports clubs and, 43-44

Objectivity
  as factor influencing reliability, 118,
    136-138
  intrajudge and interjudge, 138-139
Obstacle race test, 349-351
Obtained score, reliability and, 131-132
Ohio State University Step Test, 253-254
Olympic Health and Racquet Club, 46
1-RM test, 303-307
Ordinal scale, 68
Orthopedically impaired, tests for, 444,
    445
Overarm throwing, stages in, 400-401

P

PEAS, 382-384
PPCF, 487
PROGRAM CHANGE, 477
PWC$_{170}$ Test, 59, 259
Paraplegia, 447
Pass-fail method of grading, 469
Passing test, basketball, 202-203
Patterning, as objective in motor
    domain, 36
Patterns, movement, basic, 399-400
Pearson product-moment correlation
    coefficient, 102-104, 133, 164
Perceived exertion scale, 369, 393-394
Perceiving, as objective in motor
    domain, 36
Percent, cumulative, 72
Percentage-correct method of grading,
    465-466
Percentage method of grading, 464-465
Percentile, 71, 75-80
Percentile formula, 77-78
Percentile norms, 293-295
Percentile rank, 80-82, 109-110
Perceptual motor behavior, tests of, 419
Perfect positive correlation, 103
Performance evaluation, sex-fair, 490-491
Performance standards
  grading and, 466-467
  uninstructed/instructed approach for
    setting, 148-149
Performance testing, handicapped and,
    431
Performance, motor, in children,
    measurement of, 398-426
Peripheral, computer, 497, 500, 502
Personal computers, 496-498
Phobia, computer, 504
Physical education, grading in, 454-474
Physical Estimation and Attraction Scale,
    382-384
Physical fitness knowledge, test of, 296
Physical fitness tests
  administration of, 287-295
    data processing of results, 290-291

Physical fitness tests—cont'd
  administration of—cont'd
    norms, use of, 293-295
    preparation for, 288-290
    trials, number of, 291-293
  for impaired children, 437-444
  increase in use of, 17
Physical fitness
  athletic performance-related, 265-298
  health-related, tests of, 226-264
  tests of, 417-419
Physical performance, measures of,
    191-225
Physical performance standards for girls
    and women, reassessment of,
    16-17
Physical work capacity test, 59
Playground and Recreation Association of
    America, 12
Poole forehand clear test, 197
Poole long serve test, 194-195
Posture, measurement of, 339-342
Power, test for, 320-326
Prediction(s), test and, 8
Predictive validity, 127-128
Prescription, exercise, tests and, 7
President's Council on Physical Fitness
    and Sports, 249
Principles of test construction, 159-170
Program evaluation, 482-486
Program GRADES, 513-514
Project UNIQUE Physical Fitness Test,
    444-448
Proportion of agreement, 152
Psychomotor domain, 34-37
Pull-Ups Test, 268-270, 311-312
  modified, 271-272
Pulse Recovery Step Test, 46
Purdue Perceptual Motor Survey,
    431-432
Purpose-Process Curriculum Framework,
    487

Q

Queens College Step Test, 255-256
Questionnaire, use of to measure
    affective behavior, 369

R

RAM, 499
ROM, 499
RUN, 509
Racquetball tests, 212
Random Access Memory, 499
Range, 71, 89
  of ability, as influence on reliability,
    137
Rank difference correlation coefficient,
    104-105

Rating scale, 165-168
Ratio scale, 68
Raw score(s), 88, 108
Reactive effect, 367
Read Only Memory, 499
Real limits, 77
Rectangular distribution, 110
Refining, as objective in motor domain, 36
Reflexes, testing for, in handicapped, 431
Related abilities, measures of, 365-396
Reliability coefficient, 153
Reliability, 118, 130-138
   criterion-referenced, 151-153
   factors influencing, 136-138
   as step in development of tests, 163-165
   validity and
      of criterion-referenced tests, 143-157
      of norm-referenced tests, 118-142
Repeated throws, as aspect of softball test, 213-214
Response distortion, 367
Rogers, Frederick Rand, 12

S

SAVE, 510
SCAT-C, 374-375
Sandbagging, 459-460
Sargent, Dudley, 11
Scale, rating, 165-168
Schick softball test battery, 213-215
Schneider, E. C., 11
School-based setting, measurement in, 20-41
Score(s)
   derived, 108
   limits, 77
   raw, 88, 108
   test, summarizing, 66-85
Scoring, objectivity of, 138-139
Scott Motor Ability Test, 348, 352-353
Scott, Gladys, 12
Self-motivation, test for, 8-9
Semantic differential scale, 368-369
Sensorimotor testing, for handicapped, 431
Sentry World Headquarters, Physical Fitness Center of, 53
Set of test scores, summarizing, 66-85
Sex differences, motor performance and, 489-491
Shared variance, 108
Short-answer item, 181
Showers, as factor in grading, 461-462
Shuttle run test, 277-278
Sideward leap, modified, 333-334

Single test administration reliability, 132-135
Sit-and-Reach Test, 241, 336
Sit-ups, modified, 238-240
Sit-ups test, 268-270, 312
   flexed-leg, 275-277
Six-hundred yard run test, 283-285
Skewed distribution of scores, 95-96
Skill(s)
   components of, 161-162
   sports, tests of, 192, 225, 403-417
Skinfold caliper, 234-236
Skinfold thickness values, 46, 50
Soccer tests, 213
Soccer Wall Volley Test, 408-410
Social behavior, 367, 375-379
Softball Repeated Throws Test, 411-412
Softball tests, 213-215
Softball Throw, test for in handicapped, 441-442
Software, 500
   commercial, 507-508
   user-developed, 508-510
Spearman-Brown prophecy formula, 135, 165
Specifications, table of, 172
Specificity, task, 329, 359
Speed of service test, 216
Speed shot shooting, 199-201
Split-half reliability estimate, 133-134
Sport Competition Anxiety Test, 374-375, 376
Sports clubs, measuring skills in, 43-44
Sports skills, tests of, 192-225, 403-417
   construction of, 160-170
Sports, modification of, 14-15
Sportsmanship, 367, 385, 388-389
   as factor in grading, 462
Squat thrust test, 319-320
Standard deviation, 90-92
Standard deviation method of grading, 463-464
Standard error of measurement, 135-136
Standard score(s), 96-102
Standard score method of grading, 464
Standard score norms, 111
Standard(s)
   of performance, as attribute of behavioral objectives, 28-30
   physical performance, for girls and women, reassessment of, 16-17
Standardization of directions, in development of sports skills tests, 163
Standing broad jump test, 351
Standing long jump test, 279-281
   for handicapped, 440-441
Static balance, 330

Static strength, 301
Statistics, 66
   game, 168
   simplified, 65-116
Stem, as aspect of multiple-choice test, 177
Step test(s), 46, 250-256
Storage, data, 499
Stork Stand Test, 330-332
Strength
   dynamic, 301
   muscular, tests of, 299-328
   static, 301
Stress and anxiety, measure of level of, 372-373
Stress Inventory, 373
Students, grades and, 456-457
Subjective evaluation, 24
Subjective test, 138
Submaximal stress testing, 258
Summative evaluation, 10-11
Swimming tests, 215

T

T-scaled scores, 111
T-scores, 476-477, 513
   transformation, 99-102
Table, contingency, 150-151
Table of specifications, 172
Tally, 70
Target test, as aspect of softball test, 214-215
Task specificity, 329, 359
Taxonomy
   affective domain and, 32-34
   cognitive domain and, 31-32
   psychomotor domain and, 34-37
Tendency, central, measure of, 86-89
Tennis tests, 216-221
Tensiometer, cable, 301
Terminal behavior, identification of, 28
Test-retest reliability, 135
Test(s)
   criterion-referenced, 143-144
   knowledge, construction of, 171-189
   objective, 138
   of sports skills, 192-225
   subjective, 138
   types of, 5-8
Test administration, 173-174
Test battery, 165
Test construction, principles of, 159-170
Test length, as influence on reliability, 138
Test score(s)
   distribution of, 86-116
   individual, precision of, 135
   summarizing of, 66-85

Testing, school-based, 20-24
Texas physical fitness-motor ability test, 285-286
Three-hundred yard run-walk test, for handicapped, 443
Throw-and-Catch Test, 415-417
Throwing, overarm, stages in, 400-401
Title IX, 16-17
Tonic labyrinthine reflex, 432
Trait, use of as label, 358-359
Trials, number of, in administering physical fitness tests, 291-293
True-false item, 174-176
True score, reliability and, 131-132
Trunk extension, test of, 337-338
Tuttle Pulse Ratio Test, 11
Tuttle, W.W., 11
Twelve-minute swim test, 215

U

Unit grade
   determination of, 458-462
   testing and, 455
Universal Gym, 299
User-friendly programs, 508

V

Validity coefficient, 130, 151
Validity, 118, 119, 146-151
   content, 121-124
   criterion-referenced, 126-129
   decision, 148-151
   domain-referenced, 146-148
   logical, 124
   reliability and
      of criterion-referenced tests, 143-157
      of norm-referenced tests, 118-142
   as step in development of tests, 163-165
Variability, measure of, 89-92
Variable(s), 68-69
   graph of relationships between, 105-107
Variance, 90-91
   shared, 108
Varying, as objective in motor domain, 36
Vertical jump, 320, 325-326
Vic Tanny International of Wisconsin, Inc., 45-46

Visually handicapped, 445
Volleyball tests, 221-223
Volleyball Wall Volley Test, 406-408

W

Walk, balance beam, 334
Wall volley test, 131
Weak measure(s), 370-371
Wear Attitude Scale, 385, 386-387
Weighing, hydrostatic, 261-262
Weight-training machines, use of, 301
Weight, grade, 464, 468-469

Y

YMCA, 53, 59
Youth Fitness Test, 17, 267-268, 417-418

Z

Z-score(s), 511-512
   transformation, 97-98
Zigzag run
   ball changing, 209-210
   test for, 354